Determined To S

Chris Gregory is the author of *Be Seeing You: Decoding The Prisoner* (1997), *Star Trek: Parallel Narratives* (2000) and *Who Could Ask For More: Reclaiming The Beatles* (2008). He also writes poetry, short stories, plays and novels. More examples of his writing can be found at *From the Pen of Chris Gregory* (www.chrisgregory.org/blog)

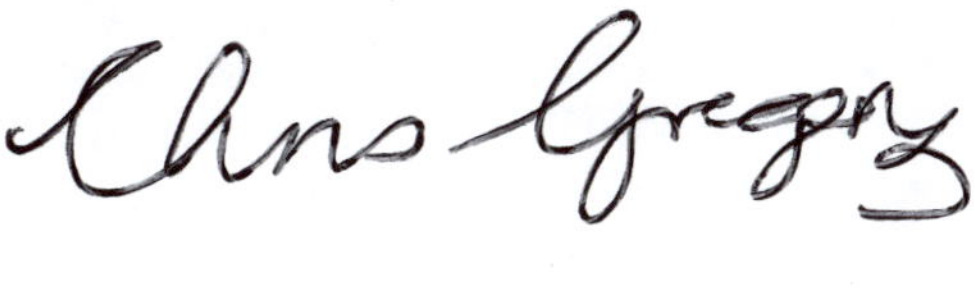

This book is dedicated to Stanley Jackson McCormack
(...*May you stay forever young...*)

DETERMINED TO STAND

The Reinvention of Bob Dylan

Chris Gregory

the plotted plain press

First published in Great Britain by the plotted plain press, 2021

Special thanks to Mark Weller, Gordon Macniven, Geoff Marshall, Ian Cooper and David McBride for their invaluable help and comments.

Cover design by Chris Gregory
Cover photo by Harry Scott

ISBN 978-0-955-7512-1-9

Contents

Prelude

...DESTINY is a feeling you have that you know something about yourself nobody else does. The picture you have in your own mind of what you're about WILL COME TRUE. It's a kind of a thing you kind of have to keep to your own self, because it's a fragile feeling, and you put it out there, then someone will kill it. It's best to keep that all inside...

Bob Dylan *60 Minutes* Interview 2004

11th March 1995. It is a cold spring evening in Prague and Bob Dylan is playing his first gig of what will be another busy year. After a couple of numbers, he abandons his guitar and mumbles something about having just caught the 'flu. For the rest of the show he will prowl the stage, microphone in hand, focused entirely on his singing. Whatever the state of his health, he sounds fresh and utterly focused. The songs are mostly familiar but have been heavily rearranged. The show begins with a riff-heavy version of *Down in the Flood* from *The Basement Tapes*, now presented as a slow, deep blues and a kind of proclamation for what will follow. The singer declares vehemently that he is not *...gonna be your best friend now...* Throughout *Just Like a Woman, Tangled Up in Blue, Mr. Tambourine Man* and *It's All Over Now Baby Blue* he stretches his vocal lines to what seems to be their limit, every song sounding deeply resonant and heartfelt.

It is on the tenth number in the set, *Man in the Long Black Coat*, that sparks truly fly. The original version on *Oh Mercy* (1989) had benefitted from producer Daniel Lanois' atmospheric 'swampy' arrangement (with added sound effects of chirping crickets) and Dylan had played the song many times in the intervening years. But here it takes on a completely new incarnation. It is a mythic tale of how a woman living somewhere in the Deep South is whisked away by a mysterious stranger - perhaps a priest or a con man (or both) who overwhelms her with an unknown, unspeakable power. Although we hear that the *...Preacher was a talkin', there's a sermon he gave/ He said every man's conscience is vile and depraved...* she chooses to 'give her heart' to this apparently demonic figure. Dylan takes the song at a sonorous pace, at first pronouncing the words in a near-whisper, then extending the final syllable of the last word of each line. The mood that is evoked shifts from eerie calm to a kind of transcendent fear, its dramatic effect heightened by the contrasts created as Dylan keeps moving out of one mode and into another.

The effect builds up throughout the song, until in the final verse the softly spoken lines ...*There's smoke on the water, it's been there since June/ Tree trunks uprooted, 'neath the high crescent moon...* are set against him almost screaming ...*Feel the pulse and vibration and the rumbling force/ Someone is out there beating on a dead horse...* He seems to fully inhabit the apocalyptic energy of the transformation that has occurred. The song deals with a kind of spiritual 'uprooting', like that of those devastated trees. The set pattern of the nameless woman's life has been destroyed and along with it many established certainties. Never has the conventionally twee 'moon/ June' rhyme been used to such a devastatingly ironic effect. But the identity of 'the man' still remains a mystery. Is he truly the Devil or is he a liberator?

Man in the Long Black Coat is Dylan's most unflinching depiction of the conflict between the settled, ordered world of conventional religion and the uncertain, often frightening, mystical space of the creative imagination. In this performance, whose varying vocal inflections portray an unforgettably anguished mental condition, showing how quickly one state of mind can 'slide' into another, Dylan himself appears to have entered an almost trance-like, shamanistic space. He is, quite literally, in a fever. And in this performance he dramatises with great eloquence the essence of the spiritual conflict that he has been caught up in for so many years. In his younger days he had been 'possessed' by the spirit of creative imagination, so much so that the poetry that was 'written in his soul' had poured out of him while he inhabited a place ...*far from the twisted reach of crazy sorrow...* Now, in this moment, by descending into the deepest hollows of his soul, he begins to glimpse that place again...

The extent of the cultural impact of Bob Dylan's work is almost impossible to measure. As a songwriter he has hugely expanded both the types of subject matter and the kinds of lyrical expression which the art of song can encompass. As a singer, his often harsh, ever-changing and always controversial vocal style - with its emphasis on the dramatic declamation of lyrics - has changed popular perceptions of how songs can be delivered. He has opened the way for many other singers with 'unconventional' voices to be heard. Thousands of cover versions of his songs have been performed by artists from almost every musical genre. He has also been a major instigator of massive shifts in the direction of popular music. Although he rose to prominence as a solo folk singer, his subsequent embrace of rock and his profound influence on The Beatles, The Rolling Stones, The Byrds and other leading musicians in the 1960s played a major role in transforming what had primarily been teenage dance music into a potent and meaningfully expressive art form.

In his long career Dylan has embraced many different styles, including country, blues, gospel and pre-rock popular music. His embodiment of various musical 'personalities' in succeeding years has been so marked that, in the 2007 biopic *I'm Not There*, director Todd Haynes employed no less than six different actors - including a woman (Cate Blanchett) and a twelve year old African American boy (Marcus Carl Franklin) - to portray him. Perhaps the most unprecedented feature of his career, however, has been the way in which, in his later years - when most of his contemporaries have been content to rely on the repetition of past glories - he has undergone a process of personal and artistic 're-invention'. The result of this has been a body of work whose thematic range and musical sensibilities encompass much of the history of American music. Many of these songs have a particular resonance with the pre-1960s era, especially the years from the 1920s, when the recording industry became a mass medium, up to the rockabilly of the late 1950s. This is largely the territory Dylan covers in his lovingly conceived *Theme Time Radio Hour* shows, in which Frank Sinatra and Louis Armstrong rub shoulders with Elmore James, Hank Williams and Muddy Waters. Dylan also tips his cowboy hat to the music of pre-rock composers like Johnny Mercer and Harold Arlen. As he sings in his recreation of the blues classic *Rollin' and Tumblin'* (2006) *...I've been conjuring up all these long dead souls from their crumblin' tombs...*

Dylan's late style makes extensive use of lyrical and musical 'quotations' from and allusions to many old pop, blues, country, folk and gospel songs. Many lines refer to, or resonate strongly with, the work of his literary precursors, especially Ginsberg, Whitman, Poe, Keats, Blake, Rimbaud and Shakespeare. The influence of ancient Greek and Roman writers, including Homer, Virgil and Ovid, has become increasingly prominent. He has also 'lifted' phrases from strangely obscure sources, such as a half forgotten Civil War poet, a Japanese detective novel, newspaper clippings and tourist guides. Some songs seem to be almost entirely composed of fragments of other songs, poems or prose works. His unique way of 'juggling' many different cultural elements gives his late work a characteristically postmodern edge. While his earlier songs had defined and expressed the tumultuous era of his youth in political, social and linguistic terms, these multilayered creations provide a characteristically oblique commentary on the complex and confusing world of the culture, society and politics of the twenty first century.

Another striking aspect of Dylan's later work has been the role of live performance in the recreation and redefinition of his songs. His approach to performing has always been unique and iconoclastic but until the late 1980s he toured only sporadically. Since 1988, however, he has spent the majority of his time and energy slogging across North America, Europe, Asia and Australasia on what has become known as the 'Never Ending Tour'. In every year up to 2019 he played between 80 and 100 live concerts, performing in venues as varied as the massive 1994 Woodstock 2 Festival, the West Point Military Academy, New York's Supper Club, London's Royal Albert Hall and casinos in Las Vegas. This remarkable level of dedication to his performing art has clearly been central to his 'reinvention' as an artist and a public figure. These shows have included an often drastically radical recreation of his own back catalogue as well as a plethora of 'covers' from a huge range of different sources. He has pursued a lifelong dedication to spontaneity in performance, as if on an endless quest for the 'Holy Grail' of the 'perfect' version of each song, which will create a unique emotional awakening in his listeners.

He has constantly experimented with and modulated his songs, in search of those elusive flashes of true inspiration.

The vast majority of Dylan's concerts and public appearances have been recorded by dedicated fans, despite the often rigorously enforced prohibition of such activities. Dylan himself has never expressed enthusiasm for the fact that new high quality 'stealth recording' techniques have made the preservation of almost all his live shows possible. Perhaps he feels that such activities may in some way destroy that 'fragile feeling' that the artist himself has striven to preserve in his relentless quest to fulfill the 'destiny' of each of his songs; thus potentially killing the spontaneity that is such a crucial element of his attitude to performing. Yet these recordings do exist and are circulated widely on the Internet and among Dylan's fan base. So it is an inescapable fact that the existence of this vast body of recordings now represents a crucial element of the 'text of Dylan', providing an opportunity for present and future listeners and scholars to follow and examine the evolution of each song. At his most inspired and spontaneous, Dylan has created what Roland Barthes calls 'texts of bliss' - moments in which the 'rewriting' of the lyrics through their rephrasing and musical rearrangement create a spontaneous process of 're-composition' in which both singer and audience participate. Such revelatory moments may sometimes occur midway through shows that are otherwise relatively unremarkable, but when they do the songs can take on new and deeper resonances. In the course of this work, by focusing on a selection of particularly distinctive live performances, I have endeavoured to bring a number of them into the light.

This bulk of this book consists of detailed commentaries on Dylan's songs of the post-1997 period, mostly derived from the albums *Time Out of Mind* (1997), *"Love And Theft"* (2001), *Modern Times* (2006), *Together Through Life* (2009), *Tempest* (2012) and *Rough and Rowdy Ways* (2020). I have also examined his prose fantasia 'autobiography' *Chronicles Volume One* (2004), along with his role as a scriptwriter and actor in the 2002 film *Masked and Anonymous* as well as his extensive work as a painter and sculptor during this period. There are also some reflections on how these 'extracurricular activities' illuminate his work as a songwriter. The first chapter attempts to define his unique style of 'song poetry', and goes on to examine the process of catharsis that he went through from the late 1980s onwards, in order to make his later 'reinvention' possible. In the second chapter I have considered the surprisingly strong influence of the popular sentimental romantic tradition on his latter day work. The third chapter is focused, in contrast, on songs of romantic disillusionment, with a particular emphasis on the influence of the blues. The fourth and fifth chapters reflect on the many songs of this period in which Dylan employs a humorous approach. These songs often present a ruefully self-deprecatory commentary on his experience of the ageing process. The sixth and seventh chapters investigate his more visionary or apocalyptic contemporary songs, through which he has held up a mirror to the dark side of American history, politics and religion. The eighth chapter focuses on his excursions into the genre of the 'murder ballad' and his late career embrace of a 'bardic' role.

The songs of Dylan's late period are full of diverse allusions and tributes to various historical and musical heroes, demonstrating how he has integrated the influence of visual arts, theatre and cinema into his compositional methods. The images in these songs are often presented from several 'angles' at once, in the manner of modern artists such as Picasso. There are many different narrative voices and it is often impossible to tell which one is 'the voice of Dylan' himself. The characters in the songs sometimes deliver self-reflexive 'speeches' which resemble Shakespearean soliloquies. The stories they tell are often subject to time-shifts and 'jump cuts' which reflect their author's interest in experimental films. The songs also depict ways in which Dylan engages in a restless and ongoing search for new inspiration; a process that becomes a kind of 'spiritual quest'. They allow audiences to become active participants in a process of interpretation in which there is often no definitive 'meaning' to be found, while inviting them to explore a multiplicity of musical and literary genres. In my commentaries I have attempted to 'open up' various routes into understanding the songs, in order to enrich listeners' experiences as they engage with this often mysterious, sometimes confusing but ultimately magical and transcendent body of work.

One: A Bargain with the Chief Commander

...I consider myself a poet first and a musician second. I live like a poet and I'll die like a poet....
Bob Dylan: interview with Robert Shelton, *Melody Maker*, 29 July 1978

12th July 2019. We are nearing the climax of the 'British Summer Time' concert in Hyde Park, London. The sun is going down now on the massive crowd of over 50,000. Bob Dylan is six songs into his performance at the biggest show of this summer's tour of Europe. A few lucky folks well off enough to pay hundreds of pounds for an 'exclusive' ticket are close enough to see the action on stage. Most of us are left with no option but to watch the big screens which for once - presumably grudgingly - Dylan has agreed to. Neil Young and Promise of The Real have just played a storming show, heavily biased towards *Harvest* and other classic '70s albums. This is the kind of gig at which most acts would present a 'greatest hits' selection but Dylan continues with the set which he has been playing throughout the tour, which is heavily slanted towards relatively new material.

He is surely aware that, after the concert, the newspapers will be full of the usual complaints about his mode of singing, the unrecognisable versions of the songs and grumbles about why he didn't play this or that hit. But Dylan, who stays behind his piano for almost the entire show tonight, appears unperturbed. He is in a very good mood, it seems. On several occasions, if you look up at the screens, you can actually see him smile. Whether or not opening the show with *Ballad of a Thin Man* is a sly comment about those in this 'mainstream' audience who *...know something is happening...* but *...don't know what it is...* is open to question. This song and *Highway 61 Revisited* have, however, at least sounded reasonably like the originals; although *It Ain't Me Babe* - another 'audience challenging' song - has been delivered with a weird syncopated beat, *Simple Twist of Fate* has featured very different lyrics and *Can't Wait* has been transformed into a 'funk' workout of which Nile Rodgers or George Clinton would be proud.

After playing a couple of notes on his grand piano Dylan launches into some familiar lyrics: *...Oh the streets of Rome are filled with rubble/ Ancient footprints are everywhere...* Although this is hardly one of his 'greatest hits', most of the fans will recognise it as a song from 1971 originally recorded by The Band, which appeared as a bonus track on the *More Greatest Hits* album. It subsequently developed a varied life in performance, becoming the opening song in the 1975 Rolling Thunder shows and in the movie of that tour *Renaldo and Clara*. Later it found a place in various Never Ending Tour set lists and was covered by the Grateful Dead, Elliot Smith, Emmylou Harris and others. It grew into a song that became emblematic of the path that Dylan had chosen, expressing a constant striving to keep experimenting with his music and singing until he finally created that elusive 'masterpiece', an effort which - as the song suggests - can never be truly fulfilled. The message of the song seems to be that it is the striving for perfection, rather than the reaching of perfection itself, that defines a great artist. In a recent exhibition at the Halcyon Gallery in London called *Mondo Scripto* ('world writing' in Latin) Dylan had exhibited witty pencil sketches to illustrate his songs. The sketch for *When I Paint My Masterpiece* featured a fairly straightforward image of a Renaissance era artist at a canvas. He is painting a self portrait.

The notion of *Masterpiece* - which began life as a relatively light hearted ditty - as being emblematic of Dylan's own career as an 'artist', is now made more explicit by the extensive lyric changes. It has always had a 'loose' set of lyrics, and even the two 'original' versions are different. The story that unfolds describes the journey of a famous and celebrated artist through various cities in Europe. En route he has to cope with exhausting journeys, the adulation of fans and crazed 'newspaper men'. Halfway through there is one short bridge section which normally runs: *...Sailin' round the world in a dirty gondola/ Oh to be back in the land of Coca Cola...* a 'throwaway' line which is, however, quite funny and distinctive.

The song is not one full of rich metaphor or poetic tropes. It is mostly written in a fairly jokey, conversational way. We hear of *...Newspaper men eating candy...* who *...Had to be held down by big police...* and *...Clergymen in uniform and young girls pulling muscles...* which is playfully rhymed with *...landing in Brussels...* There is a mysterious sense of rumination, however, as Dylan contemplates the 'ancient footprints' he sees in Rome. Naturally, he is thinking of the traces of the Roman Empire, although the reference to *...the nights we spent inside the Coliseum/ dodging lions and wasting time...* seems to mix the idea of him 'travelling back in time' (at least in his mind) to the days of cruel public spectacles with his experiences as a tourist. Similarly, in the next verse, he refers to a 'memory' of *...running on a hilltop following a pack of wild geese...* Here he appears to take on the persona of the boy who looks after geese in a famous legend about ancient Rome, in which the honking of the geese forewarned the citizens about an attack from the Gauls.

The second verse of the song is the section which has changed the most since its composition. In The Band's recording the singer tells us that he is going to go back to his hotel room because he has a date with *...a pretty little girl from Greece....* In the *Greatest Hits* version the date is with *...Botticelli's Venus...* (In some live shows this appears to become 'Botticelli's niece') so anchoring the song in the early Renaissance era; although it is difficult to take either variant particularly seriously. But the version of the song that Dylan launches into here runs: *...Got to hurry on back to my hotel room/*

Gonna wash up my clothes, scrape off all of the grease/ Gonna turn my back on the world for a while/ Gonna stay right there till I paint my masterpiece... At this point it had been all of seven years since Dylan had released an album of new songs. For many performers of his age - 78 - this might seem normal. But these personal, and perhaps rather painful lines, suggest that his dedication to his art is undimmed, even if the act of creativity itself does involve considerable self-sacrifice. It also involves 'scraping off the grease' - implying that he normally presents himself to the world like an actor on a stage. He will need to remove that 'grease paint' in order to be himself and reach out again for his creative spirit.

The lyric changes in the next verse are even more jarring. Instead of the previous references to 'larking about' in the Coliseum he is now *... Dodging lions with a mean and hungry look...* Then he tells us that *...Oh, those mighty kings of the jungle, I could hardly stand to see 'em/ I can see 'em coming, I can read their faces like a book...* The lions have now become objects of terror, as if they represent the inevitability of physical or creative death. Later, after a fairly long and sombre-sounding instrumental break, he replaces the 'Coca Cola' reference with *...sailing round the world full of crimson and clover...* an apparent reference to a largely forgotten '60s 'bubblegum hit' *Crimson and Clover* by Tommy James and the Shondells. The use of the phrase here seems to suggest a confusing world full of complete contrasts. This is followed by *...Aaah, Lord, sometimes I feel that my cup is running over...* an allusion to a line in Psalm 23:5 in which he suggests that he has achieved spiritual fulfillment. Yet Dylan still seems to be beset by doubts. If his 'cup is running over' why does he need to retreat into solitude in search of inspiration?

The performance represents a radical revision of the song, which - although it retains the slightly dreamlike and otherworldly quality of the original - is transformed from a light hearted romp into a profound meditation on the role of the artist in old age. How much of this will be picked up by the massed punters in Hyde Park, never mind the jaundiced journos who will be writing all this up later, is questionable. But the fact remains that, three decades into his Never Ending Tour, Bob Dylan remains so much more than just a 'popular entertainer'. Although he can still project his work to a mass audience, not only does he not play 'nostalgia shows' but he also continues to refuse to become complacent about his own artistic development. Despite all of his achievements over a career that now lasts almost six decades, he continues to serenade his muse, still insisting that his real 'masterpiece' is yet to come.

Yippie! I'm a poet, I know it... hope I don't blow it... Bob Dylan sings in his jokily self deprecating talkin' blues *I Shall Be Free No. 10* (1964). From the release of his breakthrough second album *The Freewheelin' Bob Dylan* (1963) onwards, his lyrics have been widely acclaimed as poetry. In his first flush of fame, between 1963 and 1967, he appeared to be consumed by inspiration, as if drunk on words, pouring forth hundreds of songs; far too many to record on his own albums. In his early years he also composed a series of lengthy, impressionistic poetic sketches which appeared on some of his album covers and on those of his most prominent interpreters like Joan Baez and Peter, Paul and Mary. Over the succeeding decades, using a variety of ever changing musical styles, he has broadened and deepened his range of poetic approaches. In 2004 his highly impressionistic memoir *Chronicles Volume One* was published to considerable critical acclaim. Acceptance by the literary establishment has, however, taken some decades to achieve. In the years after his rise to prominence, his status as a popular entertainer (some of whose songs even became 'big hits' in the charts) mitigated against his being embraced by 'grown up' commentators and academics. But since the publication of Michael Gray's groundbreaking *Song and Dance Man* (1973), an ever-expanding number of critical studies (focusing mainly on his lyrics) have appeared and he has acquired some very prominent supporters in the literary world, such as former Oxford professor of poetry Christopher Ricks and Andrew Motion, once Britain's poet laureate. Dylan has been awarded several honorary degrees, as well as a Pulitzer Prize, the Presidential Medal of Freedom and the French Officier de la Legion d'honneur. Courses on his work are now taught in universities and a major archive of his material has been established in Tulsa Oklahoma.

In 2016 Dylan received the ultimate mark of approval in the literary world when he won the Nobel Prize for Literature. The award, with its massive worldwide profile, was the subject of some controversy. A great deal was made of the fact that Dylan failed to come up with any immediate sound bites, although this would hardly be a surprise to anyone with the slightest knowledge of his lifelong wariness of the media. He declined to attend the prize giving ceremony due to what he called 'prior commitments' and dispatched Patti Smith to collect the award for him. She was so nervous at appearing at such an excessively formal occasion (attended by the King of Sweden and other notables in full Ruritanian regalia) that she fluffed the words while bravely attempting to perform *A Hard Rain's a-Gonna Fall* with an orchestra. Inevitably, a few commentators came out of the woodwork who still insisted on publicly arguing (as they had been doing ever since Dylan first appeared on the scene) that because he is primarily a songwriter, his work cannot really be called 'literature'. But the most memorable comment came from Leonard Cohen who, in one of his last public statements, commented that giving Dylan the award was "like pinning a rosette on Mount Everest for being the highest mountain".

Dylan, who has always fought shy of celebrity culture, mostly maintained a respectable distance from all of this. He made only two public statements about receiving the honour. The first was a brief speech which was read at the prize-giving banquet by Azita Raji, the US Ambassador to Sweden, while the second was the lecture he was required to give as a Laureate. In both cases, quite possibly influenced by his latter-day immersion in the study of Ancient Greek and Roman texts, he uses the rhetorical device of assuming a 'humble' persona. In the speech he confesses to being amazed at being given the award and to being thrilled to be in the company of so many literary 'greats', who he enumerates with apparent awe. Then, cleverly twisting the rhetoric around, he compares himself to no other than the most acclaimed 'literary' artist of all:

...I began to think about William Shakespeare, the great literary figure. I would reckon he thought of himself as a dramatist. The thought that he was writing 'literature' couldn't have entered his head. His words were written for the stage. Meant to be spoken not read. When he was writing Hamlet, I'm sure he was thinking about a lot of different things: "Who're the right actors for these roles?", "How should this be staged?", "Do I really want to set this in Denmark?" His creative vision and ambitions were no doubt at the forefront of his mind, but there were also more mundane matters to consider and deal with. "Is the financing in place?", "Are there enough good seats for my patrons?", "Where am I going to get a human skull?" I would bet that the farthest thing from Shakespeare's mind was the question "Is this literature?"...

While the notion of Shakespeare worrying about 'where to find a human skull' is a typical example of Dylan's wry humour, the comparison is in fact extremely apposite. Both writers' words only really come alive in performances presented to an audience. Both are first and foremost popular entertainers who are, as Dylan (with his tongue firmly in his cheek) points out here, very much concerned with the practical aspects of performance. And just as in many of Dylan's songs the lyrics may be continually changed and adapted to different musical styles, in performances of Shakespeare the text is often cut for the demands of particular productions. The playwright's words - despite their great majesty and poetic quality - are not treated as 'sacred' but can be adapted to the requirements of different dramatic interpretations.

The poetic power of 'bards' (writers with a distinctly public role) such as Shakespeare and Dylan can be measured by the extent to which some of their most evocative phrases have come to have an independent life outside their original contexts. This often enhances the poetic resonance - and the depth of meaning - of the words themselves. It has been speculated that an expression such as *...A horse! A horse! My kingdom for a horse!...* (from *Richard III)* would have quickly passed into common parlance, as a useful way of describing a situation in which a small event or circumstance can provide a crucial tipping point for a larger event. In the same way, a Dylan line such as *...You don't need a weatherman to know which way the wind blows...* can be applied (perhaps with a 'nod and a wink') to circumstances in which signs and portents exist which may make an outcome obvious - but only to 'those in the know'. It is also true that both writers have worked within pre-existing musical and rhythmic structures. Most of Dylan's songs are based on models from the world of folk, blues, country and gospel. Similarly, Shakespeare's dramatic poetry is written in iambic pentameter, a regular form of metre designed to bring about dramatic effects in performance, rather like modern rap music. Music was very important in Shakespeare's plays and Shakespeare was an accomplished songwriter. His plays are often interspersed with musical interludes, and at the Globe, each performance - even that of a tragedy - would end in the performers joining up with the audience in a 'jig', where they would all dance and sing together to musical accompaniment. Very much, in fact, like a rock'n'roll show...

One of the key qualities of what we may call Dylan's 'sound poetry' is its theatricality. In the later live shows of the Never Ending Tour he seeks to emphasise this in terms of presentation. By the early 2000s he is appearing on stage in elaborate costumes that project a deliberately stylish 'retro' look, while his backing musicians generally wear dark, matching 'uniforms'. The ritual that is enacted at the end of every show, as he and the band stand stock still, absorbing the applause without reacting, has been likened to a 'Brechtian alienation device' (*Verfremdungseffekt)*, a technique which is intended to remind audiences of the inherent artificiality of theatrical constructs. His vocal style can also be considered to be 'theatrical'. In most of his recordings and live shows he manipulates his vocal mannerisms to 'declaim' lyrics in the manner of an actor, so that they never 'merge' - like those of more conventional vocalists - into the musical background. Thus his performances demand that listeners pay full attention to his lyrics. If one plays Dylan albums in succession it can also be observed that his singing tends to change from record to record, sometimes quite radically. On 'lighter' albums like *Nashville Skyline* (1969) or *Shadows in the Night* (2015) he demonstrates that, if the songs require it, he can actually sing quite smoothly. But it is certainly true that his often harsh vocal tones have alienated many listeners and commentators over the years. In the immensely witty speech given for his 'Musicares Person of the Year Award' in 2015 he protests, using deliberately self-deprecating rhetoric, that:

... Critics have been giving me a hard time since Day One. Critics say I can't sing. I croak. Sound like a frog. Why don't critics say that same thing about Tom Waits? Critics say my voice is shot. That I have no voice. Why don't they say those things about Leonard Cohen? Why do I get special treatment? Critics say I can't carry a tune and I talk my way through a song. Really? I've never heard that said about Lou Reed. Why does he get to go scot-free?...

In the Nobel lecture, which is presented in recorded form, accompanied by soft piano music, Dylan responds to his critics with much eloquence and dry wit. He leads the listeners off in a 'merry jig' of his own. At first he teases them with some delightfully tall stories of mystical experiences in his early youth. He repeats a story he had previously recounted in interviews of being in the audience at Buddy Holly's last ever concert appearance, at which ....*He looked me right straight dead in the eye, and he transmitted something...* and then relates how Leadbelly's *Cotton Fields* introduced him to the colourful world of *...the secrets, the mysteries...* of the folk song tradition. So far, in a way, as might be expected... *Chronicles* had been full of such tributes to his musical heroes. But then he suddenly changes tack and - adopting the tone of a dutiful student who has been asked to compose an essay - unexpectedly pays tribute to what he calls his 'grammar school reading'. He mentions three works which he claims have been key influences. His choices are rather unexpected. While one might expect him to extol the virtues of Blake, Ginsberg or Rimbaud, he begins by presenting a 'scholarly' exposition of Eric Maria Remarque's *All Quiet on the Western Front* and Herman Melville's *Moby*

Dick. His commentaries are fairly lengthy, entertaining and often slyly humorous. Ever-vigilant Dylan scholars have pointed out that he has even lifted some phrases from online versions of the 'York Notes' provided for those who are studying the novels. The connections to his own work appear, however, to be somewhat tenuous. It might be argued that the anti-war message of Remarque's novel may have had some distant impact on his early 'protest' material, and that the mordant humour and epic quality of *Moby Dick* might have had some notional influence on his songs of 1965-66. *Bob Dylan's 115th Dream* (1965) even refers to a 'Captain Arab', while its hapless central character and his cohorts are *...busted for carrying harpoons...*

Far more revealing is Dylan's exposition of the third text - Homer's *Odyssey* - the themes of which he claims to have found traces of in various folk songs, including (rather bizarrely) *Home on the Range.* His colourful summary of the famous epic poem can be seen to have some close resonances with his own 'epic journey' through various potential artistic 'pitfalls':

..The Odyssey is a strange, adventurous tale of a grown man trying to get home after fighting in a war. He's on that long journey home, and it's filled with traps and pitfalls. He's cursed to wander. He's always getting carried out to sea, always having close calls. Huge chunks of boulders rock his boat. He angers people he shouldn't. There's troublemakers in his crew. Treachery. His men are turned into pigs and then are turned back into younger, more handsome men. He's always trying to rescue somebody. He's a travelin' man, but he's making a lot of stops...

Having compared the various fantastical perils that Odysseus goes through to the universal vagaries of life, Dylan reverts to his faux-naïve persona. He maintains that the sound of words can be as important as the meaning, inferring that he himself has not always 'understood' the words he has written. He insists that *...If a song moves you, that's all that's important...* Reiterating the theme of the earlier speech, he concludes:

...Songs are unlike literature. They're meant to be sung, not read. The words in Shakespeare's plays were meant to be acted on the stage. Just as lyrics in songs are meant to be sung, not read on a page. And I hope some of you get the chance to listen to these lyrics the way they were intended to be heard: in concert or on record or however people are listening to songs these days. I return once again to Homer, who says, "Sing in me, oh Muse, and through me tell the story"...

One might argue that Dylan, with his typically perverse logic, may be leading us 'up the garden path' with his summaries of his chosen texts. But by concluding with Homer - with whom the canon of Western literature can be said to begin - he is reminding us that poetry, from its ancient origins, has most commonly been communicated to audiences through music and dramatic recitation. He might have added that Romantic poets such as Burns, Blake, Wordsworth and Coleridge often based their poems on traditional ballads, just has he frequently did on his early albums. After the award of the Nobel Prize some of his critics (few of whom were really familiar with how varied his work is) maintained that the award was not justified because his lyrics 'did not work on the page'. But in fact his major achievement has been to use modern technology, music and 'dramatic recitation' to lift complex and highly literary poetry *off* the page and restore it to the kind of relationship with a popular audience which has existed through most of the history of literature. From the moment of his first breakthrough at the age of only 21, when he composed the iconic and philosophical 'protest anthem' *Blowin' in the Wind*, Dylan has been a 'public poet', whose words have been communicated through the mass media rather than in 'slim volumes'. He has often struggled with this 'bardic' or Homeric role, especially given the unwanted media attention it has brought him. Few major literary figures have ever had to struggle with the level of intrusion into their personal lives that is associated with stardom in the modern age. And Dylan is without doubt a star. Although he has made every effort to keep his private life as secret as possible, he has been forced to live with the burdens associated with such a status for his entire adult life. As he complains, rather bitterly, in *Idiot Wind* (1975) *...People see me all the time and they just can't remember how to act/ Their minds are full of big ideas, images and distorted facts...*

Dylan has achieved particular prominence because of his gift for fusing complex uses of metaphor, allusion, alliteration and other poetic techniques with the rhythms of everyday speech. As a songwriter who relies on rhythm and rhyme, he has naturally been most influenced by pre-modernist writers whose work was constructed using a more 'musical' framework. His work is deeply grounded in his deep absorption of the entire canon of English poetry. Yet he is as much in debt to the singer-songwriters who have influenced him. He appears to hold folk, blues and country singers like Leadbelly, Robert Johnson, Blind Willie McTell, Memphis Minnie, Woody Guthrie, Johnny Cash and Hank Williams in as much veneration as the great literary artists of the past. He sees them all, quite correctly, as poets.

Much of Dylan's attitude to the role of 'public poetry' is grounded in the profound influence of the 'Beat Poets' such as Allen Ginsberg, Jack Kerouac and Gregory Corso, who first came to prominence in the 1950s. These writers adopted a radically anti-establishment stance in the midst of a very conformist era of American culture. They were part of a subculture which strongly espoused 'alternative' lifestyles. Ginsberg was openly homosexual years before the term 'gay' was in common parlance and their advocacy of the benefits of illegal psychotropic drugs was no secret. Their highly controversial and outspoken work was at first generally dismissed by the literary establishment. Ginsberg's epic of urban rage *Howl* (1956) was subjected to a major obscenity trial. Dylan and Ginsberg became firm friends. In the iconic opening sequence from *Don't Look Back*, Don Pennebaker's film of Dylan's 1965 tour of Britain, where Dylan casts away various bizarre cue cards over the soundtrack of his scatological, anti-establishment 'rap' *Subterranean Homesick Blues*, Ginsberg stands in the background like a presiding uncle looking down with approval on his generational successor. In Dylan's film *Renaldo and Clara* (1978) Dylan and Ginsberg are seen together making a pilgrimage to Kerouac's grave.

The work of the Beats was radically different to much of twentieth century poetry. They rejected the modernist approach which had been promulgated by T. S. Eliot and his successors - with its experiments in form and its often obscure intellectual word games - in favour of the dramatic use of everyday language, as epitomised by the poetry of their great hero Walt Whitman. They also experimented with spontaneous composition and were influenced by the improvisational methods of bebop performers such as Lester Young and Charlie Parker. The rhythms of their language were rooted in musical structures and their work was often performed in bohemian coffee houses and bars to an accompaniment of bebop jazz. Their aim was to democratise and popularise contemporary poetry - to return it to being a public art form rather than the preserve of a few academics. In *Desolation Row* (1965) (a title which itself referred to Kerouac's novel *Desolation Angels,* published in the same year) Dylan sums up this attitude by gently mocking the progenitors of modernism, suggesting that they are too obsessed with academic rigour to empathise with real human feelings, recognise the beauty of nature or connect with the power of imaginative creativity: *...Ezra Pound and T. S. Eliot, fighting in the Captain's Tower/ While calypso singers laugh at them, and fishermen hold flowers...*

With his iconoclastic attitude and his embrace of songwriting traditions that are not conventionally considered to be 'literary', it is hardly surprising that Dylan's relationship with the academic establishment has not always been a smooth one. A university dropout himself, he has always been rather uncomfortable around caps and gowns. This is reflected rather provocatively in some of his early songs. In *Ballad of a Thin Man* (1965) he castigates the narrow mindedness of 'Mr. Jones' for associating with 'the professors' who have, as he witheringly puts it *...been through all of F. Scott Fitzgerald's books...* In the surreal 'dreamscape' of *Tombstone Blues* (1965) he refers scathingly to how *...the National Bank at a profit sells road maps for the soul/ To the old folks' home and the college...* In 1970's *Day of the Locusts* (whose title derives from Nathaniel West's satirical 'anti-Hollywood' novel of 1939) he relates his discomfort when being awarded an honorary degree by Princeton University with a mixture of comic confusion and loathing *...The man standing next to me, his head was exploding...* he sings *...I was praying the pieces wouldn't fall on me...*

The essential nature of Dylan's ever-evolving 'sound poetry' is expressed in the 'theatrical' relationship between performer and audience, within which a fluidity of poetic meaning is created. This is part of the reason why his fans have been so dedicated to 'bootlegging' his live shows and unreleased studio outtakes. They have recognised that the greatest moments in his live performances are often those in which he is driven by pure inspiration to modify his words or to place unexpected emphasis on them. He often changes lyrics in performance or presents them in different musical settings which may subtly change their meaning. Meaning, expression and emotion can thus be said to be multifaceted, multi dimensional and continually shifting. This allows the artists who 'cover' Dylan considerable scope to find new shapes and patterns within the songs. The classic example is Jimi Hendrix's incandescent version of *All Along the Watchtower,* which transforms the song from a quietly allusive 'Biblical paradox' into a stratospheric warning of a coming apocalypse.

While it is certainly true that Dylan's success in the early 1960s made possible the emergence of many other such figures in popular music, his approach differs considerably to that of most of his major contemporaries. Some of his most prominent and highly talented peers, such as Leonard Cohen, Paul Simon or Joni Mitchell have striven hard to drive the art of poetic song towards a kind of formal perfection. Cohen was a published poet many years before he made his first record. Simon's *The Sound of Silence* and Mitchell's *Amelia* are meticulously crafted poetic songs, both using a logical pattern of imagery within an intellectually satisfying and coherent structure. They are 'finished' works of art and thus are rarely altered much in live shows. In contrast, Dylan's songs tend towards random imagery and curiously shifting patterns of emotion. In performance, meaning is created as much by his intonation and phrasing as by the words themselves. His songs prominently feature lines and phrases in which the sound of the words is an important element of their poetic quality.

An example of this occurs in *Visions of Johanna* (1966) in the unforgettable phrase *...the harmonicas play the skeleton keys and the rain...* With a comma inserted, we might read the lines as a list of evocative images: *...the harmonicas play, the skeleton keys and the rain...* If we leave out the comma, we may imagine that these (apparently disembodied) 'harmonicas' are somehow playing a song called 'The Skeleton Keys and The Rain', which sounds like a rather surreal version of some ancient folk song. But when the words are sung both meanings are equally valid. In different performances, the singer may or may not insert a pause where a comma might be. The word 'keys' may refer to actual keys used for opening doors or to musical keys. The reference to 'skeleton' takes us back to the song's most memorably haunting line *...the ghost of 'lectricity howls in the bones of her face...* The imagery resonates with the sound of the song itself, which features Dylan playing the harmonica, an instrument he characteristically uses as a counterpoint to or substitute for words. The ambiguity in such transcendent poetic juxtapositions of sound, imagery and meaning allows the singer the freedom to subtly modulate the meaning of a song in different performances. 'Sound poems' can thus be said to have an extra dimension which poems that merely remain 'on the page' do not have.

In Dylan's live shows, each song is launched upon an imaginative and interpretative journey on which it may be stretched, changed, extended, edited or inverted to give it a multiplicity of meanings. This is especially true of the songs from *Blood on the Tracks* (1975) such as *Tangled Up in Blue, If You See Her, Say Hello* and *Simple Twist of Fate*, which have been performed in many different lyrical variants. Another example is *I Want You* (1966), the recording of which features Dylan joyously skipping through a colourful if apparently unrelated series of references to characters such as a 'dancing child in a Chinese suit' and 'the Queen of Spades'. In its 1978 incarnation (captured on the *Bob Dylan at Budokan* album) the song is slow, wistful and infinitely sad, as if the narrator is running through this impressionistic catalogue of youthful exuberance with the bitter perspective of experience. Such changes are not always planned and may come about spontaneously. Dylan is notorious for not rehearsing with the musicians he works with, hoping they can respond to his own methods. In many ways this stance of submission to the whims of his own inspiration - although it originates in the influence of the Beats, with their dedication to spontaneity - is consistent with a devotion to the kind of poetic ideal espoused by Romantic poets like Blake, Shelley, Coleridge and Wordsworth. The poet is consumed by (and is at the mercy of) his own imagination, to which he willingly submits. As Wordsworth puts it in a passage from *The Prelude*:

...A correspondent breeze, that gently moved
With quickening virtue, but is now become
A tempest, a redundant energy,
Vexing its own creation. Thanks to both,
And their congenial powers, that, while they join
In breaking up a long-continued frost,
Bring with them vernal promises, the hope
Of active days urged on by flying hours,
Days of sweet leisure, taxed with patient thought
Abstruse, nor wanting punctual service high,
Matins and vespers of harmonious verse!...

Such an aesthetic is, of course, not easy to sustain. For an artist whose career has been so dedicated to the 'tempest' of the imaginative spirit, those 'days of sweet leisure', where inspiration flows so effortlessly, have not always been easy to find. In some phases of his career, Dylan has produced very little, while in others he has been extremely prolific. He has always depended on catching the 'correspondent breeze' of natural inspiration. In his younger years, his connection to this ineffable source of inspiration often appeared to be completely unconscious, as if he was 'channelling' words which had come to him from some 'higher source'. But as he has grown older, he has been through many periods in which these 'channels' have not always been open. Like so many poets before him he has needed to make conscious appeals to the muses - the Ancient Greek goddesses of artistic inspiration - for assistance. Such invocations are common throughout the history of Western literature. They typically appear at the beginnings of works. *The Odyssey* (Peter Green's translation) begins:

...The man, Muse - tell me about that resourceful man, who wandered
Far and wide, when he'd sacked Troy's sacred citadel:
Many men's townships he saw, and learned their ways of thinking,
Many the griefs he suffered at heart on the open sea,
Battling for his own life and his comrades' homecoming....

Dylan makes such an invocation in *Mother of Muses*, from 2020's *Rough and Rowdy Ways.* With its stately, sonorous tune, its address to a 'higher being' and its plea for redemption, the song is constructed in the mode of a 'pagan hymn'. In some ways it bears a resemblance to Dylan's recordings of *O Come All Ye Faithful* and *Little Town of Bethlehem* on his 2009 charity album *Christmas in the Heart.* It is delivered with the same unashamed lack of irony as a sincere expression of faith - not in the Christian God but in the spirit of creativity. Its resonant melody recalls the soul classic *The Dark End of the Street*, a moving tale of 'forbidden love' written by Dan Penn and Chips Moman and originally recorded by James Carr in 1967. The musical backing is sparse - featuring a slightly Latin flavoured acoustic guitar played by Blake Mills and subdued hand-held percussion.

The song is addressed to Mnemosyne the Greek Titaness who, after mating with Zeus gave birth to nine daughters, all representing different facets of the arts: Calliope (epic poetry), Clio (history), Euterpe (music), Erato (lyric poetry), Melpomene (tragedy), Polyhymnia (hymns), Terpischore (dance), Thalia (comedy) and Urania (astronomy). Mnemosyne (which in Ancient Greek means 'memory') was also the name of one of the rivers of the underworld. She was the mother of the mythical poet Orpheus, who was worshipped in the Orphic religion, initiates of which believed in transmigration - the belief that a soul can pass from one person to another, either through reincarnation or by other means. Drinking from the river of memory would ensure that the devotee's soul could avoid such a fate in order to spend a blissful eternity with Orpheus and other great heroes. Drinking from the other river of the underworld Lethe (the river of oblivion) would wipe out all the memories and condemn the individual to more and more reincarnations within what was regarded as the 'prison house' of the human body.

In *Mother of Muses* Dylan gives thanks to the spirit who has provided him with new inspiration and humbly requests that the memory of his work be preserved. The song has six verses, each consisting of three rhyming couplets, with lines of roughly ten syllables each - the traditional metre of iambic pentameter. The language is very clear and direct. The first verse begins and the first three verses end with the invocation: *...Mother of muses, sing for me...* The first verse addresses Mnemosyne directly, imploring her and 'the women of the chorus' to sing in praise of a natural but mythical landscape, of the *...mountains and the deep dark sea...* and *...the lakes and the nymphs of the forest...* Dylan also requests that she sing of *...honor and fame and glory be...* In *The Odyssey* it is the pursuit of glory and honour that motivates Odysseus. If he can achieve these goals his fame will last beyond his death, making him 'immortal' like the gods.

Dylan humbly acknowledges his own mortality, imploring Mnemosyne and her choir to *... sing for my heart/ Sing of a love too soon to depart...* He then requests that she honour *...the heroes who stood alone/ Whose names were engraved on tablets of stone...* implying that the process of 'engraving' gave those heroes the kind of immortality he wishes to share. He then provides us with a list of such heroes. It may be surprising that the author of *Masters of War* and *With God on Our Side* now appears to venerate famous generals - firstly *...Sherman, Montgomery and Scott...* (all of whom fought for the Union against the Confederacy in the American Civil War) and then *...Zhukov and Patton...* (the leading Soviet and American generals in World War Two) but in the context of this song he appears to be defining heroism very much as the Ancient Greeks would have done. These generals are, after all, the modern equivalents of Greek military heroes such as Achilles, Hector and Agamemnon. He follows this with another somewhat unexpected assertion that these generals *...cleared the path for Presley to sing...* and *...carved out the path for Martin Luther King...* two modern 'heroes' who represented freedom of expression in very different ways. The broad sweep of history in these few lines is quite remarkable, but the verse ends almost casually, with Dylan sighing *...They did what they did and they went on their way/ Man, I could tell their stories all day...*

Dylan now makes a request to Mnemosyne: *...I've fallen in love with Calliope/ She doesn't belong to anyone - why not give her to me?...* deliberately extending the line here as he implores the mother of the muses to allow him to 'possess' the muse of epic poetry. The following highly evocative lines are whispered in awe: *...She's speaking to me, speaking with her eyes/ I've grown so tired of chasing lies...* Thus he implies that the gift of inspiration - which the ethereal Calliope (the muse of both Homer and Virgil) will supply - is transmitted in some mystical, non verbal way. He then humbles himself even more by admitting that *...I've already outlived my life by far...* It is this devotion to searching for the sources of inspiration which has kept him 'alive' artistically. He thus bows before the awesome power of Mnemosyne, asking her to *...unleash her wrath...* implying that he is prepared to withstand whatever fate she has in store for him *...Show me your wisdom, tell me my fate...* he implores her *...Put me upright, make me walk straight/ Forge my identity from the inside out....* He places his soul and his fate in her hands.

In the final verse the singer is truly down on his knees. He glories in the poetic power which his devotion to Mnemosyne (and, perhaps, his 'arranged marriage' to Calliope) has supplied him with. Having drunk from the river of memory, he begins to quote lines from songs which have inspired him. He implores Mnemosyne to *...release your charms/ Let me lay down in your sweet lovin' arms...* as if, perhaps, he wishes to conceive more muses with her. These lines recall Elvis Presley's anguished *Lovin' Arms* (1972) in which the singer imagines connubial bliss which he will never experience *...Wake me, shake me, free me from sin...* refers to a lively 1960 doo-wop song recorded by The Coasters. Drinking from the river of memory was said by the Orphics to wash away a person's sins. He asks Mnemosyne to *...Make me invisible like the wind...* so that he can be 'transfigured' into pure essence - and unified in spirit with the muses. Then his spirit - and thus his creativity - can be free to 'roam' wherever it will. He declares that he has *...Got a mind to ramble, got a mind to roam...* quoting the title of a defiantly sexual blues song by Alberta Hunter from 1950. In the final line *...I'm travelin' light and I'm slow coming home...* he pays tribute to Leonard Cohen, using the titles of three of his songs from his final three albums: *Travelin' Light* (2016), *Slow* (2014) and *Coming Home* (2012). Cohen died of cancer in 2016, just after the release of his last album *You Want it Darker* and presumably was quite aware in his final years that his end was imminent. By compressing these song titles into a single line, it seems that Dylan is suggesting that the soul of his fellow musical poet has been 'transfigured' to become a part of his own consciousness. With the help of his great contemporary, he can now 'travel light' with a new kind of poetic freedom.

In *I Contain Multitudes,* the opening track on *Rough and Rowdy Ways*, Dylan proudly presents himself as a bardic figure, while exploring many of the personal difficulties such a role implies. Like the Nobel lecture (which it resembles in tone and delivery) it explores the relationship between a supposedly insecure 'public poet' and his audience. It takes the form of a softly spoken recitation with minimal backing consisting of a repeated plucked acoustic guitar figure and some extremely restrained 'orchestration' provided by Donnie Herron's washes of pedal steel. The six verses and two linking bridges and the taut lyrical expressions build up to the repetition of the all-encompassing refrain. Dylan's delivery is restrained and dignified throughout. The song shifts back and forth between narrative voices, the most dominant being the voice of a rather self-pitying narrator, whose half-hearted appeals to a lover will inevitably fall on deaf ears, and the voice of Dylan himself. The narrator tries, at least at first, to win our sympathy. Adopting a particularly humble tone, he insists throughout that he is merely a flawed human being. He pays tribute to William Blake and Edgar Allan Poe but he does not presume to compare himself to either of them. There is, however, an implied comparison to Walt Whitman, who, in his 'American epic' *Song of Myself*, places himself in a bardic role as the personification of the American nation. In Section 51 of the poem Whitman explains that, although he - like America itself - may be full of contradictions, he is happy to embrace them:

...The past and present wilt—I have fill'd them, emptied them.
Listener up there! what have you to confide to me?
And proceed to fill my next fold of the future.

Look in my face while I snuff the sidle of evening,
(Talk honestly, no one else hears you, and I stay only a minute longer.)
Do I contradict myself?
Very well then I contradict myself,
(I am large, I contain multitudes)...

The song begins with a broad philosophical statement: *...Today and tomorrow and yesterday too/ The flowers are dyin', like all things do...* Dylan caresses the words tentatively, with a tone of wistful regret. The narrator then makes his first direct address, presumably to his potential lover. He appears to be proposing a romantic journey: *...Follow me close, I'm going to Ballinalee...* referring to an Irish village which features in *The Lass from Ballinalee*, an early nineteenth century Gaelic poem by Anthony Raftery *...I'll lose my mind if you don't come with me...* he pleads. The village is never mentioned again but it appears to represent a place of escape from the contradictions that the song will outline. We are then presented with the first of the clashing images that will dominate the narrative: *...I fuss with my hair and I fight blood feuds/ I contain multitudes...* This appears to be the voice of Dylan himself, who is indeed frequently seen 'fussing with his hair' and who has written many songs which can be said to have engaged with political or psychological 'blood feuds' *...Got a tell tale heart like Mr. Poe/ Got skeletons in the walls of people you know....* alludes to two of Edgar Allan Poe's best known gothic horror stories, *The Tell Tale Heart* and *The Cask of Amontillado,* both of which involve the victims of murders being walled up or buried under floorboards, suggesting that the narrator has some dark secrets that he would rather keep from us. He then piles on the rhetorical self-pity: *...I'll drink to the truth and the things we said/ I'll drink to the man who shares your bed...* It is obvious by now that the lover he addressed in the first verse won't be accompanying him to Ballinalee or anywhere else in the near future. In another delightfully compressed phrase he states that *...I paint landscapes, I paint nudes/ I contain multitudes...* In real life, Dylan himself is indeed an artist who has worked in both mediums.

The language of the song is crisp and carefully constructed. A distinctively visual couplet follows: *...A red Cadillac and a black moustache/ Rings on my fingers that sparkle and flash...* The reference to the Warren Smith rockabilly nugget, which Dylan covers so memorably for a Sun Records tribute compilation, is appropriate as the song being referred to relies very much on self-deprecating humour. Our narrator, like the singer in *Red Cadillac*, has apparently lost his girl to a more 'impressive' male. It appears that - despite his 'sparking rings' - he is admitting his inadequacy. He makes another appeal to his lover, but is full of uncertainty: *...Tell me what's next, what shall we do/ Half my soul belongs to you...* But the idea that he could ever be any kind of 'constant lover' is questionable. With all his inbuilt contradictions, it seems that he cannot commit more than 'half' of himself. He also freely admits that he is prone to reckless indulgence: *...I rollick and I frolic with all the young dudes...* he sighs, referring here to David Bowie's 'teen rebellion' anthem *All the Young Dudes,* a hit for Mott the Hoople in 1973. By now the narrative modes are beginning to dissolve. It is becoming impossible to tell where the voice of the fictional narrator ends and that of Dylan begins.

In the first bridge section, the narrator presents some bizarre juxtapositions: *...I'm just like Anne Frank, like Indiana Jones/ And them British bad boys the Rolling Stones...* The comparison between the mundane but terrifying reality recorded in Anne Frank's diary and the ridiculous fantasies of Steven Spielberg's blockbusters is arguably rather tasteless but here the narrator is presenting himself as a very imperfect mixture of the saintly, the adventurous and the disreputable. He admits that he can be both serious and superficial - apparently viewing fact and fantasy as equally valid: *...I go right to the edge, I go right to the end...* he tells us *....I go right to where all things lost are made good again...* He is an adventurer, and is prepared to take risks, but only up to a point. But he is proud of his embrace of his contradictions *...I sing the songs of experience like William Blake....* he states dryly *...I have no apologies to make...* This 'high minded' statement from the 'public poet' is contrasted with a very mundane 'confession': *...I drive fast cars/ I eat fast foods....* The narrator is, like Whitman, presenting himself as a very flawed 'everyman' figure *...I'm a man of contradictions...* he tells us *...I'm a man of many moods...*

We are then presented with more odd contrasts*: ...Pink pedal pushers, red blue jeans/ All the pretty maids and all the old queens... Pink Pedal Pushers* (1958) is a song by Carl Perkins, whose contemporary Gene Vincent released a song called *Red Bluejeans and a Ponytail* (1957). 'All the pretty maids' is a line from a nursery rhyme, while the reference to 'old queens' appears to refer, in a rather affectionately tongue-in-cheek way, to the aged gay men (like Whitman and Ginsberg) who have influenced him. In a bizarre narrative shift he proclaims that *...I carry four pistols and two large knives...* The reference is to a description by Ward Hill Lamon, one of Abraham Lincoln's bodyguards, to how he regularly armed himself. The narrator appears to be implying that he often becomes paranoid about the 'threat' posed by those who wish to attack him. One is reminded of the overtly cryptic and defensive stance Dylan has been known to take in interviews. Lamon's weapons did not, of course, prevent Lincoln being assassinated.

In the second bridge section, we are in 'fairy tale' territory: *...You greedy old wolf...* Dylan sings *...I'll show you my heart/ But not all of it, only the hateful part...* We may wonder if this 'wicked wolf' has been watching and listening the whole time, perhaps waiting for a moment to pounce *...I'll sell you down the river...* the narrator threatens... *I'll put a price on your head...* It is hard to know whether he is still addressing the 'wicked wolf,' who embodies his paranoia, or whether he is threatening his estranged lover with some kind of betrayal. Then, in one of the song's most remarkable lines, he confesses *...What more can I tell you? I sleep with life and death in the same bed...* This is another expressly gothic image, recalling the 'zombie' character of Life-in-Death in Coleridge's *Ancient Mariner.* The narrator's self-pity now turns to spite. Finally he addresses his lover in no uncertain terms: *...Get up off my knee/ Keep your mouth away from me...* But then he contradicts himself again, declaring that *...I'll keep the path open, the path in my mind...* and that *...I'll see to it that there's no love left behind...* Finally he ties it all up by telling us *...I'll play Beethoven's sonatas and Chopin's preludes...* Despite his equivocal response to the object of the song, whether it be a lover or a listener, he declares that can still conclude his rather contradictory and confused appeal with a considerable flourish. He thus assures us that, despite whatever self-doubts he may have, his creativity will remain intact.

In *I Contain Multitudes* Dylan uses an appeal to his anonymous lover to explain the contradictions of his role as a 'public poet'. As listeners we may imagine (at least at times) that it is us who he is addressing. After unsuccessfully attempting to entice us to join him on a magical romantic journey, he then tries to push us away. It is left to us to decide whether we can accept the paradoxes that are presented with. Dylan appears to be suggesting that, although we may admire his work (as so many of us do) to the point of adulation, he is ultimately just a flawed human being - perhaps even a spoiled, over-indulgent 'bad boy' who is uncertain about his own talents and his role as a public figure. While he appears to embrace Whitman's aesthetic, and pays fulsome tribute to Blake and Poe as his literary forebears, he also 'confesses' that he engages in many 'vulgar' pursuits and habits. The tone of the song, however, is always playfully ironic. In inhabiting this flawed persona Dylan employs a classic rhetorical trick. He may demand that we 'keep our mouths away' from him - to refrain, perhaps, from speaking so many words of praise - but he is also, with a sigh, a shrug of his shoulders and perhaps a sly wink, reaching out for reassurance, asking for our love.

3rd April 1992. A steaming hot night in Melbourne, Australia. The crowd in the beautiful old Palais Theatre is all fired up, really going for the loud, energetic rock 'n' roll being pumped out from the stage. It's a Friday night, they've sunk a few tubes and they're feeling like letting off some steam. And why not? After all, this kind of event doesn't happen that often down under. And besides, this guy is a legend. OK, he may not have had any hits for a few years and, to be honest, he looks a little bit past his sell by date. He's got this really bizarre little white trilby hat on, which kind of shades out his face, and some smelly old shapeless brown check jacket he must surely have picked up in an op shop downtown. He hasn't even bothered to say hello to the audience. But one thing is certain - his band can really kick some shit! They start with that old number Hendrix used to do *...Must be some way out of here...* Whew! From there on, you wouldn't complain. Hard to tell which song is which, though... None of 'em sounds anything like they used to. Even that slow smoochy country style one about the moons and the spoons is done really fast. The man himself doesn't move around much, except to wiggle his left leg a little now and again. He squints suspiciously and spits all the words out in a sort of sneer from the corner of his mouth, making sure that there's no way the audience can turn this into any kind of 'sing-a-long'. Ornery bugger that he is...

Now we come to the quiet bit of the show. Most of the musicians file offstage, leaving only the singer and his bass player. Time for a bit of a breather, maybe. A few people grab the chance to get to the bar. Perhaps not such a bad idea, but... an expectant silence descends. He steps up to the microphone and gives a funny little cough, ignoring all the requests being shouted out, not to mention a few aspersions on his paternity. This is Melbourne, after all. His eyes are cast down, like he's focusing on some invisible spot in front of him, as if his body's on stage but his mind is off somewhere else. He begins to strum a simple, unfamiliar chord sequence. It's a bit off-key, a bit clunky. Doesn't sound like one of the old hits, but you never know. One thing's for sure, if he does that one about the times-a-changin' everyone will go ape-shit.

When he opens his mouth, his voice rises and falls in a rather weird way with every word *...Come all you maids both near and far and listen to my ditty...* he begins, pausing before taking his final breath, putting an odd little bit of emphasis on the last word. You never heard anything quite like it. Then his voice drops almost to a whisper: *...'Twas near Gravesend there lived a maid/ She was so neat and pretty...* This time he stretches the last word over three syllables. Suddenly he sounds terribly weary, like he's pissed off with the world and he's on the verge of bursting out into tears. The whole auditorium has gone deathly quiet. The low murmur of chat that had begun after the band went off has suddenly ceased. Even those on the way to the bar have stopped to turn and stare.

Though he may look like a shabby little bastard, right now you just can't take your eyes off him.

The next line *...Her true love he was pressed away...* seems to come out very quickly. But then he lets himself linger over *...And drownded in some foreign sea...* He stretches the word 'foreign' over four syllables. He sings in a weirdly jerky way, as if he really is being tossed about in a rough storm: *...Which caused this fair maid to say/ "I'll be a rambling sailor"...* A few seconds ago, he'd sounded so bloody sad, now he sounds kind of downbeat, offhand... or maybe he's just bottling it all up. He barely pauses before he's into the next line, pronouncing each word with that weirdly random diction again, his voice going up and down like a jack-in-the-box: *...With trousers blue and jacket white/ Just like a sailor neat and tight...*

You can only say it's bizarre. With the old fashioned lingo, this is obviously some ancient sea shanty, the usual kind of stuff about girl loses boy, girl dresses up as a boy, goes off to sea, gets into a lot of fights. Eventually she slips down off the rigging and she's a goner. Bloody shame and all that. The kind of thing you get blokes with froth on their beards knocking out in pubs everywhere. But never like this... Dylan is handling it just like a jazz singer, playing around with the tempo at will. It's like he's *discovering* the words as he sings them. You really have no idea what will come next, and you get the feeling that he doesn't either. Then suddenly the line *...Never did her courage fail/ Through stormy seas and wintry gales...* seems to come out in one long, concentrated breath. Strewth! It's so bloody moving, you just can't help thinking that in some strange way he's identifying *himself* with the poor old girl. But then we come to the *really* sad part. *...Her hand it slipped and down she fell/ She calmly bid this world farewell...* there's just a tiny pause after 'calmly', a slight quaver over 'bid'. There's a sort of desperation in his voice. A kind of yearning for something utterly lost, some kind of magic that can never be recovered. Lost love, perhaps. Lost youth, maybe... Dammit, you just can't put your finger on it. But when he delivers *...The roses sweet grow at the feet/ Of the one who was undaunted...* bloody hell, God knows why, but you really just want to *cry...*

In the early years of the Never Ending Tour, during which he released no original material, Bob Dylan often tested the patience of his fans. Fronting a musically minimal three piece band, he would tear through his back catalogue at considerable speed. He rarely spoke to the audience. At times it was difficult to tell which song was which. Dressed in scruffy, ill-fitting clothes, he sometimes spent entire shows staring down at the floor while he mumbled the lyrics. The set lists, along with the quality of the performances, would vary greatly from night to night. It was not uncommon that the only songs he appeared to really focus on were cover versions, although at times he appeared to be playing them unrehearsed. The musicians were forced to try to read his whims and follow along with whatever he tried to do. In the late '80s and 1990s he tried out hundreds of covers, many of which he would only play once or twice. They consisted mainly of traditional folk, blues, rock'n'roll and country songs, along with a smattering of the work of contemporary songwriters like Leonard Cohen, Neil Young and Gordon Lightfoot. Some of these songs appeared on *Good as I Been to You* and *World Gone Wrong*, the two solo acoustic albums of traditional folk and blues material released in 1992 and 1993.

Female Rambling Sailor was one of the 'trad folk' covers, such as *Little Moses, Lady of Carlisle, The Golden Vanity* and *Trail of the Buffalo*, which Dylan tried out in the acoustic sets on the 1992 tour of Australia and New Zealand. The song was only performed six times, four of which were on this tour. On several occasions he appeared to forget the lyrics, or get them mixed up. On this particular night, however, he turns such failings dramatically to his advantage. Half way through the penultimate verse, he falters. Instead of continuing to sing, he just carries on strumming. We have reached the point in the narrative where it is revealed that the sailor who has fallen to her death is called Rebecca Young. The next lines are supposed to run ...*Come all ye maids both near and far/ And listen to my story/ Her body's anchored in the ground/ Let's hope she's wrapped in glory...* But Dylan appears to have forgotten them.

He carries on strumming uncertainly on the guitar for a few seconds, then finally he combines the second half of the previous verse with the second half of the final verse, with its somewhat downbeat conclusion: ...*On the River Thames she's known quite well/ No sailors there can she excel/ Let one tear fall as a last farewell/ To the female rambling sailor...* As the performance ends with more tentative strumming, the final chords seem to hang in the air uncertainly. The crowd seems to need to take a great collective in breath. It's almost as if they don't really know why they're responding so rapturously. In this strange moment of uncertainty, singer and audience are united in one of those rare, mysterious instances of collusion which can turn performance art into something awe-inspiring and unforgettable. And it is a fact that, at this crucial juncture in the song, Dylan has had no choice but to improvise that makes this moment so compelling. It is as if he is communicating a feeling that is so ineffable that it can never be truly put into words. A moment, perhaps, of truly spiritual grace...

Despite the apparently detached historical context of the song, Dylan seems to have chosen to perform it because it expresses particular emotions he could relate to. This was made more explicit just before he presented the song (word perfect this time) on the following night in Melbourne. Just as he strums the opening chords, he gives the audience a rare introduction: *...Ah... this is a song about a sailor...* he mumbles *...I kinda identify with this...* This might have seemed a very odd thing to say, coming as it does before a performance of an obscure eighteenth century seafaring ballad. Yet Dylan's close engagement with the song (as compared with his relative disengagement with much of his own material that night) and his sympathetic yet unsentimental delivery seems to suggest that he really does identify himself strongly with the protagonist. Here is a character in disguise, whose real identity is 'locked up neat and tight', limited by the constraints of conventional society but determined not to let this hold her back. Through her 'rambling' she has discovered the kind of freedom she presumably would never have experienced at home. Like Rebecca, Dylan seems to be abandoning himself to whatever fate will deliver. He is sailing off in disguise on a voyage to unknown lands, in search of his muse.

Female Rambling Sailor is strangely morally ambivalent, although the hesitant sentiments at the end seem to be significant. We are never told whether Rebecca is a virtuous person or not. The line *...Let's hope she's wrapped in glory...* which Dylan, on that night in Melbourne, somehow cannot bring himself to deliver, only offers hope for her salvation, rather than certainty. The 'flawed' performance, with its awkward, stuttering guitar lines and strangely uncertain delivery, eloquently conveys the sensation of a soul suspended in a strange kind of purgatorial space. This is a feeling which would later be explored in more detail on *Time Out of Mind. Female Rambling Sailor* is about courage in the face of adversity and squaring up to the ultimately tragic nature of life itself. Its protagonist accepts her fate without demur, and hopes that her virtues will eventually exonerate her. She's trying to get to heaven, perhaps, before they close the door.

Chronicles Vol. One, the bulk of which concerns Dylan's early years in Greenwich Village, cannot be taken literally as a 'factual' autobiographical text. With its non-chronological structure and highly impressionistic descriptions, it may be better described as an exploration of how memories can be reconstructed. The book took many by surprise because of its clarity and accessibility. Dylan's only previous piece of extended prose, the 'novel' *Tarantula* (written in 1965-66), was a barely comprehensible text heavily influenced by the 'cut up' techniques and prose improvisations of the Beat writers, especially William Burroughs. The prose style of *Chronicles* is, in contrast, characterised by short, punchy sentences and much ironic humour. It bears little relation to Dylan's lyric writing, although it has been shown that - as with his late period songwriting - some of the phrases used in the book have been 'borrowed' from a range of sources. There are many amusing descriptions of the characters he was hanging out with in his early, heady days, ranging from Billy the Butcher - a singer who could only perform one song - to Tiny Tim, who sang 1920s romantic standards in a high, whiny voice.

Few would expect Dylan to produce a conventional autobiography, but the amount of detail that is left out in *Chronicles* is very significant. There is little focus on his personal life. He makes a couple of fleeting references to his wives, who are never named, and none at all to his children. There is no mention of his experiences with drugs or his religious conversion or beliefs. No accounts are given of how he 'went electric' or of his tours with The Band. There are only limited allusions to his early life in Hibbing and his experiences in the folk clubs in Minneapolis. Although Dylan takes us back and forth through time and he describes many personal encounters, the main thrust of the book is devoted to explaining how he absorbed a vast amount of literary, musical and artistic influences in order to create a unique style of his own. He can, however, certainly be described as an unreliable narrator. Dylan scholars have pointed out that the characters of Ray Gooch and Chloe Keil, who he describes in some depth and claims he lived with in Greenwich Village, are almost certainly invented.

Dylan's accounts of his encounters with the playwright Archibald MacLeish and the producer Daniel Lanois in the chapters devoted to the recording of *New Morning* (1970) and *Oh Mercy* (1989) also appear to be full of colourfully 'imagined' detail. In *New Morning* little information is given about the recording of the album. Most of the chapter consists of an account of his unsuccessful attempt to write songs for a play that MacLeish had written. In *Oh Mercy* he writes about meeting producer Daniel Lanois and the recording of *Everything is Broken*, *Dignity*, *Disease of Conceit*, *Ring Them Bells* and *Man in the Long Black Coat*. But the most revealing sections of the chapter are his decidedly 'poetic' descriptions of the series of 'revelations' that led to him launching the Never Ending Tour. He is unsparing in his own depictions of the creative void he seemed to be trapped in by the late 1980s. In *New Morning*, he recounts the almost intolerable burdens that had been placed on him because of his role as a public poet. He describes how his post-motorbike-accident 'retreat' to a mostly rural area of upstate New York, which began in 1966, was an attempt to escape from the trappings of stardom. This was a period in which he had been acclaimed as an iconic hero by the burgeoning counterculture. He describes how difficult it was for him to blend in with ordinary life, even in such a relatively remote location as Woodstock. He is highly scathing about obsessive followers who turned up at his house expecting him to provide some kind of pronouncements of great wisdom and waxes lyrical about his hatred of the label of 'spokesman for his generation':

...Whatever the counterculture was, I'd seen enough of it. I was sick of the way my lyrics had been extrapolated, their meanings subverted into polemics, and that I had been appointed as the Big Bubba of Rebellion, High Priest of Protest, the Czar of Dissent, the Duke of Disobedience, Leader of the Freeloaders, Kaiser of Apostasy, Archbishop of Anarchy, the Big Cheese...

The influence of Woody Guthrie's semi-fictionalised memoir *Bound for Glory* (1943) on *Chronicles* is profound. Both books are primarily celebrations of the joys of American music. Guthrie writes in a similarly intimate way and is also extremely 'selective' about the real events of his life. Jack Kerouac's *On the Road* (1957) is also a major stylistic inspiration, especially in its ecstatic descriptions of bebop jazz as played by musicians such as Lester Young, Charlie Parker and Dizzy Gillespie. In *Chronicles* Dylan eulogises both books. He writes of *Bound for Glory* that *...I went through it cover to cover like a hurricane totally focused on every word, and the book sang out to me like the radio...* His real life meetings with Guthrie in Brooklyn State Hospital in 1961 are rather glossed over. He does, however, describe his excitement at seeing the houses in New York in which Walt Whitman and Edgar Allan Poe lived. In the long second chapter *The Lost Land*, set in Greenwich Village in the early 1960s, he describes in detail his passion for literature - and for poetry in particular - mainly through describing the contents of Ray and Chloe's extremely eclectic book shelves.

Perhaps the most memorable elements of *Chronicles* are Dylan's distinctive tributes to his musical influences. After attending a performance of songs by Bertolt Brecht and Kurt Weill he tells us he *...was aroused straight away by the raw intensity of the songs... they were erratic, unrhythmical and herky-jerky - weird visions...* He explains how Brecht's song *Pirate Jenny* motivates him to pick out stories from newspapers and begin writing topical material. When he watches folk singer Dave Van Ronk perform he feels he is *...sitting at the feet of a timeworn monument...* His early hero Hank Williams sings with *...a voice like a beautiful horn...* Woody Guthrie has a *...fierce poetic soul - the poet of hard crust sod and gumbo mud...* Roy Orbison sounds like he is *...singing from an Olympian mountain top...* In the songs of the Clancy Brothers the language is *...flash and provocative - a lot of action in the words, all sung with great gusto...* Harry Belafonte is *...that rare kind of character who radiates greatness, and you hope that some of it rubs off on you...* Songwriter Harold Arlen's songs inhabit a *...bittersweet, lonely, intense world...* Joan Baez is said to sing ... *in a voice straight to God...* while in Frank Sinatra's voice he hears *...death, God, the universe, everything...* When he comes to pay tribute to Johnny Cash, his imagination really takes flight:

...Johnny didn't have a piercing yell, but ten thousand years of culture fell from him. He could have been a cave dweller. He sounds like he's at the edge of a fire, or in the deep snow, or in a ghostly forest, the coolness of conscious obvious strength...

In expressing what his first experience of hearing Robert Johnson meant to him, Dylan sounds even more awed. He compares the great blues singer to nothing less than an Ancient Greek god:

...The vibrations from the loudspeaker made my hair stand up. The stabbing sounds from the guitar could almost break a window. When Johnson started singing he seemed like a guy who could have sprung from the head of Zeus in full armour...

Between 2002 and 2013 Bob Dylan's performances were preceded by a 'potted biography' read by his stage manager, the distinctively hirsute Al Santos:

...Ladies and gentlemen, please welcome the poet laureate of rock 'n' roll. The voice of the promise of the Sixties counter-culture. The guy who forced folk into bed with rock, who donned make-up in the Seventies and disappeared into a haze of substance abuse... Who re-emerged to find Jesus. Who was written off as a has-been by the end of the Eighties, and who suddenly shifted gears, releasing some of the strongest music of his career, beginning in the late Nineties...

The intro was taken almost verbatim from an article written by a journalist, Jeff Miers, for the *Buffalo News* in August 2002. Presumably Dylan must have picked up a copy of this paper when on tour and found it rather amusing. He never made any public comment on it, leaving the audience to decide whether its summary of his career is accurate or not. By now, as he was appearing in distinctively 'retro' stage costumes and ending his shows with the Brechtian 'stone face' device, the announcement seemed to be a good fit with his new, ironically theatrical, methods of stage presentation. Despite its use of journalistic cliché, it does present a reasonably concise summary of Dylan's career. In the decades since his emergence, Dylan has indeed filled the role of 'poet laureate of rock and roll'. His early work included many song-poems of love and loss, exploring complex emotions. In these songs - which were heavily influenced by the emotional realism of country music songwriters like Hank Williams and Johnny Cash - understatement and an economical use of language were prominent. *One Too Many Mornings, Boots of Spanish Leather* and *Mama You Been on My Mind* looked back on past relationships not with yearning or regret but with a kind of stoical acceptance. In *Girl from the North Country* and *Bob Dylan's Dream* he presents poignant romantic evocations of memory, while *Don't Think Twice, It's All Right*'s protagonist analyses a doomed relationship with philosophical grace.

The role of 'poet laureate' is a bardic one, in which the laureate is expected to write on matters of public interest. Dylan rose to fame largely because of the spellbinding impact of his songs of political and social protest of 1963-64. He was acclaimed by denizens of the left wing, anti-establishment 'folk music movement' in the USA - such as the veteran singer/activist Pete Seeger - as being the most powerful new voice expressing their world view. Against the background of the burgeoning Civil Rights movement, Dylan's *Oxford Town, Only a Pawn in Their Game* and *The Lonesome Death of Hattie Carroll* were eloquently expressed and devastatingly ironic exposes of the effects of racism in American society. In the midst of the most dangerous phase of the Cold War, his powerfully evocative and moving geo-political 'protest songs' expressed the feelings of youth in a world which was in turmoil, and possibly on the brink of ultimate destruction, with righteous anger. The deadpan black humour of *Talkin' World War III Blues* exposes the absurd logic of the Cold War era. The polemical *With God on Our Side* viciously deconstructs the conventional view of American history and the way that religion is used to justify war. *Masters of War* brings down poetic wrath on the machinations of the military-industrial complex in no uncertain terms. The anthemic *Blowin' in The Wind* asks fundamental and universal questions about political and social corruption and inequality. Most impressive of all is the epic ballad *A Hard Rain's a-Gonna Fall*, written around the time of the 1962 Cuban Missile Crisis, when the nuclear standoff between the USA and the Soviet Union reached its most dangerous point. The song's presentation of an apocalyptic scenario consists of an extraordinarily intense cavalcade of highly evocative and sometimes surreal poetic imagery. Dylan's appearances at the March on Washington in 1963 and the 1963 and 1964 Newport Folk Festivals - the major public gatherings of the folk movement - as well as his personal liaison with 'folk queen' Joan Baez - further cemented his position as the 'voice of a generation'.

It is also true that Dylan 'forced folk into bed with rock'. He was soon was to abandon the persona which had made him famous, that of a folk troubadour backed up only by his own acoustic guitar and harmonica. He had embraced that role in celebration of his idol Woody Guthrie, even though he had first been inspired to play music as a teenager by the explosive rock and roll of Elvis Presley and Little Richard. Inspired - like most popular musicians of his generation - by the fearlessly dynamic way in which The Beatles had rejuvenated rock music, Dylan began experimenting with new song forms. One of The Beatles' biggest hits in the US in 1964 was the ecstatic and incredibly catchy *She Loves You*, with its defiantly optimistic refrain of *...Yeah, yeah, yeah...* One of Dylan's first responses to the cultural explosion that the Beatles caused was a song which, on the surface, was a very spiky rejection of a cloying and over-possessive lover. As well as being an 'answer song' to *She Loves You*, it could also easily be interpreted as an impassioned denial of the role of 'saviour' that many were already attaching to him *...You say you're lookin' for someone/ Who's never weak but always strong...* he sang, in a sneering tone *...to protect you and defend you/ Whether you are right or wrong/ Someone to open each and every door/ But it ain't me, babe/ No, no, no, it ain't me babe....*

By 1965, Dylan had already begun recording with rock musicians. His subsequent tours of 1965-66, backed by a loud, scruffy, group later to find fame as The Band, were confrontational affairs at which angry 'fans' organised mass protests, booing and catcalls whenever he strapped on an electric guitar. A particular vocal minority regarded both his change of musical style and his move away from explicitly political lyrics as nothing less than a 'sell out' to commercial values. Dylan's most iconoclastic moment in popular music history occured in the legendary climax to his show at the Manchester Free Trade Hall in 1966 when a disenchanted 'fan' accuses him of being a 'Judas'. Dylan's response, which is captured at the climax of Martin Scorsese's 2005 film *No Direction Home*, is to raise the volume of the music even louder *...I don't believe you!...* he cries, then launches into a witheringly powerful version of *Like a Rolling Stone*, a song which begins as a vicious 'put down' of a spoiled and pampered starlet but then turns the pointed question *...How does it feel... to be out on your own, like a complete unknown, like a rolling stone...* into a celebration of the way that a substantial section of his generation had decided to forge a life style which was very different to that of their forebears.

The assertion that Dylan was 'the voice of the promise of the sixties counter-culture' is more problematical. His 'protest' songs had been so far reaching in their impact that he was acclaimed as being more than a poet - he was seen as a prophet or a saviour, the embodiment of youth and all its discontents. It soon became clear, however, that Dylan was becoming increasingly uncomfortable being cast in such a role. The assassination of President John F. Kennedy in November 1963 scared him. He wanted to be seen as an artist, not a politician. And he certainly did not wish to become a martyr. He gave up any direct engagement with political events. He was never glimpsed at any of the anti-Vietnam marches that grew in size as the 1960s swelled into a cultural battleground between the mainstream and the counterculture. His public stance would continue to remain defiantly in opposition both to the conventions of show business and to those who wished to pigeon hole him into a particular ideological role or musical style. From 1964 onwards he abandoned directly 'political' song writing. The songs on his 1965-66 trilogy *Bringing It All Back Home*, *Highway 61 Revisited* and *Blonde on Blonde* featured surreal and mysterious juxtapositions of imagery and casts of symbolic characters, as he explored a range of new musical styles through his collaboration with rock, blues and country musicians. In *Mr. Tambourine Man*, *Like a Rolling Stone* and *Visions of Johanna* he invites the listener to explore states of altered consciousness. In *It's Alright Ma (I'm Only Bleeding)*, *Subterranean Homesick Blues*, *Maggie's Farm* and *Ballad of a Thin Man* he mocks, teases and lambasts the denizens of the 'straight world' with an acid wit. In the epic *Desolation Row* he assembles a wide cast of archetypal characters and takes the listener on a journey into a kind of parallel dimension.

Although there was an immediate reaction against Dylan's new style by some of his followers, ultimately his refusal to compromise with outdated ways of thinking made him a hero to many. Despite abandoning the role of a 'protest singer' he became even more acclaimed by the 'counter culture'. His new more 'cerebral' songs opened up the lyrical possibilities of popular music in a revolutionary way. They provided musical and lyrical templates for the psychedelic era of 1967 and the subsequent cultural explosion of the growth of the 'alternative society', symbolised by the epochal Woodstock Festival in 1969. Ironically, however, during the late 1960s and early 1970s, when his influence was perhaps at its height, Dylan himself was largely absent from the 'scene'. Between May 1966 and January 1974 he abandoned touring altogether. After suffering a motorcycle accident, there were rumours he might have died, or was paraplegic or disfigured. In fact, he was holed up in Upstate New York, making 'secret music' with the backing musicians who had shared the abuse and catcalls of the 1966 electric tour. Over the next few years, these recordings began to seep out. They sounded nothing like the '66 tour or *Blonde on Blonde*. *The Basement Tapes* exist in an eerie linguistic and musical world of their own; a kind of drunken dream landscape peopled by a gallery of dubious characters. The songs seem suspended in time, as if they are snippets of imaginary low budget Westerns, edited together in a random order. The recordings would not see any official release for a number of years, although some leaked extracts soon began to form the basis of the burgeoning 'bootleg' industry.

As his rural idyll - and later his marriage - ended, Dylan's work of the mid 1970s moved into another distinct phase, an intensely personal form of songwriting that traced his own journey through romantic disillusionment towards a new kind of self awareness. In January 1974 he set off on a major tour of stadiums and other large venues across the USA. Most of the songs on his new album *Planet Waves* still bathed in the comparative simplicity of the rural and domestic lifestyle he had been embracing. But barely a year later, with his personal life now in turmoil, *Blood on the Tracks* (1975) combined a series of accounts of doomed romances with a new and more complex aesthetic sensibility. He claimed his poetic inspiration had been rekindled by his attendance at painting classes in New York with a teacher called Norman Raeburn. The engagement with painting techniques led to the creation of 'cubist' songs on *Blood on the Tracks* like *Tangled Up in Blue, Simple Twist of Fate* and *Idiot Wind*, in which the narrative focus continually shifts from one perspective to another and in which events often do not unfold chronologically. He followed this with the highly acclaimed *Desire* (1976) and the epochal 'Rolling Thunder Tour' of 1975 in which he and a ragged band of acolytes toured New England, making impromptu appearances in small and often rural locations. On *Desire*, mostly composed in collaboration with Canadian theatre and cinema director Jacques Levy, the inspiration is decidedly cinematic, with the action and characters in songs like *Hurricane, Joey* and *Romance in Durango* being based on the identifiable tropes of crime, gangster and Western movies.

The mid '70s period was very popular with Dylan's core audience, and Dylan became one of the biggest acts on the rock circuit, filling stadiums and topping the bills at festivals. But this phase only presaged his most controversial period of all. There are hints of what was to come in the 1978 album *Street Legal*'s lengthy, complex and mystical songs such as *Changing of the Guards, No Time to Think* and *Where Are You Tonight? (Journey Through Dark Heat)*. These songs depict elements of a personal crisis through the filter of arcane symbolism. The mysterious *Senor,* the 'twisted' love song *Is Your Love In Vain* and the gratingly harsh demonic blues of *New Pony* hinted at bleak existential terror. The album was released during a massive world tour which took up most of the year. Dylan was accompanied by a large 'show band' featuring several guitarists and musicians playing instruments such as saxophones and flutes, along with a trio of black female backing singers. But at the final gig in Hollywood Florida, audiences were mystified by the appearance of *Do Right to Me Baby*, a new song with oddly religious lyrics. Earlier on in the show, however, if they had been concentrating hard enough on *Tangled Up in Blue*, they might have noticed that when the narrator meets the girl who normally quotes *...an Italian poet from the thirteenth century...* she now refers instead to *...Jeremiah 17 verses 21 and 23....*

The reference to 'finding Jesus' is a crucial part of the account that the stage announcement presents. Religious imagery and themes have always loomed large in Dylan's work, while the influence of the Bible as both a spiritual guide and a literary text has been profound. In *When the Ship Comes In* (1964) he invokes the story of David and Goliath when demanding vengeance against old and outdated ways of thinking that he proclaims are about to be swept away. In *Highway 61 Revisited* (1965) he imagines a conversation between God and Abraham about the killing of his son Isaac, conducted in hipster jive. On the *John Wesley Harding* album (1968) much of the language deliberately imitates that of the King James Bible. But such engagements with religious themes and language seemed to be purely literary and intellectual. In 1979 most Dylan fans were wholly unprepared for what appeared to be his sudden and complete conversion to a form of 'Born Again' Christianity. After his album *Slow Train Coming* was released in August of that year, it was evident that he had undergone what he later called a personal 'experience of Christ'. In his long residency at the Fox Warfield Theater in San Francisco in November of that year he did not perform any of his older songs. At first he merely played his new religious material without comment, but soon he began to engage in long, rambling onstage 'sermons' which railed against the sins and corruption of the modern world and prophesised an imminent apocalypse. At a show in Tempe Arizona on 26th November, introducing the song *Solid Rock,* he delivered an extraordinary monologue:

... Jesus Christ is that solid rock. He's supposed to come two times. He came once already. See, that's the thing, he's been here already. Now, he's coming back again. You gotta be prepared for this. Because, no matter what you read in the newspapers, that's all deceit. The real truth is that he's coming back already. And you just watch your newspapers. You're gonna see, maybe two years, maybe three years, five years from now, you just watch and see. Russia will come down and attack in the Middle East. China's got an army of two hundred million people. They're gonna come down in the Middle East. There's gonna be a war called the Battle of Armageddon which is like some war you never even dreamed about. And Christ will set up his kingdom. He will set up his kingdom and he'll rule it from Jerusalem.....

For the great majority of Dylan's followers, his sudden fervent embrace of this particular religious brand was a terrible shock. Many of his musical heroes, like Hank Williams, Elvis Presley and Johnny Cash, had released explicitly religious material. But unlike Dylan they had been raised as devout Christians. What especially disturbed his fans was that he was now displaying the fanaticism of a convert to an extremist cult. A figure who had been associated with left wing and liberal political and social causes had now apparently embraced a fundamentalist and politically reactionary world view. In *Slow Train Coming*'s paean to the 'Precious Angel' - the woman who had facilitated his conversion - he had declared *...You either got faith or you got unbelief/ There ain't no neutral ground...* lines which, despite their sincerity, appear to contradict his previous very passionate insistence on individual freedom of thought and expression. Even more disturbingly, *Slow Train* referred to *...Sheiks walkin' around like kings, wearing fancy jewels and nose rings/ Deciding America's future from Amsterdam and to Paris...* apparently revealing xenophobic prejudices. He released another explicitly devotional album in *Saved* in 1980 and continued touring extensively throughout 1980 and 1981, presenting shows that now began with gospel performances by his backing singers. As later revealed on the official *Bootleg Series* release *Trouble No More*, the performances very often extremely powerful, reflecting the defiant intensity of his new found religious fervour. But many of his long term fans felt alienated, some permanently.

Dylan's proselytising phase turned out, however, to be relatively short lived. By the 'Third Gospel Tour' of late 1980 he had already began to include many of his older songs in his shows. The 1981 album *Shot of Love* consisted mostly of secular material, although it concluded with the explicitly Blakean *Every Grain of Sand,* which dealt in an especially powerful way with his crisis of faith. Although it features much religious imagery, this searingly emotional song confronts matters of spiritual doubt with a poetic force which had been noticeably absent from Dylan's devotional material. He acknowledges the awesome presence of a deity in no uncertain terms: *...In the fury of the moment I can see the Master's hand/ In every leaf that trembles, in every grain of sand....* but he also admits that *...Like Cain I now behold this chain of events which I must break...* The use of the name of the Biblical character of the original betrayer, rhyming as it does with 'chain' is especially powerful here. The rhyme itself is a poetic and musical link between the two words, suggesting that that singer himself is impelled to reject his faith. In the heartbreaking final verse - as he realises that his 'born again' experience may have been merely an illusion, his anguish and disillusionment are palpable: *...I hear the ancient footsteps like the motion of the sea/ Sometimes I turn, there's someone there, other times it's only me...*

The song's title is a direct reference to the brilliant 'flash of perception' in which William Blake evoked the presence of a spiritual dimension in all things and thus defined the role of a poet as *...To see a World in a Grain of Sand/ And a Heaven in a Wild Flower/ Hold Infinity in the palm of your hand /And Eternity in an hour...* The implication of this song, which is of fundamental importance to the rest of Dylan's career, is that although religious certainty may provide great spiritual solace, a poet with Dylan's restless creative spirit cannot be perpetually bound by any creed or dogma. He seems to recognise that, for him, the notion of God, or as he puts it here, 'The Master', is ultimately a *poetic* one. This frees him to engage with spiritual issues without being tied down to notions of literal truth. But letting go of the solace and spiritual comfort that his conversion had temporarily provided would not be easy for Dylan. He had been through a turbulent few years, having experienced an extremely painful divorce from his wife Sara, and it seems likely that the description of him subsequently *...disappearing into a haze of substance abuse...* is quite accurate. In this context his embrace of Christianity had clearly been a huge comfort to him.

In the years that immediately followed Dylan's overtly 'religious period' he seemed to be floundering, uncertain as to whether to write songs with direct messages or to allow his poetic sensibilities to take full flight. Although he was clearly still capable of writing songs of great depth and insight, he seemed very unsure of himself. He also seemed to be trying at times to 'hang on' to aspects of his religious faith. But songs like *Property of Jesus* (1981), a very bitter putdown of friends and followers who had rejected him during his 'Born Again' period, and *Man of Peace* (1983), in which he warned of the disguises the Devil make take when stirring up evil, lacked the unswerving conviction which his Christian material had clearly conveyed. In an apparent attempt to return to the role of a 'public poet', the *Shot of Love* (1981), *Infidels* (1983) and *Empire Burlesque* (1985) albums included a number of what might perhaps be described as 'protest songs'. But the inane anti-Vietnam dirge *Clean Cut Kid,* the Zionist diatribe *Neighborhood Bully* and the anti-globalisation, anti-trade union rant *Union Sundown,* were simplistic, confused and politically rather reactionary. The most effective material on these albums, such as the visionary songs *Every Grain of Sand, Jokerman, I and I* and *Dark Eyes* all seemed to focus on the 'dark side' of his own spiritual journey. He left several of his best songs of the period, such as the epic blues tribute *Blind Willie McTell* and labyrinthine examinations of his own spiritual confusion like *Angelina, Foot of Pride* and *Caribbean Wind*, off these albums and replaced them with relatively bland substitutes.

Dylan's collaborations with other musicians in these years were also problematical. Now without a regular touring band, he worked with a variety of session musicians. The addition of the rock solid Jamaican rhythm section of Sly Dunbar and Robbie Shakespeare on *Infidels* and *Empire Burlesque* was an imaginative move, but their distinctive sound was buried under a conventional rock mix. The rather half hearted attempt to let contemporary dance producer Arthur Baker loose on several tracks on *Empire Burlesque* was similarly unconvincing. In 1984 Dylan played a lucrative tour of packed European stadiums (captured on the album *Real Live*) backed up by former Rolling Stone Mick Taylor and other British rock veterans, but many of the arrangements of the songs were plodding and predictable and the highlights of the shows were Dylan's solo spots. Most notoriously of all, when headlining the American section of the Live Aid concert and global telethon on 13th July 1985 (watched by around two billion viewers) he contributed a shambolic, under-rehearsed three song acoustic set in which his backing musicians - the heavily inebriated Rolling Stones Keith Richards and Ronnie Wood - seemed to be struggling to stay in tune. Following this debacle, he took to playing live with established bands like Tom Petty and the Heartbreakers and The Grateful Dead who, though massively successful in their own right, were still willing to spend time as backing musicians for such a legendary figure.

By the late 1980s, Dylan's credibility as a contemporary artist was in tatters. He was indeed *...written off as a has-been...* by many commentators. His albums of 1986-88 received the greatest critical pasting of his career, especially the live *Dylan and the Dead*, drawn from his gigs backed by The Grateful Dead in 1986, which was almost universally derided. *Knocked Out Loaded* (1986) and *Down in the Groove* (1988) were albums with few original Dylan compositions, including rather listless collaborations with Tom Petty and Carole Bayer Sager, along with a ragbag of cover versions including a cover of Kris Kristofferson's cloying tribute to various martyrs *They Killed Him* which was accompanied by, of all things, an 'angelic' children's choir. *Rolling Stone* magazine called this *...the absolute bottom of the Dylan barrel...* Dylan's own compositions such as the gloomy *Death is Not the End* and the leaden *Had a Dream About You Baby*, were depressingly maudlin. He had begun to epitomise the figure of the 'burned out rock star'. His performance as one such character in the disastrous 'straight to video' film *Hearts of Fire* in 1987 was almost *too* convincing. Even the way he had begun to dress on stage, in open necked shirts with dangling medallions and ill fitting tight trousers, seemed to evoke memories of the last years of Elvis.

While the assertion in the onstage announcement that Dylan's eventual artistic resurgence was to occur suddenly in the late '90s is an obvious journalistic exaggeration, he certainly did experience a period of considerable struggle from the late '80s onwards. The release of the brilliant album *Oh Mercy* in 1989, consisting of a series of pithy songs written mostly in short, often bitter, rhyming couplets, and benefitting from the imaginative production of Daniel Lanois, appeared to herald an artistic renaissance. But 1990's *Under the Red Sky*, a collection of *Oh Mercy* leftovers and 'nursery rhyme' songs interspersed by unconvincing attempts at humour such as the notorious *Wiggle Wiggle,* rather punctured this impression. Dylan would then release no more new songs for seven years, dedicating himself entirely to performing - often in relatively small venues - with a regular touring band. The song which best expresses the what he was going through in the early years of the Never Ending Tour is a co-composition which appears on *Down in the Groove* called *Silvio,* for which Dylan reportedly did not even write the words. But Grateful Dead lyricist Robert Hunter's lyric seems to empathise particularly well with Dylan's inspirational predicament. Even though it has never been one of his best known songs, Dylan would perform *Silvio* on hundreds of occasions over the next few years. Often, these performances, which included extended instrumental workouts, would become the centrepiece of the shows. It was as if the song had taken on an invocatory role. *Silvio* is a kind of confession and a provocation, possibly to dark forces, for the rediscovery of inspiration.

Silvio appears to be a character of dubious virtue. He is a strange mixture of conman and black magician. The references to Dylan himself, with their allusions to two of his best known songs, are barely veiled: *...Honest as the next jade rolling that stone/ When I come knocking don't throw me no bone...* Silvio promises that one day he will go *...down in the valley and sing my song...* This may be the Biblical 'valley of death' or some future place of liberation. But in the meantime the song issues what sounds like an open invitation for Dylan's audience to either accompany him through the process of struggle he is going through or desert him: *....I give you what I got until I got no more/ I take what I get until I even the score/ You know I love you and furthermore/ When it's time to go you got an open door...* The chorus runs: *Silvio, silver and gold won't buy back the beat of a heart grown cold/ Silvio, I gotta go, found out something only dead men know...* The song dramatises the plight of an artist who has lost both his faith and his inspiration and who is facing a kind of 'death in life' - the truth that *...only dead men know...* During the 1990s, as the Never Ending Tour continues, Dylan will return to the song again and again, as if to continually remind himself that the struggle he has immersed himself in is, for his creative poetic soul, nothing less than a matter of life and death.

In 1997, just after the release of *Time Out of Mind* and his well-publicised near-death experience with histoplasmosis, a potentially life-threatening infection of the area around the heart, Dylan is interviewed by *Newsnight*'s David Gates for a cover story article. He relates a very strange tale about a 'revelation' he had had some ten years before, which he claims occurred when performing in Locarno, Switzerland with Tom Petty And The Heartbreakers, towards the end of the 1987 'Temples In Flames' tour:

....It's almost like I heard it as a voice. It wasn't like it was even me thinking it... I'm determined to stand, whether God will deliver me or not... And all of a sudden everything just exploded. It exploded every which way. And I noticed that all the people out there - I was used to them looking at the girl singers, they were good-looking girls, you know? And like I say, I had them up

there so I wouldn't feel so bad. But when that happened, nobody was looking at the girls anymore. They were looking at the main mike. After that is when I sort of knew: I've got to go out and play these songs. That's just what I must do...

This particular passage, which has been interpreted as being an expression of Dylan's rationale for launching the Never Ending Tour, has received much attention in the years since it was first published. The 'girls' he refers to are the Queens of Rhythm, a group of gospel-trained singers who provided backing vocals on this and the 1986 'True Confessions' tour with Tom Petty's band. They included Carolyn Dennis (who Dylan secretly married in 1986) and her mother Madelyn Quebec. Dylan's statement that this 'vision' occurred has often been taken at face value, but over the years he has frequently used interviews as a way of 'putting on' his audience, sometimes relating fictionalised or semi-fictionalised accounts of his own biography. In his first ever encounters with journalists and radio show hosts in the early 1960s he invented a colourful if very improbable account of his early life which involved travelling around the country as a circus hand and meeting a series of legendary bluesmen. His famously surreal and hilarious *Playboy* interview of 1966 was later revealed not to have been a spontaneous exchange at all. In fact, he wrote down the answers and sent them to the interviewer.

It is thus quite possible that the Gates 'interview', which mostly consists of paraphrase, was another deliberate concoction between interviewee and interviewer. Dylan has always been a notoriously elusive and difficult interviewee, and perhaps this was the only way Gates could get him to 'co-operate'. The deliberately jokey references to 'the girls' certainly supports this. The notion that Dylan himself - who is quite short sighted - could tell who the audience was looking at, is fanciful, to say the least. The idea that he would remember having had this experience in such detail and then only recall it so many years later is also open to question. There is nothing in the widely circulating bootleg recording of the Locarno gig to indicate that any sudden 'Road To Damascus' moment has occurred. It is most likely that Dylan is again using poetic license to explain his motivation for taking up such an extensive and potentially punishing touring schedule. The tone of the first part of *...determined to stand whether God will deliver me or not...* sounds very much like that of a preacher, whereas the second part suggests a questioning of faith. Perhaps Dylan (like Silvio) feels that he has been 'called' to go out and play his songs, even if that may be sinful. In being 'determined to stand' he is thus wilfully defying God's wishes. The disclaimer about whether God 'will deliver me or not' is, however, a clear indication that - in embarking on the Never Ending Tour - he has decided to pursue an independent spiritual path.

In a 2004 TV interview with Ed Bradley on the show *60 Minutes*, when asked why he was still 'out there', continually touring, Dylan replies*: ...It goes back to that destiny thing. I mean, I made a bargain with it, you know, a long time ago. And I'm holding up my end... to get where I am now...* The interviewer raises a quizzical eyebrow. *...And with whom did you make the bargain?...* Dylan laughs, his eyes twinkling mischievously: *...With the chief commander...* he drawls *...in this earth and in the world we can't see...*

In making this rather wonderfully ambiguous and playful statement, Dylan is surely winding his interviewer, and his audience, up. The notion of God as a 'Chief Commander' is quite an amusing one, although there are those (including some slightly crazed online conspiracy theorists) who believe that Dylan's 'bargain' is a similar Faustian pact to the one made by Robert Johnson, who supposedly sold his soul to the Devil in order to become a brilliant musician. After all, the Devil, as the old saying goes, is always the one with the best tunes...

Dylan later reiterates the story of his 'revelation' in a rather different way in *Chronicles*. He goes back to early months of 1987, when he was rehearsing in San Rafael, California with The Grateful Dead in preparation for a tour. In the early part of the sessions various members of The Dead declared themselves to like many of the songs which Dylan had written and recorded yet which he had never played live. Dylan recounts that at first he had no enthusiasm for playing these songs. He was finding it hard to perform at all. Then one day, taking a lunchtime break, he wanders casually into a bar and encounters a local jazz band playing and is suddenly struck by the way the singer, an old man wearing *...a mohair suit, flat cap with a little brim and shiny necktie....* is singing. Inspired by the old jazz singer to rediscover a vocal technique he claims he once knew but had now forgotten, Dylan recalls returning to the rehearsals, sailing through the old songs and then breezing through the concert tour itself. But this first revelatory experience proves to be of only temporary use. Soon he's back on tour with Petty and though he is managing to get through the concerts without too many problems, he's still feeling very disillusioned. But then, in another reference to his revelatory 'experience' during the show in Locarno, Switzerland, he claims that he *...fell into a black hole...* suddenly freezing up and becoming unable to perform. Yet despite this 'panic attack', he somehow finds a way to carry on:

...I conjured up some different type of mechanism to jump-start the other techniques that weren't working. I just did it automatically, out of thin air, cast my own spell to drive out the Devil. Instantly, it was like a thoroughbred had charged through the gates. Everything came back, and it came back in multidimension...

In this remarkably imaginative account Dylan suggests that he was undergoing a psychological crisis of confidence. But in describing how he overcomes his inner insecurities, he again assumes the persona of Silvio, the practitioner of the dark arts, the 'conjuror' who casts a spell to drive out the Devil. And by exercising (or perhaps exorcising) this power he is 'born again' in a new way. His adherence to conventional religion had led him into a creative dead end. Now it had been replaced by a more ambiguous kind of 'faith'. In a 1997 interview he stated that:

...Here's the thing with me and the religious thing. This is the flat-out truth: I find the religiosity and philosophy in the music. I don't find it anywhere else. Songs like 'Let Me Rest on a Peaceful Mountain' or 'I Saw the Light'- that's my religion. I don't adhere to rabbis, preachers, evangelists, all of that. I've learned more from the songs than I've learned from any of this kind of entity. The songs are my lexicon. I believe the songs....

No matter how fictionalised his accounts of a 'revelation' may be, Dylan appears to realise that 'pursuing his muse' cannot be separated from spirituality. He had always been a spiritual seeker, inspired by a belief in the existence of some form of higher reality. But now he appears to have turned his focus onto a humanistic devotion to the spiritual power of art. He will soon become impelled to dig ever deeper into the musical culture which had originally inspired him. He seems to have decided that setting himself a particularly gruelling live schedule was his 'destiny', or perhaps his own personal path to redemption. Years of sustained, down-to-earth hard work would follow, in which he would attempt to recover his 'lost muse' through an immense effort of sheer willpower. There would be many setbacks on the way. Following the examples of his close friends in The Grateful Dead and the veteran 'outlaw' country star Willie Nelson, he created a lifestyle for himself in which he would spend most of his life on the road. Recording albums, writing books, even making long-running radio shows, all had to be fitted into his touring schedules. He would dedicate himself to exploring the ways in which his songs could be modified and adapted, so that they could take on a new life in each performance. In order for him be able to write significant songs again, he would have to immerse himself deeply in his own musical and poetic influences. He was setting out on a long journey. At times he would find it very difficult to motivate himself. Sometimes, especially in the early days, his performances would teeter uncertainly between the incomprehensible and the inspired. But he was now committed to following his own spiritual path. He had made his own bargain with that mysterious 'Chief Commander' and, 'whether God would deliver him or not', he was 'determined to stand'.

9th February 2010. We're on Prime Time American TV. Before each of the frequent ad breaks we see a snow-bound White House, like an image on a Christmas card. Tonight, the presidential home is the venue for a concert celebrating fifty years of the Civil Rights movement. The show features a cast of ageing notables including Joan Baez, John Mellencamp and Smokey Robinson. Of course, as it's such an 'official' occasion, it's all a little stiff and formal. Black ties and tuxedos abound. Before Bob Dylan makes his appearance, he gets a special intro from Mr. President himself. Barack Obama's introductory speech quotes from *When The Ship Comes In* and, as if to show us that, despite his exalted position, he is still a 'cool dude' and a knowledgeable 'real fan', he humbly thanks Bob for being *...good enough to take a night off from his Never Ending Tour...* While he and Michele sit nodding their heads, looking for all the world like a couple of awestruck middle aged punters who've paid top dollar for a front row seat at a rock show, Dylan squints under the bright chandeliers, sometimes closing his eyes, his leg twitching ever so slightly, as he delivers *The Times They Are a-Changin'.* This is one of his signature songs from the early '60s. The lyrics eloquently express both the exhilaration and the anguish of that momentous decade. Its narrator assumes a prophetic, even vengeful, tone, warning the older generation that, unless they are prepared to relinquish their power and control of 'children' who are 'beyond their command', they will soon be swept away by a coming 'flood' of inevitable, inexorable change ... *You'd better start swimming...* he warns *...or you'll sink like a stone...*

Yet today, even though the words have not been altered, the song appears to signify something quite different. Dylan's cracked, weathered voice lends immense gravitas to the performance. The musical backing, like the singing, is precise and restrained. Dylan supplies some rather basic strumming on an acoustic guitar while his long term shadow Tony Garnier plucks slow, sonorous notes from a double bass. The arrangement is dominated by piano, played by Patrick Warren, which somehow seems to unearth a new melody which, you might say, was always present in the tune but has only now been revealed. Dylan uses rather oddly syncopated phrasing, compressing the words in the verses and leaving space for the piano to come in at the end of each chorus. Lyrics that once were declaimed so vehemently are now delivered in a measured, somewhat distanced, tone. What had been a defiant celebration of youth has become a universal statement of cyclical change and an achingly sad reminder of the inevitable effects of the passage of time ... *The first one now will later be last...* Bob whispers conspiratorially, as if he's about to share some dark secret with us ... *and the present now will later be past...*

As for Dylan himself, you'd hardly think he was performing for millions on TV. There's no hint of 'showbiz', no smiling for the cameras, no nostalgic speeches. His face is a blank canvas. In a few minutes, when the song ends, he will give the slightest of bows, shuffle forward to dispense a quick handshake to the dignitaries and be gone. You get the impression that he'd much rather be someplace else, or even that he's just stepped out of some other time... With his pencil-thin moustache and his immaculate lounge suit with the neat waistcoat and gaudy yellow dress shirt, he looks like a rather diminutive version of Vincent Price in some obscure 'B' movie set on a nineteenth century Mississippi river boat, or some dubious character in a Mark Twain short story. A serviceable villain, indeed... At other moments, as he twists his own youthful poetry into new and surprising shapes, you can perhaps imagine him as Edgar Allan Poe, the master storyteller of American darkness. There are moments when he seems to be far away somewhere, in a kind of rapture, entranced by how the familiar phrases trip from his tongue, as he teases new meanings and resonances from every word.

And if you're being particularly fanciful, you can't help but wonder if maybe... just maybe... he is remembering a summer's day, long ago in August 1963. A crowd of 200,000 people are lined up in front of the Lincoln Memorial at the March for Jobs and Freedom in Washington D.C. It is just a few minutes before Martin Luther King will deliver his epochal *...I Have a Dream...* speech. Dylan is duetting with Joan Baez on that hymn to righteous revenge that the President has just quoted from. It has to be said that they are a pretty odd couple, her voice as pure as silk and his as rough as gravel. They strain to harmonise... *There's a stillness in the wind, before the hurricane begins....*

Two: *A Date With the Fairy Queen*
Romantic Dreams

...Throughout my career, if I have done anything, I have paid attention to every note and every word I sing - if I respect the song. If I cannot project this to a listener, I fail...
Frank Sinatra

...Some people tap their feet, some people snap their fingers, and some people sway back and forth. I just sorta do 'em all together, I guess....
Elvis Presley

The *Expo '92 Guitar Legends* Festival in Seville, Spain on 17 October 1991 is a worldwide TV event, featuring a series of renowned guitarists demonstrating their chops in extended guitar solos. Bob Dylan is perhaps a strange choice for such a gathering, given that he's hardly what you'd call a 'guitar hero'. He's been allocated a forty minute slot in the show and - in deference to the theme of the evening - has already given us an extended version of *All Along The Watchtower* with Richard Thompson 'channelling Hendrix' on guitar and Jack Bruce on bass. The set will later conclude with a 'superstar jam', consisting of what might charitably be called a 'lively' duet with Keith Richards on the hoary old rock'n'roll chestnut *Shake, Rattle and Roll.* As so often on such big occasions, Bob looks rather bemused and distant, as if he is just a little embarrassed to be here. For most of the show he keeps his eyes fixed studiously down on his guitar, as if the cameras are not even present. The short acoustic session begins with a (highly appropriate) take on *Boots of Spanish Leather* and a rather perfunctory version of one of his favourite covers, *Across the Borderline.* Thompson keeps glancing rather nervously at Dylan, who has almost certainly provided him with very little guidance as to what to play. But like a true virtuoso he bravely supplies some tasteful improvised acoustic picking. It is all really a little ragged. Only in the final number of the acoustic set does the performance come alive...

After some basic strumming and a short burst of harmonica, Dylan begins enunciating some decidedly unfamiliar lyrics, in short staccato bursts *...Answer me... oh my love...* Now, for the first time, he looks up into the camera. Then with a strange wry smile, exposing his teeth a little as he does when he is enjoying playing with an audience, he poses the question *...Just what sin... ...have I been guilty of?...* As Thompson does his best to get into the spirit of the thing by supplying some fluid counterpoint melody lines, Dylan seems to take great pleasure in teasing the listeners by placing apparently random emphasis on particular words: *...If you can DO without me...* he pleads *...I'll try not to care/ But if you ever think ABOUT ME/ Won't you LISTEN to my prayer....*

Although he never announces the song to the audience, it is in fact *Answer Me, My Love*, an old Frankie Laine and Nat King Cole favourite, whose melody has (at least in their versions) some resemblance to The Beatles' *Yesterday*. As Dylan asks *...Won't you tell me where I went astray...* it is as if he is weighing each syllable carefully, challenging us to decide whether he is being serious or self-mocking. In a typically offhand way, he seems to be using the song as a direct appeal to his audience to really 'listen' to him again, while he begs their 'forgiveness'. He paces his delivery thoughtfully, as if he is considering the clichés in the lyrics and letting us decide whether the protestations he is making and the questions he is asking are serious or not. We don't get a shot of the actual audience, who are probably somewhat underwhelmed, if not confused, by all this. For all we know, they are not particularly bothered. They may well be more interested in preparing themselves for the adrenaline rush from the next guitar god. Onstage, Dylan continues to alternate between blinking myopically and flashing his lopsided grins. It is obvious that he is enjoying himself now. He gives the song his all, clearly revelling in the delicious ambiguity of the moment.

One aspect of Bob Dylan's late period - which has sometimes bewildered and divided his long term followers - is his fascination with the sentimental tradition of popular song. In the early phase of the Never Ending Tour, he included *We Three (My Echo, My Shadow and Me), Don't Pity Me, Moon River* and *Let's Learn to Live and Love Again* in his shows, alongside his many interpretations of traditional folk and blues numbers. It soon became clear that he was developing a special affection for this kind of material. Its influence on his songwriting in the 2000s, especially on *"Love And Theft"* and *Modern Times*, was obvious. In the mid 2010s he issued *Shadows in the Night* (2015), *Fallen Angels* (2016) and *Triplicate* (2017), albums consisting entirely of his interpretations of what has in recent years become popularly known as 'The Great American Songbook'. The songs were written by George and Ira Gershwin, Harold Arlen, Irving Berlin, Hoagy Carmichael, Johnny Mercer and others. Almost all had been recorded at some time by Frank Sinatra. These songs made up a significant portion of Dylan's live shows between 2014 and 2017. When performing them, Dylan would usually stand centre stage to sing without an instrument, sometimes gesticulating to illustrate particular emotions, very much in the manner of a crooner.

In his younger days, Dylan had often been scathing about this kind of music. Before a 1962 concert performance of *Blowin' in the Wind* in a small club in Toronto he mutters *...Here's a song that's in sort of a set... set pattern of songs that say... a little more than "I love you and you love me, and let's go over to the banks of Italy, and we'll raise half a family, you for me, and me for you"...*

In 1985 (in a rare moment of public egotism) he stated, with apparent satisfaction that *...Tin Pan Alley is gone. I put an end to it. People can record their own songs now...* In a 2015 interview, however, he admitted that:

...To those of us who grew up with these kinds of songs and didn't think much of it, these are the same songs that rock 'n' roll came to destroy - music hall, tangos, pop songs from the Forties, foxtrots, rumbas, Irving Berlin, Gershwin, Harold Arlen, Hammerstein. Composers of great renown. It's hard for modern singers to connect with that kind of music and song...

The songs of these 'composers of great renown' dominated American popular music during the decades before the coming of rock'n'roll in the mid-1950s and continued to be popular with older listeners through the 1960s. The songwriters were usually professional employees of music publishers. By the late 1930s the popular music industry had become an efficient and vertically integrated 'production line' in which composers, lyricists, arrangers and singers all played their separate roles. Many of the lyricists were highly accomplished writers, but their subject matter was almost entirely focused on matters of love. Their tone was generally smooth and the projection of emotion tended to be sentimentalised. Any expression of overt sexuality also had to be kept in check. Before the invention of microphones and amplifiers vocalists had to shout, wield megaphones or emote operatically to reach the back of an auditorium. But when this technology became widespread in the 1920s, a more 'mellow' method of enunciation became possible. Singers were able to project their vocals in a more subtle and nuanced way, in a style of singing that came to be known as 'crooning'. This meant that vocalists could communicate in a more intimate - and therefore sexier - manner than their predecessors. In the 1940s, crooners like Frank Sinatra became the first 'pop idols'. By the mid 1950s, on albums like *Songs for Young Lovers* (1954), *In the Wee Small Hours* (1955) and *Songs for Swingin' Lovers* (1956) - on which he worked with orchestral arranger Nelson Riddle - Sinatra took the art of song to a new level of 'adult' sophistication.

In comparison, the early rock'n'roll which was then emerging appeared to more mature music fans to be merely crude. It was dominated by repetitive rhythmic beats, with connotations of high energy excitement and sexual abandonment. For two or three 'crazy' minutes, the records of Little Richard or Jerry Lee Lewis or Gene Vincent took teenagers into a world of apparent danger, of temporary madness, of complete abandonment. Most powerfully of all, the nineteen year old Elvis Presley, chock full of testosterone and rage, preened and grunted and thrust his hips provocatively at the audience *...Baby... baby... baby... let's play house!...* he wailed suggestively. On the heart rending, career-defining *Heartbreak Hotel* (1956) the lyrics are a kind of extended metaphor in which the hotel and its staff embody the desperate feelings of lost love which the narrator is experiencing. Presley turns this into the most powerful expression of pure sexual frustration anyone had ever heard. His real power as a performer was, however, relatively short lived. Within a few years he had been thoroughly co-opted by 'the establishment'. He had quite willingly (and apparently proudly) accepted conscription into the US Army, while much of the focus of his career was directed towards his acting and singing roles in a series of forgettable 'B' Movies.

The rock'n'rollers who most influenced the next generation of performers were artists like Buddy Holly and Chuck Berry, who wrote their own songs and through whom the music became a form of *personal* expression. When The Beatles took Britain by storm in 1963, and conquered the USA in 1964, they were mostly performing their own material, a precedent which virtually all 'credible' musicians in the 1960s then had to follow. The performer who most epitomised the new approach to singing and songwriting was none other than Dylan himself. He redefined notions of what a popular singer, and a popular song, was supposed to sound like. His vocal influences ranged from Delta Blues performers of the 1920s and 30s to obscure Hillbilly mountain singers. Unlike most of the commercially successful folk singers of his day he made no attempt to sound 'pleasant' or 'smooth' in his delivery. His imaginative transformation of popular song forms in terms of subject matter, length and structure created a new template with which both his contemporaries and his audience could engage. He demonstrated most eloquently that the subject matter of popular song lyrics did not need to be restricted to boy-girl romance. Under his influence, the attempt to write poetic or meaningful lyrics which conveyed personal, truthful self-expression or political or social comment became *de rigueur* for any band or singer who wanted to be taken seriously.

To the new generation who had grown up with Elvis and his successors, the 'old music' symbolised all that was insipid, conventional, inauthentic and downright *boring* about the culture of the 'old world'. Members of the baby boomer generation - while venerating the 'people's music' of folk, blues, jazz and country - tended to view the popular songs of the pre rock'n'roll years as consisting purely of schmaltzy romantic clichés written for 'polished' performers in Hollywood musicals. This is, of course, a great oversimplification. As a very knowledgeable 'historian' of all forms of American music, Dylan was fully aware that there had been much interaction in the 'pre-Elvis' era between forms of popular music like jazz, blues and country and the mainstream. Some country and blues singers modified their style to appeal more to mainstream audiences. Even Bing Crosby, the biggest star of the early crooning era, learned much of his technique from blues and jazz vocalists. Like most teenagers in the 1950s, Dylan had grown up listening to whatever music was available on record or radio. In *Chronicles*, looking back on his youth, he reveals that:

... I used to play the phenomenal "Ebb Tide" by Frank Sinatra a lot and it never failed to fill me with awe... when Frank sang that song, I could hear everything in his voice - death, God and the universe, everything...

Dylan's late period embrace of the sentimental song tradition may partly be, perhaps, a way of accommodating themes that are more appropriate for a singer in his later years - longing, regret, awareness of mortality, even nostalgia. By focusing on the work of the most skilled lyricists and composers within that tradition, he has been able to demonstrate its validity as an authentic American art form. Between 2006 and 2009, he hosted and presented a radio show on the XM Satellite Radio Network, *Theme Time Radio Hour*, which ran for three seasons and over a hundred episodes. A two hour 'lockdown special' was also broadcast in September 2020. The normally taciturn host (who by now had adopted the practice of almost never talking to the audience on stage) adopts the persona of a cheery, chatty, avuncular 'radio personality' who, as well as introducing the music being played (none of which is by Dylan himself), tells corny jokes, reads extracts from poems, gives 'homespun' advice and household tips, relates anecdotes and tall tales and even presents recipes. The tone of the show, along with the selection of music, is quirky and nostalgic. Dylan presents himself as a decidedly apolitical 'regular guy', who enjoys baseball and boxing, a good cigar and a well-aged single malt (with a nonchalant unconcern for health issues). He relates many 'potted biographies' of the artists whose songs he plays, delighting in describing their 'colourful' exploits and many vicissitudes. He is consistently warm, funny and engaging and appears to take particular delight in unearthing obscure tracks. His characteristic 'interview persona', in which he is fond of issuing gnomic utterances and teasing his fans with misleading clues to his world view and aesthetics, is almost entirely absent.

Theme Time is a very cleverly conceived theatrical performance - a stylised, tongue in cheek homage to 1950s radio shows. Much of what Dylan says is in fact scripted by the show's writers and producers. Although the fiction is maintained that Dylan is, like an old time D. J., 'spinning these discs' himself, his voiceovers are taped separately and put together with various recorded elements such as 'period' ads, jingles and sound clips. There are various 'guest appearances' from assorted celebrities, some of whom had supposedly composed the (almost certainly faked) emails that Dylan regularly responds to. The weekly taped introduction claims that the show is being recorded live in the Abernathy Building, an entirely fictitious location. The show successfully conveys not only Dylan's encyclopedic musical knowledge but also his genuine love for a very wide range of musical forms. Many old blues, jazz and country tracks, some of which he himself had covered and many of which had clearly influenced his music, are played. There are also many rock'n'roll and rockabilly classics, a smattering of songs by Dylan's contemporaries as singer songwriters, much doo wop, calypso, gospel and the occasional rap, although (perhaps surprisingly) very little of the traditional British folk music which had inspired much of his early work. The tone is overwhelmingly American, with some British and occasional French input. There are many humorous and novelty ditties. The show is a kind of history of recorded American music, with some tracks dating back to the 1920s. The era of the Great American Songbook is thoroughly embraced, and there are many selections by Sinatra, Crosby, Nat King Cole, Dean

Martin, Billie Holiday and other crooners, whom he often praises highly as he relates their life stories.

Despite the generally light hearted and entertaining tone, the matter of lyrics very much takes centre stage. Dylan frequently quotes from the songs he is about to play. Each week's show is based, as the name suggests, on a particular theme. The first few in Season One are *Weather, Mother, Drinking, Baseball, Coffee, Jail* and *Father*. The next episode *Wedding* features music from performers as diverse as Dave Edmunds, Frank Sinatra, Ry Cooder, Darlene Love, Big Joe Turner and Fred Rich and His Orchestra. The famous and the obscure are mixed with jokes and anecdotes in a seamless whole. American music from the 1920s is presented as a kind of integrated cultural continuum. As well as being highly entertaining, *Theme Time Radio Hour* can be seen as a kind of aesthetic manifesto for Dylan's late style, as demonstrated most clearly on *"Love And Theft"* and *Modern Times*, in which deliberate homages to and pastiches of the popular music of the 1930s, '40s and '50s are integrated with contemporary language and in which the borderline that was established in the '50s and '60s between 'pre-rock' and rock (what one might call 'Before and After Elvis'), is no longer visible. Dylan uses the show to deconstruct a cultural divide which he himself had, in his younger years, done much to create.

28th April 2017. A lone steel guitar begins a mournful intro. The lighting in the grand old English Music Hall setting of the London Palladium is dim and shadowy. The show has almost reached its climax. The singer now steps to the middle of the stage, staring out at some obscure midpoint in the audience, just a microphone in hand. He wears a black suit edged with white trimmings and a white broad brimmed hat. There is a quiet strumming of guitars, the plucking of a double bass and soft washes of almost indiscernible percussion *...The falling leaves...* he begins. There is a gap of several seconds *... drift by the window... The autumn leaves ... of red and gold...* It is a song of regret, of old age reflecting philosophically on youth. Autumn days are coming to an end. Winter will soon set in. The spirit of a lost love is present, as if it is hovering in the air. The singer recalls her sunburned hands, her summer kisses. It is as if each line is falling slowly through space. The lines pile up as they land gently on top of each other. *...And I miss you... Most of all... My darling... When autumn leaves... start to fall....."*

The performance, with its elegiac, wistful tone, is a fitting climax to a show in which Dylan has alternated between his own songs and his covers of standards. In between *Highway 61 Revisited, Love Sick* and *Desolation Row* he has ruminated on his *Melancholy Mood*, demanded *All or Nothing at All* and warned of *Stormy Weather*. As the final notes fade away, he seems to melt into the shadows at the side of the stage. Of course, he will be back for the encores, when we will hear his own standard *Blowin' in the Wind,* which has been covered by hundreds of artists from every musical field, including Stevie Wonder, Neil Young, Dolly Parton, Johnny Cash, Nana Mouskouri, The

Killers, Elvis Presley and Marlene Dietrich. Tonight the version that ends the show is smooth and nuanced, bearing more resemblance to Sam Cooke's version than Dylan's original.

As the audience stream out they are entertained by a talented busker - a guy from the Czech Republic who calls himself 'Frankie' - who performs a note-perfect set of Bob Dylan songs with his guitar and strapped-on harmonica. A large crowd gathers around him and they join in enthusiastically with those songs they all know and love so well. These are mostly songs they haven't heard in the concert they've just seen. In truth, you might say that 'Frankie' sounds more like 'Bob Dylan' than Dylan himself. Also, he's unlikely to 'go electric', get converted to any religion or - despite his name - try to emulate Frank Sinatra. Soon the pile of coins in the cap he's laid down is looking pretty healthy and he's doing *Mr. Tambourine Man* for third time. By request, naturally...

In an interview conducted after the release of *Shadows in the Night* in 2015, when asked why he was covering these old songs, Dylan stated that:

...They've been covered enough. Buried, as a matter a fact. What me and my band are basically doing is 'uncovering' them. Lifting them out of the grave and bringing them into the light of day....

Dylan has often professed considerable admiration for the disciplined economy of the work of lyricists such as Johnny Mercer and Ira Gershwin, whose songs have been recorded by a multiplicity of artists but have often been 'smothered' by orchestration and over-emotive singing. His approach has been to present 'stripped down' interpretations, using his own touring band to provide very minimal musical settings in order to rescue them from over familiarity and 'scholcky' musical presentation and thus to 'uncover' the skill of these writers. By removing the music's usual framework, his aim has been to deconstruct the audience's preconceptions of mainstream pre-rock popular songs, demonstrating that they can - if presented sympathetically and sparingly - subtly convey real rather than fake emotions in a way that is just as 'authentic' as any folk song. In 'stripping down' these songs he is also able to expose and emphasise the music's roots in the jazz and blues traditions which have always formed a backdrop to his own work.

Dylan's 1993 version of the standard *You Belong to Me* - in which an anguished singer laments that his loved one is currently separated from him while she is travelling to various exotic locations - is a stylistic template for the albums he will record some two decades later. The song, mainly composed by Chilton Price, was recorded by many artists, including Sinatra. It was made particularly famous by Dean Martin in 1952, in a recording which sets his trademark 'cool', relaxed vocal style against heavy orchestration. Dylan performs a highly evocative version on acoustic guitar and harmonica with a particularly nasal vocal emphasis. The recording was taken from the sessions for *Good as I Been to You* and appeared on the soundtrack for the movie *Natural Born Killers* (directed by Oliver Stone with a script by Quentin Tarantino) in 1994. Dylan's vocal is thinly plaintive. He seems to have little chance of enticing his errant love. The lament that she is so far away, accompanied by the continued assertion that their love will survive, comes over as tragic self-deception. In the context of the 'killer lovers on the run' theme of the film, his sad, fatalistic treatment of the song helps create some sympathy for the doomed couple, despite their murderous crimes.

One romantic track which did make it onto *Good as I Been to You* was *Tomorrow Night*, which uses the standard posture of a tortured lover expressing his anguished insecurity about a potential romance. Written by Sam Coslow and Wilhelm Grosz, the first recorded big band version, by Horace Heidt and His Musical Knights (1939), features rather bland female vocals and comes across as a typically pleasant ballad of the period. The song became a big hit in 1946 when the blues singer Lonnie Johnson performed it with basic guitar accompaniment. In the version recorded by the young Elvis Presley at the Sun Sessions in 1954, the guitar figure is even more basic, with the emphasis on Presley's piercing (and fairly heavily echoed) vocals. The gradual transformation of the song can be seen as another model for Dylan's approach to, and interest in, sentimental material. Johnson (and to an even greater extent Presley) make the song far more resonant by stripping it down to its basic musical form.

In the hands of vocalists with the skill of Johnson and Presley, the audience can 'read through' their protestations, so allowing the singers to display their own vulnerability in a way that can generate real emotions, despite the indulgence in romantic clichés. The implied irony in lines like *...Will all the thrill be gone?..., ...Will it be just another memory?..., Your lips are so tender, your heart is beating fast...* and *...Will you be with me when the moon is bright?...* suggests that the answers to these questions will certainly be 'no'. It is up to the singer to convey the right kind of vulnerability to get this across. Dylan's rendition of *Tomorrow Night* (which he performed frequently in concert between 1992 and 1998) is modelled on Presley's version. The inclusion of the track on an album of 'basic covers' of blues and folk songs illustrates that the vocal styles of the crooners were sometimes very close to those of classic blues performers. Both styles attempt to establish a kind of 'intimate' communication with listeners, with a particular emphasis on the way lyrics are phrased in their delivery. In concert the song also creates a dialogue with the audience, and becomes a kind of meditation on the transience of performing art itself, as Dylan asks the poignant question *...Tomorrow night/ Will all the thrill be gone?.... Will it be just another memory?...*

Dylan's treatment of *I'm a Fool to Want You,* the opening track on *Shadows in the Night,* is an outstanding example of his 'uncovering' of a song. Sinatra's 1951 recording uses sweeping strings and extensive vocal backing, emphasising the full magnificent tragedy of the piece, in which the singer almost drowns in his own self-immolation as he confesses his 'addiction' to the object of his love. In Billie Holiday's 1958 reading, also supported by a string arrangement, she brings the full weight of her own tragic persona to bear on the sparse and evocative lyrics. In Dylan's version, Donnie Herron's steel guitar functions as a low key substitute for orchestration. The use of dramatic pauses is particularly 'theatrical'. There are moments when Dylan's voice almost cracks, but he appears to be forcing himself to hold back on the lachrymose emotions, only just keeping himself in check, which adds considerably to the drama. He is not afraid to push his voice here in a way that sometimes shows his vocal frailties. This makes the starkly confessional quality of the address to the lover more believable. The recording has a particularly haunting quality whose effect is not unlike that of an anguished blues song, minus the twelve bar structure.

Much was made of the fact that almost all of the songs on the album had previously been recorded by Frank Sinatra. But in many ways Dylan's model is Willie Nelson, whose 1978 album of standards *Stardust* (and subsequent sequels) seems to have inspired Dylan to follow a similar path. Several prominent singers of the rock generation have also covered this material. Some, like Rod Stewart in his series of *Great American Songbook* albums, have gone for the full orchestral treatment. Others have been less reverential. Bryan Ferry, for example, treats songs like *These Foolish Things* or *You Go to My Head* in a cleverly ironic manner. Nelson takes the songs more seriously. He eschews over-instrumentation and relies on understated vocal inflexion. A prime example is his version of *Some Enchanted Evening* from Rodgers and Hammerstein's 1949 musical *South Pacific*, which has been subjected to many lushly orchestrated versions. In the original production it was performed, with great aplomb, by the Italian opera singer Ezio Pinza. Sinatra's version is, not surprisingly, considerably more low key. Nelson strips the song down further, adding muted backing vocals. He uses a small studio band to imitate an orchestra, so demonstrating that this apparently maudlin tearjerker contains a core of real emotional vulnerability. The song conveys the tentative emotions of lovers' first nervous meetings with real eloquence, as its protagonist warns of the consequences of missing the key moment when a relationship might suddenly be sparked off. Dylan's version is even more 'naked', with very basic accompaniment, and as such is perhaps the most affecting and surprising of all his performances on these albums. It becomes an almost chilling evocation of loneliness, like a hazy, half-remembered dream in monochrome, as if the narrator is an old man warning a young man of the dire consequences of not taking action when the 'time is right' in his life. The tone of aching regret is decidedly moving and genuine.

The most skilful of the old songwriters could, by the crafting of simple language, achieve subtle effects whereby the authenticity of the emotions that the singers are expressing could be called into question. The effectiveness of this relies on the ability of the particular singer to convey vulnerability or uncertainty as well as longing in their interpretation of the lyrics. It also depends on the kind of musical arrangement used. Irving Berlin's *How Deep Is the Ocean* (covered by Dylan on *Triplicate*) utilises simple metaphors which emphasise the infinite nature of the narrator's love, which is *...as deep as the ocean, as high as the sky...* The song consists of a series of rhetorical questions which place the depth of the narrator's love on a cosmic level: *...How far would I travel* *to be where you are?/ How far is the journey from here to a star?...* The compactness of the language allows the singer to convey meaning through controlled intonation. In early versions by singers such as Rudy Vallee and Carmen Lombardo (both 1932) the vocal is plaintive and conventionally humble, as if the singer is down on one knee making a proposal of love. The arrangements are fulsome, as if to extract the maximum emotional effect. In Bing Crosby's recording (from the same year) the musical backing is more restrained and the vocals are more upfront. Crosby employs his deep baritone, includes some almost-spoken passages and maintains a kind of vocal discipline that effectively suggests the hopelessness of the singer's predicament without over-emoting. Frank Sinatra's rendition (1946) is more melodramatic, with his voice almost cracking in places. Ella Fitzgerald's 1958 recording is full throated and ethereal. Billie Holiday's interpretation (1954) is more upbeat, with a restrained jazzy background. She treats the lyrics more playfully. There is the hint of a laugh in her voice, as if she is using the words to tease a lover. Dylan's own reading is perhaps closest to the Sinatra version in style. As with many of his covers of standards, he emphasises the song's melancholic qualities. He treats the lyrics with great respect, singing more 'tunefully' than is normally expected of him. This was a song which he developed considerably in live shows. In a performance in Boston on 14th July 2016, he allows more jazz inflexions and variations into his vocal, in a way that resembles Crosby's version.

Dylan's main interest in 'uncovering' these songs seems to be in unearthing their tragic essence. In performance, stepping up to centre stage without an instrument, the songs operate in this deliberately theatrical setting almost as 'soliloquies' - intimate revelations of the innermost thoughts of the singer. This creates a prevailing mood of despondency which is most explicit in his rendition of *Melancholy Mood* (on *Fallen Angels*). Like quite a few of Dylan's selections, this is a relatively obscure Sinatra number, which he first recorded as the vocalist for Harry James and His Orchestra in 1939. The original has a particularly jazzy feel. It commences with an evocative trumpet solo by James, who had been schooled in the blues as a boy and was much admired by Louis Armstrong. The song became a centrepiece of Dylan's performances. Dylan's projects the brooding, ominous quality of Walter Schumann's tune and Vic R. Knight's lyrics, with their repeated admission of a jilted lover's almost suicidal depression, to the fore. Charlie Sexton plays the 'trumpet' introduction as a low-key Django Reinhardt styled flamenco blues guitar piece. Dylan's vocals are reverent, almost whispered. The minimalistic, impressionistic lyrics plunge into depths of almost gothic romanticism:

...Oh, what a lonely soul am I, stranded high and dry by a melancholy mood...
...Gone is every joy and inspiration, tears are all I have to show, no consolation
All I can see is grief and gloom, till the crack of doom...

culminating in a wonderfully stark image of loneliness, depicting a solitary dancer mourning his lost love:

...Love is a whimsy, as flimsy as lace/ My arms embrace an empty space....

A similar tone of regretful melancholia is evoked in *Where Are You?, Full Moon and Empty Arms, Nevertheless, Maybe You'll Be There, Once Upon a Time, That Old Feeling* and *My One and Only Love.* Critics of Dylan's 'crooning' albums have pointed out, with perhaps some justification, that - in contrast to the lightness of touch which Nelson often brought to his versions - this approach tends to produce a rather unvaried 'melancholy mood'. However, Dylan also covers a few more wistful, up-tempo numbers like *That Old Black Magic, Polka Dots and Moonbeams, The Best is Yet to Come* and *I Guess I'll Have to Change My Plan*, which are jazzier in their arrangements and feature more elements of self-deprecating humour. Perhaps the most effective of these songs is *Why Try to Change Me Now*, in which the singer's personal eccentricities are both mocked and celebrated. This became a staple of Dylan's concerts, and something of a 'signature song', often played at the end of a show, with its dryly humorous depiction of a character who ignores the vagaries of fashion to determinedly to do everything 'his way'. It was certainly bizarre to hear Dylan, always the least conventional of singers, pose the question:

...Why can't I be more conventional?
People talk, people stare, so I try
But that's not for me, 'cause I can't see
My kind of crazy world go passing me by...

The best of the romantic songwriters could, by skillfully manipulating sentimental conventions, suggest that their narrators were especially fallible human beings. Such songs often tend to be, as we have seen, studies of melancholy in which it is possible to 'read through' the romantic clichés in order to 'uncover' hidden psychological depths. A carefully placed word or phrase can create considerable ambiguity. In Dylan's explorations of the genre, his narrators are often sad, lonely, obsessive - or even potentially dangerous. In *Make You Feel My Love* from 1997's *Time Out of Mind*, the narrator offers the woman he is in love with a shoulder to cry on. It seems that she has suffered some emotional trauma (most likely breaking up with another lover) and he desperately tries to convince her that he could make her feel better. He professes his love for her in no uncertain terms. But, as the winsome melody suggests, there is a strong sense that the feeling is tragically one sided. This in itself is nothing unusual. Songs with narrators professing unrequited love have been a romantic staple since the days of the troubadours. What singles out *To Make You Feel My Love* is the way in which the lyric's unsettling mixing of romantic and poetic language makes us question the narrator's motives and sincerity. The opening line ...*When the rain is blowing in your face...* suggests, in a fairly obviously metaphorical way, that the woman is suffering. But this is followed by *...And the whole world is on your case...* a distinctly jarring shift in tone and a rather deliberately contrived attempt to get her sympathy ...*I could offer you a warm embrace...* also sounds rather awkward. Is this love, we may ask, or a business deal?

The desperate narrator takes his supplications to extremes. The lines *...When evening shadows and the stars appear/ And there is no-one there to dry your tears...* feature typical 'sentimental' imagery that suggests a state of sadness or even depression but the narrator insists on following this with the ridiculously exaggerated *...I could hold you for a million years...* Many romantic songs do, of course, profess love that will last 'forever' but the specific numerical reference to a 'million' suggests that the narrator is merely blurting out impossible assurances. In the first bridge he tries to reassure her in a more conventional way that, although she 'hasn't made her mind up yet' (presumably about him), he would 'never do her wrong'. But the assertion that *...No doubt in my mind where you belong...* suggests that the narrator may well be delusional about her feelings for him. There is 'no doubt' in his mind but presumably plenty in hers. But he seems determined to prostrate himself before her on an even more masochistic level: *...I'd go hungry, I'd go black and blue/ I'd go crawling down the avenue...* he cries tearfully *...There's nothing I wouldn't do....*By now it must be obvious that, whatever protestations he may make, the narrator doesn't have a hope in hell of securing this woman's love. By continuing to make such exaggerated assurances such as *...I'll go to the ends of the earth for you...* he clearly sounds much *too* desperate.

In the second bridge the narrator indulges in a series of rather clichéd metaphors, through which he attempts to represent her state of mind: *...The storms are raging on the rolling sea/ And on the highway of regret...* he begins, following this with *...the winds of change are blowing wild and free...* There is at least some consistency in the imagery here. But *...You ain't seen nothing like me yet...* comes over as another rather exaggerated and boastful claim and a rather awkward use of a common aphorism (which slightly paraphrases Al Jolson's famous catchphrase) further suggesting the narrator's emotional desperation. In a later live version Dylan replaces the last two lines with *...Put your hand in mine, and come with me/ I'll see you don't get wet...* This certainly fits with the natural imagery of 'storms' and the 'rolling sea', but only makes the narrator appear even more unconvincing. In the final verse *...I could make you happy, make your dreams come true/ There's nothing I wouldn't do...* he at least appears to be expressing sincere sentiments, but with *...I'd go to the ends of the Earth for you...* he blows his credibility again.

The song has been criticised in some quarters for its rather extreme use of romantic cliché but its highly stylised quality of exaggerated desperation - whereby the narrator's appeals are somehow too awkward-sounding to be truly romantic - is what makes it so affecting. Against our better judgement, we feel great sympathy for a narrator who appears to have good intentions but is clearly incapable of expressing them. *Make You Feel My Love* has itself become a 'standard'. It is by far the most widely covered of all Dylan's late songs. Single releases by Adele, Garth Brooks and Billy Joel have been major pop hits. It has also been recorded by Bryan Ferry, Joan Osborne, Kelly Clarkson, Trisha Yearwood and has even featured in TV talent contest shows such as *The X Factor*. Much of its wide appeal derives from its distinctive melody, which is tinged with sadness. The variations of that melody in the two bridge sections intensify the narrator's increasing expression of anxiety and hopelessness. Despite the many cover versions of the song, there are few variations in the arrangements or even the vocal tones of the performers. The same is true of Dylan's own live versions, although sometimes the song is delivered at a slower and more sonorous pace than the original. The lyrics do not lend themselves to over-emoting. Almost any singer can sound both hopeful and awkward when delivering them. The version by Adele sounds clear and strident but it is the singer's modest and somewhat mournful tone that expresses the pathos at the heart of the song. Despite the awkwardness and over-emotionalism, there seems to be genuine regret and genuine love (or at least genuine longing) here, but we are left with the uneasy feeling that the narrator is not being completely 'straight' with the object of the song, or with the listener. There is a powerful sense of there being an unspoken subtext behind all the avowals. As listeners we may imagine that we are being serenaded by someone who is tragically mistaken, not about how they feel but about how *we* feel. By using deliberately exaggerated rhetoric, Dylan creates a very distinctive and unusual 'melancholy mood'.

By the time Dylan released *"Love And Theft"*, his use of pre-rock musical styles had become more explicit. On *Bye and Bye* and *Moonlight* he again plays self consciously with their characteristics in order to create rather ambivalent narratives in which we are fundamentally unsure of the sincerity of the narrators. But while the narrator of *To Make You Feel My Love* is, despite his inarticulacy, basically innocent and an object of our pity, in these songs there are hints that the narrators are using romantic conventions to manipulate the subjects of their appeals. This gives the songs a potentially tragic or even dangerous edge. These darker elements are made even more disturbing by the prevailing mood of apparent frivolity in the musical styles being used. The apparently rather slight *Bye and Bye* is a clear homage to 1930s style ballroom dance music. It appears, at least at first, to be a conventionally 'smoochy' number. The tune, which is partly derived from *Having Myself a Time*, a 'good time' song popularised by Billie Holiday, skips rather merrily from verse to verse with the narrator quite consciously embracing its immersion in the sentimental world view *...I'm singing love's praises...* he declares gaily *...in sugar coated rhyme...* A light, humorous mood is created when it begins with one of the corny 'jokes' that are scattered randomly around *"Love And Theft"* *...I'm sitting on my watch so I can be on time...* Thus the persona of a slick entertainer who always has a line of patter is established. The narrator likens himself to the star of a Hollywood musical, coming on like Gene Kelly or Fred Astaire: *...I'm painting the town/ Swinging my partner around...*

The song has four short verses, no chorus and two bridges. At first listen it appears to be a carefree romp through romantic clichés *...I know who I can depend on, I know who to trust...* the narrator declares reassuringly. But after this brightly-lit 'top hat and tails' persona has been established, the tone begins to darken. We then hear that he is *...Watching the roads, studying the dust...* and *...making my last go-round...* Then the tone shifts dramatically. By the first bridge section his breezy self-assurance seems to have vanished. Now he is *...scuffling and shuffling....* And, more disturbingly, perhaps

...walking on briars... Then there is a sudden unexpected and rather ominously self-aware confession: *...I'm not even acquainted with my own desires...* The rhyme is partly reconstructed from lines in Shakespeare's *As You Like It* when the heroine Rosalind declares that *...How full of briars is this working day world...* but later admits that *...Let me the knowledge of my fault bear with me/ If with myself I hold intelligence/ Or have acquaintance with mine own desires...* The allusion intensifies the mood of uncertainty which has overtaken the song, as the narrator - like Rosalind - begins to question his own motives: *...I'm rolling slow, I'm doing all I know....*

By now the jauntiness of the opening of the song has vanished. Although the musical tone is still cheery, the lyrics become ever more confessional *...I'm telling myself I've found true happiness....* the narrator assures us but then confesses that *...that I still have a dream that hasn't been repossessed....* And he is still 'walking on briars': *...I'm walking slow/ Going where the wild roses go...* By now we have a picture of a narrator who seems to have no control over his own emotions. He is clearly fooling himself that he is really happy. Even his 'dreams' - his innermost desires - have been taken away from him. The use of the apparently out-of-place term 'repossessed' is particularly galling, suggesting a strong lack of emotional control.

The second bridge begins with: *...Well, the future for me is already a thing of the past...* The distinctively 'Dylanesque' use of ambiguous paradox recalls such lines as *... I was so much older then, I'm younger than that now...* (*My Back Pages,* 1964) *...When you ain't got nothing, you got nothing to lose...* (*Like A Rolling Stone,* 1965) or *...to live outside the law you must be honest...* (*Absolutely Sweet Marie*, 1966). The line has often been taken as being emblematic of the whole tone and approach of Dylan's 21st century work. In his songs, his 'Americana' themed paintings and his radio show, Dylan constantly evokes images of an 'old America' (or perhaps a kind of 'classic Americana') personified in images of 1950s automobiles, roadside motels and 'endless highways' which he finds buried just beneath the surface of today's world. The narrator may simply be being nostalgic, or refusing to adapt to change. Or, perhaps more pertinently -- and possibly more menacingly - he has already made his mind up about the steps he is going to take. The next line: *...You were my first love and you will be my last...* may seem innocent enough. In the vernacular of the sentimental tradition, it could be seen as a confession of undying 'eternal' love. On the other hand, given the suggestion of the narrator's lack of self-control, it could be viewed as being rather more sinister, perhaps even a threat.

By the final verse we seem to have jumped into that pre-ordained future referred to in the previous lines. There are intimations of tragedy *...Papa gone mad...* we are told *...Mama's feeling sad...* Then in the next, and most unnerving line, the singer suddenly comes on like a hellfire preacher, declaring that: *...I'm gonna baptize you with fire so you can sin no more.....* The transition from carefree lover to crazed revenger seems complete. Then there is a strange historical juxtaposition *...I'm gonna establish my rule through civil war...* There appears to be a definite, calculated threat here aimed at the object of the song, who is only clearly addressed in the ambiguous and foreboding final line: *...Gonna make you see just how loyal and true a man can be....* We can perhaps assume that the narrator is a jilted lover who is using the song to vent his feelings of remorse. Or maybe he is *really* creepy, like a stalker in a cheap horror flick, determined to wreak revenge. The increasingly dark lyrics are continually juxtaposed against the jauntiness of the tune, which may suggest that the implicit threat in the last few lines is merely some kind of wish fulfillment. Dylan plays rather lovingly with the tropes and conventions of sentimental song, in which the jilted lover is a stock figure. But in the final lines, he suggests a connection between these conventions and the deranged mentality of the USA's 'crazed' assassins, from the murderers of John and Robert Kennedy, Martin Luther King and John Lennon to the perpetrators of a long string of massacres conducted in schools, colleges, churches, synagogues, mosques and other institutions.

Dylan's interest in the American Civil War is well known. In *Chronicles* he describes a time in the early 1960s when he spent whole weeks in a public library examining all the articles in the *New York Times* published between 1855 and 1865. He explains that:

...The age that I was living in didn't resemble this age, but it did in some mysterious and traditional way. Not just a little bit, but a lot. There was a broad spectrum and commonwealth that I was living upon, and the basic psychology of that life was every bit a part of it. If you turned the light towards it, you could see the full complexity of human nature. Back there, America was put on the cross, died, and was resurrected. There was nothing synthetic about it. The god-awful truth of that would be the all-encompassing template behind everything I would write...

Whether Dylan *really* managed to fit this rather extraordinary piece of research into his busy schedule as a folk performer and composer is debatable. But in his late period songs he refers back to the time of the American Civil War on many occasions. As the time frame of the songs on *"Love And Theft"* and *Modern Times* shifts around, often imperceptibly, from the present day to various moments in the earlier part of the twentieth century, the legacy of the great American conflict of the previous century is a constant reference point. In a number of songs Dylan even lifts lines from Henry Timrod, a rather obscure contemporary of Whitman known as the 'poet of the Confederacy' and 'pastes' them into the songs. The reference to 'Civil War' here is rather ambiguous, suggesting that the song may be more than an anguished lover's lament. Perhaps the narrator of *Bye And Bye* is a member of the racist Ku Klux Klan, long a powerful force in the antebellum South, and his supposed 'love object' is going to be his victim. The tone of *... I'm gonna baptize you with fire so you can sin no more...* seems to be that of the kind of politico-religious fanaticism that the Klan espouses. The reference quotes John the Baptist from Luke 3:16:

...John answered, saying unto them all, I indeed baptize you with water; but one mightier than I cometh, the latchet of whose shoes I am not worthy to unloose: he shall baptize you with the Holy Ghost and with fire...

One may argue that the narrator is speaking metaphorically. But the inclusion of such aggressive and perhaps slightly crazed religiosity certainly hints at a dark fanaticism.

The phrase 'bye and bye' appears in the first line where the narrator assures us that he is ... *breathing a lover's sigh...* The phrase itself (sometimes spelt 'by and by') refers to some vague, ill defined time in the future. It is also often used in gospel songs and hymns as a synonym for 'the hereafter' or for the coming of 'Christ's kingdom on earth'. The popular hymn *In the Sweet Bye and Bye*, which promises the faithful a reunion after death, has become a standard, and has been covered by (among many others) Johnny Cash and Willie Nelson. One famed 'gospel shouter' hymn called *Bye and Bye* looks forward to the day when every day 'will be Sunday'. Another famous popular hymn *By and By When the Morning Comes* runs*:*

...We are tossed and driven
On the restless sea of time;
Somber skies and howling tempests
Oft succeed a bright sunshine;
In that land of perfect day,
When the mists are rolled away,
We will understand it better by and by...

Although the phrase only appears once in Dylan's song, its religious connotations and the hints of fanaticism may suggest that the narrator has murderous intentions. On the other hand, the phrase is a very common one and is generally used in a purely secular way. Perhaps it is just a blithe, inconsequential means for the narrator to introduce himself. There is little doubt, however, that Dylan is teasing us with both possible meanings. *Bye and Bye* is a song that purports to be an 'old style crooner' in which a jilted lover expresses his anguish. But its sly suggestions and partial allusions invite us into the intricate and subversive game that *"Love And Theft"* plays with its audience, in which history and literary references are juggled with musical and lyrical conventions, so that the future really does become ....*a thing of the past...*

Moonlight, the other obvious 'crooner' from *"Love And Theft",* also appears - on the surface at least - to be a romantic song. Its musical construction is simple. It begins with a basic guitar line, followed by a soft percussive shuffle. There are six short verses which end with the refrain ... *Won't you meet me out in the moonlight alone...* and two extended bridges. Dylan's vocals are restrained and plaintive and apparently sincere. The music clearly harks back to the romantic numbers of the 1920s and 30s. Its melody bears some resemblance to Glenn Miller's *Moonlight Serenade* (1939). Dylan stirs up a whole melting pot of allusions. The line *...my sad heart is yearning...* appears in the lament *Shepherd of the Hills,* as recorded in 1927 by the Jack Hylton Orchestra. *Meet Me by the Moonlight Alone* is the title of a song by the Carter Family from 1928. The phrase *Doctor, Lawyer, Indian Chief* is the title of a song by Hoagy Carmichael. "It takes a thief to catch a thief" is a proverbial saying originating in the seventeenth century. The reference to the plant 'Black-Eyed Susan' recalls a poem about a female sailor by the eighteenth century poet John Gay called *Sweet William's Farewell to Black-Eyed Susan*

(1720). The famous lines *...For Whom The Bell Tolls/ It tolls for you and me...* are from John Donne, as well as being the title of Ernest Hemingway's novel about the Spanish Civil War (1940). Another reference point may well be the aforementioned *Stardust,* which has a similarly elegiac, late-evening feel.

Adopting a suitably languid vocal tone, Dylan conjures up an autumnal setting - a typical location for a romantic ballad. The season is associated with sad memories and missed opportunities. We are first informed that *...The seasons they're a-turning...* (an opening line that quietly references Dylan's own *The Times They Are a-Changin'*). Later we hear that *...The clouds are turning crimson/ the leaves fall from the limbs...* and that the petals have been blown off the trees. The singer also 'yearns' to hear *...the songbird's sweet melodious tone...* In romantic songs like *Stardust* and *A Nightingale Sang in Berkeley Square,* songbirds are symbolic of love. And 'moonlight' itself is conventionally associated with romance, as in *Moonlight Becomes You*, a big hit for Bing Crosby in 1942 or Van Morrison's *Moondance* (1970), which Dylan covered in 1992. Dylan appears to revel in all these clichés. But he also begins to add some memorable poetic detail, naming specific plants (*...Orchids/ poppies/ Black-Eyed Susan...* and later *...trailing moss in mystic glow...* and *...the boulevards of cypress trees...)* in order to embellish the 'dimly lit' romantic atmosphere. Then lines begin to appear that would be unlikely to feature in traditional romantic numbers. The sunset is described somewhat apocalyptically as *...the earth and sky that melts with flesh and bone...* This suggests a possible intimation of mortality, in that the autumnal sunset may be a metaphor for ageing as well as a potential meeting place for lovers *...The air is thick and heavy/ All along the levee...* may indicate a Mississippi/New Orleans setting for the song. It seems as if a storm is about to break. Now the birds have gone. The geese, we hear, have made their autumnal migration. The tension in the air has become palpable.

In the first bridge, the song's narrator reveals himself to be a 'lover' who is prepared to use techniques of manipulation and control *...I'm preaching peace and harmony/ The blessings of tranquility...* he croons. This is in considerable contrast to the next line *...Yet I know when the time is right to strike...* Is he being threatening, or merely playful? It certainly seems that his tone is becoming more patronising as he declares *...I'll take you 'cross the river dear/ You've no need to linger here...* and then, even more ambiguously: *... I know the kind of things you like....* By telling the object of his address that he knows what is good for her, he is certainly breaching the romantic code. And yet the calm, conversational tone that the lines are delivered in can be taken merely as light persuasion. The narrator throws in the tantalising line: *...the masquerades of birds and bees...* which may be a rather elegant way of describing the game of sexual display and flirtation. But is he asking his lover to take part in some kind of 'masquerade'? Already we may suspect that the singer's romantic declarations may 'mask' more specifically poetic concerns, as he 'leads us by the hand' into the song's symbolic landscape.

We are then bombarded by an almost blinding profusion of natural imagery, including 'crimson leaves', 'shadows over stone', 'pink and white' windblown petals and 'boulevards of cypress trees'. Red, pink, white and green colours clash in the moonlight..

Although the singer maintains his 'sweet melodious tone' his emotions seem to be rising as his vivid imagination takes flight. He admits that he is over-excited. He tells us that ...*My pulse is running through my palm...* Nature now seems to have come alive in his imagination. We are shown...*trailing moss in mystic glow/ Purple blossoms soft as snow...* and ...*yellow fields with twisted oaks that groan...* And, as if to identify *himself* as an elemental force of nature, he proclaims that ...*my tears are flowing to the sea...* By now we can see that the love he is professing for a woman, or for nature, is rather frenzied. *Moonlight* appears at first to be a lover's invitation to meet in a romantic setting. But its focus on the mystical qualities of nature - and of autumn in particular - recalls the bleak landscape of Keats' *La Belle Dame Sans Merci*, which also has a symbolic autumnal setting. But here the sexual roles are reversed. Whereas Keats' narrator is entranced and beguiled by the deadly 'belle dame', here it is the narrator who is enticing and mesmerising the object of the song. Songbirds - particularly nightingales - commonly feature as symbols of romantic love in sentimental songs. But now they have been silenced. A strange and unsettling quiet settles over a landscape that seems, as in so many of the greatest poems of the Romantic era, to be alive. And no birds sing...

26th October 2014. Bob Dylan is coming to the end of a three night stand at the Dolby Theater, Hollywood, an intimate and prestigious 3,000 seat auditorium which - since 2001 - has been the venue for the Academy Awards ceremonies. It's time for the set ritual of the encore, which for the whole of this year's shows has been *All Along the Watchtower* followed by *Blowin' in the Wind.* Pretty much what you'd expect. The LA fun lovers are buzzed out and leery, no doubt expecting the familiar tunes, and are certainly not ungenerous in shouting out their love and appreciation. Right now, the lights are still dimmed. But as they slowly come up, Dylan is not behind his keyboard as usual. He is standing centre stage, in a neat brown suit with white striped trimmings and a flat topped boater, a favourite of Buster Keaton and all the rage around 1926. The strains of Donnie Herron's steel guitar come in as Dylan steps forward and sings ...*Should my heart not be humble/ Should my eyes fail to see/ Should my feet sometimes stumble/ On the way, stay with me...* The excited audience throws whoops and cheers up at the stage. Bob does not flinch. He continues: ...*Like the lamb that in springtime/ Wanders far from the fold/ Comes the darkness and the frost/ I get lost, I grow cold...* He takes a breath ...*I grow cold, I grow weary, and I know I have sinned/ And I go seeking shelter and I cry in the wind...* More cheers. They're loving the excitement of this. Bob is doing a debut performance...

Typically, there has been no introduction of this number, although it is unlikely that many of the LA concertgoers will have ever heard it before. For all they know, it might be a new Dylan song. The narrator is certainly seeking 'shelter from the storm' as he 'cries in the wind'. In fact, it was written by Jerome Moross (music) and Carolyn Leigh (lyrics) for Otto Preminger's Golden Globe nominated movie *The Cardinal*, in which it was performed by Frank Sinatra. Leigh wrote lyrics for several 'movie songs' including *Witchcraft, The Best is Yet to Come* and *Young at Heart*, the last two of which Dylan would, along with *Stay With Me*, record in 'un-covered' versions. The film, which has the two world wars as a backdrop, tells the life story of a rather heroic priest who rises up the Catholic Church hierarchy, having made some agonising moral decisions on the way. The 'religious' imagery in the simple but powerful lyrics reflects this. Sinatra's recording features his usual immaculate phrasing, set against a full string section, which build up as the song reaches its climax. Dylan's version here is shorter, with minimal accompaniment. Charlie Sexton plucks almost inaudible guitar lines and Tony Garnier scrapes his bow across the double bass. Dylan sings softly:

...And though I grope and I blunder and I'm weak and I'm wrong/
Though the road buckles under where I walk, walk along/
Till I find to my wonder every path leads to thee/
All that I can do is pray, stay with me/ Stay with me....

B*eyond the Horizon*, from *Modern Times,* is perhaps Dylan's most explicit venture into the sentimental tradition. A meditation on theme of mortality delivered with light irony, it is also a kind of pastiche of all those romantic, corny songs which tell us about a love which will 'last forever'. The song wallows unashamedly in a sepia-tinted romantic world, taking us to 'the end of the rainbow' through 'the long hours of twilight' under 'crimson skies'. The melody is derived from the old romantic weepie *Red Sails in the Sunset*, a hit for Bing Crosby, Nat King Cole and Louis Armstrong written in 1935, whose narrator mournfully pleads for his love to return from a sea voyage. There are also references to other romantic songs like *The Bells of St. Mary's* and *Round about Midnight*. Over a soft shuffle of stand-up bass and a whisper of 'Hawaiian' steel guitar, the vocals are querulous, sighing; straddling a thin line between Dylanesque harshness and appealingly innocent sweetness. In a joyfully playful romantic way, the narrator seems to suggest that his love is so strong that it will continue even beyond death.

The song begins by conjuring up an imaginary world situated somewhere *...in the long hours of twilight...* The narrator looks into the face of death with a sly shrug and a playful wink. We are presented with a vision of Paradise re-imagined as an 'all singing, all dancing' Hollywood musical; a place where *...life has only begun...* It's as if he has followed Dorothy 'over the rainbow' into a garishly coloured fantasy land. The sentiment seems to be that once our anxieties about death are cast aside, we can experience paradise on Earth, a place where *...love waits forever/ for one and for all...* and in which all earthly desires can be fully realised. The singer pines for his love, his 'wretched heart' pounding. He has been 'kissed by an angel' yet he experiences 'mortal' (rather than immortal) bliss. Now he dances with his darling, cheek to cheek: *...Every step that you take...* he declares *...I'm walking the same...* His love for his 'angel' has redeemed him 'just in time', saving him from despair. For a moment he is thrown back in time to a place where *...it's dark and it's dreary...* You can see the tear in the corner of his eye: *...I'm wounded, I'm weary...* he confesses *...my repentance is plain....* Now he is down on one knee, perhaps offering up a single red rose, thanking her for the redemption she is offering him. He marvels at his own survival, feeling that his 'life has been spared' to be fully present in this triumphant moment: *...I still can't believe...* he sighs *...that you have set aside your love for me...* The narrator plays the role of a penitent lover to the full. He refers to his 'wretched heart' which after her 'angel's kiss', is *...drowning in mortal bliss...*

Such rhetoric and imagery are common in the sentimental tradition. Women are often seen as 'angels' who will redeem their male lovers. Here, though, religious imagery is given particular emphasis. The line *...Down in the valley someone prayed for your soul...* seems to refer to the Biblical 'valley of the shadow of death' from Psalm 23. The singer appears to be suggesting that he and his lover will be together through eternity. Clearly it is the narrator who is doing the praying. But it is unclear who is being addressed here. It's tempting to imagine an ageing lothario being renewed by the caresses of some young 'precious angel', lying in bed *...in the soft light of morning...* as he watches her sleep, marvelling at how her beauty and vitality have filled him with such 'mortal bliss'. Right now he seems to be awed at the way that, 'beyond the horizon' of his expected creative life, he has been renewed once again by the creative spirit of his muse.

In the song's occasional moments of doubt, we sense a certain frustration that life may not be long enough for the singer's poetic energies to be fully realised, but in the end he rejoices in having *...more than a lifetime/ to live loving you...* so celebrating the boundlessness of the poetic spirit itself. The song can be seen as a message to Dylan's audience which might only come to full fruition after the singer's death. Here he appears to be 'confessing' to us that he has devoted his life to creating art that will give him a kind of immortality, while acknowledging that in reality such a notion is just an illusion. In some of his songs he expresses surprise at his own continued longevity. Even back in 1978 in *Where Are You Tonight* (*Journey Through Dark Heat*) he declares in tangible exaltation *...I can't believe it/ I can't believe I'm alive!....* Here the lines *...There's always a reason/ That someone's life has been spared...* seems to suggest that he feels he is living out some kind of 'destiny' ordained by a higher power.

Beyond the Horizon was performed 58 times between 2007 and 2009, during which time its lyrics and melody were varied considerably. From the first performance onwards, the verse referring to the 'angel's kiss' is replaced by *...The morning sun is risen/ On the whole human race/ I'm right out of prison/ I put on my good face...* which further emphasises the narrator's penitence and the universal theme of the song. Other new lines are even more confessional: *...I'm roaming the meadows/ I'm barefoot in pain...* the narrator tells us *...I'm trampling on shadows/ I have no shame...* On another occasion the narrator abases himself even further by switching somewhat bizarrely into 'Mexican cowboy' mode with *...My boots and sombrero/ My saddles and spurs/ If I die tomorrow/ Everything will be hers....* These lines again toy with elements of humorous pastiche, although by 2009 the song's melody has been considerably changed and the delivery is slower and more deliberate, as if Dylan is attempting to be less parodic. In the rewritten lyrics that appear on Dylan's official website, much of the religious imagery is played down. The narrator is now *....staring out the window of an ancient town/ Petals from flowers falling to the ground...* Later he states that *...I lost my true lover in the dusk, in the dawn/ I have to recover, get up and go on...* and *...Slipping and sliding, too late to stop/ Riding and gliding, it's lonely at the top....* lines that play with clichés in a rather different manner, but which de-emphasise the theme of eternal love and attempt to make the song a more straightforward declaration of determination to carry on in the face of adversity.

Spirit on the Water, also from *Modern Times*, is expressed through the tender whisper of an ageing crooner. In its amiable and self deprecatingly humorous depiction of a desperate older man begging for sexual favours from an alluring younger woman, it is reminiscent of several late-period Leonard Cohen songs. Both Dylan and Cohen deal with the problems that ageing brings with self-deprecating wit. They both use addresses to women as ways of addressing their own 'spiritual' desires, thus hoping to remain in touch with the sources of their inspiration. Cohen had played the part of romantic seducer with great eloquence in his earlier work but by the time of *I'm Your Man* (1988), as he contemplates his late middle age, he turns to professing his lust with comic desperation. He insists that he will do anything his young lover asks him to, even to the extent of telling her that if she wants to turn tricks on the street he will 'disappear' for her. He completes his self-humiliation by declaring that: *...I'd crawl to you baby and I'd fall at your feet/ I'd howl at your beauty like a dog on heat...*

Dylan's narrator never gets quite that desperate and his concerns are - at least on the surface - more ethereal. He begins by referencing the first few lines of Genesis: *...Spirit on the water/ Darkness on the face of the deep...* taking us into the moments before creation. The music rolls in a steady tempo, with deep, subdued double bass, delicate brushes on the drums, gently tinkling piano and tasteful snatches of violin and guitar. It is as if the singer's spirit is indeed hovering over the surface of the primordial ocean, gliding in air in the moment before creation. His heart, it seems, is light. He is in love, besotted with some young 'princess'. He can hardly sleep *...You got a face that begs for love...* he sighs. Yet it's clearly him who's doing the begging. Using well-worn blues imagery as sly sexual innuendo, he implores her to *...put some sugar in my bowl/ I feel like lying down... Need A Little Sugar in My Bowl* is a song recorded by Bessie Smith in 1931, in which she tells us that *...I need a little sugar in my bowl/ I need a little hot dog between my rolls...* which could hardly be more explicit. Dylan's plea is also a straightforward come-on but the cool, resigned delivery of the lines conjures up a world-weariness which suggests that, despite his apparent lustfulness and vigour, a 'lie down' is really all he needs. Certainly, it's all he's likely to get. He pictures himself fading away, the substance of his body becoming like mist and shadow *...I'm as pale as a ghost...* he sighs *...holding a blossom on a stem....* He is not even offering her flowers, but something incomplete, faded, and barely even visible. Though he tells her that he

...can't believe these things could ever fade from your mind... we can be sure that they will.

The narrator is ready to confess his deep devotion, to express his humility and to give thanks for the sheer privilege of being allowed merely to exist in the presence of his beloved. In reality, of course, it's likely that the 'princess' will use him and discard him. Yet he is determined to make the most of what he is being offered. He seems to revel in every moment. He insists that he *...can't explain/ the sources of this hidden pain...* so assuming the traditional role of the self-effacing, martyred lover: *...If I can't have you...* he breathes ... *I'll throw my love into the deep blue sea...* But we are never really convinced that he is experiencing genuine 'pain'. Like a true romantic fool he tells her *...Life without you/ Doesn't mean a thing to me...* In fact we can only pity him as the evidence accumulates that she is manipulating him for her own ends: *...You do good all day/ You do wrong all night...* We can almost see the tears of joy, mingled with the inevitable disappointment. The lines *...When you're with me/ I'm a thousand times happier than I could say...* are delivered with cute nonchalance, as is *...What does it matter/ What price I pay?...* Although the singer may wish to dismiss his own suffering, trying to make us believe that just spending any time in her presence makes the humiliation he must face bearable, the lightness of his tone betrays him.

The pleas now become increasingly hopeless. He tells her he will accept any humiliation to be with her and begins to dream of a kind of eternal union which might extend even beyond the grave. Yet the strange confession in the penultimate verse, that he cannot join her in 'paradise' because *...I killed a man back there...* (With its odd echo of Johnny Cash's iconic line in *Folsom Prison Blues: ...I shot a man in Reno/ Just to watch him die...*) suggests that he considers himself - as a miserable sinner - unworthy of her. Perhaps - as in *Every Grain of Sand* - he is identifying himself with Cain, the slayer of his brother Abel in the Genesis story, who is condemned to walk the earth thereafter, but can never escape the consequences of his 'mortal sin'. Yet he ends the song with jaunty confidence, suggesting that, even without this 'paradisiacal' union, they could still *...have a 'whomping' good time...* together. They could have their own 'moment of creation' with her spirit moving over his 'dark waters' to create a flash of blinding, inspirational light. The narrator's flower of youth may have faded but he is still holding that fragile blossom on a stem, dreaming of eternal bliss.

Here Dylan brings great assurance and optimism to his skilful manipulation of the conventions of the romantic song. Behind each sighing gasp of despair there is a touch of ironic lightness, a sense that he has been liberated from the 'hidden pain' that love so often brings. It is hard not to read the final lines as a message to his listeners about his continued vitality. Indeed, when audiences became familiar with the first lines of the final verse they would respond to the (possibly rhetorical) questions*...You think I'm over the hill?/ You think I'm past my prime...* by cheering or shouting a resounding 'No!'.

When the Deal Goes Down is perhaps the most precisely written and the least ambiguous song on *Modern Times*. The tune is based on *Where the Blue of the Night (Meets the Gold of the Day)*, a Bing Crosby number from 1931. It was performed on almost 150 occasions between 2006 and 2013, with little variation in the lyrics or melody. It deals with mortality and the fragility of existence 'in this earthly domain' with great humility and dignity. Its rich fusion of natural imagery and restrained plain speak is reminiscent of the precise and measured poetry of Robert Frost. The delivery is a breathy, almost whispered, Willie Nelson-style croon which befits its bittersweet nature. There is a sparing use of archaic language, including several lines 'borrowed' from Henry Timrod. The song is also infused with the spirit, and some of the imagery, of the blues. Yet these disparate elements are quite seamlessly combined, as the singer conducts a kind of conversation with his audience, the rest of the world and himself. The phrase 'when the deal goes down' is used in several blues songs, including *Honey Babe Let the Deal Go Down* (1931) by The Mississippi Sheiks and *Don't Let Your Deal Go Down*, first recorded by Charlie Poole and The North Carolina Ramblers in 1925 (and covered by Dylan on several occasions). The 'deal' in these songs is a gambling metaphor which the singers extend to life in general, the idea being that you have to use whatever 'hand' you are given. Here, Dylan's narrator is determined to hold onto the 'cards' he has been dealt.

The song depicts a struggle for, and perhaps a final attainment of, a kind of spiritual enlightenment, which will be achieved not through any conventional religious path but through making a personal 'deal' with the spirit of creativity. It begins like a slow country waltz, with some mournful steel guitar and tense percussive brush strokes. In the first verse the narrator describes the state of existential confusion he has found himself in, confessing that *...We live and we die/ We know not why...* Any prayers that may be offered up are like invisible clouds, floating away unnoticed. The 'pathways of life' are dark and the singer stands in the symbolic landscape of *...the world's ancient light/ Where wisdom grows up in strife...* The declaration that *...But I'll be with you when the deal goes down...* is the first statement of defiant faith, apparently contradicting what has gone before. As the band sticks to the minimal backdrop, the song shifts between the personal and the universal. The first lines of the second verse *...We eat and we drink, we feel and we think/ Far down the street we stray...* suggest that we are all fallible creatures who will inevitably 'stray' from the path of virtue. The singer is 'haunted' by his regret for *....things I never meant or wished to say...* The second half of the verse moves into more imagistic expression *...The midnight rain follows the train...* is the song's most 'Dylanesque' line, using typical blues imagery. 'Rain' is a common image in Dylan's work, frequently symbolising chaotic confusion and spiritual desolation. Here the 'midnight rain' stands as a metaphor for life's troubles, following the train which symbolises the progress of a human life.

The next line *...We all wear the same thorny crown...* delivered with a kind of light, sighing compassion, is perhaps the song's most resonant image. The vocal delivery is so moving because of the sense of dignity Dylan imparts to what amounts to an almost tearfully world-weary acceptance of the inevitability of the burden we must all bear - not of 'sin' but of the awareness of our own mortality. Despite this, the song is extremely positive in that it celebrates human potential. The next line, the exquisitely alliterative

...*Soul to soul, our shadows roll...* further emphasises the idea that although ultimately we are all equally mortal, our 'shadows' will eventually merge blissfully together in the spiritual world. Dylan caresses the words gently, with their neat internal rhyme suggesting his acceptance of a kind of universal harmony. The title refrain at the end of the verse now begins with 'and' rather than 'but'. The contradictions of the first verse have clearly, to some extent, been resolved.

The mood of reconciliation continues *...We learn to live...* he tells us ...*and then we forgive/ o'er the road we're bound to go...* The anachronistic expression gives the lines a kind of timeless quality, with the reference to the 'road' of life echoing the 'street' on which we 'stray' from the first verse. Perhaps Dylan was recalling Robert Frost's famous poem *The Road Not Taken* with its final declaration that:

...I shall be telling this with a sigh
Somewhere ages and ages hence
Two roads diverged in a wood and I
Took the one less travelled by
And that one has made all the difference...

The next lines, partly borrowed from Timrod, focus again on the fragility of life: ...*More frailer than the flowers/ These precious hours...* Dylan adds the remarkable *...that keep us so tightly bound...* suggesting that we often keep the potential 'blooming' of our lives, and of our creativity, 'tightly bound' like pressed flowers in an old book. The implication seems to be that life is infinitely precious and that it should not be wasted in futile struggle. Following this, the final lines are triumphant, with the singer greeting his muse like a revelation, a *...vision from the skies...*

Finally our 'seeker' reaffirms his newfound acceptance of life's turbulent path. Instead of following a 'road' he follows a more natural 'winding stream'. He tells us that he has picked up a rose, the Blakean symbol of love, life and death; but that, rather comically *...it poked through my clothes...* But he does not feel it pricking him now. Although he lives in *...this earthly domain/ Full of disappointment and pain...* he now fully accepts his place in the scheme of things. Despite the 'deafening noise' of life's mad confusion, he accepts the 'transient joys' of life, even though *... I know they're not what they seem...* He confesses that he 'owes his heart' to the subject of the song. And he implies that when his 'deal' finally 'goes down' he will be reunited with Calliope herself - the muse of creativity in whom he now places his faith.

20th December 2016. One of NBC's pre-Christmas specials features Bob Dylan participating in another stellar gathering. The show is *Tony Bennett Celebrates 90: The Best is Yet to Come*. Most of the show was recorded on September 5th at Radio City Music Hall. The front few rows of the theatre are packed with stars, some of whom will soon be appearing on stage. In the front row is none other than the immaculately dressed and coiffured Mr. Bennett himself, looking extremely dapper, full of vitality and naturally very pleased to be here. Perhaps you could call him a 'role model' for Dylan, a comparative youngster at only 75. Bennett has always been a stout defender of the virtues of the Great American Songbook and as such has not altered his performance style - or his set list - a great deal since his heyday in the 1950s and '60s. He has been on record as declaring that Mercer and Porter and their contemporaries were the greatest songwriters of all time and that what he performs should be regarded as 'classical' music.

In recent years Bennett has become something of a 'retro' cult figure among baby boomers and their children, having acquired a reputation as 'the last of the great crooners'. Tonight's show features members of the rock generation like Stevie Wonder and Elton John, as well as younger performers like k. d. lang, Lady Gaga and Rufus Wainwright and modern balladeers like Michael Bublé and Leslie Odom Jr. They all perform numbers that are associated with Bennett, in front of a full orchestra. Gaga, looking suitably sultry in a slinky ball gowns with slit sides, appears twice and camps up the full Judy Garland on *The Lady is a Tramp* and *La Vie en Rose*. Stars of Hollywood are also in attendance. They include Bruce Willis, who introduces Diana Kraal; Robert De Niro, who introduces Andrea Boccelli and Kevin Stacey, who does a passable job of crooning *The Very Thought of You* and *If I Ruled the World.* Jazz trumpeter Wynton Marsalis gives a thoughtful speech explaining how Bennett was a supporter of Civil Rights and marched with Martin Luther King. Several clips have been 'phoned in' by other celebrities, including rock luminaries Keith Richards and Paul McCartney. Even Homer Simpson and Miss Piggy get in on the act. Dylan's performance, which is introduced by Steve Buscemi, was recorded on 28th October in the Workplay Theater in Birmingham, Alabama when Dylan was between shows in his current tour.

Once Upon a Time, recorded by Bennett in 1962, has not yet been released by Dylan but will appear on *Triplicate* in 2017. It was composed for the rather obscure 1962 musical *All American*, written by Charles Strouse with lyrics by Lee Adams. The first recording was by the musical's lead Ray Bolger, famous for his role as the Scarecrow in *The Wizard of Oz*. Bolger is more of a comic than a singer and basically 'talks' through the song. Yet it soon became a standard. Frank Sinatra's recording (1965) uses full on orchestration, milking the nostalgia in the song for all it's worth, whereas Bennett's version is slightly more restrained. But tonight the TV audience will witness an 'uncovered' performance, with Donnie Herron's restrained steel guitar taking the place of the orchestra. Dylan stands centre stage, clad in a rather lurid green suit with yellow cuffs, and plays with the microphone stand in true crooner fashion. The lyrics conjure up a prelapsarian, childlike world *...A girl with moonlight in her eyes put her hand in mind...* he coos *...And said she loved me so/ But that was once upon a time, so long ago....* All the clichés are here. There are willow trees and stars and references to a *...world that was sweeter than we knew...* But this is a song which, because of its blatantly nostalgic tone (which is, of course, appropriate for the occasion) benefits greatly from the minimalist treatment. As usual, Bob plays it straight but, because the delivery emphasises the 'fragile' nature of the sentiments being expressed, there is just a hint of irony in the performance. By paring it down to its most basic constituents and presenting an unashamedly tearful story in its 'purest' form, he reveals the genuine but extremely delicate expression of pathos within the song. He turns it into an understated ode to the lost innocence of a musical form that was soon to be 'drowned out' by the unashamed passion of rock'n'roll.

The fortunes of Hollywood and mainstream American popular music have, since the coming of sound in the cinema in the late 1920s, been thoroughly interlinked. Popular crooners like Bing Crosby, Dean Martin and Frank Sinatra had successful parallel careers as movie stars. A few rock stars, such as David Bowie, Mick Jagger, Ringo Starr and Art Garfunkel, have had some success in this area, as have country performers like Johnny Cash, Willie Nelson and - most notably - Kris Kristofferson. Film music is, however, one area in which the musical values of the Great American Songbook era have remained mostly intact and generally immune from the dominance of rock'n'roll, rap and other rhythmic forms. Hollywood films still specialise in 'big emotions', which require massed violins on the soundtracks, so songs by modern romantic balladeers like Barbara Streisand and Celine Dion have continued to be successful.

In the 2000s Dylan took on several commissions to write songs for films. As a confirmed cineaste, he seems to have relished the challenge of composing songs that reflected on the themes of the films in question. Apart from *Things Have Changed*, these songs have remained relatively obscure, although most of them were anthologised on the *Bootleg Series* release *Tell Tale Signs* in 2008. *Waiting for You*, which was written for Callie Khouri's 2002 movie, *Divine Secrets of the Ya-Ya Sisterhood*, has not as yet appeared on a Dylan album, although it did become a staple of his live set from 2013-15. *Divine Secrets* is a wryly bittersweet and avowedly feminist tale centered on the complex relationship between a mother and daughter. The story is focused on a well known female playwright Siddalee Walker (Sandra Bullock) who engages the wrath of her eccentric and feisty mother Vivienne (Ellen Burstyn) when she appears to confess in a (somewhat doctored) interview to feeling rather unhappy about her childhood. Siddalee is subsequently kidnapped by her mothers' lifelong friends in the 'Ya Ya Sisterhood' (a kind of proto-feminist 'support group' they had originally formed together in their youth) so that mother and daughter can be confronted with each other. Eventually, with the Sisterhood's help, Siddalee comes to understand the dark side of her mother's character, so leading to an eventual rapprochement between the two. The film is a warm, lightly comedic tribute to the potential strength of female solidarity.

Waitin' for You is an exercise in rather oblique storytelling, which broadly follows the theme of the film. It is a stately country waltz, dominated by plaintive steel guitar and backed by an oddly stiff, almost military drum pattern. It uses many of the tropes of the sentimental tradition, without the hints of darkness displayed in *Bye and Bye* and *Moonlight*. Although it expresses a degree of anguish, its imagery and its delivery are playful, allusive and ultimately reassuring. Dylan's voice begins by sounding cracked and bitter, but becomes increasingly warm as the song progresses and we sense a kind of optimism building *...Hope may vanish...* he confides to us *...but it never dies...* The song is written as an address by the Ya Ya Sisterhood's anguished mother Vivienne to her estranged daughter. It deals with the dilemmas of parental love when the child has grown up. You can almost hear the parental sighs at the child's wilfulness: *...I'm letting her have her way...* the narrator insists and *...the poor girl always wins the day...*

All this is a prelude to the meeting between mother and child that forms the core of the film's story. Dylan builds this up towards the end of the first verse with some delicious allusions. As the music swirls, we seem to be in some kind of dance hall. The dance appears to be increasingly wild, erratic and drunken, with the *...whiskey flyin' into my head...* The band is playing so hard that *...the fiddler's arm has gone dead...* There is a suggestion of small-town claustrophobia: *...talk is beginning to spread...* In the second verse the narrator cries self-pityingly into her whiskey bottle: *...It's been so long since I held you tight/ Been so long since we said goodnight...* and *...The taste of tears is bittersweet/ When you're near me, my heart forgets to beat...* But the third verse rescues us from this maudlin direction with perhaps the song's most charming lines *...Well the king of them all is starting to fall/ I lost my gal at the boatman's ball...* Dylan lets his tongue linger over these lines, which allude to a nineteenth-century minstrel song *De Boatman's Ball*, written by Daniel Decatur Emmett, the composer of the civil war standard *Dixie*.

The narrator now appears to be laughing at herself, having lost her daughter to the world of fame and entertainment. The next line *...The night has a thousand hearts and eyes...* alludes to both the jazz standard *The Night Has a Thousand Eyes* and a famous short poem by the late nineteenth century poet Francis William Bourdillon. Dylan tweaks this lovelorn line slightly to emphasise the steadfastness of the narrator's 'heart', as she insists that she will *...stay on top of things...* She will keep that 'eye of the heart' open, despite her estrangement from her daughter. In the last verse she begins to empathise with the daughter more strongly: *...Another deal gone down, another man done gone/ You put up with it all, and you carry on...* Clearly she admires her courage and steadfastness, as one woman to another, confessing that *... I'd bet the world and everything in it on you...* Finally she offers humble solace in the clever couplet *...Happiness is but a state of mind/ Any time you want, you can cross the state line...* The pun on 'states' is one many American writers have used from Whitman onwards. Here you can hear her bravely brushing away the tears and wishing her daughter the best, hoping that she will be able to give her comfort. Now the band has packed away its instruments and the mother sits alone in the deserted dancehall. In her drunken state she can still hear the waltzes playing and she is picturing her little girl as she was, small and helpless. The feelings of abandonment and betrayal have been resolved. Despite her pride she is ready to give hope and comfort.

Soon After Midnight, from *Tempest*, is an explicitly 'romantic' song which would become a staple of Dylan's live set. Dylan uses a melody based on *The Moon Got in My*

Eyes, written by Johnny Burke (the lyricist of many popular tunes including *Pennies from Heaven* and *Moonlight Becomes You*) and composer Arthur Johnston. The song begins with drums and guitars kicking into a slow, languid rhythm. The language of the song is precise and compressed, the enunciation of every word clear and distinct. Dylan's vocal is dreamy, detached, almost a whisper. He pronounces the words sweetly and beguilingly. The song is addressed to another ghostly dream figure who seems to take on various different forms and who can appear and disappear at will. One of Poe's heroines, perhaps... a character in 'a dream within a dream'... certainly someone who will always be slightly out of the singer's grasp. The song mixes ethereal romantic and humorous expression with hints of the gothic horror that characterises some of the album's songs. As if to lull us into submission, we are enticed by this lovely melody into a dreamscape in which we can never quite tell the difference between poetic fantasy and harsh reality.

As Dylan delivers the first rhyme he rolls the words around his tongue, adopting the traditional posture of the humbled lover: *...I'm searching for phrases/ To sing your praises...* These lines are taken from the intro to Bing Crosby's version of the standard *Too Marvellous for Words* (1937). The singer sounds apologetic, as if he is already lapsing into cliché because the emotions he feels are rendering him almost speechless. Maybe he's down on his knees again, begging to be heard, confessing his own inadequacies: *...I need to tell someone...* he admits. Then he begins to draw us inexorably into the world of his own imagination: *...It's soon after midnight/ And my day has just begun...* Having played the penitent lover, he now he begins to explain how he has been wronged: *...A girl named Honey took my money/ She was passing by ...* The 'money/honey' rhyme appears in the 1950s standard about a 'gold digging' woman *Money Honey,* written by Jesse Stone and recorded by The Drifters, Little Richard, Elvis Presley and many others. The line 'she was passing by', and the singer's apparent detachment, as conveyed by the smooth vocal, suggest that the girl is a mere shadow, a ghostly figure or an illusion. The way Dylan draws out his delivery of 'passing' adds to this effect, which is further emphasised by *...It's soon after midnight/ And the moon is in my eye...* The singer has been 'blinded' by the girl's luminescent beauty. The imagery hints not only at madness but also a kind of reflectivity. Now we are drawn further into the narrator's consciousness, as if we can see our own image reflected in his eyes.

A key moment of transformation then occurs. The narrator's attitude changes from one of supplication to one of defiance. The calm, dreamy tone begins give way to ominous threats. The third verse begins *...My heart is cheerful/ It's never fearful/ I've been down on the killing floors...* The rhyme *...cheerful/ fearful...* echoes the earlier uses of *....phrases/ praises...* and *...money/ honey...* but here it sounds slightly 'forced'. This gives the singer's protestations an edge of tension, as if he isn't really sure what he's saying and is trying hard to convince himself. The first line recalls the Biblical proverb *...A cheerful heart is good medicine, but a crushed spirit dries up the bones...* (Proverbs 17:22). However, the reference to 'killing floors' is weirdly jarring, juxtaposing harsh blues imagery against dreamy romantic cliché. The expression features in the Howlin'

Wolf song *Killing Floor* (1964) and the much earlier Skip James number *Hard Time Killing Floor Blues* (circa 1931). The term literally refers to the slaughterhouses in which many black workers were employed when they arrived in Chicago after migrating from the Deep South in the 1920s and 30s. It was used in the blues as a metaphor for a hopeless situation, especially in a sexual relationship. The singer seems to be implying that he has been through so much pain in his love life that he has learned that he may as well always be 'cheerful'. However, we may by now begin to suspect that he is merely trying to reassure himself.

When he sings ...*I'm in no great hurry/ I'm not afraid of your fury/ I've faced stronger walls than yours...* Dylan (always the master of phrasing 'weird' rhymes) delivers 'hurry' and 'fury' without a moment's embarrassment. He seems to be gathering his own courage for some conflict to come. But the girl being addressed has placed a wall up against him, which he is determined to breach. The strange image of a lover's wall can be found in tragic story of the archetypal doomed lovers Pyramus and Thisbe, as related by the Roman poet Ovid in his *Metamorphoses*. The lovers are told by their warring families that they are not allowed to see each other and the only way they can communicate is through a crack in the wall that adjoins their houses. The two lovers later both commit suicide in a confused situation that Shakespeare adapted for the tragic ending of *Romeo and Juliet*. Shakespeare also mercilessly satirised Ovid's story for considerable comic effect in the 'play within a play' in *A Midsummer Night's Dream*. The dreamy *Soon After Midnight* takes the listener into a kind of *Midsummer Night's Dream*, a scenario in which the illusions of love are made manifest.

We are then presented with more rather oddly juxtaposed references to opposing female archetypes: ...*Charlotte the harlot dresses in scarlet/ Mary dresses in green....* The tongue in cheek internal rhymes of the first line depict a prostitute or 'scarlet woman' while 'Mary' denotes innocence. 'Charlotte the Harlot' is a character in a traditional bawdy song about a 'cowpuncher's whore'. Perhaps we may now be wondering about the earlier 'honey' who 'took his money'. Could the narrator actually be consorting with prostitutes but turning the whole thing into a dreamy romantic fantasy? Is this another deeply misogynist unreliable narrator? But then, in the song's most delicious twist, Dylan croons ...*It's soon after midnight/ And I've got a date with the fairy queen....* You can almost hear the smile as he sings. Now he sounds very pleased with himself, as he steps out of a mundane existence and into the magical world. The allusion to *A Midsummer Night's Dream* is explicit. The implication seems to be that the object of the singer's affection, his 'Titania', is a far greater 'catch' than any of the other women in the song and that his love for her is magical. But is he, like Nick Bottom, really just an 'ass' who is in the grip of an illusion?

This mood of defiance continues, as the narrator defies the prurience of others: ...*They chirp and they chatter...* he shrugs nonchalantly, asking ...*What does it matter?...* But suddenly the imagery turns mysteriously violent. Those who are opposed to the romance of this modern Pyramus and Thisbe (or Romeo and Juliet) are said to be ...*lying and dying in their blood...* And the narrator suddenly refers to 'two timing Slim', another rather jarring shift (possibly a reference to 'bad motherfucker' anti-hero of a Johnny Otis song) and declares he will *...drag his corpse through the mud...* It seems that he will be giving his enemies no quarter, despite engaging in this 'forbidden love'. The shift of tone to that of a violent Western ballad is rather shocking and disconcerting. But as the song ends the singer seems to be confidently stepping out again with his 'fairy queen'. Now his tone is soothing. The sly juxtaposition of the title of the famous Elvis song *It's Now or Never* with the shy but determined *...more than ever...* again emphasises the playful, intimate nature of the address. The ironic use of the vernacular *...When I met you/ I didn't think you'd do...* is charmingly set against the final, rather touching, protestation of true love: *...I don't want nobody but you...*

Although couched in the form of a romantic ballad, *Soon After Midnight* is also a song of defiance. Now, after so many struggles, the narrator is back in touch with the 'dream world' of his imagination. He can triumphantly assert his faith in himself and humanity. He has a dream that cannot be repossessed. The moon is in his eyes. And most importantly, *he has a date with the fairy queen.* He bows to his muse, whether she be spiritual or earthly, virgin or whore. Now that he has found her, he will not be distracted...

On the dreamily philosophical *I Made Up My Mind to Give Myself to You* from *Rough and Rowdy Ways* Dylan's understated enunciation resembles a gentle whisper. When he stretches out on the repeated refrains and at particularly emotional moments, his voice occasionally cracks slightly, giving the performance a special edge befitting the 'voice of experience' that the song is channelled through. A single male vocal provides quiet 'oohs' in the background throughout. The sound and instrumentation of the track are reminiscent of his Great American Songbook albums. Dylan's touring band provide a tasteful accompaniment, with Tony Garnier's bass pulsing out the beats of a slow waltz over touches of light percussion from Bob Britt and mandolin by Donnie Herron. The song's beautifully enticing melody is an adaptation of *Belle nuit, ô nuit d'amour*, often referred to as *Barcarolle*, from Jacques Offenbach's 1881 opera *The Tales of Hoffman*. The music has been used in films such as *Life is Beautiful* (1997) and *Midnight in Paris* (2011). In 1968 its melody was adapted by lyricists Les Reed and Jackie Ray as the song *Please Don't Go*, which was a hit for British classical singer Donald Peers.

The lyrics of *I Made Up My Mind* rely mainly on simple imagery, which is set against warm, intimate and colloquial expressions. In the six verses which end in the title refrain, a regretful narrator meditates languidly on his determination to devote himself to the object of the song. The verses are interspersed by three bridges, in which the identity of the narrative voice is sometimes less clear. Despite the rolling cadences of the melody and the narrator's apparent sincerity, the song becomes ever more ambiguous as it progresses. When 'uncovering' the Great American Songbook material Dylan had sought to bring out the emotional subtleties that had so often been hidden beneath overbearing string arrangements and cooing backing vocalists. In *To Make You Feel My Love* and the 'sentimental' tracks on succeeding albums he had frequently placed romantic clichés in the mouths of unreliable narrators, mixed confessions of undying love with expressions of doubt and injected elements of blues imagery and religious and philosophical themes. His entire foray into this area had thus been both a celebration and a subversion of its qualities. This enterprise comes to a grand and expressive climax here. Dylan inhabits the song like an experienced actor, and possibly one who is playing more than one part.

The opening couplet is precisely constructed to give an impression of languor, setting the scene in just a few words: *...Sitting on my terrace lost in the stars/ Listening to the sounds of the sad guitars...* With the repeated 's' alliteration Dylan 'slides' the words together wistfully. He sits on his front porch, staring up into the infinite spaces, perhaps slowly moving backwards and forwards in his rocking chair. The whole song is framed by this image, and it may be that all the subsequent descriptions are scenes that he is playing out in his head as he wrestles with the complexities of his life. In the background there are the barely audible 'sad guitars' and the quiet hum of the backing vocals as we are transported into the world of memory. These lines may already produce a certain sense of unease in the listener, but the following *...Been thinking it all over and I thought it all through/ I made up my mind to give myself to you....* appears to be reassuring. Again the 'soothing' alliteration is pronounced in both lines. But there is already something odd about them. The repetition in the first part of the couplet seems strangely pointless. Already we may be asking if the narrator has *really* 'thought it all through'. The elongated title line seems to be slightly awkward, as if the narrator is fumbling to express himself.

The second verse begins with short statements which Dylan lengthens as he draws them out: *...I saw the first fall of snow/ I saw the flowers come and go...* more alliterative lines which are suggestive of the passage of many seasons. *At the First Fall of Snow* is a song by Lorene Rose which was a hit for Hank Williams in 1955, two years after his death. It is a tale which relates how two fathers who have both lost infant daughters 'at the first fall of snow' commiserate with each other. The second line recalls Pete Seeger's *Where Have All the Flowers Gone,* a powerful anti-war polemic which was a staple of many folk singers' acts in the early 1960s. Both songs are laments for the death of innocence *...I don't think that anyone else ever knew...* Dylan sings, sighing, before repeating the title. Here the protagonist of the song appears to have telescoped a whole life of regret into these few short lines. The title takes on a different meaning now. What might in the first verse have signified the promise of a romantic proposal now begins to sound like a hopeless plea. We are informed that he has 'made up his mind' in such an elongated way, which matches just how long he has been prevaricating. Now it may well be too late. The first fall of snow clearly happened many seasons ago.

The first bridge interrupts the trance-like flow of the melody with Dylan - in a decidedly hoarser vocal, delivering another awkward line: *...I'm giving myself to you, I am...* which he rhymes with *...From Salt Lake City to Birmingham...* This is followed by a second geographical reference: *...From East LA to San Antone/ I don't think I could ever live my life alone...* These journeys, which criss-cross America, take us to locations which have all featured on the Never Ending Tour. It is tempting to hope that Dylan is serenading his listeners here. Perhaps the song is a declaration of love and devotion to his fans, who he now wishes to 'give himself to'. Ronnie Gilbert's introduction of Dylan at the Newport Festival 1964 was: *...Take him. You know him. He's yours....* Recalling this in *Chronicles* Dylan raged *...What a crazy thing to say! Screw that. As far as I knew, I didn't belong to anybody then or now...* Yet here he is, many decades later, offering himself to us...

Now that he has our attention he delivers the song's most remarkable lines *...My eye...* he begins *...is like a shooting star...* In *Shooting Star,* the concluding track on *Oh Mercy,* the star represents memories of his past love. Here it appears to function as a powerful metaphor for creativity. One might argue that many of Dylan's songs are indeed 'shooting stars', composed in what their author has described as a 'trance-like state', coming out of nowhere and bursting into light as they flash by. We are informed that the eye *...looks at nothing here or there, looks at nothing near or far...* The blankness of this statement, with its ambiguous double negative, recalls Zen ruminations on 'nothingness' from *The Basement Tapes* such as *Too Much of Nothing* or *Nothing Was Delivered.* In the next line the narrator quietly acknowledges this gift *...No one ever told me, it's just something I knew...* The kind of creativity being unleashed here comes from the ability to keep a steady eye.

If Dylan is boasting in these lines, then the next couplet demonstrates his humility with considerable grace *...If I had the wings of a snow white dove...* he sings *...I'd sing the gospel, the gospel of love....* Again the deliberate use of repetition suggests uncertainty. Perhaps Dylan is implying that if his soul was 'snow white' enough (like that of Disney's princess, perhaps) he would be able to deliver a pure spiritual message to his listeners. Or maybe he is just trying to tell his lover that he has *...a love so real, a love so true...* In the Bible, a dove appears to Noah to signify the end of the flood and the same bird appears in the New Testament as the Holy Spirit. The country gospel ballad *Wings of A Dove*, a 1960 hit for Ferlin Huskey and later Marty Robbins, whose first line is *...On the wings of a snow white dove/ He sends His pure sweet love...* (a paraphrase of Psalm 55:4-8) refers to this. Dylan's lines also recall the opening couplet of *Dink's Song*, a traditional folk ballad in which a woman is lamenting the fact that her lover has left her: *...If I had wings like Noah's dove/ I'd fly up the river to the one I love...* The song was performed on the 'Minnesota Hotel Tape' in 1961 and appears on the *No Direction Home* Soundtrack from *The Bootleg Series.*

The next bridge jolts us out of the narrator's fevered fantasies. It begins *...Take me out traveling, you're a traveling man/ Show me something that I'll understand...* The address to a 'traveling man' suggests a narrative shift. Perhaps this is the object of the singer's love replying to him. The second couplet *...I'm not what I was, things aren't what they were/ I'm going to go far away from home with her...* returns us to the male narrator's voice. But instead of a direct address to his love, the narrator appears to be talking to himself, again suggesting that her 'address' to him was merely in his imagination. The slightly awkward and seemingly unnecessary repetition in the first lines of each couplet reinforces the mood of tragic regret which is now becoming dominant. Perhaps he is indeed trying to reach out to God, or to some elemental aspect of himself which he has always denied.

This becomes more explicit in the next verse, in which the narrator admits that *...I traveled a long road of despair...* and laments that *...I met no other traveller there...* Again there is repetition within the line, which now feels like a confession. The narrator seems to be attempting to convey the essential isolation of the artist, who has to travel 'a long and lonely road' in search of inspiration. But in the next line Dylan whispers the achingly sad *...A lot of people gone - a lot of people I knew...* before delivering the title phrase. Now he confronts the feelings of grief which may have inspired the song. The 'you' that is being addressed has seemed at times to be a lover, Dylan's audience or God. But the overwhelming tone of regret suggests that this is the lament of a singer who, because he has felt compelled to follow the artist's lonely path, now regrets that he never gave enough time and attention to friends, lovers and compatriots who have passed away. In his late 70s, still contemplating a continuing creative future, Dylan is trying to come to terms with these losses. As with *Mother of Muses*, the ghost of Leonard Cohen seems to haunt, and to inhabit, the song. In a 2016 interview with *The New Yorker*, Dylan stated that Cohen's *... gift or genius is his connection to the music of the spheres...*

After an instrumental break, in another remarkably powerful couplet he tells us *...My heart's like a river, a river that sings/ It just takes me a while to realize things...* This time the metaphorical repetition in the first line is not awkward, but clear and assured and the second line is wonderfully warm, human and self deprecating. His calm and assured address to his 'lover': *...I'll see you at sunrise, I'll see you at dawn/ I'll lay down beside you when everyone's gone...* suggests that one day he will be joining his lost compatriots in their graves. But in the final verse he pleads that he be spared for some time yet: *...I travel from the mountains to the sea/ I hope the gods go easy with me....* Finally he addresses his lover (or his audience) again with the delightfully playful *...I knew you'd say yes - I'm saying it too/ I made up my mind to give myself to you...* Having passed through anguish, regret and grief, the final affirmation expresses the pure joy of being alive.

I Made Up My Mind is arguably the supreme achievement of Dylan's engagement with the sentimental tradition. He uses language that is in itself relatively straightforward, but which recalls the subtlety of expression of the more personal songs of lyricists like Ira Gershwin, Johnny Mercer or Oscar Hammerstein II, to take us on a journey through a range of different emotions. Despite the pain and anguish that he - like all of us - may have experienced in life, which is conveyed very eloquently in his expansive vocal performance, he expresses a wonderful positivity here. He transforms what appears to be a hopeless lover's plea into a transcendent message directed at all of creation. Now he can put his regrets behind him and ensure that every moment he has left on earth will not be wasted. Sitting on his front porch, staring up at the stars, he is now at one with the universe.

19th November 1995. The Shrine Auditorium, Los Angeles. It is the occasion of the taping of the Frank Sinatra 80th birthday tribute which, as *80 Years My Way,* will be shown on TV a few weeks later. Clad in a sharp grey suit and (unusually for him in those days) a tie, Bob looks decidedly nervous, as if he is performing in front of royalty which, in a peculiarly American way, he is. His performance is the last of a series of tributes that have been dedicated tonight to the Great Frank who sits, accompanied by his wife Barbara, in the front row. The story goes that Bob, like all the other performers, was going to do doing a Sinatra number. He and Tony, and the string section employed to back all the other performers that night, had it all rehearsed. Then, at the last moment, 'Frank's people' had communicated that they wanted Bob and the boys to do his 1964 song *Restless Farewell.* This was a song Dylan had not performed for thirty years. But, of course, you didn't mess with 'Frank's people'... It was, as Marlon Brando might have muttered, an offer you couldn't refuse. But what was Bob to make of the idea that, back in the early 60s, Frank and his Rat Pack pals had been screwing around in Vegas amusing themselves by grooving to The *Times They Are a-Changin'* album? Was this the same Sinatra who had once called rock'n'roll "the most brutal, ugly, desperate, vicious form of expression it has been my misfortune to hear"? But there is certainly no way Bob is going to junk Frank's suggestion and deliver a snarling *Maggie's Farm.* Newport '65 this is not...

The performance opens with some quiet acoustic strumming. Dylan enunciates the lyrics in a reverential near-whisper, which stands in total contrast to the showbiz pizzazz of almost all the performers who have preceded him. He pronounces every word with great care. The music gradually rises with a stately grace. Dylan's understated phrasing lets the words breathe with the power of lived experience. Soon it is clear why Sinatra himself likes the song. It is extraordinary how a lyric which Dylan had composed as a 22 year old, more than thirty years before, now stands as such an eloquent summation of Sinatra's career, the personal testimony of an old man looking back on a tempestuous life with great dignity and poise, yet with unrepentant defiance. The tune of the song is based on the traditional Irish lament *The Parting Glass,* which Dylan had picked up from The Clancy Brothers, and whose imagery of 'taking the last drink' of life Dylan develops poetically into the story of a narrator who 'did it *My Way'.* But unlike that old warhorse of a song, with its bombastic egotism, we are able to read other meanings into *Restless Farewell,* as the (possibly quite inebriated) raconteur is clearly being so defensive about his life that he may well be an unreliable narrator. We can only imagine what other stories those who had 'tangled' with him might tell...

The alcohol-related imagery in the early part of the song chimes perfectly with Sinatra's own 'hell raising' lifestyle in the past, in contrast to the fact that it will clearly soon be 'closing time' for him (He died less than three years later). Lines such as *...Ev'ry girl that ever I've hurt, I did not do it knowingly...* seem to summarise what you might imagine would be 'ol' blue eyes' ' attitude to his famously 'colourful' love life. Dylan's *...Ev'ry foe that ever I faced/ The cause was there before we came, and ev'ry cause that ever I fought, I fought it full without regret or shame...* could easily refer here to the many personal conflicts Sinatra had experienced in his life. But then the song gets darker. The narrator admits that if he thought too much about all this, he might go insane. But in the end, he redeems himself by admitting humbly that: *...It's for myself and my friends that my stories are sung...*

The final verse is a meditation on the accumulated 'dust of time', in which so many 'rumours' accumulate but then, in what is surely one of Dylan's most accomplished denouements, he declares, using a poignantly extended series of metaphors *...But if the arrow is straight/ And the point is slick/ It can pierce through dust no matter how thick...* In other words, the 'rumours' may be well be true. By now, we can clearly sense that the singer is not really the moral paradigm that he has continually professed to be. But whatever sins he may have committed, the judgement that posterity will make will not be based on any of this, but on how well he has expressed himself. It is a song, ultimately, that a man might sing when he meets his maker. It is a kind of confession, a prayer recited in the hope of redemption, and thus a meaningful statement about the relationship between life and art. Dylan delivers it with what can only be called profound reverence.

...Happy birthday, Mr. Frank... says Bob at the end and the camera cuts to Sinatra himself. It's not surprising that he has tears in those famous blue eyes.

Three: *The Door Is Closed Forever More*
Romantic Disillusionment

Feel like a broke down engine, ain't got no drivin' wheel,
Feel like a broke down engine, ain't got no drivin' wheel
You all been down and lonesome, you know just how a poor man feels
Blind Willie McTell, *Broke Down Engine*, 1933

When the train, it left the station
With two lights on behind
When the train, it left the station
With two lights on behind
Well, the blue light was my blues
And the red light was my mind,
All my love's in vain...
Robert Johnson, *Love In Vain*, 1937

17th November 1993. The Manhattan Supper Club is jam packed with a thousand whooping and jumping fans. They are *determined* to have a real good time. The place is so intimate and sweaty that you could almost reach out and touch the band, maybe to mop their brows or hand them a much needed beer. This is the kind of joint where, back in the day, if you were lucky, you might have caught Billie or Miles or Ella or Coltrane close up. Tonight's 'cabaret attraction' is playing the last of four 'secret' shows. The five musicians are pretty cramped up on the stage. The little guy at the front on acoustic with the harmonica holder round his neck, in a natty brown tweed jacket, is exchanging wide grins with the guy in the bowler on the double bass. There's another guitarist, a drummer and a steel player up there too. It's hard to make their faces out but jeez, you can tell they're enjoying themselves... By the side of the stage some tech guys have set up cameras and mikes and stuff. Maybe they're filming it for MTV or the like, but Lord knows how they'll get the sound above the hollers. But who cares? It's time to PARTY...

We're about four numbers into the set now. It's as hot as hell in here. After a few seconds of nifty finger picking we're right into it. It's the twelve bar blues with rhythm, and it really *swings*... Already heads are nodding and bodies are rocking. The singer does a little shimmy forward, not that he has much room. And he's lamenting so harmoniously ...*Lord, that weeping willow, moanin' like a dove.... ...I got a girl in the country, man, I sure do love...* His voice swoops and falls, just like that moanin' dove ...*Ain't had no lovin' since my little girl been gone...* he pines, he cries, and then he sighs: ...*Ain't no love mama, ain't no gitt'n' along...* It's such a sad song, but he's smiling so much you can see his teeth while that ol' bass player swings that big box around. And when he cries out ...*Ah, shucks!!!...* it's just such a goddam beautiful moment. You can't help but cheer. And then he tells us how the girl treats him so mean and dirty. He can't get to sleep just thinking about her ...well, not so much about *her*, more about some man who might be ...*makin' an early mornin' creep...* So he's going to ...*buy me a bullfrog...* to act kinda like an alarm clock to stop this. It's so damn funny. In the end all he can do is tell her ...*You're gonna want my love, mama, some old lonesome day....* Like he's just trying to keep from crying ...*And it'll be too late, I'll be gone too far away...* Then there's that beautiful refrain again. Now he really wrings out those rhymes, the ...*dove...* the ...*love...* And the crowd calls out in encouragement. Of course there'll be no happy ending. She really is *done gone*, no doubt about it. But the joy of the song is in the weeping, and even in the cursing, and in that hot sweet desperation in his voice...

The blues is the music of romantic disillusionment. It is also the music of resistance. In song after song, singers bewail the fact that their lovers have abandoned them. The consequent sexual tension is conveyed through various metaphors, many of them symbolic of the way that black people are marginalised in a white-dominated society. Yet the unique alchemy of the blues allows it to transform despair into a feeling of being released from one's troubles, if only for a few dizzily ecstatic moments. Much of this is conveyed through the distinct stylistic mannerisms of individual singers. As a young man Dylan declared that his ambition was to be able to 'carry himself like Big Joe Williams'. He wanted to achieve the gravitas which would allow him to convey the emotional metamorphosis which is at the heart of the form's appeal by bringing his own distinctive approach to bear. His one-off performance of Blind Boy Fuller's 1937 song *Weeping Willow* demonstrates one way in which blues songs can evolve through being adapted by different singers. Dylan thoroughly inhabits the narrator's plaintively tearful but somewhat hopeless 'loser in love' persona. He skips gaily over the delightfully suggestive lyrics, lamenting the sadly 'drooping' willow of the singer's manhood and recounting his desperate desire to place a sweaty bullfrog next to his errant lover's bed. In the background, it's possible to hear members of the audience laughing along with the singer's on-stage play acting, as an expression of sorrow and regret is transformed into a genuinely joyful experience.

Dylan is a great admirer of Delta Blues singers the Mississippi Sheiks, who achieved some popularity in the early 1930s. The Delta Blues originated in the highly segregated state of Mississippi in the early years of the twentieth century. Its most prominent stylists were Charley Patton and Blind Lemon Jefferson. By the 1920s, some blues artists were able to supplement their income with (often rather meagre) royalties from the nascent recording industry. Within a few years, the Great Depression had forced numerous singers and musicians to abandon performing. Many of them - including Muddy Waters - migrated north, especially to Chicago, where they adopted electric instrumentation, pioneering the guitar-bass-drums format which later became the foundation of rock'n'roll. The Sheiks, with their three singers and a violin player, had a uniquely jaunty and cheerful sound. Their most well known composition was *Sitting on Top of the World*, which became a blues standard and was recorded by Dylan on *Good as I Been to You*. On *World Gone Wrong* Dylan's slow and ruminative performances of two of their songs, *World Gone Wrong* and *Blood in My Eyes,* transform them into dark evocations of personal alienation. Big Joe, one supposes, would have been proud.

World Gone Wrong's narrator, who has been ejected from home by his wife or lover, laments his lack of personal control over events. His attempt to assert this power, though apparently threatening: *...If I didn't leave you, I would have to kill you dead...* is unconvincing, as is his 'advice' to anyone else in his position: *...Just tell her kindly, "there is the front door"...* The refrain *...I can't be good no more, just like I did before, honey 'cos the world gone wrong...* seems to shift the blame onto a more cosmic scale. In *Blood in My Eyes* the narrator sees a young beauty who works as a prostitute and immediately falls in love with her: *...Hey hey babe I got blood in my eyes for you...* he tells her *...I don't care what in the world you do....* But she merely smiles at him and retorts *...Hey, hey, man, can you wait a little while?...* In the face of such contemptuous disregard, he is completely powerless.

Feelings of personal desolation are expressed even more blatantly in *Ragged and Dirty* (also on *World Gone Wrong* and performed at the Supper Club) a song from the repertoire of Blind Lemon Jefferson and Sleepy John Estes. Dylan's loose and rhythmic take is similar to the 1942 recording by Willie Brown, but he also draws lyrics from other variants. The narrator describes himself as *...broke and hungry/ ragged and dirty too...* It is perhaps not surprising that the girl to whom he is (rather pathetically) appealing appears to have another lover and will not let him in her house to sleep with her. He even appeals to her just to let him *...sit down in your door....* Finally he attempts (presumably unsuccessfully) to 'guilt trip' her by telling her not to be too hard on him because he is so young. He then informs her that he'll be leaving on the next train and that he feels so desperate that he *...don't mind dyin'....* Even more powerful is the impassioned version of Blind Willie McTell's *Broke Down Engine* on *World Gone Wrong,* which uses classic blues imagery to express personal, sexual and spiritual desolation. Dylan adds tension by using the old blues singer's trick of tapping out a rhythm on the body of the guitar. The narrator's spirit is depicted as being like a train with no driver, a broken engine and *...no whistle or bell...* His depleted sexual power is contrasted with the fact that his 'hot mama', who can *...really do the Georgia crawl...* has left him. So he goes to his 'praying ground', falls down on his knees and tries to strike a bargain with the Almighty: *...I ain't cryin' for no religion...* he confesses, with disarming honesty *...If you give me back my baby, I won't worry you no more....* But he himself is another 'broke down engine' whose spirit of resistance against the impossible demands society has placed upon him has been weakened and finally destroyed. His appeal to the Lord will surely go unheard.

Time Out of Mind is a collection of bluesy songs which are focused on themes of romantic regret, despair and revenge. When the album was released, many commentators immediately decided that (as with *Blood on the* Tracks) Dylan must have been through a life-changing break-up of a relationship. There is, however, little biographical evidence for this. The album features a series of first person appeals to lovers, but we learn virtually nothing about the character of any of these women. The main focus is on the state of mind of the singer. Dylan's expressions of romantic disillusionment represent the despair a poet feels when his inspiration has apparently drained away. He allows us into the depths of his deep inner struggle to regain this inspiration. The songs can thus be seen as being directed not at 'real' women but to his elusive muse. In performance, disguised in his 'song and dance man' persona, in his 'cowboy threads' with his 'cowboy band', he delivers these songs with a mixture of foreboding and a comic, self-deprecating edge.

The opening track *Love Sick* is an intense psychological self-examination of a dark emotional world. Its identification of the 'sickness of love' with a 'sickness of the spirit' sets the tone for the whole album. The first austere metronomic beats are followed by a startlingly deep, gravelly and echoey vocal - quite different to anything previously heard on a Dylan record. The lyrics are bitter and stark, as if they have been honed and chiselled to remove all extraneous matter *...I'm walkin'....* Dylan begins ominously. There are three regular beats before he growls *...through streets that are dead...* More beats, then *...I'm walkin'... with you in my head...* This is a highly striking twist on the typically repetitive opening of a blues song. The spaces between the words seem to suggest much that is unspoken, building up an almost unbearable tension. The slow rhythm suggests the beating of an uncertain heart *...My feet are so tired...* Dylan proclaims, with world-weary grace *...My brain is so wired/ And the clouds are weeping...* The personification of nature in the last image recalls lines from Keats' *Ode To Melancholy: ...But when the melancholy fit shall fall/ Sudden from heaven like a weeping cloud...* as well as Bardolph's description of a hopeless enterprise in *Henry IV* Part 2, Scene 3*: ...a naked subject to the weeping clouds...* This is set against the rather startling use of 'wired' - a very modern expression of mental confusion which graphically represents how 'stressed out' many people feel in an electronic age.

The song's narrator then draws the listener into the scene, addressing us directly *...Did I...* he asks us, leaving that regular pause again *...hear someone tell a lie/ Did I... hear someone's distant cry...* He sounds infinitely desolate, but the fact that he has to ask his listeners to verify the reality of what has happened prepares us for the sudden shift into his memories, where innocence and cruelty are juxtaposed: *...I spoke like a child/ You destroyed me with a smile/ While I was sleeping...* The precise diction and strict rhyme scheme are maintained, as a deeply tragic sense of betrayal is evoked. The sense of a life lived in pain and frustration is agonisingly conveyed, as if the singer is

King Lear on the heath, bewailing his fate. In later live versions the lyrics strongly suggest that the betrayal has been carried out by a younger lover. At a show in Tokyo on 3rd April 2014 Dylan sings: ...*You were young and you were wild/ You looked at me and smiled/ I felt like my whole life I'd been sleeping....* In Oklahoma City on 3rd May 2015 the first two lines are: ...*You thrilled me to the heart/ Then you ripped it all apart...* The song is so direct and so (apparently) unromantic that it is clear that the narrator is examining the nature of love itself, and is doing so with what seems - at least at first - to be a kind of clinical precision.

As Dylan spits out the tongue-twisting lines that constitute the first chorus ...*I'm sick of love/ But I'm in the thick of it/ This kind of love/ I'm so sick of it...* he seems to be describing himself as - like the narrator of *Broke Down Engine* - a kind of wrecked machine. The very sound of the internal rhymes 'sick', 'thick' and 'sick' (again) convey a very real sense of being trapped in self disgust. Yet the narrator cannot escape the consequences of his involvement. He is being sucked down into a kind of slough of despond, a 'pilgrim' who is making no 'progress' at all. His utter disillusionment with the seemingly toxic force he calls 'love' seems to indicate that he has reached an overwhelming existential crisis. At this point he appears to resemble the condemned anti-hero of Camus' *The Stranger,* who positively revels in the meaninglessness of life and is thus apparently uncaring about his own fate.

The lack of 'love' here is used as a powerful representation of a dearth of inspiration, which to a poet is a kind of 'spiritual death'. Through the narrator's 'hollow eyes' we see ...*lovers in the meadow...* and ...*silhouettes in the window...* The singer tells us: ...*I watch them 'till they're gone and they leave me hanging on/ To a shadow...* Then we get a wonderfully 'well timed' explanation of the song's distinctive beat: ... *I'm sick of love/ I hear the clock tick...* But the paradoxical image of ...*Sometimes the silence is like thunder...* represents the singer's full embrace of life's contradictions. He declares that he will abandon all restraints and morality: ...*Sometimes I want to take to the road and plunder...* In later live versions this is changed to ...*Sometimes I feel like I'm being plowed under...* a very different fate, in which any kind of control is lost. He tries his hardest to purge the memory of his 'sick love'. Any faith he may have had in her has been thoroughly shaken ...*Could you ever be true...* he muses ...*I think of you and I wonder...* We are then presented with what we think will be the final denouement: ...*I'm sick of love/ I wish I'd never met you/ I'm sick of love/ I'm trying to forget you...* But then there is a final twist as Dylan adds a short coda: ...*Just don't know what to do...* which concludes, after a dramatic pause, in the admission that ...*I'd give anything to/ Be with you...* The hypnotic beat fades into the background. It seems that the narrator has been mocking us all along, 'playing hard to get'. He may be 'sick of love' but of course he is still entrapped by it. The song both celebrates and bemoans this universal dilemma.

Love Sick was performed many hundreds of times in the succeeding decades. It provided a highly dramatic musical contrast during Dylan's 'crooning years'. Its mood becomes increasingly cathartic, with the arrangements pushing towards new melodramatic limits. Yet its excoriating examination of romantic disillusionment is also leavened by an underlying suggestion of self-deprecating humour. It eloquently demonstrates Dylan's understanding of the transformative power of the blues. Despite the overwrought emotional angst that the song conveys, its anti-climactic conclusion contains a very strong element of self-mockery. A few years after its initial release, a re-recorded version was used in a *Victoria's Secret* commercial, in which Dylan made a personal appearance. In this bizarre artifact he is surrounded by slinky, seductive models clad in very expensive lingerie, while he skulks like a cackling Don Juan in the background. There was much speculation as to why he had accepted this assignment, which hardly boosted any residual image he might have as the 'voice of a generation'. He was accused, of course, of 'selling out' to commercial interests. Perhaps he really had decided to 'take to the road and plunder'. But maybe he was just trying to show us that the song really had just been one big tease.

Another darkly melodramatic song from *Time Out of Mind* is the penultimate track, the slow and heavy twelve bar blues *Can't Wait*. The song's hysterical narrator pleads with his lover in a tone of manic desperation. Dylan's voice is consistently 'ragged and dirty'. The music has a slightly choppy feel, and with jerky, intrusive, snatches of guitar suggesting the narrator's insecure state of mind. Early on he insists that he's trying to 'walk the line', a reference to Johnny Cash's classic 'morality tale' of a man who repetitively and desperately asserts that, whatever happens, he will remain faithful. The song begins *...way past midnight...* with the narrator telling us that he is becoming extremely impatient, desperately hoping that the woman who has ditched him will change her mind. The song's imagery, combined with the mysterious reference to those *...people all around/ Some on their way up and some on their way down...* and the melodramatic declaration that *...the air burns...* suggests that his torment is so great that he is literally in hell. Soon he is *...breathing hard/ Standing at the gate...* waiting, perhaps, for the gates of the underworld to open up and swallow him.

The narrator's use of emotional blackmail is unrestrained. He tells his lover that: *...my heart can't go on beating without you...* Then he wallows in self pity, declaring *...Your loveliness has wounded me/ ...I'm reeling from the blow...* The striking use of 'loveliness', which is delivered as an accusation, is especially cruel and contradictory. It is not her rejection that has hurt him, it seems, but her beauty and humanity. At this point, we begin to question the narrator's integrity, if not his sanity. He begins to speculate on what he might do if he was to meet her, admitting with rather shocking candour that *...I'd like to think I could control myself, but it isn't true...* It's hard to know whether this is an admission of vulnerability, a threat of sexual violence or a statement of potentially murderous intent. The justification he advances *...That's how it is...* (pause) *...when things disintegrate...* indicates that the narrative appears to be moving towards nothing less than a confession of mental breakdown.

...I'm doomed to love you... Dylan cries mournfully ... *I've been rolling through stormy weather....* an allusion to the Arlen/ Koehler standard *Stormy Weather* (1933) which Dylan will later cover on *Triplicate*. But in the manner of one of Edgar Allan Poe's

crazed, obsessed narrators he does not seem to *want* to recover from his 'affliction'. His declaration that *...I'm thinking of you and all the places we could roam together...* conjures up a spectral image of the two of them 'roaming' this landscape like Heathcliff and Cathy on the moors in Emily Bronte's *Wuthering Heights*, figures whose ghosts are still out there in the 'stormy weather'.

The final verse, which begins: *...It's mighty funny/ The end of time has just begun/ Oh honey, after all these years you're still the one...* is full of strange juxtapositions. The use of the light hearted rhyme 'funny' and 'honey' seems very odd, especially as it appears to refer to a 'doomsday' scenario. During Dylan's religious conversion of 1979-81 his songs and onstage pronouncements proclaimed that he now accepted the 'Born Again' Christian belief that we are living in the 'End Times'. According to the prophecies in *Revelations* these are the last years before humanity will be destroyed in a cataclysm of fire (which some believers identify with nuclear war). 'The Lord' will then return to Earth to pass judgement. Dylan's deranged narrator seems to be longing for the death of all humanity in a coming apocalypse. And he is becoming more and more impatient. The 'loveliness' that has 'wounded' him is not only that of his ghostly lost love, but also of the beauty and positivity of life itself, which now repels him. In another graphically gothic image he tells us that he is *...strolling through the lonely graveyard of my mind...* Then he piles more guilt on the woman who has rejected him: *...I left my life with you, somewhere along the line...* (a 'line' which he has supposedly always walked). One can almost imagine him sobbing as, in the final lines, he begs for forgiveness: *...I thought I would be spared this fate/ But I don't know how much longer I can wait...*

By inhabiting this character's thoughts and taking us on a terrible journey which will twist 'time out of mind', Dylan appears to be plumbing the depths of existential despair. But the narrator's obsessive appeals to the anonymous object of the song, which even appear to encompass possible mass death and destruction, are so exaggerated that he has no real credibility as a potential lover. By taking us into the 'inferno' of such a mind, Dylan pushes the convention of self-deprecatory emotional submission, which is a feature of both the blues and the sentimental tradition, to such extremes that it is impossible to take him seriously. Ultimately, the narrator is mocking himself, pushing romantic disillusionment to its furthest possible extremes, wallowing in his own insecurities. This is, as in so many blues songs, a rhetorical trick. Dylan is playing a game with his audience, portraying himself as a poet whose despair at losing his inspiration is so great that he will quite happily drag the rest of the world down 'into the pit' with him.

In order to convey this heavily parodic aspect of *Can't Wait*, the song needs to be performed in a way that carefully 'walks the line' between doom-ridden despair and humorous pastiche. The recording on *Time Out of Mind,* although it comes over as extremely dark and anguished, does not fully manage to convey such delicious ambiguities. The song was played live on hundreds of occasions after the release of the album but it took some time to become fully realised. In a performance of the song at the Alcatraz Club in Milan on 22nd June 2011, however, Dylan gives the song the full theatrical treatment it needs. Standing centre stage without an instrument, he adopts a pose of studied casualness, all the time consciously playing the lead role in this 'gothic drama'. He barks out the lyrics, playing the part of the crazed lover or gothic avenger to the hilt, deliberately prolonging the tension until he finally repeats *...I don't know...* over and over again. By the end of the number he is grinning widely. And well he might. After playing the song for more than ten years, this time he has *really* nailed it. The song is now very scary, and very funny, at the same time.

The character Dylan assumes in *Cold Irons Bound* is more 'seriously' psychotic. The way the song is played and sung reflects this. The song is built on a hypnotic, choppy, repetitive blues riff with slashing layers of guitar and some atmospheric washes of organ. It sounds like the narrator is on some dark, bumpy road as he heads 'out of town'. The vocal, as filtered through Lanois' murky echo on the album, is slightly sneering, uncaring. The live version on *Tell Tale Signs*, recorded at the Bonnaroo Festival in 2004, features more extended guitar workouts. Dylan's vocals here are now much more emotionally resonant. The song has been 'opened out' to explore the dark emotions it conveys. But perhaps the definitive reading is the one which is featured at the climax of Dylan's film *Masked and Anonymous* in 2002. Here Dylan appears in full cowboy garb, in character as the movie's taciturn anti-hero Jack Fate. The brilliantly deadpan delivery of this version sums up the film's dark and subversive take on the morality of American political life.

References to various other songs are scattered throughout the lyrics ...*The fields are turned brown...* (in verse one) is the title of a Stanley Brothers song. The Stanley Brothers, who were at their peak in the late 1950s, were masters of a particularly dramatic 'Southern gothic' style of bluegrass, in which the singers often appeared to be trembling in submission to a vengeful deity. Dylan played many of their songs, such as *Hallelujah, I'm Ready to Go*, *Somebody Touched Me*, *Stone Walls and Steel Bars* and *Searching for a Soldier's Grave* in his live shows around the turn of the millennium. Later on there is a mention of *Whiskey in the Jar,* an Irish murder ballad sung from the point of view of the felon himself, which was often performed by Dylan favourites The Clancy Brothers and was made famous in a memorably vivid rock version by the Irish band Thin Lizzy in 1972. These allusions are points of reference to the song's themes of murder, guilt and religious hypocrisy.

From the first lines *...I'm beginning to hear voices and there's no-one around...* it is made clear that the narrator is delusional, if not completely mad. Then we hear that he's *...all used up and the fields have turned brown...* We may already suspect that these 'fields' are in his mind. When he tells us that ...*My love for her is taking such a long time to die....* we may be wondering - perhaps in a ghoulish, Hitchcockian kind of way - whether (given the narrator's apparent state of 'frenzy') it was the girl he is singing to who took 'a long time to die'. The fact that this line is preceded by *...I went to church on Sunday and she passed by...* makes the character even more smoothly scary. We get the sense that the narrator has been watching the woman passively, but with considerable fascination. Although he pretends to be 'God fearing' he appears to have murderous intentions. One is reminded of the psychopathic but apparently 'holy' preacher played to such icily terrifying effect by Robert Mitchum in the 1955 'Southern gothic' movie *Night of the Hunter.* Mitchum's character, who can kill without any guilt, has 'LOVE' tattooed on one hand and 'HATE' on the other. Maybe the narrator of this song is adorned in a similar way.

In the first chorus we see how the narrator is consumed by his obsession: *...I'm waist deep, waist deep in the mist...* he breathes *...It's almost like I don't even exist...* The chorus line *...I'm twenty miles out of town/ In cold irons bound...* suggests that he has already been convicted of her murder and is now being taken away, presumably to be executed. The strong internal rhymes clearly suggest that he cannot resist one of the 'seven deadly sins': *...The walls of pride are high and wide/ Can't see over to the other side....* His lament that *...It's such a sad thing to see beauty decay/ It's sadder still to see your heart torn away...* is again eerily macabre, conjuring up images of rotting bodies and a 'ripped out' heart. But he revels in his own obsession: *...One look at you and I'm out of control...* before he projects it into almost ludicrously cosmic terms: *....like the universe has swallowed me whole...*

We are then drawn deeper into this twisted narrative, as he declares*...the winds in Chicago have torn me to shreds...* The narrator is, like one of T. S. Eliot's 'hollow men', a human being whose soul has been ripped out. The surreal personification in the next line: *...Reality has always had too many heads...* again signifies his detachment from everyday life. He seems to be becoming more and more aware that he is trapped *...Some things last longer than you think they will...* is an understatement here. His 'personal hell' will of course last for all eternity *...There are some kinds of things...* he observes *...that you never can kill...* In the concluding lines he appears to be on his bended knees, as if proposing a kind of deathly marriage pact. He swears he will remember the woman 'forever' and that he has tried to 'love and protect' her, but - in a particularly delicious couplet - declares that: *...The fat's in the fire and the water's in the tank/ The whiskey's in the jar and the money's in the bank...* Everything, he suggests has settled in its 'rightful' place. Here again Dylan leads us into the dark regions of the soul. However, as with the twisted narratives of *Love Sick* and *Can't Wait*, the use of the gothic mode may have other purposes. The juxtaposition of various allusions, colloquial sayings and bizarre observations, delivered in a non-linear mode of storytelling all contribute to the levels of ambiguity. Perhaps the narrator really is a convicted murderer who is facing his doom. Or maybe he is just inviting us into another gothic nightmare, cackling with glee as he does so.

Country music originated, like the blues, in the early twentieth century and first achieved national prominence through the recordings of The Carter Family and Jimmie Rodgers. The two forms, although apparently divided along racial lines, have much in common. They both originated among amateur musicians schooled in traditional styles. Whereas mainstream popular music had a clear separation between writers and performers, both blues and country mainly relied on performers to write (or at least 'adapt') their own songs. The importance of the individual 'authentic' styles of particular singer-songwriters was prominent. Most country music, previously known as 'hillbilly' or 'country and western', is based on a similar musical structure to the blues. It expresses the preoccupations of the poor and working class whites who make up its audience. Country singers, however, find it less necessary to disguise their feelings in metaphor and symbolism. They are more likely to employ a form of 'straight talking' which distinguishes their songs from those of mainstream 'romantic' writers. One of Jimmie Rodgers' best known songs *Waiting for a Train* (1928) relates the tale of a penniless hobo who is attempting to travel from California to his home in 'Dixie' (the Deep South) by jumping trains. Hank Williams, one of Dylan's earliest musical heroes, specialised in stark and heartrending confessions of failed love and personal inadequacy like *Cold Cold Heart* (1951) and *I'm So Lonesome I Could Cry* (1949).

Standing in the Doorway, another song from *Time Out of Mind,* is undoubtedly one of Dylan's saddest songs. It is a ballad of romantic disillusionment which is influenced by the sensibilities of the blues. But its musical form is closer to that of country. The tune is a slow waltz, dominated by double bass and plaintive steel guitar. The song has been performed fairly often in concert but Dylan has offered few musical and lyrical variations. On *Time Out of* Mind, in what is almost certainly a live studio take, he showcases his mature vocal style to near-perfection in a 'straight up' performance worthy of the great country singers. The emotions in the song are complex and ambiguous but he conveys them with great dexterity through his dramatic phrasing and detailed vocal nuances.

The narrator resembles the archetypal 'drifter' found in many country songs. Like the singer in *Waiting for a Train* he may well be 'a thousand miles from home'. He stands at the entrance to some lowlife juke joint, strumming his guitar for a few coins. There are hints that - like the protagonist of *Cold Irons Bound* and many country songs - he has committed a serious violent crime and is 'on the run'. Dylan relates all this soberly and philosophically, with great dignity. To some extent the song is reminiscent of classic country songs of heartbreak like Roy Acuff's *Blue Eyes Cryin' in the Rain,* or Dolly Parton's *I Will Always Love You*, in which the narrators do not attach blame onto the lover who has left them but accept the situation with great stoicism. *Standing in the Doorway* depicts the singer's desolation as a kind of spiritual crisis and we get the feeling that only his faith in his maker is preventing him from sinking into suicidal despair. Yet he is not attempting to present us with any moral lessons. He appears to hold out no prospect of any kind of redemption.

A sense of mental confusion is evident from the beginning. The first few lines show us that, as far as he is concerned, reality has already been distorted. It is a summer night and a juke box is playing softly in the background *...Yesterday everything was goin' too fast/ Today it's movin' too slow...* he tells us, in a mournful tone which suggests infinite regret. He delivers the 'shocking' line *...Don't know if I saw you I would kiss you or kill you...* with nonchalance, adding that *...It probably wouldn't matter to you anyhow...* Thus we can sense that the apparent threat of violence, while it may express the mixture of yearning and anger he feels, is really nothing but a form of expression of how pitiful his situation really is. Each of the five verses has *...You left me standing in the doorway crying...* as the penultimate line, but every final line is different, as if the narrator is trying to come to some kind of definite conclusion but cannot really make up his mind. Here he informs us that *...I got nothing to go back to now...* reinforcing the sense that he is hovering in front of some kind of destiny but is afraid to step towards it. Perhaps the 'doorway' opens into death, or maybe it will lead to new hope. But he seems to be caught in a kind of emotional paralysis. Thus he will never be able to open the door.

There is a suggestion that he is in some kind of drunken stupor. We hear that *...The light in this place is so bad/ Makin' me sick in the head...* but we must know it's not really the poor light that's doing this *...All the laughter is just making me sad...* he tells us, reinforcing the impression that the doorway leads into a lively bar where people are socialising and having fun. But then he seems to look upwards, as if asking for some kind of salvation. As he does so, we are presented with a series of impressionistic 'snapshots'. In one of the song's most heart stopping moments Dylan draws in a little breath and sings: *...The stars have turned cherry red... Cherry Red* is a well known blues song, recorded in 1939 by Big Joe Turner and later by many others. In a clearly sexual 'come on', Turner tells his lover to *...squeeze me pretty baby till my face turns cherry red...* But here this image is transformed. Although it retains its blues connotations, the 'red stars' are clearly another hallucinatory vision in the narrator's mind. Significantly, this reference is the only flash of colour in what is otherwise a 'monochrome' vista. The narrator, it seems, has 'blood in his eyes'.

The next two lines are quite beautifully compressed and imagistic *...I'm strumming on my Gay Guitar...* Dylan sings in a leisurely manner, before pausing to add ...*smokin' a cheap cigar...* The striking alliteration of 'Gay Guitar' is quite disarming. It appears to suggest the 'old fashioned' meaning of 'gay' as carefree and happy. In fact a 'Gay Guitar' is a specially designed instrument, often decorated ornately with flower patterns, which was popular with country singers in the 1950s and '60s. It was created by an instrument maker called Frank Gay. This contrasts neatly with the 'down and dirty' graphic image of a 'cheap cigar'. Then the narrative changes tone. Dylan draws the syllables out to create emphasis, further giving us an impression of a dream like state *...The ghost of our old love has not gone away/ Don't look it like it will anytime soon...* he muses and ends the verse in a typically romantic location *....under the midnight moon....* Now we can see a clear image of the singer, his beautiful guitar in hand, wreathed in thick smoke, like a figure in a film noir movie. The narrator then appears to share a confidence with us: *...Maybe they'll get me and maybe they won't/ But not tonight and it won't be here...* This again suggests that he may be some kind of outlaw. It is certainly not made clear who 'they' are. But from here on, he seems to be beset by feelings of approaching doom. It may be that he has killed the woman he is singing about. After all, he said he wasn't sure whether to kiss her or kill her... But given his hallucinatory state, it is difficult to be sure about this. However, the next lines seem to indicate that he fears his end will be coming soon: ...*There are things I could say, but I don't/ I know the mercy of God must be near...*

In a number of country songs, men who have committed serious offences make a full confession of their own sinfulness. In Merle Haggard's *Mama Tried* the narrator relates how he was drawn into crime at a young age despite his mother's heroic attempts to save him from such a life. Similarly, in Johnny Cash's harrowing cowboy ballad *Don't Take Your Guns to Town* the young man ignores his mother's pleas to stay away from guns and ends up being shot down. The narrator of *Standing in the Doorway* is contemplating the nature of mortality. We may speculate as to whether the phrase 'the mercy of God' as used here indicates a premonition of death or predicts possible salvation, in either an earthly or a heavenly sense. It seems that the song's protagonist may be experiencing the same confusion. When he tells us *...I've been ridin' the midnight train/ I got ice water in my veins...* is he therefore a cold blooded killer? This is hard to believe, as he angrily accuses the absent lover of leaving him *...suffering like a fool...* So the intimations of violence may be mere bravado. The much-used blues motif of 'the midnight train' may be another suggestion that the rider is travelling to imminent physical or spiritual death.

The rest of the song is dominated by a sense of encroaching doom. The narrator appears to be talking to himself and may be predicting his own death: *...When the last rays of daylight go down/ Buddy, you'll roll no more...* The colloquial use of 'buddy' is particularly affecting, as if the narrator appears to be consoling himself. Despite the overall pessimism of the lyrics, the song is characterised by a tenderness which is conveyed quite explicitly in Dylan's sweetly reflective delivery. Yet it still seems as if the narrator's fate is pre-determined. As the night closes in he is now thinking aloud about his own funeral: *...I can hear the church bells ringin' in the yard/ I wonder who they're ringin' for?...* In perhaps the most heartbreaking line the singer shares with us that *...Last night I danced with a stranger/ But she just reminded me that you were the one...* The waltz rhythm of the tune is particularly effective - helping us to picture the sad, slow dance in the rundown juke joint. The final image in the verse, when he tells us that she left him crying *...in the dark land of the sun...* is of course paradoxical, but it seems to refer back to the opening *...last rays of daylight...* The singer is trapped in that moment when the sun disappears over the horizon - a 'twilight zone' in his mind, identified here as that aching feeling of regret we experience after a gorgeous, unique sunset. Here Dylan transforms romantic disillusionment into a kind of transient ethereal beauty, leaving an aching in our hearts. Rarely has romantic regret been conveyed so graphically or so movingly.

The first lines of the final verse *...I'll eat when I'm hungry, I'll drink when I'm dry...* are borrowed from the traditional American folk ballad *(I've Been a) Moonshiner*, the song of an unrepentant liquor bootlegger which Dylan sometimes performed live in his Greenwich Village years. His impassioned delivery on the studio version of this song (recorded in 1963 and released on *The Bootleg Series Volume One*) is characterised by the way he sustains specific notes to create a compelling mixture of beauty and tension, in one of his finest ever recorded vocal performances. The narrator of the song is in many ways a 'lost soul', who makes no excuses for himself and laments his descent into alcoholism with great pathos. But he is also a philosopher, who ends by declaring that *...The whole world's a bottle/ And life's but a dram/ When the bottle gets empty/ It sure ain't worth a damn...* The spirit of that uniquely compelling performance is transmuted into *Standing in the Doorway*, with its riveting juxtaposition of graceful anguish and personal tragedy. The song ends with a confession and a testament. The imagery becomes extraordinarily graphic: *...Even if the flesh falls off of my face/ I know someone will be there to care...* Already the narrator seems to be looking beyond his own death - his immersion into 'the dark land of the sun'. Yet he seems to find some mysterious consolation. The next lines are exquisitely tender in their simplicity: *...It always means so much/ Even the softest touch...* This is contrasted with the way he suddenly pulls back emotionally in the disclaimer *...I see nothing to be gained by any explanation/ There's no words that need to be said...* In the end he remains stoical, taking us back to the refrain and ending with a common phrase which 'wraps up' his predicament neatly and shows us that he sees no way out of it: *...Blues wrapped around my head...*

On *Time Out of Mind*, Dylan showed that he had devised a new approach to his music, which was the product of his immersion in the eerie strangeness of old folk songs, the emotional honesty of country music and the sly ambiguity, stoic acceptance of fate and transformational joy of the blues. In *Standing in the Doorway* all these elements come together as Dylan uses romantic disillusionment as a path to spiritual wisdom. The magic of the song comes from the fact that, despite being devastated by events, the narrator can rise above them through the pure beauty of his expression - thus spilling out the contents of his soul. The narrator here is almost certainly a sinner, quite possibly one beyond redemption. He may even be a cold blooded killer. But the feelings he expresses can be felt quite tangibly by the listener. The song deals with universal, elemental, emotions. Although it provides no easy answers and leaves us in a kind of limbo, it confronts Dylan's crisis of inspiration with unswerving courage, by dealing with basic existential questions. It also asks whether life itself is worth living. Its narrator stands in a doorway that leads to the 'undiscovered country' of 'the world beyond'. He delivers his soliloquy like a combination of one of Clint Eastwood's hard-bittern western anti-heroes and a down-at-heel Hamlet, his face covered by a cowboy hat, strumming that Gay Guitar, forever wreathed in a cloud of dense smoke from that two-bit cigar.

12th January 2012. The audience in the Hollywood Palladium is largely made up of film stars, directors, producers and their acolytes in shiny designer suits and gravity-defying ball gowns. The occasion is the Critics' Choice Movie Awards Ceremony, at which the great director Martin Scorsese - of *Taxi Driver, Raging Bull* and *Goodfellas* fame - is being presented with one of those lifetime achievement awards that Hollywood loves to dish out in its annual orgies of self-congratulation. Bob Dylan will be performing one song as a tribute to Scorsese, who is receiving the award partly because of his record as a music documentary maker. The lights go up and there is Bob centre stage in a plain black suit, with just his trusty harmonica in his left hand. He will remain pretty much in the same space throughout the performance, illustrating his lyrics with hand movements, somewhere between a crooner and a mime artist. Although he often looks uncomfortable at 'official' events, tonight he is supremely confident, focused and self assured, even flashing the odd sideways grin. Perhaps he's had just a little lubrication. Behind him the band, also dressed in black, look as serious and dedicated as ever. Donnie Herron fingers a mean mandolin. Dylan's voice has just the right amount of gritty edge. This isn't the easiest song to sing. The vocalist needs to sound sympathetic to his subject, yet not be too po-faced about it. *...Seen the arrow on the door post/ Saying 'This land is condemned'....* This version is swinging, muscular, with Bob sharing his little gestures with us. It is a compelling dramatic recitation.

Blind Willie McTell was written and recorded in 1983, but its presence has hovered ghost-like over Dylan's late period performances and recordings, for which in many ways it supplies a kind of template. It was a last minute omission from the *Infidels* album, much to the chagrin of Dylan fans when bootlegged versions of 'piano based' and 'electric' versions emerged shortly afterwards. The song was soon acclaimed as a masterpiece by esteemed Dylan scholars such as Christopher Ricks. The 'piano version' eventually appeared on the first *Bootleg Series* release in 1991. It was, however, the recording by Dylan's old compatriots The Band (now reduced to a trio) on their album *Jericho* in the same year that seems to have rekindled his interest. He began playing it live with an arrangement based rather less obviously on the tune of the classic blues lament *St. James Infirmary.* Dylan also sticks with The Band's version of the chorus line *...I'll tell you one thing/ Nobody can sing...* as improvised by The Band's singer Levon Helm. Dylan also changes the reference to 'Jerusalem' to the distinctly Blakean 'New Jerusalem'.

The song's four verses seem disconnected in terms of any obvious narrative. There are shifting time frames and locations, taking us *...all the way from New Orleans to New Jerusalem...* presenting us with a symbolic landscape of the African American experience. It has been argued that the song does not seem to be really 'about' Blind Willie McTell. However, Dylan uses a towering figure in the history of the blues as an appropriate symbol of a form of music which signified both a resistance to and a way of coping with racist oppression in the United States. The blues has sometimes functioned as the conscience of America; a form of truth-telling countering the mainstream mythology of the 'American Dream'. *Blind Willie McTell* is a different kind of dream, reaching ever further back into American history. We are presented with the image of a lonesome *...hoot owl singing/ As they were taking down the tents...* with highly evocative imagery *...the stars above, the barren trees, were his only audience...* Are the tents being taken down after a show by Blind Willie himself? Or is this some kind of religious 'revival' meeting?

Later we are taken even further back, into the time of slavery. The narrator draws us into another graphic scene: *...See them big plantations burning...* suggests a scene from the Civil War, and *...hear the cracking of the whip...* depicts the brutality of slavery itself, presented in 'real time'. We get a little southern colour here: *...Smell that sweet magnolia blooming/ See the ghosts of slavery ships...* Then we are transported to the 1920s: *...There's a woman by the river/ With* a *fine young handsome man/ He's dressed up like a squire, bootleg whiskey in his hand...* We can hear a chain gang hollering in the distance. Dylan presents various tableaux of the black experience over time. Finally he lands in the present day, in a clear reference to the song's musical origins *...gazing out the window/ Of that old St. James hotel....*

Whereas the original recording has a certain ethereal quality, tonight's performance is thoroughly grounded. Dylan arranges the historical images of America like a movie maker using jump cuts, bringing the song to a highly dramatic climax with the final *...Nobody can sing the blues like Blind Willie McTell...* Then the harmonica is raised and he plays out another verse instrumentally. The song is one of his most impressive uses of the kind of compressed language that he began perfecting around the time of *John Wesley Harding,* combined here with the post-impressionistic narrative techniques he explored on *Blood on the Tracks.* Although it eulogises one of the great blues masters, it is not a conventional blues song. It is implicitly a song about *how* to sing the blues, about the singer's struggle to 'carry himself like Big Joe Williams' and to summon the spirit of that 'lonely hoot owl' whose voice is addressed only to the 'stars above'. Heaven, it declares, will hear Blind Willie in the spirit of that owl, even though the man himself spent much of his life in abject poverty. Blind Willie was an unrecognised genius, and Dylan here summons up all his strength to sing that genius into eternity. The song is a kind of invocation, which defiantly declares that the eternal muse of poetry will always triumph in the end. There are many twists and turns on the spectral highway on which that chain gang is always marching, but the phantoms of their cries will hover in the air forever.

Bob Dylan has recorded many different types of blues-based tunes throughout this career; some comic (like *Leopard Skin Pillbox Hat* (1966), which mercilessly mocks the pretensions of a rich socialite); some reflecting on failed relationships (like *Meet Me in the Morning,* 1975); some sweetly suggestive (like *It Takes a Lot To Laugh, It Takes a Train To Cry,* 1965) and some verging on the darkly demonic (like *New Pony* (1978). All of these songs use 'quotations' from older blues songs or refer back to them in some way. The narrators of blues songs can be notoriously unreliable and unsympathetic, often resorting to vain pleading. This creates a subtle underlying level of narrative, combining self-mocking humour and pathos. In Tampa Red's *Sad Letter Blues* (1939) the singer accepts news of his girlfriend's death with hardened stoicism. In Robert Johnson's desperately mournful *Love in Vain* (1937) the singer follows his departing love to a railway station but his attempts to persuade her to stay by 'looking her in the eye' are doomed to failure. The narrators' insecurities may be revealed in comic, or sometimes tragi-comic, ways. Blind Willie McTell's dryly hilarious *A Married Man's a Fool* (1956) recounts a dubious story in which the narrator listens to a sermon by a preacher who insists that married women will always 'play around', thus lending supposed 'scriptural authority' to his own lack of self-worth. In Leadbelly's *Shout On (Honey I'm All Out and Down)* (1947) the singer plays the part of a sadly 'put upon' male. He works as a mule skinner (or 'mule driver') describing his job as *...putting by initials, baby, on a mule's behind...* while wishing his pay day could be delayed because he knows that his 'brown skin woman' will take all his wages. This is especially ironic because a 'mule' is often used as a particularly derogatory slang term for a black woman. But it is the woman who is 'tanning' *his* behind.

On several songs on *Time Out of Mind* Dylan presents narrators whose rather pathetic appeals to lost lovers reveal nothing but their own insecurities, often to comic effect. These songs refer to many other previous songs in a way that forms a commentary on the blues itself. *Million Miles* is a slow twelve bar with a solid, chugging rhythm, which is counterposed by snatches of jittery guitar and stabbing organ that illustrate the narrator's changeable moods. The song is another hopeless plea to a lover, full of rather extreme exaggeration which makes us feel that this narrator cannot really be believed. The song is musically - and to some extent lyrically - modelled on *Tryin' to Get to You*, first released by the Washington rhythm and blues group The Eagles in 1954 but made famous by Elvis Presley in 1956, who turns it into a joyous sexually teasing romp. He wins the audience over by convincing us that he is really in control of the situation. But in *Million Miles* the narrator sounds desperately confused: *...You took a part of me that I really miss...* he tells her *...I keep asking myself how long I can go on like this...* He even accuses the girl of 'telling herself a lie'. But then he tracks back: *...But that's alright mama, I told myself one too...* He ties himself up in knots here, languishing in his self-pity. Arthur Crudup's *That's Alright Mama*, which is referenced here, is also a message of sexual submission, which Presley transformed into a breathy expression of unadulterated lust. But here Dylan turns the phrase into a lame attempt by the narrator to justify himself.

The narrator continues to try his best to win our sympathy. The extreme hyperbole of the repeated title line *...I'm tryin' to get closer, but I'm still a million miles from you...* closely resembles the studied exaggeration of *...I could hold you for a million years...* in *Make You Feel My Love*. The assertion that *...You took the silver, you took the gold/ You left me standing out in the cold...* suggests that she has left him penniless as well as bereft. *...People ask about you, I didn't tell them everything I knew...* seems to be an unsuccessful attempt to sound mildly 'threatening' *...Did so many things I never did intend to do...* appears to be a rather unspecific admission of guilt *...Maybe in the next life I'll be able to hear myself think...* the narrator bleats feebly, rather desperately hoping for reincarnation in a better situation. In his desperation, he tries to appeal to his lover by stringing several blues clichés together: *...Need your love so bad...* he declares.... *Turn your lamp down low...* lines drawn from songs popularised by Fleetwood Mac and Muddy Waters *...Rock me pretty baby, rock me all at once...* echoes the smooth sexual come on of B.B. King's *Rock Me Baby* (1964). But then he destroys the effect with the jokey *...Rock me for a little while, rock me for a couple of months....* In later live versions this is replaced by *...Rock me till everything gets real/ Rock me 'til there's nothing left to feel...* which is equally ineffective as a seduction line.

There is another tongue twister in the last verse: *...There's voices in the night tryin' to be heard/ I sit here listenin' to every mind-pollutin' word...* By now the narrator has become just plain paranoid. The final statement *...I know plenty of people who'd put me up for a day or two...* shows that he is now grasping hopelessly at straws. The song can be seen as commenting slyly on Dylan's relationship with critics and audiences, suggesting that many of those who interpret his work are often 'a million miles' away from understanding it. As with *Can't* Wait, in the context of *Time Out of Mind*'s dark themes it is rather hard to appreciate its parodic qualities. Dylan performed many live versions over the years, testing its limits with varying degrees of emotion and using it as an effective vehicle for the band to stretch out and demonstrate their 'blues chops'. By the time of the show at Milwaukee on 8th November 2012 its tone has become decidedly lighter, with Dylan's characteristically jerky piano dominating the sound. He also seems to deliberately amplify the narrator's assertions, so placing more emphasis on the exaggerated pleading in the lyrics. Only in live performance is justice done to the levels of narrative ambiguity which Dylan plays with here.

In *'Til I Fell in Love with You* the tone is more despairing. The narrator is again missing his girl, but here there is no significant attempt to win her back, despite the direct address in the repeated title refrain. The opening lines illustrate this graphically, and with considerable economy: *...My nerves are exploding/ And my body's tense/ Feel like the whole world/ Got me pinned up against the fence...* The use of slight echo and distortion adds to feeling of alienation. However, the tension in the opening lines is then somewhat dissipated as the song progresses. The narrator's mood becomes rather listless: *...I've been hit too hard, seen too much...* and rather helpless: *...Nothing can heal me now but your touch...* The pain of unrequited love as expressed in the chorus: *...I was alright 'til I fell in love with you...* is clearly there, but its edges are somewhat dulled. We are then told that his *....house is on fire...* but he appears to take a rather passive attitude to this. All he can do is bemoan his bad fortune, as if he is watching the disaster from a safe distance. *...I thought it would rain...* he tells us, sounding rather dazed and emotionally numb *...but the clouds passed by...* It sounds like he is ready to 'give up the ghost' and surrender to his fate *...I feel like I'm coming to the end of my way...* he announces gloomily. But then he stirs himself to declare, in an echo of a line from *Psalm 28*: *...But I know God is my shield and he won't lead me astray...* Despite this proclamation, it seems that he has little real faith that 'the Lord' will deliver him from his depressed state. Immediately afterwards, he admits that *...I still don't know what I'm gonna do...*

What follows is even more impressionistic, dreamy and detached: *...Boys in the street, beginning to play/ Girls like birds, drifting away...* It's as if he's staring at a street scene through some kind of opiate haze, watching the events in slow motion. Certainly he seems to be losing touch with everyday reality. He then makes an unconvincing attempt to boast rather spitefully that: *...When I'm gone, you'll remember my name/ I'm gonna win my way to wealth and fame...* But he then retreats into his own rather cluttered mindset where there is *...Junk piling up, taking up space...* Presenting us with a rather disturbingly hallucinatory image he tells us that *...My eyes feel like they're falling off my face...* It seems that he cannot see anything clearly now. Finally he confesses that *...My attempts to please you were all in vain...* a reference to Robert Johnson's anguished blues classic. But in reality he is merely world-weary. He declares that if he is still alive tomorrow he'll be *...Dixie bound....* returning to his home in the Deep South. While *Million Miles* uses exaggeration to parody the blues singer's plight, *'Til I Fell in Love with You* is more sincere and melancholic. But both songs reflect on Dylan's struggle to find inspiration. Ultimately it seems that it is only his desire to reach his poetic muse which sustains him.

Dirt Road Blues puts a more positive spin on the struggle Dylan is describing. With its swinging tune and slight rockabilly feel, it is reminiscent of Gene Vincent's version of the cheery Bill Monroe bluegrass classic *Rocky Road Blues*. The lines in the first verse are lifted almost verbatim from *Lonesome Atlanta Blues*, recorded by Bobby Grant in 1927, but while Grant's song is a slow and mournful lament, Dylan's expression is distinctly light and airy. An earlier *Dirt Road Blues* was performed by none other than Big Joe Williams, whose version is adapted from the earlier-still *Down the Dirt Road Blues*, a darkly meditative piece in which the singer seems to be contemplating the possibility of suicide. The 'dirt road' (which is emblematic of the landscape of the Deep South) is a common motif in blues songs, often representing the singer's desire for freedom or escape. The narrator is determined to keep moving, it seems, not necessarily in search of his love but in an attempt to escape from the pain of separation from her. The song begins with the repeated proclamation *...Gonna walk down that dirt road 'till someone lets me ride...* References to 'riding' often have sexual connotations, so maybe the singer here is hoping to find another woman. He tells us that if he can't find the girl who has left him he will just *...run away and hide...* But as he leads us through the sprightly tune it's hard to believe that he's really suffering that much.

The narrator then tells us he's been *...pacin' round the room, hoping maybe she'll come back...* This is neatly rhymed with *...I been prayin' for salvation/ Laying round in a one room country shack...* The 'salvation' he is seeking here, however, definitely seems to be earthly rather than spiritual. *One Room Country Shack* was a 1953 single written and performed by Mercy Walton and later recorded by Buddy Guy, Taj Mahal and others, in which the singer sings of his lost love while held up in an isolated location. In the next lines the singer will *...walk down that dirt road 'till my eyes begin to bleed...* a direct reference to *Blood in My Eyes* and a metaphor for desperate sexual longing. Dylan uses this patchwork of references in a rather teasing way. The narrator confirms his 'love sick' condition, drawing on well known blues expressions to try to support his case, but the rather carefree vocals tend to belie this. When he sings *...'Til my eyes begin to see/ Till my chains have been shattered and I've been freed...* the reference to emancipation from slavery functions as a metaphor for his own 'emancipation' from the 'chains' of his lost love.

In the most evocative lines the singer declares *...I've been lookin' at my shadow/ Watchin' the colors up above...* followed by *...I've been rollin' through the rain and hail/ Lookin' for the sunny side of love...* There is a passing reference to *Keep on the Sunny Side*, a late nineteenth century hymn which became one of the signature tunes of The Carter Family. The contrasting imagery of the narrator's 'shadow' and the 'stormy weather', set against the search in the sky for 'colours' and the sunshine of redemption is particularly effective, as Dylan places vocal emphasis on the surprising reference to the 'sunny side'. Here the inspiration for which the narrator is determined to keep searching is identified with the sun coming out from behind the clouds.

In the final verse the repeated line *...Gonna walk down that dirt road/ Till everything becomes the same...* is followed by *...I'll keep on walkin' till I hear her holler out my name...* after which the track ends rather abruptly. In the lyrics on the official Bob Dylan website the final lines have been changed to *....Gonna walk down that dirt road/ Till I'm right beside the sun...* which makes more sense in terms of the imagery of the song. This is followed by a new concluding line*...I'm gonna put up a barrier to keep myself away from every one...* This rather odd 'afterthought' seems a little out of keeping with the positivity of the recorded ending. After the dramatic declaration of spiritual isolation in *Love Sick*, which it follows on the album, the song indicates a determination by Dylan to 'carry on regardless'. At times it almost spills over into desperation but otherwise it maintains its cheerful tone right up until its sudden fade out. It is a joyful declaration of artistic freedom, in which Dylan - in celebration of his new relationship with the spirit of inspiration - can now take to the 'open road', following his muse wherever the 'rides' he hopes to be offered will take him.

12th January 1990. Toad's Place is a club and concert venue in New Haven, a small city in Connecticut which is the home of Yale University. Right now we are four songs into the longest show of Dylan's career. Tonight he is playing four one hour sets with only small breaks in between. Naturally there has been a scramble for tickets as the place only holds 700. The enthusiastic audience is jammed up against the stage, cheering and shouting requests for songs. They are certainly privileged because tonight Bob Dylan is responding to them, acting almost like an 'entertainer'. He appears to be treating the show as a live rehearsal for his upcoming tour. He even talks and jokes with the crowd. He will play fifty songs tonight, including a whole range of covers, some of which he has never played before. The set begins with Joe South's *Walk a Mile in My Shoes*. Later there will be *Everybody's Movin'*, an old rockabilly number by Glen Trout,

Kris Kristofferson's *Help Me Make It Through the Night* and a whole range of country and blues numbers. He will even attempt Bruce Springsteen's *Dancing in the Dark*, grinning as he fails to remember all the words. Later on in the evening somebody will ask him to sing the Traveling Wilburys song *Congratulations*. He will turn round, show the band a few chords and give it a go.

Whatever Dylan is 'on' tonight, it has certainly fired up his energy. The audience can't quite believe that he will just go on and on for the entire evening, as if he is truly leading a 'club band'. Somehow the musicians - G. E. Smith on guitar, Tony Garnier on bass and Christopher Parker on drums - manage to keep up the pace and respond to his whims. Occasionally it is a little sloppy but there are a few moments of true inspiration. Along with most of the songs from *Oh Mercy*, there is a heartfelt take on Leadbelly's *In the Pines* and a stunning, highly emotional version of *Tears of Rage*, that great song of generational angst from *The Basement Tapes*. When it finally all ends with *Like a Rolling Stone*, the audience have truly had an experience they can brag to their friends about.

Right now a thumping up-tempo drumbeat from Christopher Parker is pounding out and Dylan is about to perform one of the most generic blues songs, whose development reflects much of the history of the blues in the twentieth century. On the sleeves of the many bootleg versions of the show the song is listed as *Trouble No More*, credited to 'McKinley Morganfield' (Muddy Waters). But this is a song which exists in many different versions. The first known recording is a haunting acoustic country blues number called *Someday Baby Blues* by Sleepy John Estes (1937), with Hammie Nixon on harmonica. The song was adapted by piano player Big Maceo Merriweather in 1940 as *Worried Life Blues*. Merriweather slows down the song considerably to produce a soulful version which showcases his virtuoso keyboard skills and sophisticated vocal technique. Muddy Waters recorded the most well known variant in 1955, applying his trademark Chicago blues boogie stomp, with notable contributions from Willie Dixon on bass and Little Walter on harmonica.

The song has been recorded under its various different titles by many blues singers such as B.B. King, John Lee Hooker, Mississippi Fred McDowell, as well as rock performers like Eric Clapton, Jerry Garcia and The Allman Brothers Band. Almost all of these artists, while retaining the basic tune and chorus line of *...Someday baby, you ain't gonna trouble (or worry) me no more...* tend to make up their own lines for the verses. Tonight much of what Dylan sings is incomprehensible in this smoky, echoey space. He does, however, revert to Sleepy John's chorus line of *....Someday baby, you ain't gonna worry my mind any more...* Other verses seem to contain snatches of lines from Waters' version. It is hard to be certain. It's quite likely that Dylan is making them up as he goes along.

In his later music Dylan - whose voice has increasingly come to sound like that of a 'grizzled' bluesman - has gravitated more and more towards the self-deprecating humour, the lack of sentimentality and - perhaps most of all - the supremely subtle poetic fluidity of the blues. The material that blues singers perform often consists of their own versions of established songs, in which lyrics are often swapped around, changed and adapted. Many blues songs can thus be said to have various 'authors'. Even Robert Johnson, who died in 1937 and whose work languished in obscurity until it was rediscovered in the early 1960s (when it became one of the major inspirations for British blues revival musicians such as The Rolling Stones and Eric Clapton) 'borrowed' many verses in his songs from previous sources. In the early years of the blues, before the songs were being recorded, performers would learn songs from other singers by ear. Some singers mixed lines from different songs together and threw in a few of their own. As a young performer, Dylan was thoroughly schooled in this 'folk process'. Many of his early compositions utilised existing melodies from folk ballads. Some were adaptations of previously existing songs. His gorgeous adaptation of *Corrina Corrina,* which is listed on the *Freewheelin'* album as 'traditional' is his own amalgam of the traditional song *Corrine, Corrina* with the melody and some of the lyrics of Robert Johnson's *Stones in My Passway.* When performing the song live Dylan would also vary the lyrics considerably, throwing in or discarding various verses. Such practices were common among many of the performers Dylan met and learned from in the coffee houses of Minneapolis and Greenwich Village where he first plied his trade.

Three of the songs on *Modern Times* are fairly obvious 'remakes' of well known blues songs. The narrators use the language of romantic disillusionment, filtered through the inbuilt ambiguity of the metaphorical language of the blues, to attempt to keep the spirit of creativity in their sights. They all feature unreliable narrators who rely on self-deprecating wit. *Someday Baby* is Dylan's version of the blues standard he knocked out sixteen years before on that memorable evening at Toad's Place. Yet the sound of the recording and the tone of his delivery is very different. He strips the song down and adds a fast, insistent rhythm. His vocal is smooth and understated throughout, only rising in pitch slightly as he sings the chorus line ...*Someday baby, you ain't gonna worry po' me any more...* Here, in contrast to his natural gruffness, the singing is smooth and self confident. Only at the really crucial moments, where genuine questions are being asked, does he sound less assured.

The song is yet another 'my baby done left me' blues. All its variants rely on the common blues motif of the desire for eventual 'revenge' against an unnamed female who has left him bereft. But here Dylan's narrator never sounds in the least depressed. At worst he offers a shrug at the world's unfairness. The band's playing is particularly tight and disciplined, providing a tension which underlines the narrator's insistence on 'keeping his cool'. The lyrics are as plain and subdued as the singer's tone. The narrator is insistent that *eventually* the girl will come to regret leaving him in the lurch. He pleads with us to *...pity po' me...* but he sounds so cool and unconcerned that it is difficult to take this plea at face value. He then insists on providing a series of excuses for ways in which his 'revenge' will be delayed. He complains that *...Well, you take my money, and you turn me out..* his voice gliding smoothly over the words. But then, during *...You fill* *me up with nothin' but self doubt...* he hesitates just slightly on the first syllable of *...nothin'...* Given that his 'baby' has just ripped him off for all his money and thrown him out of his own home, he has *some* right to be angry. But he still seems determined to present himself as being in control.

In the next verse, however, he sounds like he might finally lose his cool *...You drive me so hard...* he asserts *...almost to the grave...* Dylan's voice becomes suddenly guttural on the final word. But the overall delivery is still so smooth that it's hard to believe he's really so hurt. This impression is confirmed after a short instrumental passage, with snatches of unflashy guitar building up the tension, when we hear that *...I'm so hard pressed, my mind tied up in knots/ I keep recycling the same old thoughts...* as if he is now admitting that his problem is not really with the woman but with himself. Thus his violent 'threat' to her that he will *...wring your neck...* in the next verse is very unconvincing, especially as he claims that he would only do it to preserve his 'self respect'. The singer *tries* to be angry, telling the girl she can *...take your clothes/ Put 'em in a sack...* and that he *...gon' drive you from your home...* but because his tone is so restrained and unemotional, this again feels like an empty boast. Finally he runs out of threats. He can only reflect that *...living this way ain't a natural thing to do...* and rather pathetically laments *...Why was I born to love you?...* It seems that Dylan is once again addressing the spirit of inspiration that he was 'born to love'. But the pressure of expectation has driven him nearly 'to the grave'. He is 'so hooked' on his muse's charms that he must continue to serenade the creative spirit, no matter how unnatural it may seem to him to continue doing so. Yet he is worried that self-doubt and lack of inspiration (those 'same old thoughts') will overwhelm him. But the lack of any convincing panic in his voice or in the music conveys the impression that this is very unlikely to happen. The singer still fears, or knows, that the woman may desert him. One day, he tells us, he will be gone, down a road from which there is no return. The tussle with his 'self-doubt' will then finally be over. But he doesn't sound too worried right now. That day still seems a very long way away.

Tell Tale Signs features a harder edged take of the song. The rhythm here is tighter, less relaxed and the vocal more uncertain and jumpy. While the message of disillusionment remains basically the same, the narrator sounds rather more bitter and vulnerable. Or at least, he's trying to fool us into thinking he feels like that... The lyrics are also somewhat more direct and self-critical. He still harbours dark thoughts about disposing of his lover: *...Gonna blow out your mind, and make you pure...* he tells her *...I've taken about as much of this as I can endure...* But the performance is still not really venomous enough for us to believe that he really *means* this, unlike the cold hearted narrator of Robert Johnson's *32/20 Blues* (a sharp and bitter Dylan cover of which also appears on *Tell Tale Signs)* who vows to shoot his woman. Whereas Johnson's threats appear to be quite serious, Dylan's narrator seems to be merely providing a safe escape route for his revenge fantasies. He pretends that he is not *really* asking for her pity, as he casts himself deliberately into abjection: *...Little by little, bit by bit...* he sings, the 'babyish' words suggesting a kind of mock timidity *...I'm becoming* *more of a hypocrite...* Then we hear how she has *...made me eat/ A ton of dust...* By now he admits to being rather scared of her: *...You're potentially dangerous...* he cries *...and not worthy of trust...* The similarly awkward *...When I heard you was cold, I bought you a coat and hat/ I think you must have forgotten about that...* sounds rather pathetically forlorn. Playing the martyr, he tells her he will 'turn the other cheek' to her insults. When he resorts to *...if all else fails, I'll make it a matter of self-respect...* he's really squirming. By now the woman has probably turned away haughtily, not impressed by this rather pathetically inadequate display of bravado.

Dylan's variation on the blues standard *Rollin' and Tumblin'* is built squarely on another Muddy Waters song with the same name, which has been recorded by prominent rock/blues acts such as Canned Heat, Eric Clapton, Johnny Winter and Dr. Feelgood. Waters' version is a development of the earliest known version, *Roll and Tumble Blues*, recorded by Hambone Willie Newbern in 1929. Robert Johnson used some of the lyrics in *If I Had Possession over Judgement Day* (1936). Many years later, Captain Beefheart used it as the basis of the 'psychedelic blues' *Sure 'Nuff 'N Yes I Do* (1967). Some performers have adapted or completely rewritten the song, retaining only the distinctive driving rhythm, which tweaks the familiar twelve bar form slightly by adding an extra beat. In Dylan's hands it becomes a kind of tribute to the many blues masters who have covered it. His exuberant and up-tempo 'rewrite' preserves most of Waters' first verse but extends the song to ten more original verses. Dylan twists and turns the words around to bring out their full ambiguity. He stretches out *...cried...* in the first two lines, lingering on the syllables, turning the line *...I cried the whole night long...* into a kind of joyful release. The last line of the verse changes Waters' *...I couldn't tell right from wrong...* to the more equivocal *...I must have bet my money wrong...* (an expression lifted from the traditional *Gamblin' Blues*). In the next verse, after the standard complaint that *...I got troubles so hard, I can't stand the strain...* he spits out the extraordinary *...Some lazy slut has charmed away my brains...* Here he adopts the hard-drinking, womanising persona that so many blues singers hide behind.

The following verses alternate between blues clichés and clever, knowing asides, which demonstrate that the narrator's macho stance is merely a front. The exaggeratedly defensive *...I ain't nobody's house boy, I ain't nobody's well trained maid...* descends into farce *...This woman so crazy, I ain't gonna touch another one for years...* is desperately self-mocking, as is *...Ain't nothing so depressing as trying to satisfy this woman of mine...* Dylan's phrasing, as he crams the words in, is immaculate *...Well I got up this morning/ Saw the rising sun return...* is followed by *...sooner or later/ You too shall burn...* But it is hard to believe that this declaration of revenge is any more than bluster. The narrator becomes even gloomier, retreating into an exaggeratedly gothic tone: *...The night's filled with shadows/ The years are filled with early doom...* which he rhymes (in another miracle of phrasing) with perhaps the song's key line: *...I've been conjurin' up all these long dead souls from their crumblin' tombs...* In order to come to terms with this woman draining away his vital energies, sapping his inspiration, it seems that he has had to summon the ghosts of Muddy Waters, Robert Johnson, Hambone Willie et al.

Finally he delivers a plea for forgiveness, suggesting to the woman that they *...forgive each other...* and for a celebration *...go down to the Greenwood Glen...* (a reference to the black district of Tulsa, Oklahoma, an important centre for jazz and blues in the pre-war era and one of the three reputed sites of Robert Johnson's grave). The last verse repeats the first, changing the last few words with what sounds, at first, like a typical 'signing off' line in a blues song: *...I think I must be traveling on...* Dylan sings *...traveling wrong...* a line which echoes *...bet my money wrong...* showing the singer's awareness of his own inadequacy. Here Dylan uses the blues itself as a metaphor for the artist's struggle with the creative imagination. This is conveyed through the song's confident, witty execution. Never does Dylan sound the least bit miserable. The tone of the song, despite its comic asides, is triumphant.

While many blues songs allude to, quote from or even 'steal' from older songs, Dylan expands the scope of the genre by using lines from wildly divergent sources. Several lines in *Rollin' and Tumblin'* are derived from Ovid, much of whose subject matter - like that of the classic blues singers - was focused on eroticism and unrequited love *...She conjures up long-dead souls from their crumbling sepulchres ...* and *...You must get yourself a houseboy, and a well-trained maid...* both appear in Peter Green's 1982 translation of *Amores.* Other lines in the song are re-phrasings of the work of Henry Timrod, whose poem *Little Willie* - recounting how his own baby, who was born at Christmas, suffers an early death - features the lines *...that early doom/ The tale which is shadowed here...* The 'long dead souls' are thus not just dead blues singers but the many poets and singers who preceded them. By 'cutting up' and inserting lines from such disparate sources Dylan shows the links between poets and singers throughout the ages, illustrating how similar their concerns are. But he is not presenting himself as any kind of musty scholar or a purveyor of existential doom. He pronounces the lyrics with a dry, comic irony which is worthy of the romantic trickster Ovid himself.

The third of these songs, *The Levee's Gonna Break,* is characterised by an insistent, repetitive, yet understated rhythm. It became a prominent feature of Dylan's live act for several years. Despite its theme it is basically a cheerful workout, often used very effectively in live performance to build up the tempo of the shows. The music and lyrics are closely based on Memphis Minnie and Kansas Joe McCoy's *When the Levee Breaks* (1929). Released two years after the Great Mississippi Flood, this was one of a several blues songs recalling this terrible event. The flood covered an area of 15,000 square miles and destroyed half a million homes, as well as causing the deaths of thousands. Its effects contributed to the mass migrations of African Americans to Chicago and other Northern cities. Despite this, singer Kansas Joe's tone is one of stoical indifference. The deft guitar picking by Memphis Minnie gives the track a lightness of tone. And though Joe tells us he's *...worked on the levee, mama both night and day...* and claims to have *...nobody to tell my troubles to...* it's almost as if the flood is merely a kind of backdrop for his complaints about the 'woman trouble' that he keeps alluding to. But rather than being angry, he seems merely resigned to his fate. It appears that the great effort he's put it to preventing the dam bursting is only important as a symbol of the impossibility of him keeping his woman.

In the blues, and in several of Dylan's songs such as *A Hard Rain's a-Gonna Fall* or *Down in the Flood*, the imagery of flooding often implies a kind of judgement - divine or otherwise - on the human condition. In the first verse we hear that *...Everybody sayin' this is a day only the Lord could make...* suggesting that the flood has been the result of divine intervention. The narrator tells us that *...I got to the river and I threw my clothes away...* suggesting some attempt at baptism or personal spiritual 'cleansing'. He tries to be optimistic, telling us that *...Riches and salvation can be waiting behind the next bend in the road...* and repeats a preacher's millenarian promise that *....Few more years of hard work, then there'll be a thousand years of happiness...* But he never really sounds convinced that such 'salvation' is at hand. It seems that he's hedging his bets on the results of Judgement Day. He expresses resentment at the unnamed forces of authority who will *...strip you of all they can take...* but he reserves his ire for the woman who has deserted him: *...I picked you up from the gutter and this is the thanks I get...* is followed by the supremely laconic *...You say you want me to quit ya/ I told ya, "No, not just yet"...*

There are also veiled hints that his lover's sexuality is rather overpowering: *...I woke up this morning, butter and eggs in my bed/ I ain't got enough room to even raise my head...* along with more conventional confessions of devotion: *...When I'm with you, I forget I was ever blue/ Without you there's no meaning in anything I do....* But perhaps the most revealing lines are *...I look in your eyes, I see nobody other than me/ I see all that I am and all I hope to be...* This recalls songs like *It Ain't Me Babe* and *Just Like a Woman*, where the 'lover' being addressed can be seen as an aspect of the narrator himself. The philosophical emphasis of the line that follows creates an ambiguous suggestion that in addressing his elusive lover, the narrator is using her as a 'mirror' for the imperfections of his own soul. As in *Someday Baby* and *Rollin' and Tumblin'*, the muse being addressed is a rather slippery figure - a kind of phantasm who does not always manifest herself in physical form.

8th April 2009. Grand Amphithéâtre, Palais de Congress, Paris. On his extensive world travels, Bob Dylan has been known to play 'one off' versions of particular songs, especially if they are related to the location he is appearing in. Tonight he is midway through a twenty three date European tour. Paris has always had an important place in his affections. The French capital has been a frequent port of call on the Never Ending Tour and on his visits he has sometimes invited Hughes Aufray - a singer noted for performing French versions of his songs - onstage with him. Tonight Dylan launches into a reverential reading of Charles Aznavour's *The Times We've Known*, a song he has only ever performed once before. In late 1989, midway through a show at Madison Square

Garden - in the days when he still occasionally introduced songs - he had mumbled mysteriously*...I usually only play these songs when I'm all by myself, but I feel like I'm all by myself now...* certainly a strange sentiment to utter in such a large and prestigious venue. Tonight there is no introduction. The audience is presumably more likely to be familiar with the work of Aznavour. The song begins with the evocative couplet *...The times we've known are slipping by/ Like vapour trails across the sky...*

Dylan 'uncovers' what would have normally been a heavily orchestrated number by using minimal instrumentation and a restrained vocal tone, although his voice is noticeably stretched when he reaches the repeated refrain. *The Times We've Known* is a nostalgically philosophical address to an unnamed lover, but its main concern is really with surviving the times when *...life was hard and chances few...* It briefly refers to the same passage from Ecclesiastes that appears in Pete Seeger's *Turn, Turn, Turn: ...The time to laugh, a time to cry/ A time to let the world go by/ And if we had some tears to pay/ No one can take those tears away...* The band's playing is a little uncertain at first. It may be they were unprepared for this sudden addition to the usual set. But soon they get on board and help Dylan build up to a rousing finale as he repeats the title line. In fact, he's fluffed the last line of that verse, changing it to *...we wouldn't pay them anyway...* which doesn't quite make sense, but nobody seems to notice. There is some polite applause, and the show moves on.

Bob Dylan has long professed an admiration for the songs of Charles Aznavour, who was a hugely successful performer throughout a career that lasted seven decades. Aznavour sold over 180 million records and was even known by some as the 'French Frank Sinatra'. He wrote around a thousand songs in various different languages and in many different modes. A number of his best known songs are uncompromisingly self-critical. In *Drinking*, the third episode of *Theme Time Radio Hour,* Dylan plays several country records that outline the consequences of drunkenness in no uncertain terms. But the revelation of the show is *I Drink*, Aznavour's shockingly stark and unstintingly graphic depiction of the evils of alcohol. Aznavour is one of the best known exponents of *nouvelle chanson*, a style in which lyrics and storytelling tend to be emphasised over musical accompaniment and which is linked to various traditions of French poetry. It has its roots in the songs of the troubadours of the middle ages, who would perform epic poems and romances to musical accompaniment. Its singers often use gesture and movement on stage to illustrate their lyrics in a theatrical manner.

In 2009 Dylan was approached by French writer/director Olivier Dahan to provide music for his upcoming American 'road movie' *My Own Love Song*, a whimsical comedy-drama starring Renée Zellweger and Forrest Whittaker. Zellweger plays Jane, a former professional singer whose life and career have been severely limited by a car crash some years before, which has left her wheelchair-bound and led to her young son Devon being adopted. Dylan co-wrote *Life is Hard* with Robert Hunter for the climactic scene of the film in which she performs the song in front of her son. A number of other songs emerged from the collaboration. These formed the basis of *Together Through Life*, an album of short, punchy songs with stripped down lyrics and catchy hooks and riffs. Much of the music has a 'Tex-Mex' feel which is appropriate for the film's Southern US location, with David Hidalgo, leader of Los Lobos, adding accordion to most of the tracks.

Life is Hard has many of the qualities of nostalgic regret and naked emotional honesty associated with Aznavour's songs. Its expression of stoicism in the face of existential pain is characteristic of modern chanson. The song conveys a similar philosophical stoicism in the face of deep adversity. The instrumentation is fairly sparse, dominated by Donnie Herron's plaintive steel guitar and Mike Campbell's mandolin, while George Receli plays a very slow shuffle on drums. Dylan pronounces the words clearly with little affectation, very much in the manner of Aznavour. As in *The Times We've Known*, the song is composed of simple, sometimes ironic, rhyming couplets. In the first verse, Jane declares*: ...The evening winds are still/ I've lost the way and will/ Can't tell you where they went/ I just know what they meant ...* Later she tearfully tells her son that *...I pass the old school yard/ Admitting life is hard/ Without you near me....* These lyrics are designed to catch the boy's attention and are made particularly poignant because she has not seen him since he was a baby, some eleven years ago, and so will not be able to recognise him instantly *...Ever since the day you went away...* she laments *...I felt that emptiness inside...* and then *...Since we've been out of touch/ I haven't felt that much....* The final verse reiterates the pain of separation: *...I feel a chilly breeze/ In place of memories...*

Another song from the album, the solo Dylan composition *This Dream Of You,* also uses the lyrical and musical modes of chanson. The version on the album is led by David Hidalgo's accordion and Donnie Herron's violin, which do much to conjure the atmosphere of a pre-war French café. One can almost see and smell the Gauloises smouldering in the ashtrays. Although it does not feature in the film it could easily have been written as an expression of Jane's predicament. Dylan's vocals are fairly low key, reflecting uncertainty and regret. The song was performed on an occasional basis between 2009 and 2012, with mandolin and harmonica generally supplying the 'ambience'. Its narrator is pictured as sitting in a 'nowhere café', and expresses great uncertainty about the future. He addresses a lost love, who he can now only see in a dream. Even then his vision seems to be rather blurred. The repeated refrain at the end of each verse ...*This dream of you which keeps me living on...* is certainly not any kind of strong declaration of faith. The singer declares that the dream is ...*All I have and all I know...* but although he sounds disillusioned he never appears to be really desperate. He wonders *...why I'm so frightened of dawn...* Later he reveals that *...There's a moment when all old things become new again...* But he admits that *...that moment might have come and gone...* Then he describes his fascination with the dream that is holding his attention: *...I look away but I keep seeing it/ I don't want to believe but I believe it...* It seems that he knows that all of this is all an illusion, but that he cannot draw himself away. In the first bridge section, in an odd, perhaps slightly awkward, use of repetition: *...Shadows dance upon the wall/ Shadows that seem to know it all...* he reveals that the truth he cannot grasp himself is clearly out there, but it is only manifesting itself to him in a way he cannot grasp.

The narrator's uncertainty continues *...Am I too blind to see?...* he asks, repeating a line from 1979's *Precious Angel ...Is my heart playing tricks on me?...* But by then he seems to have moved beyond any really deep emotions: *...I'm lost in the crowd/ All my tears are gone...* His grip on his feelings, and on reality, continues to slip and his uncertainty grows stronger *...Everything I touch seems to disappear/ Everywhere I turn, you are always here...* In another context, this might be seen as a statement of faith, but here he seems disconcerted, even slightly haunted. The final verse contains an effective contrast of images: *...From a cheerless room, in a curtained gloom/ I saw a star from heaven fall...* This last phrase is the title of a popular romantic song from 1934 by Joseph Schmidt which was later recorded by Vera Lynn and others. The image of 'curtained gloom' is a borrowing from Timrod's poem *Serenade* (1872). The contrast of imagery suggests that the falling star may be bringing faith, or hope, or some way out of the 'nowhere café'. But then he relates that *...I turned and looked again but it was gone...* Finally, he is left with just the dream.

In *I Feel a Change Comin' On,* Dylan is in rather more familiar territory. The stately melody has some resemblance to Sam Cooke's *A Change Is Gonna Come.* The song is a wistful acknowledgement of the effects of ageing which accepts the inevitability of romantic disillusionment. Like so many songs of Dylan's late period, its narrator is an older man who desires a younger woman. But here, instead of manically chasing after her, he seems to accept that he really has no chance with her. The first refrain runs *...I feel a change comin' on/ And the last part of the day is already gone...* The song - which has five verses and two bridges - begins with the line *...I'm looking the world over...* the title of a Memphis Minnie song. The narrator sees a woman who he refers to as 'my baby', although this is surely just wish fulfillment. He tells us that she is *...walking with the village priest...* This may suggest that she is arranging a marriage, although presumably not with him. At first he tries not to adopt the typically lustful approach of blues singers in favour of a more romantic 'marriage of minds'. As the song turns into a direct address, he states that *...We've got so much in common/ We strive for the same old ends...* He hopes they can become 'friends', although he does get slightly friskier in the next verse: *...Life is for love/ And they say love is blind...* he begins, trotting out the oldest cliché in the book. But then he attempts, a little half-heartedly, to win her over *...If you want to live easy/ Baby pack your clothes with mine...*

Finally he lets his lustfulness get the better of him *...You're as whorish as ever...* he suddenly (and rather surprisingly) declares, although to his credit he does try to balance this with another rather clichéd attempt at 'romance': *...We see the meaning of life/ In each other's eyes...* But in the bridge which precedes this verse he is considerably more realistic: *...Ain't no use in dreaming...* he admits *...I got better things to do...* and then he turns a romantic cliché around: *...Dreams never worked anyway/ Even when they did* *come true...* In the second bridge he sings *...I'm listening to Billy Joe Shaver/ And I'm reading James Joyce...* Dylan has expressed admiration for the work of 'outlaw country' singer-songwriter Shaver (whose songs have been recorded by both Willie Nelson and Waylon Jennings) on more than one occasion. Joyce, like Dylan, incorporated many allusions and references to other works in his writing, especially in his most acclaimed work *Ulysses*, a modern retelling of Homer's *Odyssey* - a text which has clearly been a key influence on both writers. The juxtaposition of the two names neatly sums up how Dylan's work draws upon both musical and literary influences. 'Joyce' also rhymes neatly with the next lines: *...Some people tell me/ I've got the blood of the land in my voice...* This statement, with its possible resonance with Woody Guthrie's 'alternative American anthem' *This Land Is Your Land* could certainly be applied to Dylan, whose work incorporates so many strands of American music and literature. The last verse uses simple but direct language which Hank Williams himself - the master of the plain-spoken but emotionally gut-wrenching lyric - would have been proud of: *...Everybody got all the money/ Everybody got all the beautiful clothes...* Dylan sings *...Everybody got all the flowers/ I don't have one single rose...*

Beyond Here Lies Nothin' is a much bleaker song of romantic disillusionment, stark in its imagery with possible intimations of violence. It was performed many times from 2009 onwards. The dominant riff resembles Fleetwood Mac's *Black Magic Woman* (1968), also covered by Santana on their album *Abraxas* (1970), which is itself based on Otis Rush's *All Your Love* (1958). The tune, with its slightly 'Latin' clipped rhythms, fits very well with lyrics that are sometimes ominous or even threatening. The presence of Hidalgo's accordion in the studio version also gives the song a 'borderland' feel. This helps suggest that the characters in the song are 'on the edge' in both a physical and a metaphysical sense - in a place where all that 'lies beyond' is an endless stretch of desert. There is even a certain suggestion that the narrator may be expressing nihilistic or even (very unusually for Dylan) atheistic feelings. The title phrase appears in Ovid's *Tristia and the Black Sea Letters,* in which the poet complains about his exile from Rome*: ...Beyond here lies nothing but chillness, hostility, frozen waves of an ice-hard sea....* The picture Ovid conjures up certainly chimes with the feeling that Dylan imparts. The song can be seen as the product of an existential crisis, as a recognition of mortality, or as another song of doomed, unrequited love. Dylan's performance certainly provides an air of menace, as well as a mixture of anger and vulnerability.

The song begins with a typical romantic address: *...Oh I love you pretty baby/ You're the only love I've ever known...* The next lines *...Just as long as you stay with me/ The whole world is my throne...* take the typical 'eternal devotion' of a lover to an extreme and seem to suggest that the narrator is more interested in power than love. The first refrain *...Beyond here lies nothin'/ Nothin' we can call our own...* intensifies the implication of an almost pathological possessiveness. The tone of both the music and the vocal - sung in a typically Dylanesque 'acid tongue' - is already suggestively portentous. We then enter into darker territory, an effect which is cleverly achieved by suggestion alone *...I'm movin' after midnight...* is a smoothly alliterative line which recalls both Howlin' Wolf's *Moanin' After Midnight* and Patsy Cline's *Walking After Midnight,* both songs of abandonment. This is followed by *...through boulevards of broken cars...* which conjures up a strangely apocalyptic image. It is as if some great and tragic event, like a nuclear war or an earthquake, must have happened. But the real 'apocalypse' is, it seems, in the narrator's mind. He continues to reiterate his dependence on the object of his love: *...Don't know what I'd do without it/ Without this love that we call ours...* This is a rather awkwardly phrased declaration, in contrast to the clarity of *...Beyond here lies nothin'/ Nothin' but the moon and stars....* The use of the half-rhyme emphasises the disparity between the uncertainty of the narrator's supposed 'love', which appears to be based on an obsessive possessiveness, and the way in which the second line of the refrain has expanded the scope of the song onto a 'cosmic scale'.

There are more intimations of violence to come. We are told that *...Down every street there is a window/ And every window's made of glass...* glass which could soon be shattered. The declaration that follows is far more equivocal *...We'll keep on lovin' pretty baby/ Just as long as love will last...* The earlier suggestion of an 'eternity of nothingness' has been tempered. The refrain is modulated by a powerfully suggestive image of something looming darkly over their love: *...Beyond here lies nothin'/ But the mountains of the past....* Despite trying to 'wipe out' his misdemeanours, the narrator has come to realise that the looming shadow of the past will inevitably catch up with him. It seems that escaping from the consequences of one's actions is impossible, even if one retreats to some place in some far-flung 'borderland'. In the final verse the narrator becomes strangely penitent: *...My ship is in the harbor/ And its sails are spread...* strongly implies that he wishes to escape from his predicament. He begs for mercy and healing: *...Listen to me, pretty baby/ Lay your hands upon my head...* But the answer to the final refrain seems to indicate that there *is* no escape: *...Beyond here lies nothing/ Nothing done and nothing said...* The last line moves away from the symbolism of previous verses, twice repeating the song's key word. Thus the narrator - despite his delusions of grandeur - may end up bereft, with 'nothing'. This, it seems, is where nihilism inevitably leads. As King Lear, mystified by his daughter Cordelia's refusal to prove her love for him, exclaims *...Nothing will come of nothing...*

While *Beyond Here Lies Nothing* explores the spiritual void which is depicted in the existential works of French writers like Albert Camus and Jean-Paul Sartre, the album's major tour-de-force *Forgetful Heart* takes us directly into the 'heart' of this philosophy with great eloquence, passion and power. The 'stripped down' lyrics are knife-sharp. This is a song about the effects of time, about memory, about old age looking back on youth and about how our lives can be wasted if we do not savour every single moment. It is both an address to a lover and an appeal to the singer's own emotional core: *...Forgetful heart, lost your power of recall...* Dylan begins *...Every little detail, you don't remember at all...* The next line *...The times we knew...* is a near-verbatim reference to Aznavour's song *...Who would remember better than you?...* Dylan asks. Already there is a palpable sense of loss and of great regret. This is made all the more effective because it is set against a distinctively haunting melody which allows us to almost taste the bliss whose absence the song laments. The message appears to be that, in order to truly appreciate love for another person, one must be absolutely present in the moment. Such moments, however, can easily slip away. Even in the midst of ecstatic love we can become distracted, egotistical or over-possessive. The song also grapples with the problem of what time does to human consciousness. Even if one has *really* loved, as time passes, recapturing that feeling may become impossible. 'The times we knew' cannot ever be brought back. In this deep conversation with his heart, the singer laments the impossibility of freezing those feelings in time, despite the fact that the attempt to do so is perhaps the main goal of all poetic songwriters.

The next two verses build up the tension by following a set pattern of alternating between short and long lines. The second verse begins: *...Forgetful heart/ We laughed and had a good time you and I...* In the third verse we get *...Forgetful heart/ We loved with all the love that life can give...* These are colloquial, warm reminiscences, showing that the narrator's memory is intact. But the responses in the next lines: *...It's been so long/ Now you're content to let the days go by...* and *...What can I say?/ Without you it's so hard to live...* are despairing, the short statements conveying the narrator's lack of ability to recall or reclaim those feelings. At the end of the second verse we are offered some hope: *...When you were there/ You were the answer to my prayer...* but by the end of verse three the efforts to recall the feelings that have deserted him have overwhelmed him: *...Can't take much more...* he tells us, in no uncertain terms. Then there is the pathetic rhetorical plea: *...Why can't we love like we did before?...* It is a question that nobody can answer. Time has done its work now and the feelings of the past cannot be reclaimed. Its effects are inexorable, inescapable...

Finally Dylan links the corrosive effect of time to Macbeth's famous *...Tomorrow and tomorrow and tomorrow...* soliloquy in which the protagonist, on hearing of the death of his wife, expresses the despairing notion that life is essentially meaningless: *...Life's but a poor player...* the murderous king tells us *...a walking shadow that struts and frets his hour upon the stage and then is heard no more...* Dylan encapsulates this speech and internalises it: *...Forgetful heart...* he laments *...Like a walking shadow in my brain...* The powerful image of a shadowy figure pounding the 'corridors' of the singer's brain, echoing the heart which beats ever louder and louder, leads us to the brutal reality of the narrator's confession that *...I lay awake and listen to the sound of pain...* He is a soul in torment, quite literally in limbo. But the triumph of the song is that he has somehow detached himself from his pain. Rather than feeling it, he 'listens' to it, as if it is somehow external to him. Or perhaps he all he can hear is the insistent beating of his own heart. This recalls Poe's *The Tell Tale Heart*, in which the narrator is a murderer who kills an old man merely for the thrill of doing so. He then buries the corpse under his floorboards and covers his tracks meticulously. But eventually he can hear nothing but the beating of the dead man's heart (which of course, is only in his mind). This is so overwhelming that he gives himself up to the police.

Then, in one of Dylan's most astonishing lyrical coups, everything is turned around *...The door is closed forevermore....* he declares ominously *...if indeed there ever was a door....* The conjoined word 'forevermore' is an echo of Poe's famous refrain 'nevermore' in his poem *The Raven* where the dead girl Lenore is described as *nameless here for evermore*. The 'door' being referred to might be the 'door' to hell that Dylan is trying to slip through in *Can't Wait* or the one in whose shadow the haunted narrator of *Standing in the Doorway* strums that Gay Guitar. But it can never be opened. What it represents is beyond human understanding. So there will 'indeed' be no answer to the narrator's 'prayer'. These words express an entire spiritual dilemma. They suggest that maybe in fact there is no door, and thus no heaven and no hell. Maybe 'the door' itself and what it may lead to is all a construction of the imagination. The crucial word in the line is 'indeed', which is normally a word used for emphasis, drawing our attention to the final conclusion that the great barrier that the narrator has erected is merely one he has constructed in his own mind. But in this case 'indeed' also suggests that the door might even be real.

The resolution of *Forgetful Heart* is one of Dylan's key moments of spiritual uncertainty; a paradoxical twist in which he admits the inadequacy of language when dealing with the ultimate questions. But he also suggests that, when negative emotions overwhelm us, there *is* always a way out. All we have to do is look inside ourselves and reconceptualise the way we see things, using words to create new mental structures. Then the imaginary doors we have placed in front of us will disappear. This is a very Blakean insight into the spiritual world - suggesting that by thinking 'poetically' we can go beyond the limitations of mere words in order to rearrange the images that have become fixed in our mind and reconstruct them anew. *Forgetful Heart*'s exploration of romantic disillusionment celebrates the fact that individuals can choose to cast off the *...mind forg'd manacles....* which prevent us from experiencing true creative and spiritual liberation. As Blake states in *The Marriage of Heaven and Hell: ...If the doors of perception were cleansed, everything would appear to man as it is, Infinite...*

13th November 2002. Bob Dylan and his band are playing the second of two shows at Madison Square Garden in New York. As in the other gigs on this tour, they have been performing a surprising number of cover versions of songs by contemporary song writers. These have included Van Morrison's *Carrying a Torch*, Neil Young's *Old Man*, Don Henley's *The End of the Innocence* and the Rolling Stones' *Brown Sugar.* Dylan has also regularly covered five Warren Zevon songs: *Mutineer, Accidentally Like a Martyr, Boom Boom Mancini* and *Lawyers, Guns and Money.* Such a selection is unusual for Dylan who, even in the 1990s when he played hundreds of covers, generally focused on older folk, blues, gospel and country material. The Zevon songs were being played as a response to the singer-songwriter's recent announcement that he was suffering from terminal cancer, from which he died early in 2003. Yet at no point during the tour did Dylan speak to the audience to explain his choices of songs, even though they may well have been unfamiliar to them. The tour was also notable for Dylan's almost complete switch to playing a keyboard onstage, which was soon to become a permanent feature of his performances. This was also never explained to the audience. Yet tonight, after performing his standard encores of *Blowin' in the Wind* and *All Along the Watchtower,* he surprises the audience by making an announcement:

...Thank you. There's a tribute going on, I guess it's the next week or the week after, it's over in England, for George Harrison with lots of ... I'm not sure who... But we can't make it. I just want to do this song for George because we were such good buddies...

Then we hear the familiar intro to *Something*, perhaps George's saddest and yet most beautiful song, which Dylan performs from behind his keyboard with great precision, delivering the verses with surprising gentleness and obvious loving care. Next to him, Larry Campbell plays the mandolin, which dominates the sound. Halfway through the song Dylan tilts his head slightly as a signal to Charlie Sexton, who plays a perfectly rendered version of George's sweetly measured lyrical guitar solo. When the song ends Dylan and the band stand stock still as usual. It is a moment of quite overwhelming emotion. The tribute has been executed with impeccable taste. Dylan and Harrison had indeed been close friends. They had collaborated on the wistful *I'd Have You Any Time*, the first track on Harrison's first solo album *All Things Must Pass.* Harrison had always been a vocal supporter of Dylan even when he faced the most criticism in the 1980s. Between 1988 and 1990 they collaborated on two albums by the somewhat jokey 'supergroup' The Traveling Wilburys with Tom Petty, Roy Orbison and Jeff Lynne. When George died in 2001 Dylan released an effusive and beautiful tribute:

...He was a giant, a great, great soul, with all the humanity, all the wit and humor, all the wisdom, the spirituality, the common sense of a man and compassion for people. He inspired love and had the strength of a hundred men. He was like the sun, the flowers and the moon and we shall miss him enormously. The world is a profoundly emptier place without him...

The performance of *Something*, which was repeated only once, at a show in George's home town of Liverpool in 2009, is a remarkable example of Dylan's musical dexterity and spontaneity. Judging by his onstage 'nudging' of members of the band on stage it has hardly been rehearsed at all. The song was written as a tribute to George's then wife Patti Boyd (later the subject of another classic rock song, Eric Clapton's *Layla*). It appears on the last album the Beatles recorded, *Abbey Road.* By this time the songwriting of the 'quiet one' was comparable to that of Lennon and McCartney. *Something* is generally regarded as the outstanding song on the album. Although it presents itself as an unequivocal love song, its prevailing mood is of a certain stoicism and acceptance of the frailty of human feelings and of love itself. It as if George - who had been steeped for many years in Eastern philosophies - is looking at himself, and his own love for a woman, with a serene, almost unemotional aloofness. The contrast between this existential detachment band the sincere love it expresses is a profound expression of the fragility not only of love but of life itself. Frank Sinatra called it 'the greatest love song of the past fifty years' and performed it many times in concert. The kind of universal love it celebrates is so pure and so elemental that it is almost overwhelming. But it also stands in its own way - along with McCartney's *Let It Be* - as a tearful yet dignified acknowledgement of the breakup of the most famous and successful band of all time, and with it the end of the 'sixties' and all the impossible hopes and dreams that the epochal decade signified. Dylan himself was at the centre of the cultural maelstrom of that era. He whispers his great friend's words with a kind of transcendent awe. Tonight his performance has a special quality of quiet dignity and restraint, the elements that illuminate his most powerful latter day songs of romantic disillusionment.

Four: *I'm in the Wrong Town...*
Seeing with 'New Eyes'

...O my Luve is like a red, red rose
That's newly sprung in June;
O my Luve is like the melody
That's sweetly played in tune...
Robert Burns *My Luve is Like a Red Red Rose* (1794)

11th February 2011. The tuxedos and the ball gowns have been dusted off yet again for the 53rd Annual Grammy Awards. This is a typically glitzy Hollywood affair at the Staples Center in Los Angeles. Around 26 million viewers have tuned in. In between the gushingly emotional presentations, Norah Jones has led a tribute to Dolly Parton and Mick Jagger has hosted an homage to Solomon Burke. A bunch of female vocalists have bravely attempted to pay some 'respect' to Aretha Franklin. Meanwhile, award winner Eminem has done his thing with his backing tapes, as have Katy Perry, Lady Gaga, Bruno Mars, Justin Bieber and Rihanna, not to mention Gwyneth Paltrow singing along with The Muppets. It's a slickly choreographed show with well rehearsed curtain changes. In order to fill out the whole glorious evening, there are awards for many musical sub-categories, reflecting the diversity of American popular music - there's pop, dance, R and B, rap, country, New Age, gospel, Latin, blues, bluegrass and more...

One of the newer categories is 'Americana' - a rather ill-defined combination of some of these strands of music - which had nevertheless became a recognised term by the 1990s. This is represented by Mumford and Sons and the Avett Brothers - both bands of youngish musicians on mandolins, fiddles, guitars and drums - who deliver their contributions with great enthusiasm and energy. They are decked out in 'authentic' 1930s-style work clothes - the kind of thing Woody Guthrie would have slipped into when he was off to the dustbowl or in which members of The Band would pose for some sepia-tinted photo shoots back in the day. Just as the Avetts finish their song, they stand up in unison. They are joined not only by the Mumfords but also by a bunch of dodgy looking gunslingers in dark suits, who a few of the audience might recognise as members of Bob Dylan's touring band. They all form a reasonably neat semi-circle, as if they are about to perform some kind of complicated barn dance. Then they begin to bash hell out of their instruments in a kind of mandolin-led 'manic hoedown', jumping up and down enthusiastically. Dylan, looking pretty dapper in a black suit and white spats, steps lightly into the middle of this assembly. Unusually for him, he is grinning benignly. Without further ado he launches straight into *...Well, I ain't gonna work on Maggie's Farm no more...*

Dylan spits out the famously acerbic lyrics with gravelly relish. The whole gang joins in on the chorus, as if they're singing along to a kind of 'National Anthem of Americana', which in a way they are. Many years ago, at the Newport Folk Festival on 25th July 1965, Dylan had launched into his first live appearance with a loud 'electric' band. *Maggie's Farm* was the standout performance of the three song set, with Dylan's manic, sneering vocals set against the screaming riffs of Mike Bloomfield, lead guitarist with the Paul Butterfield Blues Band. And so a musical revolution began. But there will be no booing or cutting of cables tonight. The performance is a kind of celebration of what Americana has now become - of how it has morphed out of what was once known as 'folk' and now incorporates elements of country, bluegrass, blues and other forms of 'the people's music', all filtered through a decidedly 'alternative' attitude. Surrounding Bob are a ragged bunch of its most successful modern performers, looking suitably awestruck at backing up the 'godfather' of the genre himself. Dylan stands on the spot where the cameras will catch him, spreading out his arms and swaying. This is a song he has performed many hundreds of times since that historic afternoon but tonight, possibly because there was only one rehearsal, it has a fresh and original energy.

Maggie's Farm is a surreal adrenaline rush of a song, with flashes of hilarious lyrical brilliance *...I wake up in the morning, fold my hands and pray for rain...* it begins *...I got a head full of ideas that are driving me insane...* This could be a summary of Dylan's astonishingly creative 1965-66 period, not to mention a wonderfully funny description of poetic inspiration itself. The song is built on *Down on Penny's Farm*, a complaint about corrupt landlords recorded by the Bently Boys in 1929. In a few judiciously chosen lines Dylan builds up a vivid picture of being 'imprisoned' on a farm on which he is made to 'slave' by various members of the young woman's family, who clearly delight in finding different ways of oppressing him. There is her brother, who *...fines you every time you slam the door...* her 'pa' whose *...bedroom window is made out of bricks...* and her 'ma', a scary, middle aged 'battle axe' who *..talks to all the servants about Man and God and Law...* and who *...is sixty eight but says she's twenty four...* The narrator's free spirit is contained and enslaved by these larger than life representations of 'Middle America'.

The song is an angry protest against the stifling of the creativity of youth by older generations - a kind of ruthlessly satirical *Times They Are A-Changin'*. Its merciless satire can be applied to any situation in which mindless bureaucracy or social control is being exercised. It is also Dylan's 'kiss off' to the fake authenticity of the mostly white middle class folk movement, with its 'sanctification' of American rural workers and its insistence that only acoustic music could be taken seriously. After his incendiary performance at Newport, Dylan would soon have to face down the particularly vocal animosity of some of these folk fans. But his persistence eventually led to the conceptualisation of a new musical genre, fuelled by the re-styling of various elements of traditional American music. It is no exaggeration to say that Americana was created during the recording of the legendary *Basement Tapes* in the Big Pink house in Woodstock in the summer of 1967. So it is not surprising that Dylan, having originally suffered so much abuse for this vision of American music, is beaming tonight. He is now triumphantly leading a group of devoted acolytes through a delightfully joyous rendition of the song that symbolises their entire musical raison d'être.

The 'hoedown' reaches its exultant climax in the last verse *...Well I try my best to be just like I am...* Dylan twists his head a little, and then focuses in on the microphone *...But everybody wants you to be just like them/ They say "Sing while you slave", I just get bored...* After another chorus with everyone joining in, he blows a few notes on his harmonica, bends his knee a little and waves his hand like a conductor to finish the song. He shuffles a little, stares briefly at an unknown point somewhere up above him - as if cheekily requesting a little divine blessing - then makes a quick exit into the shadows.

Since the beginning of his career, a comic or satirical perspective has profoundly informed Bob Dylan's music and lyrics, his style of performance and his public persona. When he first arrived in Greenwich Village in 1960 as a ragged, baby-faced purveyor of an encyclopedic range of folk and blues songs, he was in the habit of conversing freely and often humorously with his audiences. It was noted by some commentators that his onstage mannerisms were distinctly 'Chaplinesque'. It might be argued, however, that the other great genius of silent film, 'the Great Stone Face' Buster Keaton, has influenced Dylan's onstage style even more, especially in his later years, when his performances of songs are often delivered from behind a decidedly 'deadpan' expression. At other times, when being interviewed by straight faced journalists who continually try to pigeon-hole him, he has been capable of wisecracking like Groucho Marx. In a 1965 interview, when asked whether he thought of himself primarily as a singer or a poet, he giggled a little as he shot back *...Oh I think of myself more as a song and dance man, y'know...* When one especially naïve reporter asked him exactly how many 'protest singers' there were he answered quite straight facedly *...about 136...* When pressed to elaborate he added *...well, either 136 or 142...* Even at this early stage in his career, he seems to have adopted such responses as a kind of defence mechanism, a way of deflecting often inane or irrelevant 'celebrity questions'. When his patience became frayed, however, the comedy could slide into vicious putdowns, as can be seen in the press conference scene in *Don't Look Back*, Don Pennebaker's cinéma vérité documentary of his last acoustic tour of England in 1965.

Dylan's earliest comic songs were mostly in the 'talkin' blues' form, which he had picked up from Woody Guthrie's political and social commentaries such as *Talkin' Dust Bowl Blues*, *Talkin' Merchant Marine* and *Talkin' Fishing Blues.* Dylan covered many of these in his early performances in Greenwich Village. 'Talkin' blues' songs were one of

Woody's trademarks but were originated by Christopher Bouchillon, a white country blues singer who was known as 'the talking comedian of the south', with his 1926 song *Talking Blues* and 1928's *New Talking Blues.* The format is a fairly rigid one. Each verse has two rhyming couplets followed by a longer, non-rhyming line - often consisting of a derisive or offhand comment. One of Dylan's earliest compositions *Talkin' Bear Mountain Picnic Massacre Blues*, a tale of a pleasure cruise boat which sinks after being overloaded by unscrupulous operators, is a very close imitation of Guthrie's talkin' style. *Talkin' John Birch Paranoid Blues* is Dylan's first use of the medium for the purposes of political satire. It purports to be written from the point of view of a member of the John Birch Society (an extreme anti-communist group) who is so paranoid about 'reds under the bed' that he accuses Presidents Jefferson, Lincoln and Eisenhower of being 'commies' and is even suspicious of the *...red stripes in the American flag...* Dylan was scheduled to perform this song on what would have been his first appearance on the mass audience Ed Sullivan TV show in 1963. When told its content was unacceptable, he walked off the show, in a move that was viewed as commercial suicide at the time. The song was deleted at the last moment from *Freewheelin'.*

Two other talkin' blues numbers - *I Shall Be Free* (1963) and its 'sequel' *I Shall Be Free No.10* (1964) feature scatological comic asides which sound like they had been improvised in the studio, providing a humorous contrast to the many 'heavy' songs that surround them. In his most accomplished composition in this vein, *Talkin' World War III Blues* (1963) Dylan takes the form into realms of deathless absurdism. The narrator relates a dream to his psycho analyst in which almost everyone except himself has been killed in a nuclear war. He drives down Manhattan streets in an abandoned Cadillac, calls up the talking time clock and listens to the same time being repeated for over an hour. The dark humour turns into chilling pathos: *...I spied a girl and before she could leave/ I said, 'Let's go and play Adam and Eve'/ I took her by the hand and my heart was thumpin'/ When she said 'Hey man, you crazy or somethin' '...* Then comes the killer line: *...'You seen what happened last time they started?'...*

By the mid-60s, Dylan's humour often derives from strange or surreal juxtapositions. *Motorpsycho Nitemare* (1964) combines a 'shaggy dog' story featuring a young student hitch hiker, an ultra conservative farmer and his daughter, to which Dylan adds elements of the plot of Hitchcock's *Psycho.* In *On the Road Again* (1965) the narrator tells a girl he's leaving her as a consequence of the peculiar behaviour of her grotesque, Addams-family like relatives. *Bob Dylan's 115th Dream* (1965), which begins with a false start and the sound of laughter, is a joyously anarchic tale in which the narrator arrives on the *Mayflower* to 'discover' modern America and then races through an account of a series of farcical 'jump cuts' into a range of ludicrous situations. In *Tombstone Blues* Dylan mocks the mentality of political, military and religious leaders, including the crazed 'Commander-in-chief' who declares that *...the sun's not yellow, it's chicken...* In *Highway 61 Revisited*, money-grabbing capitalists consider selling 'ringside seats' for a third world war. *Rainy Day Women #12 & 35* is a deadpan riff on the double meaning of 'stoned', in both 'druggie' and Biblical senses. *Leopard Skin Pillbox Hat* is a deliriously joyful mockery of the superficiality of a young starlet who is obsessed by materialism. *Basement Tapes* songs such as *Please Mrs. Henry, Yea! Heavy and a Bottle of Bread, Lo and Behold* and *Don't Ya Tell Henry* play around with nonsense verse. 1968's *Ballad of Frankie Lee and Judas Priest* and 1975's *Lily, Rosemary and the Jack of Hearts* entertain us with surreal and mischievous morality parables with a darkly comic sensibility. In the wake of Dylan's religious conversion, the humorous element in his work was largely absent - and much missed. By now he had long abandoned any attempt at discourse with his audiences in live shows. In 1988, however, during his short lived membership of the Traveling Wilburys, he co-wrote fairly witty parodies of Prince (*Dirty Mind*) and Bruce Springsteen (*Tweeter and the Monkey Man*). But the humour in these songs, such as it is, lacks the teasing wit and biting comic edge of his earlier work.

It is only with the sixteen-minute epic *Highlands,* the final track of 1997's *Time Out of Mind,* that Dylan 're-invents' his comic voice. He returns to the kind of wryly humorous allusive word play that had been such a strong feature of his pre-conversion work, but from a more jaundiced, world-weary perspective. *Highlands* does, however, feature some of the dry wit that marked some of his earlier comic songs, relating its rather bizarrely uneventful story with a dry comic sensibility, seamlessly mixing conventional poetic language with a conversational tone. The musical backing is a minimalistic blues riff which continues throughout the track with little real variation Dylan sounds dreamily detached from events throughout. The 'tagline' is derived from Robert Burns' ballad of 1789 whose chorus runs:*...My heart's in the Highlands, my heart is not here/ My heart's in the Highlands, a-chasing the deer/ Chasing the wild deer, and following the roe/ My heart's in the Highlands, wherever I go...* This is usually sung to the tune *Failte na Miosg.* Like Dylan, Burns was a poet-songwriter who often set his lyrics to traditional tunes. Dylan even once declared Burns' *My Luve is Like a Red Red Rose* his favourite poem ever.

The first lines of the song establish its romantic credentials with some concerted Wordsworthian idealisation of nature: ... *Well my heart's in the Highlands gentle and fair/ Honeysuckle blooming in the wildwood air/ Bluebells blazing where the Aberdeen waters flow...* This highly evocative opening recalls another famous 'Scottish' ballad *Bluebells of Scotland,* written by Dora Jordan (an English woman) in 1801. The lines are, however, full of anachronisms. Bluebells flower in April and May in Scotland whereas honeysuckle flowers in late summer. The city of Aberdeen is on the North East coast of Scotland rather than the Highlands. It seems that the place where the narrator's 'heart' is located does not have a real geographical location. The sound of the words is especially soothing, with their alliteration of 'blooming/ bluebells/ blazing' and the idyllic sounding 'Aberdeen waters', although the words are rather parodic of conventional romantic lyricism. This is a hint that the narrator is depressed and that he refers to this pre-lapsarian world as a place where his problems will be magically solved. He tells us, rather uncertainly, that *...I'll go there when I feel good enough to go...*

As if to remind us that this is a kind of blues song, the statement ... *Woke up this morning...* is followed by a graphic description of the narrator's state of mind:*...and I* *looked at the same old page...* suggesting that he has writer's block or a dearth of inspiration. Dylan piles up the depressive imagery: *...Same ol' rat race/ Life in the same ol' cage...* The extent of his alienation from the world is made clear: *...I don't want nothing from anyone/ Ain't that much to take...* he declares, rather hopelessly, then undercuts this with the poker-faced line *...Wouldn't be able to tell the difference between a real blonde and a fake...* There may be an allusion here to *Blonde on Blonde*, which ends in another epic song *Sad Eyed Lady of the Lowlands* ('lowlands' being of course the opposite of 'highlands') *...Feel like a prisoner in a world of mystery/ I wish someone would come and push back the clock for me...* makes him sound like he is trapped in idle wish fulfilment. It also introduces the theme of ageing which will be crucial to the story that is about to unfold.

We are then transported back to the narrator's dream world, where *...the wind it whispers to the buck eyed trees in rhyme...* The presence of these 'buck eyed trees', which exist in America but not in Scotland, again indicates the imaginary nature of this place. The phrase 'buck eyed' also suggests a rather strange and twisted version of reality. The narrator admits that although his heart is in the Highlands *...I can only get there one step at a time...* suggesting that he is nowhere near reaching his destination. The next three verses veer between the prosaically comic and the dramatically poetic. A surprising contemporary allusion appears: *...I'm listening to Neil Young/ Gotta turn up the sound/ Someone's always yelling "Turn it down!"...* We presume that the narrator must be grooving to *Cortez the Killer* or *Down By the River* or one of Young's other guitar epics rather than a laid back track like *Heart of Gold* *...I feel like I'm drifting, drifting from scene to scene/ Wondering what the devil it can all possibly mean...* describes the narrator's state of mind rather delightfully. It is thus rather difficult to take the next line *...Insanity is smashing up against my soul...* entirely seriously, especially as it is followed by the prosaic *...You could say I was on anything but a roll...* and the ludicrous *...If I had a conscience, well I might just blow my top/ What would I do with it anyway?/ Maybe take it to the pawn shop...*

We then return to the pastoral fantasy. Effortlessly creating a half rhyme with his distinctive intonation, Dylan sings *...My heart's in the Highlands at the break of dawn/ By the beautiful lake of the Black Swan...* The Black Swan Odile is a character in Tchaikovsky's tragic ballet *Swan Lake*, in which she functions as the evil doppelganger of the innocent heroine Odette. Traditionally, both roles are played by the same ballerina. The allusion to the famous 'doubled' ballet suggests that the dual states of mind are merely two sides of the same coin. The other striking image in this verse *...Big white clouds like chariots that swing down low...* refers to the gospel standard *Swing Low, Sweet Chariot*, which outlines a vision of a chariot coming down from heaven to save people from oppression. Written in the late nineteenth century by Wallis Willis (a Native American songwriter) it refers to the story in *Kings* 2:11 in which the prophet Elijah is taken up to heaven in a 'celestial chariot'. This strong image of liberation made it one of the anthems of the Civil Rights movement. The contrast between the white clouds and the black swan again mirrors the two roles in *Swan Lake*, as well as reflecting the moral struggle between black and white during the Civil Rights era. The differing images also suggest the inner turmoil of the protagonist. Whereas in the previous verses, the claims of depression had been hard to take seriously, now we are being led into more emotionally resonant territory. The narrator concludes by telling us that the 'Highlands' is *...the only place left to go...*

The tone of the song then shifts rather dramatically. For the next seven verses we are placed within an often hilarious absurdist drama. This comprises an encounter between the narrator and a waitress, during which the narrator drops some knowing asides. The tale is related in the present tense, effectively transporting the listener into the scene: *...I'm in Boston town, at some restaurant...* The terse rhyme *...I've no idea what I want...* is indicative of the short exchanges of dialogue that will follow. After the 'lead up' to the encounter, we can assume that he is referring to more than just his choice of snack. He tries to qualify this but fails: *...Well, maybe I do but I'm just really not sure...* He explains that there's only himself and the waitress in the restaurant *...Must be a holiday...* he mutters *...there's nobody around...* The waitress, who has *...a pretty face and long white shiny legs...* studies him closely as he sits down, as if she recognises him. At this point it may be safe to assume that the narrator is a famous person - possibly Dylan himself - and someone who finds it difficult to have straightforward relationships due to the level of his fame.

The narrator's first words to the waitress: *...Tell me what I want...* are somewhat disconcerting. She fires back *...You probably want hard boiled eggs...* The insecure celebrity, whose attention has been directed towards the fantasy world he has been describing, is now asking a 'fan' to direct him. Her swift and cheeky response suggests that she has picked up on his 'hard boiled' mood. When he attempts to take control by ordering her to *...bring me some...* she replies tersely: *...We ain't got any. You picked the wrong time to come...* She suddenly switches tack *...I know you're an artist...* she tells him... *draw a picture of me...* This feisty girl appears to be thoroughly enjoying playing with the sexual dynamics of the situation. His replies, and the excuses he continues to give in the next verse, are disarmingly funny: *...I would if I could but... I don't do sketches from memory...* he tells her, as if she is somehow absent at that moment. He then makes the lame excuse that he does not have a drawing book or a pencil. But despite his physical presence in the diner, it is really him who is 'absent'. His heart - and his head - are still in the 'Highlands'.

The waitress continues to insist, pulling out a pencil from behind her ear and presenting him with a napkin *...You can do it on that...* she says flatly, as if the proposed drawing will be equivalent to some basic bodily function. He makes a half hearted attempt by sketching out a few lines. When she sees this she throws it back at him, declaring *...That don't look a thing like me...* He addresses her pleadingly, if rather submissively *...Oh kind miss, it most certainly does...* which only draws further scorn. The waitress rather aggressively changes the subject, again suggesting that she knows the narrator by reputation *...You don't read women authors, do you?...* He guffaws at this suggestion: *...You're way wrong...* She retorts *...Which ones have you read then?...*

He replies rather tentatively*...read Erika Jong...* pronouncing the author's surname inaccurately with a 'J'. This indicates his actual ignorance of feminist fiction. Jong's works are not generally taken very seriously by feminist literary critics. Her most famous novel *Fear of Flying*, a best seller after its publication in 1973, describes its heroine's quest for a non-emotional sexual encounter which she calls the 'zipless fuck'. But the narrator's apparent attempt at sexual innuendo certainly won't succeed here. The waitress disappears without taking any kind of order and he makes a quick and presumably embarrassed exit.

...I step outside back to the busy street... the narrator tells us, still feeling disconnected from reality *...but nobody's going anywhere...* The encounter with the waitress has made it obvious to him that he is struggling to deal with the consequences of ageing *...Some things in life...* he sighs *...it gets too late to learn...* He admits that *...I'm lost somewhere. I must have made a few bad turns...* He then walks past a park and observes *...All the young men and young women looking so good...* This is followed by the disconcertingly poignant: *...I'd trade places with them in a minute if I could...* In the final verses, however, there is a growing sense that the narrator, having plumbed the depths of despair and embarrassment, has finally begun to see a way out of his situation. First he gives us another delightful comic vignette: *...I'm crossing the street to get away from a mangy dog/ I'm talking to myself in a monologue...* a particularly smart rhyme and a hint that everything in the song may have been occurring in his imagination. This is reinforced by the desire he expresses to 'wrap himself up' in a garment that will insulate him from the attention of others: *...I think what I might need might be a full length leather coat...* which is juxtaposed in a disarmingly deadpan way with an encounter with the 'real world': *...Somebody just asked me if I've registered to vote...*

The conversation with the waitress has shown him aspects of himself he had not previously been able to recognise: *...The sun is beginning to shine on me...* he declares *...but it's not like the sun that used to be...* Although he states flatly that *...the party's over, and there's less and less to say...* he follows this with the apparently revelatory, if perhaps contradictory *...I got new eyes, everything looks far way...* He puts particular emphasis on 'new eyes', as if to indicate that this is what the whole song has been leading up to. Finally he reaffirms that his heart remains in the 'Highlands', which is still (using a familiar nursery rhyme refrain) *...over the hills and far away...* He admits that he hasn't reached his destination yet but hopes that he will 'figure out' a way *...I'm already there in my mind...* he tells us *...and that's good enough for now...* His journey towards self-realisation in *Highlands* is the culmination of the struggle to regain inspiration that Dylan depicts throughout *Time Out of Mind,* where he confronts the implications of ageing in various different ways. Having taken us through a series of dark scenarios, it is as if he has finally arrived at a place where he can assume a new comic persona.

Shortly after the release of the album Dylan came down with histoplasmosis, a rare but seriously life threatening illness about which he later quipped *...I thought I was* *about to join Elvis...* Yet within a very short time he had recovered and was back on the road, now able to continue the Never Ending Tour with a batch of new songs which he could spend several years testing out and exploring. *Highlands* was performed on nine occasions between 1999 and 2001. On *Time Out of Mind* it is slow and meandering, indicating the narrator's languorous and uncertain mood. At Chula Vista California on 25th June 1999, Dylan speeds up the tempo, having rearranged it for his live band, so that it now lasts only ten minutes. He performs the song with considerable brio, abandoning the deadpan delivery and stretching out many of the syllables for emphasis. The music also builds up to a triumphant climax. Over the course of the next two years there will also be some variations in the lyrics. By the time he reaches Madison Square Garden on 27th July 1999 (in a somewhat ragged rendition where he appears to forget several verses) he no longer wishes the waitress to 'tell me what I want' but asks her to *...tell me what's good today...* indicating the extent to which he now conveys far more self-confidence. In later shows the waitress' responses to his order also change, alternating between telling him he 'probably wants' soft boiled and scrambled eggs. In Glasgow on 17th September 2000, he replaces the reference to 'Neil Young' with 'Annie Lennox', the Scottish former Eurythmics singer and musical partner of his friend Dave Stewart. By the time of the song's final performance at Columbia Missouri on 24th April 2001 *Highlands* has become a full blown rhythmic outing.

Between 1997 and 2001, when *"Love And Theft"* was released, Dylan's performance style and his public persona were evolving rapidly. He had added the highly accomplished blues guitarist Charlie Sexton to his band. With Sexton and Larry Campbell now supplying backing vocals, there was a strong element of joyous harmonising in the performances. By 2001, he had begun to adopt a distinctly different and more consciously 'theatrical' approach. He now wore a selection of 'cowboy hats' and sported a pencil thin moustache. He began appearing in ever more elaborate stage costumes, often in imitation of classic country singers, while his band were usually dressed in dark grey suits. The performances were now billed as 'The Bob Dylan Show', and were often publicised by what appeared to be 'retro' and rather kitsch-looking bills resembling promotional posters for the variety shows of the early rock'n'roll era. Dylan appeared to be deliberately playing the part of a 'song and dance man' yet without the typically unctuous patter which such performers would normally adopt. Dressing in a variety of retro outfits and presenting himself as if he was an old cowboy movie star, he teased his audience with his unique mixture of apparent showbiz artifice and a completely anti-showbiz attitude.

This comic sensibility was reflected in *Things Have Changed* (2000), written for the movie *Wonder Boys*, directed by Curtis Hansen. Michael Douglas starred as (the ironically named) Grady Tripp, a formerly radical but now disillusioned middle-aged college professor whose personal and professional life has been plunged into turmoil. The film is a witty examination of his mid-life crisis. It reflects wryly on how he struggles to complete his latest novel while conducting an affair with his boss' wife and trying to contain his excessive alcohol habit. The song's sprightly tone anticipates the supercharged word games and sly postures that will characterise *"Love And Theft"*. Suddenly we are hearing a mischievous, giddy and joyously funny Dylan. This new brightness (and lightness) of tone is immediately signalled by the attractive rhythmic shuffle, shaded by almost Latin percussion, which opens the track. The voice is a finely judged, gravelly whisper, which perfectly fits the tone and subject matter of the song, especially in the tiny understated sighs which he uses at various dramatic moments. Dylan paints a comically self-deprecating picture of a cynical, ageing entertainer who is desperately trying to grab hold of whatever life can offer him, before it is too late.

The lyrics are sharply honed with many delightfully ironic touches, none more so than in the description of the woman sitting on his lap drinking champagne *...Got white skin...* he purrs *...got assassin's eyes/ I'm staring up into the sapphire-tinted skies...* Dylan's tongue slides around the alliteration, positively wallowing in the delicious contrast in these lines. The narrator appears to be wealthy and 'well-dressed', perhaps an ageing roué with a young, gold-digging beauty in tow *...I'm in love with a woman...* he confesses later *...that don't even appeal to me...* His mind is clearly elsewhere. Despite his wealth and status he is trapped. The song has a series of bridges, helping to lead in to the rather attractively catchy (and almost hummable) chorus. The lines in these sections represent the narrator's mind wandering off in strange directions. Firstly he pictures himself *...standing on the gallows with my head in a noose...* which may be an ironic depiction of the trap he's got himself into by following a debauched, unfocused lifestyle *...Any minute now...* he tells us conspiratorially *...I'm expecting all hell to break loose...* though he hardly sounds like he's getting himself into a sweat over it. The 'sing-along' chorus again indicates a narrator who is barely engaged with the world, suffocated by his own ennui *...People are crazy, times are strange...* he tells us, with an air of passive acceptance. But then he proceeds to confess that ...*I'm locked in tight/ I'm out of range...* He is a prisoner of his own boredom. He knows he is trapped but cannot be bothered to do anything about it: *...I used to care...* he sighs, full of world weariness *...but things have changed...*

The next verse contains the song's funniest lines. *...This place ain't doin' me any good...* he muses *...I'm in the wrong town/ I should be in Hollywood...* This makes him sound even more comically decadent, like a washed up member of Sinatra's 'rat pack'. It's as if he's leaning back on his bar stool, expecting us to give him some sympathy when he knows full well he doesn't deserve it. In his misty-eyed, drunken reverie he seems to be indulging in some bizarre pre-war Hollywood-style fantasy: ...*Gonna take dancing lessons, do the jitterbug rag/ Ain't no shortcuts, gonna dress in drag...* he declares, as if he's banging his glass of bourbon down on the bar, expecting some bored waitress to console him. But then, as the drink begins to take effect, he grows bitter *...Only a fool in here...* he tells us *...would think he's got anything to prove...* In the next bridge he indulges in rather vague clichés about how life has passed him by: *...Lot of water under the bridge, Lot of other stuff too...* he mumbles. Then he tips his hat drunkenly to his imagined audience: *...Don't get up gentlemen...* he insists (as if they would!) *...I'm only passing through...*

As our hero grows ever more maudlin the song takes a darker turn. Earlier on he had alluded to *...waiting on the last train...* Now he expands on this apocalyptic hint: *...If the Bible is right, the world will explode...* His drunken haze begins to lead him into darker moods as he seems to fear some kind of judgement from on high. Hell, it seems, is just around the corner *...Some things are too hot to touch...* he mutters darkly, confessing that *...I've been trying to get as far away from myself as I can...* By the next bridge he seems to have fallen right off his barstool. He adopts a desperately tragicomic and rather ridiculous tone: *...Feel like falling in love with the first woman I meet/ Putting her in a wheel barrow and wheeling her down the street...* In the last verse he indulges in classic country 'face in the beer glass' laments: *...I hurt easy, I just don't show it/ You can hurt someone and not even know it...* The logic of the coup-de-grace line *...All the truth in the world adds up to one big lie...* is similarly illogical and inebriated. Finally there is a random reference to *...Mr. Jinx and Miss Lucy...* who *...jumped in the lake...* The narrator declares that *...I'm not that eager to make a mistake...* 'Mr. Jinx' was a 'beatnik' cat in Hanna-Barbara's late 1950s cartoon *Pixie and Dixie*. The narrator apparently feels that his life is one long 'jinx'.

The persona Dylan adopts is, like Grady Tripp, a drunken cynic who laments his own mortality. With the apparent reference to *The Times They Are a-Changin'* in the chorus, it is tempting to think of the song as being emblematic of our 'modern times'. Times which have certainly changed, it seems, but not for the better. Yet the song breathes with wit and new life - the product, perhaps, of someone who sees through 'new eyes'. It winks dismissively at the habit of fake nostalgia. The high profile of *Wonder Boys*, and the song's release as a single, put Dylan in the 'mainstream' for the first time for many years, especially after it won the Oscar for best movie song. It was promoted by a video which featured clips from the movie, intercut with shots of Dylan outside a late night shopping mall in a Buster Keaton style flat hat, a dress suit and a walking cane, looking like some 1920s hoofer. Both Dylan and Michael Douglas are shown miming the lyrics, although they are mostly quite happily out of synch. Dylan looks like he's enjoying himself immensely as he mugs his way through this, making much 'ironic' use of his eyebrows. With his snazzy dress suit and his dancing shoes, he faces the new millennium with a sly smile, a knowing wink and a twirl of his cane.

25th November 2003. The Academy, Brixton is an intimate venue and tonight it is jam packed. Originally built as a cinema in 1929, the venue still retains its proscenium arch and 'Italian-Renaissance' décor. Three thousand fans are crammed into the standing space. Dylan has just played two nights in the smaller London venues, beginning at the Shepherd's Bush Empire and continuing at the Hammersmith Odeon. The set lists have varied every night. A few songs that Dylan has rarely played have been unearthed. At Shepherd's Bush the second number was *The Mighty Quinn*, which had only been performed a few times since the Isle of Wight Festival in 1969. At

Hammersmith *Romance in Durango* received its first airing since 1976. This is the end of a long tour and there is a sense that Dylan is kicking back, feeling a little free to experiment. After the opening *Wicked Messenger*, a melody which sounds fairly familiar to at least some members of the crowd begins to drift across the auditorium: *...The comic book and us, we caught the bus/ The poor little chauffeur, though, she was back in bed/ On the very next day, with a nose full of pus...* The nonsense rhymes can only be from *The Basement Tapes* and here, quite out of the blue, is *Yea! Heavy and a Bottle of Bread,* a song Dylan has only performed once before in the thirty six years since it was first captured on Garth Hudson's sturdy reel to reel tape recorder.

Dylan stoops slightly over his piano *...It's a one-track town, just brown and a breeze too/ Pack up the meat, sweet, we're headin' out ...* he sings. *...For Wichita in a pile of fruit/ Get the loot, don't be slow, we're gonna catch a trout ...* The song depicts a gang of ne'er-do-wells, drifting between various 'one track towns' with their dubiously won spoils. But are they on a bus or hitching a ride on a fruit wagon? The boys certainly seem to be in a drunken haze *...Pull that drummer out from behind that bottle/ Bring me my pipe, we're gonna shake it...* the singer calls out. There is even a wonderfully inventive hangover cure: *...Slap that drummer with a pie that smells!...* The geography of the song appears more than a little skewed. A few minutes ago we were in Wichita, Kansas. Now he calls out *...Take me down to California, baby...* As you might say, we're not in Kansas any more, Dorothy...

The arrangement of the song differs little from the original but a few touches of 'surf guitar' from Dylan's current (and rather flashy) lead guitarist Freddie Koella make the song sound even spookier. When the band drives on into the next number, *Tweedle Dee & Tweedle Dum,* the transition is somehow seamless. It is as if the songs on *"Love And Theft"* have taken up where *The Basement Tapes* left off, careering wildly in vintage automobiles across what the esteemed rock critic Greil Marcus famously called 'the old, weird America', with no choruses of *The Star Spangled Banner* to be heard and certainly no slices of 'mom's apple pie' available in the dusty, half-abandoned arcades.

After the dark landscapes of *Time Out of Mind, "Love And Theft"* is a revelation. Dylan the 'Jokerman' is back in full swing. The songs are bizarre, allusive and mysterious. The lyrics are a patchwork of quotations from various songs, stories and even one-liner jokes, some of which sound like they had been whispered to you by passing drunks. There are also sly innuendos, romantic trysts in the moonlight and convoluted blues parables. The album creates a world of its own, a carnival of freaks and losers and chancers. On the sleeve, Bob wears a white Stetson and proudly sports his 'villainous' 'tash. He looks like he might pigeon hole you in a bar, get you to buy him a drink and spin some pretty questionable tales. You certainly wouldn't accept a cheque from him. The title is borrowed from a 1993 book by historian Eric Lott entitled *Love & Theft: Blackface Minstrelsy and the American Working Class*. Blackface minstrelsy -

which today is viewed as racist and demeaning - was an extremely popular form of entertainment in the late nineteenth and the early twentieth century. Lott argues that the minstrel shows (which were attended largely by white male working class audiences) simultaneously celebrated and mocked black culture. Thus a self conscious white male working class culture was created, which embodied fear of and repulsion towards black people. This was ambiguously mixed with a kind of sympathetic identification with their culture, as well as a certain amount of guilt at the 'theft' of that culture. Several of the songs on *"Love And Theft"* take us back to the days of minstrelsy, reminding us that even 'light entertainment' in the USA has been touched by such racist attitudes.

The album will not, however, be any kind of socio-historical dissertation. Any doubts that it will be a 'real fun rollercoaster ride' disappear as soon as an instantly catchy rockabilly riff booms out and a voice growls, rather suspiciously *...Tweedlie Dum and Tweedlie Dee, they're throwing knives into the tree...* We may wonder if this is going to be another wacky kids' song, like *Wiggle Wiggle*. Dylan even pronounces the names in a 'babyish' way. But it soon turns out that these two characters are far from loveable. The song is a lively introduction to *"Love And Theft"*'s world of 'weird Americana' in which various 'desperadoes', outlaws and freaks compete for attention, as if they are the circus performers of *Ballad of a Thin Man* or refugees from the mad world of *The Basement Tapes*. It sets the scene for the album's many juxtapositions of roguish, sepia-tinted American characters past and present.

The song was performed some 500 times between 2001 and 2015. Dylan rarely altered the lyrics or the arrangement. But in a performance at the Brisbane Tivoli on 27th August 2014 the original's driving riff is abandoned and the song is transformed into a sad lament, led by Dylan's piano playing rather than guitars. This brings out the darker side of the lyrics, although the new arrangement de-emphasises the song's pithy and cynical humour. Both the music and many of the lyrics are 'lifted' from various obscure sources. The hypnotic, repeated riff originates from a bluegrass tune originally called *Bongos and Uncle John* by The Dixieland Drifters (1961). The song was re-recorded in the same year as *Uncle John's Bongos* by Johnny and Jack, a country/rockabilly duo consisting of Johnnie Wright and Jack Anglin. Dylan covered their songs *Searching For a Soldier's Grave, Humming Bird* and *This World Can't Stand Long* in his shows around the turn of the millennium. Tweedle Dee and Tweedle Dum appear in Lewis Carroll's *Through the Looking Glass*. They are two very fat and nasty identical twins who speak 'as one', finishing each other's sentences. The characters have often been used for satirical references to politicians or other prominent figures who appear to be corrupt.

The song is chock full of lines lifted from a range of sources. The reference to the *...stately trees...* and *...secrets of the breeze...* and the line *...A childish dream is a deathless need...* are drawn from Timrod's *A Vision of Poesy*, a mystical tale of a young boy's awakening in nature *...I got love for you and it's all in vain...* alludes to Robert Johnson's *Love in Vain ...I'll stab you where you stand...* is a line from Edgar Allan Poe's haunting doppelganger story *William Wilson*, which has obvious connections to the eponymous characters in the song. The lyrics also include unusual twists on various well known phrases. 'Nose to the grindstone' is a common way of describing someone engaged in monotonous hard work. It also appears in Merle Haggard's *Workin' Man's Blues*, a song to which Dylan would compose a 'sequel' on his next album ...*One day older and a dollar short...* is a vernacular phrase referring to someone who cannot meet their obligations...*Your presence is obnoxious to me...* and ...*I've had too much of your company...* originate from a nineteenth century music hall show entitled *Box and Cox*, a one act comic opera with a libretto by F.C. Burn and music by Arthur Sullivan, later of Gilbert and Sullivan fame. In 1856 Edward Byron Christy adapted the story into a sketch show for his Christy Minstrels, a popular blackface troupe, with 'Africanised' dialogue. The song quotes from an exchange in which 'Aunty B', an unscrupulous landlady, has rented out an apartment to Cox and Box, another pair of doppelgangers, one of whom works nights and the other days, without telling them:

Box: (Looking significantly at Aunty B.): Well, I oughter hab, dat's a fac', for I pays for it. So if you's no dejections, I'll just remark dat your presence is obnoxious to me - I wants to go to bed.

Cox: No mam! I've had too much of your company already. Vamoose!

Another source is a guidebook to New Orleans written by Bethany E. Bultman. In one review of a restaurant Bultman refers to the food as ...*dripping in garlic and olive oil...* a description which Dylan borrows. The line ...*a multimillion dollar gown...* is also found in the guidebook in a description of the clothes worn by one of the drag queens at the Mardi Gras festival. The song contains various other references to the Mardi Gras carnival ...*Throw me something, Mister please!...* are the words that spectators traditionally shout out as the carnival floats (or 'krewes' go by). Dylan name checks Tennessee Williams' famous New Orleans-set play *A Streetcar Named Desire* and refers to pecan pie, a local culinary speciality. We are also told that the 'Tweedles' have a parade permit. It seems that the two characters are performers on a 'krewe' in the Mardi Gras in New Orleans, presumably in costume as Carroll's fat boys.

Dylan uses the surreal juxtapositions and patchwork of references to create a highly ambiguous and brutally comic critique of those who abuse power. The first image we are given is of these two figures, presumably on their carnival float ...*throwing knives into the tree...* indulging, it seems, in a harmless pursuit. But the next line, the dryly monosyllabic and comically alliterative ...*Two big bags of dead men's bones...* is a brilliantly pithy description of the aftermath of a battle. This is rhymed with the heavily cynical ...*got their noses to the grindstone...* suggesting that Tweedledee and Tweedledum - who we can identify as warring politicians who may represent opposing parties but are really identical - are profiting from all this. They are today's 'Masters of War'. The language of the song is deliciously sharp: ...*Living in the land of Nod...* Dylan sneers ...*trusting their fate to the Hands of God...* It seems they are carrying out their carnage with religious justification while they themselves live in a kind of fantasy land of denial. In the Bible, the Land of Nod is where Cain is sent after murdering his brother

Abel in the first act of human violence. Tweedledee and Tweedledum are their heirs of these brothers. In their faces, as they *...pass by so silently...* on their carnival float you may see Hitler and Stalin, Bush and Saddam, Napoleon and Wellington or other murderous generals or leaders.

The ageing brothers are *...going to the country, they're going to retire/ They're taking a streetcar named Desire...* The reference to Tennessee Williams' dark tale of obsession and sexual violence (which is set in New Orleans) casts another shadow on their character. We hear of their arrogance and their blind stupidity on their road to destruction: *...Neither one's gonna turn and run/ They're making a voyage to the sun...* Tweedle Dum tells his brother that *...His master's voice is calling me...* Many dictators do indeed feel they have a personal 'hotline to God'. Their self-serving arrogance is emphasised: *...They walk among the stately trees/ they know the secrets of the breeze...* Then, as politicians do, they begin to turn on each other. As in *William Wilson*, their self-obsession becomes destructive paranoia: *...Your presence is obnoxious to me...* Tweedle Dum spits at his brother while the detached and cynical narrator tells us *...They're like babies sitting on a woman's knee...* further emphasising their childish spitefulness. The narrator also 'licks his lips' over more darkly suggestive culinary lines: *...Brains in the pot, they're beginning to boil/ They're dripping with garlic and olive oil...* Perhaps the brothers are ready to 'consume' each other.

It seems that Tweedle Dee is the victim here. In the little drama being carried out on the carnival float, we now see him *...on his hands and knees...* begging for someone in the crowd to help him. The statement *...They're living in a happy harmony...* is cruelly ironic. Here is the voice, perhaps, of a smooth politician, assuring us that all is peaceful, when in reality 'back stabbing' is the order of the day. The twins' stupidity is emphasised when we are informed that *...they're one day older and a dollar short...* but that they are being protected by the authorities: *...They've got a parade permit and a police escort...* The Mardi Gras carnival floats appear as a surreal representation of American culture and politics *...They're lying low and they're making hay...* suggests their devious motives, false modesty and continual exploitation of others. The phrase *...they seem determined to go all the way...* may be a sly reference to Lyndon B. Johnson's 1964 campaign slogan 'All the way with LBJ'. Johnson was the President most responsible for the US' disastrous and murderous involvement in Vietnam, which certainly ended in two very 'big bags of dead men's bones'.

As the song ends, the narrator's attention seems to be pulled in various different directions. He stands watching the parade with his girl, who is suitably dressed for the carnival in her *...multi-thousand dollar gown...* while he himself seems to be distracted by some philosophical reflections *...A childish dream is a deathless need...* he tells us *...and a noble truth is a sacred creed...* The grotesque twins on the carnival float are certainly obsessed by their childish dream, which Dylan rather comically juxtaposes with the faux-Buddhist reference. But there is, of course, nothing 'noble' about them. In the final verse Tweedle Dum exerts his power over his supplicant brother, now depicted as a *...lowdown, sorry old man...* Tweedle Dum, we are informed, will *...stab you where you* *stand...* Inevitably, their 'childish dream' of the pursuit of power will lead to violence, with one corrupt politician overthrowing the other. They may disguise their intent in pseudo-religious or destiny-related rhetoric but they are certainly not to be trusted.

Lonesome Day Blues is a breezily light hearted song, built around a loud, repetitive blues riff with prominent bass and drums. It is written in classic blues form with repeated lines, which - like many of the other songs on the album - link together apparently random images, allusions and references. But here almost the entire song consists of a patchwork of quotations from and paraphrases of other sources. Even the title has been used (with some slight variations) in songs by Blind Willie McTell, Jesse James, Forrest City Joe and Alger 'Texas' Alexander. The narrator's consciousness appears to be rather fractured. He is experiencing a series of apparently unconnected thoughts and memories, most of which are the product of his 'wandering mind'. Some of these reflections appear to come from his own experiences. Others are taken from a range of very disparate sources. He shares these thoughts with us while driving along a highway and - in the typical manner of blues songs - musing about a woman who has left him. However, he rarely sounds sad or morose. The use of the disparate references may indicate that he is trying to impress his former lover with his eloquence and learning. But she is, of course, not present so the dialogue he is conducting with her is sadly one-sided.

The song begins by presenting us with a picture of the narrator's state of mind. *...Today has been a sad and lonesome day/ I'm just sittin' here thinkin', with my mind a million miles away...* The exaggerated reflection is quoted, almost verbatim, from Muddy Waters' slow and ruminative blues *Lonesome Day*. Variants of these lines also appear in Odetta's *Go Down Sunshine* and the Mississippi Sheiks' *Stop and Listen Blues*. We are then transported into the first of a series of the narrator's memories. We appear to be in a rough dancehall, perhaps even a shack with a dirt floor. His memories are lively and vivid *...They're doing the double shuffle...* he reminisces *...they're throwing sand on the floor...* We are also presented with an image of the singer having left his *...long time darlin' standin' at the door...* There is no more explanation of this as the narrator's mind immediately jumps through time and space and we are presented with a little 'potted biography' of how he lost his family: *...My pa he died and left me, my brother he got killed in the war... My sister ran off and got married/ Never was heard of any more...* It can't be said, at this point, that he sounds in any way sad about this. But it prepares us for the song's main revelation.

The narrator declares that: *...Samantha Brown lived in my house for four or five months...* We have no idea who 'Samantha Brown' is and she will not be mentioned again. She does not seem to be his errant lover, as he adds that: *...Don't know how it looked to other people, I never slept with her even once...* These lines come from a very unexpected source - John Bester's translations of *Confessions of a Yazuka* (2013) by Junichi Saga, a Japanese doctor. Saga claims to have been treating Eiji Ijichi, an organised crime boss, in the months before he died. The main bulk of the work consists of the various stories that this 'Godfather' tells to Saga about his life in crime. Perhaps the narrator of Dylan's song has lived a similarly dissolute life. More, apparently random, quotations and paraphrases from the book, such as: *...My captain he's decorated, he's well schooled and he's skilled/ He's not sentimental - it don't bother him at all/ How many of his pals have been killed...* and *...He's not a gentleman at all - he's rotten to the core/ He's a coward and he steals...* appear later in the song. The book has been described as a 'novel' but it is difficult to tell where the boundaries between fact and fiction lie in the story, which has the particular dream-like quality which is characteristic of much modern Japanese fiction.

Lonesome Day Blues has a similarly otherwordly atmosphere. As with Saga's book, it is very difficult for us to tell which of the narrator's apparently random reflections are real or imagined. Much of what he says seems to be reconstructed from various 'voices' that are drifting through his consciousness. The weather, he observes as he drives on, is *...not fit for man or beast...* a lugubrious comment which is repeated constantly for deadpan comic effect by W. C. Fields in the movie *The Fatal Glass of Beer* (1933). Dylan then has a little fun pronouncing the elongated paradoxical line: ....*Funny, how the things you have the hardest time parting with/ Are the things you need the least...* which may represent the narrator attempting to 'big himself up' by pretending that he doesn't really care that his woman has left him. There is a suggestion that in reality he is in something of a panic: *...I'm forty miles from the mill...* he tells us *...I'm dropping into overdrive...* This is followed by a rare moment of personal introspection: *...Settin' my dial on the radio/ I wish my mother was still alive...* with the emphasis very much on 'mother'. It seems that the narrator, having earlier told us about his 'scattered' family, is rapidly turning over all these apparently random memories and references in an attempt to deflect his deep feelings of grief. Dylan's own mother Beatty Zimmerman, with whom he had a very close relationship, died in 2000 - the year before *"Love And Theft"* was released.

The narrator continues to reference widely disparate sources *...Last night the wind was whisperin'/ I was trying to make out what it was...* consciously echo a rather beautifully evocative passage from *Huckleberry Finn:*

...I felt so lonesome I most wished I was dead. The stars was shining, and the leaves rustled in the woods ever so mournful... ...and the wind was trying to whisper something to me and I couldn't make out what it was....

Like Dylan's narrator, Huck is clearly having a 'lonesome day' himself. The presence of the words of the youthful hero of Twain's novel - with its radical utilisation of the technique of the unreliable narrator and its often poetic approximation of the rhythms of contemporary rural American speech - is no surprise in the world of *"Love And Theft"*, with its frequent evocation of the language of the nineteenth century. The penultimate verse contains perhaps the oddest 'lift' of all *...I'm gonna spare the defeated...* Dylan's narrator exclaims. *..I'm gonna speak to the crowd/ I'm gonna teach peace to the conquered/ I'm gonna tame the proud...* These lines are a paraphrase of Allen Mandelbaum's translation of Virgil's *Aeneid,* which recounts how the noble and apparently merciful Trojan Aeneas treats his enemies during the founding of Rome. The narrator, who has been declaring his innocence throughout the song, seems to be inferring - in a perhaps rather grandiose way - that he will now 'mercifully' forgive his errant lover her infidelities. He wraps this up in the final verse, with its description of chaos and disturbance of order: *...Leaves are rustling in the wood/ Things are falling off the shelf...* and in the final comic denouement: *...You're gonna need my help sweetheart/ You can't make love all by yourself...* He is finally reduced to a kind of pleading hopelessness. But we are not fooled. This really is a 'sad and lonesome day'. Despite his worldliness and emotional self-control, in reality he is lost without his much-loved mother's guiding hand.

In the delightfully ambiguous *High Water (For Charley Patton)* many of the concerns of Dylan's late period - American history, racism, betrayals in love, the search for inspiration and religious hypocrisy - are represented in a bewildering mix of anger, confusion and apocalyptic warnings with some wacky, racy humour. The song, which again features many 'borrowed' lines, has also grown and developed in performance, having been featured in over 700 shows between 2001 and 2018. Although the lyrics have never been altered, Dylan has experimented considerably with its pacing and delivery. On *"Love And Theft"* it is a pleasant mid-paced canter, with Larry Campbell's banjo especially prominent. At Niagara Falls on 23rd August 2003, in the scorching version which is included on *Tell Tale Signs,* the song has become a fully realised hard rock number driven by some of George Recile's most powerful drumming and Freddie Koella's driving guitar solos. Dylan's vocals have become extended howls of rage. A slower and calmer piano-led version in Albuquerque on 7th October 2018 brings out the sly humour in the song more effectively. While *Blind Willie McTell* is Dylan's dignified, beautifully imagistic and resonantly poetic tribute to the musical form which has inspired him the most, *High Water* - which is conversational and visionary, meaningful and flippant - is perhaps Dylan's most successful attempt to replicate the way that blues songs can convey complex emotions while uplifting audiences with their sheer joyous intensity.

The song has seven verses, each one in traditional eight line blues form and always ending with *...High water everywhere....* Most of the lines are short and punchy, with each verse also containing one or two lines which allow tongue twisting and often humorous comments to be added. This is one of those Dylan songs which is especially hard to sing, although Barb Jungr's jazzy interpretation adds a new dimension, indicating just how well Dylan's use of line variation can be adapted to the techniques of jazz vocalists. The subtitle *(For Charley Patton)* indicates that the song is both a tribute to the primal Delta blues progenitor and a kind of 'sequel' to Patton's *High Water Everywhere,* one of the many songs about the cataclysmic 1927 Mississippi flood. In his song Patton describes his experiences of the flood and concludes that he will retreat to the 'high country'. The lyrics are fairly plain and descriptive but Patton's sometimes mumbled and unintelligible vocals, which convey barely restrained anger and vitriol, make this one of the greatest early blues classics. Patton creates a striking rhythm by hitting the side of his guitar as he plays. The Mississippi flood - which is also referenced in *The Levee's Gonna Break* - holds a prominent place in blues lore and legend. Images of the deluge are included in the song, while Dylan extends the idea of the flood as a symbol in many different ways.

In the first verse, we hear that the 'high water' is *...rising night and day...* and that *...all the gold and silver are being stolen away...* lines which resonate with any disaster and subsequent economic collapse and which hint at the intervention of unseen and unnamed 'dark forces'. We then switch to a graphic and quite extraordinary picture of another great blues singer: *...Big Joe Turner looking east and west from the dark room of his mind...* Turner's recording of his song *Shake, Rattle and Roll* was crucial to the evolution of early rock'n'roll. A cover version was the first big hit for Bill Haley and The Comets. The song was also recorded by Elvis Presley and countless others. The image of 'the dark room of his mind' is an extremely powerful description of the mentality of a blues singer, with Big Joe portrayed as surveying the entire country from coast to coast. We hear that *...he made it to Kansas City, Twelfth Street and Vine...* where he is greeted by utter desolation: *...Nothing standing there/ High Water everywhere...*

Dylan's harsh pronunciation of 'nothing', along with other key words in the penultimate lines of each verse, adds greatly to the unfolding drama. Big Joe was a native of Kansas City. He also performed a song called *Kansas City Blues*, although the reference to 'Twelfth Street and Vine' is a quote from Wilbert Harrison's 1959 hit *Kansas City.* Big Joe was only fifteen at the time of the Mississippi flood. The account of his 'arrival' in Kansas City at this time is largely fanciful. But Dylan's transposition of this figure through time - rather than being more obvious and mentioning Charley Patton himself - indicates that the song will extol the timeless nature of the blues, as well as the way in which it can make American place names sound iconic and symbolic.

We will not meet Big Joe again, but the second verse kicks off with more descriptions of the disaster: *...High water risin', the shacks are slidin' down/ Folks losin' their possessions, folks are leaving town...* What happens next represents a quite extraordinary leap: *...Bertha Mason shook it, broke it, then she hung it on the wall...* 'Bertha Mason' is the name of the renowned 'madwoman in the attic' in Charlotte Bronte's *Jane Eyre*, in which the apparently homely heroine eventually finds love with the Byronic hero Mr. Rochester. Only later does Jane discover that Rochester is already married to a woman who has gone mad and has been incarcerated for several years in his attic. What made this revelation especially shocking to its early Victorian readers was the fact that Bertha was a black woman. Bertha is also the subject of Jean Rhys' acclaimed 'prequel' *Wide Sargasso Sea*, an account of her early life in the West Indies. Dylan references another Charley Patton song, *Shake It and Break It* (1929), to describe Bertha's crazed rebellion *...You can shake it and break it, you can hang it on the wall...* The inclusion of this notoriously feisty literary character appears to widen the scope of the song considerably. Bertha's instructions *...You're dancing with whom we tell you to or you don't dance at all...* show that she certainly pulls no punches *...It's tough out there...* she tells us. By now it is clear that the 'high water' which is 'everywhere' is more than just a flood. It is a rising tide of racism and consequent civil unrest. Now a notorious literary 'victim' of white dominance is inviting us to either engage with or to 'dance' through her opposition to this tyranny - or not to bother at all.

The next verse begins with the typical kind of macho boasting that characterises many blues songs, with the narrator now addressing a young woman. *...I got a cravin' love for blazin' speed, I got a hopped up Mustang Ford...* he boasts, referring to the novelty rockabilly record *Hopped Up Mustang* by Arlen Sanders which is also quoted in *Summer Days.* The 'cheeky' internal pararhyming of 'cravin' and 'blazin' and the description of the car as 'hopped up' all contribute to the idea that the narrator is offering to take her on a wild ride, which is confirmed by the highly provocative*...Jump into the wagon, love, throw your panties overboard!...* The narrator then 'bigs himself up' in a quite hilarious way *...I can write you poems, make a strong man lose his mind...* Here, it seems, is a macho guy preening and strutting about his prowess in poetry. What chance then for a poor girl who has already 'lost her panties'? This is followed by a rather pathetic plea that sounds like it comes out of a nursery rhyme: *...I'm no pig without a wig, I hope you treat me kind...* so making himself look even more ridiculous. *...Things are breakin' up out there...* he warns her, but we can only hope that she will, if she has any sense, hang onto those panties and avoid 'jumping aboard'.

After this rather bizarre intermission, we are back in the apocalyptic flood: *...High water rising, six inches above my head/ Coffins droppin' into the street like balloons made out of lead...* But this is all, of course, exaggerated. How can the water be 'six inches above' the narrator's head? And where on earth have these coffins dropped from? A 'lead balloon' is often used as a euphemism for how a badly told joke goes down. This is followed by some apparently genuine geographical detail: *...Water pouring into Vicksburg, don't know what I'm going to do...* Vicksburg is a town which is adjacent to the Mississippi river. Then we witness what appears to be a conversation between someone who is in a boat and someone who is not. *..."Don't reach out for me," she said "Can't you see I'm drowning too?"...* Perhaps this is the girl who he has been trying to entice into his boat (or his 'Mustang') in the last verse. Or perhaps this is another conversation entirely. The song moves from scene to scene so quickly that it is impossible to tell. What is certain, it seems, is that *...It's rough out there...*

We are then catapulted back to the literary world of the nineteenth century. The next line begins as if the narrator is relating a typical corny 'Englishman, Scotsman and Irishman' joke: *...George Lewes told the Englishman, the Italian and the Jew...* George Lewes (pronounced 'Lewis') was a leading philosopher of the late Victorian age who for many years cohabitated 'scandalously' with the great Victorian novelist George Eliot (real name Marian Evans). Lewes and Evans rejected conventional Christianity in favour of a scientific rationalistic approach. Both were heavily influenced by Charles Darwin's monumental *On the Origin of Species* (1859) which postulated the theory of evolution through natural selection. The 'Englishman, the Italian and the Jew' appear to be a trio of Victorian-era intellectuals to whom Lewes says *...'Don't open up your mind, boys, to every conceivable point of view'...* This is very odd, as one would expect Lewes, as a rational philosopher, to instruct them to do exactly the opposite. But here Dylan seems to be engaging in an intellectual game with his audience - gleefully throwing out historical riddles to confuse us, such as *...They got Charles Darwin trapped out there on Highway 5/ Judge says to the High Sherriff "I want him dead or alive/ Either one, I don't care"....* Highway 5 is the road that runs from Los Angeles up to Seattle, along America's west coast. Here we see the ludicrous concept of this grand Victorian scientist, frock coat and massive beard on display - referred to as if he is a common outlaw. This seems to be a playful dig at Christian fundamentalists who to this day reject the scientific basis of Darwin's work in favour of the highly unscientific 'theory' of creationism. Thus we are invited to view narrow minded religious bigotry as part of the deluge that is swamping the characters. Dylan once stated that the 'hard rain' in *A Hard Rain's a-Gonna Fall* was not a 'nuclear rain' but a rain of lies. Here, by using elements of comic absurdity, he depicts a world being overwhelmed by a 'tide' of prejudice and dogma.

The penultimate verse begins with one of Dylan's most effective juxtapositions of a quotation from an old song with a line of his own: *...The cuckoo is a pretty bird, she warbles as she flies/ I'm preachin' the Word of God, I'm puttin' out your eyes....* The first line is from *The Cuckoo,* a popular English-American folk song with many variations which Dylan performed regularly in his early years. It was also a staple of the acts of contemporary folk singers such as Joan Baez, Anne Briggs, Shirley Collins and Ramblin' Jack Elliot. The cuckoo is nominally a bringer of good tidings; its appearance signalling the beginning of spring. But it is also often a symbol of marital infidelity, as cuckoos are known to 'invade' the nests of other birds. In the various versions, the cuckoo itself is never the subject of the song but tends to be referred to in a rather offhand way. The song is - like *High Water* - directed at a beautiful but unfaithful lover. Here the expression of anger is particularly effective as the first line tends to suggest a kind of natural innocence, in contrast to the sudden and unexpectedly cruel and violent second line. The rather shocking nature of his intended revenge conjures up another image of religious hypocrisy. The contrast is so extreme, however, that it can also been seen as an example of the song's dark humour.

The picture that has been built up of the narrator as a rather pitiful figure is further emphasised in the next lines, which take us into another one of those 'colourful' slices of Americana which litter *"Love And Theft"* (and which, many years before, had been a prominent feature of *The Basement Tapes*) where strange 'low life' characters make fleeting appearances and deliver homespun judgements: *...I asked Fat Nancy for something to eat/ She said "Take it off the shelf"/ "As great as you are man, you'll never be greater than yourself"/ I told her "I don't care"...* This certainly brings him down a peg or two. A 'Fat Nancy' is a colloquial American name for someone who gobbles up all the available food before anyone else can. The term became widespread after a famous train disaster in Virginia in 1888 in which a bridge known as 'Fat Nancy' collapsed, killing nine passengers, although the Confederate General James Longstreet survived. The bridge itself was named after a local black woman whose job it was to make sure it was safe. Here 'Fat Nancy' punctures the narrator's macho posturing, despite him pretending that this does not bother him. Finally the chastened narrator begins with a classic blues reference: *...I'm getting up in the morning/ I believe I'll dust my broom...* he tells us, reverting, it seems to 'dusting his broom' (masturbating) because he is *...Keeping away from the women/ Giving 'em lots of room...* He ends his narrative by jumping back to the beginning of the flood: *...Thunder rolling over Clarksdale, everything looking blue...* he warns us before delivering the plaintive and (given his attitude so far, frankly unbelievable) *...I just can't be happy, unless you're happy too...* This seems to be a final 'kiss off' to Dylan's listeners. In *High Water* he plays a very clever game with his audience, sinking himself deeply into the blues idiom while throwing in many unexpected references and connections. He deadpans his way through the performance like Buster Keaton in movies such as *Sherlock Jr.* or *One Week* in which, although the world around him is in a state of chaos, he never drops that great stone face.

25th September 2000. In the impressive Victorian edifice of the Guildhall, Portsmouth, Bob Dylan is playing the second of two especially vibrant shows. So far we've had the usual stomping set opener - *Hallelujah, I'm Ready to Go* - followed by a slightly snarly *Mr. Tambourine Man* and a highly energised and quite beautiful rendition of *A Hard Rain's a-Gonna Fall*, enlivened by some sterling harmonies from Larry and Charlie. Bob and the band are going through the set at a frantic pace. The crowd is buzzing as the first bars of the next song are heard, with Bob, Larry and Charlie all strumming acoustics. Just a few seconds in and we get *...Frankie Lee and Judas Priest, they were the best of friends...* This is a rare treat indeed. Dylan has only ever played this song a handful of times since its first appearance on the enigmatic and mysterious *John Wesley Harding* album in 1968. It's a surreal shaggy dog story with sacrilegious overtones. Frankie Lee is a gambler who borrows money from his friend Judas Priest. He spends 'sixteen nights and days' in a brothel which Judas refers to as 'eternity', then bursts into his friend's arms and dies of thirst.

Like most of the other songs on the album, the action occurs in an indeterminate time and place, although it does have a vaguely 'Western' feel. It may be a cowboy song, a spoof, or a symbolic existential parable. It may even be something to do with Jesus and Satan in the desert. Quite possibly it's all of these things, or none of them. The key to the song is provided by 'the little neighbor boy' who carries Frankie's coffin, who keeps his *...guilt so well concealed...* and who *...mutters underneath his breath 'nothing is revealed'...* Why the boy is guilty we will never know. The motivations of all the characters remain a mystery. Only the boy knows the real truth. Like Beckett's *Waiting for Godot, The Ballad* presents us with notions of sin and redemption but quite deliberately refuses to resolve them. Tonight Bob is relishing every word, acting out the individual parts in this absurdist tale. The tone is always light, never judgemental. He throws in as an extra line: *"Have it any way you want" said Judas Priest...* Mission bells are tolling. Frankie has made his choice, for better or worse. The singer stretches out the vowels as the song reaches its climax. Every line sounds loaded and meaningful: *...One should never be where one does not belong..., ...Don't go mistaking paradise for that home across the road...* But ultimately, of course, *..."nothing is revealed"...*

The impressionistic songs on *"Love And Theft"* take place in a timeless 'dream America' of constantly shifting historical settings. The action often moves seamlessly between the mid nineteenth century, the prohibition era, the 1950s and the present day. In a number of these songs, which reflect in a ruefully comic way on his own struggles to find inspiration and his relationship with his audience, Dylan adopts various - sometimes rather roguish - historical personas. His narrators present us with their thoughts and memories in an apparently random order, which we as listeners are left to make sense of. This may appear to be a post-modern narrative technique but it was in fact commonly used by the early blues singers, who would often change the order of the verses around in different performances of their songs. In each song, Dylan takes us inside a particular narrative or dramatic exchange, leaving many of the specific details to our imagination.

In the gently affectionate *Po' Boy* the main character seems to be a comedian, who may even be performing at an old fashioned minstrel show, although given the quality of his jokes he seems unlikely to pass any audition. A 'po' boy' is a standard figure of self personification in the blues, as well as the name of a popular local sandwich in New Orleans. The tune is gently melodic and teasing with a ragtime-infused feel and Dylan's singing is plaintively sweet. In live performance the tempo is slowed down a little, emphasising the prettiness of the melody. The overall effect tends towards wistfulness rather than laugh-out-loud humour. We can only pity the main character however, as he gives us selected extracts from his 'stand up' act: *...Man comes to the door - I say, "For whom are you looking?"/ He says, "Your wife", I say, "She's busy in the kitchen cookin'"...* This is, perhaps, the kind of intro that an old time entertainer might begin a routine with, complete with stereotypical gender roles. In the second verse he tries a little harder to raise a laugh *...I say, "How much you want for that?" I go into the store/ The man says, "Three dollars". "All right", I say, "Will you take four?"* Meanwhile he is being addressed by another unnamed character, who may be his lover, who asks*..."Po' boy - where you been?"* The 'boy' snaps back *"I already tol' you - won't tell you again"...* She tries to reassure him: *...Po' boy, never say die/ Things will be alright by and by...* He then complains that the life of a travelling entertainer is not an easy one. He has been*...workin' on the mainline - workin' like the Devil...* which is neatly rhymed with: *...The game is the same - it's just on a different level...* an injection of a distinctively modern term from computer games into the otherwise 'archaic' language.

Some details of the po' boy's life follow: *...Po' boy in a red hot town/ Out beyond the twinklin' stars...* On his travels from gig to gig, as well as having to try to avoid the police, it seems that our hapless 'entertainer' has to 'ride' trains by clinging onto their roofs: *...Ridin' first-class trains - making the rounds/ Tryin' to keep from fallin' between the cars...* We then get to hear another one of his 'jokes': *...Othello told Desdemona, "I'm cold, cover me with a blanket/ By the way, what happened to that poison wine"... She says, "I gave it to you, you drank it"...* Dylan crams in the syllables for maximum comic effect. The joke is on the po' boy, of course, as his knowledge of Shakespeare is clearly very shaky. He seems to be mixing up the endings of *Othello* and *Romeo and Juliet.* Such cod versions of Shakespeare were often included in minstrel shows. In *Huckleberry Finn* the shifty con men who call themselves 'The King' and 'The Duke' make part of their living by mangling the bard at such events. It may also be that the 'boy' and his girl are - like Othello and Desdemona - a black boy and a white girl, and thus likely to incur considerable prejudice in what is presumably a location in the Deep South. It is more likely, however, that the po' boy is actually white, but that his appearances on stage are in blackface. He may, however, quite genuinely be shivering with the cold at nights. The girl attempts to console and encourage him: *...Po' boy, layin' 'em straight - pickin' up the cherries fallin' off the plate...* which presumably refers to the 'laying out' of his repertoire of jokes.

In the next three verses, the po' boy becomes sweetly romantic, giving the girl a little 'potted biography' and again attempting rather unsuccessfully to show off his (rather limited) education: *...Time and love have branded me with its claws...* he tells her, a grammatically rather dubious but certainly poetic-sounding statement which is adapted from a description of a race horse derived from Charles Baudelaire's *Un cheval de race (A thoroughbred),* although it seems highly unlikely that the po' boy knows this. Presumably it is another line he has half-heard at another minstrel show recitation. The next line: *...Had to go to Florida, dodgin' them Georgia laws...* is derived from Blind Willie McTell's breezily comic *Kill It Kid Rag.* In both cases the allusions fit perfectly with the character of our hero. They evoke our compassion for him, summing up both his past and his present life on the edges of the law. The joke that follows, which again we may imagine he from his stage act, goes: *...Poor boy, in the hotel called the Palace of Gloom/ Calls down to room service, says "Send up a room!"...* This is at least a little funnier than his earlier efforts. It is actually one of Groucho's lines from the Marx Brothers' movie *A Night at the Opera* (1935).

The boy continues with his life story. We may or may not believe the account he gives, as he is still trying to impress the girl: *...My mother was a daughter of a wealthy farmer/ My father was a traveling salesman, I never met him...* more lines which are taken from *Confessions of A Yazuka.* The boy then recalls his kind uncle, who adopts him after his mother dies. Suddenly, and rather unexpectedly, he becomes rather romantic: *...All I know is that I'm thrilled by your kiss/ I don't know any more than this...* She responds sympathetically *...Po boy, picking up sticks...* and seems to be promising to provide him with some security: *...Build you a house out of mortar and bricks...* For a few moments we are back on stage as he relates a truly terrible 'knock knock' joke, resting on the excruciating pun *...Freddie or not....* Finally she leaves us with a cute image of her 'po' boy' *...neath the stars that shine/ Washing them dishes, feeding them swine...* This is the kind of occupation he is likely to be destined for, given his limited talents as an entertainer. We then leave the couple canoodling, presumably out 'under the stars' together, softly whispering sweet promises to each other.

This witty little exchange of dialogue can be taken as a tongue-in-cheek commentary on the often cruel nature of performance itself. The 'boy' can be seen a representation of any entertainer who is subjected to the harsh judgements of an audience. He could even be a self-mocking portrait of Dylan, who arrived in New York City in the freezing winter of 1961 and had to survive by playing for dimes in folk clubs. A po' boy himself, he told anyone who would listen extremely exaggerated stories about his supposedly deprived childhood, spinning yarns about working in circuses and meeting famous blues singers. The song may also reflect on the dire situation he found himself in during the late '80s when he was coping with a string of terrible reviews and struggling to be a credible entertainer. Like the po' boy, he pleads for our sympathy. But we should be careful not to take everything he tells us at face value...

In contrast, the slow and deliberate twelve bar blues *Cry Awhile* presents us with a bitter, twisted and cynically manipulative narrator. In typical blues fashion, it appears to be a cry for revenge against a lover who has walked out on the narrator. Dylan revels in adopting the put-upon persona of the narrator, spitting out far more syllables than would normally fit in a line, an effect which is balanced by the long drawn out pronunciation of words in the chorus, whose refrain recalls that of *I Cried For You*, a song written in 1923 by Arthur Freed, Gus Arnheim and Abe Lynam and later recorded by many artists including Count Basie, Sarah Vaughan and Billie Holiday: *...I cried for you/ Now it's your turn to cry over me....*

The first two tongue-twisting lines are accompanied by a juddering beat, over which Dylan begins breathlessly: *...Well, I had to go down and see a guy named Mr. Goldsmith/ A nasty, dirty, double-crossin', backstabbin' phony I didn't wanna have to be dealin' with...* The narrator is certainly pulling no punches here. In the second half of the verse, he relaxes into *...But I did it for you and all you gave me was a smile/ Well, I cried for you - now it's your turn to cry awhile...* This bitter twist will be repeated at the end of each verse. He certainly seems to be implying that she is in his debt *...I don't carry dead weight - I'm no flash in the pan...* he exclaims, in the first of a stream of slightly twisted popular aphorisms he uses to justify himself *...Can't you see I'm a union man?...* he cries, a line which seems to be intended to signify his dependability. But this is surely just so much bluster *...I'm letting the cat out of the cage...* he proclaims, in a somewhat twisted version of the common phrase 'letting the cat out of the bag', meaning to give voice to something previously hidden away, or in this case, 'locked up'. There may well also by a sly sexual innuendo here *...Feel like a fightin' rooster/ Feel better than I ever felt...* an allusion to Willie Dixon's *Little Red Rooster,* a song of strutting sexual braggadocio popularised by Howlin' Wolf and the Rolling Stones, which sounds like the boast of an ageing lover, preening himself before attempting a seduction.

The narrator's lack of sincerity is made obvious. The explanation *...But the Pennsylvania line's in an awful mess and the Denver road is about to melt...* appears to present a rather convoluted reason for why the narrator hasn't visited the object of his affections. Given the geographical references, he also seems to be suggesting that this would involve quite a long trip. But this is surely nothing more than an excuse. He may bemoan the end of the relationship but it seems that he isn't really committed to making it work. In reality the supposed 'distance' between the estranged lovers may be imaginary, as his next complaint is that he has heard a 'pounding on the walls'. This suggests that the lover lives next door to him. The narrator decides that this must have been *...Don Pasqualli making an early morning booty call....* Here a modern slang phrase is combined with a reference to a womanising character from a popular nineteenth century comic opera. Presumably this assumption is, however, a product of the narrator's paranoid imagination.

The narrator continues to plead for sympathy but never comes over as a sympathetic character *...To break a trusting heart was just your style...* he complains. He claims to be *...on the fringes of the night, fighting back tears I can't control...* But his assertion that he has been praying to God for her to change her mind quickly turns to sacreligious lustfulness: *...Well, there's preachers in the pulpits and babies in the cribs/ ...I'm longin' for that sweet fat that sticks to your ribs...* After descending into pathetically abject self-pity *...I'm gonna buy me a barrel of whiskey/ I'll die before I turn senile...* he becomes abusive and threatening. He gets himself tangled up in an awkward metaphor about their relationship: *...Well, you bet on a horse and it ran on the wrong way/ I always said you'd be sorry and today could be the day...* Finally he declares: *...I might need a good lawyer, could be your funeral, my trial...* dropping a reference to *Your Funeral and My Trial,* a song by Sonny Boy Williamson in which the singer appears to be making similarly empty threats.

While the narrator of *Cry Awhile* is certainly unsympathetic, the voice Dylan assumes in *Honest With Me*, which is built around a repeated driving blues-rock rhythm, is decidely edgy and disturbing. The song, which is another address to an unfaithful lover, is peppered with references which give it an uncertain and shifting relationship with geographical space and historical time. The opening line *...I'm stranded in the city that never sleeps...* seems to place us in Chicago, a city that is particularly associated with gangsters. *The City That Never Sleeps* is a 1953 film noir gangster thriller set in that city *...Some of these women...* the narrator snarls, like a low life hoodlum from such a movie *...they give me the creeps...* He reveals that *...I'm avoiding the South Side as much as I can...* referring to a particularly deprived and crime-ridden district *...These memories I got...* he complains *...they can strangle a man...* The rest of the song takes us back into these memories. The narrator continues trying to defend himself, making rather futile attempts to convince his lover of his worth. We cannot necessarily assume, however, that all of the lyrics are necessarily directed at her, especially as she is presumably one of those women who 'give him the creeps'. He alternates between appealing to her and delivering asides to his listeners. Although he delivers the repeated refrain of *...You don't* *understand it - my feelings for you/ You'd be honest with me if only you knew...* it is he who needs to be honest with himself. The song is, like many classic blues numbers, a kind of internal conversation in which the narrator is trying to convince himself of his own virtues.

The narrator appears to be relating some kind of dramatic story but only supplies broad outlines and a few specific details. He reveals, rather melodramatically, that: *...I came ashore in the dead of night...* and that *...When I left my home the sky split open wide...* These mysterious lines are followed by rather confused attempts at self-justification. He states that *...Lot of things can get in the way when you're tryin' to do what's right...* The way in which Dylan strains to fit into the song's meter makes him sound like he is inventing his rather pathetic excuses on the spot. We then hear that *...I never wanted to go back there/ I'd rather have died...* No clear explanations are ever given for these declarations, but we may speculate that some serious crime has been committed. Perhaps he has had a massive row with his lover, or has even murdered her. He is certainly becoming defensive *...I'm not sorry for nothin' I've done...* he claims *...I'm glad I fought - I only wish we'd won...* The origin of these lines in *I'm a Good Old Rebel*, a pro-Confederate song of defiance, seems to cast him in a very dubious light. Perhaps he has decided that his actions are justified because he and his lover were engaged in some kind of personal 'civil war'.

This apparent jump back in time is reinforced by another bizarre historical reference: *...The Siamese twins are coming to town/ People can't wait - they're gathered around...* Chang and Ed Bunker were conjoined twins who were born in Siam (modern Thailand) and became major attractions in variety shows in the 1830s and '40s, especially in the Southern states. Various rather contradictory accounts of their lives exist, including one by Mark Twain: *Personal Habits of the Siamese Twins* (1875). Twain's satirical account contains various unacknowledged anecdotes about the twins, delivered with his usual wry wit. Other writers pictured them as symbolising the two sides in the Civil War - having separate 'personalities' but ultimately being irretrievably 'joined at the hip'. Dylan himself - who is famously a Gemini - has used the motif of 'twinning' on several occasions. *Tweedle Dee & Tweedle Dum* is of course a song about twins. In *Street Legal*'s *Where Are You Tonight (Journey Through Dark Heat)* he sings: *...I fought with my twin, that enemy within, 'til both of us fell by the way...* In *Simple Twist of Fate* (1975) he looks back on an old lover and tells us *... I still believe she was my twin....* It may be that *Honest With Me*'s narrator even sees himself and his lover as 'Siamese twins' who will always be inseparable, despite their differences.

The narrator becomes ever more desperate to justify himself, veering between anxious appeals and insults. He tells us that *...My woman got a face like a teddy bear/ She's throwing a baseball bat in the air...* combining an insinuation that she is acting childishly with what may be a rather vague intimation of a violent threat. But the joke, it seems, is really on him *...Some things are too terrible to be true/ I won't come here no more if it bothers you...* he cries petulantly, throwing in more lines from *Confessions of a Yazuka.* He is still attempting to play the 'martyr'. But we are never given any clear indication of what these 'terrible' things are. He continues to carry on an imaginary conversation with his lover: ...*You say my eyes are pretty and my smile is nice...* he tells her, then snaps petulantly ...*Well, I'll sell it to ya at a reduced price....* At times the protestations become plain silly, as if - pretending he is a 'po' boy' - he is attempting to turn the whole situation into another corny 'minstrel show' joke: ...*I'm stark naked, but I don't care/ I'm going off into the woods, I'm huntin' bare...* Then he announces that ...*I'm here to create the new imperial empire/ I'm going to do whatever circumstances require...* which appears to be his attempt to be 'commanding' over her. This falls flat because of the ridiculously tautological expression 'imperial empire'. Finally he tries to reassure us that he is just a 'good ol' boy': ...*My parents they warned me not to waste my years/ And I still got their advice oozing out of my ears...* Despite all his pleading and self-justification, it is blatantly obvious that he has no chance of getting his woman back. As in *Cry Awhile,* Dylan creates a highly unsympathetic and unreliable narrator whose protestations we can read through quite easily. Both songs can be said to reflect in a dryly comic way on Dylan's relationship with his audience. Here he plays the part of the sly trickster to the hilt, as if he is some dubious riverboat gambler from a Mark Twain story, who attempts to win our sympathy by using every rhetorical trick he can think of. He is clearly not being honest with her - or us - at all.

Perhaps the most whimsical track on *"Love And Theft"* is *Floater (Too Much to Ask),* which is dominated by the violin which opens the song and provides some musical breaks. In live performance these were often developed into extended violin solos by Elana Fremerman (in early 2005) and Donnie Herron (from late 2005 onwards). The tune is loosely based on *Snuggled on Your Shoulder*, recorded by Bing Crosby in 1932. Dylan's vocals sound somewhat detached and a little world weary. The song has no chorus or repeated refrains. The setting is a kind of imaginative dream world of the American Deep South in some indistinct era between the Civil War and the 1930s. It places modernity in conflict with tradition in a way that echoes the work of Southern novelists like William Faulkner and Flannery O'Connor. It is almost like a compressed novel with an 'intimate' first person narrative. The song features more extensive borrowings from *Confessions of a Yakuza.* On the surface it would appear that the narrator of this song and the gangster Eiji Ichiji have little in common, but *Confessions* is also relating a story of the transition to modernity, with which its narrator has a rather ambivalent relationship. Thus phrases like ....*My old man would sit there like a feudal lord...* ....*If it bothers you so much, why don't you shove off...* ...*Age doesn't matter... Age by itself just doesn't carry any weight...* and ... *Tears or not, though, that was too much to ask...* all from Saga's book, seem to fit seamlessly into the song's narrative.

Floater is a distinctly 'cinematic' song. The first lines paint a near-idyllic picture of lazy summer days, full of ...*dazzling sunlit rays...* It is ...*another one of them endless days...* The narrator appears to be on a fishing boat, from which making a catch is no great effort ...*I fish for bullheads...* he tells us ...*I catch a lot, sometimes too many...* He mentions that he is in love with his 'second cousin' and seems content at first to imagine a life with her. But already there are intimations of discontent. A ...*summer breeze is blowin'...* and *...a squall is setting in...* The narrator reflects that *...sometimes it's just plain stupid to get into any kind of wind...* It seems that the world in which he hopes he can just continue 'floating', in his overstocked lake or river, is under threat. This is communicated by the narrator relating tales of apparently random aspects of his life. We are given various details which sound potentially threatening, although in each case the 'cool' narrator just plays them down *...The old men 'round here, sometimes they get on bad terms with the younger men...* But then *...old, young, age don't carry weight, it doesn't matter in the end...* There is a suggestion that he may be subject to the control of a corrupt hierarchy: *...One of the boss' hangers-on comes to call at times you least expect/ Tries to bully ya - strong-arm you - inspire you with fear....* But *...It has the opposite effect...* Then later, although he admits that the area has been hit by hard times, he is again stoically philosophical: *... It don't bother me - times are hard everywhere/ We'll just have to see how it goes...*

The impression we get by now is that the narrator is very much determined to retain his idyllic rural life, despite increasing social pressures. He expresses some admiration for his father, who he describes (in an apparently positive way) as being like some impassive 'feudal lord' who never argues with his mother. It seems that the narrator will be happy to marry his second cousin and remain where he is. But the forces of change seem to be threatening him. The old trees in his area are being burned down, presumably to be replaced by commercial crops such as forestry or cotton or tobacco. The narrator tells us that *...There's a new grove of trees on the outskirts of town/ The old one is long gone/ Timber two-foot-six across/ Burns with the bark still on...* Later he tells us that *...you can smell the pinewood burning...* Meanwhile it seems that many of the inhabitants have left the area, having found local conditions intolerable. They *...all got out of here any way they could...* We are informed that*...The cold rain can give you the shivers/ They went down the Ohio, the Cumberland, the Tennessee/ All the rest of them rebel rivers...* The geographical reference to 'rebel rivers' is another allusion to the Civil War, although the action of the song seems to be taking place some years after that conflict. One of the song's more bizarre asides seems to be another 'overhearing' of Shakespeare from a minstrel show: *...Romeo, he said to Juliet, "You got a poor complexion/ It doesn't give your appearance a very youthful touch"/ Juliet said back to Romeo, "Why don't you just shove off/ If it bothers you so much"...* In performance, the irreverence of these lines often draws a chuckle from the audience.

Then the tone of the song shifts. The narrator declares his potentially violent opposition to being 'shoved around' by outsiders. Suddenly he appears to be making a direct threat in no uncertain terms: *...If you ever try to interfere with me or cross my path again/ You do so at the peril of your own life...* he warns, and then tells us that *...I'm not quite as cool or forgiving as I sound/ I've seen enough heartaches and strife...* We are then taken back in time. His grandfather, it seems, was a duck trapper who could *...do it with dragnets and ropes...* while his grandmother could *...sew new dresses out of old cloth...* It appears that the narrator is clinging on to vestiges of the traditions of self-reliance in his family. But then the tone shifts and becomes mournful, almost elegiac. With regard to his grandparents he admits that *...I don't know if they had any dreams or hopes...*

In the remarkable penultimate verse we are then given some clues as to the narrator's own aspirations. While referring to 'dreams and hopes' he tells us that *...I had 'em once, I suppose...* but - in an extended line full of evocative descriptions of the traditional way of life that now appears to be under threat - he tells us that his aspirations had to compete *...with all the ring-dancin' Christmas carols on all of the Christmas eves...* This is juxtaposed against the suggestively laconic *...I left all my dreams and hopes/ Buried under tobacco leaves...* In its own way this line is equally rich and suggestive in that it appears to make us reflect on what we have been told in a different way. Tobacco is of course one of the biggest crops in the Southern states. It may be that the narrator himself is only really 'fishing' in his spare time and that he has, like so many others in the South, been drawn into the tobacco cultivation industry. The final verse strikes a tone of apparent defiance. The suggestion here seems to be that he is about to be evicted or displaced. He declares, however, that *...It's not always easy kicking someone out/ Gotta wait a while - it can be an unpleasant task...* and finally that *...Sometimes somebody wants you to give something up/ And tears or not, it's too much to ask...* It seems that the defiance he has been attempting to express is futile, and that he is in tears as his old life is about to be destroyed.

The song is a remarkable experiment in novelistic narrative, quite unlike anything else Dylan has written. Its juxtaposition of American individualism and Japanese fatalism provides a very unusual perspective on the theme of the inevitability of changing times. Its story of resistance to such change gently mocks a narrator who is struggling to cope with the consequences of modernity. In the end we may sympathise with his predicament but we must surely realise by now that his protestations will be futile. Although *Floater* is the most untypical and apparently 'obscure' song on *"Love And Theft"*, in many ways the story it tells is central to the preoccupations of all the songs on the album. Perhaps Dylan himself is the 'floater', happy to bask in his fascination with a number of periods in American history, luxuriating in the 'old weird America' that his songs mythologise, but fully aware that - unless he can breathe some life back into them - the strange, mysterious and often cryptic messages of the 'old songs' that he so venerates will soon become unintelligible to modern audiences.

The 2001 album *Good Rockin' Tonight: The Legacy of Sun Records* is a pretty obscure compilation which you'd need to dig through a good few bargain bins to find now. Yet it certainly has its share of big names. Paul McCartney does his best Elvis impression on *That's Alright, Mama.* Elton John pounds the life out of his keys on Jerry Lee Lewis' *Whole Lotta Shakin' Goin' On.* Eric Clapton, Jeff Beck, Chrissie Hynde, Sheryl Crow, Tom Petty, Van Morrison, Page and Plant and other luminaries provide their takes on various well-known rockabilly classics. Track nine begins with a resonant bass line and some chiming 'surf' guitar, before Bob Dylan comes in with some sweet, decidedly tongue-in-cheek vocals: *...Who you been lovin' since I been gone?...* he croons sweetly *...A long tall man with a red coat on?...* Typically, Dylan has gone for a more obscure choice. *A Red Cadillac and a Black Moustache* is a product of Sam Philips' Sun Records label, on which Elvis, Johnny Cash, Jerry Lee Lewis and others made their debuts in the mid 1950s, although the track was not released until it appeared on a compilation album in the early 1970s. Warren Smith was an artist who some thought could have been 'as big as Elvis' but he never achieved great commercial success. Dylan 'spun' several of his records on *Theme Time Radio Hour* and had played both *Red Cadillac* and *Uranium Rock* with Tom Petty back in 1986.

Dylan's performance is a tour-de-force. The music is cool and relaxed and, although the song is about betrayal, Bob doesn't in all honesty sound too miffed. It is as if he is singing with a smile in one corner of his mouth throughout *...Good-for-nothin' baby, you been doin' me wrong...* he complains, and then repeats *...Who you been lovin' since I been gone...* twice, stretching out the syllables lovingly. Despite the singer being usurped by a rival, he is so impressed by the guy's appearance, his mode of transport and his overall demeanour that the song becomes a tribute to this 'dastardly fellow', who is later described as *...a real cool cat with eyes of blue....* Someone has seen him with our narrator's girl *...at the break of day/ Dinin' and dancin' at the cabaret...* Clearly a pretty suave dude, but one who sadly makes the narrator feel outclassed - rather like Dolly Parton's *Jolene* in reverse. The killer line which determines his 'superior' status is delivered near the end of the song... *He was long and tall, had plenty of cash/ He had a red Cadillac and a black moustache....* This is repeated twice, culminating in the elegant denouement: *....He held your hand and he sung you a song/ 'Who you been lovin' since I been gone?'...* which reveals that she has, of course, been two-timing both of them. The way that the narrator's initial question is turned into a song which his rival sings to the 'flighty girl' is neatly ironic. Dylan caresses the lyrics with great affection, inhabiting the narrator's feelings of feigned shock, jealousy and effrontery and expressing them with immaculate comic timing.

On *Together Through Life*, the most 'lightweight' album of his late period, Dylan and co-writer Robert Hunter seem determined to have some fun. Many of the songs delight in mocking the stock macho attitudes often found in blues, country or rock songs. *My Wife's Home Town,* a heavily flippant twelve bar blues which is modelled on Willie Dixon's much-covered *I Just Want To Make Love To You*, is an exaggerated parody of the way in which male blues singers often claim rather unconvincingly that they are blameless victims. The downtrodden narrator makes a meal of complaining about his very dominant wife. As the slow rhythm grinds on almost painfully, he continues to profess his innocence as well as his desire for a 'quiet life'. But his protestations are so extreme, and so tiresome, that we can have little empathy with him

...I didn't come here to deal with a doggone thing... the song begins *...I just came here to hear the drummer's cymbal ring...* The narrator is hoping to 'lose himself' tonight at a musical show. But he is immediately nervous and defensive *...There is no way you can put me down...* he asserts *...I just want to say that hell's my wife's home town...* He struggles, however, to convince us of this assertion: *...Well there's reasons for that and reasons for this...* he tells us *...I can't think of any just now, but I know they exist...* In various ways he tries to persuade us that his 'better half' really is rather terrifying: *...She got stuff more potent that a gypsy curse...* he exclaims in mock fear *...One of these days, I'll end up on the run/ I'm pretty sure, she'll make me kill someone...* he whines, before the big beat comes back in *...Don't be looking at me with that evil eye...* he pleads, showing how scared of her he really is. But he certainly doesn't seem to have any intention of leaving this supposedly awful harridan, even though - as he now seems to hint - she is apparently controlling him by some kind of 'witchcraft'.

Shake Shake Mama is a pleasantly infectious twelve bar shuffle, with a conventional blues address using repeated lines. It takes its title, melody and much of its lyrical approach from a song with the same name by Texan bluesman Mance Lipscomb, who Dylan shared billing with in some early 1960s folk festivals. Lipscomb's original uses the classic comic blues technique of delivering a series of hopeless appeals to a girl. He promises to buy her a diamond ring, and later a 'box back' coat, but only if she will 'shake those hips' for him. He tries a few empty threats of withdrawing his own sexual favours *...Ain't gonna give you no cherry ball...* he tells her. But he soon acknowledges that she has returned to a previous lover: *...You been slippin' to your old-time used to be...* Later he appears to admit, using an extended metaphor related to the mechanics of his car, that this has killed his own sexual prowess: *...Oh, my clutch start to slippin', My carbs won't even sing/ Blues in the compression, fire my piston ring...* Dylan's song also relies on comic sexual innuendo, although he uses a slower beat with an infectious 'bumpy' rhythm. The band's playing is crisp and economical and his vocal is fairly harsh, with deliberately drawled inflexions at moments when the tone is particularly self-deprecating and he when wishes to sound convincingly 'hurt' as he outlines his rather futile complaints. He plays the ageing roué to considerable comic effect. The first repeated line is rather compelling, if hardly original: *...I got the blues for you baby when I look up at the sun...* he growls lustily *...Come back here and we can have a little fun...*

A series of droll 'come-ons' follow but it soon becomes apparent that the rather naïve narrator is being taken advantage of by a girl who is certainly no innocent and who will no doubt be laughing at him throughout. He protests that she has taken all his money and given it to 'Richard Lee', presumably her other lover (or perhaps her pimp). The first chorus line *...Shake shake mama like a ship goin' out to sea...* is a nice piece of alliteration, which is both sexually suggestive and indicative of the hopelessness of his pursuit. The song also features a corrupt magistrate, 'Judge Simpson', a figure who the narrator expresses considerable loathing for: *...Nothing shocks me more than that old clown...* he complains. There is a veiled suggestion that the girl (like the subject of so many blues songs) is a prostitute, but that he does not realise this: *...Your clothes are all* *torn and your language is a little rough...* he tells her, with slightly forced politeness. Given that his appeals to her have almost certainly fallen on deaf ears, he tries rather pathetically to gain her sympathy: *...I'm motherless, fatherless, almost friendless too...* he wails twice. Finally he attempts to deliver a rather unconvincing threat: *...If you're goin' on home, better go the shortest way...* But by now the girl has, no doubt, swanned off with Mr. Lee, leaving him chafing at the bit.

Another song which plays around with musical and romantic clichés is *Jolene*. Merely to use this title may seem impertinent; the equivalent perhaps of writing a song to a girl called 'Jude' or 'Lilli Marlene', given that Dolly Parton's song of the same name (originally released in 1973) has become so iconic. Parton's *Jolene* is an appeal by an insecure woman who feels she is relatively 'plain' to a beautiful rival with 'flaming locks of auburn hair' who she fears will steal her man. What marks it out as so distinctive is the narrator's emotional honesty, as well as its implicit recognition of how women are objectified. It is an earnest plea for solidarity between women. By using the iconic name Dylan pays tribute to Parton. The song is also a parody of the swaggering male sexuality often expressed in mainstream American rock. As in Parton's heroine, the object of Dylan's song is an idealised example of female beauty. The narrator plays the part of an extremely macho lover who will 'conquer' her: *...I am the King...* he declares in the chorus *...and you are the Queen...* Many of the lines are similar to those found in various songs by the American rock group Mink De Ville, whose material tend to focus on 'streetwise' urban romanticism in the mode of performers like Bruce Springsteen, John Mellencamp and Bon Jovi.

The crass exaggerations begin with the opening lines: *...Well you're comin' down High Street, walkin' in the sun/ You make the dead men rise and holler 'She's the one!'...* This seems to imply that the girl is so beautiful that even the dead will rise from their graves to announce the fact. *She's the One* is a Bruce Springsteen song from the *Born to Run* album which is delivered with brimming self confidence. We can imagine that Jolene herself is quite likely to be completely 'turned off' by all this, but he does not let up: *...Well, it's a long old highway, don't ever end/ I've got a Saturday Night Special/ I'm back again...* 'Saturday night special' is a popular term in the US for a cheap handgun. Here its phallic connotations are obvious. He assures her that *...I keep my hands in my pocket...* presumably to keep control of that 'Saturday night special'. He announces that *...I'm moving along...* but quickly turns rather childishly defensive, asserting that: *...People think they know, but they're all wrong...* By now, we sense that, although the narrator is more strident than the poor sap in *Shake Shake Mama*, he is equally unlikely to succeed in his ambitions. His seduction technique continues to be very unconvincing: *...You're something nice, I'm gonna grab my dice/ I can't say I haven't paid the price...* This may imply that 'Jolene' is a prostitute - who he has paid for and who he is acting out a charade with... *Those big brown eyes, they set off a spark/ When you hold me in your arms things don't look so dark...* he tells her. Maybe she is even pretending to be Dolly's character...

If You Ever Go to Houston is another tongue-in-cheek song with a 'Tex-Mex' feel, emphasised by David Hidalgo's prominent accordion. It may be a light hearted tribute to Dylan's great Texan friend Willie Nelson. Both singers have expressed considerable fascination with America's cowboy mythology. Co-writer Robert Hunter has written lyrics for several 'outlaw songs' for the Grateful Dead, perhaps the most well known being *Friend of the Devil* (which Dylan has performed live on many occasions), in which the narrator is an unrepentant drifter and womaniser. *If You Ever Go to Houston* begins with a warning, which also reminds the listener of the strict 'cowboy ethos' which dominates the song: *...If you ever go to Houston/ You better walk right/ Keep your hands in your pockets/ And your gun belt tight...* The requirement to 'keep your hands in your pockets' is, of course, to reassure the other 'gun slingers' that you are not about to 'draw' on them. Perhaps the warning suggests that the locals will certainly 'outdraw' you. We then get a mention of two intersecting Houston streets, Bagby and Lamar, clearly a dangerous neighbourhood because the narrator warns *...You better watch out for the man with the shining star...* presumably a sheriff or marshal who will be 'gunning for you' if you venture there.

This character is clearly an 'old school' cowboy, more John Wayne than Clint Eastwood. In contrast to the fast pace of some of the other songs on the album, Dylan delivers his lines in a leisurely drawl, as if he is entertaining a crowd in a local bar or cantina. The 'sentimental gunslinger' figure he portrays is a stock character in Western comic books, pulp novels and movies. The song appears to celebrate the romanticism of gun fighting - focusing on the cowboy hero's 'code of honour' - but parodies its clichés in a way that suggests that the narrator's 'advice' and 'boasting' may really be so much hogwash. It seems that, on a previous visit, he has clearly only just escaped with his life *...I know these streets/ I've been here before...* he tells us *...I nearly got killed here in the Mexican War....* This anchors the song firmly in the nineteenth century. The war between the US and Mexico took place between 1846-48, shortly after the annexation of Texas, and included the much-mythologised doomed 'last stand' by US troops at the Alamo, led by legendary American hero Davy Crockett. It was finally won by the US General and former President of Texas Sam Houston, after whom the city is named.

After a short instrumental break, the narrator offers the unnamed listener some more advice, telling him that if he ever goes to Dallas (Texas' other major city) that he should say hello to three sisters called Mary Anne, Lucy and Betsy and reassure them that *...I'm still pullin' on the trigger/ Hangin' on the best I can...* He then confesses to having a 'burning fever' in his brain which will keep driving him on as a lonesome drifter, but then - as a parting shot - tells the listeners that if they ever go to 'Austin, Fort Worth or San Antone' (other cities in Texas to which the narrator has clearly 'rambled') they should *...Find the bar rooms I got lost in/ And send my memories home...* No doubt Willie will be passing through all those places on his own 'Never Ending Tour', so he'll get the chance to kiss all the girls and raise a glass of Bourbon in honour of this 'wandering cowboy'.

The most obviously 'jokey' song on *Together Through Life* is the closing number *It's All Good,* an infectiously sarcastic riposte to the use of a conventional platitude which Dylan claimed to have heard 'one too many times'. The musical structure of the song is very simple. It is based on a repetitive riff which studio guitarist Mike Campbell 'answers' with a brief counterpoint throughout. Hidalgo's accordion is again prominent. Dylan's vocal is fairly harsh, which is appropriate for the song's bitter humour *...Talk about me, babe if you must/ Throw on the dirt, pile on the dust...* Dylan begins, reminding us that he is certainly not dead yet, but that he'd *...do the same thing if he could...* In the third line of each verse he pretends to agree with the repeated sentiment of the ubiquitous title phrase. But the irony of the title will soon become blindingly obvious. Each verse paints a generalised picture of a corrupt world. *...Big politician telling lies....* is rhymed rather gratuitously with *...Restaurant kitchen full of flies...* Dylan plays the conventional moralist in a typically deadpan manner. We hear that wives are leaving their husbands and not returning home after parties (shock, horror!). Many people 'in the country and on the land' are said to be *...so sick they cannot stand...* There are even some violent images. The mention of *...the widow's cry, the orphan's plea...* sounds vaguely Blakean. We hear that there is a *cold blooded killer, stalking the town...* and that cop cars are 'blinking', buildings are collapsing... The narrator seems to be suggesting that the long-feared San Francisco earthquake is coming soon. Perhaps this is all a punishment - not by a really jealous Old Testament Jehovah figure, but a modern urban dwelling deity, who will wreak some terrible vengeance because He is so pissed off with all this cloying positivity!

One of *Together Through Life*'s few literary allusions comes in the final verse as Dylan rather cheekily declares *...I'll pluck off your beard and throw it in your face...* The line references *Hamlet* Act 2, Scene 2; when Hamlet - trying to convince his wicked Uncle Claudius and his mother that he is mad - delivers an extended 'mad speech' which includes the passage:

..Who calls me "villain"? Breaks my pate across?
Plucks off my beard and blows it in my face?...

It's All Good is itself a kind of 'mad speech', in which Dylan mocks those who preach a rather sickly and false brand of optimism. Having lived for so many years in California - very much the centre of the 'feel good' culture he is mocking so mercilessly here - his Midwestern cynicism has kicked in. But then, as if the expression has finally - and annoyingly - stuck in his mind so that he cannot escape it, he shakes his head and shrugs *...After all, it's all good...*

A raucous party is in full swing. A white haired accordionist plays the intro to a stomping polka as the assembled guests all go a bit bonkers, dancing like crazy across the floor and up and down the stairs. In front of the balcony, an old dude in a decidedly retro black suit, a long blond wig and a white top hat - who sways a little like he's certainly knocked a few back - leads a very merry call and response sing-a-long in a gruff but cheery voice: *...Who's got a beard that's long and white?...* he calls out. The revellers respond *...Santa's got a beard that's long and white!...* The singer continues *...Who comes around on a special night...* and the response is *...Santa comes around on a special night...* We are also informed about Santa's boots, his 'suit of red', the cap on his head and his 'cherry nose'. As each verse builds up to a climax, the 'answers' to the questions are repeated in truncated forms until we reach the not unexpected conclusion that the figure in question *...Must be Santa... must be Santa Claus...* Meanwhile, one of the party guests is being chased by two of the others. He jumps on top of a book case and throws several glasses into the crowd. They pursue him through the house until he eventually jumps - in true Hollywood style - through a plate glass window and makes his exit in double quick time. The singer, who has changed headgear several times through the video clip and now wears a little red Christmas hat, is pictured watching all this while exchanging rueful glances with a full dress Santa.

The idea that Bob Dylan would one day make the Christmas album that this video clip promotes would once have seemed like a joke. Elvis, yes... Rod Stewart, yes... Johnny Cash, definitely (He made several!). But Bob... the 'voice of a generation', the subject of countless tomes of lyric analysis, the anti-establishment hero... Surely not... Yet at the end of 2009, *Christmas in the Heart* arrived. There had been a 'Christmas' episode of *Theme Time Radio Hour* a couple of years back, which mainly featured a selection of more obscure oddities such as an early Bob Seger track which changes a James Brown song into *Sock It To Me Santa,* Sonny Boy Williamson singing a *Santa Claus* blues, various Calypsonians and a bunch of more or less forgotten acts performing odd variations on festive themes. At a stretch, if Dylan was going to do a charity record like this, surely he would do something pretty left field. Yet the most bizarre thing about the album is how conventional the song choices are. It is a pastiche of the Christmas music of Dylan's childhood of the 1940s and '50s, but with the 'schmaltz level' turned down. Most of the selections are well known Christmas 'stocking fillers' such as *The Little Drummer Boy, Winter Wonderland, I'll Be Home for Christmas, Silver Bells, Do You Hear What I Hear?* and *Have Yourself a Merry Little Christmas,* interspersed with several traditional hymns. The most 'upbeat' number is *Must Be Santa*, the subject of the promotional video. This is based on a 'thumping' call and response German drinking song *Schnitzelbank,* to the tune of which composers William Fredericks and Hal Moore added festive lyrics. It was originally a hit for Mitch Miller, the 'king' of 1950s novelty hits. Dylan's version is based on a more recent adaptation by the 'folk-punk-polka' band Brave Combo, in which the names of some of the reindeer are replaced with those of recent US Presidents:

...Dasher, Dancer, Prancer, Vixen
Eisenhower, Kennedy, Johnson, Nixon
Dasher, Dancer, Prancer, Vixen
Carter, Reagan, Bush and Clinton...

However, this all tumbles out so fast that you might not notice the absence of 'Comet, Cupid, Donner and Blitzen'...

The album was recorded by Dylan with members of his touring band, augmented by David Hidalgo on accordion and Patrick Warren on piano. Essential to the sound are the backing vocals, mainly by Amanda Barrett and Abby DeWald of the Ditty Bops, a comic-theatrical 'folk swing' band who base their style on the Andrews Sisters, major singing stars of the 'swing era' of the 1940s and early '50s. Although Dylan is covering standards here (several of which had been recorded by Sinatra) he does not, as on the string of 'standards' albums he would record a few years later, modulate and discipline his singing style to 'suit' the material. Instead the gravelly 'Louis Armstrong' tones that dominate *Together Through Life* and *Tempest* are in full effect. This is an effective contrast against the 'ultra-clean' sound of the Ditty Bops' harmonies, which resembles the way in which, in the live shows of his later years, Leonard Cohen's deep bass baritone had been counterposed against the 'angelic' voices of the Webb Sisters.

The recordings anticipate the 'standards' albums in that, instead of using the kind of orchestration that features on most Christmas albums, Dylan relies on a small band. The contribution of multi-instrumentalist Donnie Herron, who substitutes steel guitar, violin, mandolin and trumpet for massed strings, is vital. David Hidalgo also plays a major role on accordion, guitar and violin. Although most of the material itself is light hearted, Dylan demonstrates great affection for the songs. His 'grizzled' voice gives the album an edge that most Christmas recordings lack. Like *Theme Time Radio Hour*, it has been described as an exercise in kitsch - the appropriation of 'sentimental' art in order to find aesthetic value in ironic terms. Yet his treatment of this material is only partly ironic. The four hymns: *The First Noel, Hark the Herald Angels Sing, O Come All Ye Faithful (Adeste Fedeles)* and *O Little Town of Bethlehem* are sincere performances, in which the contrast between Dylan and the Ditty Bops is especially effective. Dylan even sings the first verse of the third song in Latin. The soldier's lament *I'll Be Home for Christmas* delivers some genuine pathos. Here Dylan is working with lyrics and tunes that are, even more than those on the 'Sinatra' albums, *extremely* familiar. But because he 'plays it straight', he succeeds in making us hear these songs in a new way. For most Dylan fans, however, it has to said that this album is strictly a 'once a year' after dinner treat.

Five: *A Long and Narrow Way*
Tall Tales and Scary Stories

...We live in a world of fantasy where Disney has won, the fantasy of Disney. It's all fantasy. That's why I think that if a writer has something to say he should say it at all costs. The world is real. Fantasy has become the real world. Whether we realise it or not ...
Bob Dylan, Interview with David Flynn, Rome 2001

...Our breath comes out white clouds
Mingles and hangs in the air
Speaking strictly for me
We both could have died then and there...
Joan Baez *Diamonds and Rust* (1975)

23rd November 2018. Tonight, Bob is On Broadway. The Beacon Theater, New York, is one of Dylan's favourite venues. Built as a movie house in the Hollywood 'golden age' of the late 1920s, it shamelessly displays a glorious - if arguably vulgar - faux classical grandeur. Two thirty foot tall Greek goddesses hold up each side of its proscenium arch. It also boasts a plethora of gilded plaster mouldings, while its corridors are decorated with exotic scenes of Arab trading caravans, featuring many camels and elephants. This is the first performance of a seven night residency. The 'Bob Dylan Show' is a pretty slick operation, featuring almost identical set lists throughout the whole tour. Dylan is bare headed, in a plain white jacket and black trousers with thin white stripes down the legs. The extravagant stage costumes of previous years have been toned down a little. Only once, during *Scarlet Town*, has he adopted the centre stage position, standing without an instrument and showing us his moves, in a unique combination of crooner and shadow boxer. Otherwise, he has remained behind his grand piano, which is now high up in the mix. His singing, after disciplining himself on standards for several years, is tightly controlled and precise.

We have now reached the climax of the show - the last number before the encore. The band kicks into a fast, crisp rhythm. For the first few seconds the song is unrecognisable to those who only know this stuff from the records. But then Dylan delivers the familiar opening lines: *...You might be an ambassador to England or France/ You might like to gamble, you might like to dance....* A few whoops go up as the crowd, who by now are definitely in the mood to dance, recognise *Gotta Serve Somebody*, the opening track from his first 'born again' album *Slow Train Coming*. But what comes next is entirely new: *...You might be in Las Vegas, having lots of fun...* The corner of Bob's mouth creases into what can almost be called a smile *...Or hidin' in the bushes, holding a smoking gun...* The main refrain, a rather equivocal instruction that one must either serve 'the Devil or the Lord' is unchanged. This is the one song from that era that he still plays regularly. But apart from that refrain all traces of its religious origins have now disappeared. Stripped of Mark Knopfler's 'tasteful' guitar licks, you might say - at the risk of being a little blasphemous - that it 'rocks like a bastard'.

There are more surprises to come *...You might be in a honky tonk, you might be in a nursing home...* Bob sneers... *Searching through the rubble with a fine tooth comb/ They may call you Peter, they may call you Paul/ You might not even have a name, they may call you nothing at all...* 'Peter and Paul' are certainly pretty important saints, but if there is any spiritual message here it's pretty hard to fathom. Later we get: *...You might be on the highway, heading for the coast/ Maybe you're hallucinating, you might think you've seen a ghost/ They might call you Mystic, maybe call you Mr. Soul/ You might be on the wagon, might be on a roll...* There appear to be references to two contemporaries - Van Morrison famously travelled *Into the Mystic* and Neil Young once invoked *Mr. Soul.* But what is Bob trying to say here? *...You might be someone's neighbor, some sweet mother's son/ Someone's jealous husband, or someone on the run/ You may be on the borderline, holding down the fort/ Or maybe you're a lawyer, waiting for your day in court...* As poetry, it's not exactly Shakespeare, but it's certainly fun, and decidedly more so than the original, with its slightly creepy description of a *...rock'n'roll addict, dancing on the stage/ Might have drugs at your command, women in a cage...* Apart from the song's 'killer chorus' and the opening lines, the lyrics are *entirely* different. This is something that only Bob Dylan has the nerve to do. And now that his fans have come to expect it, they cheer loudly as they are reminded yet again that this is no nostalgia show.

Gotta Serve Somebody might be Dylan's most changeable song. The words have been altered many times. In a show in Portsmouth on 24th September 2000 he includes the line: *...They might call you Bono, they might call you Sting/ They might call you anything...* There is no attempt to preach, or to quote scripture, or even to bamboozle us with references, allusions or metaphor. Maybe next year the characters in the song will be completely different but the message will be the same. We may all think that we're in charge of our own destinies, and that we are free to make choices, but fate is certainly leading us all somewhere. We may or may not decide to 'go down to the crossroads' but our destinies will catch up with us all eventually. The little guy with the frizzy hair on stage who's pushing eighty knows this as well as we do, but until that happens - with that buzzing energy still flowing through him, he's determined not to waste a second.

In the blues, macho sexual boasting is frequently practised by singers who are attempting to assert themselves in a world in which they are disadvantaged by their social position. Such songs tend to be full of wild promises, bizarre symbolism and much self-deprecating humour. The joke, however, is usually on their narrators. In a number of his most energetic late period songs, Bob Dylan spins some very tall tales indeed, casting himself as an ageing roué determined to impress young and beautiful women. Occasionally it seems that we are hearing his authentic voice but this is frequently subverted by sly narrative shifts. As in Picasso's cubist paintings, we are shown images and situations from a range of different perspectives at the same time. While inviting his listeners to dance, his narrators tease them with statements that may or may not reflect his own attitudes to matters such as religion, politics and sex. In these songs Dylan plays knowing games with his audience. He shows an exuberant disregard for the ageing process and triumphantly asserts his continual vitality and resurgent creative powers. Whenever a particular pronouncement seems to be presented as a serious statement, he undercuts it with ironic humour.

The sprightly and highly energetic twelve bar 'jump blues' *Summer Days*, with its lively foot tapping rhythm, is the most immediately accessible track on *"Love And Theft"*. It is delivered with breathless energy, in an unflagging demonstration of Dylan's verbal dexterity. An instrumental break occurs after every few verses, allowing the singer to literally catch his breath. Every fourth verse is a bridge, slowing the pace down a little, before it takes off wildly again. The song became a staple of Dylan's live set for many years, with a mostly unchanging arrangement, although for a brief period in 2013-14 it was reconstituted as a fiddle-based 'hoedown'. Snatches of the lyrics have been lifted from a wide range of sources and there are plenty of jokes and comic references, expressed through the persona of an older man who is attempting to come to terms with the fact that 'things have changed'. But despite the disappointment that is inevitably coming his way, he seems determined to 'take it on the chin' and move on.

The action begins during a party or celebration, at which the apparently rather inebriated narrator is making a speech. He begins by acknowledging that he is no longer as young as he was: *...Summer days, summer nights are gone...* he declares, but immediately hints that he will be up for some 'after party action', telling us with a knowing wink that *...I know a place where something's goin' on...* He boasts that *...I got a house on the hill, I got hogs out there in the mud...* and that *...I got a long haired woman, she got royal Indian blood...* This line is, rather bizarrely, a paraphrase of a description from L. Rider Haggard's *Heart of the World* (1885), a fantasy novel about the discovery of a lost Mayan city in Mexico. The main thrust of the song consists of the narrator's doomed attempts to win back the love of this 'exotic princess'. In the process he will take us on a rather mad, careering journey which will culminate with him attempting to come to terms with his past. His initial address invites his listeners to accompany him on the journey, as if we are indeed present at the party itself. In order to prepare us for this, he proposes a toast: *...Everybody get ready...* he commands *...lift* *up your glasses and sing!...* And then, in no uncertain terms, he declares dramatically: *...I'm standing on the table, proposing a toast to the king!...*

We then cut to a scene where he is *...driving on the flats in a Cadillac car...* He now appears to be drunkenly racing around, perhaps on some deserted beach. It may well be that 'the king' he has been referring to is none other than Elvis Presley. Cadillacs were, of course, one of Elvis' favourite 'toys', although whether the automobile is pink (as in Bruce Springsteen's rip-roaring 1985 tribute) is unstated. In 2007, Dylan appeared in a commercial for the makers of the renowned classic car - who were involved in sponsoring *Theme Time Radio Hour* - in which he eulogised the joys of driving their famous high class automobile, while listening to music with the windows rolled down 'on a long drive to nowhere'. This was accompanied by the usual cries of 'sell out' from those who still expected him to be some kind of anti-capitalist 'voice of the people'. But such cars are very specific mythological symbols of the kind of America Dylan explores, not only in his songs but also in his paintings of truck stops, motels and the other paraphernalia of the road.

Dylan ramps up the energy of the song. The wonderfully flippant self-mockery of *...The girls all say I'm a worn-out star...* is followed by the carefree *...My pockets are loaded and I'm spending every dime...* and the delightfully tongue-twisting *...How can you say you love someone else when you know it's me all the time?...* But sadly the 'dialogue' he is supposedly conducting with his 'princess' now appears to consist of him talking to himself. As the car roars on through inclement weather and bitter memories of a failed relationship loom up in front of him, he seems to be lost in a thick fog of his own mind. The details are rather blurred at first, but of course he is probably considerably 'loaded' as he drives. It seems that the woman whose absence he is lamenting has been led astray by some rich competing suitor: *...What good are you anyway...* he berates himself drunkenly *...if you can't stand up to some old businessman?...* another line judiciously borrowed from *Confessions of a Yazuka*. Then he pictures a wedding, presumably of the woman, to this villainous character: *...Wedding bells ringin', the choir is beginning to sing...* He slyly infers that she will be sexually disappointed by the old man: *...What looks good in the day ...* he mutters *...At night is another thing....*

We then flash back to a conversation between the narrator and the woman, which has occurred at some indeterminate time in the past. She is looking into his eyes and holding his hand. But we will soon be in no doubt that she is giving him the 'brush off' *...She says "You can't repeat the past." I say, "You can't? What do you mean, you can't, of course you can!"...* This piece of spectacular verbal gymnastics is quoted almost verbatim from F. Scott Fitzgerald's *The Great Gatsby*. It appears in a conversation between Nick Carraway, the novel's narrator, and the deluded millionaire party animal Jay Gatsby, who seeks to achieve his 'American Dream' through displays of conspicuous wealth and consumption. Gatsby is assuring his friend Nick that he will be able to 'repeat the past' by getting back together with Daisy, his ex-girlfriend who is now married to another man. Nick tries to warn him of the futility of this but Gatsby ignores him and sets off on a path that will lead to his own destruction. The use of these famous lines infers that the narrator is also making a futile attempt to 'repeat the past'. It is striking that Dylan chooses to include such a blatant quote from the novel when (in 1965's *Ballad of a Thin Man*) he had once so scathingly decried 'Mr. Jones' - presumably a literary critic - who had *...been through all of F. Scott Fitzgerald's books....*

The narrator becomes increasingly petulant. As he drives along this 'road to nowhere' he seems to be imagining another conversation with his 'princess': *...Where do you come from, where do you go?...* he asks, borrowing the chorus of the well known barn dance tune *Cotton-Eye Joe ...Sorry, that's nothing you would need to know...* she replies. He responds by attempting to gain her sympathy: *...My back has been to the wall so long...* he complains *...it seems like it's stuck...* Then he pleads self-pityingly, laying it on thick: *...Why don't you break my heart one more time just for good luck?...* Right now, though, he is still racing towards another confrontation with her *...I got eight carburetors, boys, and I'm using them all!...* he claims defiantly (lines taken from an obscure surf-rock single *Hopped Up Mustang* (1964) by Arlen Saunders which describes a 'hot rod' race between a Mustang and a Cadillac). But this macho boast, which implies that he is still 'hot' sexually, is deflated when he has to admit that *...I'm short on gas, my motor's starting to stall...* And in lines taken from another folk standard *John Henry* he admits that *...I got my hammer ringin', pretty baby, but the nails ain't goin' down...*

When he finally reaches his destination, he gets only a scathingly sarcastic response: *...You got something to say, speak up or hold your peace...* the woman barks at him *...If it's information you want, you can get it from the police...* It seems that she has been having an affair with a rather shady politician (possibly the 'businessman' referred to earlier), who now makes a very rapid exit from the scene: *...Politician got on his jogging shoes/ He must be running for office, got no time to lose...* This is a sideswipe at politicians who try to impress the electorate with their apparent health and vigour, while concealing their rather murky personal lives. The figure of President Bill Clinton, who had recently left office after being mired in a sex scandal, certainly comes to mind. The veiled allusion continues with the gloriously alliterative *...He been suckin' the blood out of the genius of generosity....* which is (rather ironically) taken from a speech by none other than 'honest Abe' Lincoln to a temperance society.

In the final scenes, the narrator's pursuit of the woman is presented in mock-religious terms: *...Standing by God's river...* he declares dramatically *...my soul is beginning to shake...* But he undermines this with the thinly secular: *...I'm countin' on you love, to give me a break...* Yet beneath the bravado he already knows that his quest has been futile. He announces that he will be *...leaving in the morning as soon as the dark clouds lift...* before declaring (in another paraphrase of Saga) that he intends to *...break in the roof, set fire to the place as a parting gift...* This seems to be a rather desperate threat. But we know by now that this is all just blather. The final repetition of *...I know a place where something's going on...* seems to suggest that, having finally accepted that his pursuit is hopeless, he will shake off the disappointment and return to the party. He has finally learned the lesson that Gatsby did not. The past, it seems, cannot really be repeated. But right now the 'summer night' is still relatively young. There is still much fun to be had. Having learned a hard lesson, the narrator can now shake off the burden of his past and look to the future. The song maintains its manic pace to the end, while we carry on doing that jump jive.

The narrator of *Thunder on the Mountain,* the joyful rockabilly stomp which opens *Modern Times,* is another ageing roué. Sly sexual references and innuendos are liberally thrown around, with Dylan again revelling in his lascivious persona. The song became a staple of his shows from the time of the album's release until the sets became dominated by Great American Songbook material. In 2017 it returned in a faster, supercharged (and irresistibly danceable) version. It opens with a highly melodramatic instrumental flourish that is almost unique in Dylan's music. There is a 'thunderous' roll of drums. A guitarist picks out a blues groove. Then there is a pause, just for a millisecond so we can draw breath, before the whole band kicks in. The tune is driven by a speeded up version of the blues lick that Chuck Berry uses for *Let it Rock.* The rhythm keeps pounding on with little respite while the stormy conditions that are evoked in the opening lines never abate. The sky is dark and the thunder is cracking. The cosmos itself appears to be in flames: *...Thunder on the Mountain...* Dylan cries, setting up the scene *...fires on the moon...* He assumes the role of a cosmic trickster who is determined to harness the power of the coming apocalypse for his own nefarious ends. He hears the distant thunder, coming - we might imagine - from Mount Olympus and is inexorably drawn towards it. He seems to think he is Prometheus, attempting to steal fire from the gods to renew himself in his mature years.

As the apocalyptic thunder rumbles in the distance the narrator appears to revel in the panic that ensues *...Today's the day I'm gonna grab my trombone and blow...* he declares *...There's hot stuff here everywhere I go...* The line is taken almost verbatim from Memphis Minnie's provocative *Hot Stuff* (1937). Her 'stuff' appears to consist both of various forms of trouble (such as encounters with the police) and sexual opportunities. She sings: *...I went down to the butcher to get me a piece of meat/ He looked like he could knock me off my feet...* The narrator seems confident that he will be able to grab some of this kind of 'hot stuff'. He begins to fantasise: *...I was thinkin' 'bout Alicia Keys...* he sings, stretching out the last word for particular emphasis *...couldn't keep from crying/ When she was born in Hell's Kitchen, I was livin' down the line...* He tells us that he has been searching for the young soul singer *...clear through Tennessee...* The line is adapted from another Memphis Minnie song, *Ma Rainey Blues: ...I was thinking about Ma Rainey, wonder where could Ma Rainey be/ I been looking for her, even been 'n old Tennessee...* Minnie also tells us that *...When she made Bo Weevil Blues, I was living way down the line/ Every time I hear that record, I just couldn't keep from crying...* Years before, in his surreal *Tombstone Blues* (1965), Dylan had referred to the legendary blues singer Ma Rainey as sharing a 'bedroll' with none other than Beethoven.

'Hell's Kitchen' is a district of New York City where Alicia Keys was actually born. The reference hints that the narrator is looking forward to enjoying some 'devilish' temptations *...Feel like my soul is beginning to expand...* he declares jauntily *...Look into my heart and you'll sort of understand...* He proclaims that he is being inexorably drawn to the 'music' of the thunder that will give him his new powers *...I don't need any guide...* he exclaims *...I already know the way...* He appears to believe that the thunder will make him sexually irresistible. But for now he maintains a semblance of modesty. He even puts on a chivalrous act *...Remember this, I'm your servant both night and day...* he declares, and pretends that he is *...gonna forget about myself for a while, gonna go out and see what others need...* In the meantime the apocalyptic scenario appears to be approaching. The north wind appears to be 'picking up speed' and 'pistols are popping' behind him as he 'blows' out of town.

The 'key' to the song may lie not with the lovely Alicia but with the next lines, in which our pumped-up narrator informs us that *...I've been sitting down studying the art of love/ I think it'll fit me like a glove....* The joyous delight he takes in this 'discovery' is deliciously echoed in the obvious cliché (and clear insincerity) of the 'love/glove' rhyme. In fact, perhaps the line should be written *...studying 'The Art of Love'...* as he is referring to a poetic work by Ovid, which is quoted from in several songs on the album. *The Art of Love* (*Ars Amatoria*) consists of advice to young men on how to charm, seduce and make love to young women. The narrator tries to convince us that he has picked up some useful tips from the Ancient Roman poet, imagining that he will find *...some real good woman to do just what I say...* His lament that *...Everybody's got to wonder what's the matter with this cruel world today...* though delivered with considerable pizzazz, is hard to believe. But such is his *joi de vivre* that he persuades us to follow him on his journey *...Some sweet day, I'm gonna stand beside my king....* he declares merrily, suggesting rather unconvincingly (as so many blues singers do) that at some indeterminate time he may abandon this life of sin and turn to 'the Lord' (or possibly Elvis!). He avows that *...I won't betray your love or any other thing...*

Thunder's narrator may be a rascal, but he is certainly a charming one. He piles on the sexual innuendo and macho boasting, attempting to justify himself with his supposedly pious protestations: *...Gonna raise me an army, some tough sons of bitches...* he growls, coming on like some slightly demented version of Rambo, which he follows with the delightfully ridiculous (if somewhat outrageously rhymed) *...I'll recruit my army from the orphanages...* He now seems to be building up his declarations of vitality to absurd lengths. The following line perfectly sums up his fake religiosity and ludicrous sexual bravado: *...I've been to St. Herman's Church, said my religious vows/ I've sucked the milk out of a thousand cows...* Saint Herman of Alaska was an 18th Century Russian monk who is the Orthodox Church's patron saint of North America. He was renowned for his legendary meekness and gentleness. This is contrasted with the extreme lasciviousness of the following line, which references Robert Johnson's *Milkcow's Calf Blues*, in which the singer declares that his abandoned calf, who 'needs a suck', has been 'ramblin' around' and has got herself into trouble with another 'man bull cow'. When Johnson sings *...If you see my milk cow, please drive her home...* he is of course really referring to a woman in a pointedly sexual way. The song is perhaps best known in Elvis Presley's monumental version from the 1954 Sun Sessions. In mid-song Elvis transforms what begins as a slow blues into a wild rockabilly workout *...Let's get real real gone!...* 'the King' cries, and in that moment rock'n'roll is born.

In the next verse Dylan pushes the innuendo even further: *...I got the pork chops, she got the pie....* he grins, taking us into distinctly 'Mae West' territory. He follows this with a gleeful *...She ain't no angel and neither am I...* referencing the famously suggestive star's most well known movie *I'm No Angel* (1933). But the supreme self confidence of the earlier part of the song has now turned to petulance: *...Shame on your greed, shame on your wicked schemes...* Then he tells his lover *...I'll say this, I don't give a damn about your dreams...* Here he really does seem to be fingering that sexy moustache, coming on like Clark Gable in *Gone with the Wind.*

For the rest of the song he stokes up the vision of the physical and sexual chaos he is planning to cause. He announces that *...All the ladies in Washington scrambling to get out of town...* The use of the genteel term 'ladies' conjures up a rather comical image of refined nineteenth century women with their bustles and umbrellas fighting with and falling over each other in a mad scramble to evacuate the capital. This sounds more like a reference to the American Civil War era than - as some have suggested - 9/11, despite the next line being *...Looks like something bad is going to happen, you better roll your airplane down...* which is taken almost word for word from Kokomo Arnold's song *Mean Ol' Twister* (1937). The narrator's boasting is now being stretched to ludicrous lengths, as he infers that the 'ladies in Washington' appear to be in fear of his sexual prowess. The apocalyptic 'thunder' that is about to descend is supposedly a projection of his potent sexuality. However, as he confides to us, he seems ready to 'roll around' and make an exit at any moment.

The narrator now makes one last desperate attempt to win back his lover. He implores her to join him in the mass flight that is about to occur: *...Everybody's going and I want to go too...* He tries to exonerate himself for all his misdeeds: *...I did all I could...* he insists *...I did it right there and then...* But now the thunder has broken over his head. He has become convinced that the sexual power he emanates is now so great that women will flee from his presence in terror. He declares that he has no shame. *...I've already confessed...* he announces *...no need to confess again...* At first he seems happy to exploit the catastrophe that, in his fantasy, he has apparently brought about: *...Gonna make a lot of money, gonna go up north/ I'll plant and I'll harvest what the earth brings forth...* he asserts. But then, with a wicked glint in his eye, he proclaims *...The hammer's on the table/ the pitchfork's on the shelf...* Both the hammer and (especially) the pitchfork are associated with the Devil. The narrator may be asserting that he has laid the implements down, but there also seems to be an implied threat that he can pick them up again at any moment. Finally he pleads *...For the love of God/ You ought to take pity on yourself...* He has clearly wronged his loved one, and appears to have summoned up all the elements, trying to turn himself into some kind of 'super hero' in an effort to win her back. But it remains highly unlikely that he has convinced her of his good intentions.

Duquesne Whistle, the opening track on *Tempest* (co-written with Robert Hunter) is another highly allusive, metaphor-laden message of personal defiance. In contrast to the manic energy of *Summer Days* and *Thunder*, there is a deceptive lightness of touch. The track begins with a charming little vignette of a tune; a delicate, jaunty forty second 1920s ragtime 'mini-overture' played by Dylan, Charlie Sexton and Stu Kimball on electric guitars. This is derived from Jelly Roll Morton and His Red Hot Peppers' instrumental *Each Day* (1930). At first the musicians sound far away, as if we are straining to listen to an old scratchy recording of some country blues strummers, having a well needed break from work in the hot sun, sitting by the train track in their overalls. Then the amplified drums and bass suddenly explode into action and a furious swing rhythm kicks in. The basic melody is still Jelly Roll's, but it now sounds as if an express train has just rounded a sharp corner and is heading full tilt towards us. The guys on their lunch break are drowned out. And then we hear old Uncle Bob, in the uniform of the conductor, holding his whistle aloft. With his crooked smile, that peculiar twinkle in his eye and a voice that is rougher than ever before, for a few moments he sounds for all the world like Louis Armstrong.

The train is one of the key metaphorical tropes of both the blues and country music. For southern blacks it represented both freedom and escape. Trains make their appearance in countless blues songs: *...When the whistle blows I gotta go, oh mama don't you know...* begins the breathless refrain of *Freight Train Blues*, a much-recorded song written by John Lair in 1935 and covered by Dylan on his debut album in 1962. Dylan's version, like many of its antecedents, incorporates the rhythm of the train into the musical performance. The tempo is fast and the vocal delivery manic, as the narrator tells us that he was 'born by a railroad track' where *...the holler of the driver was my lullaby...* Here the passing train represents the high spirited determination of its narrator not to be held back or slowed down. In the blues tradition, trains (with their undeniably phallic qualities) can also function as sexual metaphors. In Elvis Presley's epochal recording of Junior Parker's *Mystery Train* (1955) the singer's panting imitation of a locomotive conveys rampant sexual desire. Dylan's majestic *It Takes a Lot to Laugh, It Takes a Train to Cry* (1965) slows the pace down, making the extended sexual imagery, such as *...If I don't make it, you know my baby will...* and *...Don't my gal look fine when she's coming after me...* both more subtle and more sensual. While Elvis thrusts without restraint, Bob gives his 'gal' time to 'catch up': *...I wanna be your lover baby...* he drawls *...I don't wanna be your boss...*

In gospel songs, trains often function as religious metaphors. In the traditional spiritual *This Train is Bound for Glory* (memorably recorded by Sister Rosetta Tharpe in 1935 and later modified in a more secular form by Woody Guthrie), the passengers on the train are speeding towards heaven. Curtis Mayfield's gospel classic *People Get Ready*, first recorded with his group The Impressions in 1965 - and covered several times by Dylan - develops this metaphor further, taking the holy train on a journey of liberation that symbolises the struggle of oppressed minorities for freedom and equality. Dylan's *Slow Train* (1979) seems to promise an apocalyptic revenge on the hypocrites of the world. Many blues singers alternated between performing blues and spirituals. This tension between the 'Lord's music' and the 'Devil's music' is also what energises much of early rock'n'roll. The extreme sexual expression in the music of Little Richard and Jerry Lee Lewis - both of whom later recorded gospel albums - was made even more powerful and 'dangerous' by the double-edged sense that the 'Whole Lotta Shakln' Goin' On' they were engaging in was somehow shameful.

The music of country singers is deeply informed by the spirit of the blues and the sexual/religious tension can sometimes be even more pronounced. In Hank Williams' agonised *I Heard That Lonesome Whistle Blow* (1951) the narrator recounts how he was arrested on the Georgia main train line as a result of some unstated 'trouble'. He now sits in his prison cell *...All alone, I bear the shame...* he moans *...I'm a number, not a name...* The train whistle he can now hear outside clearly represents the freedom he has lost. In *Folsom Prison Blues* (1955) Johnny Cash's tortured (and very probably condemned) narrator who has confessed to us that *...I shot a man in Reno, just to watch him die...* listens to the trains go by and imagines that *...there's rich folks eatin', in a fancy dining car/ They're probably drinkin' coffee and smokin' big cigars...* In both songs, the prison setting works as a metaphor for the sexual and emotional repression imposed on the narrators by conventional religion. The fact that both are clearly sincere in their religious beliefs only adds to the poignancy of their plight. They sincerely want to be free but the fact that they genuinely seem to believe that they *deserve* their fate only makes the songs more painfully heartbreaking.

Duquesne Whistle is a successor to these two earlier songs, but is more light hearted and positive. *Folsom Prison Blues* ends with the singer telling us that if only he could be freed from his prison *...I'd let that lonesome whistle blow my blues away...* a reference to the Williams song. In the second line of every verse, Dylan describes the whistle similarly, as a spirit of freedom, a wind that is 'blowing away' repression. At first it is *...blowin' like it's gonna sweep my world away...* In the penultimate verse, it is *...blowin' like it's gonna blow my blues away...* This is a direct reference to the Cash song, and thus to the Williams song before it, as well as all the older train songs that inspired both singers. Yet *Duquesne Whistle* is not a song of anguish. It presents another scenario in which an older man is pursuing a vigorous sexual relationship with a younger woman *...I wake up every morning with that woman in my bed...* the narrator tells us, sounding terribly pleased with himself *...Everybody's telling me she's gone to my head...*

Here Dylan references both the jazz standard *You Go to My Head* and the traditional blues intro *...woke up this morning...* In the first verse his po-faced protestation of 'innocence': *...You say I'm a gambler, you say I'm a pimp/ But I ain't either one...* paraphrases Big Joe Turner's line in his *Playboy Blues* (1946): *...Some people call me a pimp, some people call me a gambler, but I ain't neither one...* In the second verse, the narrator's lover is *...smiling through the fence at me...* which resembles a line in the traditional song *Watermelon on the Vine*, another song popularised by Bill Monroe: *...See that watermelon smiling through the fence...* The knowing line *...You old rascal, I* *know exactly where you're going...* echoes the song *You Rascal You* which was performed by Cab Calloway and later by Louis Armstrong: ...*When you dead in your grave, No more women will you crave, I'll be glad when you dead, you rascal, you!...* Dylan twists all these lines around, playing heavily on their suggestiveness. A couple of literary allusions are also dropped in. The narrator's lover is *...blowin' like she's at my chamber door...* a reference to Edgar Allan Poe's *The Raven* (a long rhythmic poem which also uses sexual metaphors) while *...the lights of my native land are glowin'...* in the final verse references Ovid's lament for his exile from Rome in *The Art Of Love* .

As the song begins, the narrator implores us to listen to the 'Duquesne Whistle'. Fort Duquesne (pronounced 'doo-cain') is a town in Pennsylvania but the song is making a direct reference to the Duquesne train route, which ran through America's industrial heartland - from New York to Pittsburgh - from the 1930s to the 1950s. Carbondale, which is also referred to in the first verse, is another industrial town in Pennsylvania. The main reason for using these names is to convey the idea that the train in the song, like the narrator, is 'of a certain vintage'. As Dylan sings at the end of the first verse *...sounds like it's on its final run...* At the end of the second verse the train whistle is *...blowin' like it ain't gonna blow no more...* Later, more explicitly, the whistle is *...blowing like it's gonna kill me dead...* The train appears to be a symbol of the narrator's sexual prowess. He is an old man, and this may be his final fling, but he's sure going out with a bang. Yet Dylan also identifies the train whistle with his young female lover. In the second verse, she is *...blowin' like she's never blowed before...* She appears at his 'chamber door' positively panting with lust: *...blue light blinking, red light glowing...* Here Dylan switches his mode of address (through his use of personal pronouns) from 'she' to 'you'. Now he addresses his lover directly, identifying her clearly as the source of his sexual rejuvenation: ...*You're the only thing alive that keeps me going...* he pants ...*You're like a time-bomb in my heart...* The suggestion seems to be that the young lover's sexual energy may be so 'explosive' that it may be the end of him.

Dylan then delivers perhaps the song's most strikingly surprising lines: ...*I can hear a sweet voice gently calling/ Must be the mother of our Lord...* The narrator's sudden switch into apparent religiosity is, however, handled with the kind of light irony that permeates the song. When Dylan sings *...blowin' like my woman's on board...* we are reassured that the narrator has not been deflected from his lustful pursuit. This is further emphasised by the line in the next verse which is surely the funniest in the song: ...*You old rascal, I know exactly where you're going/ I'll lead you there myself at the break of day...* Here, the narrator actually seems to be addressing his own penis. When he wonders *...if that old oak tree's still standing...* (a reference to the country standard *The Green Green Grass of Home,* in which the narrator's fantasy of returning home is finally undercut by the revelation that he is a condemned man waiting to be executed) he is making another playful sexual allusion, again acting the part of the self-deprecating aged lover. It is with some apparent relief that he finally admits that the whistle (or the woman) is *...blowin' right on time...*

All three of these songs confront the problems of finding inspiration in old age with tremendous energy and verve. In the ironic blues tradition, the narrators of *Summer Days* and *Thunder on The Mountain* are 'losers' whose attempts to reconnect with past lovers are unsuccessful. In *Summer Days* the narrator shows apparent disregard for the consequences of his actions, even If all his plans go awry. *Thunder's* narrator, in attempting to play the part of 'the bad guy', implores us to join him in a riotous disturbance of all the elements, perhaps in celebration of the 'devil having the best tunes'. Both songs are fractured, confessional narratives in which the unreachable lovers may be taken to represent lost sources of inspiration which the singer can no longer connect with. Their high-spirited and positive delivery suggests a determination to shrug off such setbacks and move forward. In *Duquesne Whistle* Dylan sounds calmer and more self assured. He may sometimes struggle to keep up with this new younger lover, who represents his rediscovered muse. Whatever sins he may have committed - and whatever twists and turns his career may have taken - here he stands, defiant and of course determined. He faces up to the ageing process by sticking a defiant finger up at convention. It is a stance recalling an iconic photo of Johnny Cash in which he half-jokingly 'gives the finger' to the prison authorities at San Quentin, an image which the ever-mischievous Ovid would have no doubt approved of most heartily.

27th September 1997. Dylan and his band are on stage at the Centro Agroalimentare in Bologna, Italy for a concert at the 23rd World Eucharistic Congress, a festival held by the Roman Catholic Church. This is high profile stuff. There are 'about 300,000 young Catholics' in the audience and the show is going out live on Italian TV. Bob is looking pretty spruce in a massive white Stetson hat and black suit with white piping. Sitting by the side of the stage, atop a set of white steps and surrounded by a collection of teenagers and cardinals who sit, naturally, at his feet, is none other than Pope John Paul II himself - who is, of course, an even bigger draw than Dylan. Yet it is hard to say who is topping the bill. Some of the teenagers have already recited the lyrics to *Forever Young,* translated into Italian. Then, just before Dylan's performance, they declaim *Blowin' in the Wind.* Whereupon the Pope delivers a twenty minute sermon giving his own answers to the questions posed by Dylan's song:

...You say the answer is blowing in the wind, my friend... So it is: but it is not the wind that blows things away, it is the breath and life of the Holy Spirit, the voice that calls and says, 'Come!... You ask me how many roads a man must walk down before he becomes a man. I answer: there is only one road for man, and it is the road of Jesus Christ, who said, 'I am the Way and the Life'...

It is, unquestionably, a bizarre set of juxtapositions. The pontiff had not been previously known as a Dylanologist, a commentator on the lyrics of rock music or, indeed, a warm up act for famous rock stars. However, he seems to have his own very clear interpretation of these famous words. Many of the rock press and assorted Dylan watchers around the world, meanwhile, are seething. Here is Dylan selling out again, it seems, bowing to the establishment and the forces of reaction. Meanwhile, Dylan's Christian fans - always ready to gobble up any shred of evidence that he is still 'one of them' - are naturally pleased, despite the fact that, although he had once been 'born again', that hardly makes him a Catholic. Perhaps they are hoping he will justify their faith in him by delivering *In the Garden* or *I Believe in You*. It is not to be.

He does begin, however, with a revised version of *Knockin' on Heaven's Door* (which, at a stretch, you might call a 'religious' song). In live performance he has often added extra lyrics to what had originally been a very minimal piece written in 1973 for the soundtrack of *Pat Garrett and Billy the Kid*. Now he attaches an extra verse ...*Mama wipe the tears out of my eyes/ I can't see through 'em any more/ I'm lookin' up into the skies/ And I feel like I'm knockin' on heaven's door*... Perhaps he has composed these words especially for the occasion, or maybe he's just trying to bolster the song up a bit. This is a festival gig, after all. Plenty of choruses, hand swaying and lifting your pals up onto your shoulders... The rendition of the song, and of *A Hard Rain's a-Gonna Fall*, which follows, is particularly strong. Bucky Baxter's pedal steel is especially prominent in the mix and Dylan's singing is precise and confident. Larry Campbell lets loose on a few guitar solos, and David Kemper hammers those drums. The crowd, as you might expect, goes kinda nuts...

Next up, Dylan's job is to meet with John Paul, who is rather aged and infirm and, as the TV camera reveals, unfortunately seems to be having problems staying awake during the set. Bob almost trips as he ascends the steps. Then, like the true gentleman he is, he removes his hat in a sweeping gesture, gives a delicate little bow and shakes the old chap's hand. Whatever they say to each other is inaudible, but it's unlikely that they're doing a quick bit of song analysis. Although you never know... Perhaps Karol Wojtyła *is* a secret Dylan fan. He is a singer himself and his bestselling album of Latin chants has no doubt outsold even *Time Out of Mind*. After this, he gives another short speech and leaves the stage, before Dylan finishes the show with *Forever Young*. As so often in recent years, Dylan fans are left puzzled. Does this appearance constitute some kind of 'statement'? Is he being, to put it in appropriate terminology, 'ecumenical'? Is he promoting his new album, or (God forbid!) is he only doing it for the filthy lucre? Or it this 'just another gig' on the 'Never Ending Tour?...

In her great autobiographical song *Diamonds and Rust* (1975) Joan Baez expresses not only her immense love and admiration for Dylan but also her understandable frustration at his notoriously 'slippery' qualities. She sums this up by describing him as ...*you who are so good with words/ And keeping things vague...* In his later work Dylan has embraced more and more levels of ambiguity in his songs. He has indeed become a master of 'keeping things vague'. The influence of the Mississippi Sheiks and Blind Willie

McTell - both skilled purveyors of comic irony - on his later work is particularly pronounced. As they were operating in the oppressive 'Jim Crow' days of the 1920s and '30s, they needed to be ambiguous in their lyric writing and expression. Their use of language is consistently suggestive and metaphorical. Their narrators often indulge in exaggerated boasting, in songs characterised by a highly skilful use of ironic, self-deprecating and dark humour. References to sex, religion and death are expressed in a way that purports to be comic but can sometimes be deeply subversive. The Mississippi Sheiks' *He Calls That Religion (1932)* mocks a preacher who *...used to reach just to save souls/ But now he's preachin' just to buy jelly roll...* ('jelly roll' being a euphemism for female genitalia). In Blind Willie McTell's *Lord Send Me an Angel (1933)*, the singer pleads to God to help him overcome not only his lustful urges but also his supposedly unfailing attractiveness to women: *...My baby studying evil and I'm studying evil too/ Gonna hang round here to see what my baby gon' do/ I can't be trusted and I can't be satisfied/ When the men see me coming, they go pin their womens to their side...*

Several of the songs on *Tempest* explore matters of sex, religion and death from behind a veil of such darkly ironic humour. In *Narrow Way* the narrator seems at first to be on a spiritual quest but later he appears to be addressing a very raunchy lover. Many of Dylan's later songs tread a careful line between the sacred and the profane, but here this juxtaposition is the central focus of the song. The first line of its refrain *...It's a long, it's a long and narrow way...* which is repeated at the end of each of the eleven verses, references Matthew 7:14: *...Straight is the gate, and narrow is the way, which leadeth unto life, and few there be that find it...* In contrast, the second line is built around a refrain borrowed from the Mississippi Sheiks' *You'll Work Down to Me Someday (1935) in which the* narrator sounds rather hurt and angry with his lover, adopting a rhetorically humble posture. He also appears to be attempting to address a higher power, begging for his failing faith to be restored. Dylan's stylised diction (with the cunning addition of the word 'surely') twists the words to make them sound more sexually suggestive: *...If I can't work up to you....* he drawls in the repeated chorus line *...You'll surely have to work down to me some day...*This can be seen either as a straightforward invitation to fellatio or an admission that he is just a miserable sinner who will eventually reap the wrath of 'the Lord'.

The grinding, repetitive riff that continues throughout the song suggests that the narrator is doggedly plodding through a hostile desert landscape *...This is a hard country...* he mutters darkly *...to stay alive in/ Blades are everywhere and they're breaking my skin...* Yet his preoccupations continually shift through space and time. Sometimes he appears to be addressing a particular woman and at others he merely ruminates about her. In the first verse, we meet the song's protagonist, a 'spiritual wanderer' who has apparently retreated into the desert to make some sense of his life. *...I'm gonna walk across the desert 'till I'm in my right mind...* references Allen Ginsberg's *America (1956)*, which casts scorn on the patriotic ethos of the 1950s:

...America, when will we end the human war?

Go fuck yourself with your atom bomb.
I don't feel good don't bother me
I won't write my poem till I'm in my right mind...

It seems that Dylan's narrator, like Ginsberg, needs to liberate himself from various preconceptions so as to be able to 'think straight'. He has walked away from his home and his family and has set himself on a quest of spiritual discovery. He has rejected any connection with his previous existence: *...Nothing back there that I can call my own...* The parallel with the Biblical story of Jesus' forty days and nights in the wilderness is obvious. But the narrator already appears to be struggling to ward off temptation. A voice is whispering in his ear, but he orders it to *...Go back home/ Leave me alone...* As yet we do not know whether this is the voice of God or the Devil. Neither, perhaps, does he. He is disillusioned with conventional ways of thinking and certain events have made him extremely angry. He seems determined not to 'serve anybody'.

There seems to be a clue to the nature of these events when we are presented with a sudden and unexpected allusion to American history, referring to the British burning the White House down in the war of 1814. Ever since then, the narrator declares, *there has been ...a bleeding wound in the heart of town...* This war, sometimes known as the Second War of Independence, marked the point at which the USA enlisted a professional army and thus began to assert itself on the 'world stage'. The conflict resulted in victories for the USA, especially in the battles of Baltimore, Pittsburgh and New Orleans. The reference seems to suggest that the narrator, who we may now see as representing the American nation, is carrying some kind of 'stigmata', or some unhealed or festering abrasion.

A series of weirdly fractured quasi-Biblical allusions then begins to pile up: *...I saw you drinking from an empty cup...* the narrator cries *...I saw you buried and I saw you dug up...* and then *...I kissed your cheek, I dragged your plow/ You broke my heart, I was your friend 'til now...* These appear to be allusions to the Last Supper, the resurrection and Jesus' betrayal in Gethsemene. Yet the language used is curt, almost brutal. Even more scathing are the lines *...You went and lost your lovely head/ For a drink of wine and a crust of bread...* and later *...Your father left you, your mother too/ Even death has washed its hands of you...* The references to bread and wine, the crucifixion, the resurrection and the washing of hands (as in Pontius Pilate's rejection of responsibility during Jesus' trial) are made with apparent disdain. The narrator appears to be callously rejecting the Jesus-figure who is whispering in his ear. This appears to be linked to the fact that he seems to be fleeing a war zone *...This is a hard country to stay alive in...* he tells us. There is a reference to *...the courtyard of the golden sun...* which evokes an image of the Inca capital at Cuzco. This was destroyed by Conquistadors who were acting 'in the name of the Lord'. The narrator seems to be making a link between Christianity and imperialism - and perhaps American 'imperialism' - in particular. The lines *...We looted and plundered on distant shores...* are followed by the vituperative *....Why is my share not equal to yours?...*

Having apparently rejected conventional spirituality because of its corruption, the narrator now directly addresses a *...cake walking baby....* with whom he can satiate his lust, so as to achieve his 'deliverance'. This is a reference to a popular 'dirty jazz' tune of the 1920s, *Cake Walking Babies from Home,* a favourite of Louis Armstrong, Sidney Bechet and Bessie Smith. The song begins: *...Cake walkers may come, cake walkers may go, but I wanna tell you 'bout a couple I know/ High steppin' pair, debonair/ When it comes for bus'ness not a soul can compare...* These 'cake walkers' are prostitutes who are unafraid to 'strut their stuff'. The narrator tells his woman he wants to take her on a *...roller coaster ride...* and to *...lay my hands all over you...* He declares that *...I've got a heavy stacked woman with a smile on her face/ And she has crowned my soul with grace...* The comic juxtaposition of sexual and religious imagery is explicit *...I'm still hurting from an arrow that pierced my chest...* he tells us, comparing himself to the early Christian martyr Saint Sebastian, who was tied to a tree by his Roman persecutors and shot with many arrows. But then he pushes the profanity even further *...I'm gonna have to take my head...* he growls, with great relish *...and bury it between your breasts...* He then tells his well endowed 'saviour' that *...You can guard me while I sleep/ Kiss away the tears I weep...*

These references to profane, earthly 'salvation' are supported by *...Been dark all night but now it's dawn/ The moving finger is moving on...* a reference to Edward Fitzgerald's renowned translation of the eleventh century Persian hymn to hedonism *The Rubaiyat of Omar Khayyam:* Khayyam sees life as a continual 'moveable feast':

...The Moving Finger writes: and, having writ,
Moves on: nor all thy Piety nor wit
Shall lure it back to cancel half a Line,
Nor all thy Tears wash out a Word of it...

In the final verse of *Narrow Way* the lines*...I heard a voice at the dusk of day/ Saying, "Be gentle brother, be gentle and pray"...* refer to how Khayyam discerns a spiritual meaning in an ordinary earthly process, the turning of a potter's wheel:

...For in the Market-place, one Dusk of Day
I watch'd the Potter thumping his wet clay
And with its all obliterated tongue
It murmur'd - "Gently, brother, gently, pray!" ...

The narrator thus infers that we should follow the advice of the old sage, who many years before, in *Absolutely Sweet Marie,* Dylan had referred to as 'the Persian drunkard'. Khayyam's path to spiritual fulfilment involves embracing pleasure and looking at life with a light heart:

...Here with a loaf of bread
beneath the bough,
A flask of wine, a book of verse - and thou
Beside me singing in the wilderness -

And wilderness is paradise enow...

Narrow Way is neither a statement of belief nor an explicit 'rejection' of conventional religion. It is more of a comic pastiche of notions of the search for spiritual redemption. Asking God to 'work his way down' to him is all very well but, given his merely equivocal demonstration of faith, it is hard to see why 'the Lord' should bother. In some ways its narrator resembles the lustful narrators of *Duquesne Whistle, Thunder on the Mountain* or *Shake, Shake Mama.* As he gets older he has become weary of the 'narrow way' of spiritual struggle. He strongly desires to enjoy earthly pleasures while he is still able. So he turns to the philosophy of the 'Persian drunkard', concluding that his path to 'grace' will be found in earthly pleasures.

Early Roman Kings is another song in which Dylan plays around with cleverly ambiguous verbal and historical juxtapositions. The repetitive blues riff it uses is instantly recognisable, as it is virtually identical to Bo Diddley's *I'm a Man* (1955), itself 'inspired' by Muddy Waters' *Hoochie Coochie Man* (1954). Following the success of Diddley's song, Waters released his own *Mannish Boy* (1955) as an 'answer song' in which he pretends to be offended by the younger artist usurping 'his' tune. All three songs use the riff, which features a stop time figure on a single chord, creating a powerfully 'raw' effect. This conveys an impression of strutting masculinity, modified by self-mocking humour, which the lyrics mirror. Dylan's vocal here is often reminiscent of Waters' hoarse delivery. The song became an almost ever-present fixture in Dylan's live shows from late 2012 onwards, providing an opportunity for lead guitarist Charlie Sexton to exercise his expert 'blues chops'. The original 'Early Roman Kings' were of course monarchs who reigned in Rome before the creation of the Roman Republic. The modern 'Early Roman Kings' were a violent teenage gang in late '60s and early '70s New York, known for both their tendency towards violence and their distinctive dress sense.

The gang is described in sharp, tongue-twisting phrases: *...All the Early Roman Kings in their sharkskin suits/ Bowties and buttons, high top boots....* A 'sharkskin' suit is made of a shiny woven fabric. The use of the term conveys a definite air of both menace and cool stylishness. The alliteration is especially effective, with the smooth 's' sounds in the first line contrasted against the harsher 'b' sounds in the second. The next line is somewhat surprising, however, as the 'kings' are said to be *...Driving the spikes in, blazing the rails...* It recalls some phrases used in *Mike,* a traditional railroad workers' ballad:

...A-levelin' up the road bed ain't no fun
Nor-a-drivin' down the spikes in the boilin' sun
Heat boils down, and shakes along the blazing rails,
Hangs around your head until your mind nearly fails...

It is unlikely, however, that such a gang of toughs would be employed on a railroad. The spikes they are 'driving in' would appear to be more menacing objects. The phrase 'blazing the rails' suggests 'blazing a trail', which might be closer to what the gang are actually attempting. Yet we hear very little about their activities, only that they are (in a phrase that uses more delicious internal rhyming) *...nailed in their coffins in top hats and tails...* We may presume that certain gang members may have met an early and grisly end and that they may have wished to be 'buried in style'. Dylan makes much use of suggestive language. He mentions 'spikes', 'nails' and (by inference) 'sharks' (itself the name of a Puerto Rican gang in Bernstein and Sondheim's *West Side Story*) as well as 'coffins'. The final lines are delivered in mocking contrast, with imagery suggesting an air of almost childlike innocence: *...Fly away little bird, fly away, flap your wings/ Fly by night, like the Early Roman Kings...* The term 'fly by night' has clear connotations of criminal 'dodgy dealing'. The language of the song is extraordinarily compressed, with Dylan licking his lips around the words suggestively, clearly enjoying the heady brew of humour and menace.

One of the inspirations for the song seems to be HBO's groundbreaking TV series *The Sopranos* (1999-2007) which mixes the conventions of the gangster genre with those of TV soap operas. The audience generally sympathises with the protagonist Tony Soprano (James Gandolfini) who is portrayed as a 'loveable' family man, despite his violent 'day job' as a the head of a Mafia gang and his continual extra-marital dalliances. *The Sopranos* is heavily influenced by the major crime movies of the 1970s and '80s, especially Francis Ford Coppola's *The Godfather Parts 1 and 2* and Martin Scorsese's *Mean Streets, Taxi Driver* and *Goodfellas.* These are films which also derive much of their effect by contrasting the family life of violent criminals against their 'professional lives'. *The Sopranos* is particularly known for some darkly comic 'one liners'. In the second verse of *Early Roman Kings ...You try to get away, they drag you back...* echoes a repeated line which Silvio, Tony's most faithful lieutenant, likes to amuse the other mobsters with by repeating: *...Just when I thought I was out, they pull me back in...* The other guys think this is hilarious, as Silvio is doing an impersonation of Al Pacino playing Michael Corleone in *The Godfather, Part 2. The Sopranos* frequently indulges in knowing meta-fictional references of this kind, with the gangsters modelling themselves on cinematic icons. The show also cross references rock culture. It is set in New Jersey, so Tony Soprano is naturally a huge Bruce Springsteen fan. The actor playing the part of Silvio is Steve Van Zandt, famous as the lead guitarist in Springsteen's E Street Band.

The notion that *Early Roman Kings* may be about more than a street gang is further emphasised in the second verse. The 'Kings' are seen *...in the early, early morn...* (a passing reference to Little Richard's *Good Golly, Miss Molly*, 1958) *...coming down the mountain, distributing the corn...* They appear to be assuming the role of Ceres, the Roman goddess of agriculture, who role was to feed the population. They are also described as *...speeding through the forest, racing down the track...* again suggesting that we are not in New York now *...Tomorrow is Friday, let's see what it brings...* Dylan ruminates. It seems that nobody quite knows what to expect next, despite the fact that *...Everybody's talking about the Early Roman Kings...* But in the third verse a series of warnings is delivered: *...They're peddlers and meddlers, they buy and they sell/ They destroyed your city, they'll destroy you as well...* Dylan then applies more 'doubled' characteristics to the 'Kings'. We hear that they are 'lecherous and treacherous' and that they are 'sluggers and muggers'. He also delights in the use of half-rhyme: *...Each of them bigger than all men put together...* We hear that *...All the women goin' crazy about the Early Roman Kings...* As well as being thugs and autocrats, they are now also 'superstars'.

In the second half of the song, we switch from the third to the first person. The voice is now that of a rather crazed narrator addressing a woman who has deserted him. But his entreaties are hardly seductive *...I'll dress up your wounds with a blood clotted rag...* he tells her *...I ain't afraid to make love to a bitch or a hag...* Perhaps he is promising to save her from the ravages of the 'Kings' but here he indulges in the kind of language that Tony Soprano and his cronies frequently bandy about in the Bada Bing. You can just imagine Silvio delivering this line, to much amusement. He continues to mock her mercilessly: *...If you see me coming and you're standing there...* he tells her *...wave your handkerchief in the air...* Then he declares defiantly: *...I ain't dead yet, my bell still rings...* The 'bell' may indicate his continued vivacity or it may be 'tolling' for both him and the addressee, who may even be his victim *...I keep my fingers crossed like the Early Roman Kings...* he tells her. He admires the 'Kings' from afar but cannot aspire to being as 'cool' as them.

Dylan's narrator now plays the *Grand Guignol* comic-horror card to full effect, coming on like a snarling stage villain *...I'll strip you of life, I'll strip you of breath...* he wheezes *...Ship you down to the house of death....* You can almost hear him cackling demonically. He revels in his cruelty: *...One day you'll ask for me/ There'll be no-one else that you'll want to see...* Then he appears to morph into the figure of the Emperor Nero, who famously 'fiddled while Rome burned': *...Bring down my fiddle, tune up my strings...* he commands, presumably to his imagined sycophants. *...Gonna break it all down like the Early Roman Kings...* The narrator continues to evoke the 'Kings' as the embodiment of evil, yet they are figures who he clearly admires. His continued obsequiousness towards them indicates the likelihood that he himself is still in their shadow, and that all this boasting is mere fantasy.

The final verse begins with another shift in time and space *...I was up on Black Mountain the day Detroit fell...* the narrator declares *...They killed them all off and sent them to hell...* Black Mountain is a popular recreation area in upstate Michigan, 260 miles north of Detroit. There have been two Sieges of Detroit, one in 1763, during the war between the British and the French and one in 1812 during the British-American war. This was the same conflict in which the British 'burnt the White House down'. But it may be more relevant that the city of Detroit, once the centre of the US automobile industry and the 'Motor City' which gave its name to Tamla Motown records, has declined since the 1960s along with that industry. It has lost two thirds of its population and has become an area in which poverty and violent crime have become rife.

All of these dark and suggestive allusions are subverted by the hilarious *...Ding Dong Daddy, you're coming up short/ Gonna put you on trial in a Sicilian court...* The icily sibilant rhymes 'short' and 'court' deliver a thoroughly deserved comeuppance for this particularly nasty character. *Ding Dong Daddy from Dumas* (1928) was the title of a comical song about a boastful philanderer which was popularised by Louis Armstrong and later by Bob Wills. In a notorious court case in 1945, a San Francisco street car conductor called Francis Van Wie who married thirteen wives became known as the 'Ding Dong Daddy of the D-Car Line'. 'Ding Dong Daddy' is also the name of a villainous character in the children's animated superhero TV series *Teen Titans*. Its use is especially effective as a way of mocking the apparently macho nature of the song's narrator. The 'Kings' can be identified with any group of authoritarian figures, from corporate capitalists to railroad barons. *Early Roman Kings* thus suggests, in its own rather playful way, that political corruption and violence are just as rife today as they were thousands of years ago.

Another song from *Tempest* which deals with death and destruction but which has a fantastical but also somewhat whimsical humorous quality is the title track. This is a fourteen minute 'epic' consisting of fifty verses, all sung to the tune of a vaguely 'Celtic' waltz. The song was released in 2012 - a hundred years after the sinking of the Titanic - probably the most famous and dramatic shipwreck in history. The event was a huge news sensation at the time and created massive worldwide interest. Since then many books, articles and films have related versions of a story which has always retained its power to move audiences, especially as the ship was regarded as 'unsinkable'. Its destruction by an iceberg on its maiden voyage to the USA has since become a symbol of the end of an era of deference towards the upper classes and of the kind of cultural blindness that led the world into the dreadful carnage of World War One. The 1997 blockbuster *Titanic* directed by James Cameron and starring Leonardo Di Caprio and Kate Winslet as Jack and Rose, two fictional 'star crossed lovers', became one of the most commercially successful movies of all time. The theme tune, a lachrymose power ballad belted out by Celine Dion called *My Heart Will Go On* (1997), became a huge worldwide hit.

Dylan's song uses only a few elements of the true story. It also contains a series of religious and biblical allusions which appear to explore notions of free will and predestination. And in a bizarrely comical way, it also includes several references to Cameron's film. Dylan avoids poetic language and metaphor, choosing instead the kind of language that was used in contemporary songs and newspaper reports about the disaster. The story is filtered through a fictional, ghostly character called the Watchman, who observes but has no control of events. Many of the events depicted are strange and illogical. This is enhanced by the 'dreamily' repetitive musical setting. It may even be that the whole song is a description of the Watchman's dream, as many events in the narrative follow each other with a kind of surreal logic. Many colourfully symbolic characters appear in brief cameos. Dylan switches between realism, fiction and fantasy in a kind of burlesque of disparate ideas. He contemplates the theme of mortality, and all the questions that surround it, with a serene, smiling, contemplative detachment.

The song is entirely composed of four line stanzas, each of which has exactly eight syllables. The choice of this format appears to be deliberate. In the manner of a traditional ballad, there are no choruses or bridge sections. Many such songs were written and performed, some in the immediate wake of the event, and many others over the next few decades, by popular singers as well as blues and country artists. Among the most well known was Ernest 'Pop' Stoneman's *The Sinking of the Titanic* (1926), which contains the refrain *...It was sad when the great ship went down...* This was used in several subsequent versions of the song, including one by Woody Guthrie. This version tells the story in a straightforward way, although it does emphasise that *...The rich they declared they would not ride with the poor/ So they sent the poor below...* Frank Hutchinson, a white blues singer, produced a kind of early 'talkin' blues' version. 'Hi' Henry Brown's *Titanic Blues* (1932) relates the story with a kind of po-faced relish. Many blues singers commented on the fact that *Titanic* did not allow black passengers to board; some even hinting at the sinking thus being a kind of divine retribution. A legend had grown up that the great black boxer Jack Johnson had been denied passage on the ship. This is recounted very sarcastically in Leadbelly's *The Titanic* (1948), which includes the lines: *...Jack Johnson want to get on board/ Captain said, "I ain't hauling no coal"...* What is surprising about many of these songs is that, instead of being tragic laments, they are often pithy and satirically humorous commentaries on an event which had already taken on iconic significance.

The most obvious genesis of *Tempest* lies in another song simply called *The Titanic,* popularised by the Carter Family. This was written by an obscure songwriter called Seth Newton Mize in the 1920s and was recorded by many country artists. Dylan uses a slowed down version of this song's melody. He also borrows the character of the Watchman from this source; although the Watchman in Mize's song purports to be a real character who is said to have been aboard the ship, rather than the semi-mythical figure that Dylan creates. Mize also implies that Captain Smith caused the disaster because he was drunk. It seems that the tradition of songs about the *Titanic* soon became one in which the legend, rather than the reality of the event, was emphasised. Dylan's song also begins with a slightly altered version of Mize's first verse, which runs:

...The pale moon rose in glory,
She's drifting from golden west,
She told her sad, sad story:
Sixteen hundred have gone to rest...

Dylan's song opens with the lines: *...The pale moon rose in its glory/ Over the Western town...* and continues *...She told a sad, sad story/ Of the great ship that went down...* the last line here incorporating the refrain that occurs in Stoneman and other singers' versions. The idea of the moon 'telling the story' is a rather poetically wistful one, although - in the context of Dylan's incorporation of elements of Cameron's film - the woman who relates the events here may be the character of Rose (Kate Winslet). The film begins and ends with the words of the centenarian Rose and the whole story of what happened in 1912 is presented as a flashback. Mize's first line also - by a happy co-incidence - contains the word 'rose'.

The next few verses are couched in the kind of clichés that were popular around the time of the disaster itself *...'Twas the fourteenth day of April... The night was bright with starlight.... The chandeliers were swaying...* The ship was *...sailing into tomorrow/ to a golden age foretold...* But there is already a premonition of disaster as *...all the lords and ladies...* are said to be *...heading for their eternal home...* This account sounds very much like florid journalistic description. The orchestra on board the ship is playing *...songs of faded love....* Then we are introduced to the first of the many characters who will make their entrances and exits: *...The Watchman he was dreaming as the ballroom dancers twirled...* But then there is a very odd shift of tone: *...He dreamed the Titanic was sinking into the underworld...* In his dream, the Watchman imagines the ship to be sinking not beneath the sea but beneath the earth. The references to 'the golden age' and 'the underworld' evoke elements of classical mythology. But as Dylan recounts the story to the slow waltz tune, there is no sign of panic or alarm, or even drama, in his voice. He merely sounds amused throughout.

There is an even more surprising shift in the next verse. If we are expecting the song to be any kind of serious spiritual discourse we are about to be disillusioned *...Leo took his sketch book/ He was often so inclined/ He closed his eyes and painted/ The scenery in his mind...* There is no doubt here that the character being described is one of the two main protagonists of the movie. Dylan refers to him not as 'Jack' (the character's name) but as 'Leo', a jokily abbreviated form of Leonardo (as in Di Caprio). In the film, Jack Dawson is a poor artist who in one scene sketches the beautiful and aristocratic Rose in the nude, which leads onto a 'steamy' erotic encounter. But Dylan tells a different tale. 'Cupid' (the God of love in classical mythology) shoots an arrow into 'Leo' and he immediately 'falls into the lap' of the nearest woman. Already the events of the song appear to have merged with the Watchman's dream. Events now take place with dream-like rapidity and logic. Suddenly Leo discovers that the ship is flooding, then we learn that the 'smokestack is leaning sideways' as *...heavy feet begin to pound...* while Leo *...walks into a whirlwind...* The real *Titanic* did not, of course, encounter a whirlwind or a 'tempest'.

We now hear that *...dead bodies are floating in the double-bottomed hull...* (a 'real life' detail), while the engines explode and the bow splits apart. Passengers are flung around the ship in scenes of utter mayhem *...The veil was torn asunder...* is a reworking of lines in Matthew 27 describing the destruction of the Temple in Jerusalem. The next few verses introduce us to numerous (mostly fictional) characters. The first one, Wellington (the name of a famous general and thus presumably some kind of 'stiff' military character), who sees his furniture moving around and then *...straps on both his pistols...* thinks he will need to defend himself against some kind of threat, although such an assumption is of course ridiculous. We see some the horrors of the tragedy through his eyes. 'Friends and lovers' are said to be *...clinging to each other side by side...* while *...mothers and their daughters... ...jump into the icy waters...* presumably to an almost certain death. We then see 'Mr. Astor' (John Jacob Astor IV, a multi millionaire and one of the richest people in the USA) kissing 'his darling wife'. Astor was perhaps the most famous casualty of the disaster and is mentioned in most of the songs about the event. Leadbelly's version includes a similar account of him kissing his wife. Astor also features as a character in Cameron's movie. Mance Lipscomb's *The Sinking of the Titanic* states, rather acidly, that *...Jacob Astor was a millionaire, had plenty money to spare/ But when the Titanic was sinking, Lord, he could not pay his fare....*

We are also told that *...Brother rose up against brother/ In every circumstance/ They fought and slaughtered each other/ In a deadly dance...* For a moment we seem to be transported onto a battlefield, with the description of brothers fighting each other evoking the events of American Civil War. Meanwhile, the slow waltz tune continues unabated. The dream-narrative continues to 'cut' in and out of the *Titanic* scenario. We hear that the lifeboats are being lowered, but then that *...there were traitors, there were turncoats/ Broken backs and broken necks...* none of which was reported as happening on the real sinking ship or in Cameron's film. A bishop leaves his cabin to try to help, but realises that everything is hopeless. He merely turns his eyes heavenwards and addresses God by saying *...The poor are yours to feed....* The ineffectuality of this representative of the church is contrasted with that of 'Jim Dandy', who cannot swim but gives up his seat on a lifeboat to a crippled child. 'Jim Dandy' is a fictional character who is known for rescuing others and who appears in a 1956 hit song by Laverne Baker. As Dandy sees 'the starlight from the east' he knows he will die soon but *...his heart was now at peace...*

As chaos takes over we return to our friend Leo, who can now make no sense of what is happening in this bizarre, hallucinatory scenario*: ...Leo turned to Cleo/ "I think I'm going mad"/ But he'd lost his mind already/ Whatever mind he had...* We are never told who 'Cleo' is. Meanwhile the description of Leo trying to *...block the doorway to save all those from harm/ Blood from an open wound pouring down his arm...* seems to be a version of the scenes in the movie where Jack performs heroics in order to save some of the passengers. But this is the last we will hear of Leo and we will never find out whether he shares Jack Dawson's fate. In the next verse we hear that: *...Petals fell from the flowers/ 'Till all of them were gone/ In the long and dreadful hours/ The wizard's curse played on...* The mention of the 'wizard's curse' suggests that this dream-version of the sinking of the ship is indeed a kind of Hollywood movie in which the passengers have been bewitched by an unseen manipulator. Given that the trouble with the ship appears to have been started by a whirlwind, perhaps this 'remake' of the famous movie has somehow incorporated elements of *The Wizard of Oz.* Dorothy and her friends are however, nowhere to be seen.

Various other characters now contemplate their fate. 'The host' (presumably the ship's designer, Thomas Andrews) is shown calmly drinking brandy as the ship goes down. The captain stoically remains at his post. We are told that he *...remembered bygone years....* and that *...He read the Book of Revelations and he filled his cup with tears....* Although one hardly imagines him having much time for reading as the ship sinks, in one scene in the film a Catholic priest is shown reading a passage from the final book in the Bible. Many other people perished, it seems, who would be *...Nameless here* *forever more...* (a line borrowed from Poe's *The Raven*) and that, when the Reaper's work was finished *...sixteen hundred had gone to rest...* These are described as *...the good, the bad, the rich, the poor/ The loveliest and the best...* As the crowds are pictured waiting at the landing place for the survivors to arrive, someone concludes that *...There is no understanding on the judgment of God's hand....* Finally we see the Watchman again, still dreaming, as the ship sinks and the waltz fades away. Dylan presents the story of the *Titanic* - or, more accurately - the legend of the *Titanic,* as if it is a mythical construct. He combines various aspects of songs about the disaster with a few elements from the film and some apparently random characters in a cartoon-like presentation of the tragic story which revels in its comic ambiguity.

Many Dylan fans found *Tempest* especially puzzling. It was hardly surprising that he seemed to have little interest in the historical details of the actual disaster. But on hearing that Dylan had written a lengthy song about the sinking of the *Titanic,* it was perhaps expected that he would produce a long and serious meditation on the subject - a sequel, perhaps, to *Desolation Row* in which the lines *...the Titanic sails at dawn/ And everybody's shouting "Which side are you on?"...* symbolise the futility of 'taking sides' in a political or philosophical argument when humanity is on the brink of potential disaster. Instead of this, Dylan produces a comic pastiche. Yet the story of the sinking ship will always be symbolic of the futility of attempting to defy 'the judgement of God's hand'. He illustrates this by including characters from the poem *Under Ben Bulben* by W.B. Yeats (a contemporary poet at the time of the sinking). The poem, a meditation on the possibility of an afterlife, includes the lines *...Calvert and Wilson, Blake and Claude/ Prepared a rest for the people of God...* The four figures are all visionary artists. Dylan cuts the list down to three and changes 'Calvert' to 'Calvin'. John Calvin was one of the leading founders of Protestantism and was a major proponent of the idea that human actions are predestined by God. William Blake, whose religious impulses were far more libertarian, was opposed to such a doctrine. Dylan playfully imagines these figures 'gambling in the dark' over their fate. We know, however, that these actions will be entirely futile. We are informed emphatically that *...Not one of them would live to tell the tale or disembark...* By setting this dispute on the *Titanic* Dylan implies that debates about predestination and free will are as much a waste of time as Wellington arming himself. In the context of his other comic songs about ageing, the implication here seems to be that he no longer wishes to waste his time in 'idle speculation'. Life, while you are lucky enough to still have it, is to be lived and treasured in every moment.

In 1997 the album *Songs of Jimmie Rodgers: A Tribute* was released on Egyptian Records, Bob Dylan's own record label. Dylan had devoted much time and attention to putting the album together. There are contributions by Bono, Willie Nelson, Steve Earle, Alison Krauss, Jerry Garcia, Van Morrison, Mary Chapin Carpenter, John Mellencamp and others. To many 'rock generation' listeners Rodgers is a dim and distant figure, perceived perhaps as something of a joke because of his trademark yodeling. But in Dylan's remarkably effusive sleeve notes he is determined to establish this apparently 'hokey' singer as a major figure in twentieth century music. He begins with a highly dramatic statement that *...Jimmie Rodgers is, of course, one of the guiding lights of the twentieth century whose way with song has always been an inspiration to those of us who have followed the path....* He describes Rodgers as: *...A blazing star whose sound was and remains the raw essence of individuality in a sea of conformity, par excellence with no equal...* and *...a performer of force without precedent with a sound as lonesome and mystical as it was dynamic...* and as someone who *...gives hope to the vanquished and humility to the mighty...* He also explains that Rodgers, who died from tuberculosis in 1933 at the age of only 36, was cited as a major influence by bluesmen such as Howlin' Wolf, Muddy Waters and Big Bill Broonzy as well as country singers like Hank Williams, Johnny Cash and Merle Haggard and that, in his short but highly successful career, he did much to bring the both blues and country music to national prominence: *...He has come to be known as the 'Man Who Started It All'...*

In a contemporary interview with Octopus Media Dylan asserts that Rodgers' songs *...seem really funny and bright but underneath they could be really dark and dreary...* His own contribution to the album is the relatively obscure Rodgers song *My Blue Eyed Jane*. The vocal - which he recorded several times over a backing track laid down in 1994 - is sweetly plaintive, and the backing is dominated by Bucky Baxter's steel guitar. The song, which has a light and cheerful tone, begins in a highly conventional way. We hear that the narrator and his Jane (the *...sweetest girl in all the world...*) fell in love *...like turtle doves...* under the moonlight. But when he asks her to marry him the girl replies mysteriously *...Oh dear, it seems so queer that this could happen here...* He continues to profess his love for her, requesting that they meet at sunset, when (rather ominously) *...the shadow's creeping over town...* In the final verse he bids her a sad farewell. He tells her he has to depart and he half heartedly asks her to accompany him but it is obvious that she will not. The narrator laments that *...The world is drear without you dear/ But I cannot linger here...* Why the girl has rejected him is never explained. But the 'shadow' which seems to hang over the song may reflect the fact that Rodgers knew that his own end would soon be nigh.

The title of Dylan's *Rough and Rowdy Ways* album is derived from Jimmie Rodgers' *My Rough and Rowdy Ways* (1929), an apparently cheerful song punctuated by his trademark yodelling. It begins with a series of romantic clichés, claiming that the narrator has 'settled down' with a perfect lady in *...a cottage in the old home town...* and thus is now a sober, respectable citizen. But when he meets one of his old associates, colourfully described as: *...a bounder who knew me when I was a rounder...* he then becomes involved in an all night drinking and gambling session. He confesses that *...the railroad trains are calling me away...* to his old 'sinful' life. The song tells a straightforward tale of a man who falls from the 'path of righteousness'. But its jaunty tune and self mocking tone suggests that he is perfectly happy to return to those 'rough and rowdy ways'. Despite his confession of these indulgences, made during the era of prohibition, we naturally sympathise with him because of the winning charm he conveys. On the *Rough and Rowdy Ways* album Dylan pulls off a similar sleight of hand. In three darkly comic songs *Goodbye Jimmy Reed, False Prophet* and *My Own Version of You*, the narrator's real intentions appear to be hidden behind dramatic but not always believable declarations of intent. In each song Dylan makes pronouncements that we may interpret as being direct comments on his own career, but the context in which these statements are presented often suggests that we cannot take them entirely seriously.

Goodbye Jimmy Reed, a highly spirited blues rock number, is the most upbeat track on the album. With its driving beat and its tongue in cheek lyrics, it bears some resemblance to 1966's *Leopard Skin Pillbox Hat.* In form and execution it is a jubilant demonstration of Dylan's understanding of the fluidity of blues songs, in which the logical progression from verse to verse is often dependent on the singer's random thoughts and word associations. Here Dylan demonstrates his mastery of the kind of comic address which the inbuilt ambiguity of the form makes possible. He also links gospel and blues traditions by inserting several religious allusions in a deliberately ambiguous way. In a performance of great verve and spirit, and with immaculate comic timing, Dylan presents an invocation of the spirit of the blues which invites us all to share in its great warmth and life-affirming qualities.

The song celebrates the life of Jimmy Reed, a highly influential blues man with a knack of writing catchily commercial songs. His string of hits in the early 1960s - including *Baby What You Want Me To Do* (1960) *Big Boss Man* (1961) and *Bright Lights, Big City* (1961) - were covered by Elvis Presley, The Yardbirds, The Grateful Dead and many others. Dylan himself performed *Big Boss Man* with The Dead in 2003 and *Bright Lights, Big City* as a duet with Eric Clapton in 1999. Reed was a particularly prominent influence on The Rolling Stones, who included many of his songs in their early setlists. But although the track has some similarities to Reed's musical style, it allows us only a few brief glimpses into his life. It is certainly not a straightforward homage. In many ways it can also be considered as an affectionate 'shout out' to Van Morrison, who has been heavily influenced by the chugging, stop-start rhythms of Reed's music. Morrison has, like Dylan, always been something of a spiritual seeker. At various times in his career he has shown an interest in Hinduism and Scientology. When he recorded *Whenever God Shines His Light* as a duet with Cliff Richard in 1989, it seemed as if he might be embracing Christianity. But the title track of his follow-up album *Enlightenment* clearly celebrates Zen Buddhism. Once he even declared that he was an atheist. In his songs he has often referenced his musical heroes in a highly reverential way. Like the latter day Dylan, he now appears to 'find the religion in the music'.

Throughout the song, religious references are presented in a playfully provocative way. The opening juxtaposition of the sacred and the profane *...I live in a street named after a saint/ Women in the churches wear powder and paint...* sets the tone. Already the geographical location of this description is open to question. Very many cities and towns contain streets which are named after saints. Dylan himself has lived for many years in Santa Monica, California - a town which is, of course, named after a saint. The following lines *...Where the Jews and the Catholics and the Muslims all pray...* seems to suggest a multinational, multi-faith city such as Jerusalem. But the highly disarming *...I can tell a Proddy from a mile away...* lands us very definitely in sectarian Northern Ireland, where young Van grew up as a nominal Protestant. 'Proddy' is a term most likely to be used by Catholics in a pejorative way.

Despite the presence of these references, only the invocatory lines at the end of each verse suggest a fervent espousal of real faith. At the end of the first verse Dylan sings *...Goodbye Jimmy Reed, Jimmy Reed indeed/ Give me that old time religion, it's just what I need....* with great enthusiasm. He stretches out the obvious rhyme 'indeed' for emphasis. *Give Me that Old Time Religion* is the title of a traditional Gospel song that became especially popular in black churches in the early twentieth century. Blind Willie McTell recorded a memorable version in 1940. Dylan delivers the line as if he is banging his fist on a table. But the final declaration *...It's just what I need...* is decidedly incongruous, as if the singer is espousing some new kind of fizzy drink. Certainly it sounds rather profane, which is appropriate as the narrator appears to be declaring that it is the blues itself which is his 'religion'.

In the next verse, this quasi-religious tub thumping is carried even further: *...For thine is the kingdom, the power and the glory...* Dylan sings *...Go tell it on the mountain, go tell the real story...* The line from the *Lord's Prayer* is known as a 'doxology' and only appears in Protestant versions of the recitation. *Go Tell It on the Mountain* is an African American spiritual dating from the nineteenth century. There is also a hint of Van Morrison's *One Irish Rover*, a beautifully reticent expression of aching regret which Dylan covered around twenty times in concert between 1989 and 1993, and which begins *...Tell me a story...* Dylan then delivers the supposedly serious line*...Tell it in that straightforward puritanical tone...* with a straight face, as if he is a protestant preacher from Belfast, following it with *...In the mystic hours, when a person's alone...* One of Morrison's most powerful early compositions is *Mystic Eyes* (1965) while the beautifully mysterious *Into the Mystic* from 1970's *Moondance* takes the listener on a somewhat indeterminate spiritual journey. This is, however, a rather comical juxtaposition, as 'straightforward puritanism' is generally thought to be the polar opposite of 'mystical' religious practice. Then Dylan declares *...Goodbye Jimmy Reed, God speed/ Thump on the Bible, proclaim a creed!...* With his tongue firmly in his cheek, he celebrates this new 'cult' as if it is a sectarian branch of Protestantism - the branch, perhaps, that 'Van the Man' might choose to follow.

We then switch to a different narrative voice. This may be an intervention by the ghost of Jimmy Reed himself, who now seems to be preoccupied in explaining the ways in which he differs from his disciple. We hear that he was told he would never 'make it' because he failed to use flashy tricks like playing his guitar behind his head. In rock music lore such showmanship tends to be associated with Jimi Hendrix, but it was a common stage technique in the early 1960s, which The Monarchs - the teenage Van's first band - were known to use. The narrator boasts that he *...Never took off my shoes, throw 'em in the crowd...* which also refers to the peculiar way in which Morrison used to end his live shows *...They threw everything at me, everything in the book...* suggests the fate of a particularly unpopular stage performer *...I had nothing to fight with...* he claims *...except a butcher's hook...* But he remains defiantly proud in defence of the authenticity of his music: *...I can't sing a song that I don't understand...*

In the final verses, the song veers into rather more tragic territory. We are presented with what appears at first to be a particularly crude address to a *...transparent woman in a transparent dress...* The narrator declares his intention to *... break out your grapes, suck out your juice...* but is immediately forced to admit that *...I need you like my head needs a noose...* If (like the narrator of *Narrow* Way) the singer is trying to 'proclaim the gospel' by indulging in the pleasures of the flesh, he falters rather comically here. It may be, however, that the 'transparent woman' is actually a bottle of booze. Reed was not known to be religious but he was severely alcoholic, which led to his early death at the age of 50 in 1976. After all this satirical over-emotionalism, the final verse is decidedly restrained and respectful. We now seem to have reverted to the original narrator, who is welcomed to Jimmy's home state by a kindly priest: *...God be with you, brother dear/ If you don't mind me asking, what brings you here?...* The narrator replies rather casually: *...Oh nothing much. I'm looking for the man/ Need to see where he's lying in this lost land...* We are now at Jimmy's graveside. The final refrain is: *...Goodbye Jimmy Reed and everything within ya/ Can't you hear me calling from down in Virginia?... Down in Virginia* is one of Jimmy Reed's best known songs.

Goodbye Jimmy Reed is a triumphant distillation of several musical traditions. By eulogising a distinctly secular figure in mock-religious terms, it parodies gospel music in an affectionate way. Dylan's offhand references to his friend and fellow singer-songwriter Van Morrison's history and background are comically provocative but never bitchy or sniping. One can imagine Van having a good laugh over them. By waving goodbye to one of the most prominent blues men of the electric blues era, Dylan is acknowledging that the blues itself is largely music of the past. Yet the celebratory tone of the song also demonstrates that it is a musical form which is infinitely renewable. Despite its intimations of the tragedy of Reed's death, the song is a declaration of the healing power of music itself. Its main message seems to be that a form of music that specialises in turning despair into hope can effectively unite its 'followers' in a joyous affirmation of life itself.

In the grinding twelve bar 'dirty blues' *False Prophet* Dylan conducts another playful discourse, flirting with and satirising various notions that have been attached to him over the years. As with *My Wife's Home Town* and *Early Roman Kings,* he adopts his best Muddy Waters snarl. The main guitar riff and much of the musical arrangement is derived from *If Lovin' is Believin',* a 1954 'B' side by Billy 'The Kid' Emerson. The song is constructed very much in Waters' style, which includes frequent use of dramatic pauses, allowing the singer to make provocative pronouncements. The first and third lines of each verse include pauses in the middle, and consist mainly of short, punchy statements. The second and fourth lines give the singer the opportunity to take off at more length, with lyrical extensions that frequently strain against the formal structures of the music. This slight stretching out of the typical blues format allows Dylan to create space for a series of eye-opening ironic pronouncements. At times the narrative voice appears to be that of Dylan himself, while at others it seems to be a hopeful lover, albeit one with a decidedly 'ghostly' presence. Perhaps we might even imagine it to be the voice of that mysterious 'Chief Commander of the world we cannot see'.

We begin, as so many blues songs do, with a statement of problems, although what the singer describes appears to be a rather unspecific malaise *...Another day that don't end, another ship going out/ Another day of anger, bitterness and doubt...* But already the narrator claims to have some esoteric knowledge which will presumably help him to overcome this *...I know how it happened...* he tells us *...I saw it begin...* As Dylan sings the last line the guitarist 'follows' him with a riff: *...I opened my heart to the world and the world came in...* This is something of an unexpectedly transcendental statement for a blues song. It might be seen as Dylan describing how he was reunited with his poetic muse in his later years. The song describes the process by which the troubles recounted earlier in the verse are overcome. Much of the humour works because of Dylan's unique way of combining poetic and colloquial language. In the second verse he is - in successive lines - flippant, allusive, romantic and down to earth. First of all he gives us a little classical learning - summoning up some unusual 'muses' and then declaring them to be his 'winged messengers': *...Hello Mary Lou, Hello Miss Pearl...* he sings, referencing the 1961 Ricky Nelson hit *Hello Mary Lou* (written by Gene Pitney) followed by *Miss Pearl*, an obscure rockabilly number by Jimmy Wages which was recorded in Sun Studios in 1957. Both songs are examples of 'teen pop' in which the girl is a rather mysterious and unreachable figure. In the next line they are transformed into *...my fleet-footed guides from the underworld...* as the narrator identifies them with Hermes and Iris, the messengers of the ancient Greek gods *...No stars in the sky shine brighter than you...* he declares, emphasising in his serenade that they come 'from below' rather than 'from above'. It seems, however, that the 'messenger girls' may not be the innocent teens of the songs they are derived from *...You girls mean business...* he tells them in the pay off line, with just a hint of lasciviousness *...and I do too...*

The narrator continues to boast about his powers *...I'm the enemy of treason, the enemy of strife...* He follows this with a particularly personal statement *...I'm the enemy of the unlived meaningless life...* This could be taken as a kind of aphorism describing Dylan's entire attitude to his life and art, although it is not really to be taken at face value here as it is being voiced in such an exaggerated way *...I ain't no false prophet...* the narrator reassures us *...I just know what I know, I go where only the lonely can go...* The mention of yet another winsome pop song from the early '60s (Roy Orbison's majestically tearful *Only the Lonely*) tends to undercut all this grandiose postulation. But the boasting continues unabated: *...I'm first among equals...* the narrator exclaims, referring to the concept of 'princeps' first used by Augustus and then by his successors as Roman Emperors - a piece of political 'spin' if ever there was one. By the time we get to *...I'm second to none/ The last of the best, you can bury the rest...* his boastfulness almost takes him into 'Muhammad Ali' territory. This process of 'bigging himself up' reaches a climax when he finally appears to speak directly to his woman. At first, however, he seems to be somewhat aggressively addressing the doubters or enemies who he has just promised to 'bury naked with their silver and gold': *...What are you looking at?...* he begins - a typical way of 'breaking the ice' that aggressive thugs who are spoiling for a fight use. But this is followed by another remarkable flight of fancy: *...There's nothing to see/ Just a cool breeze that's encircling me...* This appears to be the ultimate boast - the narrator is so 'cool' that he is not even visible to 'ordinary eyes'. There is now a suggestion that he is not really there in the ordinary sense, as if he has only a kind of supernatural presence.

The narrator now proposes a romantic 'walk in the garden' so that he and his lover can *...sit in the shade by the fountain side...* The rest of the song appears to consist of a conversation between the two lovers in this cool and restful setting. In an apparent attempt to convince her of his virtues, he tells her *...I search the world over for the Holy Grail/ I sing songs of love, I sing songs of betrayal...* This could be taken as another description of Dylan's working methods, with particular reference to him being an eternally questing (and rigorously questioning) spiritual seeker. But the narrator now stretches his boasting to the absolute limit, claiming that *...Don't care what I drink, don't care what I eat/ I climbed the mountains of swords on my bare feet....* quoting a line from a well known Zen koan. He now appears to presenting himself as some kind of mythical 'superhero'. But he is becoming a little desperate as all his boasting has still not won the woman over*...You don't know me darling...* he pleads with her *...You never would guess/ I'm nothing like my ghostly appearance would suggest...* Again he tries to reassure her that he is 'genuine': *...I ain't no false prophet, I just said what I said/ I'm here to bring vengeance on somebody's head...* Now he seems to be threatening to use his supernatural powers on 'anyone', just to impress her.

The narrative then switches perspective. The voice we hear in the next two verses appears to be that of the woman, who now delivers a riposte to all his exaggerated chest beating. It is as if she has seen through him and has realised that, despite all his proclamations of his great powers, he has no actual substance *...Put out your hand...* she tells him *...There's nothing to hold...* Then she becomes rather bitterly sarcastic *...Open your mouth. I'll stuff it with gold...* she says, mocking all his fulsome boasts. Then she really lets him have it: *...Oh you poor devil, look up if you will...* she cries *...The City of God is there on the hill...* The reference is from the Sermon on the Mount in *Matthew* 5:4 *...Ye are the light of the world. A city that is set upon a hill cannot be hid...* But our 'poor devil' is not capable of seeing that the 'light of salvation' is directly above him *...Hello stranger...* she continues, referring to the Carter Family song, whose narrator is willing to extend love and acceptance to someone he or she has just met. But here this is followed by *...a long goodbye/ You ruled the land. But so do I...* She continues to disillusion him *...You lost your mule...* she tells him *...You got a poison brain/ I'll marry you to a ball and chain...* She seems to be suggesting that any liaison between them would be disastrous.

By the final verse, the voice of the false prophet appears to have reasserted itself. He now makes one more futile attempt to win her over: *...You know darling... the kind of life I live/ When your smile meets my smile, something's got to give...* Then the identities of the narrators seem to merge *...I ain't no false prophet...* is clearly the voice of the main narrator. But *...No, I'm nobody's bride...* appears to be the woman speaking. The final line *...Can't remember when I was born. And I forgot when I died...* is more ambiguous. In *Spirit on the Water* Dylan sings: *...I'm as pale as a ghost, holding a blossom on a stem...* Like the narrator of that song, our 'false prophet' - despite his arrogant and exaggerated claims for himself - appears to be 'fading away'. We may even ask whether he exists at all or whether he is merely a ghost, a shadow without substance. *False Prophet* may be seen as a comment on how certain individuals can be so egotistical that they become mere 'shadows' (who may perhaps only be able to 'strut and fret their hour upon the stage'). Yet the 'false prophet' is not really an evil or devilish character. He is merely fallible, with a tendency to get carried away with his own thoughts. It may be that Dylan - who has on many occasions reacted with horror to the idea that he is a prophet - is portraying himself here as a 'ghostly' figure who is just as 'transparent' - and thus fallible - as any other human being. But the narrative ambiguity in the song suggests that we could all, if given the chance, be 'false prophets'.

In *My Own Version of You* Dylan assumes a comic-gothic persona in a song that can be seen as a kind of 'manual' for his late period songwriting. By the time *Rough and Rowdy Ways* was released, the fact that his songs were partly constructed of quotations from and references to other songs, works of literature and even obscure informational texts had become common knowledge. Now he turns this method of 'reconstruction' into a far-fetched fantasy full of sharp one-liners. There are echoes of the surreal logic of early comic romps such as *Bob Dylan's 115th Dream* or *Tombstone Blues*, but as the narrator becomes more crazed and meglomaniacal, the song takes on a sombre and ambiguous tone. It is packed with allusions to gothicism, Shakespeare, the Bible and classical literature, along with knowing references to popular culture. With his tongue very firmly in his cheek, Dylan presents himself as a Dr. Frankenstein figure, engaged in a search for 'body parts', which he declares that he will soon assemble into a new creation. The music resembles the incidental filler in old horror films or TV shows dealing with 'unknown forces' such as *The Twilight Zone* or *The X-Files*. The repeated monotonous chord sequence is led by an ominous bass pattern which accelerates towards the ends of verses. In style and tone it also recalls Screamin' Jay Hawkins' 'supernatural' hell raiser *I Put a Spell on You* (1956).

The song has a variable verse and chorus structure, which Dylan uses to build up and release tension. Each two line chorus begins with a variant on the narrator stating his intention to 'bring someone to life'. The second half of the first line and the second line are different in each case. Two four line verses are followed by three eight line verses, two more four line verses and one final marathon twenty line verse. This unpredictability helps to maintain a distinctly edgy ambience, as we are drawn into the meandering narrative. The first verse immediately establishes the ghoulish ambience. Dylan's near-whispered semi-spoken vocal and the macabre, alliterative lyrics create an effectively icy 'mad scientist' tone. It sounds as if he is licking his lips in anticipation: *...All through the summers into January/ I've been visiting morgues and monasteries/ Looking for the necessary body parts/ Limbs and livers and brains and hearts...* Already we can tell he is up to no good. The first chorus: *...I want to bring someone to life - is what I want to do/ I want to create my own version of you...* is spookily parodic. The fact that the narrator seems to be addressing a lover, as he does throughout the song, suggests that he is rather desperately deranged. The scenario recalls Alfred Hitchcock's *Vertigo* (1958) in which the disturbed protagonist Scottie (James Stewart) attempts to turn a young woman called Judy (Kim Novak) into the dead Madeleine - who he is obsessed with - by making her adopt Madeleine's clothes and hairstyle.

The song includes a couple of very well known Shakespearean allusions. The narrator declares *...It must be the winter of my discontent...* rephrasing Richard III's opening speech from Shakespeare's play. The mention of 'winter' reflects on the reference to 'summers' and 'January' in the previous verse. Richard is a cackling villain, determined to take revenge on the world for cursing him with a physical deformity. He may be stuck in the 'snows' of his discontent but the clear implication of his opening statement is that his 'winter' will soon be over. Come the spring, he will enact his bloody revenge. The character has been parodied many times, most notably by Peter Sellers, whose hilarious 1964 'recitation' of The Beatles' *A Hard Day's Night* imitates Laurence Olivier's film portrayal of the evil, scheming king (1955). Thus it is hard to take the narrator seriously here, as he is clearly indulging in high melodrama.

The declaration is followed by a series of vaguely threatening statements *...I wish you'd taken me with you wherever you went...* is mysteriously beguiling. But soon it is clear that the narrator is becoming ever more paranoid: *...They talk all night, they talk all day/ Not for a second do I believe what they say...* he tells us, without revealing who 'they are'. This is reinforced by the next chorus: *...I want to bring someone to life, someone I've never seen/ You know what I mean, you know exactly what I mean...* The music rises in tempo slightly here and Dylan pretends to sound just that little bit alarmed, placing slight emphasis on the word 'exactly'. One is reminded of one of the key lines from Joseph Heller's hilarious anti war novel *Catch 22* (1961), beloved of so many 'stoners': *...Just because you're paranoid doesn't mean they aren't after you...*

The narrative then spirals into comic absurdity. As the narrator begins to explain how his monster will be put together, Dylan delivers one of his sharpest couplets ever: *...I'll take Scarface Pacino and the Godfather Brando...* followed by the deadpan *...Mix 'em up in a tank and make a robot commando...* This is so funny not only because of the tongue-twisting diction and the outrageous rhyming but because it undercuts the narrator's supposedly threatening tone so definitively. The gangster films *Scarface* (1983) and *The Godfather* (1972) and the performances of their lead actors Al Pacino and Marlon Brando are iconic examples of popular culture. *Robot Commando* is the name of a children's toy from 1961 game play book and a tabletop game from 1986. But here the reference seems to be to a 'transformer', a popular children's toy in which one kind of figure can be changed into another, just as the narrator is supposedly threatening to transform his errant lover. The next lines twist this all around even further: *...If I do it upright and put the head on straight/ I'll be saved by the creature that I create...* Here the God-like meddling with nature is reduced to the farcical level of the playground.

The rest of the verse spirals off in strange and apparently random directions as the narrator vows to make use of his new 'powers of creation' for magical effects. He makes very spurious claims of being able to get 'blood from a cactus' and 'gunpowder from ice'. The so called 'blood' that appears on a cactus is made up of tiny insects that can be crushed to make cochineal. In Jonathan Swift's great satire *Gulliver's Travels* the members of the 'Grand Academy' are engaged in trying to make gunpowder from ice. The narrator also tells us that he does not gamble with cards or dice - an unusual claim in a Dylan song. Then he seems to address his 'monster' directly: *...Can you look in my face with your sightless eye/ Can you cross your heart and hope to die...* Perhaps the monster, like Frankenstein's creation, is only half-finished. 'Cross your heart and hope to die' is a common phrase often used by children when they require a friend to pledge allegiance to them. There may also be an allusion here to Shakespeare's *Sonnet XLIII*, where the poet enters a dreamy reverie, a world of shadows in which the natural order of things is inverted:

...When in dead night thy fair imperfect shade
Through heavy sleep on sightless eyes doth stay!
All days are nights to see till I see thee,
And night's bright days when dreams do show thee me...

It now seems as if the narrator may be talking to himself, as if he is looking in a mirror. He is clearly becoming increasingly desperate. He explains that he is trying to bring forth a creation which is a mirror image of himself: *...I'll bring someone to life, someone for real/ Someone who feels the way that I feel...* He declares that *...I study Sanskrit and Arabic to improve my mind...* This is a direct reference to events in the novel, when Victor Frankenstein's friend Clerval encourages him to study languages to distract him from his obsession with science. The narrator also promises us that *...I want to do things for the benefit of all mankind...* Thomas Paine's treatise *The Rights of Man* (1791), a key text of the Enlightenment and influence on the French Revolution and the Romantic movement, is subtitled *For the Benefit of All Mankind.* This is also Victor's stated intention in the creation of his disastrous experiment. The narrator then retreats into a moment of self-pity: *...I say to the willow tree "Don't weep for me'"...* Weeping willows' are a staple of many self-pitying romantic songs, including Blind Boy Fuller's *Weeping Willow* (1937), Johnny Cash's *Big River* (1958) (in which the narrator claims he

...taught the weeping willow how to cry, cry, cry....) and the mournful standard *Willow, Weep For Me* (covered by Frank Sinatra on the 1958 album *Only The Lonely).*

The narrator is now apparently in a state of romantic despair. He *has ...no place to turn, no place at all...* But then Dylan delivers another one of his distinctively gnomic comic utterances: *...I pick a number between one and two/ And ask myself 'What would Julius Caesar do'...* Julius Caesar was, of course, no defender of the Rights of Man. His ascension to power brought about the end of Roman democracy. The reference to 'a number between one and two' could be read as a somewhat obscure allusion to the binary concept on which all computer operating systems are based. It can also stand as an image of futility, although strictly speaking there are an infinite number of fractions between one and two. Thus the narrator may think he has no options when in reality he has unlimited choices.

The narrator does, however, seem determined to create - or remake - new life: *...I'll bring someone to life in more ways than one...* he tells us in the next chorus *...Don't matter how long it takes, it'll be done when it's done...* He then proceeds to explain some of the 'tricks' he will get his new creation to carry out. Firstly: *...I'll make you play the piano like Leon Russell...* Russell collaborated with Dylan on several recordings in 1970-71 and backed him at George Harrison's Concert for Bangladesh in 1971. He died in 2016, so Dylan may be paying a small tribute here. But then we get a decidedly odd juxtaposition: *...Like Liberace, like John the Apostle...* The outrageously camp Liberace was a famous piano player and entertainer, while St. John the Apostle was one of Jesus' disciples and was traditionally thought to be the author of both the *Gospel of St. John* and the *Book of Revelations.* He instructs his creation to *...Play every number that I can play...* and then, with a nod and a wink, throws in *...I'll see you, baby, on Judgment Day...* In the lines that follow he extends an invitation *...After midnight, if you still want to meet/ I'll be at the Black Horse Tavern on Armageddon Street...* He ends the verse with a casual invitation to this supposedly Satanic location: *...Two doors down, not that far to walk/ I'll hear your footsteps - you won't have to knock...*

Dylan is now thoroughly enjoying teasing us with both Biblical and Shakespearean allusions: *...You can bring it to St. Peter, bring it to Jerome/ You can move it all over, bring it all the way home...* is another neat series of 'sacred and profane' comic juxtapositions. St. Peter was another one of Jesus' disciples and by tradition the first Bishop of Rome, the forerunner of the Popes. St. Jerome was the first scholar to translate the Bible into Latin. But Jerome is not 'sanctified' here and the phrase 'Bring it to Jerome' is the title of a song by Bo Diddley (1955) written by his bass player Jerome Green. Its refrain is *...Bring it on home, bring it to Jerome...* which seems to be referenced in the second line here. *Move It All Over* (1947) is a comical song by Hank Williams in which an errant husband is refused entry to his house after a drunken evening by his shrewish wife and is forced to spend the night sharing the dog kennel with his hapless hound. The verse ends with *...Bring it to me on a silver tray...* which may be a reference to the death of John the Baptist, whose head was supposedly presented to King Herod in such a manner. This is certainly something of a

'Frankenstein's monster' of a verse. In the chorus which follows, however, he keeps a straight face: *...I'll bring someone to life, spare no expense/ Do it with decency and common sense...* despite the fact that there is little 'common sense' on display here.

We are then presented with another well known Shakespearean allusion: *...Can you tell me what it means to be or not to be....* As with the earlier reference to Richard III, the lines from *Hamlet* - in which he questions the very purpose of existence - are recontextualised. The narrator aspires to be a God-like creator but he is as confused as Hamlet about whether life itself is worth living. He asserts that *...You won't get away with fooling me...* but we know that he is fooling himself. As his paranoia grows we may well conclude that he is talking to himself - and thus is trying to 'reassemble himself'. He then makes two rather hopeless appeals: *...Can you help me walk that moonlight mile/ Can you give me the blessings of your smile... Moonlight Mile (1971)* is a very 'druggy' Rolling Stones ballad about how life on the road can drive one to distraction. The reference suggests, if we did not suspect this already, that the narrator himself is not quite in a 'normal' state of mind. In the chorus that follows he appears to be taking a breath before delivering the extended denouement of the song. He is concentrating hard now: *...I want to bring someone to life, use all my powers/ Do it in the dark in the wee small hours... In the Wee Small Hours of the Morning* (1955) is a moody and atmospheric Frank Sinatra track in which he laments the absence of his lover. The reference helps to establish the narrator as a character who is essentially alone and isolated and whose determination to 'bring someone to life' is a demented fantasy.

In the extended final verse the narrator gives full rein to these fantasies, taking us on an impressionistic trip through history in which the events he relates are only really connected through his own mad logic. The opening couplet, with its very memorable rhyme, sets the tone: *...I can see the history of the whole human race/ It's all right there, it's carved into your face...* We may speculate now that perhaps the narrator is addressing some ancient statue - probably of an idealised naked female - fantasising that he can bring her back to life. This 'gazing into history' is a prominent feature of *Rough and Rowdy Ways*, in which the narrators frequently juxtapose elements of ancient and modern worlds. Or perhaps the narrator is merely staring into a mirror, delivering a desperate appeal to himself. He wonders whether he should bow down in subjection: *... Shall I break it all down - should I fall on my knees/ Is there light at the end of the tunnel?/ Can you tell me please?...*

We are then taken on an extraordinary visionary journey through the 'history of the whole human race'. We are commanded to *...Stand over there by the cypress tree/ Where the Trojan women were sold into slavery...* This is a reference to the aftermath of the mythical Trojan war, in events that were depicted in Homer's *Iliad* and Euripides' play *The Women of Troy*. This is immediately contextualised as being *...long before the First Crusade, long before England and America were made...* Here the tempo of Dylan's voice raises a little, as if the narrator is experiencing some kind of feverish dream. We are now being taken well beyond the bounds of the comic juxtapositions of the earlier verses, as we are swept through thousands of years of history. We are led into the darkest place imaginable *...Step right into the burning hell...* the narrator commands, as if he is the ancient Roman poet Virgil, who appears in *Inferno* - the first part of Dante's 14th Century epic *The Divine Comedy* - as the guide to Dante's own journey into potential perdition and possible madness. *Burning Hell* (1959) is, in contrast, a very powerful blues song by John Lee Hooker in which the singer unequivocally denies the existence of either heaven or hell and declares laconically that *...When I die, where I go, nobody know...*

The narrator is taking us into hell for a particular purpose - to introduce us to two figures who he presents as humanity's mortal enemies: *...Mister Freud with his dreams, Mister Marx with his axe...* He then directs us, with considerable relish, to *...See the raw hide lash the skin from their backs...* Dylan builds up the picture of a completely crazed narrator here with great intensity, using a series of monosyllables to emphasise the delirium in his voice. The insertion of these key historical figures into the narrative in this way is certainly unexpected. We may speculate that the narrator seems to blame all modern ills on the inventors of psychoanalysis and socialist political philosophy. Perhaps he is a raving 'right winger'. Or maybe, giving that he seems to be mentally disturbed, can it be that he has been subjected to some psychoanalysis himself? It may be that he is now recounting his own dreams. One might certainly wonder what 'Mister Freud' himself might make of all this. Karl Marx famously stated that *...religion is the opium of the masses...* and there is little doubt that the narrator is possessed by a kind of religious mania. Both Freud and Marx were (like John Lee Hooker in *Burning Hell)* professed atheists.

In the climactic lines, the narrator seems to be imagining himself as a God-like figure. As his mania rises to a pitch, here the address seems to be most clearly directed at himself: *...You got the right spirit, you can feel it, you can hear it/ You got what they call the immortal spirit...* he proclaims *...You can feel it all night, you can feel it in the morn/ Creeps into your body the day you were born...* He is firing himself up towards the moment at which his act of creation will take place. Now he fully identifies himself with Dr. Frankenstein, declaring that *...One strike of lightning is all that I need/ And a bolt of 'lectricity that runs at top speed...* All of this, however, is clearly just a fantasy. The narrator will never create his 'monster'. In the final lines of the verse he appears to be contemplating murder, or perhaps suicide: *...Show me your ribs, I'll stick in the knife/ I'm gonna jump start my creation into life...* The use of 'jump start' - a metaphor taken from the method of starting a dormant car battery - reveals that his understanding of the technology required for the creation of life is laughably primitive.

After the long final verse the last chorus is decidedly and quite deliberately anti-climactic: *...I want to bring someone to life: turn back the years/ Do it with laughter, do it with tears...* Then the song, rather than coming to a juddering climax, merely fades away. The narrator's mania has now subsided and that he is back on the treadmill of his everyday existence. The first line summarises his intentions and repeats his insistence on taking us back in time, whereas the second emphasises the tragic-comic nature of the song, and of his own situation. The woman to whom the song is addressed cannot, like Judy/Madelaine in *Vertigo*, be 'remade' into the woman he wants her to be. In any case, she has no doubt stopped listening to him long ago.

My Own Version of You is one of Dylan's most effective and ambiguous comic creations. He toys with his listeners throughout, jerking us sometimes violently between comic and tragic perspectives. The narrator may be an amalgam of Frankenstein and Hamlet, fantasising about creating new life but unsure as to whether life is worth living. Or maybe he is some kind of crazed fascistic fanatic, engaging in a Neitzscheian fantasy of bringing to life the first of a 'super race'. Perhaps he is on 'a mission from God' or a servant of the Devil. He may even be a materialist atheist like Dr. Frankenstein himself, who nevertheless tries to 'play God'. Thus the song may - like Shelley's *Frankenstein* itself - be both a warning about the consequences of human scientific aspirations and a cautionary tale about the consequences of both religious and materialistic obsessionalism. However, Dylan's deadpan delivery suggests that it is, like *Desolation Row* or *The Ballad of Frankie Lee and Judas Priest*, essentially a comic or satirical expression of the dilemmas implicit in the artist's position as a 'God-like' creator. As Polonius comments after one of Hamlet's most apparently mad (or 'feigned mad') speeches: *...Though this be madness, yet there is method in it...*

In 2002 Bob Dylan played the main role, supplied the music and co-wrote the script (under the pseudonym 'Sergei Petrov') for the satirical black comedy *Masked and Anonymous.* The film, which was originally conceived of as a slapstick comedy, takes place in a 'parallel USA' which is re-imagined as a 'banana republic' beset by violence and corruption. Images of the country's military dictator are ubiquitous. We learn that there has been a bloody revolution and a counter-revolution. Meanwhile, headband-clad and heavily armed honchos guard every location. In many ways the film can be considered to be a cinematic equivalent of one of Dylan's more complex and lengthy songs and is more like a European 'art movie' than a product of Hollywood. Yet it features a long list of very well known Hollywood stars, many of whom appear only in bit parts. These include John Goodman, Jeff Bridges, Jessica Lange, Penelope Cruz, Mickey Rourke, Luke Wilson, Val Kilmer, Angela Bassett, Christian Slater, Cheech Marin, Bruce Dern, Ed Harris and Chris Penn. All of these actors were persuaded by director and co-writer Larry Charles to appear for basic union rates, in order to have the chance to work with Dylan. Charles was known for his work in the more sophisticated American TV comedies, having been a scriptwriter and director on *Seinfeld* and *Curb Your Enthusiasm.* He later achieved considerable success working with the British 'character comedian' Sacha Baron Cohen in the films *Borat* (2006), *Bruno* (2009) and *The Dictator* (2012).

Dylan himself is not, of course, a professional actor but like other rock stars who have made successful movies (such as Mick Jagger in *Performance* or David Bowie in *The Man Who Fell to Earth*) he is most effective in roles which reflect his own iconic persona. As Jack Fate, he appears in the kind of ornate stage suits that he now favoured as his onstage costumes, complete with his pencil thin moustache and Hank Williams-style 'cowboy hat'. Although he plays the central role he has relatively few lines and generally responds to the longer speeches of others with laconically ambiguous utterances. It was rather predictable that the film received many negative reviews from mainstream critics, who tended to view it as 'incomprehensible' or a 'vanity project'. Although the musical sequences were generally praised, there were many disparaging comments about Dylan's acting ability. Yet few of these reviews appeared to comprehend the essentially comic nature of the film, and of Dylan's performance, whose 'stone faced' persona again shows the influence of Buster Keaton. Like Keaton, his character functions as a kind of reflection of the anarchic and often cruel craziness that surrounds him.

Dylan's particularly idiosyncratic view of American history, in which the American Civil War appears to be a constant presence, is reflected in the movie, which is set in the middle of a present day civil war. The film also satirises various aspects of the rock music business and American media corporations. In a scenario in which there is just one such corporation, controlled by state-sponsored gangsters and known simply as 'The Network', the plot centers around a scheme by a crooked, fast-talking, alcoholic entrepreneur known as 'Uncle Sweetheart' (played with considerable relish by the brilliant comic actor John Goodman) to mount a supposedly massive 'benefit concert' under the guise of raising money for the orphans of the recent fighting. In reality, he is intending to swindle any profits to pay off his gambling debts. Sweetheart tries to convince the gangsters that he will attract the top names in the rock industry such as Bruce Springsteen and Billy Joel, but in reality the only 'star' he can get is Jack Fate. Fate, whose career has nose dived after having been a big name in some indeterminate past era, is currently incarcerated in one of the regime's particularly nasty prisons. Most of the action takes place on a sound stage (which is inside a compound guarded by armed militia) during the preparation and rehearsals for the show. This is depicted as the kind of carnival setting that Dylan alludes to in several of his songs (including *Desolation Row*, *Ballad of a Thin Man* and *Tweedle Dee & Tweedle Dum*) in which various symbolic characters appear and disappear before our eyes. Fate is badgered constantly by a hard-bitten, forceful and very cynical rock reporter Tom Friend (played by Jeff Bridges) who subjects him to a series of 'interviews' in which Friend rambles on in pretentious speeches about the mythology of rock music, including references to Janis Joplin and Jimi Hendrix playing *The Star Spangled Banner* at Woodstock. Fate refuses to respond to any of this, but Friend still claims that he 'has his story'.

The film features several live musical performances by Dylan and his touring band, including a unique and particularly spirited rendition of the Southern Civil War anthem *Dixie*. A moving performance of 1985's *I'll Remember You* is used as a backdrop to flashbacks to his earlier life. A harsh, tense and dramatically stuttering version of the mythic-apocalyptic *Down in the Flood* is counterposed against scenes of violent conflict. There is a sprightly version of the traditional *Diamond Joe*, a lugubrious comic song about a corrupt wheeler dealer not a million miles from the character of Uncle Sweetheart. The climactic and dramatic version of the deathly *Cold Irons Bound* (discussed in more detail earlier) at the climax of the 'benefit concert' presages the new reign of terror of the latest military coup led by the villainous 'Edmund' (named, perhaps, after the usurping bastard in *King Lear*) played with relish by Mickey Rourke.

Masked and Anonymous satirises the media and public perception of Dylan as a 'protest singer' and reflects many of the quasi-historical thematic concerns of the near-contemporaneous *"Love And Theft"*. Despite the action taking place in a military dictatorship, Jack Fate performs no political protest songs. *The Times They Are a-Changin'* is however, performed a capella in a movingly sweet version by a ten year old girl (later to find fame as R 'n' B singer Tinashe) who is presented to Fate by her mother during the band rehearsals. A portion of *Blind Willie McTell* including the lines *...this land is condemned...* is used as an effective backdrop to scenes of homeless people on the streets. In one bizarre sequence Jack Fate encounters the ghost of a blackface minstrel (Ed Harris) who - while strumming his banjo - claims to be Oscar Vogel, a musician who the country's dictator (Jack Fate's father) has had killed for speaking out against him. Vogel delivers this account cheerily, displaying his exaggerated 'gleaming teeth' smile. Fate merely tells him that he has to get back to the stage *...Aah, the stage....* Vogel smiles *...the whole world's a stage...* alluding to Jacques' famous speech in *As You Like It*. Here Vogel plays the part of the ultimate 'protest singer' - one prepared to give his life for a cause. This is not a role which the disillusioned Jack Fate is willing to play. Although Vogel is clearly a ghost, Jack Fate seems to treat him with same insouciance as he does everyone else.

Masked and Anonymous deals with religious and political ideas and beliefs throughout, in ways that are often ambiguous and teasingly provocative. The film simultaneously plays around with various aspects of the Dylan persona. A live performance of *The Drifter's Escape* from *John Wesley Harding* is interspersed with ironic interjections by the supporting characters, providing a sardonic commentary on the kinds of discussions that surround Dylan songs. The song is an enigmatic morality tale with few specific details about a 'drifter' who is 'carried from a courtroom' after a trial. As the judge steps down the courtroom is suddenly struck by lightning and while everybody 'kneels to pray' the drifter makes a swift exit. The first reaction we get is from Tom Friend's girlfriend Pagan Lace (played as a religiously obsessive ingénue by Penelope Cruz) who, sitting in between two mute 'support acts' (dressed as Pope John Paul II and Mahatma Gandhi) explains that *....I love his songs 'cause they're not precise. They're completely open to interpretation...* A debate follows between Uncle Sweetheart and Fate's faithful friend Bobby Cupid. Cupid puts forward a straightforward religious interpretation *...It's about trying to get to heaven. You've got to know the route before you start out...* Sweetheart advances a rather dubious literary and moralistic viewpoint, claiming that the song has a 'Jekyll and Hyde quality' and is written from Hyde's point of view *...It's about doing evil and trying to kill your conscience if you can... It's not like those other songs of his about faithless women and booze and brothels and the cruelty* *of society... It's about doing good by manipulating the forces of evil....* Meanwhile the Pope and Gandhi are seen nodding in agreement with Pagan Lace.

In the next scene, Tom Friend examines a 'sacred relic' - a guitar which Cupid has brought to give to Fate, which he claims used to belong to Blind Lemon Jefferson. Then we see the louche concert promoter Nina Veronica (Jessica Lange) in her trailer, drunkenly turning on a radio news broadcast about the actual physical discovery of hell:

> *.....Geologists in Trenton are digging the world's deepest hole and have reached the depth of thirty miles. Scientists have measured the temperature down there as 3,000 degrees. They have lowered microphones and heard the sounds of millions of suffering souls. Dr. Samosa, at the project management center, has determined that the center of the earth is hollow. "Hopefully", he says, "Whatever is down there will stay down there"...*

The newsreader then blithely continues with the latest weather reports. Dylan's script for the film is, like many of his late period songs, full of religious references, but it is impossible to link these to any specific or conventional system of belief. What can perhaps be discerned, though, is the notion that human beings appear to be controlled by a God - which they themselves have invented - who is relentlessly cruel and pitiless. The powerful opening sequence of the film depicts scenes of violence in unnamed countries, while on the soundtrack a cacophony of voices can be heard in many languages. As the intro to *My Back Pages* begins, a voice emerges that appears to be a rather crazed radio preacher (played by Jeff Bridges). The full text is a little buried in the mix of the film itself but can be heard clearly at the beginning of the soundtrack album. It begins with the statement that *...Man has the mind of God but the body of dust...* This is a clear reference to Hamlet's famous question:

> *...What a piece of work is a man! How noble in reason, how infinite in faculty! In form and moving how express and admirable! In action how like an angel, in apprehension how like a god! The beauty of the world. The paragon of animals. And yet, to me, what is this quintessence of dust?...* (Act 2: Scene 2)

The 'preacher' continues with his crazed pronouncements:

> *...All human kind is a slave race... it was meant to be from the beginning... God does not suffer... He does not feel pain... He is not a courageous God... Human beings can be courageous or cowardly... Neither of these make up any of God's nature. Will Man destroy the earth to move on?... Is that his destiny?... ...Ask yourself a question people... Are you humble before God?...*

At that moment the up-tempo version of *My Back Pages* kicks in, sung in Japanese by the Magokoro Brothers. The song itself, with its memorable refrain *...I was so much older then, I'm younger than that now...* (perhaps the most famous example of 'Dylanesque' paradox) is one which Dylan asserted his disillusionment with his role as a 'protest singer'. We then see a montage of shots of desperate homeless people and the voice of the preacher returns, this time apparently even more demented:

...Or do you not - believe in the one true God? Do you believe God created the slave race? Ezekiel saw the wheel? But what kind of wheel? The cigar shaped hubcap things in the sky? Are these the gods that created mankind? People, there are many gods. It is written in the Bible that there are many gods. Does the Bible lie? These gods left before the Bible was written...

Now the preacher seems to be advocating the theories once popularised by best-selling 'historical investigator' Erik Von Daniken in *Chariots Of The Gods* (1969) in which the prophet Ezekiel's vision of a giant chariot in the sky containing angels was interpreted as evidence of intervention in human affairs by ancient aliens. The rant continues:

...Would you swear on a Bible? I'd swear on a Bible. A book of treachery and murder and genocide. Of course I'd swear on that. And I'll tell you why. The false Christianity that you subscribe to is nothing more than the cult of the virgin... People, it's time to evaluate and reflect on your lives. God has turned his back on this nation. Think about it. What did Martin Luther King get out of the whole thing? A boulevard?...

The diatribe is unfortunately a little hard to make out as it is set against the loud opening theme, but it establishes the blackly comic tone of the whole movie. The vision of America that Dylan and Charles create is certainly one in which the nation has been 'abandoned by God'. This recalls the final lines of *Chronicles,* in which Dylan, having described 'the national psyche' in the 1960s when he was starting out as 'resembling *The Night of the Living Dead'* (a reference to George Romero's 1968 comic-horror 'gore fest') declares that the road he is about to embark on is 'wide open': ...*One thing for sure* ...he concludes ...*not only was it not run by God, but it wasn't run by the Devil either...* Such statements underline the philosophical and aesthetic sensibility of Dylan's twenty first century work in music, film, print and painting. Whereas as a young man he had angrily and eloquently challenged conventional views on race, war and social inequality in 'finger pointing' songs, he now deals with such issues by assuming the 'mask' of a comically self-deprecating persona, such as the cynical barfly in *Things Have Changed* or the desperate party-goer in *Summer Days*.

Perhaps the most bizarre comic scene in *Masked and Anonymous* takes place midway through the movie. Jack Fate has just entered the compound where the concert rehearsals are taking place, in which various 'market stalls' are placed. He encounters one stall holder, an 'animal wrangler' (played by Val Kilmer, in his only appearance in the film), who has various sheep, goats and birds on his stall. Fate stops for a moment and comments: ...*Beautiful animals...* The wrangler then delivers a lengthy reply:

...I'll thank you. But it's God that deserves the credit. They have no time to bother with success or getting rich. They have no fantasies of glory. They don't borrow money to buy things that decrease in value while they own it. See, they're beautiful 'cause they just are. They do what they do. A lion don't try to be a tiger. A rabbit don't do an impression of a monkey. They don't try to be what they're not. Unlike us... us human beings... The cheetah, the tiger, the snake, the monkey, the baboon, the muskrat, the bobcat... the pig that's fat, the hippo, the rhino, the dodo, the honey badger, the slithy toad... each one, each perfect in their own original forms...

This character is clearly another kind of 'preacher', launching into a diatribe which is more about human 'sin' and corruption than the supposed 'innocence' of animals. The wrangler describes man's cruelty to animals in graphic detail, calling zoos and aquariums 'prisons' and lambasting humans as murderers of these 'innocents'. Despite this, throughout his 'rant', he sharpens two large knives, as if he is about to slaughter one of the animals. He continues, without waiting for Fate to respond:

...I avoid looking at human beings. They disgust me so much with all their atom bombs and blow dryers and automobiles. They build hospitals as shrines for diseases they create. Human beings? Alone with their secrets. Masked and Anonymous. No one truly knows them. I see a crack in the sidewalk, a crack in the mud at the bottom of a sun dried dead lake. I count them more beautiful than any human being. You know what I mean?...

Fate nods in agreement:

...Kinda like a curse, isn't it, being born?...

But the wrangler is not done:

...You got that right. That's because we live in fear. Because we know we're gonna die. Animals don't know they're going to die. They have no fear. They live content in the moment....

He now picks up a particularly gorgeous looking fluffy white rabbit, cuddling it and stroking it *...Holds us back, knowledge of death. I say amazing grace indeed...* He places the rabbit behind what appears to be some kind of cooking equipment and swiftly brings a knife down. Fate winces. The wrangler continues:

...I'll tell you something else. Ancient cultures, civilisations, used to sacrifice animals like cattle and rabbits and goats and such instead of human beings. Today we do it the other way around, we sacrifice the human being. Like the Aztecs, like the Incas, like the big corporations. Amazing grace indeed...

At this point Uncle Sweetheart appears and he and Fate depart *...What was that all about?...* Sweetheart asks. Fate delivers the hilariously deadpan *...Guy's into animals, I guess...* and they disappear into the distance.

The scene is a parody of the conventional Christian notion of original sin. The wrangler insists that animals exist in a pure Edenic mental state, as they lack the knowledge of death which comes with 'The Fall' after Adam is tempted by Eve. He also suggests that it is this basic human corruption which has led to the scenes of war and destruction that feature so heavily in the movie. He uses the title of the famous spiritual hymn of salvation and redemption *Amazing Grace* in a rather viciously ironic way, which is supported by his apparently emotionless 'murder' of the rabbit. It seems that the wrangler represents the murderous hypocrisy of humanity. Yet this all proves to be a tease. The camera pans back across to the wrangler, who picks up the unharmed rabbit, cuddling it lovingly, smiling and whispering *...I'm not gonna kill ya...* into its ear.

The scene has little to do with advancing the plot of the movie. It is more akin to a dramatic interlude in a stage play. Yet it does much to convey the film's absurdist and tragi-comic vision of the modern world. As with the earlier rant by the deranged 'preacher' and the radio reports of the 'discovery' of hell, the wrangler's bizarre monologue mocks the religious fanaticism of Christian fundamentalist preachers who can be found on many of America's airwaves, linking this to the continually corrupting power of the 'masters of war'. The wrangler's disgust with human beings as being tainted by original sin is certainly a parody of populist American preachers, conveyed by the comic juxtaposition of 'atom bombs, blow dryers and automobiles' and the ludicrously over the top deprecation of humans as being less 'beautiful' than cracks in a sidewalk or the bottom of a dried out lake. But the speech also includes the line that sums up the whole movie and gives it its title: *...Human beings? Alone with their secrets. Masked and anonymous...* This could in itself be a description of the character of Jack Fate, itself an expression of Dylan's public persona. But now there is a suggestion that the continued corruption of humanity itself is a product of false consciousness.

Here, as in so many of the songs of his mature period, Dylan examines conventional religious notions and finds them to be fundamentally flawed. Yet he does not attempt to provide any answers to such conundrums. As Jack Fate's remarkable voiceover tells us at the end of the movie, as he sits impassively while being escorted back to prison by the military police:

...I was always a singer and maybe no more than that. Sometimes it's not enough to know the meaning of things. Sometimes we have to know what things don't mean as well. Like, what does it mean to not know what the person you love is capable of? Things fall apart, especially all the neat order of rules and laws. The way we look at the world is the way we really are. If we see it from a fair garden, everything looks cheerful. Climb to a higher mountain, and you see plunder and murder. Truth and beauty are in the eye of the beholder....

There is just the tiniest hint of a miniscule Keatonesque movement of his eyes, the ghost of a smile. And then Dylan delivers the final line:

...I stopped trying to figure everything out a long time ago...

This is followed by a recent live (and rather 'gospel flavoured') version of *Blowin' in the Wind* (recorded at Santa Cruz on 16th March 2000), with its eternally unanswerable questions, on the soundtrack.

Jack Fate's final statement is teasingly and comically paradoxical, like a Zen riddle. It suggests that the only way one can 'figure anything out' nowadays is by allowing the struggle for meaning to cease, in order to understand 'what things don't mean'. In the modern world, with its confusing plethora of messages, there is no one definitive truth but only a series of distinct individual perceptions, all which all exist simultaneously. *Masked And Anonymous'* concluding 'soliloquy' thus conveys a particular kind of post modern existential philosophy which is as much in tune with our times as 'protest songs' like *Blowin' in the Wind* were in the early '60s. However, the notion that such a statement represents Dylan's actual view of the world can certainly be challenged. Jack Fate is no role model or philosopher. By assuming the cynical and nihilistic 'mask' of Jack Fate or of the narrators of his twenty first century songs, Dylan may be pointing out that it is the nihilism and cynicism itself that is really the problem.

Six: *I Shook the Sugar Down*
Monstrous Dreams and Twilight Visions

...You want to live forever, right Allen? Huh? In order to live forever you have to stop time. In order to stop time you have to exist in the moment, so strong as to stop time and prove your point. So that you have stopped time. And if you succeed in doing that, everyone who comes into contact with what you've done, whatever it might be, whether you've carved a statue or painted a painting will catch some of that; they'll recognize that you have stopped time. They won't realize it, but that's what they'll recognize, that you have stopped time. That's a heroic feat!...
Bob Dylan, Unpublished interview from 1977 found in Allen Ginsberg's papers.

8th September 1993. The Filence Center at the Wolf Trap National Park for the Performing Arts near Vienna Virginia is a strikingly designed wooden amphitheater - all sharp angles - with a state of the art sound rig. It is partly enclosed but even if you are sitting in the cheaper sections on the grass at the back on this balmy evening you can still hear every note clearly. Bob Dylan is performing for two nights to around 13,000 people in this beautiful National Park setting. He is midway through a 31 date tour with Santana, beginning in Portland, Oregon in late August, then zapping across the country, down the East Coast and ending up in California in early October. The two acts are swapping who plays first on a nightly basis. Tonight Santana have opened the show. Virtuoso guitarist Carlos will not, however, be coming out to jam with Bob. Not that he is really needed. Dylan and his band are on quite a roll tonight. The acoustic songs (two from *Good As I Been to You: You Gonna Quit Me* and *Black Jack Davey*, and two Dylan 'classics', *The Lonesome Death of Hattie Carroll* and *Boots of Spanish Leather*) are played with great power and precision. Dylan's vocals are crisp and focused. Later, on *All Along the Watchtower* he stretches out the vowels with great emphasis as he swaps guitar licks with John Jackson while the song accelerates to a dramatic conclusion. This particular touring band had sometimes been criticised for Winston Watson's drums being mixed up too high but in this venue the 'heavy rock' approach works like a dream.

Watson's drums are prominent on the first ever live version of *Series of Dreams*, to which they provide a thunderous backdrop. The song had been recorded for the *Oh Mercy* sessions in 1989, but was not included on the album. When it appeared on the first *Bootleg Series* release in 1993 there was much speculation as to why this musically unusual and lyrically tantalising track had been omitted. In *Chronicles* Dylan complains that producer Daniel Lanois had wanted him to sing the entire song as if it was a bridge section and that he had therefore abandoned it. He reports that he found this musical arrangement 'not healthy'. Tonight's version is certainly full of vitality, with Watson's frantic bongo playing forming a backdrop to one of Dylan's most enigmatic and surreal songs. The verses take us through a series of dream visions. Initially the dreams appear to be buried: *...Nothing comes up to the top/ Everything stays down where it's wounded/ And comes to a permanent stop...*

The use of the term 'wounded' has unusual connotations. It is as if the dreams themselves are somehow alive, like angry beasts trying to come to the surface of consciousness. On the studio recording Dylan sounds rather detached and aloof from the proceedings but here he attempts to beef up the song by stretching out his vowel sounds. At times he seems to forget the words and has to improvise. He tells us that in one dream *...The time and the tempo fly/ They do not exist in any one direction/ Except the one you can see with your eyes...* which does not, perhaps, entirely make sense. But despite the mistakes (if they are mistakes) he succeeds in conveying the essential strangeness of the song. The bridge section is only sung once here, although it does appear twice in some versions. This sends the song off in some 'unearthly' directions: *...Dreams where the umbrella is folded/ Into the path you are hurled/ And the cards are no good that you're holding/ Unless they're from another world...* The imagery is somewhat resonant of the paintings of Rene Magritte, who was particularly fascinated by umbrellas. Dylan uses gambling metaphors frequently in his work, but rarely in such an apparently metaphysical way. The 'other world' is of course the world of dreams, of the unconscious. He then throws a series of apparently random dream images: *...In one, the surface was frozen/ In another, I witnessed a crime/ In one, I was running, and in another/ All I seemed to be doing was climb....* Finally he throws in a boxing metaphor: *...I'd already gone the distance...*

The strangeness of the language, and the narrator's apparent lack of interest in what he observes, give the song a particularly 'alien' quality, as if the narrator is Mr. Spock, unemotionally recounting a series of bizarre events. The contrast between the frenetic drumming and the bizarre nature of what is being recounted marks out *Series of Dreams* as unique in Dylan's catalogue. It is as if the resonant images in the song are very much like a pack of cards which has been randomly shuffled. Dylan gives the impression of not quite understanding what the images signify. Perhaps he is hoping that by performing the song those images will come alive and give us - and himself - some kind of insight into the 'other world' from which they spring.

Many of Bob Dylan's most evocative and original compositions are reflections of his personal dreams and visions. These songs invite us into a dimension where past, present and future merge. They tend to be rich in wildly associative and luminous imagery and often feature symbolic characters and surreal situations. Their most powerful lines have an unforgettable resonance, as in *Mr. Tambourine Man* (1965) when Dylan leads us *...down the foggy ruins of time...* to a place where *...memory and fate are driven deep beneath the waves...* At other times he appears to use such songs to confront, or even to exorcise, his own personal demons. In *I Dreamed I Saw St Augustine* (1968), after describing the famous saint and scholar as having *...a blanket underneath his arm and a coat of solid gold...* he imagines himself as one of those *...who put him out to death...* Sometimes we are not sure whether he is describing heaven or hell, a dream or a nightmare. In a number of his late period songs Dylan uses such dream narratives in a range of different ways - to examine his own inspirational crisis, to reflect on his own mortality and to deliver some profound reflections on modern life in the late twentieth and early twenty first centuries.

Tryin' to Get to Heaven (Before They Close the Door) from *Time Out of Mind* is a beguiling song with a strikingly attractive melody. Dylan has performed it hundreds of times since its release, with a number of varying arrangements. The song is deeply rooted in the suggestive language of blues and folk traditions. The title is a paraphrase of a line from *The Old Ark's a-Movering*, a spiritual hymn from the Civil War era. The narrator tells us that *...I've been walking through the middle of nowhere...* which recalls a lively song of lost love that was delivered with great passion by Dusty Springfield in 1965. We are told that *...When I was in Missouri, they would not let me be/ ...I had to leave there in a hurry, I only saw what they let me see...* lines that resemble the opening of Furry Lewis' *Turn Your Money Green* (1928) *...You broke a heart that loved you/ Now you can seal up the book and not write any more...* refers to the traditional blues-spiritual *John the Revelator ...I've been walkin' that lonesome valley...* alludes to Mississippi John Hurt's spiritually bleak song which uses that phrase as a title. The references to these songs help create a symbolic dream landscape in which - as in *Mississippi* - American geography functions as a setting in which external conditions and internal emotions are merged.

The song is in many ways Dylan's most evocative illustration of the struggle he has gone through in his later years to regain inspiration. The remarkable opening couplet establishes the sticky, oppressive atmosphere in which his narrator is trapped: *...The air is getting hotter, there's a rumbling in the skies/ I've been wading through the high muddy water with the heat rising in my eyes...* The reference to 'muddy water' seems to indicate that we are back in the 'mighty Mississippi'. The narrator desperately tries to recall a time when he had a thriving creative life. But he fears that his connection with the sources of his inspiration will soon have faded away forever. He tells us that *...Every day your memory grows dimmer...* but admits that *...It doesn't haunt me like it did before...* He is struggling to regain even the memory of being inspired. The song proceeds, with the logic of a dream, on a journey through the narrator's memories - some real, some imagined. As he desperately tries to reclaim these memories, the images that appear before his eyes take us deeper and deeper into the heart of his despair.

The state of spiritual numbness that the narrator is experiencing is most movingly illustrated when the action shifts to a railway station, in which he now manifests himself. He stands watching the crowds pass by. With haunting directness he describes how having the gift of being able to pick up on the emotions of others can be a terrible burden *...People on the platform, waiting for the trains...* is followed by the extraordinarily*...I can hear their hearts a-beatin', like pendulums swinging on chains...* Each human being seems to be so 'hollow' inside that the creaking of each 'pendulum' can be heard in this echoey space. This creates another strong image of aesthetic vacuity - of blankness, of the creative spirit being numbed, a feeling of hopelessness which is summed up by the cuttingly incisive ...*When you think you've lost everything/ You find out you can always lose a little more...* which sounds like a common aphorism or perhaps a Zen koan *...I'm going down the road feeling bad...* the title of a traditional song often performed by both Woody Guthrie and The Grateful Dead, further emphasises the state of detachment a creative artist feels when inspiration is completely lacking.

These declarations, however, are so extreme that we may sense a slightly self-mocking tone. Although the narrator is 'trying to get to heaven', it seems, perhaps, that he is not trying hard enough. He now becomes more active in moving towards a resolution. He tells us that *...I'm going down the river, down to New Orleans...* in search, it seems, of inspiration at the source of the blues. He remains full of self doubt: *...They tell me everything is gonna be all right...* he complains *...but I don't know what 'alright' even means...* But then he experiences a vision which transports him across the country into a very dreamy fantasy: *...I was riding in a buggy with Miss Mary-Jane/ Miss Mary-Jane got a house in Baltimore...* These lines recall those of the traditional song that runs *...Ridin' in the buggy with Miss Mary-Jane/ I'm a long way from home...* which also states that *...Sally got a house in Baltimore...* The dream seems to inspire him. His confidence begins to grow *...I been all around the world boys...* he declares, using the refrain of another folk standard *Hang Me, Hang Me*. He tells us that he now intends to 'relive his dreams'. He has begun to move on from his dreadfully 'frozen' state: *...I'll close my eyes and wonder whether everything is as hollow as it seems...* indicates that he is beginning to believe that, by truly immersing himself in the song traditions which have now become his 'religion' he can overcome his creative drought.

Finally he is transported back into the railway station where could hear all those hearts beating. He muses that *...Some trains don't pull no gamblers, no midnight ramblers like they did before...* lines that recall Woody Guthrie's *This Train (Is Bound For Glory)* which proclaims *...this train don't carry no gamblers/ Liars, thieves, no big shot ramblers...* Now, by immersing himself in the mysterious dream world of the old songs, he can ride one of those trains to his final destination. He declares triumphantly that *...I've been to Sugar Town/ I shook the sugar down...* lines that originate in *Buck Eye Rabbit*, another nineteenth century folk song. Dylan seems to be revisiting the state of mind he was in during the mid 1960s, when he could channel poetic inspiration with minimal effort. The notion of 'Sugar Town' as 'a place of inspiration' is suggested by the pronounced use of alliteration. Merely by invoking its memory he has made a massive leap forward. He now realises that by immersing himself in the old songs there is a chance that he can 'open the door' to a new era of creativity. He has achieved the triumphant realisation that everything is not, in fact, as hollow as it seems.

In *Sugar Baby*, another dream narrative from *"Love And Theft"*, Dylan again immerses himself in the argot and locations associated with the blues. 'Sugar baby' or 'sugar babe' is a common mode of address to a lover in blues songs, but is often used in an ironic or less than complimentary way. The 'sugar' that the 'babe' delivers usually consists of sexual favours. The implication of such an address is that the relationship is rather false, based on material gain rather than any kind of love. If she is his 'sugar babe', then by implication he must be her 'sugar daddy'. Thus the term is often employed by singers in a rather scathing way, to indicate a relationship based on exploitation. In Mance Lipscomb's unashamedly misogynistic *Sugar Babe* he complains that his 'sugar babe' - who he is pimping out - is no longer 'delivering the goods' either sexually or financially. So he 'whups' her as punishment. In *Sugar Baby* by the taciturn white Appalachian 'Mountain singer' Dock Boggs (1927), the narrator laments that his lover has left him to bring up their baby on his own. In Dylan's song the repeated and oddly dismissive chorus: *...Sugar baby, get on down the road/ You ain't got no brains no how/ You went years without me/ Might as well keep going now...* suggests that the narrator realises that he can get by perfectly well without her. Throughout the song, he pretends that he is ambivalent about the way she has treated him, but as listeners we are not convinced by this, as his tone suggests bitter anguish and regret.

The remarkable opening couplet: *...I got my back to the sun, 'cause the light is too intense/ I can see what everybody in the world is up against...* pictures the narrator's silhouette being outlined by a halo of sunlight. This suggests that, although he is a very perceptive observer of life, his awareness of the condition of the world may sometimes be too much for him to bear. It is as if he has tried to look back into his past but has realised that it is too painful to contemplate *...You can't turn back, you can't come back...* he tells us *...Sometimes we push too far...* However, the verse does end on a positive note, as he says (apparently to himself): *...One day you'll open up your eyes and you'll see where you are...* Despite being 'blinded by the light' he is still optimistic that he will eventually be able to adjust to the situation he now finds himself in - as an older but not necessarily wiser man. The luscious melody, which is derived from *The Lonesome Road (1927)*, an emotional ballad recorded by Gene Austin and later covered by Frank Sinatra, Bing Crosby, Sam Cooke, Stevie Wonder and many others, helps Dylan inject great longing and self-awareness into these lines.

We are then transported into the historical setting in which the song appears to be taking place. It seems that we are back in the 1920s, during the era of prohibition. We are in a speakeasy, in which stashes of bootleg liquor are hidden. The narrator drawls *...Some of these bootleggers, they sure make pretty good stuff....* Then he adds, mischievously *...Plenty of places to hide things here if you want to hide them bad enough....* We are also told that: *...I'm staying with Aunt Sally, but you know she's not really my aunt...* There is an apparent reference here to *Huckleberry Finn*. Towards the end of Twain's novel Huck lives for some time with Tom Sawyer's Aunt Sally, who wishes to adopt him. Here we may assume, however, that this 'Aunt Sally' is the narrator's new lover, who may well also be the madam of a brothel - which may be where the bootleg liquor can be obtained. He then comments rather sardonically that *...Some of these memories you can learn to live with, and some of them you can't...* The reference to 'bootleggers' is another 'knowing' line which has often drawn a cheer from audiences when the song is performed live, as it can also be taken to refer to the adventurous fans who record Dylan's concerts, often using 'undercover' means to avoid detection.

The following line further anchors the song in the early twentieth century *...The ladies in Darktown, they're doing the Darktown strut...* refers to *The Darktown Strutters Ball* (1917), a popular dance tune made famous by artists such as Sophie Tucker and the Original Dixieland Jazz Band. Its lyrics are innocent enough, with a young man imploring his girl to attend a popular dance competition with him, which he seems very confident they will win. But Dylan's slow, mannered delivery makes the actions of the 'ladies' sound rather more ominous. Perhaps, as this line is rhymed with *...You've always got to be prepared but you never know for what...* these 'ladies' are 'bar girls' who are planning some kind of revenge on him. Or maybe the 'feds' are about to burst into the speakeasy *...There ain't no limit to the amount of trouble women bring...* he complains, now apparently taking refuge in a rather drunken misogynist rant. The following lines *...Love is pleasing, love is teasing/ love's not an evil thing...* are taken from the traditional Irish ballad *Love is Pleasing* (which also contains the line *...I wish, I wish, I wish in vain....* which appears in *Bob Dylan's Dream).* Now perhaps he has sobered up a little and is trying to find some philosophical compensation. But the prevailing emotions being conveyed here are still those of anguish and regret. He may appear to dismiss his 'Sugar Baby' in the chorus but we are given the impression that she has left him high and dry.

The narrator practically begs for our sympathy *...Every moment of existence...* he complains *...seems like some dirty trick...* because *...Happiness can come suddenly and leave just as quick...* He stares down at yet another drink, telling himself *...Try to make it better for someone/ You end up making it a thousand times worse...* He tries to justify all this wallowing in self pity by declaring that he is not the only 'victim' of this 'troublesome' woman: *...Your charms have broken many a heart and mine is surely one/ You've got a way of tearing the world apart, love.... See what you've done....* But then, using lines lifted from *Lonesome Road,* he demands that his 'sugar baby' face a definitive 'last judgement': *...Look up, look up, see your maker, 'fore Gabriel blows his horn....* In these final lines he insists that he will be able to separate himself from the negativity which has been 'tearing his world apart'. The 'sugar baby' may represent some kind of addiction, to drugs or sex. Perhaps, as her name suggests, she comes from 'Sugar Town'. Or she may represent the way in which the narrator has made too many compromises in his life. Although he knows she has gone now, he still misses the 'easy life' she represented for him. But perhaps soon his eyes will readjust and he will be able again to stare into the blinding light which is now behind him and accept that it is truly time to move on from the negative habits of mind which have held him back from happiness.

Scarlet Town, from *Tempest,* is distinguished by a particularly hypnotic repeated melody line which is enhanced by some atmospheric banjo playing from Donnie Herron and David Hidalgo's swirling violin. Dylan's vocal has a pronounced tone of foreboding. The song is strongly related to the traditional *Barbara Allen* - which Dylan performed on many occasions in the early 1960s and which later featured in his acoustic sets in the 1990s. This ancient ballad - which Dylan has performed on many occasions throughout his career - and of which many different versions exist, tells a tragic story of two lovers who 'die for each other'. The two stems planted on their graves, a rose and a briar, grow up and become entangled. *Scarlet Town* is named after the location of *Barbara Allen* and features the character of the heroine's dying lover 'Sweet William'. But 'Barbara' herself is absent. There is no magical or symbolic romantic denouement. The focus is on the town itself, which appears to be a hopelessly corrupt place, of which the narrator is thoroughly ashamed. The colour scarlet is often associated with shame, especially with regard to female sexuality. In *The Scarlet Letter* (1850), set in an early American Puritan settlement, Nathaniel Hawthorne's protagonist Hester Prynne is forced by the religious elders to wear a scarlet 'A' on her dress to mark her as an adulterer. The narrator plays the role of an observer rather than a participant in the action. We are given the impression that he is both 'present and not present' in a place which is partly real and partly imaginary.

The first line *...In Scarlet Town where I was born...* replicates the opening of *Barbara Allen.* But from the outset, images of corruption and decay are foregrounded *...There's ivy leaf and silver thorn...* mentions two plants that will eat away at buildings, giving an apparently pleasing impression, but which will eventually cause destruction. Despite this being the narrator's birthplace it seems oddly unfamiliar to him. Perhaps he is revisiting it after being away for some time. He tells us that *...The streets have names that you can't pronounce...* while its economy appears to be in ruins: *...Gold is down to a quarter of an ounce...* The dreamlike narrative that follows is reminiscent of a film in slow motion. The lines *...The music starts, and the people sway/ Everybody says "Are you going my way?'...* create a bizarre impression of a town in which the population has been brainwashed or mesmerised. One is reminded of David Lynch's surreal portrait of small town America *Blue Velvet,* or Peter Weir's satirical parable *The Truman Show,* in which the main character is being filmed throughout his life without his knowledge in the ultimate 'Reality TV show'.

The suggestion that we are in a twisted version of contemporary America is further underlined by the line *...Uncle Tom's still working for Uncle Bill...* 'Uncle Tom' is a character in Harriet Beecher Stowe's anti-slavery novel *Uncle Tom's Cabin* (1852). He is a virtuous slave who is subjected to terrible punishments by his master yet retains his deferential attitude. The phrase 'an Uncle Tom' has become a notorious way of describing black people who 'kowtow' to the white establishment. 'Uncle Bill' is more ambiguous, but the term is often taken to refer to a rather 'creepy' and untrustworthy relative - the brother, perhaps, of 'Uncle Sam'. 'Uncle Bill' was also a nickname for the Beat novelist - and notorious heroin addict - William Burroughs. *When Uncle Bill Quit*

Dope, which Johnny Cash performed in 1969 on one of his TV shows, is a strangely humorous tale in which the singer's uncle locks himself in a room to confront the horrors of cocaine addiction. Thus the song not only suggests that black Americans are still 'working for the man', but also that they are frequently enslaved by becoming involved in the trade in hard drugs. Sweet William, who we now encounter on his deathbed, may well be a drug addict. Mistress Mary is weeping for him profusely *...Kissing his face, heaping prayers on his head...* But these prayers will not work in this soulless land. The narrator's lament that *...So brave, so true, so gentle was he/ I'll weep for him as he'd weep for me...* strongly suggests that he is in a similar predicament. It may be that 'Scarlet Town' is in fact the US capitol Washington DC, a city which - despite epitomising American democracy - is also a major centre of the crimes associated with the drug trade. In modern America the economy of organised crime merges seamlessly with the established order. *Scarlet Town...* as we are informed tersely *...is under the hill...* Perhaps that 'hill' is actually Capitol Hill.

Having established Scarlet Town as a 'fallen paradise' there is heavy irony in Dylan's use of some of John Greenleaf Whittier's lines from *To Avis Keene,* a highly romantic 'hymn to beauty': *...The palm-leaf shadow for the hot noon hours, And on its branches dry calls out the acacia's flowers...* Dylan's paraphrase of these lines *...Scarlet Town, in the hot noon hours/ There's palm leaf shadows and scattered flowers...* shifts their connotations to suggest that the narrator is calling for 'divine help', with the imagery of 'palm leaves' suggesting Jesus' entrance to Jerusalem, as commemorated on Palm Sunday. We hear that there are *...beggars crouching at the gate....* The narrator confesses - in an obvious reference to Jesus - that *...I touched the garment but the hem was torn...* But any hope that a 'saviour' may arrive to provide redemption is short lived *...Help comes...* we are told tersely *...but it comes too late...*

The narrative continues to shift between historical periods *...In Scarlet Town the end is near/ The seven wonders of the world are here...* the narrator tells us *...The evil and the good living side by side/ All human forms are glorified...* The sub-Biblical language and the reference to the 'seven wonders of the world' seem to anchor us in ancient times, while the last line appears to suggest that Scarlet Town is indeed an ancient city full of Romanesque 'larger than life' statues which celebrate the beauty of the human form. The description could also apply to any contemporary city, full of 'technological marvels', flashing neon signs and giant billboards. 'The evil and the good living side by side' is certainly an appropriate description of modern America. There is a strong sense of individuals being trapped here. Violence, it seems, in cities controlled by organised crime families, is endemic: *...In Scarlet Town you fight your father's foes/ Up on the hill, a chilly wind blows...* But the 'fighting' is entirely futile: *...You fight 'em on high and you fight 'em down in / You fight 'em with whisky, morphine and gin...*

We are then transported into a scene in a 'lowdown' bar in a 'scummy' part of town where perhaps, in reality, we have been all the time. The narrator looks around and makes some suitably lewd comments at the girl to whom he may well have been directing this entire deranged drug-fuelled rant of fake religiosity at *...You got legs that* *could drive men mad...* he slavers, but he seems to be easily distracted - instantly beginning to dwell on missed opportunities: *...A lot of things we didn't do but I wish we had....* After this, the narrator seems to drop all pretence. There is no doubt that we really are in a seedy bar *...Set 'em up Joe, play 'Walking the Floor'* he cries drunkenly, referencing the 1988 Verne Gosdin song *Set 'Em Up, Joe* which itself refers to *Walking the Floor over You*, a hit for country star Ernest Tubb in 1941. Then, in the song's most profane lines he cries *...Play it for my flat-chested junkie whore...* The narrator has finally shown us the depravity of his condition.

The contrast between this description and the imagery in the next lines is striking: *...I'm staying up late and I'm making amends/ While the smile of heaven descends...* All things, it seems, can be 'sanctified' - even a corrupt 'sinner' like himself with his 'flat chested junkie whore'. 'The smile of heaven descends' is a borrowing from Whittier's *The Merrimac*, in which the poet uses the phrase to describe a beautiful lake. It is also reminiscent of the surreal scene in *Alice in Wonderland* in which the Cheshire Cat gradually fades away, leaving only its smile. The notion of the 'smile of heaven' seems to embody the hope that such poor sinners will still be 'smiled upon' come judgement day. Or it could signify something far more sinister and potentially violent. Maybe our amoral narrator is contemplating some act of violence in order to sustain his habit.

The final verse summarises the themes of the song. The importance of beauty, which Whittier's *Avis Keene* dwells on, is questioned philosophically. The insoluble riddle *...If love is a sin then beauty is a crime...* is followed by another ironic use of a line from Avis: *...All things are beautiful in their time....* Here the narrator seems to suggest that beauty - and therefore virtue - can be found even in the depraved state that living in this corrupt town may lead to. The final lines: *...The black and the white, the yellow and the brown/ It's all right there for you in Scarlet Town...* can be taken as another description of the USA, a land of immigrants 'of all shades'. The statement that 'it's all right there for you' may suggest that this land is a place that is open and welcome to all comers. But it may also imply that members of all these races are available to be exploited. In many ways *Scarlet Town* updates the themes of earlier Dylan songs like *It's Alright Ma, I'm Only Bleeding* or *Highway 61 Revisited*, which examined the way in which religion and violence were inexplicably linked in American culture. It presents a surreal, skewed vision of modern America - a land which politicians and movie stars have been known to refer to as 'God's country' but in which, two thousand years after Jesus' entry to the 'Holy City', beggars still 'crouch' on the streets.

16th February 1991. It is the seventh gig in Bob Dylan's eight day residency at London's Hammersmith Odeon. Around 30,000 tickets have been sold for these shows, and many punters will be coming back more than once. Downstairs, the seats have been removed and the crowd jostles forward. Those of us in the balconies crane forwards, but Bob never looks up to acknowledge us. The centre of all this attention is in a particularly reticent mood tonight. Although the lighting is dim we can just about see that he is sporting an outsize green and black check shirt and a rather shapeless white trilby. For most of the evening he hunches over the microphone and his guitar, occasionally mumbling something inaudible in between numbers. On *The Man in Me* he slurs the vocals. Guitarist John Jackson plays a few tasteful solos, but otherwise much of the music tends to plod along. The sound leaves much to be desired, with Ian Wallace's drums mixed up way too high. But the audience does not let up in its enthusiasm, especially those down below who are now getting the chance to see him in a smaller venue than on his previous tours. Even *Wiggle Wiggle*, which gets a fairly energetic outing, gets a cheer. Later on, Ronnie Wood will guest on guitar and the show will climax in the band rocking out with considerably more fervour.

We are just coming up to what we will all later agree is the outstanding part of the show - the acoustic set. For the first two numbers Dylan is accompanied only by Cesar Diaz, who supplies tasteful licks on second guitar. The first song commences with them both strumming away, and the audience can only guess at what they are about to play. It could be any one of a dozen numbers, as the melody line is not clear yet. But when Dylan sings *...While riding on a train goin' west/ I fell asleep for to take my rest...* there are plenty of whoops and hollers. *Bob Dylan's Dream* has been included in set lists since the beginning of the tour but before that he had not played it for twenty eight years, since it appeared on the *Freewheelin'* album. In some of the previous shows he had forgotten whole verses, and muffed and mixed up lines. Tonight his memory is a little better, although he renders *...Many a year has passed and gone/ Many a gamble has been lost and won ...* as *...Many a road has been lost and won/ Many a battle has been lost and won...* Otherwise, he more or less gets through it.

Despite the errors, there is great warmth in the performance. The audience can tell Bob is struggling but they egg him on with cheers. *Bob Dylan's Dream* is a very intimate song. It uses the beautiful traditional melody of *Lord Franklin* (the tragic tale of a brave but reckless eighteenth century explorer who does not return from his quest to find the North West Passage) along with some lines from other folk songs, to express a nostalgic but powerful longing for 'times past' and to lament the loss of friendships. Its narrator is an older man who is looking back wistfully on the joys of his youth. As such, it is an astonishing song for a twenty one year old to compose. But right now the crowd can clearly relate strongly to it. The singer, along with many members of his audience, is now hitting middle age, so the nostalgic mood is especially poignant. If a few words get a little jumbled here and there, that just adds to the effect. After all, 'many a battle *has* been lost and won' over the past three decades...

We remember our own lost friends and missed opportunities, sympathising wholly with Bob as he concludes *...I wish, I wish, I wish in vain/ That we could sit simply in that room again/ Ten thousand dollars at the drop of a hat/ I'd give it all gladly if our lives could be like that...* Dylan 'reclaims' the song in a performance of great tenderness, as if he has had to wait all this time to give true voice to it. Only now, it seems, can he really feel all the sadness being conveyed. He has clearly being going through some difficult times, but is using his engagement with his audience to keep him going by inviting them to share a rare glimpse into his own emotional fragility. Tonight he seems to be drawing considerable strength from them, as he invites us into his personal 'dream world'.

Not Dark Yet is one of the best known and most acclaimed songs of Dylan's late period. Yet it is hardly typical of the style of much of *Time Out of Mind* or subsequent albums. It avoids allusive wordplay and conveys its message in short, direct rhyming couplets. And while so many of Dylan's later songs feature 'hidden' or highly unreliable narrators, here the narrator wears his heart on his sleeve. He is quite prepared to admit his own 'mortal fears'. But while the song takes us to some particularly dark places, the narrator displays an 'open hearted' attitude which draws the listener in inexorably. Using direct and purposeful language, it combines the sensibility of a confessional Shakespearian soliloquy with the poise and elegance of classic romantic songwriters like Gershwin or Porter. Performed in a tender whisper over a repeated pattern led by a quiet little drum shuffle, a chiming guitar and washes of organ, its narrator adopts a tone of weary resignation as he contemplates his situation. At one point he tells us of a letter he has received from a lover, which is presumably one of rejection. We may take this to be the cause of his depressed mood.

The song conjures up feelings of helpless lassitude, tinged with regret and sadness, which have rarely been conveyed so explicitly in song. At times there is a suggestion of hopelessness but - despite the 'shadowy' nature of the emotions that are revealed here - the narrator never seems to despair. The 'darkness' which is alluded to always seems to be some way off. This is reinforced by the music, which suggests a 'dance of shadows' in the late afternoon. The narrator invites us to share feelings which - despite the confrontations with 'pain', 'scars' and 'lies' - are very alluring. The song was performed several hundred times from 1997 onwards. In 1999 it was given a haunting new musical arrangement, together with what was virtually a different tune. It was presented with dramatic pauses, sounding more than ever like a soliloquy - a deep exposition of the narrator's inner thoughts, fears, desires and visions.

Not Dark Yet conveys complex emotions by using simple, suggestive language, including a very careful use of repetition. In the first verse we are lulled into a half-sleepy mood by the alliteration of soothing 's' sounds - 'shadows', 'sleep', 'soul', 'steel', 'scars', 'sun'. The opening couplet sets the scene: *...Shadows are falling and I've been here all day/ It's too hot to sleep and time is running away...* Whereas many romantic songs and poems are set in the evening under the moonlight, here we are in the late afternoon. The narrator is drowsy. He is almost - but not quite - dreaming. He is restless, turning over in bed as he twists many thoughts around in his mind. He seems to be actively seeking the oblivion that sleep will bring. But first he must try to identify what is keeping him awake. The weather, it seems, is 'too hot', but so is the tension in his mind. Time is not 'running out' but 'running away'. He is passing into a seemingly timeless space in which he will replay the events that have brought about his agitated state. Using a plethora of 's' sounds he declares: *...Feel like my soul has turned into steel/ I've still got the scars that the sun didn't heal...* The first image suggests not only that he has 'hardened his heart' but that his inner consciousness is somehow 'shiny' and reflective of his experiences. In his mind he stares into that reflection, ruminates on the 'scars' he has accumulated in his life and regrets that the hot sun - which is now dimming as the 'shadows fall' - has not healed them. He seems to be stuck in this 'late afternoon' of his life, coping with a legacy of bitterness.

Each of the four verses follows a set pattern. In four imagistic lines the narrator's imagination projects him back into many situations in his personal history. Then, just before the concluding line *...It's not dark yet, but it's getting there...* there is a more abstract comment on the narrator's current situation, as he contemplates his past and his future. The first of these penultimate statements *...There's not even room enough to be anywhere...* is a rather awkward, indistinct, utterance. But it conveys how his life and his world have hemmed him in and made peaceful rest impossible. Using a common colloquial phrase signifying a waste of potential, he continues to self-analyse: *...My sense of humanity...* he confesses *...has gone down the drain....* Then he becomes philosophical, delivering what is perhaps the song's most heartbreaking line: *...Behind every beautiful thing lies some kind of pain...* Here Dylan confronts the great dilemma of any artist - the struggle to create beauty out of adversity. In *Ode on a Grecian Urn* Keats famously declares *...Beauty is truth, truth beauty - that is all/ Ye know on earth, and all ye need to know...* In the *Blonde On Blonde* outtake *She's Your Lover Now* the disillusioned lover cries *...Pain sure brings out the best in people, doesn't it?...* Much of the 'beauty' of art - its ability to make us gasp, to 'stop time', comes out of the transformation of pain into beauty. In *Not Dark Yet* the listener comes to feel that Dylan is truly opening his heart up to the world, even if it means exposing some painful 'scars'.

We are then presented with some context: *...She wrote me a letter and she wrote it so kind...* Dylan sings *...She put down in writing what she had in her mind...* We are never told exactly what it is that this lover, who has presumably written the narrator a 'Dear John' letter, has said to him. But his summary of her words is compassionate and sympathetic. He does not seem to blame her for rejecting him. When maintaining this façade becomes too difficult, he tries to stifle his tears, telling himself: *...I don't see why I should even care...* clearly indicating that he is determined to bear the pain. The narrator may pretend that he no longer cares, but the sad, knowing, tone of his voice tells us otherwise.

The first line of the third verse begins by using a fanciful tone which echoes that of the sentimental romantic tradition *...I've been to London...* Bob croons *...I've been to gay Paris...* 'Paris' is pronounced in the 'correct' French manner as 'Gay Paree'. This was a common phrase (in the days when 'gay' retained its original meaning) expressing the idea that Paris is a city in which love, fun and freedom can be experienced. Cole Porter's musical *Can Can* (1953) includes *Who Said 'Gay Paree'*, a song which depicts a lovelorn narrator who, having been deserted by his lover, is very miserable and does not find Paris to be 'gay' at all. Here Dylan's narrator contrasts the 'Two Cities' of Dickens' famous 'Tale' to indicate the kinds of extremes that his life has followed - dark, rainy 'London' representing serious study and 'gay Paree' representing hedonism and artistic freedom. This is succeeded by the succinct *...I followed the river and I got to the sea...* It is unlikely he is referring to either the Thames or the Seine here, but rather to the 'river' of artistic inspiration or 'flow'.

These lines, with their beautifully unforced symbolism, recall the perfect simplicity of the 'throwaway' couplet Dylan once donated to Roger McGuinn to use in *The Ballad of Easy Rider*: *...The river flows, it flows to the sea/ Wherever that river goes, that's where I want to be...* The song was recorded by The Byrds to be played over the end credits of the movie *Easy Rider*. But the most powerful version is undoubtedly that of Fairport Convention from 1969 - with Sandy Denny on vocals and Richard Thompson on guitar giving one of their most impassioned performances. These lines perfectly encapsulated the attitude of the doomed heroes of the 'hippie odyssey' movie of 1969 and, by implication, their whole generation. Dylan never bothered to claim a co-composer credit for the song, having supposedly scribbled the couplet on the back of a napkin without much thought. But these apparently 'random thoughts' may be the most expressive lines he ever wrote, perfectly describing not only the 'spiritual journey' of 60s youth but his own resolve to follow that river - of life, of discovery and of inspiration - wherever it may take him.

In *Not Dark Yet* the watery metaphors are extended as the narrator explains how he has suffered: *...I've been down to the bottom of a whirlpool of lies...* before stating that *...I ain't lookin' for nothing in anyone's eyes...* one of those ambiguous double negatives he is so fond of, conveying a strangely opaque and emotionally distant attitude. This is followed by the song's most openly confessional line *...Sometimes my burden is more than I can bear....* Finally we are taken into the place where his most intimate inner thoughts can be found *...I was born here and I'll die here, against my will...* he whispers. This is followed by the apparently self-deprecatory, perhaps slightly tongue-in-cheek *...It might look like I'm moving, but I'm standing still...* a memorable visual metaphor for the 'stopping of time' that he is experiencing. He is now in a place where his feelings are completely frozen: *...Every nerve in my body is so naked and numb...*

The 'nakedness' he refers to here is very much like the nakedness of the president in the famous line from *It's Alright Ma, I'm Only Bleeding*. It is a state in which all pretence is 'stripped away'. Here Dylan carries the physical metaphor even further, suggesting that it is his 'steely soul' that is now exposed. In order to reach this place, where time and space are irrelevant, he has had to strip himself of his own identity and purpose: *...I don't even know what it is...* he admits *...that I came here to get away from...* In this transcendent state, he is beyond redemption, beyond morality: *...I don't even hear the murmur of a prayer....* Nobody can help him now. He must reconnect with his muse urgently, before the darkness closes in.

Not Dark Yet has often been said to be 'a song about death'. Certainly the 'darkness' which has not yet arrived can be interpreted this way, but it is more appropriate to call it a song about the struggle against 'spiritual death' - which Dylan, using a word beloved of Jack Kerouac, identifies in *Desolation Row* through the doomed figure of Ophelia as the malaise of 'lifelessness'. *Not Dark Yet* is the most direct expression of the catharsis he has gone through in confronting the fear of losing his poetic 'soul'. The song touches a universal chord, allowing us to share the overwhelming feelings of existential dread and doubt that it confronts. Yet Dylan manages to do this in simple but suggestive language. He invites his listeners into a private space where we can share the naked intimacy of his feelings, even if we - as well as the singer himself - may be uncertain as to what those feelings really are.

Red River Shore was perhaps the major revelation among all the tracks released on *Tell Tale Signs*. An outtake from the *Time Out of Mind* sessions, it had been unheard since its recording some eleven years before. Two takes, which are almost identical lyrically, are presented. But although the song may be 'unfinished' in terms of production - the sound effects that characterise Daniel Lanois' 'atmospheric' techniques are absent - this is not, like some of the other *Time Out of Mind* outtakes that appear on the collection, a 'work in progress'. It is a fully realised piece, one of the most enigmatic and moving of Dylan's later songs and a truly visionary work which conveys intense sexual and spiritual yearning. The version on Disc One may be just a 'run through', beginning with sparse guitar accompaniment and building gradually with the addition of more drums, bass and a particularly atmospheric accordion played by Augie Meyers. But as with the early version of *Mississippi*, the essence of the song is captured most effectively in its 'first take'.

Dylan's singing here is breathily tender and restrained, reminiscent of the intimacy of the original 'New York Sessions' for *Blood on the Tracks*. The effect is beautifully matched to the tone of humility that underscores the unfolding narrative, tinged with a sense of aching regret. Though it is a kind of 'love song', its concerns are ultimately far more transcendent. In many ways it is a classic piece of romanticism, which echoes the nature poems of Burns, Keats and Wordsworth. The girl in the song seems more elemental than real, a kind of spirit of nature who may be taken to symbolise the poetic imagination itself. Dylan uses an authentically mature voice here to create a kind of mystical reflection on the power that memory has on our lives as we grow older.

There are two major 'Red Rivers' in the US, one in the south between Texas and Oklahoma and one in the north that runs from Minnesota to North Dakota. The 'Red River' referred to in the 1949 Howard Hawks/ John Wayne movie is the southern one, while the other is near Dylan's home state of Minnesota. But there does not seem to be any attempt to use US geography in any metaphorical way here. The 'Red River' seems to be an entirely symbolic location, with its name also suggesting blood flowing. 'Red rivers' are referred to in several folk and country songs such as *Red River Valley*, in which a young girl laments that the cowboy she loves will soon have to leave her. This dates from around 1870 and was first popularised in recorded form in Jules Verne Allen's 1929 version (known as *Cowboy Love Song)*. It has since been recorded by Jimmie Rodgers, Roy Acuff, Gene Autry, Bill Haley, Woody Guthrie, The Sons of the Pioneers and many others. Another traditional song called *Red River Shore* was popularised by

The Kingston Trio (who, despite their rather sanitised approach to folk music, Dylan cites in *Chronicles* as an early influence). This is a cowboy ballad in which the sharpshooting hero's love for the girl who lives on the shore is thwarted by her highly disapproving relatives. Although he kills thirteen of them, their manpower eventually overwhelms him and he has to retreat. Dylan's narrator does not face such problems, though he comes no closer to 'getting the girl'.

The song begins with a collocation of extraordinary imagery: *...Some of us turn off the lights and we live/ In the moonlight shooting by/ Some of us scare ourselves to death in the dark/ To be where the angels fly...* Dylan presents life as a choice between accepting the chaotic nature of existence and letting it overwhelm us. The implication seems to be that if we want to live blissfully ('where the angels fly') and fulfill our inner longings, we need to accept the 'darkness' which surrounds us and learn to accept *...the moonlight shooting by...* This highly evocative phrase suggests that a life lived to its full personal and spiritual potential must include an awareness of the impermanence of everything. This is a song about choices, but it is not one in which the narrator necessarily makes the right choice. It is a treatise on infatuation and on entrapment, focused on the narrator's intense love for an unreachable object. He describes a life spent reaching out for someone who is less a real person than a poetic ideal, perhaps a muse, but one who he never has any real chance of getting close to. As the stately tune progresses, Dylan's subdued and poignant performance conveys his sense of ineffable regret in every breath.

The narrator tells us that despite the *... pretty maids all in a row lined up/ Outside my cabin door...* he has not been distracted from pursuing his love. The use of 'pretty maids' from the nursery rhyme *Mary, Mary, Quite Contrary* next to the reference to 'my cabin door' creates an oddly archaic resonance. *Pretty Maids All in a Row* is also a song by the Eagles lamenting the death of childhood illusions. 'My cabin door' is a direct allusion to the celebrated nineteenth century American songwriter Stephen Foster's *Hard Times.* Dylan's sparing and suggestive use of such terms seems to locate the song somewhere in Foster's time, when the log cabin itself became a key symbol of the pioneer spirit - Abraham Lincoln was only one of the presidents who made much of their log cabin origins. *Red River Shore* is also somewhat reminiscent of the wistfully romantic but mournful tone of many of Foster's songs, such as *Jeannie with the Light Brown Hair.* Like the girl from the Red River shore, Foster's *Jeannie* is a kind of lost dream-lover, who is *...borne like a vapor on the sweet summer air...* The lines *... Now the nodding wild flowers may wither on the shore/ While her gentle fingers will cull them no more...* clearly suggest that poor Jeannie is dead. Dylan's language in this song hints at such an elegiac tone, though ultimately he buries even this assumption in mystery. Foster's longing for the dead girl is, like that of Edgar Allan Poe in poems such as *Lenore* and *Annabel Lee,* a stylised approach which is characteristic of nineteenth century romanticism and its preoccupation with transcendent death.

Despite his apparent immersion in this 'far away' world, Dylan constantly takes us back into everyday reality. His narrator is locked into the romantic illusion of 'love at first sight'; experiencing a love so powerful that no other attachment can ever match it *...I knew when I first laid eyes on her...* he laments... *I could never be free...* However, unlike Foster's Jeannie, this girl seems to have no defining physical characteristics. Despite this she has, it seems, something of an acid tongue. After all the narrator's wooing she advises him, rather bluntly, to *...go home and lead a quiet life...* Then we hear that his dream of her *...dried up a long time ago...* He piles on the romantic disillusionment, telling us he's living under a 'cloak of misery', that he can't 'escape from her memory' and that *...the frozen smile upon my face fits me like a glove...* The awkwardness of the metaphor is another one of the song's odd lyrical twists. Here he seems to suggest that he has willingly submitted to the state of paralysis that his memory has locked him into.

The narrator tells us he's *...trapped in the fires of time...* and *...living in the shadows of a fading past...* but admits he *...never did know the score...* and has tried to *...stay out of a life of crime...* He seems to be simultaneously far away from the shore and standing at its edge *...I'm a stranger here in a strange land...* he declares *...but I know I've stayed here before....* and remembers being here with the girl *...a thousand nights ago...* He seems to be trapped in a romantic fantasy, in love with a memory which he is unwilling to let go of. But then the narrative takes some very unexpected turns. He tells us he went back to see the girl once to *...straighten it out...* but that all the people he talked to had no memory of her. Increasingly it seems as if she may have been a figure in a dream. But there is still one more shadow from the past that the singer apparently has to exorcise. In the song's oddest twist of all we are presented with what appears at first to be a reference to Jesus: *...I've heard about a guy who lived a long time ago/ A man full of sorrow and strife/ That if someone around him died and was dead/ He knew how to bring him on back to life...* This may be an allusion to the prophecy of the coming Messiah in Isiah 53:3:

> *...He is despised and rejected of men; a man of sorrows, and acquainted with grief: and we hid as it were our faces from him; he was despised, and we esteemed him not...*

Yet this is not any kind of conventional religious revelation. The weirdly detached language in which it is presented to us - especially the phrase 'died and was dead' - suggests that the 'guy' being referred to is some kind of magician. The lines remain ominously mysterious. Does the singer want 'the guy' to bring 'the girl' back to life? Or is he merely grasping at straws? The way 'the guy' is introduced and then dismissed in no way indicates any leap of faith. All we are left with in the end is an enigma: *...Well, I don't know what kind of language he used/ Or if they do that kind of thing any more/ Sometimes I think nobody ever saw me at all/ 'Cept the girl from the Red River Shore...*
The girl, it seems was a mere chimera - perhaps a product of the narrator's own imagination. But in these last few lines, the entire veracity of the narrative is challenged. Was any of it real? Was it just a dream? Can we really trust our memories? Can we bring them back to life? The singer has obviously been inspired by 'the girl'. She seems to have always been his muse. But whenever he tries to conjure her up she slips

through his fingers, like a ghost. A ghost of a memory... The implication seems to be that only by accepting the truth of the past can we be free from it. Then we can avoid *...scaring ourselves to death in the dark...* and live in fullness of the present moment.

Perhaps the most prominent theme in Dylan's late work is that of the shadows the past casts on the present. Some of his most powerful early songs commented directly on such historical parallels. *With God on Our Side* (1964) presents a polemical and scathing view of how 'religious' propaganda has been used throughout history to justify carnage on a vast scale, ending with the unambiguous conclusion that*...If God is on our side/ He'll stop the next war...* In his later songs Dylan adopts a more fatalistic view of history. By constantly referring to images and phrases from various stages of the past, he contextualises what is happening in the present as a kind of inevitable repetition of deeply inbuilt patterns, as if we humans are acting out some kind of horribly predestined series of negative and destructive impulses.

This is not to suggest that *'Cross the Green Mountain*, another 'dream narrative' composed by Dylan for the 2003 American Civil War epic *Gods and Generals*, is a song about the 'War on Terror' or any of our other modern wars. It adheres strongly to a historical narrative. It progresses slowly, like a stately funeral march, with a sadly reflective narrative and tone. Events are recounted with humility, even tenderness. The narrator does not appear to cast judgements. But a potent and ultimately highly disturbing view of the basic corruption of human morality is presented in heartrending detail. The song is a kind of slow, deathly waltz, dominated by violin (played by Larry Campbell), military-style drums, swirling organ and Dylan's carefully paced, underplayed vocal. At times we can imagine him singing with eyes closed, completely enraptured in this meditation on death and spiritual transcendence. The ragged edges of that ancient-sounding voice set up a tension against the smooth, unhurried progression of the song's distinctive and evocative melody. The voice is of this world, yet somehow not of it. This is highly appropriate as the events the song describes are simultaneously a depiction of grim reality and a terrible dream.

The American Civil War was the first really modern war; the first to feature trench warfare on a major scale and the first in which new technologies such as mines, torpedoes, rifles and ironclad ships were used. Railways speeded up the movement of troops and the telegraph sent news and communications rapidly across the country. It was also the first war to be photographed. War now became a truly industrialised process, resulting in far more widespread and efficient methods of slaughter than had previously been possible. Industrialised warfare creates the opportunity for highly merchandised war-related industries and vast profits for the 'masters of war' who own and control them. Perhaps this is why Dylan appears to view all modern wars as extensions of this model. By immersing his narrative in this period Dylan sets up poetic and historical resonances that make the feelings he expresses equally relevant to the conflicts of today.

The poetry of the song is precise and very carefully constructed. Each line is short and perfectly regular, without any of Dylan's characteristic metre-bending. The language

Dylan uses often recalls that of those late nineteenth century American poets who wrote about the Civil War itself. Walt Whitman's exquisite post-Civil War poem *When Lilacs Last in the Dooryard Bloom'd* might be seen as a model for the deathly dreamscape of *'Cross the Green Mountain*:

...Come lovely and soothing death
Undulate round the world, serenely arriving, arriving,
In the day, in the night, to all, to each,
Sooner or later delicate death.
Prais'd be the fathomless universe,
For life and joy, and for objects and knowledge curious,
And for love, sweet love- but praise! praise! praise!
For the sure-enwinding arms of cool-enfolding death...

'Cross the Green Mountain is laced with quotations from Civil War poets. The phrase *...dim Atlantic line...* occurs in Timrod's *Charleston* (1861) *...The foe had crossed from the other side...* can be found in Nathaniel Graham Shepherd's *Roll Call ...Something came up/ Out of the sea...* recalls Longfellow's poem *Daybreak*, which begins *...A wind came up out of the sea...* Dylan's references to the 'Captain' as *...the great leader laid low...* seems to be a deliberate reference to Whitman's lament for the murder of Abraham Lincoln *O, Captain, My Captain!* The lines in the song's penultimate stanza, where the mother is offered false hope about the son's recovery directly recall Whitman's *Come Up From the Fields Father:*

...A strange hand writes for our dear son -
O stricken mother's soul!
All swims before her eyes- flashes with black- she catches the main words only;
Sentences broken - gun-shot wound in the breast, cavalry skirmish, taken to hospital,
At present low, but will soon be better.
Alas poor boy, he will never be better.
While they stand at home at the door he is dead already...

Other non-Civil War references pepper the song *...Stars fell over Alabama...* refers to the title of a 1934 jazz standard which was recorded by Louis Armstrong, Ella Fitzgerald, Frank Sinatra and Ricky Nelson. The phrase recalls a meteor shower which occurred in 1833. It has now been incorporated into Alabama license plates. Dylan's *...Heaven blazing in my head...* recalls W. B. Yeats' poem *Lapis Lazuli*, written about the coming of World War One, which includes the line *....Heaven blazing into the head....* There are also several Biblical allusions. A beast 'rises from the sea' in *Daniel* 7 and another, the 'Great Beast' in *Revelations* 13. The phrase *...all must yield/ To the Avenging God...* recalls Nahum 1:2:

... The LORD is a jealous and avenging God; the LORD is avenging and wrathful; the LORD takes vengeance on his adversaries and keeps wrath for his enemies...

'Cross the Green Mountain places us within a ruined, devastated landscape. Although the narrator - a soldier on a battlefield in his death throes - has very pious hopes and dreams, the God which rules his world is an explicitly cruel one. Only death, like the 'lovely and soothing death' in Whitman's poem, will provide relief. All civilised behaviour is being swept aside by the hand of a malicious deity. Yet the tone is wistful, regretful, without a shred of anger. The narrator sounds like he has accepted his inevitable fate. But this otherworldly detachment only adds to the power of the bitter indictment of human corruption that the song presents. There are no graphic descriptions of carnage, but much betrayal and disillusionment. As the narrator descends into the spirit world beyond the 'green mountain' his hopeless resignation to his destiny only throws the harsh revelations he experiences into sharp relief.

We begin with the narrator lying by a stream, having already 'crossed the green mountain', which may be a real or a symbolic geographical feature. He now appears to be separated from his comrades. As he awaits his end, he is in a state of fevered delirium *...Heaven blazing in my head/ I dreamt a monstrous dream...* This remarkable and perhaps contradictory image sets the tone, as normally fire is associated with hell, not heaven. It seems that the soldier is fully expecting to 'meet his maker' but is terrified that 'heaven' will be no different to the burning hell he has been exposed to on earth. The use of 'monstrous' suggests that whatever it is that *...came up out of the sea....* is some kind of Great Beast or Leviathan that has *...Swept through the land of the rich and the free....* The USA is often referred to patriotically as the land of 'the brave and the free'. The choice of words here suggests great cynicism about how the ideals of America's founding fathers have been corrupted. The Great Beast we see rising here can also be taken to symbolise the 'monsters' that humanity's folly may create.

In the following lines the narrator's closeness to death is made explicit. He is begging for its sweet release *...I look into the eyes...* he tells us *...of my merciful friend...* Death, with its 'cool enfolding arms', is that 'merciful friend' who will soon release him, not only from his physical pain but also from his sickening awareness of the awful nature of the great insanity that rages around him. He can taste the *...sad yet sweet...* memories of his life on his tongue, but already he is looking forward to a release into heaven. Yet right now he seems to be subsumed in a kind of hellish scenario where *...altars are burning...* The line *...the foe has crossed over from the other side...* while it may on one level be a description of the movements of the enemy, also seems to suggest that the Devil is walking the Earth *...We can feel them come...* he tells us, as if this is an enemy 'within' as well as without.

The fourth verse is perhaps the most graphic and evocative and suggestively powerful in the song *...Across the dim Atlantic line/ The ravaged land lies for miles behind...* conjures up a vision of a line of troops in the distance with a devastated landscape behind them *...The light's coming forward and the streets are broad/ All must yield to the avenging God...* conveys deep existential fear. Is this 'avenging God' the same 'Great Beast' which comes out of the sea in the first verse? Is it a kind of 'God of War'? It certainly seems to be the kind of God that the pious narrator believes in - one whose main purpose is to enact vengeance and destruction. The final line seems to be the key to the whole song. It is suggested that the state of war is one which has been brought about by human belief in a vicious, unforgiving deity who accepts and even justifies mass murder. The Old Testament Jehovah, perhaps, who slaughters the first born... or the perverted version of Allah who rewards suicide bombers with an eternity of bliss for destroying the infidel... The fact that the narrator seems to accept such a deity so calmly only adds to how chilling these lines are, especially in the post-9/11 context.

The narrator prepares for death with a great degree of self-possession *...The world is old/ the world is gray...* suggests that he knows there is no black and white morality here. At no point does he say that one side in the war is more evil than the other. We do not even know which side he is fighting for. He begins to wax philosophical: *...Lessons of life/ Can't be learned in a day...* he tells us, as he begins to drift into listening to *...the music that comes from a far better land...* Already, heaven is calling him. His consciousness begins to drift and splinter. In the next verse he tells us the story of the 'Great Leader' who is killed by his own men. The reference seems to be to the Confederate General 'Stonewall' Jackson - the main character in *Gods And Generals* - who in real life was the accidental victim of so-called 'friendly fire' *...Close the eyes of our Captain, peace may he know...* the narrator prays. In the next four verses we hear him continuing to prepare himself to meet his maker *...I feel that the unknown world is so near...* he tells us.

As if staking out his place in 'the above' (or at least reassuring himself that this is where he's headed) the narrator asserts that he was always *...loyal to truth and to right...* and that *...virtue lives and cannot be forgot...* He contrasts himself against those who have *...blasphemy on every tongue...* and tells himself, despite his predicament to *...Serve God and be cheerful...* while paying tribute to his brave companions, who *...never dreamed of surrendering/ They fell where they stood...* Thus, in a very conventional way, he associates salvation with martial virtues. He tries to picture himself ascending to heaven *...Stars fell over Alabama/ I saw each star/ You're walking in dreams/ Whoever you are...* contrasting this with a description of the frozen ground he lies on and his knowledge of the finality of defeat: *...the morning is lost...*

In the penultimate - and surely the most tragic - verse, a mother receives a telegram saying her son is wounded but that he will recover soon. Given the context of where the verse comes, however, we can be pretty sure that this is the soldier's own mother *...But he'll never be better...* he tells us mournfully, now so detached that he appears to be looking down upon his own body *...He's already dead...* The last verse sees our hero ascending into heaven, being *...lifted away/ In an ancient light/ That is not of day...* The final, rather strange and ambiguous lines: *...They were calm, they were blunt/ We knew them all too well/ We loved each other more than we ever dared to tell...* seem to imply that the war has been fought between members of the same family (which in the American Civil War was often the case). This adds a poignant coda to the epic lament, suggesting just how unnecessary the entire conflict was.

It may seem odd that such a major piece of work was hidden away on a relatively obscure film soundtrack. But *'Cross the Green Mountain* was, like Dylan's other 'soundtrack songs', specifically written for a purpose - to illustrate the theme of a particular film.. Although it could be called 'anti-war', this is certainly not a 'protest song'. It may have resonances with current events but it is more concerned with deep, universal themes. On one level it is a meditation on death. The narrator's humble piety is immensely moving, as is his awe at the power of the 'avenging God'. The biggest tragedy here is that the soldier dies, like so many before him, believing that what he has taken part in has been a virtuous and worthwhile exercise. His inherent goodness as a person and his faith in 'divine justice' has been twisted and perverted in the service of those whose cause he has died for. But the question this 'monstrous dream' of a song poses is whether this is a cruel, vengeful war God, who rewards military virtue and who glories in mass carnage, or a merciful God who will reward him for his humility and simple faith. Whether 'God is on his side' is up to the listener to decide.

18th November 2005. Outside it's a grey, drizzly evening on the outskirts of Birmingham, Britain's second metropolis. The National Exhibition Centre has been described by waggish locals as 'a bit of a bloody shed'. Opened in 1973, at the height of the period of what some unkind critics called 'brutalist' architecture, it looks a little bit like a cross between a football stadium and a giant warehouse. Most people arrive on buses from the city centre, which spew them out into vast corridors that lead to even vaster corridors. To say it's not exactly a funky venue would be an understatement. The concert hall itself is cavernous and echoey. It holds 15,000 seated punters and is rigorously policed by uniformed security guards who are almost all squat, bald and notoriously aggressive if you should as much as step an inch away from your allotted seat. They stand facing away from the stage, surveying the crowd in case anyone tries to take a photo, record the show or get too excited and jump to their feet in enthusiasm. There will be no dancing in the aisles tonight, by order of the management.

Despite this, Bob Dylan and his band have played a lively set, including a string of '60s favourites. Bob crouches over his electronic keyboard, which is very low down in the mix, swaying slightly from side to side as he sings. He is dressed in an immaculate black suit with neat red rings on the cuffs, a white shirt and a studded black trilby. When the band kicks into an acoustic number and he sings *...Ain't it just like the night to play tricks when you're trying to be so quiet...* the audience respond with delight. *Visions of Johanna*, which appeared on *Blonde on Blonde* in 1966, has long been acclaimed by critics and fans as being one of Dylan's greatest songs. It is a tour de force of resonant imagery with some stunningly surreal poetic leaps - one of Dylan's most 'visionary' compositions. But because of the many extended, tongue twisting lines it contains it is a difficult song to sing. There have been few outstanding cover versions and it has dropped in and out of Dylan's shows over the years. It is not a song that he would wish to attempt every night.

Tonight, however, everything clicks into place. Dylan's vocals are focused and precise and full of little nuances that add emphasis in all the right places. While many of his longer songs are often shortened for live performance, here not a syllable is missed. He plunges straight into four long verses with only a tiny musical break between each one. Before the final verse Denny Freeman adds some highly lyrical guitar licks. But it is Dylan's phrasing that carries the performance. We hear that *...The ghost of 'lectricity HOWLS in the bones of her face...* He stretches out the word *...infinity...* and then gives us a slight pause before*...goes up on trial...* after which, the delivery of *...voices echo this is what salvation must be like after a while...* sound smoothly paced and natural. When he gives us that great line about the Mona Lisa he places a pronounced emphasis on certain words *...Mona LISA musta had the highway* BLUES (pause) ... *you can tell by the way she* SMILES... It is one of those mesmerising performances when Dylan reaches out, grabs a song and breathes new life into it. It lasts for eight and a half minutes but while we are in the grip of this master storyteller, consummate actor and unique singer, time really does appear to dissolve.

Two of the songs from *Rough and Rowdy Ways, Crossing the Rubicon* and *Key West*, have particularly pronounced dream-like qualities. The identities of their narrators seem to be constantly shifting in space and time. On occasions it appears that Dylan's authentic voice is coming through. At other times we hear the voice of a historical character. The narratives of the songs take us in and out of various geographical locations, but the real journeys being undertaken are in the minds of the narrators. *Crossing the Rubicon* is a slow twelve bar blues which depicts an intense internal struggle. Its narrator wrestles with uncomfortable and sometimes contradictory emotions. In contrast *Key West*, which is the next track on the album, is a trance-like, meandering and meditative piece whose narrator seems to have found some kind of personal resolution. The two songs depict Dylan's own inner struggles with his inspirational muse and his eventual coming to terms with her essential nature.

Crossing the Rubicon is constructed in a very regular pattern, with nine verses of four lines each. Dylan's vocal is especially nuanced, depicting the conflicting extremes of decisiveness and indecision between which the narrator is continually being thrown. The narrator appears to be planning some kind of revenge, which he describes in particularly bloody terms. He seems to be experiencing considerable trepidation with regard to the decisions he needs to make but continually stresses that his actions have been forced upon him. In the first three lines of every verse he struggles with his conscience and tries - with varying degrees of success - to justify himself. He is forever brooding on the potential consequences of his actions. His continual insistence that he has 'crossed that Rubicon' is so overstated, however, that it may be that he is merely indulging feverish fantasies.

The title refers to a well documented historical event when Julius Caesar made the decision to cross the river that marked the boundary of the territory ruled directly by Rome. Caesar knew that his decision would lead to civil war. The triumph of his troops over those of Pompey led to the extinction of the Roman republic, which had existed for over 400 years, and the creation of a dictatorship which later became a massive and long lasting empire. Thus the crossing over the river came to represent a crucial moment at which the future destiny of Rome and its dominions was decided. The phrase has since come to symbolise any situation in which a potentially life changing decision has to be made. The first lines of the song: *...I crossed the Rubicon on the 14th day of the most dangerous day of the year/ At the worst time, at the worst place, that's all I seem to hear...* are delivered in Dylan's characteristic 'blues snarl'. The way he crams in the syllables in the first line indicates a certain level of panic, as if he is worried that his actions may have indeed been rather rash. In the second line he slows down a little while he complains that others have been trying to persuade him that the time is not right to act. Thus the song begins with a deliberate statement of defiance. In reality five years passed between the crossing and the murder. Caesar was, however, killed on the Ides of March (the 15th) so perhaps historical time has been collapsed here for dramatic purposes. The implication seems to be that the narrator will be in some kind of imminent danger as soon as he takes his 'fatal action'.

When Dylan follows this with*...I got up early so I could greet the Goddess of the Dawn...* he makes an odd little 'gulping' sound in anticipation. So far his pronouncements have been consistent with the 'Julius Caesar' persona. One might well imagine Caesar beginning his campaign with an invocation to Aurora, the Roman Goddess of the Dawn. But soon the narrator is already adding various mythical and literary associations: *...I painted my wagon, abandoned all hope and I crossed the Rubicon...* To 'paint one's wagon' is an expression of readiness for action, popularly associated with the 1969 movie of the same name, adapted from Lerner and Loewe's 1951 musical. In Dante's *Inferno* the words *...Abandon all hope ye who enter here...* are inscribed on the Gates of Hell. It is already clear that the Rubicon is a symbolic rather than a real location. In a couplet rich in alliteration, we are informed that *...the Rubicon is a Red River, going gently as she flows/ Redder than your ruby lips and the blood that flows from the rose...* The first line, with its capitalised 'Red River', sets up an association with *Red River Shore*'s mysteriously indefinable heroine. The second line associates the image of 'ruby lips' - a common cliché in romantic songs - with Blake's paean to sexual corruption *The Sick Rose.* The narrator seems to be clearly stating that the river he has crossed represents a torrent of sexual jealousy. He also seems to be suggesting that the river will one day run with the blood of his enemies. This recalls Macbeth's confession that:

...I am in blood
Steeped in so far that, should I wade no more,
Returning were as tedious as go o'er...

The following lines are among the most resonant in the song, mixing wry humour with terror of the unknown: *...Three miles north of purgatory - one step from the great beyond...* takes us back into 'hellish' territory *...I prayed to the cross, I kissed the girls and I crossed the Rubicon...* is a memorable juxtaposition of the sacred and the profane. Now the narrator seems to be a soldier again, preparing to go off to war. One can almost imagine him as a medieval Crusader. But Crusaders were meant to kiss the cross, not 'the girls', before battle. The lightly ironic tone of the line is more suggestive of a GI departing for World War Two. We may already suspect that the narrator's positioning himself as some kind of military figure is a fantasy. In the manner of so many blues songs, a pattern of loose associations is set up. The narrator is trying to convince us that he is a powerful figure capable of wreaking revenge on his enemy. But we sense that the boasting and strutting will have no effect.

The narrator positively wallows in his own degradation, while continuing to mutter threats. At first he is relatively calm and philosophical *...What are these dark days I see in a world so badly bent?...* he asks. The phrase 'badly bent' appears in Little Walter's 1964 tongue in cheek lament *Dead Presidents* (written by Billy 'the Kid' Emerson and Willie Dixon) which mentions the death of William McKinley, whose assassination in 1901 begins *Key West*. The narrator appears to be sinking into a mood of regret: *...How can I redeem the time - the time so idly spent...* The tempo of the song increases as the narrator then sinks into a fit of jealousy: *...I feel the bones beneath my skin and they're trembling with rage...* he tells us. Then he becomes especially petulant: *...I'll make your wife a widow, you'll never see old age...* and growls his general disillusionment with all humanity: *...Show me one good man in sight that the sun shines down upon...* He tries to convince us that he is ready for the coming battle with his usurper: *...If I survive then let me love, let the hour be mine...* before apparently attempting to set up a meeting place for the coming confrontation: *...Take the high road - take the low - take the one you're on...* But these lines, which come from the Scottish ballad *The Bonnie Banks o' Loch Lomond*, tend to undermine the seriousness of his declarations.

At the end of each verse the narrator maintains his determination to 'cross the Rubicon'. He states that *...I embraced my love and put down my head... ...I pawned my watch and I paid my debts...* and *...I poured my cup and I passed it along...* This suggests that the narrator is steeling himself for some kind of transformation. It is as if his soul, or his inner conscience, is at war with itself. At times he appears to take on the persona of an ancient Roman general, whereas at others he slips into the realm of the mundane. His 'crossing' may be taken to symbolise various difficult decisions. The mention of sharing a cup references the Last Supper, as if the narrator is comparing himself to Jesus before his trial and crucifixion. But the earlier statements of intent, such as 'pawning a watch' have already undercut such intimations.

The narrator continues to attempt to summon up the courage to take the decisive step that he seems to be finding so difficult. He makes a particularly strong accusation: *...You defiled the most lovely flower in all of womanhood...* which he follows with *...Others can be tolerant, others can be good...* strongly inferring that the object of his revenge is a vicious rapist to whom he will show no mercy. He gets down to some gruesome specifics: *...I'll cut you up with a crooked knife and I'll miss you when you're gone...* But he does not sound angry here, merely world weary *...I stood between heaven and earth...* he sighs *...and I crossed the Rubicon...* Meanwhile, the insults continue: *...You won't find any happiness here, no happiness or joy...* is hardly surprising in this context. But the object of the address appears to have shifted: *...Go back to the gutter and try your luck...* he sings *...find yourself some nice young pretty boy...* It seems that he is now addressing the woman who has left him, but in a tone that is almost childishly spiteful. By now we have heard many threats, but there is little evidence that any of them have been, or really will be, carried out.

The tone of weariness is sustained until the end of the song, even as the narrator tries desperately to summon up some much needed courage: *...I feel the holy spirit inside...* he declares *...and see the light that freedom gives/ I believe it's in the reach of every man who lives...* He appears to have got the threats out of his system but now he is clutching at straws. There is little likelihood of him wreaking the revenge he is promised. He sounds broken, defeated *...Keep as far away as possible...* he mutters, as if giving himself an instruction that negates everything he has said so far *...it's darkest 'fore the dawn...* In quoting this well known if entirely fallacious proverb, which also appears in *Meet Me in the Morning* on *Blood on the Tracks,* he now appears to be in fear of the consequences of his actions. At the end of the line Dylan mutters a tiny and almost inaudible *...Oh Lord!...* which sounds like a cry of despair. The line that follows tells us that *...I turned the key and broke it off. And I crossed the Rubicon...* as if he is indeed attempting to open a gate rather than cross a river.

In the last verse the narrator finally addresses a character by name: *...Mona baby, are you still in my mind, I truly believe that you are...* This is a considerable surprise, given that Mona is a character who is briefly mentioned in 1966's surreal odyssey *Stuck Inside of Mobile (With the Memphis Blues Again)* where she advises the singer to avoid the 'railroad men' who *...drink up your blood like wine... Stuck Inside of Mobile* consists of a stream of consciousness of bizarrely comic images, all relating to its narrator being trapped 'in the wrong place at the wrong time'. In that song Mona seems to represent ungrounded fears or paranoia. Now it seems she is standing at the singer's shoulder again. Perhaps the entire discourse of the song has been a product of the narrator's paranoia. After all, as he tells us *...Couldn't be anyone else who's come with me this far...* It may be tempting to believe that this is the voice of Dylan himself, looking back over his inner emotional and creative life. In order to begin to be creative one must always be prepared to 'cross the Rubicon'. On the other side of that river one may find inspiration or love or merely despair. But sometimes it seems that one may need an 'army' in support to have the strength to make the crossing. In the final haunting lines of the song Dylan sounds almost unbearably fatigued, as if he is about to drift into a very troubled 'series of dreams': *...The killing frost is on the ground...* he sighs *...and the autumn leaves are gone...* Then there is a return to 'looking east' where the sun will rise, although by now darkness has clearly descended: *...I lit the torch and I looked to the east and I crossed the Rubicon...*

While *Stuck Inside of Mobile* - which was written during a period when Dylan found that inspiration could come easily to him - is a playful series of surreal jests about not being able to escape from a 'hellish' situation, in *Crossing the Rubicon* Dylan - like the protagonist of *Can't Wait* - trembles at the entrance to a hell of his own making. In *Mississippi* Dylan had written about the fear of 'drowning' in doubts about his own abilities. Here he again confronts his fear of losing touch with his sources of inspiration. No longer so sure that he can summon up the 'freewheeling' imagery of songs like *Stuck Inside of Mobile*, he confronts a kind of existential terror. He is still 'three miles north of purgatory', contemplating the mysteries of the 'undiscovered country' in which new creations can be forged. He realises that he has no choice but to continue crossing that river to explore 'the great beyond'. To fail to do so would be a kind of spiritual and creative death. So he will have to wake up every morning, pay his respects again to the goddess of the dawn and continue to make that crossing over and over again, no matter how difficult and painful that process may be. The track ends with a tortured blues guitar solo from Charlie Sexton which expresses the struggle that the song communicates.

Key West (Philosopher Pirate) provides a complete contrast in mood. It is delivered in a soft, almost whispered, voice over a slow, dreamy melody. The instrumentation is low key, with washes of minimal percussion and acoustic guitars behind an almost ever-present accordion. Despite the unequivocal ending of the previous song, its protagonist, who declares that he is *...searching for love and inspiration...* appears to have made a final crossing of his Rubicon and has ended up in what appears to be a sun-kissed paradise, a place where his dreams will become real. Key West is an island at the tip of Florida and is located at the southernmost tip of the continental United States, marking the dividing line between the Atlantic Ocean and the Gulf of Mexico. As well as being a major tourist attraction it was adopted as a home by Ernest Hemingway, Tennessee Williams, Wallace Stevens, Shel Silverstein and many other writers who had also come 'looking for inspiration'. Like his distinguished predecessors, the 'Philosopher Pirate' (which could be an apt name for Dylan himself) appears to be contemplating how he might be seen by posterity. As the first chorus proclaims: *...Key West is the place to be/ If you're looking for immortality...*

The details we are given of Key West are highly impressionistic. Time and space seem to bend in miraculous ways. The song meanders through its fourteen verses, as if the narrator is throwing out random thoughts at us as he drives through the streets, sometimes taking on the role of a 'tourist guide'. He informs us that he is listening to a 'pirate radio station' which is *...coming out of Luxembourg and Budapest...* It is highly unlikely that he could be picking up European radio stations from Florida and neither Radio Luxembourg or Radio Budapest - though both famous broadcasting institutions - are illegal 'pirates'. But this, of course, is a dream. The 'pirate radio station' is an imaginary construct, a channel through which our protagonist picks up signals that may emanate from anywhere in the universe. The first song being played on his car stereo appears to be *White House Blues*, first recorded in 1926 by Charlie Poole and the North Carolina Ramblers, which includes the lines *...McKinley hollered, McKinley squalled/ Doc said to McKinley "I can't find that ball'*... In *Chronicles* Dylan recounts how he meets the owner of the Greenwich Village Folklore Center, Izzy Young, who plays him this song. The narrator hears these words, which describe the murder of President William McKinlay at the 1901 World's Fair in Buffalo, New York by the anarchist Leon Czolgosz, slightly differently:*...McKinley hollered, McKinley squalled/ Doctor says to McKinley 'Death is on the wall'...*

....Key West is fine and fair... the narrator assures us *...If you lose your mind, you can find it there...* The island is thus not only a place to rediscover inspiration but also to regain sanity. What follows seems to be the authentic voice of Dylan himself *...I was born on the wrong side of the railroad track...* he sighs*...like Ginsberg, Corso and Kerouac...* so identifying himself clearly with the Beat poets, 'philosopher pirates' all. Then he recounts some musical heroes: *...Like Louis and Jimmie and Buddy and all of the rest...* He seems to be referring to Louis Armstrong, Jimmie Rodgers and Buddy Holly, all of whom he has paid much tribute to in the past. He assures us that, like these 'mythical heroes', he has a firm grip on reality: *...I got both my feet planted square on the ground...* But this is just a rhetorical trick *...Got my right hand high with the thumb down...* he asserts, as if he is a Roman Emperor making a negative judgement during gladiatorial games *...Such is life...* he cries wistfully *...Such is happiness...*

As the narrator drives on, he continues to alternate between giving random snatches of 'tourist information' and making philosophical pronouncements *...Key West is the place to go, down by the Gulf of Mexico...* is fairly straightforward, but this is followed by: *...Beyond the sea, beyond the shifting sand/ Key West is the gateway key to innocence and purity/ Key West is the enchanted land...* 'Innocence and purity' are clearly qualities that he is trying to recover in his life. Yet he denies that he is indulging in fantasies: *...I've never lived in the land of Oz...* he insists *...or wasted my time with an unworthy cause...* Yet he recounts how he is becoming increasingly intoxicated by elements of the flora and the climate: *...Hibiscus flowers grow everywhere here..* he tells us *...If you wear one, put it behind your ear...* The image is both colourful and sensuous. He is becoming overwhelmed by the sights and smells of this 'magical' place. He insists that *...It's hot down here and you can't be overdressed...* and then claims that *...The tiny blossoms of a toxic plant, they can make you dizzy....* and *...The fishtail palms and the orchid trees/ They can give you that bleeding heart disease....*

The floral imagery and the references to the region's sticky heat increase, until we are almost 'drowning' in the sights and sounds of this tropical dream landscape. In reality what is known locally as the 'bleeding heart disease' only affects plants but the narrator seems to be increasingly convinced that the exotic flora of Key West, although beautiful and enticing, can also be dangerous. As the dreamscape of the song envelops him, he begins to fear that he will 'lose himself' *...People tell me I ought to try a little tenderness...* he muses, referring to a song that was a hit for Bing Crosby in 1932 before being transformed into a raging soul classic by Otis Redding in 1966. This rhymes neatly with a line in the next verse: *...People tell me that I'm truly blessed...* The narrator's feelings towards this 'earthly paradise' certainly seem to become more tender as he finds himself increasingly under its hypnotic spell.

The narrator then abandons his car and walks through the streets of the city of Key West: *...Amelia Street, Bay View Park/ Walking in the shadows after dark...* His musings become increasingly fantastical, as if he is an invisible presence who is merging with the city itself *...I play the gumbo limbo spirituals...* he declares *...I know all the Hindu rituals...* 'Gumbo limbo' are trees which are indigenous to the area, which has a sizeable Hindu community. But the narrator seems to have little concern for realism as he is enfolded and 'blessed' by the local flora: *...Bougainvillea bloomin' in the summer and spring/ Winter here is an unknown thing...* He seems increasingly to be trying to entice us into his visionary world: *...Feel the sunlight on your skin...* he commands *...And the healing virtues of the wind...* before making the unequivocal declaration that *...Key West is the land of light....* He thus identifies Key West as his spiritual home *...Wherever I travel, wherever I roam...* he tells us *...I'm not that far from the convent home...* referring to the Convent of Mary Immaculate, the centre of Catholic education in the area. He casually mentions that he is passing *...Mystery Street off Mallory Square...* and drops in the interesting fact that *...Truman had his White House there...* The street locations are accurate. The 'Little White House' in Key West was indeed used by President Harry S. Truman during the winter months in the late 1940s and has been an occasional official venue in succeeding years.

The next verse is the oddest in the song and seems at first to have little to do with the rest of the narrative. It begins: *...Twelve years old and they put me in a suit/ Forced me to marry a prostitute...* We may now be expecting some kind of tale of tragic abuse, but what follows is merely gently mocking and decidedly light hearted: *...There were gold fringes on her wedding dress/ That's my story but not where it ends/ She's still cute and we're still friends...* Here, it seems, is the twelve year old Dylan at his Bar Mitzvah, the Jewish ceremony that proclaims a boy's manhood. After the boy has donned the teffillin, a small black leather box attached by a strap to the head, he recites the words of the prophets from the Torah. In this case the boy appears to be reading the prophet Hosea who, as Dylan mentions in *Chronicles*, was married to a prostitute. The 'gold fringes' may refer to the decorations often traditionally attached to the Torah itself. In this bizarre if rather charming transposition Dylan appears to give a fleeting glimpse of his relationship with Judaism, a religion he seems to have been 'forced' to adhere to as a boy but which he still seems to have some lingering affection for. Finally the narrator appears to be back in his car, as he has again tuned into his pirate radio station. It seems that his trip to Key West has freed him from the shackles of thought that have previously weighed him down. He has found the key to eternal bliss, not in the tenets of any particular religious dogma but in a location which he now proclaims is *...on the horizon line...* The song then trails off without any dramatic denouement.

The location Dylan evokes here is clearly a symbolic one, which could well be taken to represent his view of mortality and the afterlife. The narrator he speaks through is, as we have seen, partly a version of himself. It is important to remember - as has been stressed throughout this book - that Dylan consistently aligns his religion with his art and creativity. In many of his late period songs he uses a symbolic language to discuss these matters. In *Can't Wait* he pictures himself standing at the gates of Hell. In *Standing in the Doorway* he seems frozen in uncertainty about 'the great beyond'. In *Forgetful Heart* he questions whether there is 'indeed' a door through which the soul can walk into the afterlife. But in *Key West* the 'key' to that 'door' has been found. The 'paradise' of Key West - a 'dream land' where immortality can be glimpsed - is *...on the horizon line...* In other words, it is right in front of us. All we have to do is look into the distance. We do not necessarily have to follow any specific path to reach it. On the complex, revelatory, sometimes shocking but often darkly humorous *Rough and Rowdy Ways* Dylan confronts mortality with a wink and a shrug. He refers to Christianity, Judaism, Hinduism and Buddhism but he neither proselytes for nor rejects any of these religions. Instead he presents us with shifting narratives and parallel perspectives, emphasising that the many ways human beings have devised to explain the mysteries of existence can all be said to have a poetic truth of their own.

14th December 1995. The Beacon Theater, New York City. It is the sixth date of the short 'Paradise Lost' tour, on which Dylan is supported by Patti Smith and her band. We are at the end of the acoustic section of the gig, and Dylan - accompanied by John Jackson on guitar - has just played stark and intimate versions of *Mr. Tambourine Man, Masters of War* and *Mama You Been on My Mind.* Quite a treat for the fans. But an even more special moment is about to occur *...Mmm... I'd like to ask Patti to sing a song with me....* Bob mumbles. And there she is, in a long red dress, her dark hair shaken loose, looking like a shamanic priestess. As she sings she raises her hands to her face and closes her eyes: *...Oh, the gentlemen are talking, and the midnight moon is on the riverside/ They're drinking up and walking and it is time for me to slide...* You can tell that she is absolutely cherishing every word, and that as a poet herself she is being transported by delight to be conveying these sparkling, magical images.

Dark Eyes is one of the great hidden gems in Dylan's catalogue. Tucked away on the end of one of his most hit-and-miss 1980s albums *Empire Burlesque*, and apparently written 'off the cuff' in the studio, this is a song that appears to have come to Dylan entire, in a vision (much like songs like *Mr. Tambourine Man* or *It's Alright Ma* had back in the '60s) in the middle of a period when he was struggling for inspiration. The studio version, a brief solo acoustic number, is in stark contrast to the rest of the album, with its rather overblown 80s production. Tonight's rendition, with Smith taking the first two lines of every verse and Dylan joining in with the last two, takes the song to new heights.

The song is a dream-vision reminiscent of the greatest work of the romantic poets. It has four verses and no choruses and each verse ends with the title. It takes us quite explicitly into a fantasia of the poetic imagination: *...I live in another world...* Bob and Patti sing together*...where life and death are memorised...* It is as if all creation is passing before him. Being able to picture this is the gift of the true visionary. But it is not, as we will soon hear, an easy one to bear. This line is followed by one of staggering radiance: *...Where the earth is strung with lover's pearls and all I see are dark eyes...* 'Lover's pearls' is simultaneously an image of purity and sexual intimacy - the 'pearls' being both manifestations of immeasurable beauty and drops of glistening semen, ready to fertilise the world. Not this world or heaven or hell - but the world of the poetic imagination...

Patti's voice is soaring and pure but quavering in wonder. Bob's is harsher, darker. It seems that there is something he knows about this 'other world'. The luminescent images keep coming: *...A cock is crowing far away and another soldier's deep in prayer...* Patti sings. Then *...Some mother's child has gone astray, she can't find him anywhere...* It is as if she is channelling the voice of Blake, summoning up an emanation of his poetic spirit. The little boy is lost. A mother wails. Then Dylan joins her for the apocalyptic lines: *... I hear another drum beating for the dead that rise/ Whom nature's beast fears as they come, and all I see are dark eyes....* The day of judgement is at hand. The 'beast' of Revelations is about to manifest itself, in fear of the rising dead. The contrasts in the song are extreme - from absolute beauty and perfection to utter terror and destruction. In this 'other world' the poet sees it all. Dylan muses on how painful it can be to be privy to these visions, for others can never see what he sees. These 'others' mock him and abuse him *...They tell me to be discreet for all intended purposes/ They tell me revenge is sweet, and from where they stand I'm sure it is....* But he is determined not to flinch: *...But I feel nothing for their game/ Where beauty goes unrecognised...* As a poetic 'seer' he must bear the pain - or perhaps the awful numbness - of living in a world in which such visionary 'seeing' is dismissed, perhaps as madness. It is as if he is experiencing hell itself: *...All I feel is heat and flame/ And all I see are dark eyes....*

The final verse throws a series of astonishing 'jump cuts' at us *...Now the French girl, she's in Paradise and a drunken man is at the wheel... The French Girl* is a song by Ian Tyson about a beautiful but enigmatic muse. Dylan recorded an impassioned version for *The Basement Tapes*. The phrase also conjures up an image of Joan of Arc - a visionary who was labelled as being mad - being consumed by the 'heat and flame' as she is martyred. Because of her faith, she can feel no pain. She is already in paradise. Meanwhile, a 'drunken man' is in charge of a world spinning out of control *...Hunger pays a heavy price to the falling gods of speed and steel...* uses a powerful double alliteration in another apocalyptic clash of images, as the industrial world is consumed in the flames. Finally the bow of Cupid, the Ancient Roman god of love, is stretched out to express his perception of how fleeting the joys of life are *...Oh, time is short and the days are sweet and passion rules the arrow that flies...* Then, in a haunting denouement, he summons up the burden of the visionary *...A million faces at my feet, and all I see is dark eyes...* The poet with a huge international audience 'at his feet' stares into the multitudes but those 'dark eyes' - those precursors of disaster, of failure, of death - are inescapable. Whatever success we have been achieved in the material world, and even as that world crashes around us, those eyes, which Blake called *...this life's dim windows of the soul...* will continue to watch us. It is thus crucial, given one's brief sojourn on earth, to make sure that each one of those 'sweet days' is savored. One must engage with the 'passion' that lifts the experience of those days to another level during the swift 'arrow flight' of our lives. The job of the poet, therefore, is to use this 'passion' to leap into the 'other world' of the imagination - to make a futile but heroic attempt at achieving immortality - to step outside of time...

Seven: *The Devil's in the Alley...*
Journeys on Dark Roads

...And just for a moment I had reached the point of ecstasy that I always wanted to reach, which was the complete step across chronological time into timeless shadows, and wonderment in the bleakness of the mortal realm, and the sensation of death kicking at my heels to move on, with a phantom dogging its own heels, and myself hurrying to a plank where all the angels dove off and flew into the holy void of uncreated emptiness, the potent and inconceivable radiances shining in bright Mind Essence, innumerable lotus-lands falling open in the magic mothswarm of heaven...
Jack Kerouac: *On the Road*

The canvas is sixty feet wide and ten feet high. It is so massively imposing that a whole room in London's Halcyon Gallery has been devoted to it. That's just as well, as you have to stand several yards away to give it your full appreciation. In fact, the further you move back, the more the impressionistic splodges of acrylic paint begin to take the form of a landscape. There are no human beings in the picture. As you stare into the vista, you may imagine that your vehicle is speeding over the bump in the road which dominates the lower half of the image. You will go up a little, then down and you will get smaller and smaller as you recede into the distance. Soon you will be indistinguishable from the terrain - just a tiny blob of colour - before you disappear entirely into the line of mountains. Telegraph poles and tall, spindly trees line your route, all diminishing in size during your journey. The colours are bold, dramatic... lines of bright yellow in the foreground, purple mountains in the distance, a swirling crimson sunset. If you happened to be standing here at the end of the day, there might be a window of just a few seconds when the setting sun would produce exactly these colours. It would be a moment so fleeting that if you blinked you might miss it. But if you meditate on the painting, which is called *Endless Highway*, for a while, you could be perpetually frozen in that moment.

In an interview with the *New York Times* in 1997 Bob Dylan stated:

...A lot of people don't like the road, but it's as natural to me as breathing. I do it because I'm driven to do it ... It's the only place you can be who you want to be...

Endless Highway is the largest and most ambitious painting that he has exhibited. It is part of a group of works called *The Beaten Path* (2016) which, like those of his first collection *Drawn Blank* (2008), grew out of his experience of the road. Dylan's sometimes garish images create a unique individual vision of the country - not only one of glorious sunsets, huge bridges and skylines but also of a non-corporate, distinctive American identity. Motels and hamburger joints, donut shops and roadside diners stand out against bright blue skies and starry nights. The automobiles are classic 1940s and '50s models, gleaming in the sun. The focus is on elements of a 'classic' American past - the era of Dylan's childhood, when the identity of modern America was formed. One can easily imagine the colourful rogues, itinerant bluesmen, wasted country singers and other denizens of the mythic land who populate Dylan's late period songs passing through these places. In the introductory essay to *The Beaten Path* he writes:

...The works were done from real life, literature, films, songs and poetry and a certain outlook all scrambled together in one form or another... These paintings are up to the moment realism - archaic, most static, but quivering in appearance. They contradict the modern world... ...The common theme of these works having something to do with the American landscape - how you see it while criss-crossing the land and seeing it for what it's worth. Staying out of the mainstream and traveling the back roads, free-born style....

Among the most striking paintings in *The Beaten Path* are those of motels - a feature of life on the road that all travelling musicians are particularly familiar with. In one of these the entire focus of the picture is a neon sign, with the words 'ROY'S' in large letters, over a vee shaped garish orange background. The painting is of a renowned motel, café and gas station in the Mojave Desert town of Amboy, California, which is located on Route 66 - possibly the famous American road of all. It originally ran from Chicago to Santa Monica, California and was immortalised in *(Get Your Kicks On) Route 66*, written by Bobby Troup and later recorded by both Chuck Berry and the Rolling Stones. In *Blue Swallow Motel*, a painting of another location on Route 66, the use of vivid blues, reds and oranges make the building look at if it is glowing (or, as Dylan might have it, 'quivering') in some kind of unearthly light. In *Motel in New Mexico,* the scene appears to be lit by sunlight but the mountains in the background are snow-covered. The use of sharp lines and bright contrasting colours in paintings like this has been compared to the work of British artist David Hockney, although the subject matter is very different. Among the other scenes depicted in *The Beaten Path* are a classic car show in Ohio, an amusement arcade on Coney Island and views of the Manhattan Bridge in New York and the Golden Gate Bridge in San Francisco - all iconic 'retro' American images.

There is no doubt that Dylan has developed his technical skill as an artist over the years. The vividness and boldness of the *Beaten Path* collection - in contrast to the more derivative work in *Drawn Blank* - indicates that he has evolved a distinctive style of his own. This has won over many art critics who were at first suspicious that Dylan - not the first rock star to have a parallel career as a painter - was merely engaging in a series of vanity projects. Dylan's painting style is primarily influenced by nineteenth century expressionists and post expressionists such as Van Gogh, Manet, Matisse and Gauguin.. Many of Dylan's paintings exist in multiple versions, all based on the same basic line drawings but presented in diverse colours. Thus there are several different *Endless Highways* and *Manhattan Bridges.* Often they are exhibited next to each other. The use of different colours suggests both the ever-changing effects of light on the landscapes and the artist's ever-varying perception of them. Thus no one painting remains fixed. New interpretations can be created at any time. Yet the underlying reality of the scenes remains the same. This technique is reminiscent of the way Dylan reinterprets and re-imagines his own songs in concert - the music, rhythm, vocal expression and sometimes even the lyrics can change but each song retains its distinctive identity. Such an approach allows individual works to be infinitely renewed.

It soon emerged that - by claiming that his paintings were based on his travels to many different places around the world - Dylan was only being partially truthful. *Blue Swallow Motel*, for example, bears an uncanny resemblance to a photo which appears on the front of a Route 66 tourist guide book. It seems that here - and in many other cases - Dylan has based his paintings on photographs rather than his own sketches. This tendency was even more pronounced in the two exhibitions he mounted in 2011, *The Asia Series* and *The Brazil Series.* These collections have a very different visual style to *Drawn Blank* and *The Beaten Path*, using darker shades rather than bright colours, although they are also based on him daubing over his own line drawings. Several of the images are clearly derived from the work of famous photographers of the early twentieth century such as Leon Busy and Henri Cartier Bresson. Although the Never Ending Tour has taken him to many parts of the world, Dylan could hardly have been in a 1920s opium den in Hanoi where Leon took the original photograph. In his written introductions to his exhibitions, he seems to be playing a game with those who follow his work, as if deliberately taunting them to challenge his authenticity.

The first indications that Dylan was interested in becoming a visual artist began to appear during his Woodstock retreat in 1967, when his painting of a man with a guitar - a rather amateurish imitation of Picasso - was used as a magazine cover. The Band's first album *Music from Big Pink* (1968) was adorned by a 'faux naive' painting by Dylan depicting the members of the group playing their instruments, accompanied by a large grey elephant. This 'primitive', child-like style, with an emphasis on scatological humour, was also evident in *Writings and Drawings* (1971), the first official collection of his lyrics, in which some of the songs were accompanied by his line drawings. The illustration for *This Wheel's on Fire* features two cartoon figures jumping away from a burning wheel with speech bubbles showing them shouting "Look out!" and "Yikes!", while another character in the foreground responds with "Holy Cow!".

Dylan also contributed the impressionistic paintings of himself for the covers of *Self Portrait* (1970) and *Planet Waves* (1974). It was not until 1992, however, that he published *Drawn Blank*, his first book of art work. This was a collection of line drawings mainly depicting various people and scenes he had encountered on his travels. By 2007 he had produced over 200 paintings based on these original images. Since then, in a period when he has been more prolific as an artist than a songwriter, he has mounted a series of exhibitions and published eight books of his artwork. His approaches to art have also diversified considerably, with experimentation in a range of methods including pastel drawings, sketches, sculpture and conceptual pieces. *Face Value* (2013) is a series of 'head and shoulders' portraits in charcoal and *Mondo Scripto* (2018) is a group of witty line drawings illustrating some of his best known songs. 2016's *Revisionist Art* collection consists mainly of mock-ups of magazine covers from the 1950s and '60s, to which he has added absurdly parodic headlines. In the 2016 exhibition *Mood Swings*, four walls are mounted with bullet-hole spattered vintage car doors, each of which is dedicated to a different 20th century gangster, with a brief biography attached. Also on show are various metal sculptures in which household tools and objects are incorporated into designs for large gates. In his introductory notes Dylan links this work to his childhood in the Iron Range in Minnesota. He combines this with an almost metaphysical discourse on the significance of the work which you might - at a stretch - even interpret as referring to his highly symbolic 1965 song *Gates of Eden*. But it is hard to know, as with so many of his pronouncements, how seriously we should take this:

...I've been around iron all my life ever since I was a kid. I was born and raised in iron ore country, where you could breathe it and smell it every day. Gates appeal to me because of the negative space they allow. They can be closed but at the same time they allow the seasons and breezes to enter and flow. They can shut you out or shut you in. And in some ways there is no difference...

There are many direct connections between Dylan's 'late period' productions as a song writer, film maker, writer of prose and visual artist. His merging of elements of the past and present, fact and fiction and original and 'found' elements in these mediums invites us to view his work from a postmodern perspective. *Time Out of Mind* and its successors were consciously influenced by the practice in modern art of using found materials in unusual juxtapositions. It was in the art world that the original concepts of modernism, and later postmodernism, were first developed, before they influenced literature, music, poetry and film. Many conceptual art pieces, such as Tracey Emin's famous 'bed' exhibit, consist entirely of 'found' materials. Despite this, in his approach to both painting and music Dylan remains in many ways a traditionalist. The influence on his work in all these fields of established 'masters' - be they Homer, Shakespeare or Poe; Hank Williams, Woody Guthrie or Muddy Waters; Truffaut, Matisse or Picasso - is obvious. His late musical style is deeply influenced by a lifetime of very wide reading of literature and appreciation of visual art, along with an encyclopedic knowledge of American music. In his art, his writing, his songs and his radio shows he focuses strongly on those elements from the past which he marks out as being relevant to the present day. Despite his acknowledgement of the postmodern condition, his immersion in the sensibilities of the past is central to his working methods. As he writes in his introduction to the *Beaten Path* exhibition:

...I believe that the key to the future is in the remnants of the past. That you have to master the idioms of your own time before you can have any identity in the present tense. Your past begins the day you were born and to disregard it is cheating yourself of who you really are...

Since the beginning of the Never Ending Tour in 1988, Dylan has been constantly on the move. His late period songs can be said to take the listener with him down a series of 'dark roads'. Many of his songs can, like his paintings of 'classic Americana', be identified with particular places or landscapes within the USA. In American literature, film and popular song the 'sense of place' has always been a dominant motif, from the Long Island of *The Great Gatsby* to the 'endless highways' of *On the Road,* the dustbowl of *The Grapes of Wrath* and the landscapes of Monument Valley in John Ford's westerns. Songs like Chuck Berry's *The Promised Land* (1964) and Dylan's tongue-in-cheek 'travelogue' *Wanted Man* (written for Johnny Cash in 1969) include a delicious roll call of place names. In the work of poets like Whitman and Ginsberg, and painters like those of the Hudson River School in the nineteenth century and Edward Hopper and Georgia O'Keeffe in the twentieth century, elements of the vast and varied American landscape have frequently been used to express ideas of metaphorical or mystical significance. This geographical sensibility is also highly important in the lyrics of blues and country musicians, who often refer to - and thus mythologise - their places of origin in the Southern states. The natural feature which has been mentioned most in both song traditions is the Mississippi - the largest river in the United States, which originates in the hills of Northern Minnesota (where Dylan grew up) and runs down to New Orleans. The Mississippi 'Delta' is also famously the 'cradle of the blues' and its relevant place names feature heavily in the expansive canon of blues material on which Dylan so often draws. The river figures large in American history, culture and literature. Mark Twain's brilliantly mischievous 'Great American Novel' *Huckleberry Finn* is centered around a journey down river by its boy hero and a runaway slave.

Mississippi, which appears on *"Love And Theft"* but which was originally recorded at the *Time Out of Mind* sessions, is framed, like most blues songs, within a 'lost love' scenario, but also reflects on Dylan's crisis of inspiration. The lyrics express the narrator's regret regarding his own bad timing in blowing his chances with a woman. Central to all of this is the use of the 'Big Muddy' river as a motif. Here, as in the songs of the great blues artists, natural speech patterns slide with apparently effortless ease into poetic metaphor and alliteration. The 'state' of Mississippi (to use a Whitmanesque pun) represents a 'state' of immersion in the imagery and mentality of the blues itself. The song consists of three long verses, each one culminating in a repeated refrain. In the first verse Dylan begins with a simple statement of his intention to pursue his faith in his muse, combined with clear intimations of mortality. The use of the pronoun 'we' involves the listener intimately in this process *...Every step of the way, we walk the line...* he sings, pointedly alluding to Johnny Cash's *I Walk The Line*, a powerful statement of a lover's *intention* to remain faithful which is so intense in its declaration of determination to be 'true' that we begin to doubt whether the singer can really remain on this path.

We are instantly cast into the arena of self-doubt: *...Your days are numbered...* Dylan sings *...And so are mine....* a line which echoes the fatalistic overtones of his earlier *...every hair is numbered...* from *Every Grain of Sand* (1981). The next few wonderfully compressed lines use short, concise statements and taut rhymes to convey the feeling of being entrapped by the constraints of time and ageing *...Time is piling up/ We struggle and we scrape/ All boxed in/ Nowhere to escape...* The 's' alliteration recurs throughout the song, most notably in the hissing sound of the title word itself. The repetition of that sound helps to pile on the angst being conveyed by the song's narrator, as if he is continually sighing - a wonderful example of 'sound poetry'. The next lines begin to explore the classic blues dichotomy between city and countryside, which here takes on a symbolic dimension. The city is seen as a 'jungle' in which both singer and audience are trapped, but from which they are continually trying to escape. The country in which the singer was raised seems to be a place of freedom and inspiration. The singer tells us, in a highly resonant phrase (again using the's' alliteration) that his problems come from being trapped in the city: *...I've been in trouble since I set my suitcase down...*

The nature of the inspirational crisis that Dylan describes is deepened in the next lines: *...Ain't got nothin' for you/ Had nothin' before/ Don't even have anything for myself anymore...* The expression is clipped, terse, and world-weary *...Sky full of fire, pain falling down...* intensifies this effect. Here the elements are magically transformed by the changing of one syllable. It is 'pain' that is 'falling down' from the sky, not 'rain' - though of course, the sky itself is 'on fire'. The singer's suppressed, burning anger leads him to the cynicism of *...There's nothing you can sell me/ I'll see you around...* the cursory brush-off suggesting that he is trapped in an inspirational void. This becomes more explicit in what follows *...My powers of expression and thoughts so sublime/ Could never do you justice/ In reason or rhyme...* The narrator laments a decline in his own poetic abilities - he cannot do justice to his muse.

This refrain *...Only one thing I did wrong/ Stayed in Mississippi a day too long...* is taken from *Rosie*, an old work song from the notorious Parchman Farm prison in Mississippi state. This was an ironic chorus that the inmates would sing on work details, indicating the oppressive nature of laws and punishment in a region where racism was rife. The implication seems to be that if only they had left the state on time (and moved to somewhere less racist), they would have avoided punishment. Dylan also uses the Mississippi as a symbol of entrapment. The suggestion seems to be that his inspirational blockage has been caused by hesitancy, a fear of moving on from one 'state' to another. A great 'rolling river' seems to yawn between the narrator and the freedom to be inspired that he so desires. Thus the 'state of Mississippi' symbolises 'the state of the blues' that the narrator finds himself drowning in.

The second verse begins with some quintessential blues imagery indicating the singer's mind set: *...The Devil's in the alley, mule's in the stall...* There are references to two well known songs here. In Porter Waggoner's *The Devil's Alley,* the 'alley' represents the road to damnation. *Mule Kicking in My Stall* is a song by Muddy Waters, first recorded by Otis Spann in 1969. In Waters' song the 'mule' clearly represents a woman whose 'kicking' suggests she is having sex with someone else. Dylan's 'mule' - perhaps a degraded form of his muse - is not 'kicking' here, but is merely trapped. These lines, with their rich patterns of association, again symbolise the narrator's feeling of being 'stuck' for ideas: *...Say anything you wanna/ I have heard it all...*

For a few moments, in his distraction, he enters a kind of dream state: *...I was thinking about the things that Rosie said/ I was dreaming I was sleeping in Rosie's bed...* This is the only direct reference to 'Rosie' in the song. In *Rosie* the name is used to indicate a fantasy woman into whose arms the inmates can dream of escaping. Here the narrator briefly glimpses the freedom that 'Rosie' offers. But in the next lines he again sounds lost and dejected: *...Walking through the leaves falling from the trees/ Feel like a stranger nobody sees....* The symbolism of the leaves falling, suggesting a dying relationship, is again contrasted with colloquial language. Now he addresses the subject of the song again, in words which, with their emphasis on those 'sighing' 's' sounds, seem to hold out little hope: *...So many things we never may undo...* he laments. He then complains, rather pitifully: *...You say you're sorry, I'm sorry too...*

Like the narrator of *Standing in the Doorway,* he seems lost in existential despair: *...Some people will offer you their hand and some won't...* he cries *...Last night I knew you, tonight I don't...* The sense of loss and anguish here is palpable *...I need something strong...* he hints darkly *...to distract my mind...* hinting that he may try to blot the feelings out with drugs. But then, in one of the song's most achingly moving and uplifting couplets, he declares that he was guided towards the subject of the song by a cosmic or heavenly force: *...I got here following that Southern star/ I crossed that river just to be where you are...* He has bravely followed his muse across the wide river into 'the state of Mississippi' - but having stayed just one day too long he has lost everything. Now he is a soul crying out in the wilderness. In the climactic final verse he graphically depicts the feeling of being beyond pain, when the soul has suffered so much that nothing else can touch it or make things worse. He is now broken, yet strangely carefree, as if - having absorbed the pain fully - he has somehow transcended it. It is suggested that he has almost 'drowned' in this pain, as if he has reached a point of semi blissfulness, in a near-death state where the pain has finally begun to ebb away. Employing more 's' alliteration he begins: *...My ship's been split to splinters/ I'm sinking fast...* He tells us he's sunk into a kind of timeless void *...I'm drowning in the poison/ Got no future, got no past....*

Just as the waters of the great river overcome him, the process of awakening begins. As soon as he is able to express how he feels in such an eloquent way, the pain is numbed. Now he feels calm, reflective *...My heart is not weary...* he sighs *...it's light and it's free...* Neatly completing the analogy he tells us: *...I got nothing but affection for all those who sail with me...* In this moment of inspiration his 'heavy' self pity and anguish is replaced by 'light' compassion. A feeling of peaceful calm overcomes him. He can now survey the frantic stressfulness of modern life from a place of detachment: *...Everybody's movin' if they ain't already there/ Everybody's got to move somewhere....*

Having ceased struggling, he begins to float to the surface. He reaches out his hand to his lover: *...Stick with me, baby/ Stick with me anyhow...* Then he declares, with beautifully measured understatement: *...Things should start to get interesting right about now...* so drawing us into the present moment.

Dylan's use of the classic blues technique of resorting to self-deprecating wit to fight despair has rarely been so refined: *...My clothes are wet/ Tight on my skin...* he sings *...Not as tight as the corner I've painted myself in...* The 'drowning' metaphor is continued here, and is compressed into two 'tight' phrases; then counterposed against a version of the expression 'painting oneself into a tight corner'. Thus we are jolted out of one kind of metaphorical language into another. The narrator is in a 'tight spot'. This is a crucial moment of acceptance and self-realisation. But now that he has taken full responsibility, it seems that his salvation is at hand: *...I know that fortune is waiting to be kind...* he tells his lover *...So give me your hand and say you'll be mine...* This sounds like a typical declaration of affection but it also suggests that he wants her to pull him out of the 'great river'. Using a double alliteration, he reflects back on the turmoil he has been going through - a state of 'living death' in which he is starved of inspiration: *...The emptiness is endless, cold as the clay...*

The final line before the last chorus, the deliciously enigmatic *...You can always come back, but you can't come back all the way...* sounds like another colloquial epigram. Dylan leaves us in suspense here. His narrator may sink or swim. Will we stretch out a hand to save him from drowning? In his final words, he seems to be suggesting that he can be saved from the torturous 'emptiness' of losing his creativity. He is giving us the chance to help him do this. But he warns that, even if he is rescued, things will never be the same again. He is under no illusion that he will be able to replicate the spontaneous poetic explosion of his youth. But from the point of self-awareness he has reached, with his 'new eyes', he has found a way of 'painting himself out of' the corner he had found himself in. *Mississippi* is a song about growing older and struggling to recapture the spirit of youth. At the same time it reflects on the human potential for 'salvation', without relying on any religious dogma. The chorus echoes the desperate wailing of the chain gang as they lament their loss of freedom, finding the deepest spiritual meaning in their desire to reach 'Rosie's bed' ('a bed of roses'). Dylan transforms that cry of defiance into one of his most powerful demands for the liberation of the spirit. He tells us of his own descent into 'the Devil's alley' without holding back from describing the pain he experienced. But it is the act of writing - or, more properly of *singing* - about this pain, which allows him to realise that he has the inner power and strength to rise above it.

Mississippi has much in common with Dylan's great celebration of the power of the imagination *Mr. Tambourine Man*. Both songs were rehearsed and demoed for one album but held back for the next one. *Mr. Tambourine Man* was originally tried out for *Another Side of Bob Dylan* in 1964 but was not released until *Bringing It All Back Home* the following year. In the meantime it was recorded by The Byrds in a truncated 'rock version' and became a huge hit single. Similarly, *Mississippi* was worked on in the *Time*

Out of Mind sessions but was not released until *"Love And Theft"* came out four years later. The first recorded version was by Sheryl Crow, whose upbeat rendition sounds a little like The Byrds. It seems that, in both cases, Dylan valued the song so much that he was determined to present it in the right setting. This is somewhat unusual for him, as he has often discarded great songs in the past and has rarely given thought to re-recording them. *Mississippi* certainly shares some of the themes of *Time Out of Mind* in that it plumbs the depths of the singer's personal despair, but its resolution is perhaps too 'upbeat' for the tone of that album. The version on *"Love And Theft"* is delivered with the kind of musical 'uplift' that characterises a collection of songs which, in great contrast to its predecessor, is zestfully energetic and playfully humorous. Dylan's voice sounds appropriately world weary, almost cracking in places. The stately tune, which features prominent, almost military 'quick step' sounding drums, builds up to an impressive climax at the end of the verses, each of which is followed by a short coda featuring Larry Campbell on mandolin. The song was performed over seventy times between 2001 and 2012, without any substantial changes to its arrangement.

Tell Tale Signs revealed no less than three alternate versions of the song from the *Time Out of Mind* sessions. The stunning, heart-stopping first take features Dylan on acoustic guitar and vocals, backed up by Daniel Lanois on second guitar. The rhythm is supplied by Lanois tapping a simple beat out with his foot. The repeated blues riff they play throws the nuances of Dylan's vocals, which alternate between pained harshness and whispered transcendence, into sharp relief. The recording is so intimate that you can hear the singer's breath between the lines and catch his moments of hesitation. The combination of all this produces spine-tingling moments of great intensity as we are taken on a roller coaster ride through the different emotional states that the song depicts. Dylan's mastery of vocal phrasing captures the absolute essence of how the blues can be a channel for the most sincere, playful and meaningful forms of poetic expression.

The second version adds bass and drums. It features a partly whispered vocal and longer instrumental interludes between the verses, with a buildup of pace towards the end of each verse. In the third version the rhythm is slightly jauntier, almost veering towards reggae in places, with Augie Myers' organ prominently featured. Dylan's vocal is more expansive, as he stretches out phrases confidently. The lyrics have been altered and the tone is more obviously confessional: *... I'm standing in the shadows with an aching heart/ I'm looking at the world tear itself apart...* The second verse now begins *...Well I been loving you too long, I know you ain't no good/ It don't make a bit of difference to me, don't see why it should...* There is an echo of the title of an Otis Redding song (*I've Been Loving You Too Long*, 1965) and a more direct reference to the 'my woman done me wrong' theme. The most memorable change of lyric is in the final verse, where the singer depicts himself as so spiritually bereft as to be 'invisible': *...Winter goes into summer, summer goes into fall/ I look into the mirror, don't see anything at all...*

Another song which focuses on particular aspects of the American landscape is 2005's *Tell Ol' Bill*. This was written for the film *North Country* (directed by Nick Caro in 2005), a drama set in the 1970s in Dylan's home territory of the Minnesota Iron Range, which was graphically portrayed in his early songs *Girl From the North Country* (1963) and *North Country Blues* (1964). It is a fictionalised account of the true story of how Josey Aimes (played by Charlize Theron), a mine worker and single parent, fights the first successful action against sexual harassment in the USA after being abused and attacked by male co-workers. The story is in the tradition of American liberal social realism established by films like *Mr. Deeds Goes to Town* (1936), *To Kill a Mockingbird* (1962) and *Silkwood* (1983). The song attempts to get inside the mind of the main character, describing her frustrations at the position she finds herself in. It shows how she eventually resolves to tackle the problem head-on. Dylan uses the film's scenario as a starting point for exploring wider concerns, turning an individual's struggle for freedom and justice into a profound meditation on human willpower.

The version of the song which appears on *Tell Tale Signs* is different to the more subdued take on the movie soundtrack. Though Dylan's singing remains gently understated throughout, the drums are more pronounced, making the song more rhythmic and the whole performance more passionate. The song seems to have been tried out in various different ways, as revealed in a bootleg tape of the sessions during which it is tried out as a slow blues, a country lament and a pained ballad. The lyrics remain virtually the same throughout the twelve different versions on the tape, suggesting that Dylan composed the piece as a poem first. Both released versions tend to tread something of a middle ground between the more extreme musical forms being played with in the studio. The version on *Tell Tale Signs* is full of subtle, querulous phrasing. The singer inhabits the voice of a modest but brave narrator and conveys a sense of quiet courage without ever falling into over-emotionalism.

The song balances pastoral imagery with determined emotion. Dylan is careful to pronounce each word clearly. The correlation between the images of the natural world and the narrator's thoughts is carefully and skilfully built up. While the scene being depicted is undoubtedly chilly and harsh: *...The rocks are bleak, the trees are bare/ Iron clouds go floating by....* there is a certain magical, dreamlike quality to this harsh North Country landscape, with its *...tranquil lakes and streams...* and *...snowflakes falling in my hair....* What is most impressive about the use of language is the expansiveness of the imagery within a disciplined, compressed format. One of the best examples is the opening verse: *...The river whispers in my ear/ I've hardly a penny to my name/ The heavens have never seemed so near/ All my body glows with flame...* The narrator seems to be in a kind of trance, as the spirits of nature converse with her. Out here in the cold North Country she feels lifted up, enraptured. The contrast between material poverty and spiritual enrichment is achieved with admirable economy and precision. The beautiful and mysterious line *...the tempest struggles in the air, and to myself alone I sing...* with its echoes of both Shakespeare and Whitman, is perhaps the most impressive example of symbolist writing in the song. There are times when Dylan can demonstrate an innate feeling for the placement of a particular word and here the use of 'struggle' following 'tempest' creates a memorable metaphorical resonance. The lone singer is engaged in a kind of tempestuous struggle with herself, trying to face up to the darkness within.

The next verses take us further into this mysterious space. The narrator searches for *...one smilin' face/ to drive the shadow from my head...* She cries *...Why must you torture me within?...* and rages *....Why must you come down off your high hill?/ Throw my fate to the clouds and wind....* It is as if she has been twisted up by the struggling tempest - the wild spirit of the bleak land - which exists both outside and inside her. This spirit which tortures her causes her to have *...secret thoughts...* which are *...hard to bear...* Now she is left alone with *... emotions we can never share...* One of the key moments in the film occurs when it is revealed that Josey's child was conceived when she was raped by her teacher. The lines in the next verse *...You trampled on me as you passed/ Left the coldest kiss upon my brow...* express the emotional aloneness of one who has experienced such an ordeal with withering clarity. Yet from this point onwards, the narrator begins to gather the inner strength she will need for the oncoming struggle *...All my doubts and fears have gone at last...* she confesses *...I've nothing more to tell you now...* She arrives at the realisation that *...the enemy is at the gates...*

From here on, the scenery is transformed. In another remarkable transposition of colloquial and figurative language Dylan contrasts the raging incoherence of the oppressed spirit: *...Beneath the thunder-blasted trees/ The words are ringin' off your tongue...* with symbolic descriptions of nature which reflect on the narrator's new, hard-won determination *...The ground is hard in times like these...* she declares. Now she is standing on solid, firm earth. And, even more remarkably *...stars are cold, the night is young...* contrasting in a single short line an image of her own fortitude with an ironic reworking of a common cliché.

In the final verses her determination to enact revenge grows. Darkness begins to fall on the landscape, reflecting the corruption she has to face up to: *...The woods are dark, the town is too/ They'll drag you down, they run the show/ Ain't no tellin' what they'll do....* But she is ready to face up to these 'enemies at the gates'. When, in the penultimate verse, the mysterious Ol' Bill arrives, she shows herself to be fully prepared: *...Tell him that I'm not alone/ That the hour has come to do or die...* She declares that *...All the world I would defy...* She is ready to take on the elements now, and to still the raging torrent that surrounds her. She stares her enemy directly in the face with a final expression of compassion: *....I look at you now and I sigh/ How could it be any other way...* Her enemy may have tried to 'throw her fate to the clouds and wind' but she has now taken control of her own destiny. Dylan turns his girl from the North Country's struggle with her inner and outer 'tempest' into a profound expression of the triumph of an individual spirit against great adversity.

But who is Ol' Bill, the apparent subject of the song, who makes only a fleeting appearance here as the narrator's helper? A folk song from the Golden Isles of Georgia runs: *...Old Bill the rollin' pin, he had a hog eye and a double chin...* Dylan seems to have taken the title from a traditional song called *Tell Old Bill* which appeared in Carl Sandburg's compendium of American folksongs *American Songbag*, first published in 1927. The song was later recorded by Dave Von Ronk on his second album. Its chorus runs ...*Tell Old Bill when he gets home/ Leave them downtown gals alone...* But Old Bill meets a sorry fate: ...*They brought up poor dead Bill, his toes were a-draggin'...* The phrase 'thunder blasted trees' is derived from Poe's poem *To Iolanthe in Heaven.* The centrality of the image of the 'tempest' also recalls Shakespeare's play of the same name, wherein the tempest itself has a similar symbolic significance. The song's narrator struggles, like Prospero, to control the 'spirits of the air'. The way that natural imagery is used as a metaphorical representation of inner turmoil here is also reminiscent of Shakespeare's poetic methodology. Who better a 'helper' than 'Ol' Bill' Shakespeare himself?

The enigmatically charming *Huck's Tune* was written in 2007 for director Curtis Hansen's 'gambling tale' *Lucky You* and later released on *Tell Tale Signs.* Like *Tell Ol' Bill, Huck's Tune* refers - if somewhat obliquely - to the characters and action in the film. Although it has only been performed on a handful of occasions (in early 2014) it is a supreme example of Dylan's late romantic style - a funny, touching and quite beautiful piece with a delicate, otherworldly quality and a dream-like meditation on fixation and compulsion. The movie is set in Las Vegas and tells the story of Huck Cheever (Eric Bana), a down-on-his-luck professional gambler who has to compete with his father (Robert Duvall) in a World Series poker tournament and win the love of Billie Offer (Drew Barrymore) who, despite being attracted by his apparent vulnerability, is suspicious of his character. Her suspicions are confirmed when, after their first night together, he steals money from her to use in the casino. Eventually the conflicts with his father and his lover are resolved when - against the habit of a lifetime - he deliberately loses the big poker game. The movie was not as successful as Hansen's other films such as *L.A. Confidential* and *Wonder Boys*. It lacks pace and suspense and features perhaps too many rather 'drawn out' poker sequences. As with *Wonder Boys* the film uses rock songs, including Bruce Springsteen's *Lucky Town* and *The Fever,* to counterpoint the action. Dylan's new song appears over the closing credits.

Dylan has always been fascinated by gambling, which looms large in American literary, film and song traditions. One of his earliest known recordings is an adaptation of the traditional *Rambler, Gambler* - which appears on *The Bootleg Series Vol. 7* - that he probably first heard in a version by the Clancy Brothers. In this song the narrator defines himself as a defiant outsider: ...*I'm a rambler, I' m a gambler and I'm far from my home/ And if you don't like me, you can leave me alone...* reflecting the figure of the gambler as the 'lone adventurer' who appears in many Westerns - the typical American 'outsider' who lives by his wits. Dylan has also performed *The Roving Gambler* (another traditional song) on many occasions. This has a very similar theme but here the gambler ends up dead in a shoot-out. It featured in some of his earliest coffee house performances in Greenwich Village and between 1997 and 2002 was performed in a rousing 'bluegrass' style as a set opener, often featuring strong harmony vocals by Larry Campbell and Charlie Sexton.

An early Dylan song *Rambling Gambling Willie*, which is heavily based on *Brennan on the Moor*, another ballad from the Clancy Brothers' repertoire, eulogises the 'gambling man' as a kind of folk hero. This rake and rogue has *...twenty seven children but he never had a wife....* We are reassured, however, that he supports them all. In the end, poor Willie meets the same fate as the Roving Gambler - getting shot after a card game gets out of hand. The notion of gambling as a metaphor for a certain kind of artistic freedom recurs through Dylan's work. In his 1965 song *It's All Over Now, Baby Blue* he declares that *...The highway is for gamblers/ Better use your sense/ Take what you have gathered from coincidence...* an invocation of the kind of spontaneous, inspirational creativity he was then relying on. 1975's *Lily, Rosemary and the Jack Of Hearts* is a surreal Western 'shaggy dog story' in which the eponymous and ever-elusive 'Jack of Hearts' is both a character in the song and a playing card. Indeed, the whole song can be seen a bizarre card game, rather like certain scenes in *Alice's Adventures in Wonderland.*

Each verse of *Huck's Tune* ends in the refrain *...I'm gonna have to put you down for a while....* The narrator repeatedly asserts that he will have to let her pass through his hands. In the movie, Huck Cheever is far from being a freewheelin' folk hero like *Rambling Gambling Willie*. He is such a compulsive gambler that he is prepared to betray both his girlfriend and his father to secure success at the table. Gambling now represents not freedom, but addiction and obsession. The film, however, does deliver a conventional happy ending. This is reflected in Dylan's approach to the song. The music is a dreamy waltz and his vocals here are understated, with the lyrics being delivered in a gently reassuring manner. The song is full of mischievous whimsy, balanced against a knowing, cautionary tone - very much the 'voice of experience', tinged with a certain regretful sadness.

The language of *Huck's Tune* strongly recalls that of the Romantic poets and the King James Bible. Its opening line *...I wondered alone through a desert of stone...* recalls both Wordsworth's *Daffodils* (which begins *....I wondered lonely as a cloud...*) and Shelley's *Ozymandias* (*...Two vast and trunkless legs of stone/ Stand in a desert...*). When the narrator announces that *...My sword's in my hand and I'm next in command/ In this version of death called life....* there are echoes of Blake's *Jerusalem* (*...Nor shall my sword sleep in my hand...*) and Coleridge's *Ancient Mariner* (*...The nightmare LIFE-IN-DEATH was she....*). Other lines in the first verse seem to have Biblical connotations *...My plate and my cup/ Are right straight up...* echoes Matthew 23:25: *...Woe unto you, scribes and Pharisees, hypocrites! For ye make clean the outside of the cup and of the platter, but within they are full of extortion and excess...* At the end of the verse he cries: *...When I kiss your lips/ The honey drips....* lines which resonate with *The Song Of Solomon* (Ch. 4, Verse 11): *...Thy lips, O my spouse, drop as the honeycomb: honey and milk are under thy tongue; and the smell of thy garments is like the smell of Lebanon...* and the final lines of Coleridge's celebrated opium dream *Kubla Khan: ...For he on* *honey-dew have fed/ And drunk the milk of paradise...* The song's most striking and memorable line, which scans perfectly with its waltz-time, is *...I took a rose from the hand of a child...* This may be a further declaration of innocence, although whether the 'child' has handed over the rose voluntarily is not stated. Perhaps this is a symbol of beauty or a manifestation of Blake's *Sick Rose* - the embodiment of corruption. Dylan's delicate delivery allows it to remain ambiguous.

The following four verses do not perhaps have the compressed poetic power of the first verse, which invites us into the dream-world of the song and depicts a narrator who has been lured into a 'honey trap'. But they develop the idea of compulsion in different ways, alternating between humour and dark intimations. The narrator seems fixated on the object of the song, who is in her *...girlish prime...* He seems to want to 'step out' with her to a 'ball' *...Behind every tree/ There's something to see...* he tells us *...The river is wider than a mile...* These lines recall the Johnny Mercer/ Henry Mancini standard *Moon River* (which Dylan has covered in concert on a couple of occasions). This begins: *...Moon river, wider than a mile/ I'm crossing you in style some day/ Oh, dream maker, you heart breaker/ Wherever you're going, I'm going your way...* Its mysterious 'dream river' is a symbol of romantic compulsion. In both songs the river may be either the 'river of life', which is always flowing with surprises, or the river of death. The link between the two songs becomes even stronger in the later lines in *Moon River* which run *...We're after the same rainbow's end/ My huckleberry friend and me...* A 'huckleberry' is a nineteenth century Southern American expression meaning 'the right person for the job'. It is an expression which Mark Twain was undoubtedly aware of when he named the eponymous hero of *The Adventures of Huckleberry Finn.* So here the 'three Hucks' are cleverly linked. Perhaps the river is, yet again, the mighty Mississippi, which at its widest spans more than eleven miles.

In the third verse the poker metaphor is stressed. We are introduced to the 'ladies and men' who have come to play the game, including a *...nurse with money in her purse...* The narrator admits that he will commit everything to his obsessive compulsion, despite the hopelessness of his position: *...You push it all in and you've no chance to win/ You play 'em on down to the end...* A poker player who has committed himself to a 'push in' has committed all his chips - his remaining stake - to the current game. Meanwhile, the narrator's 'dream visions' are multiplying. Various metaphorical descriptions of how he is playing the game follow. At one point he is merely observing the other players *...laying in the sand/ Getting a sunshine tan...* In another he is preparing to 'play his hand' *...moving along, riding in style...* In a nicely compact rhyme he tells the girl that *...From my toes to my head, you knock me dead...* 'You knock me dead' is a colloquial phrase, which occurs in blues songs such as John Lee Hooker's *Boom Boom*, signifying just how much the singer has been 'bowled over' by the object of his love. But here it may also have a darker significance, suggesting that the player may be being lured to his doom by this elusive Queen of Hearts. To 'knock' in a poker game means to decide not to play one's turn by knocking on the table, possibly forcing the other player to reveal a weak hand which he has been using as a bluff. The life of poker players, or addicts in general, may be characterised by the compulsion to bluff both others and themselves, as they are drawn towards playing a disastrous final hand.

The narrator becomes a little more honest in the fourth verse: *...I count the years and I shed no tears...* he tells us. *...I'm blinded to what might have been...* He searches around for some compensation: *...Nature's voice makes my heart rejoice...* he cries in anguish; words that recall those of *Country Home,* a nineteenth century hymn which is heavily influenced by romanticism:

...Quietly, quietly pass away my days
While a holy light of gladness ever round me plays
A light within the spirit
Which those happy ones inherit
Who hear nature's voice
Bidding their souls arise
From earth unto the skies
Making the heart rejoice...

In his desperation he implores the spirits to *...Play Me the Wild Song of the Wind....* which sounds like some old Irish ballad. He confesses that his love for his 'Queen' is 'hopeless'. Then he addresses her again, attempting to convey his sincerity: *...You're as fine as wine/ I ain't handing you no line...* But he will still 'have to put her down'. He is, it seems, about to play his last card. In the final verse he reaches the limits of bluffing, expressed in a curiously humorous and defiant cry of despair: *...All the merry little elves can go hang themselves...* He declares that *...my faith is as cold as can be...* Despite having a pile of chips next to him (He is *...stacked high to the roof...*) he insists that *...In my words you'll find no guile...*

Finally he asserts (twice) that *...the game's gotten old/ the deck's gone cold...* suggesting that the pack he is using has been tampered with. Thus the whole 'game of life' he has been describing may be declared invalid. Or perhaps this, or indeed the entire song, is an elaborate bluff. Throughout *Lucky You* we see Huck constantly staring at his fellow players, trying to figure out their motives. Perhaps the narrator of the song may merely be 'leading us on'. This is suggested by the playful tone that Dylan adopts throughout, as if he is singing with a 'merry twinkle' in his eye. Poker, as a game of bluff, is of course all about ambiguity - which is in many ways the most essential quality of Dylan's lyricism. The song is an extended 'tease' with the singer 'winking' at us, suggesting that all of this - and perhaps life itself - is just a kind of game. However, in the last couple of live performances of the song on the Japanese tour of Spring 2014, the 'playful' tone is turned down and Dylan pronounces the words rather more harshly. In this version he plays down any pretensions of nobility. He now has a 'whip' rather than a 'sword' in his hand. In this context the references to the 'nurse with the money in her purse' and the 'merry little elves' sound scathing rather than soothing. The tone of the song now suggests that treating life as a game has a considerable cost.

It is easy to see why Dylan was attracted to the subject matter of *Lucky You.* Over his long career, beset by reporters, critics and fans expecting him to provide 'profound' answers to their questions and having to live with the burden of being acclaimed as a 'spokesman' or a 'prophet', he has learned that avoiding straightforward answers is generally the best policy. Just as his songs have grown more ambiguous as his career has progressed, he has twisted and turned his own words in live performance around so that you can never quite pin down exactly what they mean. This is perhaps the reason why, at the end of every performance, he faces a cheering, adoring crowd with a stoically, steadfastly blank 'poker face'.

3rd October 1997. The Cardiff International Arena is a gloomy, echoey 'barn' of a place. The seats have been stripped out tonight and the 'groundlings' in the downstairs 'pit' hustle forward, trying to get the best view - if not the best audio balance - between the speakers. It is only four days since the release of *Time Out of Mind*, Dylan's first album of new songs for seven years and many of us have spent much of the last few days digesting its dark intimations of cold irons, lone figures at the gates of hell and smoke-wreathed cowboys in doorways. Tonight we are expecting - well, hoping - that we will be treated to an early live exposure of these songs. In that we will be largely disappointed.

Instead Bob and his band - with Larry Campbell on guitar and a prominent Bucky Baxter, mostly on pedal steel - play a solid, serious set including a smattering of songs from *Blonde on Blonde*, a surprise outing for *Tough Mama* from *Planet Waves* and an extended version of *Silvio*. We even get a live cover of *Stone Walls and Steel Bars*, a confessional murder ballad originally recorded by the Stanley Brothers in 1953. It is only in the first encore that we are presented with *Love Sick,* the opening number of the new album. This draws a considerable cheer from fans who already know it well. But the highlight of the evening, as everyone seems to agree, is *This Wheel's on Fire*, a song from *The Basement Tapes* which we have never heard live in this country before. Despite its being written some thirty years earlier, Dylan has only recently begun playing it in concert. With its rousing chorus and mysterious, enigmatic verses, it is a perfect choice for arena rock shows, allowing the guitarists to indulge in some dynamic solos.

It may even be that some of the less dedicated members of the audience think that Dylan is singing another cover. *This Wheel's on Fire* could perhaps be called the 'best known Dylan song which many people don't know he wrote'. This is partly because his original version was not released until 1975. Meanwhile, it had already become a 'pop standard' - having been a hit in Britain for Julie Driscoll with Brian Auger and the Trinity. Their version was illuminated by Auger's swirling organ and Driscoll's perfectly pitched, icy-cold delivery of the ominous lyrics. In the US, a powerful reading by The Byrds (1968) began with an actual explosion. The song also charted some twenty years later for Siouxsie and The Banshees, whose version is modeled on Driscoll's. The story told at the time was that Siouxsie - with her iconoclastic punk attitude still fully intact - actively hated 'old fart' Dylan's music and recorded the song without even realising who its author was. In 1992 it became the theme tune for Jennifer Saunders' spicily satirical 'generational reverse' British sitcom *Absolutely Fabulous*, with vocals by Adrian Edmonson.

The first recorded outing of *This Wheel's on Fire* was by The Band on *Music from Big Pink* (1968), in a restrained but rather subtly funky interpretation sung by bass player Rick Danko. Danko wrote the music for the song, after Dylan presented him with a typed sheet of lyrics. This was one of the first examples of Dylan collaborating with another writer. Danko probably did not take long to knock the tune together, as Dylan's lyrics already have a strongly musical quality which carries the song forwards. Dylan wrote the lyric after retreating to Woodstock as an escape from the intense 'rock'n'roll lifestyle'. The song is a rather bitter riposte to a lover who is living 'close to the edge' *...No man alive will come to you with another tale to tell...* the narrator says mysteriously. Later he informs her that *...I had to confiscate your lace/ And wrap it up in a sailor's knot and hide it in your case...* and then *...You called on me to call on them to get you your favors done...* The lines about the 'lace' and the 'knot' may be associated with heroin use, suggesting that the woman is an addict. The imagery in the chorus depicts a dramatic road accident such as the one Dylan suffered in 1966. The phrase *...If your memory serves you well...* begins and ends each of the three verses and in each case the repeated rhyming of 'tell' with 'well' is delayed until the final line. Several of the lines do not rhyme with anything, which makes the delayed rhyme even more effective with each repetition. The music and lyrics do not require a 'showy' vocal performance. Tonight's rendition, featuring Dylan's rather abrasive but somehow offhand vocals, is especially effective.

The way the perilous journey at the heart of the song is dramatised by the driving music suggests that it is a warning about the allure of the 'live fast and die young' lifestyle, which was much romanticised in the 1950s and 60s. Whereas in *My Generation* (1965) The Who's Roger Daltrey spat out the alarming message *...Hope I die before I get old...* Dylan's song is written from the detached point of view of one who has (only just) survived. The narrator rejects temptation but warns of possible imminent disaster. The repeated line *...If your memory serves you well...* is also the first line of Wallace Fowlie's definitive translation of Arthur Rimbaud's *A Season in Hell*, which proposes that a poet can only achieve greatness through a systematic derangement of the senses :

...I have withered within me all human hope. With the silent leap of a sullen beast, I have downed and strangled every joy. I have called for executioners; I want to perish chewing on their gun butts... ...I have called for plagues, to suffocate in sand and blood. Unhappiness has been my god. I have lain down in the mud, and dried myself off in the crime-infested air. I have played the fool to the point of madness....

The image of a fiery wheel in *This Wheel's on Fire* suggests the Biblical 'wheel of Ezekiel', in which the prophet is overcome and humbled by the immense power of Jehovah. It also reminds us of King Lear's desperate pronouncement about the certainty of the fate he has brought about for himself through his foolish and egotistical actions.

He says to his 'ideal daughter' Cordelia: *...Thou art but a soul in bliss/ But I am bound upon a wheel of fire...* The lyrics also recall the Johnny Cash song *Ring of Fire*, which is concerned with the 'demonic' power of obsessive desire. There are even echoes of Vera Lynn's stirringly patriotic World War Two song *We'll Meet Again,* which was used to such devastatingly ironic effect by Stanley Kubrick in the final scene from his brilliantly scathing black comedy *Dr. Strangelove* (1964) which depicts nuclear Armageddon. Tonight, as Dylan finally takes possession of his 'pop classic', the performance seems to encapsulate all the themes of an album which takes us into similar emotional territory. The screaming guitars create a particularly chilling 'vibe' which sends shivers down our spines, as we are drawn towards the inexorable, thrilling but very scary explosion which comes at the end of each chorus. Although Dylan is yet to play *Time Out of Mind*'s opening number, we are 'love sick' already.

W*orkingman's Blues #2* from *Modern Times* is a song whose intertextual nature is quite explicitly signposted. It is presented as a 'follow up' to Merle Haggard's 1967 celebration of blue-collar pride, *Workin' Man Blues*, although it uses only the chorus line: *...Sing a little bit of these workin' man's blues...* from Haggard's song. And while *Workin' Man Blues* is a straight twelve bar shuffle, Dylan's song is not (in the musical sense) a blues at all. Distinguished by a shimmering arrangement and heartfelt vocals and crammed with memorable poetic twists, it has a decidedly anthemic and elegiac quality. Its focus is on the difference between the sensibilities of our 'modern times' and the historical moment in which the original song was written. In the late 1960s, country music - which is primarily an expression of the culture of white southerners - tended to be viewed by the denizens of the 'alternative society' as a reactionary force, despite the fact that country influences were clearly discernible in the 'country rock' bands of this period. A song such as The Byrds' sublime *I Wasn't Born to Follow*, which appears on the *Easy Rider* soundtrack, mixes a country sound with the 'psychedelic' effects of phased guitars. At this time, however, a song like *Workin' Man Blues* would have been seen as terminally unhip. Yet from today's perspective it is more likely to be viewed as a minor classic of Americana; in its own way as much a product of the late '60s as the psychedelic songs of the Jefferson Airplane.

As a prominent country singer and something of a spokesman for working class Americans, Haggard's rather ornery response to the rise of the hippie generation was to write songs which pointed out that 'ordinary folks' did not have the luxury of 'dropping out'. Perhaps the most famous of these was his 1969 hit *Okie from Muskogee,* sung from the perspective of a returning Vietnam vet, who is dismayed and rather bewildered by what has happened to his country while he has been away. Its famous opening lines *...We don't smoke marijuana in Muskogee/ We don't take our trips on LSD...* sets the tone for a song which then proceeds to list all the 'hippieish' things that 'ordinary folks' from this rural location pointedly do *not* do - burning their draft cards, making a *...party out of lovin'...* growing their hair *...long and shaggy...* or wearing sandals.

In *Workin' Man Blues,* Haggard's narrator defines himself as an upstanding member of the 'proletariat' who has been *...a workin' man dang near all my life...* supporting nine kids and a wife with his 'working hands'. He's determined to keep working *...as long as my two hands are fit to use...* and declares (twice in the song, so we can't fail to get the point) that he *..ain't never been on welfare/ That's one place I won't be...* However, as he mulls over his beer in a tavern, he does confess that sometimes he has fantasised about doing *...a little bumming around...* But the responsibilities he carries mean that he has never had the chance to do this. His moment of doubt is quickly excised as he reiterates his intention to *...keep on workin'...* In fact, both songs are, despite their apparently 'redneck' approach, slightly tongue in cheek. Even when a relatively 'clean cut' Haggard performs *Okie* on a 1969 TV show you can almost see a slight smile on his face as he delivers the apparently 'reactionary' lines. *Okie* was even covered rather affectionately in concert by James Taylor, one of the quintessential 'alternative' singer-songwriters.

Although the narrator of *Workin' Man Blues* is undoubtedly proud of his stance, we are left in little doubt that his life is gruelling and unrewarding. He has to keep on working simply because he has no choice. No doubt he's in that tavern a lot, downing a great deal of beer. And although he proudly asserts his social distance from the hippies, he does seem rather jealous of them. In fact Haggard himself was known to be a prolific marijuana smoker, as well as later being a close pal of legendary unrepentant 'toker' Willie Nelson. Around the time Haggard released his songs, Dylan was publicly and very controversially embracing country music with the release of albums like *Nashville Skyline* and *Self Portrait.* By 2006 a decidedly 'scruffy haired' Haggard could be found touring in support of Dylan, interspersing his songs with sneering references to George W. Bush's right wing policies and spinning droll tales about hanging out with - and getting very 'wrecked' with - his good buddy Willie.

Workingman's Blues #2 evokes both bitter nostalgia and defiant dignity. The singer could be the narrator of Haggard's song, now grown old. The desperate plight of the hard pressed 'workin' man' is presented here in an especially moving way. But this is not the kind of militantly anti-capitalist 'protest song' that Woody Guthrie once sang so eloquently. Despite its winning tune and lush presentation, the emotions it conveys are ambivalent, complex, and sometimes confused. In the context of modern economic times, the straightforward values that Haggard's narrator espouses now seem sadly irrelevant. Lines from Ovid's latter day work *Tristia* are quoted throughout. *Tristia* was written when Ovid had been sent into exile and takes the form of a series of letters imploring the Emperor Augustus to allow him to return to Rome. Dylan identifies a strange congruence between this condition of exile, the plight of a modern working man and his own position as another kind of 'working man' who is distinctly distanced from much of contemporary life.

The recording of the song on *Modern Times* begins with Dylan's own haunting piano intro, underpinned by Donnie Herron's understated viola and George Receli's clipped, military-march style drumming. The voice is warm and resonant, gentle and welcoming. The first image is of sunset: *...There's an evening haze settling over town/ Starlight at the edge of the creek...* The words and the singing style create an idyllic picture. We are then transported into 'political' territory: *...The buying power of the proletariat's gone down/ Money's getting shallow and weak...* The use of the term 'proletariat' sounds oddly archaic and strangely nostalgic here. At the end of the verse the narrator, still calm and reflective, comments that *...They say low wages are a reality/ If we want to compete abroad...* To some extent this recalls Dylan's 'Guthriesque' concern for the American working man, as expressed in his 1964 song *North Country Blues* in which the mines are shut because foreign workers will *...work almost for nothing...* or *Heartland,* his 1994 collaboration with Willie Nelson which lamented the fate of American farmers left high and dry by the big corporations. But here the narrator delivers the lines with a sense of stoical acceptance. There is no real anger or attempt at political analysis. The narrator is concerned not with rebellion but with survival.

After the initial situation is outlined, the backdrops against which the narrator sings begin to shift. The narrative is gradually transformed into this dispossessed working man's dream vision. He closes his eyes while *...listening to the steel rails hum...* (a reference to the traditional *Hobo's Lament,* which Dylan would have first heard performed by Woody Guthrie) suggesting he is now a vagrant himself, reduced to riding a freight train. But he is not doing this because, like Haggard's working man, he dreams of attaining the freedom to 'bum around'. Like the migrant workers of the Great Depression, he has no choice. The great irony here is that he is no longer a working man at all. His work has been taken away. The hunger he is fighting to stop *...creeping its way into my gut...* may be real hunger or a hunger for 'what has been lost'. In any case he sounds tearful, and resigned to his fate, telling us (in a phrase borrowed from *Tristia*) that he has now hung up his 'cruel weapons'.

The song takes us inside the mind of the protagonist who, squashed into a narrow space in his box car, now finds his memories overcoming him. He is clearly in a very desperate situation. Past, present and future now seem to be jumbled up in his mind. The figure he addresses, whom he implores to *...come sit down on my knee...* seems to be one of his children, now grown to adulthood, who he dearly wants to enfold with love. But his mind is continually restless. He knows there are still battles to be fought. In each chorus he fantasises that, together with this child, he will again fight the bosses. The first part of the chorus seems to express a determination not to be defeated: *...Meet me at the bottom, don't lag behind/ Bring me my boots and shoes...* is a direct lift of a phrase that occurs in various blues songs, such as Bumble Bee Slim's *I'll Meet You in the Bottom* (1936), later rewritten by Willie Dixon for Howlin' Wolf. It is as if he is preparing for a 'war', declaring that *...You can hang back or fight your best on the front line...* The final line of the chorus *...Sing a little bit of these workingman's blues...* quotes Haggard's modest refrain as if it is a sacred call to arms. But the tone of the song, and Dylan's resigned delivery, suggests that the traditional values being celebrated in his chorus are now sadly outdated.

The narrator's dark visions begin to overwhelm him. He imagines dragging those who have dispossessed him down to hell and lining them up against a wall to have them shot. He is weary, confused, his consciousness *...tossed by the wind and the seas...* But the stirring tune, which at times recalls an old Irish lament, conveys only sadness and regret. Already he is sinking into an apathetic sleep, resigned to his redundancy in this cruel world that has rejected him: *...Sometimes no one wants what we got/ Sometimes you can't give it away...* In a phrase which is used in Robert Johnson's *Hot Tamales (They're Red Hot)* (1936) he tells us that he *...sleeps in the kitchen with my feet in the hall...* But of course he has no house - only this tiny freight train carriage where the 'kitchen' and the 'hall' exist in the same location. He imagines himself confronted by countless faceless enemies, who are crowding in on him. And he senses that death itself may not be far away. Sleep is comforting to him because it is *...like a temporary death...* In the darkness he feels a *...lover's breath...* a phrase borrowed from Timrod depicting a force which will awaken the spiritual life within. But it is too late for that 'breath' to work on him. He feels *...the night birds call...* He knows that the end will soon be nigh. Yet there is no sense of panic, or despair. The music remains stately and unstressed. The band are subdued and disciplined behind the singer's masterful control of his breath.

The narrator is exiled (like Ovid) from his land and his children. He knows that *...the sun is sinking...* on his life. In a direct quotation from *Tristia,* he cries: *...Tell me now, am I wrong in thinking/ That you have forgotten me...* He mourns the fact that the child has 'wounded him' with his words. In the final verses he tries to heal the rift between them but he then becomes possessed by a disturbing vision of what will happen to the child: *...All across the peaceful sacred fields they will lay you low/ They'll break your horns and slash you with steel...* He implores the lost child to look into his eyes one final time. And then, as his life begins to ebb away, he fantasises that the child will (in another phrase drawn from Ovid) *...lead me off in a cheerful dance...* Everything will be remade anew. He sees himself with *...a brand new suit and a brand new wife...* and declares that he can live well on a meagre diet of 'rice and beans'. In the final moments he restates his pride in being a 'working man' by telling us that he is ready to work again, unlike those who *...never worked a day in their life/ Don't know what work even means...* But in the end, as the sun sinks on his life, and although circumstances have overwhelmed him, he does have something solid to cling to. His pride, in the end, is his salvation.

Workingman's Blues #2 was performed in over 150 shows between 2006 and 2010. When it returned to the set list in 2015 it had a much more subdued melody and extensively rewritten lyrics. In a performance in Hamburg in July 2015, the narrator's desire to get revenge on his enemies by 'dragging them down to hell' is replaced by the fear that *...If I stay here I will lose it all/ The bandits will rob me blind...* In the next verse - which is almost completely rewritten - the narrator appears to meet his father (who is presumably long dead) on the street *...At least I think it was him...* he tells us. *...If I told you my whole story you'd weep....* The dream-like quality of such lines is emphasised even more in the new, and very resigned *...It's a cold black night and it's midsummer's eve/ And the stars are spinning around/ I still find it so hard to believe/ That someone would kick me when I'm down...*

In later verses he appears to have answered the 'call to arms', with the Ovidian remorse replaced by an attempt at Homeric 'valour': *...I'll punch my spear straight through/ Halfways down your spine...* But his efforts are still all in vain. Dylan's resigned delivery assures us that this is all mere fantasy, although the narrator declares his willingness to take the consequences: *...I'll lift up my arms to the starry skies/ And pray the fugitive's prayer...* This may be a reference to Haggard's song *The Fugitive,* a song which pays tribute to Dylan by declaring that *...a fugitive must be a rolling stone...* The rewritten final verse has a rather hopeless tone: *... The battle is over up in the hills/ And the mist is closing in/ Look at me, with all of my spoils/ What did I ever win....* Now the expectation of being led off in a 'cheerful dance' has gone. The narrator portrays himself as a tragic figure, whose battles have left him feeling merely empty.

Workingman's Blues #2 laments the death of a certain kind of American ethos, as expressed in Woody Guthrie's songs of working class solidarity and in novels such as *The Grapes of Wrath,* John Steinbeck's tragic epic about the dispossession of Oklahoman farmers. It emphasises how, in the modern world, the pride that working men have traditionally had in their labour has been ground down by the coming of a more complex economic and social environment in which the 'enemies' of working people are much harder to identify. It is also worth mentioning that Dylan himself has publicly declared himself a 'working man'. Through the decades of the Never Ending Tour he has pursued the goal of reasserting his position as a musical force and reinvented his art through a policy of constantly dedicating himself to his 'day job' as a working musician, without any thought of slowing down or retiring. Thus we can hear Dylan's authentic voice in the struggle of his song's protagonist as he fights to maintain the 'dignity of labour'.

In *Ain't Talkin',* the concluding track on *Modern Times,* Dylan takes us down another, even darker road. This song is set in an unremittingly bleak moral universe. The cruel and vengeful narrator is as morally compromised as the protagonist of Poe's most horrific short stories. All the action, consisting as it does of a series of personal confessions, appears to occur in his mind. Although he presents himself as a traveller, and the relentlessly slow burning rhythm suggests someone who is doggedly plodding across difficult terrain, by the end of the song he does not seem to have moved beyond the 'mystic garden' where he began. It is as if he is circling around a limited space, talking to himself, brooding on his own misery and suffering and vowing to enact his vengeance. One might think of Hitler in prison, dictating *Mein Kampf* and planning to unleash his doctrines on the world. The song is a study of how corrupted the human heart can become.

Dylan's vocals are delivered in a husky whisper that remains steady and unwavering throughout, reflecting the unyielding logic of the narrative. The narrator never becomes over emotional, which makes the tale he relates even more chilling. The track begins with an ominous flourish of piano, acoustic guitar and mournful viola before muted drums and acoustic bass take us into the verses, keeping up a repetitive beat over which snatches of guitar and viola occasionally surface. This creates a feeling of continual tension and dark menace. Even after the music ends its echoes seem to be fading away into the distance. The version on *Modern Times* is longer and slower than in subsequent live performances. It begins with a mournful sounding flourish of piano, bass and viola before launching into an unhurried but insistent rhythm. Much of the effect of the song is achieved through the resonances it creates. It makes judicious use of lyrics from traditional Irish and Scottish ballads and includes several 'quotations' from Ovid.

The opening line *...As I walked out in the mystic garden...* may be derived from the Irish ballad *As I Roved Out*, one of several wanderers' songs' that are referenced here. The 'garden' is certainly no Eden. It may be a symbolic representation of the narrator's disturbed mind, in which *...the wounded flowers are dangling from the vine...* an image resonant of Blake's ironically titled *Garden of Love*, a place where *...Priests in black gowns were walking their rounds/ And binding with briars, my joys and desires...* The next two lines counterpose the deliberately archaic *...I was passing by yon cool crystal fountain...* with the explicitly contemporary *...someone hit me from behind...* an abrupt juxtaposition of formal and colloquial tones in which the natural imagery is immediately interrupted by (a probably imaginary) act of violence. The verses follow an AB, AB rhyme scheme but in the 'A' endings Dylan 'rhymes' 'garden' with 'fountain'. This makes the 'B' sounds of 'vines' and 'behind' more vivid and direct, emphasising the harshness of the violence which exists in the corrupted 'garden' of the narrator's mind. The phrase *...yon cool crystal fountain...* is lifted from the traditional Scottish ballad *Wild Mountain Thyme*, a highly romantic celebration of the beauty of the Scottish Highlands with their summer covering of 'purple heather'. Dylan has performed this on several occasions over the years - most memorably during his acoustic set at the Isle of Wight Festival in 1969.

Judicious use is also made of rhyme in the song's nine choruses, each of which also contain four 'ABAB' lines. In each case the 'A' line *...Ain't talkin', just walkin'...* is rhymed with *...Heart burnin' still yearnin'...* a phrase taken from the Stanley Brothers' *Highway of Regret.* This is a lively bluegrass tune played on banjo and guitar, whose sentiments are those of a young lover who laments losing his girl. But Dylan upturns the 'innocent' phrase to make the psychopathic nature of the narrative more pronounced. The second and fourth lines are varied in every chorus *...Through this weary world of woe...* is rhymed with *...No one on earth would ever know....* emphasising the 'secret' nature of the narrator's confession *...Weary world of woe...* is from *Wayfaring Stranger,* a traditional ballad which Dylan performed in the early days of the Never Ending Tour. It is an uplifting account of a poverty-stricken wanderer's journey through the world. He contrasts his lot with a vision of the bliss of heaven to come, to which he is sure his journey will lead him. The direct opposite, in fact, of *Ain't Talkin'.*

It seems clear by now that the narrator's soul has been thoroughly blighted by self pity and self loathing. For a few brief moments in the second verse he appears to be aware of this and begs for assistance *...They say prayer has the power to help, so pray for me, mother...* This appeal for aid recalls such sentimental tunes as *Mother Dear, O Pray for Me,* a hymn asking for the Virgin Mary's protection, which was recorded by Bing Crosby (1951) or *Pray for Me, Mother of Mine* (1985) by country crooner Marty Robbins. But this is immediately demolished by the narrator's unequivocal, Poe-like admission that *...In the human heart an evil spirit does dwell...* The narrator then protests that *...I'm trying to love my neighbor and do good unto others/ But oh mother, things ain't goin' well...* Again Dylan uses the 'ABAB' rhyme scheme to devastating effect, contrasting such apparently conventional Christian sentiments with snarling denials. In the second chorus he declares that *...I'll burn that bridge before you can cross...* and *...there'll be no mercy for you once you've lost...* As far as we know he is alone in the garden but he can now turn his ire upon his potential victims.

In the next verse he attempts to win our sympathy by describing his own suffering: *...I'm all worn down by weepin'/ My eyes are filled with tears, my lips are dry...* But he quickly reveals his true intentions: *...If I catch my opponents ever sleepin'...* he snarls *...I'll just slaughter them where they lie...* The nonchalance with which Dylan delivers the lines, the first of several quotations from Ovid (in this case from *Amores*) makes their effect especially chilling. We can be in no doubt now that this is a soul in great torment, slogging his way through an increasingly murky landscape which he now describes as *...mysterious and vague...* He is *...walkin' through the cities of the plague...* like a character in one of Poe's 'medieval' stories *King Pest* or *The Masque of the Red Death.*

The narrator then rails against an unknown 'they' (presumably the 'enemies' he referred to earlier) who seem hell bent on victimising him and who will (in a phrase taken from Ovid's *Black Sea Letters*) *...tear your mind away from contemplation...* This seems to imply that the narrator's 'enemies' are an opposing sect, suggesting that he may be part of some fanatical religious group. In the middle ages, many saw the plague as the punishment of a (highly cruel and vengeful) deity. It is clearly this vengeful God which the narrator is in thrall to. He appears to be revelling in being surrounded by so much death and destruction. In the next chorus the narrator refers to *...eating hog-eyed grease in a hog-eyed town...* as if he is in a Mexican cantina in some weird Spaghetti Western. The line derives from the rather bizarre sea shanty *Hog-Eye Man*, which was often adorned by many obscene verses and which was originally sung by sailors to disparage the captains of 'hog-eye' barges used in rivers in the US in the nineteenth century *...Some day you'll be glad to have me around...* the narrator growls menacingly.

Soon the narrator's paranoia seems to have taken over: *...They will crush you with wealth and power...* he tells us conspiratorially *...Every waking moment you could crack...* Then *...I'll make the most of one last extra hour...* may suggest that he himself is under a 'death sentence'. Perhaps the whole song is the ramblings of a condemned man in his final hour. In the verse's final line he reveals that *...I'll avenge my father's death and I'll step back...* He is determined to do this even if it costs him his own life. But now he seems to be 'on his last legs': *...Hand me down my walking cane...* he commands in the next chorus (using the title of a well known minstrel song, which is also referenced in some versions of *Hog-Eye Man*), as if he needs physical assistance to complete his task. Now he rails at his victim, crying out *...Got to get you out of my miserable brain...* as if he is trying to stop himself reliving a crime he has committed.

In the succeeding verses, the narrator grows ever more crazed, increasingly spouting 'religious' justifications for his apparent crimes. Despite its suggested historical and Biblical contexts, *Ain't Talkin'* taps into perhaps the most pressing of our contemporary fears. To say it is a 'song about a suicide bomber' would be too simplistic, although this could be another interpretation of the line indicating that the narrator only has an hour left. The insistent rhythm he sings over could represent the ticking of a bomb set to explode when his time is up. In the next - and perhaps the most mysteriously enigmatic - verse, he expresses angry self-righteousness: *...All my loyal and much-loved companions...* he scowls *...they approve of me and share my code...* The last word of the line is particularly challenging. Does the narrator possess, or think he possesses, some arcane numerical formula that perhaps only his 'loyal and much-loved' followers understand? There is certainly a suggestion here that he is some kind of extremist cult leader *...I practice a faith that's been long abandoned...* is deliberately and teasingly ambiguous, indicating a certain type of 'religious' mentality which justifies and even promotes intolerance and extreme violence, and which arrogantly assumes it alone possesses the 'secret codes' that tell us all how to live. The narrator's *...long and lonesome road...* lacks any 'altars' or formal religious institutions. He does not need them. He is walking - it seems - across a barren landscape towards some place where he can enact his revenge. But he seems to have lost his way. Even his mule is 'sick'. And his horse, like the one belonging to the 'little boy' in Dylan's quirky ecological nursery rhyme *Under the Red Sky* (1990), is blind.

The narrator now gazes upward for inspiration, seeing the heavens lit up by 'flying wheels'. He appears to view himself as some kind of 'chosen one'. This, of course, is what all fanatically-driven mass murderers choose to believe. Yet the 'wheels on fire' he refers to have been extinguished *...The fire has gone out...* he tells us *...But the light is never dying...* In another line taken from Ovid's *Tristia* he asks, rhetorically *...Who says I can't get heavenly aid?...* But as he continues to will himself towards his final 'confession' he is determined to let us know about his own sacrifices. He tells us that he is *...carrying a dead man's shield...* and is suffering pain that is 'unending', with a *...toothache in my heel....* (a reference to *Old Dan Tucker,* another nineteenth century minstrel song, whose protagonist is said to have died from the complaint). He is determined to proclaim that he has no doubts and is serious about his task: *...I'm not playin', I'm not pretendin'...* he warns us *...I'm not nursing any superfluous fears...*

And then, suddenly, we are back in the 'mystic garden'. But instead of being in darkness, we are in bright sunlight. It seems that *...there's no one here/ the gardener has gone...* The narrator has entered the 'Gates of Eden' once again, to find that its creator has disappeared. The 'mystic garden' is described as *...the last outback at the* *world's end...* This is another line from Green's translation of Ovid. 'Outback' is an Australian term suggesting an endlessly stretching desert, baked by the sun. As we see the narrator disappearing into the distance we are left here, high and dry, in a place where all vegetation has withered and all hope has gone. The track ends with a final despondent burst of viola, as we are presented with an apocalyptic vision of desolation. This, the song appears to imply, is the possible fate of the world if such religious fanatics get their way.

The *Modern Times* version of the song is a slow building rumination, which lasts for almost nine minutes. The 'alternate version' (almost certainly an earlier take) on *Tell Tale Signs* is almost three minutes shorter. It is punchier with considerable lyrical variation and a faster, more pronounced rhythmic pulse which suggests a mood of panic and despair rather than grim resignation. The near-spoken vocals strain against the compelling 'open heartbeat' that drives the song onwards. *Ain't Talkin'* was performed over a hundred times between 2007 and 2013. Musically, this earlier take is closer to the way Dylan presented the song in live performance, although it retains the 'later' lyrics. In the *Tell Tale Signs* version the narrator places more emphasis on his abandonment by a lover and there is a less apocalyptic tone. The narrator is more breathless, and is so stressed that he has become ill *...I've got no time for idle conversation...* he tells us *....I need to find a doctor in this town...* He is careworn and stressed, declaring that *...I'm all worn out with public service, I'm beginning to crack...* There is none of the steely determination which prevails in the climax to the *Modern Times* version *...I'm goin' to throw myself upon your loving breast...* he wails, either to his lover or his saviour (though there is much less explicitly 'religious' imagery here).

In the most remarkable verse of the *Tell Tale Signs* version the narrator is cowed by a vision before which he can only tremble. Here the 'mystic garden' is bathed in bright autumnal light and illuminated by resonant, allusive symbolism. The faster rhythm and pronounced alliteration emphasises the singer's terror: *...It's the first new day of a grand and a glorious Autumn...* he breathes *...The Queen of Love is coming across the grass...* In this version he bows down before this Amazonian figure, obviously a beautiful and very powerful woman *...None dare call her anything but 'Madam'/ No one flirts with her or even makes a pass...* he tells us in awe. This vision seems to be the 'main event' of the song at this point. Here he confronts what appears to be the source of his distress. The Queen of Love (Virgil's name for Venus in *The Aeneid)* has conquered him. He kneels at her feet, bowed into submission. In the next variation on the chorus we see him *...standing outside the Gates of Wrath...* The last phrase is a direct reference to Blake's *Daybreak*, which runs: *...To find the western path/ Right through the Gates of Wrath/ I urge my way...* Blake's poem presents a vision of earthly peace and reconciliation but Dylan's narrator stands 'outside' those gates, excluded from redemption. In a rather charming ironic touch, we hear that instead of entering the gates he has to *...take a little trip along the primrose path...* Here the allusion is to *Hamlet* (1:3) where Ophelia, challenged by her brother Laertes over her attraction to

Hamlet, makes a sarcastic aside referring to Laertes' own dalliances: *...Himself the primrose path of dalliance treads...* she says, scornfully.

Dylan's hero, like Shakespeare's, has been driven half mad by love. But he must follow that 'primrose path' to whatever part of the 'mystic garden' it leads. This version ends with a repetition of the song's first lines, bringing us back full circle, followed by the enigmatic *...Ain't talkin', just walkin'/ You ride 'em high and down you go...* Along with the earlier reference to *...all rails leading to the west...* this seems to suggest more of a frontier/cowboy scenario than the final version. The imagery points towards a mythic past and the song seems to be more focused on the idea of the 'mystic garden' as a kind of Edenic vision of 'frontier America'. Dylan's 'mystic traveller' is still ruthless, still ready to 'slaughter his enemies', but now he rides off into the sunset in the time-honoured way, following that 'primrose path' wherever it will lead.

12th March 2004. The 70th Anniversary Benefit Concert for the Apollo Theater in Harlem is being filmed tonight. It will be featured on TV in a few weeks as NBC's *A Hot Night in Harlem*. The auditorium only seats 1500, but for seven decades it has played a prominent role in African American culture. In the 1930s it was one of the first major theatres to open its doors to black audiences. Since then it has been a proving ground for generations of performers, from Billie Holiday and Dionne Warwick to Lauryn Hill and Michael Jackson. Both Ella Fitzgerald and Jimi Hendrix won its legendary talent contests as teenagers. In 1963 the 'Godfather of Soul' James Brown recorded his legendary *Live at the Apollo* album here. When he died in 2006, Brown's body was brought back to the theatre before burial so that his fans could pay tribute. Tonight's show includes appearances by Natalie Cole, Patti Austin, Ice-T, Herbie Hancock, and Patti LaBelle. Bob Dylan is one of a small number of white performers who have been honoured by being invited to appear.

The acts are introduced by prominent black public figures, including Denzel Washington and Al Sharpton. Dylan's contribution is preceded by a short speech by the veteran actor and director Ossie Davis, once a leading figure in the Civil Rights movement, whose stentorian tones convey considerable gravitas:

> *...At the end of the '50s the Civil Rights movement was growing very insistent - hot and heavy. My generation was involved in challenging America's deep racial divide. We marched, we prayed, we preached and fought for freedom. Music became a significant force in bringing those issues to light and bringing the people together. A young singer by the name of Sam Cooke was dominating the charts. Sam heard a song that asked a mighty important question....*

At this point a screen behind him shows a clip of Sam Cooke singing *Blowin' in the Wind.* Davis continues:

...It prompted him to write what is perhaps his most heartfelt and moving work 'A Change Is Gonna Come', a song which became an anthem for the Civil Rights movement. To perform this for us tonight is someone I've had the pleasure of introducing before...

Davis gives a knowing smile.

...when we were together once on that historic day in Washington DC in 1963 when Dr. Martin Luther King told us about 'the dream' he wanted to share with all America. I'm pleased... nay happy... to reintroduce this artist again tonight...

Since Sam Cooke recorded *A Change is Gonna Come* in 1964 it has become a modern standard and a vocal showcase for many leading black singers, including Otis Redding, Al Green, Aretha Franklin, Jennifer Hudson and Beyoncé. In 2008 Barack Obama quoted from the song in his first speech after becoming President. It was performed at his inauguration ceremony by Jon Bon Jovi and Bettye LaVette. The song was written after Cooke and his wife were denied entrance to a whites-only motel in Louisiana, despite the fact that Cooke was a famous star who had been scoring chart hits for over five years. After he protested, he was arrested by the police for 'disturbing the peace'. By the time the song was released as a single in late 1964, he was dead, having been killed in a controversial shooting in another motel.

The recording features a massive number of musicians and progresses like a classical piece through three 'movements' - the first verse being based on horns, the second on strings and the third on timpani. The lush arrangement is enhanced by Cooke's clearly enunciated vocal. The melody bears some resemblance to *Ol' Man River* (from which it also borrows a few lines), written in 1927 by Jerome Kern and Oscar Hammerstein for the musical *Showboat* as a vehicle for Paul Robeson, then the USA's most prominent African American performer and a leading civil rights activist. The opening lines *...I was born by the river in a little tent/ And just like that river I've been running ever since...* are highly expressive in the way they modify the symbol of the 'river', while the lack of conventional rhyme suggests discord. The experience of a 'hard life' is expressed as spiritual doubt: *...It's been too hard livin'/ But I'm afraid to die/ 'Cause I don't know what's up there/ Beyond the sky...* These lines are particularly powerful because their expression of uncertainty is set against a melody and chorus that are deeply rooted in the kind of religious music that emphasises the importance of faith. For the first six years of his career, Cooke (whose father was a minister) had been a member of the Soul Stirrers, a prominent gospel group. The great power of the song lies in the fact that the singer is prepared to make a declaration of faith in the future, despite knowing that that faith alone will not be enough to bring about the change.

Dylan and his touring band perform an underplayed reading of a song which is often used as a vehicle for unrestrained emotion. Against a sparse musical backdrop, Dylan's vocal delivery is - in contrast to the song's stirring melody - especially harsh. He also reinserts the third verse which appears in Cooke's original album version of the song but which was cut out for the single so as not to 'offend' listeners: *...I go to the movie/ And I go down town....* he sings coolly *...Somebody been tellin' me/ Don't hang around...*

Whereas other performers often allow the song's winsome melody to carry it through to a triumphantly hopeful climax, Dylan ends the song with a brief affirmation: *...It's been a long time comin'/ But a change is gonna come... Yes it will...* and then curtails the performance with brutal abruptness. He is given a huge standing ovation by the overwhelmingly black audience but as usual he does not smile or respond. He stands stock still behind the keyboard he has been crouching over during the performance, his face expressionless. His stripped-down reading of the song has emphasised that, whatever we may hope for, the 'change' has certainly not come *yet*.

Pay in Blood, from *Tempest*, is a strident and riff-heavy rock track, whose amoral, strutting, arrogant tone has been compared to the more 'demonic' songs of the Rolling Stones. It certainly dispenses some violent imagery and appears to have definite political overtones, as well as intimations of Old Testament-style vows of vengeance. The notion of 'paying in blood' is often invoked in discussions about the 'sacrifices' made by soldiers in wartime, but the song's payoff line twists this around in several ways. By the 2010s the phrase 'pay in blood but not my own' might be taken to have become the dominant slogan of America's foreign policy. US involvement in the wars of other countries had reached a new level of cynical detachment. Most US ground troops were withdrawn from war zones around the world and 'conflicts' were now conducted remotely. Computer-controlled drones were used to 'take out' specific targets, often contributing to large scale 'collateral damage' among innocent people but resulting in no loss of US personnel. At the same time the weapons industry, which Dylan had once castigated in *Masters of War*, naturally continued to prosper.

The song is also an angry diatribe about oppression within America which appears to straddle past, present and even future. Although it appeared several years before Donald Trump's election to the presidency in 2016, its presentation of confused and dangerous rhetoric is eerily prescient of the 'post truth' mentality and racial tension that dominated the latter years of the 2010s. In the era of Trump, an egotistical business mogul and former Reality TV star - known for his xenophobic attitude towards foreigners, his blatantly sexist and racist rhetoric and his open support for militant right wing paramilitary elements - Dylan's notion that the legacy of the American Civil War still loomed over the condition of modern American life took on new relevance. In a 2012 interview with *Rolling Stone* he commented:

...The United States burned and destroyed itself for the sake of slavery. The USA wouldn't give it up. It had to be grinded out. The whole system had to be ripped out with force. A lot of killing. What, like, 500,000 people? A lot of destruction to end slavery...This country is just too fucked up about color. It's a distraction. People at each other's throats just because they are of a different color... It's the height of insanity, and it will hold any nation back or any neighborhood back. Or any anything back. Blacks know that some whites didn't want to give up slavery and that if they had their way, they would still be under the yoke... It's a country founded on the backs of

slaves... It's the root cause. If slavery had been given up in a more peaceful way, America would be far ahead today...

Pay in Blood presents a vivid snapshot of the attitudes of certain elements within a nation in which racial inequality persists on a huge scale and where negative attitudes towards those from other countries have become more prominent. Its imagery and modes of address are often ambiguous, as if a kind of 'civil war' of meaning is going on within the angry and violent exchanges. It is not just a song 'about' war or racial inequality - the two issues which Dylan addressed most often in his early 'protest' songs - but one which explores the entire mentality of human cruelty, hypocrisy and the desire for revenge. Despite Dylan delivering the lyrics in his bitterest snarl, it is often hard to tell whether the angry pronouncements are coming from the mouth of just one narrator or whether there is a dialogue going on between two or more speakers. Such confusion can be said to be reflective of the current media-drenched age, in which the plethora of information that we are continually bombarded with can make it very difficult to separate one voice from another, or truth from fiction. Whereas early songs like *The Death of Emmett Till, Only a Pawn in Their Game, Oxford Town* or *The Lonesome Death of Hattie Carroll* had dissected instances of racial violence by placing them in the context of an analysis of the corruption in American society, in *Pay in Blood* Dylan confronts the sickness in the body politic by using an ambiguous and often confusing 'play of voices' to demonstrates how the rhetoric of violence eats away at its soul.

The song has six verses of eight lines each and no choruses, and the harsh refrain *...I Pay in Blood, but not my own...* occurs at the end of every verse. In performance the song has been shortened to five verses with some significant lyrical revisions. Six of the eight lines in each verse follow a regular rhythm, but lines five and six shift keys and verbal phrasing, adding dramatic tension. In concert, the harsh vocals are softened somewhat as Dylan plays with the ambiguous lyrics, as if he is deliberately shifting 'personalities' in different performances. The character who appears to enunciate most of the vitriol appears to be a sociopath, but one who justifies his actions in the name of 'religious' virtues. In Christian belief, Jesus willingly accepted his death to 'pay in blood' for the sins of others. Here, using the brutal language of bigotry, Dylan demonstrates how this credo has been perverted to justify the continuous application of hatred within a society at war with itself. 'The laws of God' which the bigoted narrator is 'sworn' to enforce are more like the Old Testament laws of Moses or the 'medieval' laws of the Taliban in Afghanistan - both of which include the use of cruel and violent punishment for minor 'crimes' - than the teachings of Jesus.

The opening lines of the first verse are full of rage and anguish: *...I'm grinding my life out, steady and sure...* Dylan growls, against the menacing musical backdrop *...Nothing more wretched than I must endure...* as he spits out the words 'grinding' and 'wretched' *...I'm drenched in the light that shines from the sun...* he continues. We could easily see this as an image of a slave being forced to work in the hot climate from dawn to dusk. In crying *...I could stone you to death for the wrongs that you've done...* the narrator appears to wish for 'Biblical' vengeance to descend on his tormentor: *...Sooner* *or later you'll make a mistake...* he continues angrily *... I'll put you in a chain that you will never break...* thus, in his fantasy, reversing the process of enslavement. The repeated refrain is a brilliantly constructed series of 'sharp' one syllable words: *...Legs and arms and body and bone/ I'll pay in blood, but not my own...* It is as if the victim is thoroughly enjoying every moment of his revenge, as he destroys his oppressor's body, bit by bit.

It is possible to read the voice in these lines as being that of the oppressor, who somehow seems to feel - as members of racist groups often notoriously allege - that the demands for equality that racial minorities make are a threat to their 'way of life'. Perhaps the speaker is a white supremacist or a Klansman who is paranoid about black people 'taking over' and who is just waiting for the first opportunity to punish them by 'clapping them in irons' or applying a suitably barbaric or Biblical method of execution *...Night after night, day after day/ They strip your useless hopes away/ The more I take, the more I give/ The more I die, the more I live...* could also be voiced by either party. But the next lines - which are perhaps the most graphic and threatening in the song: *...I got something in my pocket make your eyeballs swim/ I got dogs that could tear you limb from limb...* are more obviously those of a vicious oppressor who takes great pleasure in inflicting violence. The ominous line before the refrain *...I'm circling around the Southern zone...* suggests that the speaker is from the 'Deep South'. We can imagine him 'cruising around' in a pickup truck, rifle at the ready, searching for victims. Oddly enough, the line is borrowed from *A Winter Idyll*, a rather peaceful meditation on nature by John Greenleaf Whittier. But Dylan transforms this 'innocent' line into something far more threatening.

In the next verse we appear to return to the voice of the victim. Dylan uses a gambling metaphor: *....Low cards are what I've got/ But I'll play this hand whether I like it or not....* But *...I'm sworn to uphold the laws of God/ You can put me out in front of a firing squad...* appear to come from the mouth of the oppressor. This narrator thinks he is on a 'mission from God' - so much so that he is willing to die for his 'cause', a Southern racist, who is still 'circling around' in search of victims *...My head's so hard...* he boasts *....it must be made of stone...* The vicious sarcasm of *...Another politician pumping out the piss...* may be the voice of an omniscient narrator, especially given Dylan's frequent attitude of contempt towards the 'political world'. Or it could be the voice of the angry bigot railing against liberal politicians *...Another ragged beggar blowing you a kiss...* seems to express resentment against the way such figures are sometimes seen as 'mollycoddling' the feckless. The diatribe continues, with the narrator appearing to indulge in 'drunken and dirty' insults: *...You got the same eyes your mother does/ If only you could prove who your father was...* This may, however, be the voice of the 'oppressed' character snapping back.

In performance these lines are replaced by *...Life is short and it don't last long/ They'll hang you in the morning and sing you a song...* another violent threat, which again could be either narrator talking *..Someone must have slipped a drug in your wine/ You gulped it down and you crossed the line...* though equally scathing, seems to be addressed to the racist bigot. But the implication that he has been 'intoxicated' by hateful rhetoric is contrasted against the highly ambiguous use of the Biblical homily *...Man cannot live by bread alone...* which derives from the words of Jesus in Matthew 4:4: *...Man shall not live by bread alone, but by every word that proceedeth from the mouth of God...* This oft-repeated phrase is usually meant to imply that spirituality is more important than materialism. But here, rhymed with *...I pay in blood, but not my own...* its apparent delivery from the mouth of a pious bigot is particularly chilling, suggesting that the narrator has twisted words of spiritual wisdom into a justification for 'vengeance'. Perhaps he thinks that his threatened revenge against others will help him, as the Southern saying goes, 'Get right with God'.

The penultimate verse appears to shift again into the voice of the victim: *...How I made it back home nobody knows/ Or how I survived so many blows...* suggesting, perhaps that he has survived an attempt to 'stone him to death'. He tells us that he has 'been through hell' and then delivers an especially nasty riposte: *...You bastard! I'm supposed to respect you...* which reflects on the earlier *...if only you could prove who your father was...* Both lines were pulled in the live performances of the song, as if Dylan found them a little too crude. But the rage and moral indignation which inspires the rest of the verse is clear: *...I'll give you justice, I'll fatten your purse/ Show me your moral virtues first/ Hear me holler, hear me moan...* This sounds very much like the voice of the oppressed. The reference to the term 'holler' is especially resonant of the cries of slaves, and is frequently used in blues songs. It may be that the threat to 'pay in blood' has been reversed.

In the final verse the violent tone continues unabated: *...You bit your lover in the bed/ Come here, I'll break your lousy head/ Our nation must be saved and freed/ You've been accused of murder. How do you plead?...* The statement about 'freeing the nation' could come from either party. There is now an implication of sexual violence to add to the oppressor's crimes. In the final lines we seem to be listening again to the voice of the violent bigot: *...This is how I spend my days...* he declares proudly. The assertion that *...I come to bury, not to praise...* is another ironic use of a well known Shakespearean phrase - that of Mark Antony in *Julius Caesar* - in which a politician is asserting that violence can be justified if it destroys tyranny. But in the mouth of our 'redneck friend' it becomes merely another justification of violence. The final couplet *...I'll drink my fill and sleep alone/ I pay in blood, but not my own...* is unremittingly and defiantly self satisfied. The narrator is glorying in the violence he is promising to commit, through which he claims to be enforcing 'the laws of God'.

As in many of Dylan's late period songs, Biblical references are counterposed against allusions to classical sources *...Nothing more wretched than I must endure...* comes from *Tristia* while *...They strip your useless hopes away...* is from *The Black Sea Letters.* Ovid's expressions of frustration about his exile from Rome are transposed here to depict the suffering of modern Americans. The use of such texts is part of a general implication in Dylan's songs that modern America has many similarities with ancient Rome, as it is the centre of a huge 'empire' built on violence and slavery but poisoned by the political and moral corruption which is likely to bring about its eventual downfall. The other implication is that the culture of violence which is embedded in American society has been extended by the US' treatment of the rest of the world. Thus the portentous *...I come to bury, not to praise...* becomes, like the title of the song, a reflection of the 'imperial' arrogance of post war US foreign policy. It might also serve as an epitaph for the victims of the American 'pax imperium' in Korea, Vietnam, El Salvador, Iraq, Afghanistan, Nicaragua and many other places in which the American 'emperors' have chosen to 'Pay in Blood' - but not their own. Despite the bloody anger being expressed here, *Pay in Blood* is not, however, a 'finger pointing' protest song. Although it certainly expresses disgust at the mentality of violent racists, its use of an ambiguous narrative framework suggests that, in the 'post truth' world, both oppressors and the oppressed may use the same language to express completely opposite meanings.

In *Long and Wasted Years*, also from *Tempest*, Dylan presents us with another complex and sometimes confusing narrative. The narrator appears to be lurking in the shadows of some unknown landscape. We hear that he has abandoned, or been abandoned by, his family. He hears his love muttering dark, murderous thoughts in her sleep. He worries that, when she steps into the light, the sun might 'burn her brains right out'. He begs her to come back to him, even though their love appears to have been doomed from the start. Dylan incorporates many apparently random lyrical elements and characters, 'jumping about' in time as if shuffling through a collection of fading photographs which depict the course of a relationship. The emotions being evoked are particularly direct and raw. Apart from a vague reference to 'the Eastern line', no place names are referenced. The action of the song could thus be happening anywhere, at any time. We do not even know whether the narrator is addressing one woman or several. The imagery is spiky and sometimes violent, the delivery gravelly and the music disconcertingly raw and jumpy.

The song is dominated by a repetitively hypnotic descending guitar figure, over which Dylan intones rather than sings the lyrics. The heartbreak being expressed is set against what may be unreliable memories and features several moments during which the singer almost (but not quite) loses control. This unsettling effect is emphasised by the fact that the song appears to end very abruptly, with the singer's dramatic and tragic 'discovery' of the crushing finality of the title line. In many Dylan songs (including, most memorably, *Like a Rolling Stone)* what appears at first to be an address to a lover can also be interpreted as the singer staring into a mirror, attempting to peel off the layers of his own inner masks. Here the singer declares *...I wear dark glasses to cover my eyes/ There are secrets in 'em that I can't disguise...* For a moment, despite the narrator hiding behind layers of temporal and emotional obfuscation, we can almost glimpse the iconic 1966 image of Dylan, 'the ghost of electricity' personified, as portrayed so coolly by Cate Blanchett in *I'm Not There*. Yet the clichéd *...eyes/ disguise...* rhyme, along with Dylan's deliberate delivery, emphasises a certain world-weariness which characterises the whole song. No matter how clever he may be at juxtaposing and manipulating images, this does not seem to lessen the pain and the sense of futility he is expressing.

The regretful tone is immediately established as the narrator plays around with hollow-sounding romantic clichés. The opening line ....*It's been such a long, long time...* is the title of a Bing Crosby hit from 1945 (written by Sammy Cahn and Julie Styne), a conventional and sentimentally nostalgic piece popular with those who were welcoming loved ones back from World War Two. Yet although the rest of the song (including the final revelation of the title) emphasises that its subject has been in a very long relationship, the narrator identifies the authentic moment of love between the characters in the song as having only really occurred within a short, specific moment in the past: *...One time, for one brief day I was the man for you...* We then jump into the immediate present, with the revelation that *...Last night I heard you talkin' in your sleep...* This clearly suggests that the relationship is continuing. Rather bizarrely, the narrator appears to have overheard his lover saying incriminating things in her sleep, for which she ....*might have to go to jail someday...*

The implication of this may seem threatening, but Dylan's tone is plaintive, as if he is uncertain as to how to express his embitterment and cannot really find the words to convey the complexity of his feelings. As with the equally spiky *Love Sick* we sense that, despite the apparently angry tone, the singer feels hopelessly (and helplessly) in thrall to the woman. Thus the outbursts of indignation and despair that punctuate the song when he appeals directly to her sound awkward, ill judged, uncertain: ...*Maybe it's the same for you as it is for me...* he suggests, rather tentatively. And later he pleads ...*Come back baby/ If I hurt your feelings, I apologise...*

In an apparent, but still uncertain, attempt to mock his lover, the narrator tries to get her attention by throwing in lines from a classic early rock screamer: *...Shake it up baby, twist and shout...* but he delivers them in an oddly cold way, without any of John Lennon's anguish and fervour. Indeed, he sounds thoroughly miserable. Later he invokes the old blues metaphor of *...two trains running side by side...* (as used in the Muddy Waters song with this title, which he covered in 1962) to symbolise a relationship in which the lovers' paths never truly meet. The use of these allusions seems to suggest that, although he is trying hard to locate ways of expressing his disillusionment, he cannot quite manage to find the right words. The musical clichés, in other words, just don't cut it here. There is a strange, apparently random, reference to a family he hasn't seen in twenty years, since they 'lost their land'. And as the song rises to its climax, there is an apocalyptic, yet uncertain suggestion *...I think...* he begins ...*that when my back was turned, the whole world behind me burned...* This is followed by a reference to the couple's marriage which echoes the song's first line by referring to a *... long, long aisle...* This remarkable image of a marriage as a painfully slow and drawn out journey, with the protagonists still 'walking down the aisle' after all these years, suggests that they are trapped in an inescapable cycle of despair . This further emphasises the song's bitter languor.

Appropriately for such a weirdly disjointed narrative, *Long and Wasted Years* employs a very irregular pattern of rhyming, in which the first two lines of each verse may or may not take the form of a rhyming couplet. As the narrator's anger rises, the rhyming becomes more frequent. The narrator rages at his mysterious 'enemy' who *...crashed into the dust/ Stopped dead in his tracks as he lost his lust...* Then we hear that: *...He was run down hard and he broke apart...* and *...He died in shame/ He had an iron heart...* The tone has now become stark and brutal. The image of an 'iron heart', as used by Shakespeare in both *Timon Of Athens* and *A Midsummer Night's Dream*, is drawn from the description in Ovid's *Amores* of a woman who has cut off her beautiful locks *... A crime to burn/ Locks pretty on their own - advice you'd spurn/ You iron heart! What violence! Don't scorch such hair!...* Dylan's harsh delivery of the phrase expresses great anger towards this unnamed 'enemy'. But is the narrator describing a man with whom his lover betrayed him? Or is this an 'internal enemy', an aspect of the narrator himself that, despite his best efforts and his 'dark glasses', he just *...can't disguise...*

This verse has been subjected to multiple variations in performance. While the first couplet has usually been retained, the second has presented various, and often increasingly vituperative, versions of the enemy's demise: *...He stopped dead in his tracks and he got pinned down/ Run down hard and he sank into the ground...* (Newark New Jersey 12/11/14) or *...He was run down hard, hit clean in the side/ No one can say with certainty where he died...* (Durham 25/4/15) or *...A dangerous player, he stepped out over every scalp/ He had an iron heart but it didn't help...* Or (perhaps most memorably) *...He crossed his arms, and his legs were bent/ Down to the Garden of Death he went...* (Ljubljana, Slovenia, *25/6/15).* Sometimes the enemy is addressed directly: *...What you say about anyway, you weren't there/ You can die and be damned for all I care...* (Nashville 27/4/15).

Later, the whole verse is replaced. In Austin Texas on 6/5/15 we get: *... Well, you're a murderous fool, and you've been doomed from the start/ I'll cripple your legs and I'll strike you square in the heart/ Then I'll tell your Ma and Pa/ That the vultures ate your body raw...* In Torino (2/7/15) the imagery becomes spectral: *...I met my enemy with a ruthless force/ He lost his lust and he lost his horse/ And then the light broke through/ I saw skeletons of men that I knew...* As with *Tangled up in Blue,* there are many other variations. Both songs appear to be 'unfixed' narratives; descriptions of relationships that cannot entirely be pinned down, represented by narratives within which time, place and meaning are constantly shifting.

With its disparate, confusing imagery, its ironic use of song clichés and its 'tangled' narrative, *Long and Wasted Years* can be seen as a both a 'cubist' examination of the medium of the 'love song' itself and, more obliquely, a reflection on the nature of stardom. Throughout his career, Dylan has had to balance the continuing need to please his audience with his own struggle to remain relevant. In order to do so it is necessary to make a continual effort to slay the dragon of complacency, to destroy the 'enemy within', with his 'iron heart'. So he takes us back to the *one brief day,* many long years ago, of his own pop stardom. He mocks the critics who mutter murderous thoughts about him, laments his lack of contact with his 'family' and rejoices as his 'enemy' is defeated. He returns to *that cold and frosty morn* at the beginning of his career when he and his audience joined together to hear (in *A Hard Rain's a-Gonna Fall*) *...the sound of a clown who cried in the alley....*

One might expect the lines in the final verse to be performed in a solemn or sad manner *...We cried on a cold and frosty morn...* Dylan sings *...We cried because our souls were torn...* Yet the phrasing, particularly on the second 'cried' and 'torn', makes him sound surprised, as if he has only just remembered what has happened. The next phrase *...So much for tears...* would normally indicate a kind of weary resignation. But as he delivers the title phrase, he appears to be challenging the meaning of the title, as if he is in fact posing a question *...So much for those long and wasted years...* he cries, as if questioning how 'wasted' they really were. Despite the anger that permeates much of the song, it concludes in a somewhat ambivalent way. In the hundreds of live versions that followed, this grew into a kind of triumphant self-mockery. In using the song as the climax to live shows which often juxtaposed the blood-drenched anger of the *Tempest* material against the bittersweet romance of selections from the Sinatra songbook, the singer asks us to look back on our own lives, and to question whether 'these years' have really been wasted at all.

Black Rider, from *Rough and Rowdy Ways*, consists of a direct address to an ominous figure which Dylan performs against the sparse but highly atmospheric backing of a single, flamenco-flavoured acoustic guitar. The track is reminiscent of some of the more intimate cuts on his 'Sinatra' albums such as *Melancholy Mood* or *Some Enchanted Evening* (which is referenced here). It is a near-spoken recitation, with judicious use of dramatic pauses. Subtle variations in tone are used to convey confusion, surprise, jealousy, shock, sarcasm and anger. It sounds like it has been recorded in a large and empty room, using natural echo on the vocals. At one point one can hear what sounds like a penny dropping to the ground in the distance. This creates a suitably eerie effect, as if what we are really listening to is a conversation which is being amplified within an echoey 'cavern' of the narrator's mind.

There has naturally been much speculation over the identity of the 'rider'. It may be tempting, given the frequent apocalyptic references in Dylan's work, to identify him with the third horseman of the apocalypse from *Revelations*, the bringer of famine who rides a black horse. Perhaps he is even the third 'rider' who did not appear in *All Along the Watchtower*. Some commentators have concluded that Dylan is conducting a conversation with death. Or perhaps the narrator could be addressing the Devil, contemplating a Faustian pact. The song is not, however, a comic gothic fantasia like *My Own Version of You*. The language used is surprisingly straightforward, with only very sparing use of metaphor or symbolism. As the character and nature of the 'rider' shifts continually, Dylan uses subtle variations in tone to convey confusion, surprise, jealousy, shock, sarcasm and even anger, without ever over-emoting.

At first, this dark figure does not seem to have a particularly threatening presence. The first lines of the song: *...Black rider, black rider, you been livin' too hard/ You been* *up all night, have to stay on your guard...* depict the narrator, feeling worse for wear after a 'rough night', staring into a mirror and examining the lines under his eyes. *...The path that you're walking is too narrow to walk...* he warns *...Every step of the way, another stumblin' block...* But then the background of the image in the mirror suddenly changes *...The road that you're on, same road that you know...* the narrator tells him *...Just not the same as it was a minute ago...* Dylan's use of dramatic pauses creates an impression of uncertainty, as if the narrator is unsure whether he should feel pity or fear. The rest of the song appears to consist of a conversation between the narrator and this haggard, hung over version of himself. The black rider is a kind of shape shifter, reflecting the narrator's changing moods. Every time the narrator looks in the mirror, the image of the rider changes.

In the second verse, there are no pauses within the lines. Dylan's tone is now a little more assured: *...You've seen it all...* he tells the rider *...You've seen the great world and you've seen the small...* The diction is a little awkward here, as if the narrator is nervous in the figure's presence. But then he becomes rather fevered: *...You fell into the fire and you're eating the flame...* and then even slightly apprehensive: *...Better seal up your lips if you want to stay in the game...* The image he now sees in the mirror, as he realises the extent to which the 'black rider' has damaged himself, is literally hellish. He pleads for mercy: *...Be reasonable Mister, be honest, be fair...* In the final line of the verse he seems to be closing his eyes and trying to wish the vision away: *...Let all of your earthly thoughts be a prayer...* Dylan emphasises the last three words by slowing down and stretching out the syllables, conveying what sounds like real fear for the first time.

Despite the narrator's efforts to 'walk away' it is clear now that he is under the rider's spell *...I'm walking away...* he declares *...You try to make me look back...* He continues, rather pathetically to plead: *...My heart is at rest, I'd like to keep it that way/ I don't want to fight, at least not today...* Then he becomes decidedly petulant: *...Go home to your wife, stop visiting mine...* he tells him. Then he whispers: *...One of these days, I'll forget to be kind...* The threat is barely veiled, if rather unconvincing. But it is clear by now that the black rider is a version of himself which he is ashamed of - the one who goes home to his wife. There are strong intimations that the wife may be being abused or mistreated and that the narrator is trying to avoid responsibility for indulging in this fantasy. There is a short instrumental break, with the Spanish guitar helping to create an atmosphere of intrigue and tension, as if we are in some bar in Mexico awaiting a shoot out. The narrator begs the rider to release him from the 'spell' he has cast on him: *...Tell me when, tell me how/ If there ever was a time then let it be now...* he cries *...Let me go through...* he implores him... *open the door...* confessing that *...My soul is distressed, my mind is at war...* The rider is whispering smooth reassurances in his ear, but he attempts to resist: *...Don't hug me, don't flatter me, don't turn on the charm/ I'll take out a sword and hack off your arm...* We can tell that the singer is, like the narrator of *Standing in the Doorway*, afraid to 'go through the door' that is in front of him. Or, like the narrator of *Forgetful Heart*, he may be wondering *...if indeed there ever was a door...*

In the final verse, the narrator sobers up. He decides to face up to the rider. He begins by insulting his manhood: *...Black rider, black rider, hold it right there/ The size of your cock will get you nowhere...* For a moment, the image in the mirror changes. The black rider has become Priapus, a mythical figure from Greek mythology who is cursed by Hera, the wife of Zeus, to have to carry a permanent (and extremely outsize) erection. Anyone who has ever been to Greece will have seen 'rude pictures' of Priapus depicted in post cards or on 'souvenir' ash trays. But the narrator is not cowed by this. *...I'll suffer in silence, I'll not make a sound...* he promises *...Maybe I'll take the high moral ground...* He still sounds uncertain. But perhaps he will be able to acquire the moral strength to resist the rider's allure. In order to do so he will 'summon up' help from songs he puts trust in. Dylan delivers two allusions in quick succession: *...Some enchanted evening, I'll sing you a song....* refers back to the tragically haunted ballad that Dylan covered on *Shadows in the Night ...Black rider, black rider...* he concludes *...You been on the job too long...* The last phrase is the refrain of the traditional murder ballad *Duncan and Brady.* It seems to suggest that the narrator now realises that he may be able to rid himself of this spectre that stares back at him from this dark mirror of his soul. But there is no obvious resolution here. The narrative is frozen, and we are left with the image of the narrator and the black rider still staring at each other, as the final syllable of 'long' slowly fades away into a ghostly 'Sun Studios' echo.

5th October 2001. Spokane Arena, Washington State. It is the first night of the Summer Tour of 2001, which will take Dylan and his band down the West Coast from here to LA, before zooming across the country via Denver Colorado to Sioux City Iowa and then to all points east. Tonight Dylan will unveil four songs from his recently released album *"Love And Theft"*, which had been recorded towards the end of May, a few months before his 60th birthday. The album had been released on 11th September - the day of the momentous attack on the 'Twin Towers' of the World Trade Center in New York, forever known to history as 'nine-eleven'. Just over three weeks later, the country is still in a state of panic and confusion. Security is tight everywhere. In just a few days, the invasion of Afghanistan and the 'War on Terror' will be launched, along with countless new conspiracy theories.

The crowd which fills the massive sports arena is ready for something special and there is a buzz of anticipation in the air. Bob will not disappoint. The show is especially energised tonight, with a smattering of 'greatest hits' - *Desolation Row, The Times, Knockin' on Heaven's Door, Rolling Stone* and *Blowin' in the Wind* - all performed with great passion. *Masters of War* is delivered slowly and deliberately on acoustic guitars, with every word clearly audible, with the first verse repeated for emphasis. There is also a moving rendition of Jim Anglin's *Searching for a Soldier's Grave*, a mournful lament which had been recorded in the 1950s by the Louvin Brothers and Hank Williams, among others, and which is sung from the point of view of a grieving father of one of the American dead of World War Two. This had been included in many of Dylan's set lists over the last year or so, but it clearly strikes a chord with the audience. Charlie Sexton and Larry Campbell supply bluegrass-style supporting vocals.

The opening song is another number which is unfamiliar to most of the crowd. After Aaron Copland's rousing *Hoedown* is played over the speakers, our man (attired in a white shirt and a neatly tailored black suit, and sporting that new moustache) and his band are immediately into *Wait For the Light to Shine*, a song written by country entrepreneur Fred Rose in the early 1950s for his protégé Hank Williams. Whereas Hank's version is slow and reflective, Dylan soups the number up so it becomes frenetic and celebratory. The song has a simple message, encouraging us to help friends and neighbours in trouble and to have faith that everything will be OK in the end. Tonight Dylan races through the verses and mumbles a few of the words, but nobody notices or cares. The main point of the song is its exultant chorus, simply consisting of joyous repetition of the title line, to which Larry and Charlie lend sterling support. The crowd soon responds. They may not have heard the song before, but it's easy enough to join in with. Dylan will continue to use it as his set opener on most of the stops on his nationwide tour. He will make no onstage comments about 9/11, the 'war on terror', George W. Bush, Osama Bin Laden, the Taliban or Saddam Hussein. At this pivotal moment in American history, with a new crisis about to unfold, wars about to erupt and the threat of terrorism about to become the major preoccupation of politicians across the world, this joyous opener supplies no analysis and provides no answers. For a few glorious moments, though, the audience can revel in this message of hope for the new century.

Eight: *O Wolfman Howl!*
Murder Ballads and Epic Heroes

...I've always believed that the first rule of being subversive is not to let anybody know you're being subversive....
Bob Dylan, *Theme Time Radio Hour, Trains (Part 1), 14th March, 2007*

13th September 2000. Vicar Street Dublin is what you might call a small but funky venue. Tonight it is jam packed with a thousand sweaty bodies and the Guinness is flowing. We all strain to get as close to the stage as we can. You don't get acts like this on here every day. Showbands, maybe. Irish comedians like Tommy Tiernan, certainly. But big stars like this guy... hardly ever. When we get the intro: *...Ladies and gentlemen, will you please welcome Columbia recording artist Bob Dylan...* the crowd really kicks off, shouting and whistling "Bobby!" Naturally our man doesn't say hello. Nobody expects him to. He's not the one for such nonsense. Some of the punters are already calling out for *Blowin' in the Wind*, *Heaven's Door, Rolling Stone....* But those in the know are expecting something a bit more rousing as a starter. Not an old Irish drinking song, though he's been known to do a few of those. But maybe a gospel shouter or a bluegrass number, to get us all warmed up. As the band gets into a kicking rhythm, we're able to clap along merrily, even though this is a song we've never heard him do before *...Twinkle, twinkle, little star...* it begins. But this is no Christmas carol. Tony on the bass has got his crooked smile on. The band are really up for the crack, especially on the choruses, with Larry and Charlie leaning into their mikes and supplying some sweet harmonies.

The song is *Duncan and Brady* - a 'bad man murder ballad' - a bit of a grisly tale based, so they say, on a true story - the murder of a policeman, James Brady, by a bartender called Harry Duncan in a saloon in St. Louis in 1890. In truth, nobody knows what *really* happened on that day. But some of the locals later swore that Brady and a few of his lads were only called in to break up a bar room fight. But then everything kicked off. Chairs flying around, jaws getting broken, that kind of thing... Tonight Bob appears to fluff some of the words. But we get the gist of the song pretty well. It seems that Brady was this big mouthed, trigger-happy cop, with a *...mean look all round his eye...* who was 'riding around in his 'lectric car', just looking for trouble. Then we hear that he wants to *...shoot somebody just to see them die!...* What an arse! So that's where Johnny Cash got that line from, the sneaky get...

So Brady comes into the bar and arrests Duncan, whereupon Duncan shoots him dead. That's the way it goes. But lo and behold, Brady now appears to be a bloody hero. When the women in the neighbourhood get wind of his sorry fate they all go home, dress in red and come out for his funeral. Hard to see what they saw in him. Could be he was putting it about quite a bit, the old rascal. The way Bob tells it *...They come a snifflin' and a shufflin' down the street/ In their big Mother Hubbards and their stockin' feet* ...'Mother Hubbards' were those long dresses our grandmas used to wear around the turn of the century. Why the women took their shoes off is a bit of a mystery. But nobody cares about that tonight. The main point of the song seems to be the refrain *...He been on the job too long...* which some of the folks at the front are already joining in with. You can see that Larry and Charlie are having fun stretching out and messing around with that line. Even ol' Bob, who you have to say is looking his age these days, and rarely gives anything away, sneaks a little grin now and again. By the end of the song, we get the joke. But do *we* really think Bob has 'been on the job too long'? The way he and the band attack the song and get us all jumping, he's certainly given the lie to that....

Murder ballads have long been a key part of the repertoire of folk singers, just as tales involving violence, death, betrayal and detection have always been staples of fiction. In his early days as a folk singer Dylan performed many such songs, including *Pretty Polly* - in which the narrator kills a girl because she refuses to marry him - and *Omie Wise,* where a young man murders his lover for no apparent reason. *Duncan and Brady*, whose author is unknown, had been circulating for some time before being recorded by 'old time string band' Wilmer Watts and the Lonely Eagles in 1929. It later became a favourite of blues singers who tended to add their own details to embellish the story. Leadbelly performed his version of the song on many occasions. Dylan may well have first heard it being played by his early mentor Dave Van Ronk in Greenwich Village. By then it had taken on a very dramatic shape, with touches of darkly ironic humour. Dylan recorded a very lively version with David Bromberg and his band in 1992 which was eventually released on *Tell Tale Signs*. It was performed over 80 times between 1999 and 2002, always as a set opener. At that time Dylan was under the influence of bluegrass legends The Stanley Brothers and often used his guitarists Larry Campbell and Charlie Sexton as counterpoint vocal harmony singers.

Country and blues singers found that they could excite their audiences, and perhaps even scare them a little, by performing murder ballads. Many were originally based on true stories, although the specific details were often considerably enhanced and dramatised over the years by different singers, who would also add pithy or humorous comments. On his acoustic albums of the early 1990s Dylan recorded several such tunes, all of which originated from early twentieth century African American sources. In *Frankie and Albert*, the murder of an unfaithful young man by his girlfriend is related in a curiously offhand and fatalistic way: *...She was her man/ But he done her wrong...* In *Stack-O-Lee*, the singer insists that he killed a man because of a dispute over a *...John B. Stetson hat...* Even in the relatively mournful *Delia* there are snatches of dark, offhand humour. We glimpse the murderer Curtis, whose actions are again described quite dispassionately. We hear that he is *...in the jailhouse/ Drinking from an old tin cup...* while Delia herself is *...in the graveyard...* from where *...she ain't getting' up...* The murders - or threatened murders - in many of these songs tend to be recounted rather coldly. The deaths often occur as a result of relatively trivial matters and the murderers often seem to have put little thought into their actions.

The murder ballads Dylan composed in his early days tended to be didactic and moralistic protest songs. One of his earliest compositions, the crude but righteously angry *Death of Emmett Till* (1961) tells the story of the lynching of a 14 year old black boy in graphic detail. The highly dramatic *Lonesome Death of Hattie Carroll* (1964) explains how a judge gives a rich young white man a minimal sentence for the murder of a black servant. The unremittingly bleak *Ballad of Hollis Brown* (1964) relates how a desperate farmer kills his wife, his five children and himself when his crops fail. In his later years Dylan's approach to the form is very different. His narratives are ambiguous and complex lyrical 'puzzles', drawing on a range of varying musical traditions and placing the murder stories within broad historical, social and political contexts. He frequently alters narrative perspectives, rarely relates events chronologically and avoids any direct moral judgements. At times he also appears to be interjecting his own voice, as if he is acting as a kind of 'shadow narrator'.

Tin Angel, from *Tempest*, plays around with the conventions of the form at will. Although it depicts a particularly gory scene at its climax, its depiction of violence is cartoonish. It features two dimensional characters whose motives are unclear and about whom we care little. The song is a pastiche of several particularly bloody British folk songs, some with medieval origins, and their American variants. It has 28 verses, with each line consisting of two sets of iambic pentameter - and recounts the commonly told tale of a wife running away from a powerful husband. Perhaps the most well-known ballad based around this theme is *The Raggle Taggle Gypsies*, a song of considerable antiquity describing how a noble lady escapes the confinement of a castle to live a romanticised 'free life' among the gypsies. There are many variants such as *Seven Yellow Gypsies*, *The Whistling Gypsy* and *Lizzie Lindsay.* An Americanised version *Black Jack Davy* was recorded by Dylan on *Good as I Been to You* and was performed by him on several occasions in 1993. Woody Guthrie rewrote the song again as *Gypsy Davy*, which Dylan also performed in his early 'coffee house' days. Another model is the English folk standard *Matty Groves* (sometimes called *Little Musgrave)* which was popularised in a riveting and groundbreaking 'electric folk' version by Fairport Convention on their *Liege and Lief* album in 1969. In this bloodthirsty yarn the wife of the powerful Lord Donald, who is away working on his land, spots 'young Matty' in church and invites him into her bed. But a servant informs Lord Donald, who rushes back to discover the couple in flagrante, whereupon he supplies Matty with his best sword, fights a very unequal duel and kills him. Thinking that he has proved his manhood he then asks his wife who she prefers. She is unrepentant, claiming she still prefers her dead lover. Enraged, the Lord puts his sword through her. He orders a grave for the two lovers but ends by declaring that his wife should be placed on top because ..."*she was of noble kin*"...

These ancient ballads remain popular with audiences not only because they tell stirring tales of adventure but also because they challenge gender stereotypes and class boundaries. Our sympathies are clearly with the women, who are presumably in loveless, arranged marriages but who are determined to express their sexuality (especially when choosing their own lovers) despite the hierarchical class positions they are caught up in. But the story Dylan relates in *Tin Angel* confounds any generic expectations. Although the song is an engaging - if sometimes confusing - melodrama, it also has a strange, almost hallucinatory quality. The characters' emotions are supercharged but their motivations are never fully explained. The song seems to exist in an oddly timeless space. Even its title, which appears to have nothing to do with the story that unfolds, is a mystery. It replicates many of the plot elements of traditional ballads and uses phrases from them prominently, but in a rather random way. It follows the typical plot line of an Elizabethan 'revenge tragedy' but lacks a heroic protagonist. And like such tragedies, it ends in a bloody mess.

Dylan spits out the lyrics fiercely over an insistent, hypnotically grinding beat. The repetitive rhythm of the language is highly suggestive of a galloping horse with a rider kicking his spurs. The first line *...It was late last night when the boss came home...* is drawn directly from *Gypsy Davy.* The tense musical backing draws us into a cinematic narrative embellished by Hitchcockian 'gallows humour'. From the outset, there is little attempt at historical realism. The word 'boss' is an American word which only became widespread in the nineteenth century. But by the second line, we hear that he has arrived at *...a deserted mansion and a desolate throne...* although presumably we are meant to assume that the 'throne' is merely metaphorical. The boss soon discovers that his wife has left him. His servant informs him that *...Old Henry Lee, chief of the clan, came riding through the woods and took her by the hand...* The name 'Henry Lee' is one which appears in another old murder ballad, in which the protagonist is killed by his lover. Nick Cave recorded a haunting version in a duet with P. J. Harvey on his album *Murder Ballads* in 1996. Dylan included *Love Henry,* a rather gentler variant on the theme, on *World Gone Wrong.* But it is unclear whether this is the same character. In fact, his name is never mentioned again. The statement that he is 'chief of the clan' is also hard to place historically and is never explained.

Having paused for thought, the boss sets off on a mission of revenge, instructing his servant to provide him with *...the cheapest labor money can buy...* (another relatively modern phrase). The servant is instructed to fetch the boss' coat and tie - certainly rather odd apparel for such a potentially bloody mission. In another lift from *Gypsy*

Davy, the servant is also instructed to *...saddle me up my buckskin mare...* We are then told - in a line from *Black Jack Davy* - that *...they rode all night and they rode all day....* We also hear, without explanation, that before he reaches his destination his hired men have deserted him. He arrives at Henry Lee's house alone but still clearly bent on revenge. The language becomes extremely melodramatic. We are told that his *...heavy heart was wracked with pain/ Insomnia raging in his brain...* and then that*...he threw down his helmet and his cross handled sword/ He renounced his faith, he renounced his Lord...* lines that are drawn almost verbatim from Walter Scott's poem *The Fire King,* which is set in a romanticised version of the middle ages. Now our protagonist seems to have been transformed into a medieval knight, albeit one who has rejected any kind of chivalric code.

Henry Lee's house seems to be well protected as the boss is said to have *...leaned down, cut the electric wire...* to enter it. The modern reference is contrasted with the description of him lowering himself down *...on a golden chain...* as if he is a character in a fairytale. Presumably he is descending down the wall of some kind of mansion or castle. He is described as having *...all the nobility of an ancient race...* as if he is some Ancient Greek avenger. After he spies the lovers lying by the fire, naked and so intertwined that *...it was hard to tell who was who...* he then appears from behind a curtain, crosses the room and bolts the door. If we are familiar with ballads like these, we are surely expecting him, as Lord Donald does in *Matty Groves*, to take his revenge. But then the form of the narrative, which has already been disconcerting, becomes even stranger. For the next fourteen verses we alternate between the voices of the three characters, without so much as a 'he said' or a 'she said' - as if they are reading from a dramatic script.

The first part of this 'theatrical' sequence consists of the boss and his wife throwing colourful insults at each other. He calls her a 'greedy lipped wench', tells her that she makes his 'heart feel sick' and that she has 'made a monkey' out of him. She sneeringly calls him a 'silly boy' and a 'reckless fool' and says she has had enough of his 'sweetest lies' *...Get up, stand up!...* he then commands her, in a rather anachronistic reference to a Bob Marley song. He demands that she should get dressed and threatens to kill her if she does not comply. She responds by claiming that her new lover is *...dearer to me than gold...* and demands that he leave them alone. In language as vicious as that of a Jacobean tragedy, the boss calls Henry Lee a *...a gutless ape with a worthless mind...* But she remains defiant *...You've had your way too long with me...* she tells him *...Now it's me who will determine how it will be...*

At this point, we are no doubt still expecting the boss to murder the lovers. But there is a gunshot and it seems that it is the boss who has been hit. We are informed that the *...first bullet grazed his ear/ Second ball went straight in...* This now seems to place us in the seventeenth century, as the reference to a 'ball' suggests that the gun is a weapon of that period such as a flintlock. The boss staggers back, 'as good as dead'. But then there is an even more unexpected twist. The wife now turns on her lover crying *...You shot my husband down, you fiend!...* He responds, using phrases drawn from Jeremiah

15:10, by telling her that her husband was *...a man of strife, a man of sin....* Then she pulls a knife out from under her robe. Declaring that *...all husbands are good men, as all wives know...* she stabs him. Then, crying out *...You died for me, now I'll die for you...* she touches his lips, kisses his cheek, and then stabs herself. We are left with the image of *...all three lovers, together in a heap...*

The ending seems to 'cobble together' elements of the tragic resolutions of *Macbeth, Romeo and Juliet* and *Othello*. Why the wife turns on her lover is never explained. It is as if the characters' actions themselves could easily be switched around. In the second part of the song, because of the lack of 'stage directions', it is quite difficult to know who is speaking. Dylan makes no attempt to 'voice' the different characters. It is even possible that it is Henry Lee who is shot first and that the wife kills the boss in revenge, claiming that Lee was her 'true husband'. Whereas murder ballads traditionally have a moral point to make, *Tin Angel* portrays a scenario in which we have no moral compass. We are, of course, expecting the wife - who we naturally presume to have run away from an oppressive, violent husband - to approve of the boss being killed and to celebrate her freedom with her new lover. But in the inverted and confused moral universe of the song, the conventions of traditional murder ballads are quite deliberately flaunted. By ripping up all the rules, as he does here, and by presenting the characters as two dimensional ciphers, Dylan produces a burlesque of the conventions of such songs. In doing so, he seems to be making a statement about the true nature of violence. There are many songs, stories, novels and films in which violence is romanticised in favour of the 'good guys'. This is especially true in the various genres of American popular culture such as westerns, sci-fi, war and superhero movies. But in real life, especially in a society in which the 'freedom' to carry a deadly weapon is enshrined in the federal constitution, violence merely leads to more violence and ends up consuming itself. Whatever the old songs might say...

Nettie Moore, from *Modern Times,* is a confessional song written from the point of view of a man who is facing a death sentence for the murder of his lover. The narrative is delivered through the scattered and random thoughts of the unnamed perpetrator of this crime of passion, who continually stresses his absolute devotion to his lover. In order to get inside the mind of the protagonist Dylan switches pronouns and perspectives throughout. In some instances it seems hard to believe that what is being expressed is being delivered in the narrator's voice, as if the psychological effect of committing the crime has fractured his consciousness. But the song still communicates emotion in a very visceral way. The prevailing feelings of grief and regret are conveyed with great dignity and restraint. The details of the actual murder are never revealed, as if the narrator cannot bear to confront the horror of what has happened. The song is a profound meditation on the nature of sin, expressing how a generally 'decent' person with pure and loving emotions can - through one transgressive act of violence - destroy his and another human being's life.

The musical construction of the song is quite unique in Dylan's work. It is dominated by two powerful but strongly contrasting elements. A constant heavy drum beat is supported throughout the verses by a throbbing bass, like a desperate heart that may be beating its last or the slow and steady 'drum roll' which precedes a military execution. The chorus, however, has a sweet, yearning melody which expresses the murderer's feelings with great pathos. The title and the basic melody of the chorus are derived from *Gentle Nettie Moore,* otherwise known as *The Little White Cottage,* in which a male slave whose lover was sold 'down the river', laments that he will never see her again. His only consolation is the thought of being reunited with his Nettie in heaven. This sentimentalised account of the lives of black people was written in 1857 by two white songwriters. The lyrics were by the then-renowned poet Marshall S. Pike, with music by James Pierpoint, a composer whose most famous tune was the Christmas standard *Jingle Bells*. *Gentle Nettie Moore* would mainly have been performed by 'blacked up' white performers in minstrel shows. The chorus runs:

...Oh, I miss you Nettie Moore,
And my happiness is o'er,
While a spirit sad around my heart has come;
And the busy days are long,
And the nights are lonely now,
For you're gone from our little cottage home...

Dylan's song borrows the first two lines of the older ballad. It follows them with a little snatch of symbolic pastoral imagery, which sounds almost hopeful. We hear that *...Winter's gone, the river's on the rise/ I loved you then, and ever shall...* But these hints of positivity are quickly crushed as...*there's no-one here left to tell/ The world has gone black before my eyes...* The devastating final line suggests deep regret at a life wasted. The contrast between the strangled sweetness of this mournful chorus and the repeated tense drum beat behind the verses creates an almost unbearable tension as the tragic story unfolds. The narrative moves in a cinematic way from scene to scene, as the doomed narrator's mind races from one memory to another. At times we appear to be in the nineteenth century, while at others the voice of a present day narrator seems to break through. The effect is often very disconcerting, especially as the hopes of the narrator are continually being crushed.

The first verse opens with a present tense description of an archetypal character in a quintessential American scene: *...Lost John's sitting on a railroad track...* a peaceful image which is immediately undercut by the colloquial phrase *...something's out of whack...* The unnerving rhyme suggests a sudden violent motion. *Lost John* is the title of a traditional ballad, variants of which have been recorded by Roy Acuff, Merle Travis and many others and which usually begins by picturing a rather pitiful hobo waiting to catch a ride on a freight train. We may assume that 'John' is the narrator of the song, who becomes 'lost' when he commits his crime. This is underlined by the line *...blues this morning falling down like hail...* a direct quote from Robert Johnson's *Hellhound on My Trail* in which the legendary blues singer, who was himself murdered at the age of 27, sings of being haunted by his own personal demons. This is rhymed with *...Gonna leave* *a greasy trail....* as if the heavy rain falling from the sky is somehow dirty or polluted - suggesting the 'unclean' state of the narrator's conscience.

'Lost John' then declares, in one of his more 'positive' pronouncements, that he has an urge to travel around the world and then to return to his love. This is of course nothing more than a fantasy. He admits that *...All I ever do is struggle and strive/ If I don't do anybody any harm I might make it back alive....* lines that paraphrase Hank Williams' bitterly ironic *I'll Never Get Out of This World Alive*, indicating that the narrator is quite aware that he is indulging in wishful thinking. He continues to attempt some light hearted banter: *...I'm the oldest son of a crazy man...* he tells us *...I'm in a cowboy band...* This is another one of those lines which draws cheers from the crowd in Dylan's live shows. The song was performed almost 150 times over the six years after the album's release, with very few variations. At this time Dylan would often perform in stylised 'western' get up, in apparent imitation of musical heroes such as Williams. It is thus hard to disconnect these lines from the persona Dylan was adopting in the 2000s.

Nettie Moore continually shifts us out of one mood, or one scenario, into another, as illusion is juxtaposed with reality. In a desperately convoluted vocal line, cramming those syllables in as if he has little time left to really express how he feels, the narrator admits that *...Got a pile of sins to pay for and I ain't got time to hide/ I'd walk through a blazing fire, baby, if I knew you was on the other side...* This recalls a passage in Dante's *Inferno* in which the protagonist (Dante himself), who is being guided by the Roman poet Virgil, has to walk through a fire in order to reach his dead lover Beatrice, who represents grace and redemption from sin. The allusion suggests that Nettie is the narrator's Beatrice. The narrator is now contemplating whether he will need to walk through the fires of hell to redeem himself.

We then switch into an entirely different scenario. The narrator now appears to be a in a library. Perhaps we might imagine him poring over the medieval manuscripts he was alluding to in the previous verse. But his next thoughts seem to be couched in very modern language, as if Dylan himself is again temporarily taking over the narrative: *...The world of research has gone berserk...* he ruminates *...Too much paperwork...* Some commentators have interpreted this as a sly dig at critics who 'over analyse' Dylan's work. This is particularly ironic because *Nettie Moore* is a densely allusive text which requires considerable 'research' to fully understand. But then the narrator relates the results of his studies: *...Albert's in the graveyard/ Frankie's raising hell...* is a reference to the famous murder ballad. It seems that, at least in the narrator's fantasy, the murderess Frankie is still alive. Or maybe she is already in hell. The next line*...I'm beginning to believe what the scriptures tell...* is especially portentous. It is eerily reminiscent of a line from Blind Lemon Jefferson's *See That My Grave Is Kept Clean* (covered by Dylan on his first album in 1961) whose narrator, sensing the imminent approach of death, declares *...Now I believe what the Bible told...* The implication is that he had previously doubted the 'scriptures' but that now he realises, with a growing sense of dread, that it may be too late to redeem himself.

There is then a flashback to the opening scene of the song. 'Lost John' is now sitting *...where the Southern crosses the Yellow Dog...* This is an allusion to W. C. Handy's *Yellow Dog Blues* (1922), which describes a point in a small town where two railways - the 'Southern' and the 'Yellow Dog' cross. The reference, which Handy himself first heard being sung by an unknown blues troubadour, reappears in many other blues songs, such as Charley Patton's *Green River Blues* (1929) and Big Bill Broonzy's *Southern Blues* (1935). Now Lost John is, as in Robert Johnson's *Crossroads*, at the junction of two possible paths in his life. He is 'lost' in his memories of his lover *...Those bad luck women...* he complains *...they stick like glue... Bad Luck Women* is a witty song by Memphis Minnie, in which she rebels against the prevailing misogyny in blues songs, defiantly declaring herself to be one of those 'women' herself.

We are now transported to a scene in the past when the narrator and his 'bad luck woman' were dancing and drinking and having fun: *..."Look out daddy, don't want you to tear your pants"...* she laughs at him drunkenly. But this apparently jocular comment becomes ominous, as she warns him that *..."You could get wrecked in this dance"...* She follows this with *..."They say whiskey will kill you but I don't think it will"...* This is especially ironic, given that the narrator has presumably murdered her in a fit of drunken rage. But as he imagines watching the trains head off in different directions he tries hard to focus on the good times. He uses the symbolic language of the blues to remember the sexual ecstasy they once shared *...I'm riding with you to the top of the hill...* he tells her fondly. Then he shares a little aside with us, suggesting that she had great sexual energy: *...She been cooking all day, it gonna take me all night...* he sighs happily *...I can't eat all that stuff in a single bite...* In these moments he is reunited with Nettie, if only in his memories.

This fond reverie is rudely interrupted, as we are thrust into the present tense of the song. Only now does the reality of what has occurred become evident. This is revealed in some very simple but highly dramatic lines, beginning with: *...The judge is coming in, everybody rise...* In some performances Dylan replaces 'everybody rise' by 'all rise', the standard phrase uttered by a bailiff when a judge enters the room. This is followed by the slow, drawn out instruction to *...Lift up your eyes...* Now the narrator urges himself to confront the consequences of his actions. But first he delivers a cautionary warning to both the judge and his listeners: *...You can do what you please, you don't need my advice...* he begins humbly *...'Fore you call me any dirty names, you'd better think twice...* There is a passing allusion to Dylan's *Don't Think Twice, It's All Right* in which he reassures himself that he should not feel guilty about breaking up with the girl. But here the inference seems to be that any one of us could make the mistake that the narrator has made, and that we should not rush to judgement.

These lines could, however, also be interpreted as the narrator reliving the drunken argument with Nettie that led to the murder. It may be that lust has given way to anger, as he drunkenly accuses her of calling him 'dirty names'. As the slow drum beat continues, the narrative becomes even more disturbing *...Getting light outside, the temperature dropped/ I think the rain has stopped...* And then *...I'm gonna make you* *come to grips with fate...* followed by the very threatening: *...When I'm through with you, you'll learn to keep your business straight...* Perhaps these are the threats that he makes to Nettie before the murder. Or maybe this is the judge talking, warning the narrator of what is to come. Both narrative strands are possible, and in the narrator's confused consciousness, it may be that both can be said to exist simultaneously.

In the final verses, we may imagine that the narrator (truly a 'Lost John' now) is standing with that hangman's hood over his head and the noose around his neck. He tells us that the *...bright spark of the steady lights/ Has dimmed my sights...* and then delivers one final, but deathly ironic, tribute to his lost love: *...When you're around me all my grief gives way/ A lifetime with you is like some heavenly day...* He now appears to have 'given up the ghost'. His only hope is to be reunited with Nettie in eternity. He is forced to admit (in another tongue-twisting admission) that *...Everything I've ever known to be right has been proved wrong...* And in the process of confessing his love for Nettie he reveals his murder weapon: *...No knife could ever keep our love apart...* In his last moments the reality of his impending fate finally overwhelms him. He attempts to repent, wishing to *...stand in faith and raise the voice of praise...* He claims he is 'standing in the light', but it is too late now for redemption. In the song's most heartrending line he finally cries *...I wish to God that it were night....* He knows that the 'endless night' is just a step away and there will be no divine intervention to save him.

Nettie Moore investigates the consequences of sin in a very moving way. It weighs a lifetime of good intentions against a moment of madness, when passion turns to violence. Despite 'standing by his faith', religion will offer the narrator no consolation. Yet the song aches with compassion, edging just this side of tears throughout, balancing deep grief against unnameable dread. The bleak fatalism that is conveyed is deeply rooted in the world view of the blues. Just as Robert Johnson's *Hellhound on My Trail* presents a narrator whose stance appears to be beyond any sense of 'everyday' morality - an unrepentant sinner simultaneously dreaming lustfully and experiencing extreme paranoia - so *Nettie Moore* stares unequivocally at the face of death. We realise that the narrator will never be reunited with Nettie, who he has both idealised and violated. Sweet talking will not do the trick. As with *Hellhound on My Trail*, a kind of terror lurks behind the song, a fear of a chaotic universe in which there is no divine mercy.

In *Roll on John,* the concluding track on *Tempest*, the murder that is central to the narrative is never described. Yet that murder is one of the most tragic results of the USA's 'gun culture'. The song is an elegiac tribute to John Lennon which 'rolls' its anguished but celebratory message over a stately melody. Dylan was reported to have taken the custodians of the 'Liverpool Beatles industry' by surprise in 2009 by appearing unannounced on a tour of Lennon's childhood home in Menlove Avenue. It may well be that the song was written around this time. Dylan and Lennon were not, however, close personal friends. They never collaborated musically, and met each other on just a handful of occasions. The mutual influence of Dylan on The Beatles and vice versa has, however, long been acknowledged. Dylan prompted them to write more imaginative, poetic lyrics, while their success encouraged him to play with an 'electric' band. This confluence had a huge effect on the rapid explosion and development of rock music in the 1960s. Here Dylan presents an impressionistic view of Lennon's life, depicting him as a flawed human being who nevertheless displayed distinctly heroic qualities. It is undoubtedly a heartfelt tribute, not to Lennon as a friend but as a cultural icon.

As John Lennon began to write more personal, meaningful songs it became obvious that he was struggling with many personal demons. In one of his most profound works, *Strawberry Fields Forever,* he relives aspects of his troubled childhood against a backdrop of complex and innovative psychedelic music. In the late 1960s and early 70s, as The Beatles were breaking up, and he was conducting a very public relationship with the Japanese-American conceptual artist Yoko Ono, he worked out many of his own psychological problems through his songs. This was especially true on the stark and sometimes brutally honest post-Beatles album *John Lennon/ Plastic Ono Band* (1970). He later relocated to New York City and took up residence with Ono in the Dakota Building, where he remained until his murder by a crazed fan in 1980. For five years he abandoned public performance and recording, living life as a 'house husband' while Yoko took care of business.

Lennon had courted notoriety in many ways, especially in his often forthright public pronouncements. The most notorious of these, his assertion that The Beatles were 'bigger than Jesus' in Britain, was - though taken out of context - the stimulus for him to be publicly vilified in the USA, when elements of the religious right organised mass burnings of Beatles records and memorabilia. On their final tour of America in 1966 he and the other Beatles were genuinely afraid that they might be killed. They had already incurred death threats by upsetting religious sensibilities in Japan when they played the Budokan, a sacred martial arts temple. In the Philippines the army had chased them out of their country following a perceived snub to the First Lady, Imelda Marcos. They then abandoned their extensive tours, in which their music was largely being drowned out by hysterical screaming fans. Lennon's assassin Mark Chapman later pronounced that the 'Bigger than Jesus' statement was one of the reasons he shot him. Lennon's life was thus both heroic and tragic. On the one hand he was seen as a kind of prophet. His most famous solo song *Imagine* asked the listener to conjure up a world without war, hatred and religious dogmatism. On the other hand, his personal problems and his wayward behaviour - about which he was often disarmingly honest - plagued him throughout his life.

Roll On John examines both sides of Lennon, recasting him as a modern flawed hero in the mould of Homer's Odysseus and portraying his life as a turbulent 'journey' through stormy seas. Each of its eight verses culminate with the 'anthemic' chorus *...Shine your light/ Move it on/ You burned so bright/ Roll on John...* The song begins: *...Doctor, doctor, tell me the time of day/ Another bottle's empty, another penny's spent...* Dylan's vocal here is especially harsh. At various times in his career Lennon was known for his heavy indulgence in drink and drugs. Now, it seems, we are catching him during his 'lost weekend' of 1974, when he had temporarily split from Yoko Ono and was 'hanging out' in Los Angeles with self-destructive 'party animal' rock stars like Keith

Moon and Harry Nilsson. He is depicted here as being in an alcoholic delirium. The lyrics refer to the English expression 'to spend a penny', meaning to urinate. We can picture Lennon staggering through the streets with his pals, pausing to piss against the nearest wall. Hardly the most 'heroic' of openings, but indicative of the depths the subject of the song could sometimes descend to.

Then we hear that *...He turned around and he slowly walked away....* After these indulgences, Lennon returned to Yoko and became a devoted father. But the scene being described here could also show him giving his autograph to a fan, turning around and walking towards the doors of the Dakota building, as if we are now watching his last moments in slow motion. This was a place where fans often besieged him. Earlier in that day, one of those autograph hunters (for whom Lennon signed an album cover) had been Mark Chapman. We hear that *...They shot him in the back and down he went...* There is no mention of any individual assassin - just the generic 'they'. Perhaps Dylan is asserting that Lennon's killer could have been any one of those crazed Americans who had somehow assumed that Lennon was trying to deify himself and would therefore have to be eliminated. In one of his last songs for The Beatles, *The Ballad of John and Yoko*, Lennon recounts details of his and Ono's public 'demonstrations for peace' such as their week long 'bed-in' in an Amsterdam hotel where they recorded his optimistic 'anthem to the world' *Give Peace a Chance*. But *The Ballad* is a deeply cynical song. After complaining about his vilification by the press, its chorus drily observes: *...The way things are going/ They're gonna crucify me...* This was a sarcastic reference to the way the media had blown his 'bigger than Jesus' comment out of proportion. In his choice of pronouns, Dylan echoes Lennon's statement. 'They' have killed him, thus implying that his 'crucifixion' has at last come to pass.

The next verse takes us back in time to Lennon's youth and the Beatles' early engagements: *...From the Liverpool docks to the red light Hamburg streets...* In the next line we are *...Down in the quarry with the Quarrymen...* The implication seems to be that Lennon's rise to fame came out of great hardship and social deprivation, although this is a considerable exaggeration. Dylan correctly name checks 'the Quarrymen' as Lennon's pre-Beatles group. But he is surely having a little joke on us here, as we can hardly be expected to believe that he thinks Lennon ever worked in a quarry. This is followed by another affectionate light hearted jest: *...Playing to the big crowds, playing to the cheap seats...* refers not only to the Beatles' stadium gigs in the US between 1964 and 1966 but also to Lennon's quip at the 1963 Royal Variety Performance in London (in the 'presence' of the Queen Mother) that *...those of you in the cheap seats can clap your hands. The rest of you can rattle your jewellery...* Despite having accepted manager Brian Epstein's proviso that they swap their Hamburg leathers and quiffs for smart 'Beatle suits' and uniform haircuts, Lennon hated having to fawn to royalty and wound up Epstein by telling him that that his introduction to *Twist and Shout* would include the words *...rattle your fucking jewellery...* As it was, he carried off the introduction with a cheeky grin, much to Epstein's relief.

Roll on John is unstinting in its portrayal of Lennon as a troubled soul who is engaged in a difficult, if not impossible, journey through life that seemed destined to end tragically: *...Another day in the life on your way to your journey's end...*. Dylan sings, referencing The Beatles' *A Day in the Life*, which begins with a senseless death and ends with a vast cataclysm of noise. Lennon told producer George Martin that they wanted 'a sound like the end of the world'. But Dylan carries the line off with touchingly sympathetic sadness, as if that monumental track was indeed a metaphor for Lennon's own tragic life. Lennon was drawn towards celebrity by his inexorable desire for wealth and fame but even when he achieved this, after the whirlwind of sex, drink, drugs, meditation and therapy he put himself through, he still often felt - as one of his later songs put it - 'crippled inside'.

From here we shift in time and space as Dylan identifies Lennon with the great mythic heroic figure of Odysseus, linking his struggles to the Greek hero's battles with supernatural beings. He begins to interject lines that he has taken directly from Robert Fagle's translation of Homer's *Odyssey* (1996), such as *...Sailing through the trade winds, bound for the south/ Rags on his back like any other slave...* During his journey, Odysseus is trapped for several years by the nymph Calypso, who wishes to make him immortal and so forces him to become her lover. Despite achieving the kind of worldwide fame that ensured his 'immortality', Lennon still felt trapped and 'enslaved' by the pressure to conform to his image as a 'loveable mop top'. In the early years of his fame, he had to hide his true personality behind his image as the cheeky, slightly cynical Beatle. This meant that he was unable to express his political or personal opinions. *...They tied your hands and they clamped your mouth...* Dylan sings *...wasn't no way out of that deep dark cave...* Having set up Lennon as a 'mythical hero', his troubles are compared to those of Odysseus. In the *Odyssey* the hero is trapped in a cave by the one-eyed Cyclops Polythemus, who eats several of his men, but Odysseus is cunning enough to trick his way out. Lennon did indeed escape from the 'trap' that The Beatles were in. After renouncing touring they spent most of the next few years in the studio creating masterpieces like *Sgt. Pepper, The 'White Album'* and *Abbey Road.*

The next verse is concerned with the public reaction to Lennon's death. Since taking up residence in New York, he had become something of a 'local hero'. He would stroll around the city alone, without a disguise or a bodyguard. The first line *...I read the news today, Oh boy...* quotes the haunting opening of *A Day in the Life* and applies it to the news of Lennon's murder. In the next line Lennon is again the trapped Homeric hero: *...They hauled your ship up on the shore...* is another line from Fagles' translation. And then, with a voice that has now softened considerably, Dylan intones, in the song's saddest lines *...Now the city gone dark, there is no more joy/ They tore the heart right out and cut him to the core...* After Lennon's murder, devastated fans kept vigil outside the Dakota for several days. As the world mourned a lost hero, it seemed that the 'heart' of the city - in which Lennon had, perhaps naively, trusted the people - had been torn out. A section of Central Park was later named 'Strawberry Fields' in his honour.

In the next three verses, which are mainly focused on Lennon's final years, Dylan appears to travel back through time to speak to Lennon directly, as if he is giving him helpful advice which we know he will never listen to: *...Put down your bags and get 'em packed/ Leave right now, you won't be far from wrong...* Dylan advises *...The sooner you go, the quicker you'll be back/ You've been cooped up on an island far too long...* The fourth line here is another direct quotation from *The Odyssey*, referring to Odysseus' entrapment by Calypso. The earlier lines refer to Lennon's stated desire, after his years being 'cooped up' in the Dakota, to revisit his native island (Britain) again; an ambition which he sadly never achieved. Lennon had been afraid to leave the USA in case he was not allowed back in the country, due to a minor marijuana bust he had suffered in London in 1968. The narrator now appears to be imploring Lennon to take that journey, which might have meant he would have avoided being murdered. Despite the fact that by 1980 he was again making new music - his album with Yoko, *Double Fantasy* had just been released - he never travelled the world on his own 'Never Ending Tour'. He never reunited with The Beatles to head up Live Aid in 1985. Like so many mythical heroes, he never grew old. Perhaps the most moving moment in the Live Aid show was a stripped down, solo acoustic rendition of *All You Need Is Love*, performed by an impassioned Elvis Costello, who seemed to be channelling Lennon's ghost, which somehow appeared to be hovering over the whole event. Costello prefaced his performance by telling the crowd: *...I'd like to sing an old Liverpool folk song...*

In the sixth verse Dylan quotes from three songs performed by Lennon *...Slow down, you're moving way too fast...* paraphrases the Larry Williams number that The Beatles recorded a sparkling cover of in 1964 *...Come together right now, over me...* quotes directly from 1969's *Come Together,* Lennon's rather surreal appeal to members of 'the underground' to be more focused in their drive for 'revolution'. These lines also function as sadly futile attempts at persuading Lennon to take a different path. But the third line *...Your bones are weary, you're about to breathe your last...* takes us forward to Lennon's final moments *...Lord, you know how hard that can be...* is lifted directly from *The Ballad of John and Yoko.*

This is followed by another rather strange diversion: *...Roll on John, through the rain and snow/ Take the right hand road and go where the buffalo roam...* The first line's depiction of adversity recalls the cry of the despairing, long-suffering lover in the Grateful Dead's *Cold Rain and Snow.* The second echoes Walt Whitman's *Song of The Open Road,* which looks philosophically at life's choices *...The earth expanding right hand and left hand/ The picture alive, every part in its best light...* as well as the famous 'cowboy ballad' *Home on the Range* (which begins *...Oh give me a home where the buffalo roam...*) which Dylan later insisted, in his Nobel Prize Lecture of 2017, was 'influenced' by Homer's *Odyssey.* This is presumably because the *Odyssey* is focused on a long and difficult journey to an idealised home. Here Dylan, having previously advised Lennon to 'slow down', appears to approve of his decision to 'stay home' with Yoko for several years in the late '70s. He himself had experienced a similar period of domesticity a few years before. Still addressing Lennon as Odysseus, he warns that *...They'll trap* *you in an ambush before you know/ Too late now to sail back home...* but of course the warning will be futile.

The concluding verse carries Dylan's tribute to an exultant, even ecstatic, conclusion. Interweaving lines from William Blake's *The Tyger* with those of a nursery rhyme, he bids farewell and makes a final tribute. Blake was, of course, like Lennon and Dylan, a poetic songwriter. It is said that he would publicly perform his songs, some of which were later set to music by Hubert Parry (the composer of the music to *Jerusalem*, the 'unofficial' English national anthem), Ralph Vaughan Williams, Allen Ginsberg and many others. *The Tyger*, which is certainly one of the most powerful poems in the English language, eulogises the magnificent if fearsome beast in a celebration of life energy, blending beauty and danger in unforgettable couplets, encapsulating both the heroic promise of liberation of the French Revolution and its destructive force. By using such a well-known allusion, Dylan celebrates Lennon's irrepressible energy - as a fellow musician and poetic lyricist and indeed as an outspoken revolutionary - while showing us where his journey into those 'dark forests' led him *...Tyger, tyger, burning bright...* Dylan sings, contrasting this with *...I pray the Lord my soul to keep...* from the nursery rhyme. He celebrates the energy-force of both Blake's 'Tyger' and Lennon and prays that he be allowed to channel some of that force - the spiritual power of inspiration and the imagination - himself.

The final lines are immensely touching in their quiet humility: *...In the forest of the night...* is taken directly from *The Tyger*. This is followed by *...Cover him over and let him sleep...* as if 'little John' has been 'reborn' as an innocent child - recalling the climactic birth of the 'Star Child' at the end of the 'psychedelic sequence' of Stanley Kubrick's *2001- A Space Odyssey.* When Lennon saw this film he is said to have declared that a temple should be built in which it should be shown on a continual 24 hour loop. By means of this prayer, Dylan identifies his own poetic spirit with both Lennon and Blake. 'Experience' and 'innocence', which Blake called 'the two contrary states of the human soul' are now reunited. This is the same tortured soul who once uttered the ultimate cry of anguish in one of his songs: *....Mother, you had me, but I didn't have you/ I wanted you, but you didn't want me...* The 'star child' 'John' (the most common English name and sometimes used as a euphemism for 'the average man') is thus returned to innocence and, despite the pain he has suffered in his life, has now achieved a kind of immortality, by creating songs that will (in the words of Lennon's ultimate acolyte Noel Gallagher) 'live forever').

If any one song can be said to justify Dylan's recurrent use of allusion - of 'lifting' the words of other writers - which is such a prominent feature of his 'late style', this is it. Despite the apparent obscurity of some of its lines, it is very carefully crafted, with each quotation from Lennon reflecting on aspects of his life. The allusions to Blake in the last verse work as a perfect summary of the qualities of Lennon as a 'heroic' figure in the classical sense - one who, like Odysseus, has to confront a life of struggle against apparently insuperable difficulties. The song-chorus verse structure has a simple repeated ABAB rhyme scheme, but it is only in the last verse that the first two lines 'bright' and 'night' rhyme with the final corresponding lines in the chorus - 'light' and the repeated 'bright', emphasising how John's light will keep burning eternally. It is as if the chorus has been 'waiting' for this final verse. *Roll On John* is a deeply sincere tribute to perhaps the only person in rock music history who can be said to rival Dylan as its most influential figure. It is also a kind of secular prayer - a paean to an artist who was decidedly *not* - as *The Ballad of John and Yoko* makes clear - any kind of 'Jesus figure'. He certainly did not want to be 'crucified', but he was brave enough to expose his own inner turmoil and suffering to the world in the most unequivocal terms.

20th February 1991. Far away in northern Kuwait, as the defeated Iraqi army attempts to retreat to Baghdad, the fires from hundreds of oil wells light up the night sky in lurid colours. Soon the American bombers will rain down death on the now defenceless lines of troops. Meanwhile, under the sixty foot high proscenium arch of New York's famous Radio City Hall, in front of a live audience of well heeled celebrities and 29 million TV viewers, here is the one of our favourite villains - not Bush or Saddam but the Joker himself, Jack Nicholson, wearing that permanent trademark sideways grin, resplendent in his tuxedo and bow tie, his eyes glinting mischief. The Grammy Awards Ceremony, the US music industry's equivalent of the Oscars, has been - as usual - a rather bland event. Sinead O'Connor, who has been nominated for 'best vocal performance' for her achingly emotional cover of Prince's *Nothing Compares To U*, has refused to appear and the award has instead been given to Phil Collins for his mawkish 'comment' on homelessness *Another Day in Paradise.*

There have, not surprisingly, been a few underhand mutterings about that. Even the follically challenged former Genesis drummer has admitted that the rebellious Irish diva should have been given the award. But nobody has - to paraphrase Basil Fawlty - 'mentioned the war'. Meanwhile, in a tribute to the 'rock aristocracy', both John Lennon (obviously posthumously) and Bob Dylan have been given 'lifetime achievement awards'. Nicholson - who, judging by his very 'cheerful' demeanour, appears to have taken full advantage of whatever 'hospitality' has been provided - waits for the gushing audience response to die down and then begins a slightly convoluted ramble, confessing that he is rather overawed by the task of having to introduce 'Uncle Bobby'. He says that he has looked in the dictionary and found that *...all the words applied to him....* although he finally settles on 'paradox' and 'disturber of the peace'. After a montage of vintage clips of Dylan in performance, Jack finishes his introduction by declaring *...Well, this guy's a riot in more ways than one...*

Radio City's art deco curtains open to a cacophony of noise. Bob's band are all sporting natty black fedoras. Dylan himself - clearly playing the 'good guy' tonight - is wearing a white one. He makes no attempt to smile or communicate with the crowd or the TV audience. He leans into the mike, his eyes closed. At first it may be unclear to the uninitiated which of his 'famous hits' he is performing. The lyrics to his most angry and bitter protest song *Masters of War*, which he had once enunciated so carefully - and with so much righteous wrath, backed by a stark acoustic guitar - are spat out with sheer insouciance. The song proceeds at a frenetic pace through the first four verses. If you strain you can just about make out *...You put a gun in my hand and you hide from my eyes/ And you turn and run farther when the fast bullets fly...*

Masters of War has often been called an 'anti-war' song. It was composed in the wake of the Cuban Missile Crisis, when the world came close to nuclear annihilation *...A world war can be won/ You want me to believe...* Dylan sings with obvious sarcasm; the implication being that - in the era of Mutually Assured Destruction ('MAD') - such a war cannot possibly be won by anybody. However, the main point of the song is an indictment not of war itself, but of the gross hypocrisy and cowardice of the profiteers of the weapons industry. The first four verses are followed by an instrumental passage, in which lead guitarist John Jackson takes a solo. Verses five to seven (in which Dylan had once decried the fact that the 'masters' had made people *...fear to bring children into the world...*) are omitted. But the utterly uncompromising final verse, in which the narrator declares that he hopes that the 'masters' - now personified as a single figure - will die soon, and that he will *...stand over your grave 'till I'm sure that you're dead...* remains. After another 'explosive' blast of guitars, the song ends in less than four minutes.

This dark, angry and sometimes almost incomprehensible arrangement of *Masters of War* had not been specifically tailored for the performance. Dylan and his band had only just flown in after an eight night engagement at the Hammersmith Odeon in London, during which they had performed the song regularly in a similar way. There is no question, however, that Dylan - who could have picked any of his songs to perform here - deliberately chose *Masters of War* because the ceremony is being held during the first Gulf War of 1990-91, soon after the 'Desert Storm' massacre of the Iraqi army. Dylan's performance works as a powerful comment on the nature of the war itself - the first major engagement involving US troops since the debacle and national humiliation of Vietnam. This was a war which was conducted mostly by advanced technological means; so that - despite the death toll of Iraqis being in the tens of thousands - the US and their 'coalition' allies lost only a few hundred troops. Meanwhile, the American news media - led by the CNN network - turned the whole event into a supposedly compelling but actually very stage-managed 'TV show'. While much of the reporting of the Vietnam War had exposed the futility and horror of the conflict, CNN presented the use of 'precision bombing' in the Gulf War as 'scientific', even humane. Naturally, the use of expensive weaponry ensured massive profits for the 'masters of war'. In this performance - amidst the 'apolitical' glitz of a commercial awards ceremony - Dylan's offhand delivery of the lyrics suggests that even though the dominance of the 'masters of war' is greater than ever, the public has been hoodwinked into a kind of bland acceptance of the true horror of what is happening. The 'heavy' sound of the screeching guitars provides a 'soundtrack' to this, as if it is 'drowning out' the noise of the weapons being fired - just as the media itself had glossed over and obscured the true nature of the slaughter being perpetrated.

Dylan's acceptance speech turns out to be one of the most bizarre moments in the history of awards shows. The audience rises to its feet and cheers exultantly and Dylan - who looks decidedly uncomfortable, as he usually does in such situations - claps back and shuffles around, nervously removing and replacing his hat like Charlie Chaplin. In his lead up to the presentation of the award Nicholson pays tribute to Dylan for *...living your creative life fearlessly and without apology...* Dylan turns away, apparently hoping to 'escape', but two rather tall big haired showgirls suddenly appear to block his way. He then appears to realise that he is required to say something meaningful. Staring downwards and still not making eye contact with the audience, he begins with what appears to be an intro to the kind of 'thank you' that a humble 'down home' God-fearing country star might give: *...Well, my daddy... you know... he didn't leave me much... you know... ...He was a very simple man, he said "Son"...* At this point he stares down at the bauble, still apparently uncertain about what he is about to say *...He said so many things, you know...* As he adjusts his hat nervously, the audience laughs in sympathy, obviously expecting some meaningful or humorous homily - and perhaps relieved that he is clearly not about to deliver some kind of 'political' comment. But then he finally looks them in the eye *..."You know, it's possible to become so defiled in this world that your own mother and father will abandon you, and if that happens God will always believe in your ability to mend your ways"...*

A second later, he swivels around and - still clutching his hat - he is gone. The audience claps politely and the ceremony moves swiftly on to the next act. As Nicholson himself implied in his introduction, Dylan has always been a contrarian. But his statement here is nothing less than bamboozling. Had he planned this all along? Was there some coded message in this strange pronouncement? Was he commenting on the war? It was highly unlikely, of course, that Abraham Zimmerman, who died in 1968, had ever said such a thing to him. In fact, as ever-diligent Dylanologists soon pointed out, Dylan had referred to a commentary made by a nineteenth century Orthodox Jewish scholar, Rabbi Samson Raphael Hirsch, on a line from Psalm 27 which runs *...When my father and mother forsake me, then the Lord will take me up...* Despite Dylan's apparent hesitation, it may even have been that he fully intended to deliver this message, which seems to imply that, despite the 'degradation' that the war profiteers had sunk to, there was still some way in which - if they changed their ways - they could be forgiven. Perhaps this was a replacement for the 'missing lines' in the song that he no longer performed: *...Even Jesus would never forgive what you do...* suggesting that, for the 'masters of war', redemption was still possible. Possible but, given the way things were in the US' supposed 'moment of triumph' in 1991, highly unlikely...

At midnight on 27th March 2020, just as the whole of the USA and Europe was going into lockdown due to the Covid 19 pandemic, a new Bob Dylan song - the first for eight years - suddenly appeared. In the midst of a very unfamiliar kind of chaos, the release, delivered for free on You Tube, took the world by surprise. *Murder Most Foul* clocked in at almost seventeen minutes, and a host of breathless commentators immediately declared it to be the longest track he had ever recorded. Within days, countless online pundits were delivering transcriptions of the lyrics, instant reviews and analyses - some of them thoughtful, some rather more dubious - of a song whose scope and breadth clearly proclaimed itself as a major new work. Despite the entire world being focused on the latest information about the virus, the release itself was suddenly big news. Many reviewers were quick to proclaim it as a timely response to the crisis, despite its apparently unrelated subject matter. The posting received several million hits within days.

As we listened to the long, winding verses and stared at the iconic image of the eternally-young President on the screen, there was no doubt that the 'murder' referred to was that of John F. Kennedy - one of the most controversial events in twentieth century American history. With the descriptions of the assassination being interspersed with, and then overwhelmed by, references to nearly a hundred popular songs, films and books, it was clear that this was a major statement. The words 'epic' and 'bardic' were bandied about at will and many reviewers concluded that this mammoth evocation of the spirit of great American music was intended to soothe a traumatised nation. Here was Dylan, it seemed, playing the role of 'poet laureate' of America. Or, as Bruce Springsteen had once called him, 'the father of the nation'... The posting was accompanied by a brief statement, which over the coming weeks would be analysed almost as much as the song itself

...Greetings to my fans and followers with gratitude for all your support and loyalty across the years. This is an unreleased song we recorded a while back that you might find interesting. Stay safe, stay observant and may God be with you...

Dylan's 'fans and followers' around the world soon began ending all their emails with 'stay observant'; which was certainly an appropriate motto for 'the time of Coronavirus' itself.

Murder Most Foul takes the key elements of Dylan's late style: allusiveness, quotation, reference, fractured narratives and ambiguous narrators, classical structure and Shakespearean scope - not to mention his characteristic 'obsessions' with jazz, blues and sentimental songs, Biblical references, minstrelsy and the American Civil War - and cooks them up into a massive 'gumbo' which encourages his listeners to investigate the origins of virtually every word and phrase he uses. It invites us all to become 'Dylanologists'. The song has a very loose and subdued musical arrangement based on piano, violin and drums, and is perhaps the closest Dylan has come to recording a jazz track. It is reminiscent of the work of the Beat poets, who would frequently recite their work to a jazz accompaniment. There are no choruses but four 'sections' or verses, each of which ends in the rhyme 'murder most foul'. The first section consists of 22 lines, the second has 32, the third 38 and the fourth 72. As we listen we wait for the familiar phrase to be repeated, but on each occasion we have to wait longer.

Dylan's vocals are surprisingly gentle - almost 'soothing' - which is in great contrast to the unstinting descriptions of violence that are recounted. The narrative stance shifts continually, sometimes from line to line. In some instances there appears to be an omniscient voice. At other times it appears that Kennedy himself is speaking from beyond the grave (like the ghost of Hamlet's father, from whom the title phrase originates). On occasions the voice seems to be that of Dylan himself. The lyrics constantly flip like cinematic jump cuts between details of the Kennedy murder and its attendant conspiracy theories and the words and titles of songs and movies, in a kind of associative intertextual meta-narrative. The song begins in a basically descriptive mode, but the flood of allusions and references - a multiplicity of voices - gradually 'overwhelms' the narrative.

Murder Most Foul has, like other long Dylan songs, routinely been described as an 'epic'. In this case the term is highly appropriate, as the song conforms to many of the conventions of the epic form as practiced by classical authors. As with the *Odyssey* and the *Iliad* it uses a 'universal' global-historical canvas and focuses on a tragic 'hero' who was thought to possess apparently 'superhuman' powers. It begins, like classical epics, 'in medias res' ('in the middle of things'), taking us straight into the action and using flashbacks to illuminate the narrative. It is also structured as an invocation to a series of muses, at first merely referencing famous pieces of music and then positively demanding that they be played by the legendary D. J. Wolfman Jack. It then develops into an 'enumerato' - a long litany of references which place the finite action of the epic within a broader historical context, expanding from mentions of pop songs to allusions to a whole range of cultural artifacts. And it uses several 'epithets' - stock phrases which audiences will be familiar with. All of these poetic conventions can be said to be 'musical' - in the sense of a musical construction like a symphony or an extended piece of jazz - and although they may be subject to complex variations, they always return us to the original theme or a recognisable turn of phrase. This is because the epic form itself is the product of an oral culture, in which the works would be performed publicly with musical accompaniment (and dramatic vocalisation) rather than being merely read 'on the page'. Dylan thus adopts the role of the 'American Homer', the 'bardic' figure who weaves his tale through the magic of sound poetry.

Murder Most Foul is a long rumination on a typical mythological scenario - that of the murdered king - around whom many tales have been woven, some true and some false. Over the last six decades the assassination has become a prime focus for conspiracy theorists who have strongly challenged the notion that Kennedy was killed by a crazed, communistic lone gunman. The consensus seems to be that his murder was a set up by the joint forces of the CIA and the Mafia, who wanted to remove him because they saw him as an obstacle to their continuing agenda of war, violence and exploitation within the expansion of 'the American Empire'. Many books, movies and documentaries have taken up this theme; perhaps most famously Oliver Stone's 1992 film *JFK*, which dramatises the efforts of public prosecutor Jim Garrison (portrayed by Kevin Costner as the kind of honest American hero previously personified by actors such as James Stewart in *Mr. Smith Goes to Washington* or Gregory Peck in *To Kill a Mockingbird*) to prove that the President was the victim of just such a conspiracy and that Lee Harvey Oswald was, as he famously declared after being arrested, just a 'patsy' (a convenient scapegoat) for darker forces.

The evidence to support such assertions has accumulated over the years and similar conspiracy theories have been applied to the subsequent murders of Malcolm X in 1965, Robert Kennedy and Martin Luther King in 1968 and even John Lennon in 1980 - all supposedly by 'lone assassins'. The notion that Kennedy was a 'peace loving hero' who - in a counterfactual history - would have prevented the escalation of the Cold War and the terrible conflict in Vietnam is a dubious one. However, as in his earlier protest songs such as *The Lonesome Death of Hattie Carroll* and *Hurricane*, Dylan is less interested in the facts of the case than in the mythic qualities of the victims he is lionising. In *Murder Most Foul*, the assassination of Kennedy is used as a grand historical metaphor for the corruption not only of America but of modern political life in general. The song is full of specific historical and geographical detail and clearly asserts that Kennedy was the victim of a conspiracy, through which the corruption of the American state and security apparatus is made manifest.

Much of the dramatic impact of the song is achieved by the subtle inflexions of the vocals being illuminated by the low key 'background music'. Dylan appears to delight in engaging in a feast of wordplay, juxtaposing common phrases, clichés and song titles with the actual details of the crime in a way that acknowledges the mythical qualities of the story he is unfolding. He uses the repeated rhyming couplets to comment on the 'myth of Kennedy' in a multiplicity of ways, teasing the listener with apparent anger which often slides into sly humour. Rarely has he used the medium of rhyme so effectively and to such ironic effect. This is demonstrated in the opening lines *...'Twas a dark day in Dallas - November '63/ The day that will live on in infamy...* which, with its rather pointed alliteration and its deliberately archaic use of language, immediately gives us the impression that the narrator is going to be relating an old fashioned story. In fact the second line - which has an epigrammatic familiarity - is lifted straight from the words of another President, Franklin D. Roosevelt, in his speech following the attack on Pearl Harbor as he announced the US entry into World War Two. This immediately gives the narrative a broader historical context. The lines are delivered in a slightly arch, knowing way, inviting us to see the historic parallels.

A series of piled-up epigrams follows: *...President Kennedy was a-ridin' high/ A good day to be livin' and a good day to die/ Being led to the slaughter like a sacrificial lamb...* The tone is still that of a cosy narrator, despite the disturbing nature of the subject matter. But we then find ourselves 'listening in' to a weirdly melodramatic conversation between Kennedy and his assassins, as if they are characters in a Greek drama *...Wait a minute boys, you know who I am!...* the hero protests, addressing the killers almost affectionately. The first half of the line is a direct lift from *Hurricane* (1976), in which the 'bent cop', who is trying to find a corruptible witness in order to frame the boxer for murder, cries triumphantly: *...Wait a minute boys, this one's not dead!...* The bad guys reply like comic-opera villains *...Of course we do. We know who you are....* And later *...We're gonna kill you with hatred without any respect....*

Despite this, the narrator maintains his cool *...We'll mock you and shock you, we'll grin in your face...* the bad guys cry. You can almost see them twirling their moustaches. But then comes the real 'killer' line: *...We've already got someone to take your place....* the shocking implication being that Vice President Lyndon B. Johnson was a tool of these shadowy forces. Dylan delivers the lines of both parties in the same rather sad, philosophical way, reciting them slowly and deliberately as the mournful violin surges into prominence. We have already heard a dry account of how the killers *...blew off his head...* and that he was *...shot down like a dog...* Now we hear that *...The day that they blew out the brains of the king/ Thousands were watching, no-one saw a thing...* The narrator's pace speeds up a little and the lines become more broken up and tense *...It happened so quickly, so quick by surprise/ Right there in front of everyone's eyes...* We are left in no doubt that the killing was the result of a carefully co-ordinated conspiracy. It was the *...Greatest magic trick ever under the sun/ Perfectly executed, skillfully done...*

Now that the spirit of 'magic' has been invoked, we are then treated to our first 'magical' invocation: *...Wolfman, O Wolfman, O Wolfman howl!...* the narrator cries, 'conjuring up' the spirit of the famous disc jockey. The cry has a very special resonance, implying that 'the Wolfman' is an unearthly, mythical creature, who will 'howl' out the hidden truth on our behalf. There is an implied allusion to the great blues singer Howlin' Wolf (from whom Wolfman Jack took his name) as well as a nod to Allen Ginsberg's 'epic' poem *Howl*, one of the defining texts of the 'Beat Generation', and an extended cry of rage against the deadening conformity of 1950s America. The rhyming of this line with *...Rub a dub dub - it's a murder most foul...* is the song's first real masterstroke, lifting it out of mere melodrama. The half-comic, half-menacing use of 'rub a dub dub' (a reference to a well known card trick) is a 'magical' way of 'calling up' the ghostly character who will later become central to the song. From the second section onwards we may well imagine that it is he who is playing the records that the narrator refers to.

As we move into the second section, the narrative structure becomes more complex, as we begin to cut between recollections of the 1960s and the (often rather gruesome) details of the murder. The first line *...Hush little children, you'll understand...* a quotation from a nursery rhyme recited over tinkling piano, perfectly echoes the lullaby-like nature of the music. Then, in a softly spoken leap forwards slightly in time, Dylan sings *...The Beatles are coming, they're gonna hold your hand...* It has become something of a cliché to say that the Beatles' arrival in America in early 1964, just weeks after the assassination, was a 'therapeutic' experience for a shell-shocked country. But the event was certainly one of the most startling turning points in post war American popular culture. In the US, which had invented rock'n'roll, the music itself had become rather passé, with the charts now dominated by bland 'manufactured' teenage crooners. But The Beatles achieved a phenomenal, unprecedented level of almost instant success. They completely transformed American rock music, as thousands of American artists scrambled to form the 'beat groups' that just three years later would become the leaders of the 'psychedelic revolution'. The breathlessly thrilling *I Want to Hold Your Hand*, a flamboyant paean to teenage sexual energy, was the record that broke them in the US. With a little ironic wit, Dylan compresses musical history into just a few words; but with the sly implication that the public were being shielded from the ugly truth of the political 'coup' that had just occurred by the media's obsession with the 'fab four'. Yet the line is not delivered with any trace of cynicism, but affectionately, as if the narrator is genuinely reaching out to sympathise with the way in which the group's deeply humanistic songs provided succour to a grieving American public.

The rest of the first part of this section alternates between musical references and 'cut up' details of the murder, sometimes delivered in rather oddly coded forms. The couplet: *...Slide down the banister, go get your coat/ Ferry 'cross the Mersey and go for the throat...* appears to be in part a reference to FBI agent Guy Bannister and anti-communist activist David Ferrie, both of whom were accused by Jim Garrison of involvement in the conspiracy to murder Kennedy. *Ferry 'Cross the Mersey* was one of the best known songs by Gerry and the Pacemakers, one of the leading 'Mersey Beat' groups and contemporaries of The Beatles, although their success in America was limited. This is followed by a reference to the 'three bums' who were briefly arrested after the shooting and who conspiracy theorists also linked to the killing. It seems a little odd for Dylan to include such obviously coded references to specific conspirators, as if he is deliberately throwing a bone to the 'Dylanologists'. But the effectiveness of these lines lies in the contrast between the reassuring warmth of Gerry Marsden's tribute to the people of Liverpool and the brutally specific details of the murder - Kennedy was indeed shot in the throat.

Several musical/cultural references follow, as we jump in time to the end of the '60s: *...I'm going to Woodstock, it's the Aquarian age/ Then I'll go over to Altamont and sit near the stage...* As Dylan delivers these lines he lowers his voice a little, so that there is a slight hint of parody. In *Chronicles* he had railed rather angrily against hippies invading his house, which was near the famous festival site in Woodstock, in August 1969. The contrast between the 'three days of peace, love and music' of Woodstock (as the hugely successful movie of the festival proclaimed it to be) with the disastrous Altamont Festival in California of a few months later has often been seen as being emblematic of the 'end of the hippie dream'. At Altamont a murder occurred near the stage during the Rolling Stones' performance of *Sympathy for the Devil*, which contains the highly ambiguous lines *...I shouted out "Who killed the Kennedys?" when after all it was you and me...* signalling that - even by 1969 - the murders had become huge cultural signifiers.

Dylan's juxtaposition of key symbolic cultural and political moments of the 60s may thus be taken to suggest that the love generation's faith in the essential goodness of humanity would inevitably be tragically exposed - thus linking the shootings at Altamont to those of the Kennedys. Dylan's delivery is sadly suggestive here, but the song becomes increasingly ambiguous in terms not only of meaning but of narrative intent. We may ask exactly who the 'I' is in these lines. Is it a kind of disembodied 'dream version' of Dylan himself (who pointedly did *not* appear at Woodstock) or is the voice of the ghost of a mythologised 'heroic' Kennedy, a ghost which haunts American cultural and political history, hovering over these milestones of the counter culture?

Dylan continues to play with such ambiguity as the narrative unfolds, using ironic rhyming to increasingly powerful effect. In the couplet *...Put your head out the window, let the good times roll/ There's a party going on behind the grassy knoll...* he refers to *Let the Good Times Roll*, a much covered rhythm and blues standard first recorded by Louis Jordan in 1946 and *There's a Party Going On* (1961), a song by one of his favourite rockabilly singers Wanda Jackson. Both of these energetic rocking numbers implore listeners to forget their troubles and have a good time. The dryly humorous notion of there being 'a party' behind the famous grassy knoll - which much evidence points to being the location of the real assassins - again seems to be a sly suggestion that the hedonism of 1960s youth culture masked the real brutality of the political reality of those times.

As the first part of the second section 'speeds' to a conclusion, more real life details of the historic events rack up the tension. The wife of Texas Governor John Connally, who was riding in the car with Kennedy, says *...Don't say Dallas don't love you, Mr. President...* and instructs the driver of the car to *...Try to make it to the triple underpass...* One of the song's most devastating lines, with its mixture of deadpan humour and cutting social comment, follows: *...Black face singer - white face clown/ Better not show your faces after the sun goes down...* so linking the murder to the racism that African-Americans were routinely exposed to, especially in areas of the Deep South where virtual 'curfews' were often imposed on their movements. Perhaps the 'black face singer' is Sam Cooke and the 'white face clown' is Lenny Bruce (who Dylan lionises in one of his songs); both of them tragic victims of brutality and oppression in the 1960s.

The second part of the second section transposes the narrator into the persona of a cop on the beat in Deep Ellum, the poverty stricken red light district of Dallas. Dylan had performed the traditional *Deep Ellum Blues* - a song which warns the wary visitor to 'keep your money in your socks' - in his early years in Greenwich Village. Now he adapts that line in ironic contrast to one of Kennedy's most famous pieces of rhetoric: *...If you're down in Deep Ellum, put your money in your shoes/ Don't ask what your country can do for you...* teasingly placing an index of the poverty and deprivation experienced by most American urban blacks next to Kennedy's pronouncement in his inauguration speech: *...Ask not what your country can do for you/ Ask what you can do for your country...* a statement which celebrates the ideals of American individualism. In this context, however, the notion of Kennedy as a heroic saviour is already being questioned.

The next line *...Cash on the barrel head, money to burn...* references two country songs; one by the Louvin Brothers and the other by George Jones. The first song laments the fact that money appears to override justice for poor people in the United States and in the second, a rich man realises that money cannot buy him love. The implied critique of US materialism in the references to these songs is set against more instructions to the driver of the car taking Kennedy to the hospital: *...Dealey Plaza, take a left hand turn...* The next couplet begins with a verbatim quote from Robert Johnson: *...I'm going down to the crossroads, gonna flag a ride...* referring to the place where the singer supposedly sold his soul to the Devil, followed by *...That's the place where faith, hope and charity died....* The notion of a 'crossroads' already has a double meaning in blues songs - it is the place where the singer meets the Devil, but it is also a place where 'two roads meet'; where the singer can then choose to follow the path of good or that of evil. Here the 'crossroads' may also be part of Kennedy's driver's route. The use of the term suggests that Kennedy's assassination was a 'crossroads' in American history.

More voices crowd in on us now. That of the 'criminal mastermind' behind the killing appears to cry *...Shoot 'em while he runs boy, shoot 'em while you can/ See if you can shoot the Invisible Man...* But are we still in Dallas, or have we leapt forward in time? In the next couplet we are not sure if it is the 'mastermind', an arms manufacturer or an American racist who is speaking. But *...Goodbye Charlie, goodbye Uncle Sam/ Frankly Miss Scarlet, I don't give a damn...* widens the context of the song further. 'Charlie' was the name used by US troops for the Viet Cong soldiers. 'Goodbye, Uncle Sam' may refer to the ignominious exit the US finally made from Vietnam in 1973. The second half of the couplet is a paraphrase of the famous words Clark Gable as Rhett Butler says to Vivien Leigh's Scarlett O'Hara in the ultimate Hollywood Civil War epic *Gone With the Wind*, a film which, for all its status as a classic movie, romanticises the American Deep South and presents slaves as being passively content with their lot. Dylan's transposes this familiar phrase - with which Butler famously and tragically rebuts his wayward lover - into a cynical expression of the amorality of those who control a corrupt political and economic system. Thus he both defamiliarises and 'weaponises' a very familiar saying and turns it into a powerful expression of disgust. Yet in his delivery of the line, he remains steadfastly, and almost spookily, cool.

The final couplets of the second section take us back to the Kennedy assassination: *...Where is the truth and where did it go?/ Ask Oswald and Ruby, they ought to know...* Lee Harvey Oswald, the supposed lone killer of Kennedy, was murdered (live on television) by night club owner and renowned Mafia associate Jack Ruby, just two days after he had been taken into custody. The conspiracy theorists have asserted that Oswald was a CIA stooge and that Ruby - who very dubiously claimed that he killed Oswald to save Jackie Kennedy the pain of having to witness his trial - was ordered to silence Oswald by the Mafia. The final lines answer this with a nod and a knowing wink: *...'Shut your mouth' said the wise old owl/ 'Business is business, and it's a murder most foul'...* The 'wise old owl' is a character from a nursery rhyme:

...A wise old owl lived in an oak
The more he saw the less he spoke
The less he spoke the more he heard.
Why can't we all be like that wise old bird?...

Now the narrator appears to be reporting the words of a Mafia hitman. 'Business is business' is a phrase commonly associated with gangsters, who are renowned for 'putting business first'. This echoes the famous line from *The Godfather* when Michael Corleone (Al Pacino), explaining to his compatriots his plan to kill a policeman, states that *...It's not personal. It's strictly business...* The gangsters in Coppola's seminal films are in fact highly patriotic. Their values are quintessentially American - 'business', which refers to their form of brutal capitalism, always comes first. The implication is that the American system itself is fundamentally corrupt - that unrestrained capitalism rules everything and that the criminals are as much a part of the American system as the politicians. This system is controlled by brutal violence, with the gun lobby and the arms manufacturers profiting at every stage of the process. In just a few cryptic lines Dylan draws us into this territory, placing the murder of Kennedy in a broad historical context that encompasses modern America, in which these forces still rule.

The third section - which is organised into three 'subsections' - continues to provide ever more gruesome details of the assassination, while the song references continue to accumulate. The first subsection again shifts between several different narrators. It begins strikingly with a paraphrase of lines from the Who's *Tommy*: *...Tommy can you hear me, it's the Acid Queen...* another evocation of the dark side of the hippie dream. The Acid Queen is an evil character who manipulates the 'deaf, dumb and blind boy' for her own ends. The hallucinogenic visions that she will provide us with will be dark ones indeed. We immediately switch to the 'ghostly' voice of Kennedy himself, who is said to be riding in a 'long black Lincoln limousine' - the car in which he was shot. The song *Long Black Limousine* was recorded by Elvis Presley in 1969. The car in that song is part of a funeral cortege for the singer's friend who was killed in a car crash after a party. Elvis tearfully laments the fact that only now has his friend finally achieved his ambition to 'ride in a limousine'. Elvis' performance is made especially powerful by its resonance with the then-recent murders of Robert Kennedy and Martin Luther King - and by implication with that of John F. Kennedy.

'Kennedy's ghost' then describes how he was riding *...straight on into the afterlife...* from where he now presumably speaks. Taking us into the 'present tense' of the key moments of the shooting, he tells us *...I'm leaning to the left/ got my head in her lap...* We then shift abruptly into the voices of the killers: *... We ask no quarter, no quarter do we give/ We're right down the street, from the street where you live...* asserting that the members of what is apparently a joint secret service and Mafioso conspiracy are 'everywhere', controlling America with violence. The last two couplets of this 'sub-section' take us back into the omniscient narrative, supplying graphic but historically accurate details: *...They mutilated his body and they took out his brain...* Kennedy's brain was removed and examined by pathologists within days of the assassination. Some conspiracy theorists later asserted that another brain was substituted in order to provide evidence given to the Warren Commission, which ruled that Oswald was the lone killer, and to cover up the fact that Kennedy was shot from several angles *...What more could they do? They piled on the pain...* Dylan sings ruefully. But then he delivers another devastatingly and darkly funny denouement *...But his soul was not there where it was supposed to be at/ For the last fifty years they've been searchin' for that...* The rhyme itself is slightly contrived, but this is only adds to the pathos, as if the narrator is slightly incredulous and cannot quite express the gravity of what he is saying. Dylan's voice drops a little here, as if he is whispering a dread secret. The notion that Kennedy's soul was a 'portion' of his brain that pathologists should have found is a rather bizarre idea. But the symbolism is clear. Kennedy's 'lost soul' represents (as a later line in the song reveals) 'the soul of the nation'. *Murder Most Foul* questions what kind of nation America is - the 'land of the free' (as patriots love to call it) or a corrupt 'empire' which controls both its own people and the rest of the world through violence and racism.

In the next subsection the narratives continue to shift. Sometimes Kennedy seems to be speaking but other voices keep intervening. The first couplet features another 'deadly' juxtaposition: *...Freedom, oh freedom, over me/ Hate to tell you Mister, but only dead men are free...* The first line is taken directly from *Oh Freedom!* a post Civil War gospel-style song closely associated with the Civil Rights movement, which has been recorded by Harry Belafonte, Joan Baez and many others. 'Only dead men are free' is a common epithet which closely resembles a famous line which has been attributed to Plato: *...Only the dead have seen the end of war...* The President's ghost then appears to plead for some kind of reversal of time, so that the murder will never happen: *...Send me some lovin', tell me no lie/ Throw the gun in the gutter and walk on by...* Two 'soul classics' are referred to here - Little Richard's *Send Me Some Lovin'* (1957) and Dionne Warwick's *Walk On By* (1963). Both songs are, significantly, cries of hopeless love. We then get an obvious reference to the Everly Brothers: *...Wake up Little Suzie, let's go for a drive/ Cross the Trinity River, let's keep hope alive... Wake up Little Suzie* (written by Felice and Boudleaux Bryant) tells a tale of teenage lovers who (apparently chastely) fall asleep in each others' arms all night but then wake up worried about the girl's reputation. But the reference may also have some autobiographical significance. Suze (pronounced 'Suzie') Rotolo was Dylan's girlfriend in 1963. She appears - in what has become something of a historically iconic image - with a fresh faced young Bob in a snow-covered Greenwich Village street on the cover of his 'breakthrough' *Freewheelin'* album. A talented artist herself and undoubtedly Dylan's muse for such songs as *Boots of Spanish Leather* and *Ballad in Plain D*, she encouraged him to write the kind of political material that first made him famous. These lines may depict him waking up with her on the morning of Kennedy's assassination and 'going for a drive', hoping that the President would pull through. The Trinity River, however, is near Dallas - although this may be yet another example of shifting perspectives. The next line: *...Turn the radio on, don't touch the dials...* may still depict Bob and Suze on their drive. But the following

...Parkland Hospital, only six more miles... seems to take us back, as if in a cinematic 'dissolve', into the 'long black limousine' carrying Kennedy to the hospital.

This is followed by some lines which mix more allusions to songs with details of the assassination *...You got me dizzy Miss Lizzy, you filled me with lead/ That magic bullet of yours has gone to my head...* refers to *Dizzy Miss* Lizzy, an energetic rock'n'roll stomper recorded by Larry Williams in 1958 and The Beatles in 1965 and *You Go to My* Head, a romantic standard which was a favourite of Billie Holiday and Frank Sinatra. The 'magic bullet' refers to the official explanation that one of the bullets that killed Kennedy supposedly entered his body, exited it and struck Governor Connally. The fact that this is clearly impossible has been cited as proof that Kennedy could not possibly have been shot by a lone assassin. What follows appears to be the voice of Oswald *...I'm just a patsy like Patsy Cline/ Never shot anyone from the front or behind...* The renowned country singer Patsy Cline also died in 1963, in a plane crash. The next couplet *...Got blood in my eyes, got blood in my ear/ Never gonna make it to the New Frontier...* seems to be the voice of the dying Kennedy. *Blood in My Eyes* - which has an obvious relevance here - is the Mississippi Sheiks song which Dylan covers on *World Gone Wrong*. The 'New Frontier' was a phrase used by Kennedy in his acceptance speech to the Democratic Convention when nominated to run for President in 1960. It came to symbolise the 'new hope' he claimed to represent.

The third subsection begins with an angry and disgusted reaction by the narrator to the viewing of the famous Zapruder film, a home movie shot by a bystander, which the conspiracy theorists claim is further proof that Oswald could not have been the killer. The narrator recoils from the apparent revelation of the truth that the film reveals: *...It's vile and deceitful, it's cruel and it's mean...* he cries *...They killed him once, they killed him twice/ Killed him like a human sacrifice...* The narrator, who claims he has watched the film 'thirty three times or more', seems to be reeling in shock, having realised what the film (which was not released for public viewing for several years after the assassination) reveals. It may be that this narrator is some ordinary representative of the public, who now knows that he has been lied to. Perhaps it is the ghost of Kennedy again. Or maybe it is the young Dylan himself. It certainly seems to be a young man who then relates the ominous and portentous anecdote *...The day they killed him, someone said to me, "Son/ The age of the antichrist has only just begun"* ... Dylan immediately switches to a detached present tense commentary, delivered rather like a news report, to which his taciturn delivery lends a rather chilling air of inevitability: *...Air Force One coming through the gate/ Johnson sworn in at two thirty-eight...* The historical details are precisely accurate, which makes the chilling warning that preceded them even more prescient, even if the 'Biblical prophecy' is not necessarily meant to be taken literally. The narrator appears to be addressing the authors of the endless conspiracy theories when he asks, rather scathingly *...Let me know when you decide to throw in the towel...* Then the section comes to a curt conclusion, which appears to assert that, whatever conspiracy theory one might believe, the 'foul' nature of the murder cannot be denied *...It is what it is...* Dylan whispers *...and it's murder most foul...*

The long fourth section of the song includes fewer references to the murder, as the 'playlist' takes over. The section begins with an ironic question. The first line *...What's new pussycat, what'd I say...* contrasts the rather frothy and silly title song of the 1965 comedy movie (sung by Tom Jones in full 'Las Vegas' mode) with the 'deep soul' of the Ray Charles classic, presenting both frivolous and serious questions about what conclusions could be drawn about the effect of the murder. The unequivocal response *...I said the soul of a nation has been torn away...* reinforces the previous reference to Kennedy's 'missing soul'. This is followed by *...It's beginning to go into a slow decay/ And it's thirty six hours past judgement day...* But this apparent declaration of fatalism should not be taken as mere apathy. Having got these fears out of his system, the narrator is now getting ready to summon up 'spiritual' help. This help comes in the form of Wolfman Jack - to whom we have already, of course, been introduced. Dylan tells us that the D. J. is 'speaking in tongues': *....He's going on and on at the top of his lungs...* a pretty fair description of Wolfman's technique which is generally applied to a supplicant in the grip of religious ecstasy. Then the invocation begins: *...Play me a song, Mr. Wolfman Jack/ Play it for me in my long Cadillac...* Dylan pronounces the lines slowly, with genuine affection.

As Dylan reels off the titles of the songs, we may assume that he is merely asking the Wolfman to play his favourite tunes. But, although there seems to be a little free association in places, the titles are carefully chosen and juxtaposed. The songs often question traditional religious morality and American justice. He begins with *...Play that Only the Good Die Young / Take me to the place Tom Dooley was hung...* Billy Joel's *Only the Good Die Young* seems to be an obvious reference to Kennedy's death. *Tom Dooley* is a nineteenth century folk song (which was a hit for folk-pop combo The Kingston Trio in 1958) about a former Confederate soldier who was hung for the murder of his girlfriend in 1868. The execution was controversial as many people considered Dooley to be innocent. *St. James Infirmary,* which is referred to in the next line, is another meditation on death. Its narrator - a notorious gambler - laments the demise of his girlfriend and predicts that his own funeral will soon follow. Dylan then throws in a little word-association. Suddenly we are in 'the court of King James'; presumably James I. When he came to the throne James I co-opted Shakespeare's theatre company - previously known as the Lord Chamberlain's Men - so that they became 'the King's men' and were thus required to perform their works at court. One of the plays that they performed was *Macbeth,* whose subject is the brutal murder of a king.

The word-association game then takes us to another soul classic, Etta James' *I'd Rather Go Blind*, which is rhymed rather curiously with *...Play it for the man with the telepathic mind...* Dylan is being especially playful here. In the *X-Men* series of comics Kennedy appears as a character who possesses superhuman qualities, including that of telepathy. In real life Kennedy did suffer from a 'genetic mutation', Addison's disease, an adrenal gland deficiency. He frequently experienced severe back pain, for which he had several major operations. Thus the next line *...Play John Lee Hooker, Play "Scratch My Back"...* is not a random choice. *Baby Scratch My Back* is a well known blues song by

Slim Harpo. It is rhymed with *...Play it for that strip club owner named Jack...* a reference to Oswald's killer Jack Ruby. The next request is for Guitar Slim's *Goin' Down Slow*, which is an address to a lover by a dying man. If some of these references may seem a little obscure for the casual listener, the next line *...Play it for me and for Marilyn Monroe...* is devastatingly obvious. The iconic film star was strongly rumoured to have had affairs with both Kennedy brothers. Her tragic death in 1962 at the age of only 36 - supposedly from suicide - later became the subject of more conspiracy theories.

The invocation continues: *...Play Please Don't Let Me Be Misunderstood* is a reference to yet another soul gem which was a hit for both Nina Simone (1964) and The Animals (1965). This song is, as its title suggests, a plea to a lover to try to reassure him that she is *...just a soul whose intentions are good...* Our ghostly narrator requests Wolfman to *...play it for the First Lady, she ain't feeling any good...* After the mention of Monroe, this may be a plea from 'Jack' to 'Jackie' to forgive him for his infidelities. Then, perhaps surprisingly, we are in the world of mainstream Californian '70s rock. First we get *...Play Don Henley, play Glen Frey* (pronounced 'Fry')/ *Take it to the limit and let it go by...* and then *...Play it for Carl Wilson, too. Looking far, far away down Gower Avenue... Take it to The Limit* (1975) was one of the Eagles' biggest hits, written by Henley and Frey with bass player Randy Meisner, who sings vocals on the original recording. This song is a lament for a potential lover who the narrator missed out on, but the title here has obvious connotations. The second reference is more obscure, referring to the fact that the Beach Boys' singer performed backing vocals on Warren Zevon's song *Desperados under the Eaves,* another bitter-sweet Californian lament in which the narrator feels that he can never escape from the previous mistakes in his life. Wilson's contribution is particularly evocative when he joins Zevon in the harmonies on the final lines *...Look away down Gower Avenue...* where the image of 'gazing into the distance' becomes equivalent to 'gazing into the past'. Dylan seems to be inviting us to share in the emotion of those final lines. It seems that the 'spirit' of Kennedy - who was denied a final shriving by a priest - may now be trying to use these songs of regret as confessions of his sins from beyond the grave.

As the requests mount up, the presence of the president's ghost seems to fade away. Dylan's omniscient narrator invites more and more voices into the song. He takes us back and forth through time, capturing musical moments that will inspire us and lift us out of despair. The references pile up in quick succession *...Play 'Tragedy' and play 'Twilight Time'...* refers to two 'doo wop' ballads of the late 50s (by Thomas Wayne and the Delons and The Platters respectively) both of which express romantic regret in tearful tones. This is rhymed with *...Take Me Back To Tulsa to the scene of the crime... Take Me Back to Tulsa* is a rather jolly song by Bob Wills whose narrator repeatedly confesses that he is 'too young to marry'. 'The scene of the crime' appears to refer to the fact that Tulsa in Oklahoma was the location of a notorious massacre of over 300 black residents by whites in 1921, renowned as the worst such incident in American history. This and the succeeding requests hint at the violence that remains endemic in American society. Queen's *Another One Bites the Dust* - a song that rides on a much-sampled central riff - laments the prevalence of murders on American streets. *Ride the Pink Horse* is a 1947 Film Noir movie in which the protagonist travels to Mexico to seek violent revenge. *That Long Lonesome Road* is a country song by C. W. McCall detailing the hard life of a trucker. These references are contrasted with mentions of two hymns, *The Old Rugged Cross* and *In God We Trust.* In *The Old Rugged Cross* (written by the evangelist George Bennard in 1912) the narrator clings to an old crucifix he has been given to remind him of Jesus' suffering. *In God We Trust* is also the official motto of the United States which, to the chagrin of secularists, has appeared on bank notes since 1957.

As more and more cultural icons are mentioned, the singer appears to gain moral authority by invoking them. The songs, films and plays being referenced now seem to represent the idea that such great artistic achievements can transcend the history of corruption and violence which has dominated the succeeding decades. By now we might expect the song - if it was to follow the patterns of previous sections - to end, but it will continue until the last mention of the title line, as if Dylan is making one great final effort to summon more and more help in his search for the lost 'soul of the nation' *...Play "Mystery Train" for Mr. Mystery*... links Junior Parker's darkly suggestive rhythm and blues classic - most memorably covered by Elvis Presley in 1956 - with another reference to a popular comic character, quite possibly a favourite of Dylan in his childhood. This is counterposed with a striking image of Kennedy's death: *...The man who fell down dead like a rootless tree... A Rootless Tree* is the title of a book of poems by Zhang Sanfeng, a thirteenth century Taoist monk who is said to have invented several martial arts. The Wolfman is now asked to play *Mystery Train* for some mysterious figures: 'the reverend' (presumably Martin Luther King), 'the pastor' (which may well refer to Pastor Dietrich Bonhoeffer, a heroic German opponent of the Nazis in World War Two) and then 'the dog who has no master'. This may be a reference to the 'Mu Koan', in which the Zen master Joshu answers a question from a student as to whether a dog can have Buddha nature with a curt 'no'.

Dylan follows this with a list of life-affirming music and musicians, now delighting in his own word play as he does so: *...Play Oscar Peterson and play Stan Getz...* he cries *...Play 'Blue Sky', play Dickie Betts...* beginning his list of great jazz musicians while pausing to refer to a stirringly attractive and hopeful song by The Allman Brothers Band. And then he rather mischievously rhymes *...Play Art Pepper, play Thelonius Monk...* with *...Play Charlie Parker and all that junk...* a riff on Parker's heroin addiction which is extended to *...All that junk and all that jazz...* referring perhaps to the problems with 'junk' that affected so many stars of the bebop era. *All That Jazz* is a popular 'show tune' from the 1975 musical *Chicago* which was a hit for Liza Minnelli in 1981. It is also the title of Bob Fosse's film of the same name (1979). This is rather delightfully (and surprisingly) rhymed with *...Play it for the Birdman of Alcatraz...* The 'Birdman' was a convicted murderer called Robert Stroud who, despite his incarceration, became a leading ornithologist. He was portrayed by Burt Lancaster in a somewhat romanticised movie in 1962. Stroud died on November 22nd 1963, the day before Kennedy's assassination. The reference here seems to present him as a symbol of forlorn hope. Unlike his birds, and like Kennedy, he will never escape. We are then thrown back in time to the 1920s: *...Play Buster Keaton, play Harold Lloyd/ Play Bugsy Siegel, play Pretty Boy Floyd...* The reference to the silent film stars appears to be a purely celebratory one. Bugsy Siegel was a famous mobster, while Pretty Boy Floyd was a notorious outlaw who was mythologised as a 'folk hero' in Woody Guthrie's song of the same name, which Dylan recorded a stunning version of for a tribute album in 1988.

The litany continues to become more and more wide ranging, imaginative and fanciful as Dylan delivers some more carefully measured couplets. Gambling metaphors: *...Play all the numbers, play all the odds...* and *...Play number six, play number nine...* are set against the rather grandiose *...Play 'Cry Me a River' for the King of The Gods...* juxtaposing the Julie London tearjerker (a particular favourite of Dylan's which he included in *Theme Time Radio Hour*) with the truly 'epic' power of Zeus. The second line is rhymed with a rather more prosaic tribute to *Rumours*-era Fleetwood Mac: *...Play it for Lindsay and Stevie Nicks...* We then get more tributes: *...Play Nat King Cole,* play *Nature Boy/ Play Down in the Boondocks For Terry Malloy...* referencing one of the crooners who Dylan particularly admires and the 1954 movie *On the Waterfront,* in which Terry Malloy is the defeated dockworker played by Marlon Brando who emits the famous cry "I could-a been a contender!" *Down in the Boondocks* is a 1965 song by country singer Billy Joe Royal in which the narrator laments being too poor to call on a rich girl he loves. *It Happened One Night*, the 1934 Frank Capra comedy starring Clark Gable and Carole Lombard, is requested, along with *One Night of Sin* - a song with a similarly risqué theme recorded by Elvis Presley in 1957. A lustful Elvis, mixing sex and religion as only he can, 'prays' to be allowed to spend the night with the object of his desire. Then there is an impassioned appeal to the Wolfman: *...There's twelve million souls listening in...* as if the D. J. is some kind of evangelist or preacher.

The 'dark side' of the song then reasserts itself, as we are jolted out of the mode of joyous celebration into a violent Shakespearean context: *...Play The Merchant of Venice, play Merchants of Death/ Play Stella By Starlight for Lady Macbeth....The Merchant of Venice* explores the limits of materialism through Shylock's demands for his 'pound of flesh'. *The Merchants of Death* by H. C. Engelbrecht and F. C. Hanighen (1934) is not a song but one of several books published in the 1930s which sought to expose the way in which US arms manufacturers had made huge profits out of the carnage of World War I, the Spanish Civil War and other bloody conflicts. Conspiracy theorists have asserted that Kennedy was eliminated by elements who saw him as a threat to the continuing profits of the huge industrial enterprise which Dwight D. Eisenhower - in his final speech as President before giving way to Kennedy - identified as the 'military-industrial complex', citing the US arms manufacturers' continuing involvement in many wars that have raged across the world. *Stella by Starlight* is a rather grandiose romantic jazz standard written by Victor Young in 1944 in which the 'stellar' object of the song is compared to 'a great symphonic theme'. Many of the bebop jazz players developed instrumental versions and it became a favourite of Miles Davis. Dylan's juxtaposition of romance and deadly materialism in these lines is particularly cutting and effective.

We are now presented with another imagined dialogue which takes us back to the moments after the shooting: *...Don't worry, Mr. President...* a soothing, disembodied voice reassures him *...help's on the way. Your brothers are coming, there'll be hell to play...* Then we hear the sneering tones of the murderers: *...Brothers? What brothers? What's this about hell?/ Tell 'em we're waiting - keep coming - we'll get them as well...* Kennedy's brothers Robert and Edward both became Presidential contenders. Robert was assassinated and Edward's career was ruined by a scandal involving the death of one of his interns. Conspiracy theorists have long argued that these events were the result of deliberate acts by their enemies. The next two couplets return to the historical details: *...Love Field was where his plane touched down/ But it never did get back up off the ground...* 'Love Field', with its obvious ironic resonance, was the name of the airport in Dallas where Kennedy landed. This is followed by *...Was a hard act to follow, second to none/ They killed him on the altar of the Rising Sun...* a reference to *The House of The Rising Sun,* an evocative New Orleans whore's lament which was covered by Dylan on his first album and later 'electrified' in the classic version by The Animals. The reference to the 'altar' seems to link these lines to a traditional Catholic practice known as 'ad orientam' in which the priest offers mass on the same side of the altar as the congregation. Some churches were built to facilitate this practice, so that both priest and followers were required to face the east, where the sun rises. This again suggests that Kennedy was a 'human sacrifice'.

More song titles and film references follow: *...Play Misty for Me and That Ol' Devil Moon/ Play Anything Goes and Memphis in June/ Play Lonely at the Top and Lonely are the Brave...* The first four songs are well known jazz standards. *Misty* is a 1954 song composed by Errol Garner and Johnny Burke. *Play Misty for Me* also refers to the 1973 film in which Clint Eastwood plays a D. J. who is stalked by an obsessive female fan. *That Ol' Devil Moon* was one of Sinatra's 'showstoppers'. *Anything Goes* is a somewhat risqué take on modern morals written by Cole Porter in 1934. *Memphis in June* was composed by Hoagy Carmichael in 1945 for the film *Johnny Angel.* The other two titles have obvious connotations with Kennedy. *Lonely at the Top* is a rather plaintive Randy Newman song about the limitations of fame, while *Lonely are the Brave* is an acclaimed 1962 'social conscience' themed Western starring Kirk Douglas. In one of the song's most inspired pairings, this is rhymed with *...Play it for Harry Houdini, spinning around in his grave...* The image of the great escapologist perpetually 'spinning around' in a location that even he cannot escape from powerfully evokes the situation that the 'soul of America' is trapped in.

The song ends with eight lines in which twelve more requests are made. The jazz pianist Jelly Roll Morton is name checked, as are Little Richard's screaming proto rock'n'roll song *Lucille, Deep In a Dream* (a song which features on Sinatra's *In the Wee Small Hours* album) and *Driving Wheel,* a blues standard first recorded by Roosevelt Sykes in 1936. Another remarkable couplet: *...Play Moonlight Sonata in F Sharp/ Play*

Key to the Highway by the King of The Harp... links Beethoven's melody with Little Walter's definitive 1958 version of one of Dylan's favourite blues songs, which in his 2015 *Musicares* speech he claimed was the inspiration for *Highway 61 Revisited.* Two American Civil War songs are mentioned: *Marching through Georgia* and *Dumbarton's Drums.* The first of these, written by William Henry Clay in 1865, commemorated General Sherman's bloody and triumphant 'march to the sea' at the end of the war, and the second is a traditional Scottish tune which was popular with Civil War marching bands. 'Dumbarton's drums' is rhymed with *...Play Darkness and death will come when it comes...*

The final couplet*...Play Love Me or Leave Me by the great Bud Powell...* references another jazz instrumental version of a popular standard. This is rhymed with *...Play The Blood Stained Banner, play Murder Most Foul... The Blood Stained Banner*, as well as being a popular hymn, was the name given to the flag of the Confederate States, which is still flown with apparent pride by some right wing groups. Here, as on so many occasions in his late work, Dylan implies that a 'civil war' is still being fought in the USA, a society in which racism still exists and violence - especially in the form of gun shootings - remains tragically prevalent. Finally the narrator asks the D. J. to play *Murder Most Foul* (the song) itself. This is a neat, self-referential twist but it also implies that the violence and corruption that the song describes will continue unabated. By focusing on a major event in modern history which occurs at the beginning of his own long career as a 'public poet', Dylan reflects with righteous anger, sadness and melancholy on the continuing corruption, prejudice and violence which marrs life in his country.

Nara, Japan, 22nd May 1994. The 'Great Music Experience' is a major series of concerts being held outside the Buddhist Temple of Tōdai-ji, the aim of which is to showcase a mixture of Japanese and Western artists in order to 'spread happiness and promote harmony between nations'. Western musicians, including Joni Mitchell, Jon Bon Jovi, Ry Cooder and The Chieftains, are alternated with Japanese acts such as Hasedera Temple Shomyo, Hiroshi Hori and the spectacular Leonard Eto and his drummers. This is the third and final night of the show. It will be broadcast to a worldwide TV audience and later released on DVD. A band of top class studio musicians have been provided to back the singers, who are performing three or four songs each. Bob Dylan is topping the bill, and has presented the same set every night. The evening will end in a general sing-along of *I Shall Be Released.* What is especially unusual about the show is that Dylan - for the first and so far the only time - is performing live with an orchestra - in this case the renowned Tokyo Philharmonic. Their conductor tonight is the flamboyant Michael Kamen, a prolific film composer who had also previously arranged orchestrations for The Who, Pink Floyd and Kate Bush.

The collaboration between Dylan and Kamen could have been a disaster, especially given Dylan's patchy record at such 'official' international events and his usual commitment to musical spontaneity. This will, however, not be a repeat of the *Live Aid* debacle. Everyone is suitably sober, straight faced and almost formally dressed. Dylan, who is attired in a plain black suit, will not be throwing in any 'gnomic' comments or making speeches from obscure theological sources. He has clearly 'learned his lines' and has rehearsed the numbers with the orchestra. *A Hard Rain's a-Gonna Fall* is a key song in Dylan's history, representing the moment at which he truly metamorphosed from a folk singer into a poet. It is built on a refrain derived from *Lord Randall*, a traditional Scottish ballad but it develops a haunting melody of its own because of the ecstatic poetic rush and natural rhythm of the lyrics. The original performance on *Freewheelin'* with stark acoustic guitar accompaniment is quite mesmerising. Here is a twenty one year old poet who, on that iconic cover shot with Suze, looks like he is barely shaving, pouring forth image upon fantastical image, burrowing deep into his imagination to bombard the listener with a vision of an apocalypse which is marked by sudden moments of exquisite beauty such as *...I met a young girl/ she gave me a rainbow...* Dylan did not perform the song on his mid '60s tours, and it seemed to be unequivocally linked to his early acoustic style. But Bryan Ferry's startling 1973 rock version, featuring female backing vocalists, ringing guitars, sound effects and arch, almost parodic vocals demonstrated that this was a song one could *dance* to. Since then Dylan has performed it hundreds of times in concert, using many different arrangements and vocal styles.

Each of the five verses begins with a question and builds to a climax with a repeat of the refrain. The orchestra creates a kind of tsunami of sound, building in intensity with each verse and going into 'full flood' mode on the refrains. The performance lasts for over seven minutes and includes all five long verses. Dylan's vocals are extremely measured and every word is delivered with great clarity. Although he softens his tone at times, his voice still has a harsh edge. This provides an appropriate contrast to the sweeping strings. The song's formal structure means that it works surprisingly well as a 'classical piece'. But, given the context of the venue and the nature of the occasion as an international event designed to promote cross cultural understanding, the performance has a very special significance. *A Hard Rain's a-Gonna Fall* was written in mid 1962, around the time of the Cuban Missile Crisis. Dylan had previously written the much more directly 'finger pointing' protest song *Let Me Die In My Footsteps*, a naive but powerful attack on the mentality of those in the US who at that time were planning to use fallout shelters, which would of course have been pathetically useless in the event of a nuclear cataclysm. But *Hard Rain* goes much further. Although it will always be linked to this momentous point in history, it is far more than an anti-war protest. It presents a series of often terrifyingly graphic images related to some unknown apocalyptic scenario and ultimately becomes a song of defiance - which could be applicable to any historical calamity - against the mentality which has created the disaster. And of course the fact that Dylan is performing tonight in the only country to have suffered nuclear attacks - promulgated, of course, by members of the nation he comes from, gives the performance a very special resonance *...I'll tell it and think it and speak it and breathe it...* Dylan sings *...and reflect from the mountain so all souls can see it...* As the orchestra brings the song to its climax, the performance becomes an unequivocal and heartfelt plea not only for international peace, but also for its audience to see past the 'hard rain' of lies and deceit that prevent this happening. Despite his constant denials of being 'the voice of his generation' there is no doubt that here Dylan is here quite consciously taking up the stance of a prophet - standing on a high mountain and surveying what is below.

Dylan's art has always involved the spontaneous communication of direct and authentic emotion through the medium of a form of sound poetry that he has distilled himself from a plethora of influences. Tonight he won't be able conjure up any odd chords or change the tempo half way through with a nod and a wink to Tony Garnier. But the orchestration, thankfully, is never syrupy. Dylan's voice is mixed up high. You can hear every word, ringing out clearly in the night. Not one word has been missed out in this staggeringly powerful performance, which encapsulates his entire journey from scruffy folk singer to international cultural icon. What was originally a stark solo plea - a voice crying out alone in a desolate wilderness - has become a kind of conversation between Dylan and the world. He once stated (allowing himself considerable poetic licence) that every line is the title of a song which he did not think he would ever be able to write. Tonight *Hard Rain* somehow seems to contain *all* of the songs he has ever written. He has *...walked and crawled through six crooked highways...* and has *...been out in front of a dozen dead oceans....* He has *...walked ten thousand miles in the mouth of a graveyard...* And it is we, the audience, who can now ask *...Where have you been, my blue eyed son?...*

We can leave it to Dylan himself to answer this question. Many years later, in his 2017 interview with Bill Flanagan, he would relate a story about his first meeting with Frank Sinatra:

> *...He was funny, we were standing out on his patio at night and he said to me, "You and me, pal, we got blue eyes, we're from up there" and he pointed to the stars. "These other bums are from down here". I remember thinking that he might be right....*

Bob Dylan Discography

Studio Albums

All songs by Bob Dylan unless stated

Bob Dylan (1962) You're No Good (Jesse Fuller)/ Talkin' New York/ In My Time of Dyin' (trad. arr. Dylan)/ Man of Constant Sorrow (trad. arr. Dylan)/ Fixin' to Die (Bukka White)/ Highway 51 Blues (Curtis Jones)/ Gospel Plow (trad. arr. Dylan.)/ Baby Let Me Follow You Down (trad. arr. Ric Von Schmidt)/ House of the Rising Sun (trad. arr. Dave Van Ronk)/ Freight Train Blues (John Lair)/ Song to Woody/ See That My Grave is Kept Clean (Blind Lemon Jefferson)

The Freewheelin' Bob Dylan (1963) Blowin' in the Wind/ Girl From the North Country/ Masters of War/ Down the Highway/ Bob Dylan's Blues/ A Hard Rain's a-Gonna Fall/ Don't Think Twice, It's All Right/ Bob Dylan's Dream/ Oxford Town/ Talkin' World War III Blues/ Corrina Corrina (trad. arr. Dylan)/ Honey Just Allow Me One More Chance (Henry Thomas/ Bob Dylan)/ I Shall Be Free

The Times They Are a-Changin' (1964) The Times They Are a-Changin'/ Ballad of Hollis Brown/ With God on Our Side/ One Too Many Mornings/ North Country Blues/ Only a Pawn in Their Game/ When the Ship Comes In/ Boots of Spanish Leather/ The Lonesome Death of Hattie Carroll/ Restless Farewell

Another Side Of Bob Dylan (1964) All I Really Want to Do/ Black Crow Blues/ Spanish Harlem Incident/ Chimes of Freedom/ I Shall Be Free No. 10/ To Ramona/ Motorpsycho Nitemare/ My Back Pages/ I Don't Believe You/ Ballad in Plain D/ It Ain't Me Babe

Bringing It All Back Home (1965) Subterranean Homesick Blues/ She Belongs to Me/ Maggie's Farm/ Love Minus Zero - No Limit/ Outlaw Blues/ On the Road Again/ Bob Dylan's 115th Dream/ Mr. Tambourine Man/ Gates of Eden/ It's Alright Ma (I'm Only Bleeding)/ It's All Over Now, Baby Blue

Highway 61 Revisited (1965) Like a Rolling Stone/ Tombstone Blues/ It Takes a Lot to Laugh, It Takes A Train to Cry/ From a Buick 6/ Ballad of a Thin Man/ Queen Jane Approximately/ Highway 61 Revisited/ Just Like Tom Thumb's Blues/ Desolation Row

Blonde on Blonde (1966) Rainy Day Women #12 & 35 / Pledging My Time/ Visions of Johanna/ One of Us Must Know (Sooner or Later)/ I Want You/ Stuck Inside of Mobile with the Memphis Blues Again/ Leopard Skin Pillbox Hat/ Just Like a Woman/ Most Likely You Go Your Way (And I'll Go Mine)/ Temporary Like Achilles/ Absolutely Sweet Marie/ Fourth Time Around/ Obviously Five Believers/ Sad Eyed Lady of the Lowlands

John Wesley Harding (1967) John Wesley Harding/ As I Went Out One Morning/ I Dreamed I Saw St. Augustine/ All Along the Watchtower/ The Ballad of Frankie Lee and Judas Priest/ The Drifter's Escape/ Dear Landlord/ I Am a Lonesome Hobo/ I Pity the Poor Immigrant/ The Wicked Messenger/ Down Along the Cove/ I'll Be Your Baby Tonight

Nashville Skyline (1969) Girl from the North Country (with Johnny Cash)/ Nashville Skyline Rag/ To Be Alone With You/ I Threw It All Away/ Peggy Day/ Lay Lady Lay/ One More Night/ Tell Me That It Isn't True/ Country Pie/ Tonight I'll Be Staying Here With You

Self Portrait (1970) All The Tired Horses/ Alberta No. 1 (trad. arr. Dylan)/ I Forgot More Than You'll Ever Know (Cecil A. Null)/ Days of '49 (trad. arr. Dylan)/ Early Morning Rain (Gordon Lightfoot)/ In Search of Little Sadie (trad. arr. Dylan)/ Let it Be Me (Gilbert Becaud/ Mann Curtis/ Pierre Delano)/ Little Sadie (trad. arr. Dylan)/ Woogie Boogie/ Belle Isle (trad. arr. Dylan)/ Living the Blues/ Like a Rolling Stone (live)/ Copper Kettle (Albert Beddoe)/ Gotta Travel On (Paul Clayton)/ Blue Moon (Richard Rodgers/ Lorenz Hart)/ The Boxer (Paul Simon)/ The Mighty Quinn (live)/ Take Me As I Am (Or Let Me Go) (Boudleaux Bryant)/ Take a Message to Mary (Felice and Boudleaux Bryant)/ It Hurts Me Too (trad. arr. Dylan)/ Minstrel Boy (live)/ She Belongs to Me (live)/ Wigwam/ Alberta No. 2 (trad. arr. Dylan)

New Morning (1970) If Not for You/ Day of the Locusts/ Time Passes Slowly/ Went to See the Gypsy/ Winterlude/If Dogs Run Free/ New Morning/ Sign On the Window/ One More Weekend/ The Man in Me/ Three Angels/ Father Of Night

Dylan (1973) Lily of the West (trad. arr. Dylan)/ Can't Help Falling in Love (George Weiss/ Hugo Peretti/ Luigi Creatore)/ Sara Jane (trad. arr. Dylan)/ The Ballad of Ira Hayes (Peter La Forge)/ Mr. Bojangles (Jerry Jeff

Walker)/ Mary Ann(trad. arr. Dylan)/ Big Yellow Taxi (Joni Mitchell)/ Spanish is the Loving Tongue (Billy Simon/ Charles Badger Clark)/

Planet Waves (1974) On a Night Like This/ Going. Going, Gone/ Tough Mama/ Hazel/ Something There Is About You/ Forever Young (1)/ Forever Young (2)/ Dirge/ You Angel You/ Never Say Goodbye/ Wedding Song

Blood on the Tracks (1975) Tangled Up in Blue/ Simple Twist of Fate/ You're A Big Girl Now/ Idiot Wind/ You're Gonna Make Me Lonesome When You Go/ Meet Me In the Morning/ Lily, Rosemary and the Jack of Hearts/ Shelter From the Storm/ Buckets of Rain

The Basement Tapes (1975) (with The Band) Odds and Ends/ Orange Juice Blues (Blues For Breakfast (Richard Manuel)/ Million Dollar Bash/ Yazoo Street Scandal (Robbie Robertson)/ Goin' to Acapulco/ Katie's Been Gone (Robbie Robertson/ Richard Manuel)/ Lo and Behold/ Bessie Smith (Robbie Robertson/ Rick Danko)/ Clothes Line Saga/ Apple Suckling Tree/ Please Mrs. Henry/ Tears of Rage (Bob Dylan/ Richard Manuel)/ Too Much of Nothing/ Yea! Heavy and a Bottle of Bread/ Ain't No More Cane (trad.) / Down in the Flood/ Ruben Remus (Robbie Robertson/Richard Manuel)/ Tiny Montgomery/ You Ain't Goin' Nowhere/ Don't Ya Tell Henry/ Nothing Was Delivered/ Open the Door Homer/ Long Distance Operator/ This Wheel's on Fire (Bob Dylan/ Rick Danko)

Desire (1976) Hurricane/ Isis/ Mozambique/ One More Cup of Coffee (Dylan)/ Oh, Sister/ Joey/ Romance in Durango/Black Diamond Bay/ Sara (Dylan) (all songs by Bob Dylan and Jacques Levy unless shown)

Street Legal (1978) Changing of the Guards/ New Pony/ No Time to Think/ Baby Stop Crying/Senor/ Is Your Love in Vain/ Senor/ True Love Tends to Forget/ We Better Think This Over/ Where are You Tonight (Journey Through Dark Heat)

Slow Train Coming (1979) Gotta Serve Somebody/ Precious Angel/ I Believe in You/ Slow Train/ Gonna Change My Way of Thinking/ Do Right to Me Baby (Do Unto Others)/ When You Gonna Wake Up/ Man Gave Names To All the Animals/ When He Returns

Saved (1980) A Satisfied Mind (Red Rhodes/ Jack Hayes)/ Saved (Bob Dylan/ Tim Drummond)/ Covenant Woman/ What Can I Do For You/ Solid Rock/ In the Garden/ Saving Grace/ Are You Ready

Shot of Love (1981) Shot of Love/ Heart of Mine/ Property of Jesus/ Lenny Bruce/ Watered Down Love/ The Groom's Still Waiting at the Altar/ Dead Man, Dead Man/ In the Summertime/ Trouble/ Every Grain of Sand

Infidels (1983) Jokerman/ Sweetheart Like You/ Neighborhood Bully/ License to Kill/ Man of Peace/ Union Sundown/ I and I/ Don't Fall Apart on Me Tonight

Empire Burlesque (1985) Tight Connection to My Heart/ Seeing the Real You At Last/ I'll Remember You/ Clean Cut Kid/ Never Gonna Be The Same Again/ Trust Yourself/ Emotionally Yours/ When the Night Comes Falling From The Sky/ Something's Burning Baby/ Dark Eyes

Knocked Out Loaded (1986) You Wanna Ramble (Junior Parker)/ They Killed Him (Kris Kristofferson)/ Driftin' Too Far From the Shore/ Precious Memories (trad. arr. Dylan)/ Brownsville Girl (Bob Dylan/ Sam Shepard)/ Got My Mind Made Up (Bo b Dylan/ Tom Petty)/ Under Your Spell (Bob Dylan/ Carole Bayer Sager)

Down in the Groove (1988) Let's Stick Together (Wilbert Harrison)/ When Did You Leave Heaven (Walter Bullock/ Richard Whiting)/ Sally Sue Brown (Arthur Alexander/ Earl Montgomery/ Tom Stafford)/ Death is Not the End/ Had a Dream About You Baby/ Ugliest Girl in the World (Bob Dylan/ Robert Hunter)/ Silvio (Bob Dylan/ Robert Hunter)/ Ninety Miles an Hour Down a Dead End Street (Hal Blair/ Don Robertson)/ Shenandoah (trad. arr. Dylan)/ Rank Strangers to Me (Albert E. Brumley)

Oh Mercy (1989) Political World/ Where Teardrops Fall/ Everything is Broken/ Ring Them Bells/ Man in the Long Black Coat/ Most of the Time/ What Good Am I/ Disease of Conceit/ What Was it You Wanted/ Shooting Star

Under The Red Sky (1990) Wiggle Wiggle/ Under the Red Sky/ Unbelievable/ Born in Time/ TV Talking Song/ 10,000 Men/ 2 X 2/ God Knows/ Handy Dandy/ Cat's in the Well

Good As I Been to You (1992) Frankie and Albert (trad. arr. Mississippi John Hurt)/ Jim Jones (trad. arr. Dylan)/ Black Jack Davey (trad. arr. Dylan)/ Canadee-i-o (trad. arr. Nic Jones)/ Sittin' on Top of the World (Walter Vinson/ Lonnie Chatmon)/ Little Maggie (trad. arr. Dylan)/ Hard Times (Stephen Foster)/ Step it Up and Go (trad. arr. Dylan)/ Tomorrow Night (Sam Coslow/ Will Grosz)/ Arthur McBride (trad. arr. Paul Brady)/ You're Gonna Quit Me (trad. arr. Dylan)/ Diamond Joe (trad. arr. Dylan)/ Froggie Went A-Courtin' (trad. arr. Dylan)

World Gone Wrong (1993) World Gone Wrong (Walter Vinson)/ Love Henry (trad. arr. Dylan)/ Ragged and Dirty (Willie Brown)/ Blood in My Eyes (Bo Carter)/ Broke Down Engine (Blind Willie McTell)/ Delia (trad. arr. Dylan)/

Stackolee (trad. arr. Dylan)/ Two Soldiers (trad. arr. Dylan)/ Jack-A-Roe (trad. arr. Dylan)/ Lone Pilgrim (Benjamin Franklin White/ Adjer M. Pace)

Time Out of Mind (1997) Love Sick/ Dirt Road Blues/ Standing in the Doorway/ Million Miles/ Trin' to Get to Heaven (Before They Close the Door)/ Till I Fell In Love With You/ Not Dark Yet/ Cold Irons Bound/ Make You Feel My Love/ Can't Wait/ Highlands

"Love And Theft" (2001) Tweedle Dee and Tweedle Dum/ Mississippi/ Summer Days/ Bye and Bye/ Lonesome Day Blues/ Floater (Too Much to Ask)/ High Water (for Charley Patton)/ Moonlight/ Honest With Me/ Po' Boy/ Sugar Baby

Modern Times (2006) Thunder on the Mountain/ Spirit on the Water/ Rollin' and Tumblin'/ When the Deal Goes Down/ Someday Baby/ Workingman's Blues #2/ Beyond the Horizon/ Nettie Moore/ The Levee's Gonna Break/ Ain't Talkin'

Together Through Life (2009) Beyond Here Lies Nothin'/ Life is Hard/ My Wife's Home Town (Bob Dylan/ Robert Hunter/ Willie Dixon)/ If You Ever Go to Houston/ Forgetful Heart/ Jolene/ This Dream of You (Bob Dylan)/ Shake Shake Mama/ I Feel A Change Comin' On/ It's All Good (All songs by Bob Dylan/ Robert Hunter unless stated)

Christmas in the Heart (2009) Here Comes Santa Claus (Gene Autry/ Oakley Haldeman)/ Do You Hear What I Hear? (Noel Regney/ Gloria Shine Baker)/ Winter Wonderland (Felix Bernard/ Richard B. Smith)/ Hark the Herald Angels Sing (Felix Mendelssohn/ Charles Wesley)/ I'll Be Home for Christmas (Buck Ram/ Kim Gannon/ Walter Kent)/ Little Drummer Boy (Katherine K. Davis/ Henry Onorati/ Harry Simeone) The Christmas Blues (Sammy Cahn/ David Jack Holt)/ O' Come All Ye Faithful (Adeste Fideles) (trad. arr. Dylan)/ Have Yourself A Merry Little Christmas (Hugh Martin/ Ralph Blane)/ Must Be Santa (William Fredericks/ Hal Moore)/Silver Bells (Jay Livingston/ Ray Evans)/ The First Noel (trad. arr. Dylan)/ Christmas Island (Lyle Moraine)/ The Christmas Song (Mel Torme/ Bob Wells)/ O' Little Town of Bethlehem (trad. arr. Dylan)

Tempest (2012) Duquesne Whistle (Bob Dylan/ Robert Hunter)/ Soon After Midnight/ Narrow Way/ Long and Wasted Years/ Pay in Blood/ Scarlet Town/ Early Roman Kings/ Tin Angel/ Tempest/ Roll On, John

Shadows in the Night (2015) I'm A Fool to Want You (Frank Sinatra/ Jack Wolf/ Joel Herron)/ The Night We Called It a Day (Matt Dennis/ Tom Adair)/ Stay With Me (Jerome Moross/ Carolyn Leigh) Autumn Leaves (Jacques Prevert/ Joseph Kosma/ Johnny Mercer)/ Why Try to Change Me Now (Cy Coleman/ Joseph McCarthy)/ Some Enchanted Evening (Richard Rodgers/ Oscar Hammerstein II)/ Full Moon and Empty Arms (Buddy Kaye/ Ted Moss/ Sergei Rachmaninov)/ Where Are You (Harold Adamson/ Jimmy McHugh)/ That Lucky Old Sun (Haven Gillespie/ Beasley Smith)

Fallen Angels (2015) Young at Heart (Johnny Richards/ Carolyn Leigh)/ Maybe You'll Be There (Rube Bloom/ Sammy Gallop)/ Polka Dots and Moonbeams (Jimmy Van Heusen/ Johnny Burke)/ All the Way (Jimmy Van Heusen/ Sammy Cahn)/ Skylark (Hoagy Carmichael/ Johnny Mercer)/ Nevertheless (Harry Ruby/ Bert Kalmar)/ All or Nothing at All (Arthur Altman/ Jack Lawrence)/ On a Little Street in Singapore (Peter De Rose/ Billy Hill)/ It Had to Be You (Isham Jones/ Gus Kahn)/ Melancholy Mood (Walter Schumann/ Vick R. Knight Sr.)/ That Old Black Magic (Harold Arlen/ Johnny Mercer)/ Come Rain or Come Shine (Harold Arlen/ Johnny Mercer)

Triplicate (2017) I Guess I'll Have to Change My Plans (Arthur Schwartz/ Howard Dietz)/ September of My Years (Jimmy Van Heusen/ Sammy Cahn)/ I Could Have Told You (Carl Sigman/ Jimmy Van Heusen)/ Once Upon a Time (Charles Strouse/ Lee Adams)/ Stormy Weather (Harold Arlen/ Ted Koehler)/ This Nearly Was Mine (Richard Rodgers/ Oscar Hammerstein II)/ That Old Feeling (Sammy Fein/ Lew Brown)/ It Gets Lonely Early (Jimmy Van Heusen/ Sammy Cahn/ My One and Only Love (Guy Wood/ Robert Mellin)/ Trade Winds (Cliff Friend/ Charles Tobias)/ Braggin' (Jimmy Shirl/ Robert Marko/ Henry Katzman)/ As Time Goes By (Herman Hupfeld)/ Imagination (Jimmy Van Heusen/ Johnny Burke)/ How Deep is the Ocean? (Irving Berlin)/ P.S. I Love You (Gordon Jenkins/ Johnny Mercer)/ The Best is Yet to Come (Cy Coleman/ Carolyn Leigh)/ But Beautiful (Jimmy Van Heusen/ Johnny Burke)/ Here's That Rainy Day (Jimmy Van Heusen/ Johnny Burke)/ Where is the One? (Alec Wilder/ Edwin Finckel)/ There's a Flaw in My Flue (Jimmy Van Heusen/ Johnny Burke)/ Day In, Day Out (Rube Bloom/ Johnny Mercer)/ I Couldn't Sleep A Wink Last Night (Harold Adamson/ Jimmy McHugh)/ Sentimental Journey (Les Brown/ Ben Homer/ Bud Green)/ Somewhere Along the Way (Jimmy Van Heusen/ Sammy Gallop)/ When the World Was Young (Philippe-Gerard/ Angele Vanier/ Johnny Mercer)/ These Foolish Things (Eric Maschwitz/Jack Strachey)/ You Go to My Head (John Coots/ Haven Gillespie)/ Stardust (Hoagy Carmichael/ Mitchell Parish)/ It's Funny to Everyone But Me (Jack Lawrence)/ Why Was I Born (Jerome Kern/ Oscar Hammerstein II)

Rough and Rowdy Ways (2020) I Contain Multitudes/ False Prophet/ My Own Version of You/ I Made Up My Mind To Give Myself to You/ Black Rider/ Goodbye Jimmy Reed/ Mother of Muses/ Crossing the Rubicon/ Key West/ Murder Most Foul

The Traveling Wilburys

The Traveling Wilburys (1988) Handle With Care/ Dirty World/ Rattled/ Last Night/ Not Alone Any More/ Congratulations/ Heading for the Light/ Margarita/ Tweeter and the Monkey Man/ End of the Line

(All songs by the Traveling Wilburys - Bob Dylan, George Harrison, Tom Petty, Jeff Lynne, Roy Orbison)

Traveling Wilburys 3 (1990) She's My Baby/ Inside Out/ If You Belonged to Me/ The Deviil's Been Busy/ 7 Deadly Sins/ Poor House/ Where Were You Last Night/ Cool Dry Place/ New Blue Moon/ You Took My Breath Away/ Wilbury Twist

(All songs by the Traveling Wilburys - Bob Dylan, George Harrison, Tom Petty, Jeff Lynne)

Film Soundtracks

Pat Garrett & Billy the Kid (1973) Main Title Theme/ Cantina Theme (Workin' for the Law)/ Billy 1/ Bunkhouse Theme/ River Theme/ Turkey Chase/ Knockin' on Heaven's Door/ Final Theme/ Billy 4/ Billy 7

Hearts of Fire (1987) includes: The Usual (John Hiatt)/ Night After Night/ Had A Dream About You Baby

Masked and Anonymous (2003) includes: Down in the Flood/ Diamond Joe (Jack Elliott/ Cisco Houston)/ Dixie (Dan Emmett)/ Cold Irons Bound

Live Albums

Before the Flood (1974) with *The Band* - Most Likely You Go Your Way (And I Go Mine)/ Lay Lady Lay/ Rainy Day Women #12 & 35 / Knockin' on Heaven's Door/ It Ain't Me Babe/ Ballad of A Thin Man/ *Up on Cripple Creek* (Robbie Robertson)/ *I Shall Be Released/ Endless Highway* (Robbie Robertson)/ *The Night They Drove Old Dixie Down* (Robbie Robertson)/ *Stage Fright* (Robbie Robertson)/ Don't Think Twice, It's All Right/ Just Like A Woman/ It's Alright Ma (I'm Only Bleeding)/ *The Shape I'm In* (Robbie Robertson)/ *When You Awake* (Robbie Robertson/ Richard Manuel)/ *The Weight* (Robbie Robertson)/ All Along the Watchtower/ Highway 61 Revisited/ Like A Rolling Stone/ Blowin' in the Wind

Hard Rain (1976) Maggie's Farm/ One Too Many Mornings/ Stuck Inside of Mobile with the Memphis Blues Again/ Oh Sister (Bob Dylan/ Jacques Levy)/ Lay Lady Lay/ Shelter From the Storm/ You're a Big Girl Now/ I Threw It All Away/ Idiot Wind

Live at the Budokan (1978) Mr. Tambourine Man/ Shelter from the Storm/ Love Minus Zero - No Limit/ Ballad of a Thin Man/ Don't Think Twice, It's All Right/ Maggie's Farm/ One More Cup of Coffee (Valley Below)/ Like a Rolling Stone/ I Shall Be Released/ Is Your Love In Vain?/ Going, Going, Gone/ Blowin' in the Wind/ Just Like a Woman/ Oh, Sister/ Simple Twist of Fate/ All Along the Watchtower/ I Want You/ All I Really Want to Do/ Knockin' On Heaven's Door/ It's Alright Ma (I'm Only Bleeding)/ Forever Young/ The Times They Are a-Changin'

Real Live (1984) Highway 61 Revisited/ Maggie's Farm/ I and I/ License to Kill/ It Ain't Me Babe/ Tangled Up in Blue/ Masters of War/ Ballad of a Thin Man/ Girl from the North Country/ Tombstone Blues

Dylan and the Dead (1989) (with the Grateful Dead) Slow Train/ I Want You/ Gotta Serve Somebody/ Queen Jane Approximately/ Joey (Bob Dylan/ Jacques Levy)/ All Along the Watchtower/ Knockin' on Heaven's Door

The 30th Anniversary Concert Celebration (1993) (*with Various Artists*) *Like a Rolling Stone/ Leopard-Skin Pill-Box Hat (John Cougar Mellencamp)/ Blowin' in the Wind (Stevie Wonder)/ Foot of Pride (Lou Reed)/ Masters of War(Eddie Vedder and Mike McCready)/ The Times They Are A-Changin' (Tracy Chapman)/ It Ain't Me Babe (June Carter Cash and Johnny Cash)/ What Was it You Wanted? (Willie Nelson)/ I'll Be Your Baby Tonight (Kris Kristofferson)/ Highway 61 Revisited (Johnny Winter)/ Seven Days (Ronnie Wood)/ Just Like a Woman (Richie Havens)/ When the Ship Comes In (The Clancy Brothers, Robbie O'Connell and Tommy Makem)/ You Ain't Goin' Nowhere (Mary Chapin Carpenter, Rosanne Cash and Shawn Colvin)/ Just Like Tom Thumb's Blues/ All Along the Watchtower (Neil Young)/ I Shall Be Released (Chrissie Hynde)/ Don't Think Twice, It's All Right (Eric Clapton)/ Emotionally Yours (The O'Jays)/ When I Paint My Masterpiece (The Band)/ Absolutely Sweet Marie (George Harrison)/ License to Kill/ Rainy Day Women #12 & 35 (Tom Petty and the Heartbreakers)/ Mr. Tambourine Man (Roger McGuinn with Tom Petty and the Heartbreakers)/* It's Alright, Ma (I'm Only Bleeding)/

My Back Pages (*with Roger McGuinn, Tom Petty, Neil Young, Eric Clapton and George Harrison*)/ Knockin' on Heaven's Door (*All*)/ Girl from the North Country

MTV Unplugged (1995) Tombstone Blues/ Shooting Star/ All Along the Watchtower/ The Times They Are A-Changin'/ John Brown/ Rainy Day Women #12 & 35/ Desolation Row/ Dignity/ Knockin' on Heaven's Door/ Like A Rolling Stone/ With God on Our Side

Bob Dylan Live 1961-2000: Thirty Nine Years of Great Concert Performances (2001) Somebody Touched Me (trad. arr. Dylan)/ Wade in the Water (trad. arr. Dylan)/ Handsome Molly (trad. arr. Dylan)/ To Ramona/ I Don't Believe You/ I Don't Believe You/ Grand Coulee Dam (Woody Guthrie)/ Knockin' on Heaven's Door/ It Ain't Me Babe/ Shelter from the Storm/ Dead Man, Dead Man/ Slow Train/ Dignity/ Cold Irons Bound/ Born in Time/ Country Pie/ Things Have Changed

Live at the Gaslight 1962 (2005) A Hard Rain's a-Gonna Fall/ Rocks and Gravel (trad. arr. Dylan)/ Don't Think Twice, It's All Right/ The Cuckoo (trad. Arr. Dylan)/ Moonshiner (trad. arr. Dylan)/ Handsome Molly (trad. arr. Dylan)/ Cocaine (trad. arr. Dylan)/ John Brown/ Barbara Allen (trad. arr. Dylan)/ West Texas (trad. arr. Dylan)

Live at Carnegie Hall 1963 (2005) The Times They Are a-Changin'/ Ballad of Hollis Brown/ Boots of Spanish Leather/ Lay Down Your Weary Tune/ North Country Blues/ With God on Our Side

In Concert - Brandeis University 1963 (2011) Hone Just Allow Me One More Chance (Henry Thomas/ Bob Dylan)/ Talkin' John Birch Paranoid Blues/ Ballad of Hollis Brown/ Masters of War/ Talkin' World War III Blues/ Bob Dylan's Dream/ Talkin' Bear Mountain Picnic Massacre Blues/

The 1966 Live Recordings (2016)

Sydney 13/4, Melbourne 20/4, Copenhagen 1/5, Dublin 5/5, Belfast 6/5, Bristol 10/5, Cardiff 11/5, Birmingham 12/5, Leicester 14/5, Leicester15/5, Sheffield 6/5, Manchester 17/5, Glasgow 19/5, Edinburgh 20/5, Newcastle 21/5, Paris 24/5, Royal Albert Hall London 26/5, Royal Albert Hall London 27/5, White Plains 25/2, Pittsburgh 6/2, Hempstead 26/2, Melbourne 19/4, Stockholm 29/4

SETLIST: She Belongs To Me/ Fourth Time Around/ Visions of Johanna/ It's All Over Now, Baby Blue/ Desolation Row/ Just Like A Woman/ Mr. Tambourine Man/ Tell Me Momma/ I Don't Believe You/ Baby Let Me Follow You Down/ Just Like Tom Thumb's Blues/ Leopard Skin Pillbox Hat/ One Too Many Mornings/ Ballad of A Thin Man/ Like a Rolling Stone PLUS Positively Fourth Street (Sydney 13/4, Pittsburgh 6/2) To Ramona, Love Minus Zero - No Limit (White Plains 25/2, Pittsburgh 6/2)

Rolling Thunder Revue: The 1975 Live Recordings (2019)

S.I.R. REHEARSALS: Rake and Ramblin' Boy (trad. arr. Dylan) / Romance in Durango (Bob Dylan/Jacques Levy) /Rita May (Bob Dylan/ Jacques Levy)/ I Want You/ Love Minus Zero-No Limit/ She Belongs to Me/ She Belongs to Me/ Joey [Bob Dylan/ Jacques Levy)/Isis (Bob Dylan/ Jacques Levy)/ Hollywood Angel / People Get Ready (Curtis Mayfield)/ What Will You Do When Jesus Comes?/ Spanish Is the Loving Tongue (Charles Badger Clark/ Billy Simon)/ The Ballad of Ira Hayes (Peter La Farge) / One More Cup of Coffee/ Tonight I'll Be Staying Here with You/ This Land Is Your Land (Woody Guthrie)/ Dark as a Dungeon (Merle Travis) She Belongs to Me/ A Hard Rain's a-Gonna Fall/ Isis (Bob Dylan/Jacques Levy)/ This Wheel's on Fire (Bob Dylan/ Rick Danko)/ Hurricane (Bob Dylan/ Jacques Levy)/ All Along the Watchtower/ One More Cup of Coffee/ If You See Her, Say Hello/ One Too Many Mornings/ Gwenevere/ Lily, Rosemary and the Jack of Hearts/ Patty's Gone to Laredo/ It's Alright Ma (I'm Only Bleeding) SEACREST MOTEL RECORDINGS: Tears of Rage (Bob Dylan/ Richard Manuel)/ I Shall Be Released/ Easy and Slow (trad. arr. Dylan)/ Ballad of a Thin Man/ Hurricane (Bob Dylan/ Jacques Levy)/ One More Cup of Coffee/ Just Like A Woman/ Knockin' on Heaven's Door

Worcester MA 19/11, Cambridge 20/11, Boston 21/1 (aft) Boston 21/11 (eve) Montreal 4/2

SETLIST: When I Paint My Masterpiece/ It Ain't Me Babe, The Lonesome Death of Hattie Carroll/ It Takes a Lot to Laugh, It Takes a Train to Cry/ Romance in Durango (Bob Dylan/ Jacques Levy)/ Isis (Bob Dylan/ Jacques Levy)/ Blowin' in the Wind/ Wild Mountain Thyme (trad. arr. Dylan)/ Mama You Been on My Mind/ Dark as a Dungeon (Merle Travis)/ I Shall Be Released/ Oh Sister/ Hurricane (Bob Dylan/ Jacques Levy)/ One More Cup of Coffee/ Sara/ Just Like A Woman/ Knockin' on Heaven's Door/ This Land is Your Land (Woody Guthrie) 4/2) A Hard Rain's A Gonna Fall (Boston 21/11 aft)/ The Times They Are a-Changin' (Boston 21/11 aft)/ I Dreamed I Saw St. Augustine (Boston 21/11 aft), Never Let Me Go (Joseph Scott) (Boston 21/11 aft, Montreal 4/2) The Water is Wide (trad. arr. Dylan) (Boston 21/11 aft)/ Tangled Up in Blue (Boston 21/11 aft, Montreal 4/12) Tonight I'll Be Staying Here With You (Montreal 4/2) Love Minus Zero - No Limit (Montreal 4/12) RARE PERFORMANCES: One Too Many Mornings/ Simple Twist of Fate/ Isis (Bob Dylan/ Jacques Levy)/ With God on Our Side/ It's Alright Ma (I'm Only Bleeding)/ Radio Ad/ The Ballad of Ira Hayes (Peter La Farge)/ Your Cheatin' Heart (Hank Williams)/ Fourth Time Around/ The Tracks of My Tears (Smokey Robinson)/ Jesse James (trad. arr. Dylan)/ It Takes a Lot to Laugh, It Takes A Train to Cry

The Bootleg Series

The Bootleg Series: Vols 1-3 (1993) Hard Times in New York Town/ He Was a Friend of Mine (trad. arr. Dylan)/ Man on the Street/ No More Auction Block (trad. arr. Dylan)/ House Carpenter (trad. arr. Dylan)/ Talkin' Bear Mountain Picnic Massacre Blues/ Let Me Die in My Footsteps/ Rambling, Gambling Willie/ Talkin' Hava Negilah Blues/ Worried Blues (trad. arr. Dylan)/ Kingsport Town (trad. arr. Dylan)/ Walkin' Down the Line/ Walls of Red Wing/ Paths of Victory/ Talkin' John Birch Paranoid Blues/ Who Killed Davey Moore?/ Only a Hobo/ Moonshiner (trad. arr. Dylan)/ When the Ship Comes In/ The Times They Are a-Changin'/ Last Thoughts on Woody Guthrie/ Seven Curses/ Eternal Circle/ Suze (The Cough Song)/ Mama You Been on My Mind/ Farewell Angelina/ Subterranean Homesick Blues/ If You Gotta Go, Go Now/ Sitting on a Barbed Wire Fence/ Like A Rolling Stone/ It Takes a Lot to Laugh, It Takes a Train to Cry/ I'll Keep It With Mine/ She's Your Lover Now/ I Shall Be Released/ Santa-Fe/ If Not For You/ Wallflower/ Nobody 'Cept You/ Tangled Up In Blue/ Call Letter Blues/ Idiot Wind/ If You See Her Say Hello/ Golden Loom (Bob Dylan/ Jacques Levy)/ Catfish (Bob Dylan/ Jacques Levy)/ Seven Days/ Ye Shall Be Changed/ Every Grain of Sand/ You Changed My Life/ Need A Woman/ Angelina/ Someone's Got a Hold of My Heart/ Tell Me/ Lord Protect My Child/ Foot of Pride/ Blind Willie McTell/ When the Night Comes Falling From the Sky/ Series of Dreams

Vol. 4: Live 1966: The 'Royal Albert Hall 'Concert (1998) She Belongs To Me/ Fourth Time Around/ Visions of Johanna/ It's All Over Now, Baby Blue/ Desolation Row/ Just Like A Woman/ Mr. Tambourine Man/ Tell Me Momma/ I Don't Believe You/ Baby Let Me Follow You Down/ Just Like Tom Thumb's Blues/ Leopard Skin Pillbox Hat/ One Too Many Mornings/ Ballad of A Thin Man/ Like a Rolling Stone

Vol. 5: Live 1975: The Rolling Thunder Revue (2002) Tonight I'll Be Staying Here With You/ It Ain't Me, Babe/ A Hard Rain's a-Gonna Fall/ The Lonesome Death of Hattie Carroll/ Romance in Durango (Bob Dylan/ Jacques Levy/ Isis (Bob Dylan/ Jacques Levy)/ Mr. Tambourine Man/ Simple Twist of Fate/ Blowin' in the Wind/ Mama You Been on My Mind/ I Shall Be Released/ It's All Over Now Baby Blue/ Love Minus Zero- No Limit/ Tangled Up in Blue/ The Water is Wide (trad. arr. Dylan)/ It Takes A Lot to Laugh, It Takes a Train to Cry/ Oh Sister (Bob Dylan/ Jacques Levy)/ Hurricane (Bob Dylan/ Jacques Levy)/ One More Cup of Coffee/ Sara/ Just Like A Woman/ Knockin' on Heaven's Door

Vol. 6: Live 1964: Concert at Philharmonic Hall (2004) The Times They Are a-Changin'/ Spanish Harlem Incident/ Talkin' John Birch Paranoid Blues/ To Ramona/ Who Killed Davey Moore?/ Gates of Eden/ If You Gotta Go, Go Now/ It's Alright, Ma (I'm Only Bleeding)/ I Don't Believe You/ Mr. Tambourine Man/ A Hard Rain's a-Gonna Fall/ Talkin' World War III Blues/ Don't Think Twice, It's All Right/ The Lonesome Death of Hattie Carroll/ Mama, You Been on My Mind/ Silver Dagger (traditional)/ With God on Our Side/ It Ain't Me, Babe/ All I Really Want to Do

Vol. 7: No Direction Home: The Soundtrack (2005) When I Got Troubles/ Rambler, Gambler (trad. arr. Bob Dylan)/ This Land Is Your Land (Woody Guthrie)/ Song to Woody/ Dink's Song (trad. arr. Bob Dylan)/ I Was Young When I Left Home/ Sally Gal/ Don't Think Twice, It's All Right/ Man of Constant Sorrow (trad. arr. Bob Dylan)/ Blowin' in the Wind/ Masters of War/ A Hard Rain's A-Gonna Fall/ When the Ship Comes In/ Mr. Tambourine Man/ Chimes of Freedom/ It's All Over Now, Baby Blue/ She Belongs to Me/ Maggie's Farm/ It Takes a Lot to Laugh, It Takes a Train to Cry/ Tombstone Blues/ Just Like Tom Thumb's Blues/ Desolation Row/Highway 61 Revisited/ Leopard-Skin Pill-Box Hat/ Stuck Inside of Mobile with the Memphis Blues Again/ Visions of Johanna/ Ballad of a Thin Man/ Like a Rolling Stone

Vol. 8: Tell Tale Signs: Rare and Unreleased 1989-2006 (2008) Mississippi/ Most of the Time/ Dignity/ Someday Baby/ Red River Shore/ Tell Ol' Bill/ Born in Time/ Can't Wait/ Everything is Broken/ Dreaming of You/ Huck's Tune/ Marching to the City/ High Water (for Charley Patton)/ Mississippi/ 32-20 Blues (Robert Johnson)/ Series of Dreams/ God Knows/ Can't Escape from You/ Dignity/ Ring Them Bells/ Cocaine Blues (trad. arr. Dylan)/ Ain't Talkin'/ The Girl from the Greenbriar Shore (trad. arr. Bob Dylan)/ Lonesome Day Blues/ Miss The Mississippi (Bill Halley)/ The Lonesome River (Ralph and Carter Stanley)/ 'Cross the Green Mountain/ Love Sick/ Duncan and Brady/ Cold Irons Bound/ Mississippi/ Most of the Time/ Ring Them Bells/ Things Have Changed/ Red River Shore/ Born in Time/ Tryon' to Get to Heaven (Before They Close the Door)/ Marchin' to the City/ Can't Wait/ Kart and the Soldier (trad. arr. Dylan)

Vol. 9: The Witmark Demos: 1962-1964 (2010) Man on the Street/ Hard Times in New York Town/ Poor Boy Blues/ Ballad for a Friend/Rambling, Gambling Willie/ Talking Bear Mountain Picnic Massacre Blues/ Standing on the Highway/ Man on the Street/ Blowin' in the Wind/ Long Ago, Far Away/ A Hard Rain's a-Gonna Fall/ Tomorrow Is a Long Time/ The Death of Emmett Till/ Let Me Die in My Footsteps/ Ballad of Hollis Brown/ Quit Your Low Down Ways/ Baby, I'm in the Mood for You/ Bound to Lose, Bound to Win/ All Over You/ I'd Hate to Be You on That Dreadful Day/ Long Time Gone/ Talkin' John Birch Paranoid Blues/ Masters of War/ Oxford Town/ Farewell

Vol. 10: Another Self Portrait (1969 1971) (2013) Went to See the Gypsy/ Little Sadie (trad. arr. Dylan/ Pretty Saro (trad. arr. Dylan)/ Alberta No. 3/ Spanish is the Loving Tongue (Charles Badger Clark/ Billy Simon)/ Annie's Going to Sing Her Song (Tom Paxton)/ Time Passes Slowly/ Only a Hobo/ Minstrel Boy/ I Threw It All Away/ Railroad Bill (trad. arr. Dylan)/ Thirsty Boots (Eric Anderson)/ This Evening So Soon (trad. arr. Dylan)/ These Hands (Eddie Noack)/ In Search of Little Sadie/ House Carpenter/ All the Tired Horses/ If Not For You/ Wallflower/ Wigwam/ Days of '49 (trad. arr. Dylan)/ Working on a Guru/ Country Pie/ I'll Be Your Baby Tonight/ Highway 61 Revisited/ Copper Kettle (Albert Frank Beddoe)/ Bring Me a Little Water (trad. arr. Dylan)/ Sign on The Window/ Tattle O'Day/ If Dogs Run Free/ New Morning/ Went to See the Gypsy/ Belle Isle (trad. arr. Dylan)/ Time Passes Slowly/ When I Paint My Masterpiece LIVE AT THE ISLE OF WIGHT 1969: She Belongs to Me/ I Threw It All Away/ Maggie's Farm/ Wild Mountain Thyme/ It Ain't Me, Babe/ To Ramona/ Mr. Tambourine Man/ I Dreamed I Saw St. Augustine/ Lay, Lady, Lay/ Highway 61 Revisited/ One Too Many Mornings/ I Pity the Poor Immigrant/ Like a Rolling Stone/ I'll Be Your Baby Tonight/ The Mighty Quinn (Quinn the Eskimo)/ Minstrel Boy/ Rainy Day Women #12 & 35

Vol. 11: The Basement Tapes Complete 1967 (2014) Edge of the Ocean/ My Bucket's Got a Hole in It (Clarence Williams)/ Roll on Train/ Mr. Blue (Dewayne Blackwell)/ Belshazzar (Johnny Cash)/ I Forgot to Remember to Forget (Charlie A. Feathers/ Stanley A. Kesler)/ You Win Again (Hank Williams)/ Still in Town (Hank Cochran/ Harlan Howard)/ Waltzing with Sin (Sonny Burns/Red Hayes)/Big River (Take 1) (Johnny Cash)/ Big River (Take 2) (Johnny Cash)/ Folsom Prison Blues (Johnny Cash)/ Bells of Rhymney (Idris Davies/Pete Seeger)/ Spanish is the Loving Tongue (Charles Badger Clark/ Billy Simon)/ Under Control/ Ol' Roisin the Beau (trad. arr. Dylan)/ I'm Guilty of Loving You/ Cool Water (Bob Nolan)/ The Auld Triangle (Brendan Behan)/ Po' Lazarus (trad. arr. Dylan)/ I'm a Fool for You (Take 1)/ I'm a Fool for You (Take 2)/ Johnny Todd (trad. arr. Dylan)/ Tupelo (John Lee Hooker)/ Kickin' My Dog Around (trad. arr. Dylan)/ See You Later Allen Ginsberg (Takes 1 and 2)/ Tiny Montgomery/ Big Dog/ I'm Your Teenage Prayer/ Four Strong Winds (Ian Tyson)/ The French Girl (Takes 1 and 2) (Ian Tyson and Sylvia Tyson)/ Joshua Gone Barbados (Eric Von Schmidt)/ I'm in the Mood (Bernard Besman/ John Lee Hooker)/ Baby Ain't That Fine (Dallas Frazier)/ Rock, Salt and Nails (Bruce Phillips)/ A Fool Such As I (William Marvin Trader)/ Song for Canada (Pete Gzowski and Ian Tyson)/ People Get Ready (Curtis Mayfield)/ I Don't Hurt Anymore (Donald Robertson/ Walter Rollins)/ Be Careful of Stones That You Throw (Benjamin Lee Blankenship)/ One Man's Loss/ Lock Your Door/ Baby, Won't You Be My Baby/ Try Me Little Girl/ I Can't Make It Alone/ Don't You Try Me Now/ Young but Daily Growing (trad. arr. Dylan)/ Bonnie Ship the Diamond (trad. arr. Dylan)/ The Hills of Mexico (trad. arr. Dylan)/ Down on Me (trad. arr. Dylan)/ One for the Road/ I'm Alright/ Million Dollar Bash (Takes 1 and 2)/ Yea! Heavy and a Bottle of Bread (Takes 1 and 2)/ I'm Not There/ Please Mrs. Henry/ Down in the Flood (Takes 1 and 2)/ Lo and Behold! (Takes 1 and 2)/ You Ain't Goin' Nowhere (Takes and 2)/ I Shall be Released (Takes 1 and 2)/ This Wheel's on Fire (Bob Dylan/ Rick Danko)/ Too Much of Nothing (Takes 1 and 2)/ Tears of Rage (Takes 1 to 3) (Bob Dylan/Richard Manuel)/ The Mighty Quinn (Quinn the Eskimo) (Takes 1 and 2)/ Open the Door Homer (Takes 1 to 3)/ Nothing Was Delivered (Takes 1 to 3)/ All American Boy (Bobby Bare)/ Sign on the Cross/ Odds and Ends (Takes 1 to 3)/ Get Your Rocks Off/ Clothes Line Saga/ Apple Suckling Tree (Takes 1 and 2)/ Don't Ya Tell Henry/ Bourbon Street/ Blowin' in the Wind/ One Too Many Mornings/ A Satisfied Mind (Joe Hayes/ Jack Rhodes)/ It Ain't Me, Babe/ Ain't No More Cane (Takes 1 and 2) (trad. arr. by Bob Dylan)/ My Woman She's A-Leavin'/ Santa-Fe/ Mary Lou, I Love You Too/ Dress it up, Better Have it All/ Minstrel Boy/ Silent Weekend/ What's it Gonna Be When it Comes Up/ 900 Miles from My Home (trad. arr. Dylan)/ Wildwood Flower (A. P. Carter)/ One Kind Favor (trad. Arr. Dylan)/ She'll Be Coming Round the Mountain (trad. arr. Dylan)/ It's the Flight of the Bumblebee/ Wild Wolf/ Goin' to Acapulco/ Gonna Get You Now/ If I Were A Carpenter (Tim Hardin)/ Confidential (Dorinda Morgan)/ All You Have to Do is Dream (Takes 1 and 2)/ 2 Dollars and 99 Cents/ Jelly Bean/ Any Time/ Down by the Station/ Hallelujah, I've Just Been Moved (trad. arr. Dylan)/ That's the Breaks/ Pretty Mary/ Will the Circle Be Unbroken (A. P. Carter)/ King of France/ She's on My Mind Again/ Goin' Down the Road Feeling Bad (trad. arr. Dylan)/ On a Rainy Afternoon/ I Can't Come In with a Broken Heart/ Next Time on the Highway/ Northern Claim/ Love is Only Mine/ Silhouettes (Bob Crewe/ Frank C. Slay Jr.)/ Bring it on Home/ Come All Ye Fair and Tender Ladies (trad. arr. Dylan)/ The Spanish Song (Takes 1 and 2)/ 900 Miles (trad.arr. Dylan)/ Confidential (Dorinda Morgan)

Vol. 12: The Cutting Edge 1965-66 (2016) Love Minus Zero/No Limit - Takes 1 and 2/I'll Keep It With Mine/ t's All Over Now, Baby Blue - Take 1/ Bob Dylan's 115th Dream - Takes 1 and 2/ She Belongs To Me Take 1/ Subterranean Homesick Blues - Take 1/ Outlaw Blues - Take 1/ On The Road Again - Take 1/ Farewell Angelina/ If You Gotta Go, Go Now - Take 1/ You Don't Have to Do That/ California/ Love Minus Zero/No Limit - Take 3 remake/ She Belongs To Me - Take 2 remake/ Outlaw Blues - Takes 1 and 2 remake (1/13/1965)/ Love Minus Zero/No Limit - Takes 1 to 3 remake/ Subterranean Homesick Blues - Takes 1 to 3/ Outlaw Blues - Takes 1 to 3 remake/ She Belongs To Me - Takes 1 and 2 remake/ Bob Dylan's 115th Dream - Takes 1 and 2/ On The Road Again - Takes 1 to 4/ Maggie's Farm - Take 1/ On The Road Again - Takes 2 to 13 remake/ It's Alright, Ma (I'm Only Bleeding) - Takes 1 and 2/ Gates Of Eden - Take 1/ Mr. Tambourine Man - Takes 1 to 6/ It's All Over Now, Baby Blue - Take 1 remake/ If You Gotta Go, Go No - Takes 1 to 4/ It Takes A Lot To Laugh, It Takes A Train To Cry - Takes 1 to 9/ Sitting On A Barbed-Wire Fence - Takes 1 to 4/ It Takes A Lot to Laugh, It Takes A Train To Cry - Take 1 remake (6/15/1965)/ Sitting On A Barbed-Wire Fence - Takes 4-6/ Like A Rolling Stone - Takes 1-15/ It Takes A Lot To Laugh, It Takes A Train To Cry - Takes 1 to 3, remake/ Tombstone Blues - Takes 1 to

12, It Takes A Lot To Laugh, It Takes A Train To Cry - Takes 1 to 4/ Positively 4th Street - Takes 1-12/ Desolation Row - Take 1 (7/29/1965)/ From A Buick 6 - Takes 1 to 5/ Can You Please Crawl Out Your Window? - Takes 1-17/ Highway 61 Revisited -Takes 1 to 9/ Just Like Tom Thumb's Blues - Takes 1 to 16/ Queen Jane Approximately - Takes 1 to 7/ Ballad Of A Thin Man - Takes 1 to 4/ Desolation Row - Takes 1 to 5/ Desolation Row - Take 3 remake/ Tombstone Blues - Takes 1 to 3/ Desolation Row - Takes 1 to 7 remake/ Tombstone Blues - Take 1 Harmonica overdub/ Medicine Sunday - Takes 1 and 2/ Jet Pilot/ I Wanna Be Your Lover - Rehearsal/ Can You Please Crawl Out Your Window? - Take 1s and 2 fragments/ I Wanna Be Your Lover - Takes 1 to 6/ Instrumental Takes 1 and 2/ Visions Of Johanna - Takes 1 to 14/ Can You Please Crawl Out Your Window? - Takes 1 to 10/ She's Your Lover Now-Takes 1 to 16/ Leopard-Skin Pill-Box Hat - Takes 1 and 2/ One Of Us Must Know (Sooner Or Later)-- Takes 1 to 28/ Lunatic Princess/ Leopard-Skin Pill-Box Hat - Takes 1-2/ I'll Keep It With Mine - rehearsal/ Fourth Time Around - Takes 1 to 19/ Visions Of Johanna - Takes 1 to 4/ Leopard-Skin Pill-Box Hat - Takes 1-13/ I'll Keep It With Mine (instrumental) - Takes 1 to 9/ Sad-Eyed Lady Of The Lowlands - Takes 1 to 4/ Stuck Inside Of Mobile With The Memphis Blues Again - Takes 1 to 15/ Absolutely Sweet Marie - (3/07/1966) Takes 1 to 3/ Just Like A Woman - Takes 1 to 4/ Pledging My Time - Takes 1 to 15/ Just Like A Woman - Takes 5 to 18/ Most Likely You Go Your Way (And I'll Go Mine) - Takes 1 to 6/ Temporary Like Achilles - Takes 1 to 4/ Rainy Day Women #12 & 35 (3/10/1966) - Rehearsal and Take 1/ Obviously Five Believers - Takes 1 to 4/ Leopard-Skin Pill-Box Hat - Take 1/ I Want You - Takes 1 to 6/ Remember Me (Scott Wiseman)/ More And More (Webb Pierce/ Merle Kilgore)/ Blues Stay Away From Me (Alton Delmore, Rabon Delmore, Wayne Raney/ Henry Glover)/ Weary Blues From Waitin' (Hank Williams)/ Lost Highway (Leon Payne) / 'm So Lonesome I Could Cry (Hank Williams)/ Young But Daily Growing (trad. arr. Dylan)/ Wild Mountain Thyme (trad. arr. Dylan)/ I Can't Leave Her Behind [1] and [2]/ On A Rainy Afternoon/ If I Was a King [1] and [2]/ 14. What Kind Of Friend Is This/ Positively Van Gogh [1] to [3] / Don't Tell Him, Tell Me/ If You Want My Love/ Just Like a Woman/ Sad-Eyed Lady Of the Lowlands

***Vol. 13: Trouble No More* 1979-81** (2017) LIVE: Slow Train/ Gotta Serve Somebody/ I Believe in You/ When You Gonna Wake Up?/ When He Returns/ Man Gave Names to All the Animals/ Precious Angel/ Covenant Woman/ Gonna Change My Way of Thinking/ Do Right to Me Baby (Do Unto Others)/ Solid Rock/ What Can I Do for You?/ Saved/ In the Garden/ Slow Train/ Ain't Gonna Go to Hell for Anybody/ Gotta Serve Somebody/ Ain't No Man Righteous, No Not One/ Saving Grace/ Blessed Is the Name/ Solid Rock/ Are You Ready?/ Pressing On/ Shot of Love/ Dead Man, Dead Man/ Watered-Down Love/ In the Summertime/ The Groom's Still Waiting at the Altar/Caribbean Wind/ Every Grain of Sand RARE AND UNRELEASED: Slow Train (Soundcheck)/ Do Right to Me Baby (Do Unto Others) (Soundcheck 1978)/ Help Me Understand/ Gonna Change My Way of Thinking (Rehearsal)/Gotta Serve Somebody/ When He Returns/ Ain't No Man Righteous, No Not One/ Trouble in Mind/ Ye Shall Be Changed/ Stand by Faith/ I Will Love Him/ /Jesus Is the One/ City of Gold/ Thief on the Cross/ Pressing On/ Slow Train (Rehearsal)/ Gotta Serve Somebody (Rehearsal)/ Making a Liar Out of Me/ Yonder Comes Sin/ Radio Spot/ Cover Down, Pray Through/ Rise Again (Dallas Holm)/ Ain't Gonna Go to Hell for Anybody/ The Groom's Still Waiting at the Altar/ Caribbean Wind (Rehearsal)/ You Changed My Life/ Shot of Love/ Watered-Down Love/ Dead Man, Dead Man/ Every Grain of Sand (Rehearsal) LIVE IN TORONTO 1980: Gotta Serve Somebody/ I Believe In You/ Covenant Woman/ When You Gonna Wake Up?/ When He Returns/ Ain't Gonna Go To Hell For Anybody/ Cover Down, Pray Through/ Man Gave Names To All The Animals/ Precious Angel/ Slow Train/ Do Right To Me Baby (Do Unto Others)/ Solid Rock/ Saving Grace/ What Can I Do For You?/ In The Garden/ Band Introductions/ Are You Ready?/ Pressing On LIVE EARLS COURT 1981: Gotta Serve Somebody/ I Believe In You/ Like A Rolling Stone/ Man Gave Names To All The Animals/ Maggie's Farm/ I Don't Believe You/ Dead Man, Dead Man/ Girl From The North Country/ Ballad Of A Thin Man/ Slow Train/ Let's Begin/ Lenny Bruce/ Mr. Tambourine Man/ Solid Rock/ Just Like A Woman/ Watered-Down Love/ Forever Young/ When You Gonna Wake Up/ In The Garden/ Band Introductions/ Blowin' In The Wind/ It's All Over Now, Baby Blue/ Knockin' On Heaven's Door

Vol. 14: More Blood, More Tracks (2018) If You See Her, Say Hello (Takes 1 and 2)/ You're a Big Girl Now (Takes 1 and 2)/ Simple Twist of Fate (Takes and 2)/ You're a Big Girl Now (Take 3)/ Up to Me (Rehearsal and Take 1)/ Lily, Rosemary and the Jack of Hearts (Takes 1 and 2)/ Simple Twist of Fate (Takes 1 to 3)/ Call Letter Blues (Take 1)/ Meet Me in the Morning (Take 1)/ Call Letter Blues (Take 2)/ Idiot Wind (Takes 1 to 6)/ You're Gonna Make Me Lonesome When You Go (Rehearsal and Takes 1 to 8)/Tangled Up in Blue (Take 1)/ You're a Big Girl Now (Takes 1 to 2)/ Tangled Up in Blue (Rehearsal and Take 2)/ Tangled Up in Blue (Take 2, Remake)/ Spanish is the Loving Tongue (Charles Badger Clark/Billy Simon) (Take 1)/ Call Letter Blues (Rehearsal)/ You're Gonna Make Me Lonesome When You Go (Take 1, Remake)/ Shelter From The Storm (Take 1)/ Buckets of Rain (Take 1)/ Tangled Up in Blue (Take 3, Remake)/ Buckets of Rain (Take 2)/ Shelter From The Storm (Takes 2 to 4)/ You're Gonna Make Me Lonesome When You Go (Takes 1 -2, Remake 2)/ Buckets of Rain (Takes 1 to 4, Remake)/ Up to Me (Takes 1 and 2, Remake)/ Buckets of Rain (Takes 1 to 4, Remake 2)/ If You See Her, Say Hello (Take 1, Remake)/ Up to Me (Takes 1 to 3, Remake 2)/ Buckets of Rain (Rehearsal)/ Meet Me in the Morning (Takes 1 and 2, Remake)/ Meet Me in the Morning (Take 2, Remake)/ Buckets of Rain (Take 5, Remake 2)/ Tangled Up in Blue (Rehearsal and Takes 1 to)/ Simple Twist of Fate (Takes 1 to 3)/ Up to Me (Takes 1 and 2)/ Idiot Wind (Takes 1-4)/ You're a Big Girl Now (Take 1)/ Meet Me in the Morning (Takes 1 to 3)/ You're a Big Girl Now (Takes 3-6, Remake 2)/ Tangled Up in Blue (Rehearsal and Takes 1-3, Remake 3)/

Idiot Wind/ You're a Big Girl Now/ Tangled Up in Blue/ Lily, Rosemary and the Jack of Hearts/ If You See Her, Say Hello

Vol. 15: Travelin' Thru, 1967-69 (2019) Drifter's Escape/ I Dreamed I Saw St. Augustine Take 2/ All Along the Watchtower Take 3/ John Wesley Harding Take 1/ As I Went Out One Morning Take 1/ I Pity the Poor Immigrant Take 4/ I Am a Lonesome Hobo Take 4/ I Threw It All Away Take 1/ To Be Alone with You/ Lay Lady Lay Take 2/ One More Night Take 2/ Western Road/ Peggy Day Take 1/ Tell Me That It Isn't True Take 2/ Country Pie Take 2/ WITH JOHNNY CASH: I Still Miss Someone Take 5/ Don't Think Twice, It's All Right/ Understand Your Man (Johnny Cash) Rehearsal/ One Too Many Mornings/ Mountain Dew (trad. arr. Dylan/Cash) Takes 1 and 2/ I Still Miss Someone (Johnny Cash/ Roy Cash Jr.) Take 2/ Careless Love (trad. arr. Dylan) Take 1/ Matchbox (Carl Perkins) Take 1/ That's All Right, Mama (Arthur Crudup) Take 1/ Mystery Train/ This Train Is Bound for Glory (trad. arr. Dylan) Take 1/ Big River Take 1/ Girl from the North Country Rehearsal/ Girl from the North Country/ I Walk the Line (Johnny Cash)Take 2/ Guess Things Happen That Way (Jack Clement) Rehearsal and Take 3/ Five Feet High and Rising (Johnny Cash)Take 1/ You Are My Sunshine (Jimmy Davies/ Charles Mitchell) Take 1/ Ring of Fire (June Carter/ Merle Kilgore)/ Studio Chatter/ Wanted Man Take 1/ Amen (trad. arr. Dylan/ Cash) Rehearsal/ Just a Closer Walk with Thee/ Jimmie Rodgers Medley No. 1 (Based on Blue Yodel No. 1 (T for Texas), The Brakeman's Blues (Yodeling the Blues Away) and Blue Yodel No. 5 (It's Raining Here) (Jimmie Rodgers)/ Jimmie Rodgers Medley No. 2 (Based on Waiting for a Train, The Brakeman's Blues (Yodeling the Blues Away) and Blue Yodel No. 1 (T For Texas)Take 2/ I Threw It All Away Johnny Cash Show/ Living the Blues Johnny Cash Show/ Girl from the North Country Johnny Cash Show/ Ring of Fire (June Carter/ Merle Kilgore)/ Folsom Prison Blues (Johnny Cash)/ Earl Scruggs Interview/ WITH EARL SCRUGGS: East Virginia Blues (A. P. Carter) / To Be Alone with You/ Honey, Just Allow Me One More Chance (Henry Thomas/ Bob Dylan)/ Nashville Skyline Rag

Limited 'Copyright Extension' Releases

50th Anniversary Collection 1962 (2012) Going Down To New Orleans (X2)/ Sally (X2)/ Rambling Gambling Willie (X2)/ Corrina, Corrina (trad. arr. Dylan) (X2)/ The Death Of Emmett Till/ (I Heard That) Lonesome Whistle (Hank Williams/ Jimmie Davis)/ Rocks And Gravel (trad. arr. Dylan)/ Sally Gal (X2))/ Baby, Please Don't Go (Big Joe Williams)(X2)/ Milk Cow (Calf's) Blues (Good Morning Blues)(Robert Johnson) (X2)/ Wichita Blues (Going To Louisiana) (trad. arr. Dylan)/ Talking Bear Mountain Picnic Massacre Blues/ Milk Cow (Calf's) Blues (Good Morning Blues) (Robert Johnson)/ Wichita Blues(Going To Louisiana) (trad. arr. Dylan)/ Baby, I'm In The Mood For You/ Blowin' In The Wind (X2)/ Worried Blues (trad. arr. Dylan)/ Baby, I'm In The Mood For You/ Bob Dylan's Blues (X2)/ Corrina, Corrina (trad. arr. Dylan) (X2)/ That's All Right, Mama (Arthur Crudup) (X3)/ Mixed Up Confusion (X6)/ That's All Right, Mama (Arthur Crudup)/ Rocks And Gravel (trad. arr. Dylan)/ Ballad Of Hollis Brown/ Kingsport Town/ Whatcha Gonna Do/ Hero Blues/ Whatcha Gonna Do/ I Shall Be Free (X2)/ Hero Blues (X2)/ Hard Times In New York Town/ The Death of Emmett Till/ I Rode Out One Morning (trad. arr. Dylan)/ House Of The Rising Sun (trad. arr. Dave Van Ronk)/ See That My Grave Is Kept Clean (Blind Lemon Jefferson)/ Ballad Of Donald White/ Honey, Just Allow Me One More Chance (Henry Thomas/ Bob Dylan)/ Talkin' New York/ Corrina, Corrina (trad. arr. Dylan)/ Deep Ellum Blues (Joe & Bob Attlesay)(trad. arr. Dylan)/ Blowin' in the Wind/ The Death of Emmett Till/ Stealin' (trad. arr. Dylan)/ Hiram Hubbard (trad. arr. Dylan)/ Blowin' In The Wind/ Rocks And Gravel (Solid Road)/ Quit Your Low Down Ways/ He Was a Friend Of Mine (trad. arr. Dylan)/ Let Me Die In My Footsteps/ Two Trains Runnin' (Muddy Waters)/ Ramblin' On My Mind (Robert Johnson)/ Muleskinner Blues (Jimmie Rodgers/ George Vaughan) (X2)/ Sally Gal/ Highway 51 (Curtis Jones)/Talking John Birch Paranoid Blues/ The Ballad Of Hollis Brown/ A Hard Rain's a-Gonna Fall/ See That My Grave Is Kept Clean (Blind Lemon Jefferson)/ No More Auction Block (trad. arr. Dylan)/ Motherless Child (trad. arr. Dylan)/ Kindhearted Woman Blues (Robert Johnson)/ Black Cross (Lord Buckley)/ The Ballad of Hollis Brown/ Ain't No More Cane (trad. arr. Dylan)

50th Anniversary Collection 1963 (2013) Eternal Circle (Take 4)/ Percy's Song (Take 1)/ That's All Right, Mama/Sally Free and Easy (Take 1)/ Hero Blues (Take 3)/ East Laredo Blues (Take 1)/ Bob Dylan's New Orleans Rag (Take 2)/ Lonesome River Edge (trad. arr. Dylan)/ Back Door Blues(trad. arr. Dylan)/ Bob Dylan's Dream/ You Can Get Her/ Farewell/ All Over You/ Instrumental in Gerde's Basement/ Jam/ Keep Your Hands Off Her (Leadbelly)/ Honey Babe/ Goin' Back To Rome/ Stealin' (trad.arr. Dylan)/ Ballad of Hollis Brown/ Girl from the North Country/ Only A Hobo/ Ramblin' Down Through the World/ Bob Dylan's Dream/ Talkin' New York/ Hiding Too Long/ Ballad of Hollis Brown/ Walls of Red Wing/ All Over You/ Talkin' John Birch Paranoid Blues/ Boots of Spanish Leather/ Hero Blues/ John Brown/ A Hard Rain's a-Gonna Fall/ Dusty Old Fairgrounds/ Who Killed Davey Moore?/ Seven Curses/ Highway 51 (Curtis Jones)/ Pretty Peggy-O (trad. Arr. Dylan)/ Bob Dylan's New Orleans Rag/ Don't Think Twice, It's All Right/ With God On Our Side/ James Alley Blues (Richard 'Rabbit' Brown)/ Long Time Gone/ Only a Hobo/ Untitled Blues Jam/ A Hard Rain's a-Gonna Fall/ Honey, Just Allow Me One More Chance/ Talkin' John Birch Paranoid Blues/ Bob Dylan's Dream/ Ballad of Hollis Brown/ Talkin' World War III Blues/ A Hard Rain's a-Gonna Fall/ With God on Our Side/ Farewell/ A Hard Rain's a-Gonna Fall/ Bob Dylan's Dream/ Boots of Spanish Leather/ John Brown/ Who Killed Davey Moore?/ Blowin' in the Wind/ Blowin' in the Wind/ Only a Pawn in Their Game/ When the Ship Comes In/ Only a Pawn in Their

Game/ Blowin' in the Wind/ Percy's Song/ Seven Curses/ Walls of Red Wing/ Talkin' World War III Blues/ Don't Think Twice, It's All Right/ Only a Pawn in Their Game/ Masters of War/ The Lonesome Death of Hattie Carroll

50th Anniversary Collection 1964 The Times Are A-Changin'/ Talkin' World War III Blues/ The Lonesome Death Of Hattie Carroll/ A Hard Rain's A-Gonna Fall/ Restless Farewell/ The Lonesome Death 0f Hattie Carroll/ ERIC VON SCHMIDT SESSION: Bob And Eric Blues (Bob Dylan/ Eric Von Schmidt)/ Black Betty (Leadbelly)/ Come All You Fair And Tender Ladies (trad.)/ Florida Woman (Eric Von Schmidt)/ Johnny Cuckoo (trad.)/ Money Honey (Jessie Stone)/ More And More (Webb Pierce/ Merle Kilgore)/ Mr. Tambourine Man/ Susie Q (Dale Hawkins/ Stanley Lewis/ Eleanor Broadwater)/ Harmonica Duet/ Glory, Glory(trad.) /Dr. Strangelove Blues (Eric Von Schmidt)/ Stoned On The Mountain (Eric Von Schmidt/ Bob Dylan) (X2)/ Walkin' Down The Line/ Joshua Gone Barbados (Eric Von Schmidt)/ With God On Our Side/ Don't Think Twice, It's All Right/ The Times They Are A-Changin'/ Girl From The North Country/ Who Killed Davey Moore?/ Talkin' John Birch Paranoid Blues/ Ballad Of Hollis Brown/ It Ain't Me Babe/ Walls Of Red Wing/ Chimes Of Freedom/ Mr. Tambourine Man/ Eternal Circle/ A Hard Rain's a-Gonna Fall/ Talkin' World War III Blues/ Don't Think Twice, It's All Right/ Only A Pawn In Their Game/ With God On Our Side/ The Lonesome Death Of Hattie Carroll/ Restless Farewell/ When The Ship Comes In/ Denise/ It Ain't Me Babe/ Spanish Harlem Incident (X2)/ Ballad In Plain D/ I Don't Believe You/ I Don't Believe You/ Chimes Of Freedom/ Chimes Of Freedom/ Mr. Tambourine Man/ Black Crow Blues/ Black Crow Blues/ I Shall Be Free No. 10/ I Shall Be Free No. 10/ I Shall Be Free No. 10/ I Shall Be Free No. 10/ It Ain't Me Babe/ All I Really Want To Do/ To Ramona/ Mama, You Been On My Mind/ It Ain't Me Babe/ With God On Our Side/ The Times They Are-A Changin'/ Girl From The North Country/ Who Killed Davey Moore?/ Talkin' John Birch Paranoid Blues/ To Ramona/ Ballad Of Hollis Brown/ Chimes Of Freedom/ I Don't Believe You/ It's Alright, Ma (I'm Only Bleeding)/ Mr. Tambourine Man/ Talkin' World War III Blues/ A Hard Rain's A-Gonna Fall/ Don't Think Twice, It's All Right/ Only A Pawn In Their Game/ With God On Our Side/ It Ain't Me Babe/ The Lonesome Death Of Hattie Carroll/ All I Really Want To Do/ Gates Of Eden/ If You Gotta Go, Go Now/ It's Alright, Ma (I'm Only Bleeding)/ Talkin' World War III Blues/ Don't Think Twice, It's All Right/ Mama, You Been On My Mind/ The Times Are A-Changin'/ Talkin' John Birch Paranoid Blues/ To Ramona/ Gates Of Eden/ If You Gotta Go, Go Now/ It's Alright, Ma (I'm Only Bleeding)/ Mr. Tambourine Man/ A Hard Rain's a-Gonna Fall/ Talkin' World War II Blues/ Don't Think Twice, It's All Right

50th Anniversary Collection 1969 To Be Alone With You - Rehearsal and Takes 2-5/To Be Alone With You - Takes 2-5/ To Be Alone With You - Take 3-5/ To Be Alone With You - Takes 4 and 5/ One More Night - Takes 1-3/ Lay, Lady, Lay - Rehearsal and Take 1 and 2/ Peggy Day - Take 2/ Tell Me That It Isn't True - Takes 1-3/ Lay, Lady, Lay - Takes 1-3/ One Too Many Mornings - Rehearsal/ One Too Many Mornings - Takes 1-3,/ I Still Miss Someone (Johnny Cash/ Roy Cash Jr.) - Rehearsal and Takes 1-4/ Don't Think Twice, It's All Right/ Understand Your Man (Johnny Cash)- Take 1/ One Too Many Mornings - Take 2/ I Still Miss Someone (Johnny Cash/ Roy Cash Jr.) - Takes 1-4/ Matchbox (Carl Perkins) - Rehearsal and Take 2/ Big River (Johnny Cash) - Take 2/ I Walk The Line (Johnny Cash) - Take 1/ Ring Of Fire (June Carter/ Merle Kilgore) - Takes 2 & 3/ Guess Things Happen That Way (Jack Clement) - Takes 1, 2 and 6/ Waiting For A Train (Jimmie Rodgers) - Take 1/ Running/ Take A Message To Mary (Felice and Boudleaux Bryant)/ Blue Moon (Richard Rodgers/ Lorenz Hart) (X2)/ Ring Of Fire (June Carter/ Merle Kilgore)

5oth Anniversary Collection 1970 I Can't Help but Wonder Where I'm Bound (tom Paxton)/ Universal Soldier - Take (Buffy Sainte Marie) / Spanish Is the Loving Tongue - Take 1 (Charles Badger Clark/ Billy Simon)/ Went to See the Gypsy - Take 2 Went to See the Gypsy - Take 3/ Woogie Boogie/ Went to See the Gypsy - Take 4/Thirsty Boots (Eric Anderson) - Take 1/ Little Moses (trad.) - Take 1/ Alberta (trad.) - Take 2/ Come All You Fair and Tender Ladies - Take 1/ Things About Comin' My Way - Takes 2 & 3 (Lonnie Chatmon/ Walter Vinson/ Went to See the Gypsy - Take 6/ Untitled 1970 Instrumental #1/ 15. Come a Little Bit Closer - Take 2/ Alberta (trad.) - Take 5/ Sign on the Window - Take 2/ Sign on the Window - Takes 3, 4 & 5/ If Not for You - Take 1/ Time Passes Slowly - Rehearsal/ If Not for You - Takes 2 and 3/ Song to Woody - Take 1/ Mama, You Been on My Mind - Take 1/ Yesterday (John Lennon/ Paul McCartney) - Take 1/ Just Like Tom Thumb's Blues - Take 1/ I Met Him on a Sunday (Owens/ Lee/ Harris/ Coley) - Take 1/ One Too Many Mornings - Take 1/ Ghost Riders in the Sky (Stan Jones)- Take 1/ Cupid (Sam Cooke)/ All I Have to Do Is Dream (Felice and Boudleaux Bryant) - Take 1/ Gates of Eden - Take 1/ I Threw It All Away - Take 1/ I Don't Believe You - Take 1/ Matchbox (Carl Perkins)- Take 1/ Your True Love (Carl Perkins) - Take 1/ Telephone Wire - Take 1/ Fishing Blues (Henry Thomas) - Take 1/ Honey, Just Allow Me One More Chance (Henry Thomas/ Bob Dylan) - Take 1/ Rainy Day Women #12 & 35 - Take 1/Ain't Me Babe/ If Not for You/ Sign on the Window - Takes 1-3/ Alligator Man (Jimmy C. Newman)(1-3)/ Day of the Locusts - Take 2/ 25. Sarah Jane (trad.) 1/. Sign on the Window/ Sarah Jane (trad.) 2/ If Not for You - Takes 1 and 2/ Jamaica Farewell (Irving Louis Burgie)/ Can't Help Falling in Love (Hugo Peretti/ George Weiss/ Louis Creatore)/ Long Black Veil (Marijohn Wilkin/ Danny Dill)/ One More Weekend/ Bring Me Little Water, Sylvie (trad.) - Take 1/ Three Angels/ Tomorrow Is a Long Time - Takes 1 and 2)/ New Morning Untitled 1970 Instrumental #2/ Went to See the Gypsy/ Sign on the Window - Stereo Mix/ Winterlude/ I Forgot to Remember to Forget (S. Kesler/ C. Feathers) Takes 1 and 2/ Lily of the West (trad.) - Take 2/ Father of Night - Rehearsal/ Lily of the West (trad.)/If Not for You - Takes 1-3)/ Song to Woody - Take 1/ Mama, You Been on My Mind - Take 1/ Yesterday (Lennon/McCartney) - Take 1

Compilations with otherwise unreleased Dylan tracks

More Greatest Hits (1971) Watching the River Flow/ When I Paint My Masterpiece, I Shall Be Released, You Ain't Goin' Nowhere, Down in the Flood

Biograph (1985) Abandoned Love/ Heart of Mine (live)/ Forever Young (demo)

Singles with otherwise unreleased Dylan tracks

Mixed Up Confusion / Corrina Corrina (trad. arr. Dylan), 1962
Watching The River Flow / Spanish Is the Loving Tongue (Charles Badger Clark/ Billy Simon), 1971
George Jackson (Big Band Version)/ George Jackson (Acoustic), 1971
Rita May (Bob Dylan/ Jacques Levy) / Stuck Inside Of Mobile With the Memphis Blues Again (live), 1976
Gotta Serve Somebody / Trouble In Mind, 1979
Union Sundown/ Angel Flying Too Close to the Ground (Willie Nelson), 1983
Band Of The Hand / Theme From Joe's Death, 1986
Dignity/ John Brown (live)/ It Ain't Me, Babe (live), A Hard Rain's a-Gonna Fall (live), 1995
Love Sick/ Love Sick (live), 2000
Things Have Changed/ Blind Willie McTell (live), 2000
Most Likely You Go Your Way (And I Go Mine) (Mark Ronson remix)/original version, 2007
Dreamin' of You/ Down Along the Cove (live), 2008

Albums with otherwise unreleased Dylan tracks

John Brown, Let Me Die in My Footsteps, Talkin' Devil, Only A Hobo, *Broadside Ballads, Vol. 1*, 1963
Wallflower, Blues Stay Away From Me (Henry Glover/ Alton Delmore/ Rabon Delmore/ Wayne Raney), Me and Paul (Willie Nelson), with Doug Sahm, *Doug Sahm and Band*, 1973
Buckets of Rain, with Bette Midler, *Songs for the New Depression*, 1976
Sign Language, with Eric Clapton, *No Reason to Cry* (1976)
We Are the World (Lionel Ritchie/ Michael Jackson) with Various Artists, *USA For Africa*, 1985
Sun City (Steve Van Zandt) with Various Artists, *Artists United Against Apartheid*, 1985
Street Rock, with Kurtis Blow (Kurtis Blow) *Kingdom Blow*, 1986
Pretty Boy Floyd (Woody Guthrie), *Folkways: A Vision Shared - A Tribute to Woody Guthrie & Leadbelly*, Various Artists, 1988
Love Rescue Me (U2/Bob Dylan), with U2, *Rattle and Hum*, 1988
People Get Ready (Curtis Mayfield), *Flashback - The Original Motion Picture Soundtrack*, Various Artists, 1990
Nobody's Child (trad.) with Traveling Wilburys, *Romanian Angel Appeal*, 1990
This Old Man (trad. arr. Dylan), *For Our Children*, Various Artists, 1991
Heartland, with Willie Nelson (Bob Dylan/ Willie Nelson), *Across the Borderline*, 1993
You Belong To Me (Chilton Price/ Pee Wee Ellis/ Redd Stewart) *Naural Born Killers soundtrack*, 1994
Chimes of Freedom (1994 version), *Third Annual Farewell Reunion*, Mike Seeger/Various Artists, 1994
Boogie Woogie Country Girl (Doc Pomus/ Reginald Ashby), *Till the Night is Gone: A Tribute to Doc Pomus*, Various Artists, 1995
Ring of Fire (Merle Kilgore, June Carter) *Feeling Minnesota Soundtrack*, Various Artists, 1996
My Blue Eyed Jane (Jimmie Rodgers), *The Songs Of Jimmie Rodgers - A Tribute*, Various Artists, 1997
I Can't Get You Off Of My Mind (Hank Williams) *Timeless: Hank Williams Tribute*, Various Artists, 2001
Roll on John (trad.) (1962): *There Is No Eye: Music For Photographs*, Various Artists, 2001
Red Cadillac and A Black Moustache (Lillian May/Willie Bea Thompson) *Good Rockin' Tonight: The Legacy of Sun Records*, Various Artists, 2001
Return to Me (Carmen Lombardo/ Danny Deminio), *The Sopranos: Peppers & Eggs*, Various Artists, 2001
Waiting for You: *Divine Secrets of the Ya-Ya Sisterhood Soundtrack*, Various Artists, 2002
Train of Love (Johnny Cash), *Kindred Spirits: A Tribute to the Songs of Johnny Cash*, Various Artists, 2002
Knockin' on Heaven's Door, with Calcutta Sabera Foundation *Girls Voices of Hope*: Various Artists, 2002
Change My Way of Thinking (new version) *Gotta Serve Somebody: The Gospel Songs of Bob Dylan,* Various Artists, 2003
Mutineer (Warren Zevon), Enjoy Every Sandwich: *The Songs of Warren Zevon*, Various Artists, 2004
Tell Ol' Bill, *North Country Soundtrack*, Various Artists, 2005
Do Re Mi (Woody Guthrie) *The People Speak soundtrack*, 2009
Don't Ever Take Yourself Away, *Hawaii 5-0 soundtrack*, 2011
The Love That Faded (Hank Williams/Bob Dylan) *The Lost Notebooks of Hank Williams*, 2011

Things We Said Today (John Lennon/ Paul McCartney) *The Art of McCartney*, 2014
He's Funny That Way (Neil Moret/ Richard Whiting) Universal Love: *Wedding Songs Re-Imagined*, 2018

Unreleased Bob Dylan songs

One Eyed Jacks, Talking Hugh Brown (1960)/ Talkin' Folk Lore Center Blues/ I Was Young When I Left Home, Bonnie Whyd'ya Cut My Hair (1961)/ Ballad of a Gliding Swan (1962) Troubled and I Don't Know Why (1963)/ Love is Just a Four Letter Word (1965)/ Nowhere to Go, I'd Have You Any Time (both with George Harrison) (1969)/ Champaign Illinois (with Carl Perkins) (1969)/ Ballad of Easy Rider (with Roger McGuinn) (1969)/ Vomit Express (with Allen Ginsberg) (1971)/ Rock Me Mama (Wagon Wheel)/ Goodbye Holly/ Sweet Amarillo (1973) Money Blues (with Jacques Levy) (1975)/ If I Don't Be There By Morning, Walk Out in the Rain, Coming from the Heart, Stop Now, The Wandering Kind, More than Flesh and Blood, I Must Love You Too Much, Tell Me the Truth One Time (all with Helena Springs, 1978)/ Stepchild/ You Don't Love Me No More/ This-a-way That a-way/ Take it or Leave It/ Daddy's Gonna Take One More Ride/ Legionnaire's Disease (1978)/ Is it Worth It?/ Almost Persuaded/ Borrowed Time/ On a Rocking Boat/ Fur Slippers/ Give Him All/ Hallelujah/ High Away/ Wind Blows on the Water/ Magic (1981)/ Julius and Ethel (1983)/ I Once Knew A Man/ Who Loves You More/ I See You Around and Around/ Dirty Lie/ Enough is Enough/ Almost Done/ Go 'Way Little Boy/ New Danville Girl/ I'm Ready for Love (1984)/ Tragedy of the Trade, Masquerade (with Gerry Goffin) (1985)/ Steel Bars (with Michael Bolton) (1985)/ Well Well Well/ Howlin' at Your Window/ All the Way Down/ Moving on the Water/ Worth the Waiting For/ Nothing Here Worth Dying For/ 26 Storeys High, Won't Go Back 'Til They Call Me Back, Straight A's in Love/ The Very Thought of You/ Baby Coming Back From the Dead, Waiting to Get Beat, Shake, Find Me, Right Hand Road Blues (1985)/ Rock 'em Dead/ To Fall in Love With You, Ride This Train (1986) Jammin' Me (with Tom Petty) (1986)/ You Can Blow My Mind If You Want To (1987)/ Like A Ship (with Traveling Wilburys) (1987)/ As We Sailed into Skibreen (with Jackie Leven) (1987)/ King of Kings (2001)/ Waiting for the Morning Light (with Gene Simmons) (2005)/ Gone But Not Forgotten (2016)

Bob Dylan's Appearances in Films

Don't Look Back 1967 (filmed in 1965)
Eat the Document filmed in 1966
Renaldo and Clara 1978 (filmed in 1975)
The Last Waltz 1978
Hearts of Fire 1987
Masked and Anonymous 2003
No Direction Home 2005
Rolling Thunder Revue- A Bob Dylan Story 2019

Selected Bibliography

Books by Bob Dylan

Tarantula (1971). Macmillan
Writings and Drawings (1973). Jonathan Cape
Chronicles: Volume One (2004). Simon & Schuster
The Lyrics: Since 1962 (2014). ed. Christopher Ricks, Lisa Nemrow, Julie Nemrow Simon & Schuster
The Nobel Lecture (2017). Simon & Schuster

Art books by Bob Dylan

Drawn Blank (1994). Random House
The Drawn Blank Series (2008). Prestel
The Brazil Series (2010). Prestel
The Asia Series (2011). Gagosian Gallery
Revisionist Art: Thirty Works by Bob Dylan (2013). Halcyon Gallery
Bob Dylan: Face Value (2014). National Portrait Gallery
The Beaten Path (2016). Halcyon Gallery
Mondo Scripto (2018). Halcyon Gallery
Mondo Scripto 2020 (2020). Castle Fine Art

Interviews with Bob Dylan

Younger Than That Now: The Collected Interviews with Bob Dylan (2004). Thunder's Mouth Press.
Cott, Jonathan (ed.) *Dylan on Dylan: The Essential Interviews,* (2006). Hodder & Stoughton.
Burger, Jeff (ed.) *Dylan on Dylan: Interviews and Encounters,* (2018). Chicago Review Press.

Biographies of Bob Dylan

Bell, Ian (2012) *Once Upon a Time: The Lives of Bob Dylan.* Mainstream Publishing.
Bell, Ian (2013) *Time Out Of Mind: The Lives of Bob Dylan.* Mainstream Publishing.
Cott, Jonathan (1984) *Dylan.* Rolling Stone Press. ISBN 0-09-158750-6.
Epstein, Daniel Mark (2011) *The Ballad of Bob Dylan: A Portrait.* HarperCollins.
Heylin, Clinton (1996) *Bob Dylan: A Life In Stolen Moments: Day by Day 1941-1995.*
Heylin, Clinton (2011) Bob Dylan: *Behind the Shades*: 20th Anniversary Edition. Faber and Faber.
Scaduto, Anthony (1972) *Bob Dylan.* Sphere.
Shelton, Robert (1986) *No Direction Home: The Life and Music of Bob Dylan.* New English Library
Sounes, Howard (2001) Down the Highway: The Life of Bob Dylan. Grove Press.

Books about Bob Dylan

Barker, Derek (2008) *The Songs He Didn't Write: Bob Dylan Under The Influence.* Chrome Dreams.
Bauldie, John, ed. (1992) *Wanted Man: In Search of Bob Dylan.* Penguin
Corcoran, Neil, ed. (2002) *Do You, Mr. Jones? Bob Dylan with the Poets and Professors.* Chatto & Windus.
Dettmar, Kevin J., ed. (2008) *The Cambridge Companion to Bob Dylan.*

Cambridge University Press.
Goss, Nina, ed. (2018) *Tearing the World Apart: Bob Dylan and the Twenty-First Century.* University Press of Mississippi.
Gray, Michael (2000) *Song & Dance Man III.* Continuum.
Gray, Michael (2006) The Bob Dylan Encyclopedia. Continuum International.
Griffin, Sid (2014) *Million Dollar Bash: Bob Dylan, the Band, and the Basement Tapes* (Revised & updated ed.). Jawbone.
Heylin, Clinton (2009) *Revolution In The Air: The Songs of Bob Dylan*, Volume One: 1957-73. Constable.
Heylin, Clinton (2010) *Still On The Road: The Songs of Bob Dylan*, Volume Two: 1974-2008. Constable.
Heylin, Clinton (2016) *Judas!: From Forest Hills to the Free Trade Hall: A Historical View of Dylan's Big Boo.* Route Publishing.
Heylin, Clinton (2018) *No One Else Could Play That Tune: The Making and Unmaking of Bob Dylan's 1974 Masterpiece.* Route Publishing.
Hinchey, John (2002) *Like a Complete Unknown: The Poetry of Bob Dylan's Songs, 1962-1969.* Stealing Home Press.
Humphries, Patrick (1991) *Oh No! Not Another Bob Dylan Book.* Square One Books.
Kinney, David (2014) *The Dylanologists: Adventures in the Land of Bob.* Simon & Schuster.
Marcus, Greil (1991) *Mystery Train: Images of America in Rock'n'Roll Music.* Penguin Books.
Marcus, Greil (1997) *Invisible Republic: Bob Dylan's Basement Tapes.* Picador.
Marcus, Greil (2005) *Like a Rolling Stone: Bob Dylan at the Crossroads.* Public Affairs.
Marcus, Greil (2013) *Bob Dylan by Greil Marcus: Writings 1968-2010.* Public Affairs.
Marshall, Scott (2017) *Bob Dylan: A Spiritual Life.* BP Books.
McGregor, Craig (1972) *Bob Dylan: A Retrospective.* William Morrow & Co.
Mellers, Wilfred (1984) *A Darker Shade of Pale: A Backdrop to Bob Dylan.* Faber and Faber.
Muir, Andrew (2003) *Troubadour: Early & Late Songs of Bob Dylan.* Woodstock Publications.
Muir, Andrew (2013) *One More Night: Bob Dylan's Never Ending Tour.* Create Space.
Muir, Andrew (2019) *The True Performing of it: Bob Dylan & William Shakespeare.* Red Planet Books.
Porter, Cathy (2006) *Bob Dylan and Philosophy* Open Court Publishing Co.
Polizzotti, Mark (2006) *Highway 61 Revisited.* Continuum.
Ricks, Christopher (2003) *Dylan's Visions of Sin.* Penguin/Viking.
Riley, Tim (1992) *Hard Rain: A Dylan Commentary.* Knopf/Vintage.
Rotolo, Suze (2008) *A Freewheelin' Time.* Aurum Press.
Santelli, Robert (2005) *The Bob Dylan Scrapbook.* Simon & Schuster.
Scobie, Stephen (1991) *Alias Bob Dylan.* Red Deer College Press.
Shepard, Sam (1978) *Rolling Thunder Logbook.* Penguin Books.
Sloman, Larry (1978) *On the Road With Bob Dylan: Rolling With the Thunder.* Bantam Books.
Thomas, Richard (2017) *Why Bob Dylan Matters.* Dey Street Books.
Thomson, Elizabeth, ed. (1990) *The Dylan Companion.* Macmillan Publishers.
Wald, Elijah (2015) *Dylan Goes Electric!: Newport, Seeger, Dylan, and the Night That Split the Sixties.* Dey Street Books.
Williams, Paul (1980) *Dylan - What Happened?.* Entwhistle Books.
Williams, Paul (1991) *Bob Dylan: Performing Artist The Early Years* 1960-1973. Underwood-Miller.
Williams, Paul (2004) *Bob Dylan, Performing Artist: The Middle Years (1974-1986).* Omnibus Press.
Williams, Paul (2005) *Bob Dylan, Performing Artist: Mind Out Of Time (1986-1990 & beyond)* Omnibus Press.
Wilentz, Sean (2009) *Bob Dylan In America.* The Bodley Head.
Williamson, Nigel (2004) *The Rough Guide to Bob Dylan.* Rough Guides.

Other Relevant Books

Blake, William (2008) *Complete Poetry and Prose.* University Of California Press
Bronte, Charlotte (2006) *Jane Eyre.* Penguin
Bronte, Emily (1999) *Wuthering Heights.* Nelson Thornes
Burroughs, William (2013) *Naked Lunch.* Grove Press
Charters, Samuel (1963) *Poetry of the Blues, The.* Dover Publications
Ciardi, John (2003) *Dante's The Divine Comedy.* Indiana University Press
Constantine, David and Kuhn, Tom (2018) (trans.) *Collected Poems of Berthold Brecht.* Liveright
Fagles, Robert (2009) *Odyssey, Iliad and Aenied.* Penguin
Fitzgerald, Edward (trans.) (1952) *Rubaiyat of Omar Khayyam, The.* Collins
Fitzgerald, F. Scott (2018) *Great Gatsby, The.* Om Books
Fowlie, Wallace (trans.) (1967) *Arthur Rimbaud: Collected Poems.* University of Chicago Press
Frost, Robert (1979) *Complete Poems.* Henry Holt and Co.
Ginsberg, Allen (2007) *Collected Poems 1947-1997.* Harper Collins
Gray, Michael (2008) *Hand Me My Travelin' Shoes: In Search of Blind Willie McTell.* Chicago Review Press
Green, Peter (trans.) (2005) *Homer's Odyssey and Iliad* University of California Press
Ovid's Tristia and the Black Sea Letters. University of California Press
Gregory, Chris (2008) *Who Could Ask For More? Reclaiming the Beatles.* plotted plain press.
Guthrie, Woody (1983) *Bound For Glory.* Om Publications
Hawthorne, Nathaniel (2004) *Scarlet Letter, The.* Digireads
Heller, Joseph (2011) *Catch-22.* Simon and Schuster
Hilburn, Robert (2014) *Johnny Cash: The Life.* W and N
Keats, John (1977) *Complete Poems, The.* Penguin
Kerouac, Jack (1999) *On the Road.*Penguin
Lewinsohn, Mark (2013). *The Beatles - All These Years: Tune In.* Little Brown
Malone, Bill and Laird, Tracey, E. W. (1960) *Country Music USA.* University of Texas Press
Melville, Herman (2016) *Moby Dick.* Macmillan
Michie, James (2002) *Ovid's Art of Love, The.* Modern Library
Oliver, Paul (1990) *Blues Fell This Morning: Meaning in the Blues.* Cambridge University Press
Palmer, Robert (2001) *Deep Blues.* Penguin
Poe, Edgar Allan (2011) *Complete Poems and Stories.* Canterbury Classics
Raeburn, David (trans.) (2004) *Ovid's Metamorphoses.* Penguin
Shakespeare, William (2016) *Complete Works.* Oxford University Press
Shelley, Mary (1994) *Frankenstein.* Dover Publications
Shelley, Percy Bysshe (2017) *Selected Poems and Prose.* Penguin
Steinbeck, John (2000) *Grapes of Wrath, The.* Penguin Classics
Timrod, Henry (2020) *Poems.* Blurb
Twain, Mark (2015) *Adventures of Huckleberry Finn, The.* Create Space
Ward, Matthew (2016) *Albert Camus: Stranger,The.* Vintage
Wheen, A. W. (trans.) (1996) *Erich Maria Remarque: All Quiet on the Western Front.* Vintage
Whitman, Walt (1995) *Leaves of Grass.* Wordsworth Poetry Library
Wordsworth, William (2005) *Collected Poems.* Penguin

Index

Song, album, film, TV show, poem and book titles in italics. Material written or directed by Bob Dylan and artwork by Bob Dylan in bold italics.

Dylan albums in bold italic capitals